Mental Health Care
Issues in America

Mental Health Care Issues in America

AN ENCYCLOPEDIA

VOLUME TWO: N–W

Michael Shally-Jensen,
Editor

 ABC-CLIO

Santa Barbara, California • Denver, Colorado • Oxford, England

Copyright 2013 by ABC-CLIO, LLC

All rights reserved. No part of this publication may be reproduced, stored in a retrieval system, or transmitted, in any form or by any means, electronic, mechanical, photocopying, recording, or otherwise, except for the inclusion of brief quotations in a review, without prior permission in writing from the publisher.

Library of Congress Cataloging-in-Publication Data

Mental health care issues in America : an encyclopedia / Michael Shally-Jensen, editor.
   v. cm.
Includes bibliographical references and index.
ISBN 978–1–61069–013–3 (hard copy : alk. paper) — ISBN 978–1–61069–014–0 (ebook)
1. Mental health—United States—Encyclopedias. 2. Mental health services—United States—Encyclopedias. 3. Psychiatry—United States—Encyclopedias. 4. Mental illness—United States—Encyclopedias. I. Shally-Jensen, Michael.
RC437.M46   2013
362.19689003—dc23   2012023911

ISBN: 978–1–61069–013–3
EISBN: 978–1–61069–014–0

17 16 15 14 13   1 2 3 4 5

This book is also available on the World Wide Web as an eBook.
Visit www.abc-clio.com for details.

ABC-CLIO, LLC
130 Cremona Drive, P.O. Box 1911
Santa Barbara, California 93116-1911

This book is printed on acid-free paper ∞

Manufactured in the United States of America

Contents

Alphabetical List of Entries

Topical List of Entries

Children and Youth

Adolescence and Mental Health

Attention Deficit/Hyperactivity Disorder

Autism Spectrum Disorders

Campus Life and Mental Health

Children and Mental Health

Depression

Drug Abuse and Mental Health

Eating Disorders

Family and Mental Illness

Gender Identity Disorder

Genetics and Mental Health

Impulse Control Disorders

Intellectual Disability

Internet Gaming Addiction

Learning Disabilities

Lesbian, Gay, Bisexual, and Transgender (LGBT) Mental Health Issues

Residential Treatment for Young People

School Mental Health

Self-Injury and Body Image

Suicide and Suicide Prevention

Ethnicity, Race, and Culture

African Americans and Mental Health

American Indian and Alaskan Native Mental Health

Asian American and Pacific Islander Mental Health Issues

Culturally Competent Mental Health Care

Latinos and Mental Health

Institutions, Settings, and Social Contexts

Campus Life and Mental Health

Community Mental Health

Creativity and Mental Health

Disasters and Mental Health

Psychiatry, Psychology, and Pharmaceuticals

The Public Sphere

N

Narcissism

Jerrold Lee Shapiro

The modern term "narcissism" is employed to describe both a psychiatric disorder and an evolving social norm in individualistic (as opposed to collectivist) cultures. In common parlance, it is a pejorative term for selfishness. The primary focus here is on the psychiatric syndrome.

It is named after the Greek myth of Narcissus, a youth described as being most beautiful and as so obsessed with his appearance that he was ever-fearful of finding the slightest personal imperfection. He was even more disdainful of any faults in others. Indeed, he was cruel to the maidens and nymphs who deigned to love him. Displeased by Narcissus's hubris, the gods punished him by causing him to fall in love with his own image in a reflecting pond. Believing that the image was a beautiful water nymph, the youth repeatedly tried to approach her, only to have her image fade away. Devastated by the perceived rejection, he became unable to leave the reflection and ultimately pined away.

Thus exist two major components of a modern day affliction: (1) obsessive self-involvement, marked by feelings of grandiosity and entitlement coincident with a desperate fear of defects; and (2) a lack of empathy toward others (Shapiro & Bernadett-Shapiro 2006).

A Working Understanding of Narcissism

To understand the syndrome, it is essential to recognize that the true narcissistic personality is less about love of self *than love of a reflection or an image*. Indeed at deeper levels, the narcissist feels quite unlikable and insecure. He or she[1] is a person lacking a consensual measure and holds perfection as the only acceptable norm. In a futile attempt to enhance and project the ideal image, the narcissist expends extraordinary energy, building and perfecting his façade. Ironically, with depleted psychic energy, he is increasingly vulnerable to perceived slights or criticism.

Shapiro and Bernadett-Shapiro (2006) conclude that "to the narcissist, love is indistinguishable from admiration, fear or even awe. When he feels feared or

---

[1]Narcissists can be male or female, but in this discussion, the male pronoun is used.

'respected' by others, he believes that he is loved. Sadly, when respect is derived from the image, rather than the person, he must constantly live up to this projection. In this way, he becomes progressively divorced from his inner self and married to the illusion. Any 'true self' that he may have, becomes solely a slave to the image" (27).

With the surfeit of energy spent on perfecting the image and an aversion to others' flaws, the narcissist lives a life of emotional loneliness. Any vulnerability, the very traits that allow others to connect at an emotional level, is met by intense fear and revulsion.

Because loneliness may be seen as a deficit, it is transformed psychologically into a presentation of fierce individualism that zealously protects personal turf from others' dependency. This perfectionistic illusion of emotional independence is seen in psychotherapy as a defense that protects a fragile ego, but ironically also blocks it from needed emotional nourishment from others.

A second characteristic is a paradoxical drive to please others, but solely to support the image as a truly wonderful person. The true narcissist lacks empathy for others and indeed for himself. He is unattuned to any personal needs other than admiration.

The true narcissistic personality believes himself entitled to inordinate rewards. Surely, one as powerful, skilled, and special as he (or, more properly, his image) deserves to be treated better than normal people. When the narcissist is regarded as if he were an equal to others, he takes that as a betrayal, often feels cheated, or the object of discrimination. As an entitled person, he believes that he should get the lion's share, and his anger at such a slight can be quite formidable. Clinicians often refer to any attack on the image as a "narcissistic wound." Thus the narcissist seeks constant praise as evidence of his superiority. Others exist primarily as instruments for personal gratification

Believing that he (at least his image) is superior, he acts as if he is unaccountable to average people and will justify any consequences his behavior has on others' lives. Although he is often aware of his impact on others, he does not care, because his relationships are limited to adoration, which enhances his group status.

Perils of Narcissism

Anyone dependent on reflected glory is constantly vulnerable. A simple negative perception or minor criticism can seem to the narcissist a devastating threat. A professor who evaluates his work as A–, rather than A, can generate an emotional injury that could result in threats, tears, or lawsuits to "right this terrible wrong." The true narcissist does not see the 3.9 GPA as positive, only the 0.1 that interferes with his illusion of perfection.

A narcissist has a dichotomous experience of the world. Because his psyche cannot allow for any shades of gray, he lives his life on the emotional edge.

Generation Me

Personality and social psychologist Jean Twenge reports a long-term trend toward increased narcissism among college students. Twenge led a survey team that examined more than 16,000 college students who took the Narcissistic Personality Inventory (NPI) between 1982 and 2006. The results showed a significant increase in self-centeredness during this period. In her report, "Egos Inflating over Time," Twenge found a 30 percent rise in narcissism as a character trait based on NPI scores. Twenge refers to today's young adults as "Generation Me" and notes that, while members of this generation may be more "confident, assertive, and entitled" than previous generations, they are also "more miserable than ever before." In fact, says Twenge, Generation Me'ers can often feel frustrated and insecure, which commonly translates into impulse control problems and generally bad behavior.

—*Editor*

Source: J. M. Twenge, S. Konrath, J. D. Foster, W. K. Campbell, and B. J. Bushman, "Egos Inflating over Time: A Cross-Temporal Analysis of the Narcissistic Personality Inventory," *Journal of Personality* 76 (2008): 875–901; J. M. Twenge, *Generation Me: Why Today's Young American Are More Confident, Assertive, Entitled—and More Miserable Than Ever Before* (New York: Free Press, 2006); J. M. Twenge and W. K. Campbell, *The Narcissism Epidemic: Living in an Age of Entitlement* (New York: Free Press, 2009).

He cannot have even a minor disagreement without activating his "fight or flight" (sympathetic nervous system) response. This level of reactivity leads to an almost paranoid quality in the way he relates to others;—questioning their motives and searching out any potential criticism or disapproval. His extreme responses to minor or imagined slights often come across as bullying and blaming.

Although he is wont to hold others accountable to his personal standards of proper behavior, he cannot accept personal blame, because accepting responsibility for an imperfection would constitute an injury to his image. Once wounded so, no apologies, save humiliation, full acceptance of all responsibility by the other person, and extraordinary recompense are acceptable. Forgiveness is not part of the narcissistic life.

He is particularly vulnerable to others who have previously held high status (for their successes, position, or what they can offer). Once hurt by an individual whom he had initially idealized, his fury is almost boundless—like a child's tantrum. In reaction to such a slight he will devalue the person, often quite publically and destructively. Falling from the narcissist's grace renders a person "unsupportive," thereby useless in providing resources. Because such a fall presents a glimpse of a frightening picture of his underlying personal vulnerability, it is greeted with abhorrence, denigration, and rage. Because the flip from idealizing to denigrating is so precipitous and because he is so needy, long-term relationships are likely to fail and new people brought in continuously to pick up the adoring slack.

Narcissism as a Clinical Syndrome

It is not a simple matter to distinguish between narcissistic character traits, cultural patterns of narcissism, and narcissistic personality disorder (NPD). Only the last is a clinical syndrome. As defined in the *Diagnostic and Statistical Manual* (*DSM*), published by the American Psychiatric Association, the syndrome is an AXIS II, or personality, disorder—i.e., one considered a relational rather than a thought, mood, or anxiety disorder. Generally, the etiology is considered to be based on early developmental (attachment) deficits.

It is important to note that there is currently a controversial debate about the viability of all Axis II disorders, particularly NPD. There is a movement to replace, in the forthcoming fifth edition of the *DSM* (due out in 2013), the syndrome and the prototype approach generally favored by clinicians with a series of scales that measure deviance from the norm on multiple dimensions. This is a response to the current mantra from both academic researchers and third-party health care providers regarding the need for evidence-based approaches. At the time of this writing, no final decision has been rendered. But regardless of how the disorder is identified, described, and measured, treatment for individuals with NPD is unlikely to be altered much in the foreseeable future.

The Etiology of Narcissism

What could produce an individual whose regular demeanor is often but a single step away from instability and whose need for acceptance can produce tantrums and bullying? How could a person have gotten this way? What goes into the making of narcissistic personality disorder?

Freud (1913/1955) originally viewed narcissism as the normal developmental stage between the auto-eroticism of the infant and capacity for the developing child to love others. In his theory of the self, Kohut (1984) illuminates both normal and clinical narcissism. For Kohut, the self, or "center of the of the individual's psychological universe," forms through relationship with primary caregivers. The child's sense of self evolves as a result of the interaction between the child's innate potentials and the empathic responses of adult caregivers. This includes two distinct needs: mirroring (see below) and availability of an ideal adult image with whom the child can identify and internalize.

Mirroring occurs when a caregiver attends to a child, listens to him, reflects his accomplishments, extols his positive qualities, and spends time (including quality time) with him. A child learns to feel appreciated when a caregiver notices him smiling, walking, coming when called, or treating a pet kindly. Over time, children internalize this valuing and begin to appreciate themselves.

Mirroring also involves reflecting mistakes in a manner that promotes healthy self-knowledge and self-esteem—acknowledging the error, without disparaging the person. Such nontraumatic failures foster development of the child's "self." He grows emotionally as he internalizes these parental functions and meets successively new challenges, relying on his budding internal self (ego structure). On this base, the self grows when confronted with age-appropriate challenges. As the child matures, an initial sense of grandiosity ("when I cry, milk is produced") is transformed into energy, ambition, and self-esteem. A reliable internal self evolves from interaction with reliable empathic caregivers.

Hence, the idea of *internalization*. In addition to parental mirroring, caregivers also provide a model to emulate. As parents exhibit ethical behavior, justice, and compassion, the child begins to find and develop those qualities in himself. This maturing self-image can become internalized as a healthy idealized self. In short, the caregivers provide a mature adult image with whom the child can identify and subsequently internalize as his own idealized self.

Problems can occur, however. When there is a consistent failure of mirroring, the child's "grandiose self" is pushed underground, where it is unavailable for continued development and modification. Unintegrated, childhood grandiosity generates a paradoxical combination of low self-esteem and bravado. St. Clair (1986) calls this being "mirror hungry" and observes that it produces individuals who are compelled toward "empty accomplishments" in order to bolster low self-esteem.

Similarly, without a proper ideal image for identification, a child will search for an idealized "other" to build out his ideal self. This seeking can take the form, for example, of joining pro-social groups, or, conversely, of becoming involved in gangs or cults. In a milder form it can lead to naive trust in powerful, charismatic leaders and the need to follow celebrities or other figures as if they were royalty.

If we consider narcissistic pathology to be a result of repeated empathic failure of caregivers, it is likely that the parents also have a somewhat underdeveloped self. They may be preoccupied with their own needs for grandiosity and may expect the child to be the source of satisfactory mirroring instead of the recipient. For such parents, children are extensions of themselves rather than separate beings.

Children who have experienced neglect that comes from a failure of mirroring and ideal parent internalization or abuse (dehumanization) could be predisposed to most personality disorders. A frustrated or abused child quickly learns that the only reliable "object" he can trust and love is himself. However, once a child eschews the untrustworthy others, his development of a model/ideal self becomes severely limited.

Thus the adult narcissist holds onto a more primitive grandiosity, one of omnipotence and omniscience. Unchecked by reality, he believes himself entitled to special treatment as an adult. What is not learned are mature relational traits such as empathy, compassion, perseverance to reach a goal, fair comparisons with others' skills and boundaries, and the ability to postpone gratification.

Instead, he feels as if he has a birthright and is preordained to be part of the ruling class. Yet in the real world, there is a brittle susceptibility to criticism. Having suffered from repeated empathic failure by his caregivers, he replicates this lack of empathy for others as an adult. Lacking a realistic self, he is "struck to the core" by disagreement or slight disapproval. His worst fear is to be exposed as a phony. In part this fear reflects his unconscious feelings of inadequacy and low self-worth (fluctuating with exaggerated, yet fragile, overvaluation of self-worth) that result directly from the unconscious fears of a repeated emotional abandonment.

Treatment

NPD is a developmental and historical disorder. To repair it in the present, the patient would have to experience in psychotherapy the mirroring he missed as a child—an emotionally corrective relationship that supercedes the failure of the original parental one. In the role as a new parental figure, the therapist needs to set limits, be present, and be engaged with enough integrity to be experienced by the patient as an ideal other.

Psychodynamic therapists have done the majority of the research on NPD. Consistent with psychodynamic theories, the most commonly recommended treatment is long term, insight oriented, and centered around the relationship with the therapist. Masterson (1981) underscored the salience of the patient's emotional fragility and the need for an extrasupportive therapeutic alliance to heal the developmental arrest.

Kohut (1977) stressed the importance of conveying to the patient a deep emotional understanding—a joining at deep unconscious (process) levels—which he called "temporary indwelling." This is a level of empathy that allows the therapist to experience the world from the patient's own frightened and fragile perspective.

The essential therapeutic alliance may be quite volatile. Because of their emotional fragility, these patients continuously test the therapist's level of safety. Often the therapist will inadvertently activate the narcissistic constellation, which will lead to anger and demeaning of the therapist. For Masterson (1981), successful therapy evolves from the therapist's management of these breakdowns. The goal is a sort of holding similar to swaddling an infant or containing a four-year-old's tantrum. By handling, containing, and empathizing with these protective maneuvers, the therapist gains the patient's trust. If she fails to pass the tests, the patients will often feel wounded and may act out by dropping out of therapy.

Any treatment that demands adequate mirroring and empathy requires a strong *here-and-now* presence by the therapist. The therapist will also have to be firm in the face of the patient's inability to face rather than act out underlying fragility, fear, and depression. Thus early on in therapy, when a patient informs the therapist that he does not trust her, it is important for the therapist to support the lack of trust, thus operating as if through the patient's eyes.

Once the therapeutic alliance has been established by mirroring and working within the patient's frame of reference, the therapist may be able to interpret the narcissistic vulnerability (and subsequently depression) as it appears during the therapeutic sessions. When gentle interpreting activates the narcissistic defenses of anger, the therapist accepts and contains the outburst, thus rebuilding the alliance until the next misstep into painful experiences (and greater vulnerability) for the patient.

The wounded narcissistic patient can be threatening to the therapist's psyche, especially when he questions her competence. Yet the core of effective treatment involves the therapist opening herself to the patient's frightening internal vulnerabilities. The most effective way to do this involves, ironically, self-awareness and interpretation from within the psyche of the therapist. Diamond (2011), for example, describes the importance of the psychoanalyst's heuristic internal free association during sessions as a way to better comprehend the patient's deeply unconscious internal struggles. Existential therapists focus instead on a deep awareness of personal internal experiences, intimate joining, and empathy, connecting with the client's process, in a here-and-now, "I-Thou" relationship (this last term from Buber 1971). Basically, the internal thoughts and feelings of the therapist are an essential component of understanding of and empathizing with clients who are most in need and mostly unaware of their own dysfunction.

Although the focus on the here and now in therapy may initially be more threatening, because it renders ineffective the characteristic defensive maneuvers of the client, it also provides a method of gaining entrance without undue narcissistic injury. Interpretations within this empathic, accepting, noncritical frame can identify the pain and need for protection (defense) in the moment.

This form of deep connection, or temporary indwelling, provides a bond that may withstand the fear of abandonment, at least in the moment. It also opens the door for the patient to internalize the idealized identification with the therapist. Of course, the narcissist had frequently idealized relationships only to have them come crashing down and become permanently broken. Here is where the therapist's skill at staying empathic even when under attack allows for a different kind of internalization. This process is repeated at ever deepening levels of intensity until the patients can explore relatively safely their sensitivity and disappointment at relational failures and gain insight into their defensive reactions to the fear and subsequent depression around abandonment.

Because of the need for repetition, treatment is almost always long term—a minimum of one year and frequently two years or more. The goal for the end of treatment is a patient whose real self is strengthened. However, because of the developmental damage, the patient remains vulnerable to separation stress. Termination must be done carefully and slowly, because this separation may reactivate abandonment vulnerability and a narcissistic defense. Thus during termination patients must be warned to be vigilant to such vulnerability and the near automatic defense of devaluation.

Conclusion

Narcissism is a normal stage in child development that does not entirely vanish in adulthood. In a healthy individual, infantile narcissism is gradually transformed to energy, ambition, self-care, self-growth, and the extension of self to family and community. Pathological narcissism is the result of repeated empathic failure during childhood and the lack of adult figures for idealization, identification, and internalization. Specific factors contributing to empathic failure may include the isolation of the nuclear family; single-parent families; lack of social supports such as high-quality, affordable child care, preschools, and elementary schools; and cultural values such as individualism and materialism. Treatment involves providing appropriate empathy, mirroring, and a model for internalization.

See also Humanistic Theories and Therapies; Paranoia; Psychoanalysis; Psychodynamic Psychotherapy; Psychopathy and Antisocial Personality Disorder

Bibliography

Brown, N. W. 2006. *Coping with Infuriating, Mean, Critical People: The Destructive Narcissistic Pattern*. Westport, CT: Praeger.

Buber, M. 1971. *I and Thou*. New York: Scribner's.

Diamond, M. J. 2011. "The Impact of the Mind of the Analyst: From Unconscious Processes to Intrapsychic Change." In M. J. Diamond and C. Christian, eds., *The Second Century of Psychoanalysis: Evolving Perspectives on Therapeutic Action* (pp. 205–236). London: Karnac Books.

Dobbert, D. L. 2007. "Narcissistic Personality Disorder." In D. L. Dobbert, *Understanding Personality Disorders* (pp. 87–104). Westport, CT: Praeger.

Freud, S. 1913 (1955). *Totem and Taboo*. London: Hogarth Press (Standard Edition Vol. 13).

Kohut, H. 1977. *The Restoration of the Self*. Chicago: University of Chicago Press.

Kohut, H. 1984. *How Does Analysis Cure?* Chicago: University of Chicago Press.

Lackhkar, J. 2008. *How to Talk to a Narcissist*. New York: Routledge.

Masterson, J. F. 1981. *The Narcissistic and Borderline Disorders*. London: Brunner-Routledge.

Pinsky, D., and S. M. Young. 2009. *The Mirror Effect: How Celebrity Narcissism Is Seducing America*. New York: Harper.

Ronningstam, E. 2005. *Identifying and Understanding the Narcissistic Personality*. New York: Oxford University Press.

Shapiro, J. L., and S. T. Bernadett-Shapiro. 2006. "Narcissism: Greek Tragedy, Psychological Syndrome, Cultural Norm." In T. Plante, ed., *Mental Disorders of the New Millennium* (, Vol. 1, pp. 25–52). Westport, CT: Praeger.

St. Clair, M. 1986. *Object Relations and Self Psychology: An Introduction*. Belmont, CA: Brooks/Cole.

Nature versus Nurture

See Genetics and Mental Health

Native Americans

See American Indian and Alaskan Native Mental Health

Neurodiversity

Dana Lee Baker

The term "neurodiversity" has two definitions. The first refers to perceived differences in the human brain observed as significant in a given social, political, legal, economic, or cultural context. This use of the term describes a human characteristic; after all, diversity in the population depends on the identification of multiple subgroups (Baker 2011). The second definition, the one that is the main focus of the present entry, refers to a political and social movement dedicated to advancing the human and civil rights of individuals with neurological differences. Formal articulation of neurodiversity in this sense has been led primarily by autistic self-advocates (see, for example, the Autistic Self-Advocacy Network).

Neurodiversity, then, is a natural condition of humanity related to, but nevertheless distinct from, neurological difference. Whereas neurological difference originates in the biological reality that no two brains are identical, neurodiversity involves a choice to recognize differences as a fundamental component of identity and, often, to deliberately identify with a particular neurodiverse group or community (Baker 2006).

Although a neurotypical (or "normal") brain is as much a social construction as s a neurologically different one, differences recognized as sufficiently distinct from the accepted norm tend to be associated with a multitude of difficulties for individuals. Most of these difficulties result from factors external to the individual, particularly social, economic, cultural, and political factors (Griffin & Pollak 2009; Grinkler 2008). Moreover, some neurological differences constitute a threat to individual comfort or survival. As a result, each individual retains the right to consider a significant neurological difference as personally undesirable and to pursue palliative care or a cure. Given this, although objections to the use of "people first" language (e.g., in defense of individuals with disabilities) are rightly raised by those embracing neurological difference as a core, positive element of identity (Ortega 2009), use of such language in law, policy, and academic discourse can be considered as a means to include the expressed interests of all people with neurological differences.

At the group level, neurodiversity describes an inherently positive characteristic and a natural experience (Armstrong 2010; Griffin & Pollak 2009). Traditional classifications drawn from the fields of medicine and education are employed to describe neurodiverse groups. For example, categories and conditions defined in the American Psychiatric Association's *Diagnostic and Statistical Manual of Mental Disorders* (*DSM*) and in the World Health Organization's International Classification of Functioning, Disability and Health (ICF) are routinely employed in discussions of neurodiversity. Similar to discussions about other forms of diversity, much of the discourse on neurodiversity focuses on conditions understood as connected with minority groups that have historically been excluded, ignored, oppressed, or otherwise systematically disempowered. Examples of such conditions include autism, attention deficit hyperactivity disorder (ADHD), bipolar disorder, and dyslexia (Armstrong 2010). Political activity surrounding neurodiversity involves efforts to restore basic human rights, promote acceptance of neurological difference, and reduce the effects of neurotypical privilege wherever possible (Ortega 2009).

Origins and Development of the Concept

The history of discrimination against those with disabilities is less well known than the histories of oppression toward other groups. While members of the general public are exposed to information about discrimination against racial and ethnic minorities, religious groups, and women, for example, information about disability is largely absent from public education programs and general public discourse (Baker 2011). Justification of discrimination against individuals with disabilities is, unfortunately, not yet fully taboo.

The disability rights movement grew steadily over the course of the twentieth century, resulting in significant changes in public policy such as deinstitutionalization, or the move toward community mental health, and the creation of rights-based, inclusionary special education. The neurodiversity movement is part of the larger disability rights movement. For example, the mission statement of the Autistic Self-Advocacy Network (ASAN) ends with one of the main disability rights mantras, "Nothing about Us, without Us!" (http://www.autisticadvocacy.org/).

The term neurodiversity began appearing in the media, on the Internet, and in gray literature (i.e., technical reports, working papers, policy statements) in the late 1990s, usually with reference to autistics. By the latter half of the first decade of the twenty-first century, the concept was being examined and articulated in the academic literature. Though use of the term in law and political discourse remains sparse, by 2011 it had appeared in legislative testimony and court proceedings in

Half Measures

Mike Stanton, an autism activist, reports that at a recent International Autism Conference in London he heard a talk by Professor David Amaral, a psychiatrist heading the MIND Institute at the University of California, Davis. At the conference Amaral told the story of a young man with Asperger syndrome who, when asked what he would do if a pill were developed that eliminated autism symptoms, replied that he would take half the pill.

As Stanton continues,

I think this illustrates a real difference within the autism community. There are many who pathologize autism as a disorder that afflicts an otherwise healthy individual. If you hold this idea you naturally look to understand the causes of autism in order to find that "autism pill."

The idea of Neurodiversity was developed by autistic people in opposition to the pathologizing model. According to them autistic people are not disordered. They have a different sort of order. Their brains are differently wired. They think differently. They do not want to be cured. They want to be understood.

—*Editor*

Source: Mike Stanton, Action for Autism, http://mikestanton.wordpress.com.

several countries, including Australia, Canada, France, Great Britain, and the United States. In the United States, one of the catalytic events of the neurodiversity movement was the so-called ransom notes campaign of 2007, in which poorly conceived advertisements seeking to raise awareness of childhood neurological and behavioral health issues represented autism, Asperger syndrome, and other conditions as roughly equivalent to being kidnapped by an outsider (Kaufmann 2007). A protest led by Ari Ne'eman, the president of ASAN, led to a cessation of the campaign and expanded awareness of questions of rights associated with neurological difference (Kras 2009). A key concern of this campaign was the unapologetic portrayal of autism and Asperger as "totally debilitating" (Kras 2009). By mid-2011, "neurodiversity" had been used in a cover story in the *New York Times*, lost its designation as a neologism on Wikipedia, been taught as a college course at a research university, and served as a theme for an academic symposium.

Boundaries of the neurodiversity movement are debated. At the time of this writing, some continue to object to use of the term expanded beyond the experience and rights of autistics (Jaarsma & Welin 2011). This concern raises fundamental questions of the diversity component of neurodiversity, which will likely be more fully addressed in coming years. Modern concerns also surround even more basic issues of respect (Ortega 2009). For example, words describing neurological differences continue to be employed as colloquial insults, and adverbs or adjectives intended to add a negative connotation (such as "autistic economics") appear in the popular media and elsewhere (Jurecic 2007).

Finally, debate remains as to whether or not neurodiversity can be attributed to differences in neurology or to psychological differences (Ortega 2009). Despite stunning recent progress, our understanding of human neurology is still in its infancy. Even whether or not a human brain should be considered a single entity or a kind of "team of rivals" remains unknown (Eagleman 2011, 109). Many neurological differences continue to rely on behavior-based diagnoses rather than on actual knowledge of underlying physiology. While such fundamental gaps in understanding are likely to continue for the foreseeable future, more relevant from the perspective of the politics of neurodiversity are the implications of this form of diversity as a characteristic of community (Baker 2011).

Controversies and Open Questions

All expressions of human diversity involve various controversies and open issues. The concept of neurodiversity is no exception. A brief discussion of some of the ongoing controversies and open questions follows. Many of these are structurally similar to (if not identical to) conversations surrounding other forms of human diversity.

Right to Claim, Right to Pass

One such complication involves the (public) identification of individuals with neurological differences. One question in this area is whether neurodiverse groups have the right to claim individuals with neurological differences who have not publically identified. Naming particularly successful public figures in one's ranks has obvious benefits in terms of public acceptance and possible advantages in achieving policy goals. As such, the claiming of well-known individuals, both living and dead, has occurred. Whether (and under what circumstances) it is appropriate to speculate on the neurological difference of another individual remains a somewhat unsettled question, one similar, for example, to the question of "outing" others when it comes to diverse sexualities.

A similar question surrounds the issue of whether an individual with a neurological difference has a right to "pass" as neurologically typical if he or she has the ability to do so. This option is, of course, not equally distributed across the population of individuals with neurological differences. To the extent that neurological privilege and disability-based discrimination continue to exist, the advantages to passing as neurologically typical exist as well. Moreover, an individual right to retain previous identity arguably deserves protection, especially in the case of acquired or degenerative neurological difference. Finally, particularly when it comes to children, it is hotly debated whether behavioral therapy designed to force development away from neurological difference should be pursued. In Canada, this question rose to the level of a Supreme Court case. In part, this controversy surrounds the interest that many parents express in teaching their children to pass as neurologically typical.

Disinterest and Noninvolvement

Another identity-related source of discussion and controversy involves whether or not an individual has the right to remain disinterested or uninvolved in political and policy questions surrounding neurodiversity. One group to whom this question might be posed is individuals with neurological differences who enjoy relative success in society. This issue of the "tension of attention" (Baker 2011) remains similarly unresolved in politics surrounding other forms of diversity (e.g., that of if, and to what extent, it is acceptable for women to be unconcerned about women's issues). An uneasy consensus appears to have formed around the notion that in a democracy, each individual retains a right to select which, if any, political issues he or she wishes to be involved in. That being said, however, utter indifference to discrimination-based suffering, particularly when experienced by another who shares one's own personal characteristic, appears morally questionable. Along similar lines, professionals who work directly with individuals with neurological difference might have even less of a right to indifference given the power dynamic inherent in many such client-practitioner relationships.

Whether professionals working in fields related to neurological difference with *indirect* involvement with individuals with neurological differences enjoy a similar right to disinterest or indifference is also open to question. For example, the goal of eliminating autism through (purportedly) genetic testing, or Down syndrome through current technologies, involves issues such as net losses in human genetic diversity and, potentially, increased pressure to abort fetuses found to be neurologically atypical (Silverman 2008). Specification of genetic normalcy is both a scientific and political act (Bumiller 2009). At the most basic level, public involvement in scientific progress constitutes an undesirable threat to basic scientific research, one similar to introducing politics into science. At the same time, indifference among scientists to the political ramifications of science can be equally costly.

Accommodations, Services, and Infrastructures

Controversy also surrounds the question of services and accommodations in the context of neurodiversity and neurological difference. For many observers, the assertion of disability rights accompanied by a demand for disability services appears contradictory at first glance. Typically, such impressions fail to take into account the existence of exclusionary infrastructures (such as access points, functionality of utilities, etc.). In any case, the denial of some individuals' needs above and beyond the making of infrastructure changes can be harmful to those incapable of self-care or in need of targeted services in order to participate in society even under conditions of full inclusion.

Neurotypical privilege continues to be broadly accepted. If, for example, a noise commonly irritating to those considered neurologically typical is present in an enclosed space (such as the sound of fingernails run down a blackboard), then a level of urgency around removing the source of the noise almost always develops. Stopping a noise similarly irritating to an individual identified as having a neurological difference would often be considered a low-level priority, with greater attention commonly paid either to removal of the individual or toward encouraging him or her to develop greater tolerance of the sound. Social norms and standards are, of course, a necessary condition of society. In fact, as Ann Jurecic (2007) has noted, one disabling but presumably well-intentioned response to the awareness of neurodiversity would be to relieve those with neurological difference of the expectation of conformity to social norms or standards of achievement expected of those considered neurologically typical (Jurecic 2007). However, much in the area of neurological privilege remains unexamined. Considerable deliberation will be required to distinguish between such privilege and expectations surrounding social norms and standards necessary for the functioning of society.

Stakeholders

Since diversity implies a level of interdependence, the direct effects of neurological difference on family members and other intimates of individuals with neurological differences also present dilemmas. The negative effects often experienced by parents of children with autism, for example, include financial suffering, social stigma, disempowerment, unfounded suspicion of deviancy, and marital strain (Baker & Drapela 2010; Silverman 2008). Significant improvement in this area could reasonably be expected as a result of substantial changes to exclusionary infrastructures and discriminatory attitudes. Nevertheless, the desire for a normal life achieved through a separate peace with society appears to be a common one among families living with neurological differences. A related issue is that of decline or suffering experienced as a result of living with neurological differences—especially when associated with increased risk of suicide, violence, homelessness, or incarceration. Many observers argue for limits to the tolerance of expressions of neurodiversity. In other words, the question of at what point behavior becomes dangerous or risky is a difficult one but one that must be discussed all the same.

There is also the issue of posttraumatic growth and increased sense of meaning that family members and intimates with neurological difference routinely experience (Grinkler 2008; Kras 2009). Part of this controversy surrounds the question of who gets to speak for people with neurological differences. This is a core identity-politics issue, common to all forms of diversity. On the one hand, there may be little reason to expect that an individual with a neurological difference is better equipped to speak for others, particularly those with different neurological conditions, simply by virtue of being considered neurologically atypical (Ortega 2009). On the other hand, any individual who has taken the time to learn about the implications of neurological difference has a level of expertise that is potentially relevant to political discourse surrounding neurodiversity, regardless of that individual's own neurological status. Thus the matter of who can speak for whom remains a work in progress.

Conclusion

It now appears that if human neurology were somehow simple enough for human beings to understand it, we would, paradoxically, not be intelligent enough to understand it (Eagleman 2011). Full recognition of neurodiversity, in both senses of the word, originates in a more mature understanding of the human brain than now exists or has existed in the past. Substantial use of that very same human brain, however, will be necessary in order to manage the opportunities and challenges posed by neurodiversity in coming years.

See also Attention Deficit Hyperactivity Disorder; Autism Spectrum Disorders; Bipolar Disorder; Creativity and Mental Health; Ethical Issues; Genetics and Mental Health; Medical Model of Psychiatric Illness; Neuropsychiatry; Public Awareness and Public Education

Bibliography

Armstrong, Thomas. 2010. *Neurodiversity: Discovering the Extraordinary Gifts of Autism, ADHD, Dyslexia and Other Brain Differences*. New York: Da Capo Lifelong Books.

Autistic Self-Advocacy Network (ASAN). http://www.autisticadvocacy.org/.

Baker, Dana Lee. 2006. "Neurodiversity, Neurological Disability and the Public Sector: Notes on the Autism Spectrum." *Disability & Society* 21: 15–29.

Baker, Dana Lee. 2011. *The Politics of Neurodiversity: Why Public Policy Matters*. Boulder, CO: Lynne Rienner.

Baker, Dana Lee, and Laurie A. Drapela. 2010. "Mostly the Mother: Concentration of Adverse Employment Effects on Mothers of Children with Autism." *The Social Science Journal* 47: 578–592.

Bumiller, Kristin. 2009. "The Geneticization of Autism: From New Reproductive Technologies to the Conception of Genetic Normalcy." *Signs* 34: 875–899.

Eagleman, David. 2011. *Incognito: The Secret Lives of the Brain*. New York: Pantheon.

Griffin, Edward, and David Pollak. 2009. "Student Experiences of Neurodiversity in Higher Education: Insights from the BRAINHE Project." *Dyslexia* 15: 23–41.

Grinkler, Roy Richard. 2008. *Unstrange Minds: Remapping the World of Autism*. Philadelphia: Basic Books.

Jaarsma, Pier, and Stellan Welin. 2011. "Autism as a Natural Human Variation: Reflections on the Claims of the Neurodiversity Movement." *Health Care Analysis* 20(1): 20–30.

Jurecic, Ann. 2007. "Neurodiversity." *College English* 69: 421–442.

Kaufmann, Joanne. 2007. "Ransom-Notes Ads about Children's Health Are Canceled." *New York Times*, December 20.

Kras, Joseph F. 2009. "The 'Ransom Notes' Affair: When the Neurodiversity Movement Came of Age." *Disability Studies Quarterly* 30(1). Retrieved from http://dsq-sds.org/article/view/1065/1254.

Neurodiversity: A Symposium. Retrieved from http://neurodiversitysymposium.wordpress.com/.

Ortega, Francisco. 2009. "The Cerebral Subject and the Challenge of Neurodiversity." *BioSociteties* 4: 425–445.

Shift, Journal of Alternatives: Neurodiversity and Social Change. http://www.shiftjournal.com/.

Silverman, Chloe. 2008. "Fieldwork on Another Planet: Social Science Perspectives on Autism." *BioSocieties* 3: 325–341.

Neuropsychiatry

William H. Wilson

The term "neuropsychiatry" is used in two rather different senses. In its broader sense, "neuropsychiatry" refers to the diagnosis and treatment of psychiatric disorders with an emphasis on the role of the brain in causing the disorder and in being the target of treatment, which is usually medication. In this sense, "neuropsychiatry" is synonymous with "biological psychiatry" and subsumes the study and practice of psychopharmacology, the study and use of psychiatric medication. This definition is useful in delineating the scope and utility of brain-based evaluation and treatment as differentiated from more psychologically or socially based approaches. All three of these domains—neuropsychiatric, psychological, and social—may need to be addressed for effective treatment of severe psychiatric disorders (Wilson 2011).

There is, however, a second, more restrictive definition of neuropsychiatry, which is the focus of the present entry. In this narrower sense, neuropsychiatry (also known as "behavioral neurology") refers to the subspecialty of psychiatry or neurology that addresses the emotional, cognitive, and behavioral aspects of neurological disorders. While the major psychiatric disorders such as schizophrenia and bipolar affective disorder are now known to have correlates in brain structure and function, these disorders, and others that have traditionally been called "mental illnesses," are not the focus of neuropsychiatry. Rather, the subspecialty of neuropsychiatry deals with those aspects of illness that have a more clearly defined brain pathology, that is, illnesses that are usually diagnosed and treated by neurologists. In the United States, the primary professional organization is the American Neuropsychiatric Association. The United Council for Neurologic Subspecialties administers a professional certification examination in Behavioral Neurology and Neuropsychiatry, which is open to qualified neurologists and psychiatrists.

Major Disorders and Treatment Approaches

The list of neurological disorders that are accompanied by psychiatric symptoms is lengthy. These disorders are detailed in textbooks of neuropsychiatry (Moore 2008; Yudofsky & Hales 2010) and online by the National Institute of Neurological Disorders and Stroke (NIDS). The illnesses affect various areas of and processes within the brain. The type of psychiatric symptoms that occur in each disorder correlate with the areas and/or processes that are affected (Filley 2011). The discussion of disorders in this entry is intended as a general overview of the scope of neuropsychiatry, and so is not exhaustive.

Brain Tumors

Psychiatric symptoms frequently accompany brain tumors. Brain tumors occur throughout the life span but are more common in adulthood, particularly in old age. Tumors may arise from the brain tissue itself or may have spread from cancer elsewhere in the body, especially from the breast, lung, or kidney. A tumor causes changes in brain structure and function by direct invasion of brain tissue, by putting pressure on other structures, by provoking edema (fluid buildup) and swelling, or by impinging on the circulation of cerebrospinal fluid and thereby increasing intracranial pressure. Such changes are often accompanied by personality changes, cognitive difficulties, and mood abnormalities such as depression, anxiety, and mania. At times, these changes may precede physical symptoms.

MRI (magnetic resonance imaging) scanning may be used in the evaluation of new-onset psychiatric symptoms to assess the presence or absence of tumor. The primary treatment of the psychiatric symptoms is treatment of the tumor through surgery, radiation, or chemotherapy. Medication may mitigate psychiatric symptoms caused by the tumor or that arise as side effects of treatment.

Degenerative Dementia

Degenerative dementias are characterized by deficits in cognition and by abnormal behavior. The most familiar form is Alzheimer's disease, which is caused by a gradual loss of brain tissue accompanied by deposition of abnormal materials (amyloid plaques and neurofibrillary tangles) within brain cells. The prevalence of Alzheimer's disease increases with age; nearly 50 percent of people above the age of 85 are affected. The onset of symptoms is gradual, with a slow decline in memory, orientation, problem solving, and language skills. At present there is no cure, and the illness eventually leads to death.

Evaluation includes brain imaging with CT (computerized tomography), MRI, and/or SPECT (single photon-emission computed tomography) scanning. As the illness progresses, personality change, anxiety, depression, delusions, and hallucinations are common. Psychiatric medications, if used, need to be prescribed and monitored with care. Treatment effects are often modest, and medications may worsen rather than ameliorate behavioral symptoms. The antipsychotic medications have been associated with a small but real increase in death from medical illnesses in Alzheimer's disease.

The so-called anticholinesterase medications (donepezil, rivastigmine, galantamine) slow the expression of symptoms in mild to moderate dementia but do not affect the actual progression of the illness. Memantine, a medication that blocks a particular receptor for the neurotransmitter glutamate is similarly useful in more advanced illness. Other degenerative dementias include Lewy body dementia and frontotemporal dementia, which occurs earlier in adulthood.

Stroke

Stroke refers to the death of brain tissue owing to problems with blood supply. In hemorrhagic stroke, there is bleeding directly into brain tissue. In ischemic stroke, tissue death occurs because of insufficient oxygen delivery due to poor blood supply. The consequences of stroke depend upon what area or areas of the brain are affected. Marked cognitive deficits occur when several areas of the brain are affected, through multiple small strokes. This condition, known as "vascular dementia," mimics Alzheimer's disease except that the onset is often sudden and stepwise, rather than gradual and continuous. The medications used in Alzheimer's disease are also of some benefit in vascular dementias. Depression following stroke is common, and often responds to antidepressant medication.

Parkinson's Disease

Parkinson's disease is a condition resulting from gradual loss of dopamine producing cells in the brain's basal ganglia, which usually occurs in people over the age of 50. Symptoms are progressive, and include tremor, slowed movement, muscle stiffness, and impaired postural stability. These motor symptoms are frequently accompanied by depression and sleep disturbance. Diagnosis is based largely on history and neurological examination, with brain scanning and other laboratory tests to rule out other causes. Advanced cases are accompanied by Lewy body dementia, which has symptoms that are similar to those of

Alzheimer's disease. Anticholenesterase medications, sometimes used with stimulant medications, are often helpful. Other medications may help with emotional symptoms.

Chronic Pain

Chronic pain is a common cause of suffering and disability. Various types of headaches that are usually episodic can occur on a daily basis. Chronic migraine headache is especially disabling (Lee 2011). Chronic pain elsewhere in the body is a feature of many illnesses, such as joint pain with arthritis, neuropathic pain with diabetes, and the generalized muscle pain of fibromyalgia. Chronic pain also may follow injury, and may cause continuing disability after the physical injury appears otherwise to have healed.

The neurological basis of pain is complex, and is an active subject of neurological research. The nervous system adapts to ongoing pain stimuli, in ways that may actually amplify pain perception (Antonaci et al. 2011). The psychological aspects of chronic pain are also complex. Some individuals are able to find adaptive ways to live productively with the condition, while others lapse into dysfunction and dependency seemingly out of proportion to their condition. Dysphoria, depression, and irritability are common. The fact that pain is a totally subjective phenomenon may make it difficult for family members, coworkers, and professionals to distinguish real from feigned pain, and vice versa, leading to numerous misunderstandings.

Medication treatment of pain brings its own set of complications as medications that are effective in acute pain may become ineffective or counterproductive in chronic pain. Opiate pain relievers are highly addictive and prone to be abused or diverted for sale or misuse by other people.

Care of individuals with chronic pain is best approached from a perspective that takes into account all of these aspects of pain, including the assessment and treatment of the physical aspects of injury or illness, physical therapy if needed, and medication management, along with cognitive-behavioral psychotherapy focused on adaptive responses to ongoing pain, and interpersonal approaches to maintaining and enhancing social role performance.

These diverse needs are best met by an interdisciplinary team of professionals. Neuropsychiatrists may be valuable members of the team, as psychiatry's "bio-psycho-social model" encompasses the varied dimensions and complexity of pain disorders.

Epilepsy

Epilepsy is characterized by various forms of seizures that occur spontaneously and repeatedly. Anticonvulsant medications are used to reduce the intensity and frequency of seizure activity. Co-occurring psychiatric symptoms are common. Various emotional states may occur just prior to, during, or following seizure activity. Depression and anxiety are common between seizures, with rates of suicide reported to be considerably higher in people with epilepsy than in the general population. Delusions and hallucinations may accompany seizures; and in a relatively small number of patients these symptoms persist between seizures, mimicking schizophrenia. Recognition and treatment of psychiatric symptoms may lead to improved social function and quality of life.

Multiple Sclerosis

Multiple sclerosis (MS) is an auto-immune illness of the central nervous system, and is second only to trauma as the leading cause of neurological disability in adults aged 20 to 40. Women are affected twice as often as men. In MS, the body's immune system attacks white matter in the optic nerve, brain, and spinal cord, causing inflammation, scarring, and disruption of nerve cell function. Rather than attacking the entire nervous system, lesions are small and localized. In some cases these lesions occur sporadically over time, scattered though the brain, and may cause little disability. In other cases, the occurrence of multiple lesions is rapid, relentless, and devastating. Acute attacks are treated with steroids to reduce inflammation; the course of the illness may be ameliorated through reduction of auto-immune activity by treatment with natalizumab or glatiramer.

Psychiatric problems in multiple sclerosis include demoralization and adjustment reactions due to the unpredictability of the illness and the havoc it causes in young adults who are trying to achieve their interpersonal and vocational goals. MS appears to predispose individuals to major depression and other affective disturbances. In advanced cases, cognitive function is affected and psychosis may occur. Psychiatric treatment focuses on careful assessment of these varied problems and flexible treatment planning, including medication, psychotherapy, and practical support based on the particular patient's needs.

Huntington's Disease

Huntington's disease is a genetically transmitted progressive and ultimately fatal neurodegenerative disease. The initial symptoms may appear in childhood or in late life, but usually are first evident between the ages of 30 and 50. Impairment in voluntary and involuntary movement is progressive. As the illness progresses, the symptoms of subcortical dementia progressively become more prominent. In contrast to Alzheimer's disease, the initial deficits are not in memory, word finding, or other aspects of cognition but rather in decision making, planning, impulsivity, and loss of inhibitions. Depression is common. Genetic transmission is what is called autosomal dominant, meaning that a child has a

50-50 chance of having the illness if either parent has the disorder. Genetic testing for the genetic defect is available through a simple blood test, or prenatally through amniocentesis. There is no cure and no way to slow the progression of the illness. Psychiatric medications, however, can ameliorate some symptoms.

Psychiatric issues include not only the biologically based symptoms mentioned above but also the myriad of psychological, family, and social consequences of living with a relentlessly fatal disease, or of knowing that one is at a risk of developing the disease in the prime of life. Neuropsychiatrists need to be sensitive to these adjustment factors as well as to biologically based symptoms. Psychotherapy and family counseling may be useful.

Traumatic Brain Injury

Eighty thousand new cases of disability from traumatic brain injury (TBI) occur annually among civilians in the United States. Vehicular accidents are the leading cause. Such injuries due to explosions are common in disabled veterans of the wars in Iraq and Afghanistan. Disability from TBI is frequently permanent. Cognitive problems (memory, attention, difficulty shifting from one task to another, problem solving) and emotional problems (anxiety, depression, and impulsivity) are common. Medications may ameliorate the emotional symptoms but have little effect on cognitive symptoms.

Controversies

Neuropsychiatry, taken in its broad sense, is fraught with the same controversies that permeate psychiatry in general, including disagreement over the definitions of mental illness versus variations in normalcy; the benefits versus the risks of medication; what influence of the pharmaceutical industry should or should not have on medical practice; the appropriateness of pharmacological treatment versus psychotherapy and social planning; and the obligation of society to care for individuals who cannot care for themselves versus preservation of their rights to privacy and autonomy. Taken in the narrow sense, however, there seems to be less controversy over the treatment of behavioral aspects of established neurological diseases, perhaps because the physical nature of the underlying disease process is so clearly evident.

Conclusion

Taken broadly, neuropsychiatry contributes a perspective that complements psychological and social approaches to understanding and treating mental illness. In a narrower sense, neuropsychiatry attempts to alleviate the dysfunction and suffering caused by the emotional, cognitive, and behavioral symptoms that frequently accompany neurological illness.

See also Alzheimer's Disease and Other Dementias; Electroconvulsive Therapy; Genetics and Mental Health; Medical Model of Mental Illness; Memory and Disorders of Memory; Mind and Body Approaches to Mental Health; Neurodiversity; Psychiatry; Rehabilitation Services

Bibliography

American Neuropsychiatric Association. http://www.anpaonline.org/home.php.

Antonaci, Fabio, Giuseppe Nappi, Federica Galli, Gian Camillo Manzoni, Paolo Calabresi, and Alfredo Costa. 2011. "Migraine and Psychiatric Comorbidity: A Review of Clinical Findings." *Journal of Headache Pain* 12: 115–125.

Filley, Christopher M. 2011. *Neurobehavioral Anatomy* (3rd ed.). Boulder: University Press of Colorado.

Lee, Yvonne C., Nicholas J. Nassikas, and Daniel J. Clauw. 2011. "The Role of the Central Nervous System in the Generation and Maintenance of Chronic Pain in Rheumatoid Arthritis, Osteoarthritis and Fibromyalgia." *Arthritis Research & Therapy* 13(2): 211.

Lyketos, Constantine G., Peter V. Rabins, John R. Lipsey, and Phillip R. Slavney, eds. 2008. *Psychiatric Aspects of Neurological Diseases, Practical Approaches to Patient Care*. New York: Oxford University Press.

Moore, David P. 2008. *Textbook of Clinical Neuropsychiatry* (2nd ed.). New York: Oxford University Press.

National Institute of Neurological Disorders and Stroke. http://www.ninds.nih.gov/index.htm.

Wilson, William H. 2012. "Neuropsychiatric Perspectives for Community Mental Health Theory and Practice." In Jessica Rosenberg and Samuel Rosenberg, eds., *Community Mental Health: New Directions in Policy and Practice* (2nd ed., pp. 238–252). New York: Routledge.

Yudofsky, Stuart C., and Robert E. Hales. 2010. *Essentials of Neuropsychiatry and Behavioral Neurosciences* (2nd ed.). Washington, DC: American Psychiatric Publishing.

Nutritional Therapies

Gretchen Reevy

Nutritional therapies involve using dietary regimens or supplements to treat various conditions, including mental health disorders. Dietary supplements may include vitamins, fish oils, minerals, amino acids, herbs, or other botanicals. Dietary regimens may include functional foods, such as chocolate, cranberries, soy, or nuts, for their specific properties or functions. Whole-diet therapy may involve restricting or eliminating certain foods (e.g., saturated fats, carbohydrates, gluten, sugar, caffeine) or increasing intake of other foods (e.g., protein). Nutritional therapies may be employed instead of, or in addition to, standard pharmaceutical treatments. Mental health disorders that have been treated nutritionally include major depressive disorder (MDD), bipolar disorder, obsessive-compulsive disorder (OCD), anxiety disorders, insomnia, fatigue, and schizophrenia. Nutritional therapies have also been used to treat conditions such as autistic spectrum disorders and attention deficit hyperactivity disorder (ADHD) and to improve cognitive function (e.g., memory).

Background

In 1968, renowned chemist Linus Pauling published a controversial article about orthomolecular psychiatry, a biochemical model that explored nutritional therapies for mental diseases (Hoffer 2008). Pauling's theories led to the popular megavitamin therapies of the 1970s. While orthomolecular psychiatry was dismissed by mainstream mental health professional organizations (e.g., American Psychiatric Association), the theory sparked interest and further exploration into nutritional therapies for mental health disorders. Some of these therapies include supplemental vitamins or glycine for schizophrenia, kava kava (*Piper methysticum*) for anxiety, valerian (an herb) and melatonin (a pineal hormone) for insomnia, ginseng and ephedra for fatigue, and ginkgo biloba to improve memory (Elkins et al. 2005).

The neurotransmitters (chemical messengers in the brain) serotonin, dopamine, noradrenaline, and gamma-aminobutyric acid have been implicated in depression, bipolar disorder, and schizophrenia. Some individuals with mood disorders (e.g., depression, bipolar disorder) have been shown to have deficiencies of some of these neurotransmitters (Lakhan & Vieira 2008). Chemicals or substances that the body converts into other substances (e.g., neurotransmitters) are known as *precursors*. The amino acid tryptophan is a precursor to the neurotransmitter serotonin. Tryptophan is found naturally in foods such as milk and turkey. Tyrosine (and sometimes its precursor, phenylalanine) is converted into dopamine and noradrenaline. Dietary supplements containing tyrosine and phenylalanine increase arousal and alertness. Methionine is a precursor of S-adenosylmethionine (SAMe), which facilitates the production of neurotransmitters in the brain (Lakhan & Vieira 2008). Utilizing dietary supplements with the goal of increasing neurotransmitter production is known as *neurotransmitter precursor therapy*. For some neurotransmitters, use of dietary supplements may influence neurotransmitter synthesis, affecting mood and behavior (Young 1996).

Applications

Some studies have found that omega-3 fatty acids, which naturally occur in fish, may alleviate symptoms of MDD, bipolar disorder, and schizophrenia (Freeman et al. 2006). Omega-3 fatty acids can cause some side effects (e.g., gastrointestinal distress) and may not be suitable for individuals taking anti-blood-clotting medications.

Individuals with bipolar disorder or depression have been found to have deficiencies in vitamins C and B (folate), magnesium, taurine, and omega-3 fatty acids

(Lakhan & Vieira 2008). Increasing tryptophan intake has been suggested as a means to treat symptoms of depression and OCD (Lakhan & Vieira 2008).

St. John's wort (*Hypericum perforatum*) is an herb that has been much studied for the treatment of depression. It may be useful in the treatment of mild to moderate depression but not of severe depression, though some recent studies have indicated that it is no better than placebo even for mild depression (Mayo Clinic 2011). St. John's wort has also been used to treat fatigue and increase energy. St. John's wort has been associated with exacerbation of psychosis in individuals with schizophrenia and onset of manic episodes in individuals with bipolar disorder. Symptoms of mania may include abnormally high levels of excitement and energy, racing thoughts, and inappropriate or impulsive behavior (Lal & Iskandar 2000). When combining St. John's wort (or other substances that increase serotonin) with standard antidepressant medications (e.g., selective serotonin reuptake inhibitors), there is a risk of causing a potentially severe reaction known as *serotonin syndrome* (Natural Standard Research Collaboration 2009). Several herbs and dietary supplements have been found to interfere or interact with prescription medications, including St. John's wort, garlic, glucosamine, ginseng, saw palmetto, soy, and yohimbe (National Center for Complementary and Alternative Medicine 2007).

Food allergies and food sensitivities have been implicated in emotional, behavioral, and developmental disorders including learning disabilities, ADHD, depression, and autism. Some diets used to treat these conditions include eliminating sugar, caffeine, processed foods, food additives, food colorings, or fruits and vegetables. A gluten-free, casein-free (GFCF) diet—sometimes used to treat individuals with autism—eliminates all dairy products (which contain casein) and wheat products that contain gluten. Studies of the effectiveness of nutritional therapies show mixed results (Shaw 2008).

Cautions

Claims about natural treatments or miracle cures for certain conditions may be appealing to people who are seeking relief or are disenchanted with the mainstream medical establishment. Some people try nutritional interventions because they do not like the side effects associated with pharmaceutical medications. Others may use nutritional interventions because they are perceived as more natural, because they may cost less than pharmaceutical medications, or because of lack of access to health care services. There is considerable controversy about the risks and benefits of nutritional therapies. The U.S. Food and Drug Administration (FDA) classifies herbs (such as St. John's wort) as dietary supplements. FDA requirements for testing dietary supplements differ from those of pharmaceutical drugs. Dietary supplements can be sold without requiring studies on dosage, safety, or effectiveness. Possible risks of utilizing nutritional therapies include difficulty regulating dosage, lack of supervision by a health care professional, side effects, or interaction with other medications. In an attempt to treat symptoms, an individual may not be pursuing treatment for the correct diagnosis or may neglect to consider using established treatments. While more medical and mental health practitioners are being trained in integrative approaches—combining standard medical and pharmaceutical treatment with complementary and alternative medicine (CAM)—not all health practitioners are familiar with CAM. This may make it difficult to recommend effective dosages of nutritional supplements.

It may be difficult to avoid dangerous drug interactions when combining CAM (including nutritional supplements) with standard pharmaceutical treatments.

See also Mind and Body Approaches to Mental Health; Popular Remedies and Quackery; Self-Help

Bibliography

Elkins, G., J. Marcus, M. H. Rajab, and S. Durgam. 2005. "Complementary and Alternative Therapy Use by Psychotherapy Clients." *Psychotherapy: Theory, Research, Practice, Training* 42: 232–235.

Freeman, M. P., J. R. Hibbeln, K. L. Wisner, J. M. Davis, D. Mischoulon, M. Peet, P. E. Keck Jr., L. B. Maranqell, A. J. Richardson, J. Lake, and A. L. Stoll. 2006. "Omega-3 Fatty Acids: Evidence Basis for Treatment and Future Research in Psychiatry." *Journal of Clinical Psychiatry* 67: 1954–1967.

Hoffer, L. J. 2008. "Vitamin Therapy in Schizophrenia." *Israel Journal of Psychiatry and Related Sciences* 45: 3–10.

Lakhan, S. E., and K. F. Vieira. 2008. "Nutritional Therapies for Mental Disorders." *Nutritional Journal* 7(2): doi:10.1186/1475-2891-7-2.

Lal, S., and H. Iskandar. 2000. "St. John's Wort and Schizophrenia." *Canadian Medical Association Journal* 163: 262–263.

Lesser, Michael. 2002. *The Brain Chemistry Diet*. New York: G. P. Putnam's.

Mayo Clinic. 2011. St. John's Wort (*Hypericum perforatum* L.). Retrieved from http://www.mayoclinic.com/health/st-johns-wort/NS_patient-stjohnswort.

National Center for Complementary and Alternative Medicine. 2007. Biologically Based Practices: An Overview. *NCCAM Backgrounder*. Retrieved from http://nccam.nih.gov/health/whatiscam/overview.htm.

Natural Standard Research Collaboration. 2009. St. John's Wort (*Hypericum perforatum* L.). Retrieved from http://www.nlm.nih.gov/medlineplus/druginfo/natural/patient-stjohnswort.html.

Pauling, L. 1968. "Orthomolecular Psychiatry: Varying the Concentrations of Substances Normally Present in the Human Body May Control Mental Disease." *Science* 160: 265–271.

Shaw, S. R. 2008. "Complementary and Alternative Therapies: An Evidence-Based Framework." *NASP Communiqué* 37(3): 1, 27–30.

Young, S. N. 1996. "Behavioral Effects of Dietary Neurotransmitter Precursors: Basic and Clinical Aspects." *Neuroscience and Biobehavioral Reviews* 20: 313–323.

O

Obsessive-Compulsive Disorder

Rudy Nydegger

Obsessive-compulsive disorder (OCD) is a frequently discussed topic that often finds its way into jokes and stories, and is believed to affect so many people that each of us probably knows someone who lives with it. Persons with OCD typically experience persistent, upsetting thoughts that produce anxiety as well as rituals they use to control their anxiety, but it is these very rituals and thoughts that end up controlling a significant part of these persons' lives. Obsessions are uncontrollable, unwanted thoughts that make a person feel uncomfortable but that "force" the person to do something to keep away the thoughts and the resultant anxiety. Maintaining a sense of control is the most significant issue for all anxiety disorders, with sufferers frequently feeling as though they are on the verge of losing control and being overwhelmed by anxiety and/or the things they fear. As a result, they often have an all-consuming need to control things related to their anxiety, making it difficult for them to function.

Understanding OCD

In order to understand the nature of OCD, one can break it down into three components. People with the disorder cannot control their thoughts or the resulting anxiety (the obsessive part), so they engage in ritualistic behaviors to give them a sense of managing (the controlling part) the repetitive thoughts and anxiety (the compulsive part). Compulsions can include rituals such as checking, counting, performing specific tasks in a specific order, and touching things; but even if these compulsive behaviors temporarily relieve the feelings of anxiety, those feelings will always return. Such rituals are similar to strong superstitions: one can be aware of the irrational nature of the acts, but *not* performing them can produce a fear of something terrible occurring, so they are performed anyway.

Many people have obsessions, or even exhibit compulsive behavior patterns, but that does not always mean that they have OCD. To qualify for an OCD diagnosis, behavioral patterns have to exist over a long period of time (e.g., months or years) and intrude into the person's daily life—someone with OCD will have good and bad days, but his or her symptoms are always present. Obsessions and compulsions can also accompany other psychological disorders, for example, obsessive-compulsive personality disorder (OCPD). A person with OCPD must learn to live with obsessions and compulsions as physical and mental habits, though these habits may not be as intrusive as those in the case of OCD. Further, OCPD lacks an anxiety component. Persons with OCPD will become annoyed at experiencing obsessions, but will not necessarily experience feelings of anxiety, even if they are prevented from fulfilling their compulsions. Obsessions and/or compulsions exist in other anxiety disorders as well, such as panic disorder or generalized anxiety disorder (GAD), but in those cases, too, the obsessions/compulsions are not as deeply ingrained or as intrusive as in the case of OCD. Even patients with eating disorders and body dysmorphic disorder (severe discomfort with one's body) will present obsessive and, perhaps, compulsive features. To qualify for an OCD diagnose, however, the symptoms cannot be a component of another disorder.

Most adults with OCD know that their ideas and behaviors are senseless; they say that they feel "crazy" and try to hide their behaviors from others, often very creatively. However, some adult patients and most children with OCD feel that their behavior is perfectly reasonable and understandable; these patients are diagnosed with "OCD with poor insight." OCD affects approximately 2.2 million American adults, many of whom live with comorbid conditions (that is, they have more than one disorder at the same time), which further complicate their problems. Patients with OCD will also frequently suffer from depression, other anxiety disorders, or other psychological problems, and some sufferers also self-medicate using alcohol or drugs—which obviously creates additional problems. The rates of OCD in men and women are similar (unlike most other anxiety disorders,

---

"Obsessive-compulsive disorder rose to greater public attention in the 1990s, becoming one of the dominant forms of mental distress. A cavalcade of books on OCD have appeared in the past ten years, along with more books on antidepressants like Prozac and their use with OCD. More and more characters in television shows and film are people with OCD. In addition, anorexia, bulimia, and other obsessive and compulsive behaviors, like addiction, stalking, compulsive shopping, compulsive eating (or noneating) are plaguing and at the same time defining us. These are the ... darker sides of obsession—the rooted-in-the-blood, bone, and mind forms of the fascination our culture has for the obsessive.

"But was it always this way? ... It is easy to say that people have always been obsessed or that the desire to find something and focus on it is a universal feature of human life. You couldn't build the pyramids or come up with *The Iliad* unless someone were obsessed enough to do so. True enough, but there is a moment in the Western world [beginning in the middle of the 18th century in Europe] when obsession becomes itself something so problematic that people begin to write about it, study it, turn it into a medical problem, and then try to cure it."

—Lennard J. Davis

Source: Lennard J. Davis, *Obsession: A History* (University of Chicago Press, 2008), 7–8.

where women tend to predominate), and OCD may emerge in childhood, adolescence, or young adulthood. Some evidence points to a genetic link in this disorder, but even if one accepts the linkage, genetics alone cannot not explain the full range of OCD symptoms. OCD can be relatively mild to quite severe, and effective treatments usually include both medication and psychotherapy; one without the other is not likely to be as successful (National Institute of Mental Health [NIMH] 2009).

Obsessions and Compulsions

OCD exists within all cultures and has been described in a variety of ways throughout history. It also appears that the basic types of obsessions and compulsions are fairly consistent across cultures (Rasmussen & Eisen 1991). The most common types of obsessions are:

1. Fear of contamination (dirt and germs)
2. Pathological doubt
3. Need for symmetry
4. Aggressive obsessions (NIMH 2009)
5. Other obsessions
   a. Sexual
   b. Hoarding or collecting
   c. Religious
   d. Need to know something or remember things
   e. Fear of saying certain things
   f. Fear of not saying the right thing
   g. Intrusive (but neutral) images
   h. Intrusive nonsense sounds, words, or music
   i. Somatic

The most common types of compulsions are:

1. Checking
2. Washing
3. Symmetry
4. Need to ask or confess
5. Counting (First & Tasman 2004)
   a. Repeating rituals
   b. Ordering or arranging

   c. Mental rituals other than counting or checking

   d. Touching certain things

   e. Measures to prevent causing harm to self, others, or things

Among children most symptoms are similar to those of adults, although washing compulsions followed by repeating rituals are the most common (Swedo, Rapoport, Leonard, Lenane, & Cheslow 1989). Most people with OCD develop multiple obsessions and compulsions over time, with a particular fear or concern dominating at any given time, and the presence of obsessions without compulsions or vice versa is unusual (First & Tasman 2004).

Many believe that OCD and Tourette's syndrome (a disorder involving involuntary tics and vocalizations) frequently exist comorbidly (i.e., at the same time) or with other tic disorders, but the relationship is not clear. Some researchers report a 5 to 10 percent comorbidity rate with OCD and Tourette's, and a 20 percent rate with other tics (Leonard et al. 1992). In addition, approximately 30 to 40 percent of those who already have Tourette's have a high probability of developing OCD. In patients with Tourette's or tics, there is a greater probability of developing childhood-onset OCD, as well as OCD symptoms of greater severity (Robertson, Trimble, & Lees 1988).

Some people confuse impulse control disorders (ICDs) with OCD, since persons with ICDs similarly obsess over what they do or want to do and may seem compulsive in terms of their inability to control the behavior. However, if someone exhibits kleptomania, trichotillomania (hair pulling), pathological gambling, sexual compulsions, or other such disorders, they do not necessarily have OCD. People with impulse control disorders actively enjoy, or at least desire to perform, the behavior in question; in contrast, those with OCD do not necessarily *want* to perform the behaviors they do but rather do so in order to decrease anxiety. Fear and anxiety drive the compulsions behind OCD, which is not the case with ICDs.

Prevalence and Possible Causes

Until the mid-1980s, OCD was considered a relatively rare disorder, but at that time a study known as the Epidemiologic Catchment Area Study found OCD to be the fourth most common mental disorder, with a lifetime prevalence rate of 2.5 percent (meaning that 2.5% of the population can be expected to have OCD at some point in their lifetime; Myers et al. 1984). The reported age of onset is usually during late adolescence; however, those who suffer from OCD will often report memories of childhood difficulties.

Swedo, Rapoport, Leonard, Lenane, and Cheslow (1989) have described a type of OCD that begins before puberty and is characterized by an episodic course of the illness with intense exacerbations (i.e., intermittent but severe occurrences). This has been linked with a certain type of streptococcal infection, leading to the subtype designation "pediatric autoimmune neuropsychiatric disorders associated with streptococcal infections" (PANDAS). In more typical forms of OCD, the course tends to be characterized by waxing and waning ("ups and downs") depending upon a number of factors (Rasmussen & Eisen 1991).

Issues of etiology (causal factors) are complex and sometimes confusing in OCD, and some studies have found structural and functional abnormalities in the brains of OCD patients (Saxena et al. 1998). Other neurobiological studies suggest that there is an abnormality in the serotonin system (i.e., specific neurotransmitters; Pigott 1996). Notable here is that all of the antidepressants that effectively treat OCD in fact affect serotonin levels (Griest et al. 1998). However, although the evidence of a role for the serotonin system in OCD is compelling, the exact nature of that role is unclear. In some forms of OCD, especially OCD with Tourette's, the balance of serotonin and dopamine (another neurotransmitter) may be important; in such cases, dopamine antagonists (or blockers) may work to improve therapeutic response (First & Tasman 2004).

As noted, there is some support for a genetic aspect of OCD. In identical twins, for example, a 63 percent concordance rate has been recorded; however, because the concordance is not 100 percent, the results mean that environmental factors must be at work as well (Rasmussen & Tsuang 1986). Pauls, Alsobrook, Goodman, Rasmussen, and Leckman (1995) studied first-degree relatives of OCD patients, and found that 10.3 percent of such relatives had OCD, with another 7.9 percent exhibiting what is termed subthreshold OCD (OCD-like behaviors that do not qualify for the diagnosis). The same researchers also reported higher relative rates of OCD in families of persons with Tourette's. Conversely, Leonard and colleagues (1992) found higher relative rates of Tourette's in families of persons with OCD. Thus although there is ample evidence pointing to a role for genetics in OCD (and, to a lesser extent, in linkages with Tourette's), it nevertheless seems unlikely that this disorder is primarily a genetic disease (Pauls 1999).

Current Status and Treatment Options

A variety of psychological factors have been proposed for the understanding and treatment of OCD. In recent years, most of the attention has focused on learning approaches, with the cognitive and behavioral perspectives predominating. Baer and Minichiello (1990), for example, have presented a model for OCD that involves the negative reinforcement of compulsions. This means that, to the extent that compulsions can reduce anxiety (short of confronting the feared stimulus), it is those compulsions that are continually being reinforced at the expense of the individual's ability to address his or her anxiety more directly. Other models are being developed that seek to integrate biological (including genetic) factors with environmental, psychosocial, and even evolutionary elements (Cohen & Galykner 1997).

OCD is one of the most challenging anxiety disorders to treat because of its complexity and because of the resistance to treatment that many patients exhibit—they often prefer to be left alone in their "comfort zone," getting by from day to day. However, a number of effective treatment options are available, often involving both medication and a behavioral component. Children and older adults seem to do very well with behavioral treatments and tolerate most of the medications, although at somewhat lower doses than adults. The goals of treatment for OCD patients are to reduce the frequency and intensity of symptoms as much as possible and to reduce or eliminate the amount of interference that the symptoms create in the person's life. Typically, most patients do not experience a complete remission but can expect significant improvement. Since OCD frequently requires longer episodes of treatment, it is frequently undertreated because insurance carriers refuse to pay for the longer courses of treatment. This can be regarded as both short-sighted and uneconomical. A person with OCD who is not treated will continue to develop symptoms that can create difficulties for the person on a daily basis and lead to continued interference in his or her life and overall health. Such conditions frequently result in higher utilization rates of other health care services. Thus appropriate, early, and thorough treatment is generally the best and most cost-effective option.

See also Genetics and Mental Health; Impulse Control Disorders

Bibliography

American Psychiatric Association. 2000. *Diagnostic and Statistical Manual of Mental Disorders* (4th ed., text rev.). Washington, DC: American Psychiatric Publishing.

Baer, L., and W. E. Minichiello. 1990. "Behavior Therapy for Obsessive-Compulsive Disorder." In M. A. Jenike, L. Baer, and W. E. Minichiello, eds., *Obsessive-Compulsive Disorders: Theory and Management* (pp. 203–232). St. Louis, MO: Year Book Medical.

Bell, Jeff. 2007. *Rewind, Replay, Repeat: A Memoir of Obsessive-Compulsive Disorder.* Center City, MN: Hazelden.

Cohen, I. J., and I. Galykner. 1997. "Towards an Integration of Psychological and Biological Models of Obsessive-Compulsive Disorder: Phylogenetic Considerations." *CNS Spectrums* 2(10): 26–44.

Eisen, J. L., D. A. Beer, M. T. Pato, T. A. Venditto, and S. A. Rasmussen. 1997. "Obsessive-Compulsive Disorder in Schizophrenia and Schizoaffective Disorders." *American Journal of Psychiatry* 154: 271–273.

First, M. B., and A. Tasman. 2004. "Anxiety Disorders: Social and Specific Phobias." In M. B. First and A. Tasman, eds., *DSM-IV-TR Mental Disorders: Diagnosis, Etiology, and Treatment* (pp. 867–901). Chichester, England: Wiley.

Griest, J. H., J. W. Jefferson, K. A. Koback, D. J. Katzelnick, and R. C. Serlin. 1998. "Efficacy and Tolerability of Serotonin Transport Inhibitors in Obsessive-Compulsive Disorder." *Archives of General Psychiatry* 52: 53–60.

International OCD Foundation. http://www.ocfoundation.org/index.aspx.

Kant, Jared D., with Martin F. Franklin and Linda Wasmer Andrews. 2008. *The Thought That Counts: One Teenager's Experience with Obsessive-Compulsive Disorder.* New York: Oxford University Press.

Leonard, H. I., M. C. Lenane, S. E. Swedo, D. C. Rettew, E. S. Gershon, and J. L. Rapoport. 1992. "Tics and Tourette's Disorder: A 2- to 7-Year Follow-Up of 54 Obsessive-Compulsive Children." *American Journal of Psychiatry* 149: 1233–1251.

Moyer, M. W. 2011. "A New Look at Obsessive-Compulsive Disorder." *Scientific American Mind*, May.

Myers, J. K., M. M. Weissman, G. L. Tischler, C. E. Holzer III, P. J. Lear, J. Orvaschel, J. C. Anthony, J. H. Boyd Jr., J. D. Burke, M. Kramer, and R. Stoltzman. 1984. "Six-Month Prevalence of Psychiatric Disorders in Three Communities, 1980 to 1982." *Archives of General Psychiatry* 41: 959–967.

National Institute of Mental Health. 2009. *Anxiety Disorders*. Washington, DC: National Institute of Mental Health.

Nestadt, G., J. Samuels, M. Riddle, O. J. Bienvenu III, K.-Y. Liang, M. LaBuda, J. Walkup, M. Grados, and R. Hoen-Saric. 2000. "A Family Study of Obsessive-Compulsive Disorder." *Archives of General Psychiatry* 57: 358–363.

Obsessive Compulsive Disorder. Mayo Clinic. Retrieved from http://www.mayoclinic .com/health/obsessive-compulsive-disorder/DS00189.

Pauls, D. L. 1999. "Phenotypic Variability in Obsessive-Compulsive Disorder and Its Relationship to Familial Risk." *CNS Spectrums* 4(6): 32–48.

Pauls, D. L., J. P. Alsobrook, W. Goodman, S. Rasmussen, and J. F. Leckman. 1995. "A Family Study of Obsessive-Compulsive Disorder." *American Journal of Psychiatry* 152: 76–84.

Pauls, D. L., K. E. Towbin, J. F. Leckman, G. E. P. Zahner, and D. J. Cohen. 1986. "Gilles De La Tourette's Syndrome and Obsessive-Compulsive Disorder: Evidence Supporting a Genetic Relationship." *Archives of General Psychiatry* 43: 1180–1182.

Pigott, T. A. 1996. "OCD: Where the Serotonin Selective Story Begins." *Journal of Clinical Psychiatry* 57(Suppl. 6): 11–20.

Rasmussen, S. A., and J. L. Eisen. 1991. "Phenomenology of Obsessive-Compulsive Disorder." In J. Insel and S. Rasmussen, eds., *Psychology of Obsessive-Compulsive Disorder* (pp. 743–758). New York: Springer-Verlag.

Rasmussen, S. A., and M. T. Tsuang. 1986. "Clinical Characterstics and Family History in DSM-III Obsessive-Compulsive Disorder." *American Journal of Psychiatry* 1943: 317–382.

Robertson, M. M., M. R. Trimble, and A. J. Lees. 1988. "The Psychopathology of the Gilles De La Tourette's Syndrome: A Phenomenological Analysis." *British Journal of Psychology* 152: 283–290.

Saxena, L., A. L. Brody, J. M. Schwartz, and L. R. Baxter. 1998. "Neuroimaging and Front-Subcortical Circuitry in Obsessive-Compulsive Disorder." *British Journal of Psychiatry* 173(Suppl. 35): 26–37.

Swedo, S. E., J. L. Rapoport, J. Leonard, M. Lenane, and D. Cheslow. 1989. "Obsessive-Compulsive Disorder in Children and Adolescents: Clinical Phenomenology of 70 Consecutive Cases." *Archives of General Psychiatry* 46: 335–341.

P

Panic Disorder

Rudy Nydegger

One of the most challenging and well-known types of anxiety disorders is panic disorder (PD). People who suffer from panic attacks experience severe and frightening symptoms such as pounding heart, trouble breathing, dizziness, chest pains, and nausea, and usually report being in poorer physical health than the general population (Amir et al. 2009). Characteristics of PD include being frightened by one's own physical symptoms and feeling as if one is going to die or go crazy. Panic attacks are the product of catastrophically misinterpreting the autonomic arousal sensations that occur in the context of nonpathological anxiety, as well as the overreacting to other sources of arousal such as physical illness, exercise, and the ingestion of certain substances (Markowitz et al. 1989). Experiencing an acute anxiety attack during or in association with a real, actual physical threat is considered a fear reaction, and it is not the same as having a panic attack; a true panic attack occurs in the absence of any real danger (Clark 1986). Patients are rarely able to reliably predict when a panic attack will occur, although there are occasions when an attack may be expected and does occur. A panic attack can strike at any time, even during sleep, and usually lasts 15 to 30 minutes. The symptoms will peak at about 10 minutes, although some of the residual symptoms may last longer. This unpredictability of an attack is quite significant to patients, since the fear of the having another attack can also be disabling.

General Description

Anyone can experience a panic attack under the right circumstances, but to be diagnosed with panic disorder one must have experienced more than the occasional panic attack and must meet specific diagnostic criteria, although most people who experience a panic attack will never go on to develop PD. One study found that the one-year prevalence rate for any type of panic attack (either unexpected or situational) was about 28 percent, which means that over one-quarter of the population will experience an attack during a given year; the majority, however, will never develop panic disorder (Norton 2009).

PD occurs in 6 million Americans annually, affecting women about twice as frequently as men, although the clinical features, such as number and severity of symptoms, are much the same across the sexes (Brown & Deagle 1992). PD often

"Panic has always been considered a symptom of larger psychiatric illnesses. Yet, only recently has it come to be considered a disorder of its own. The whole panic story is interesting as an example of how symptoms wax and wane in the history of psychiatry, treated as one among many at one point, and the focus of . . . [new research] . . . at the next. There may be good scientific reasons for the fluctuation historical courses of symptoms, yet commerce plays a role as well, for if industry needs a symptom for a compound [or drug] it has developed, one may be sure that entities such as panic will stand in good service."

—Edward Shorter

Source: Edward Shorter, *A Historical Dictionary of Psychiatry* (New York: Oxford University Press, 2005), 203.

appears in late adolescence or young adulthood, and a genetic connection suggests that relatives of PD patients will be more likely to develop this disorder than someone else in the population who is not related to the patient. This does not mean, however, that if someone in your family has been diagnosed with panic disorder, you will develop it; however, you might be slightly more at risk than someone who is unrelated to the patient.

Some of the current models of panic disorder focus on the "fear of anxiety" construct, suggesting that there is a learned component to the disorder (Oei, Wanstall, & Evans 1990). In the expectancy model of fear, panic attacks result from having the predisposition to catastrophically misinterpret and to respond with fear to benign sensations of arousal and from possessing a learned fear of anxiety, which is continually maintained by experiencing panic episodes (First & Tasman 2004). Some believe that this "vicious cycle" first begins with anything that causes arousal and then leads to a misinterpretation of emerging physical symptoms; then, anxiety emerges and accelerates to the point of panic; and, finally, the person learns to fear the original cause of arousal as well as any other situations where similar arousal might occur (Oei, Wanstall, & Evans 1990).

Panic disorder is diagnosed in about 10 percent of patients seen at mental health clinics and between 10 and 60 percent seen in various medical specialty clinics (e.g., cardiology and pulmonology) (Reiss & McNally 1985). The National Comorbidity Study found a lifetime prevalence rate of PD in the general population of 3.5 percent (Rouillon 1997), although most other studies found lifetime prevalence rates in the range of 1 to 2 percent. Generally, however, the prevalence rates are fairly consistent around the world (Eaton, Kessler, Wittchen, Magee 1994). The age of onset of PD is distributed bimodally—that is, typical onset occurs in the age groups 15–19 years and 25–30 years (Weissman et al. 1997). To complicate the clinical picture, many people with PD suffer from agoraphobia, or the fear of being in unfamiliar or "unsafe" situations. From the sparse data collected, it appears that agoraphobia affects about 0.6 percent of older adults in any 12-month period and usually in the 55–65 age group, although most patients report that it begins earlier. PD is rarely found in ages over 65, and, as in younger sample populations, it affects twice as many older women as older men. Married people are less likely to develop agoraphobia, but the loss of a spouse and the onset of other health and/or psychological problems may precipitate PD (Ballenger & Fryer 1996).

The frequency of attacks varies considerably among individuals with panic disorder, and those who experience repeated panic attacks can become disabled by restricting their activities and avoiding situations for fear of a having a panic attack. This pattern can continue, leading to the development of agoraphobia; in clinical samples, PD with agoraphobia is more common than PD without it. If panic disorder is diagnosed early, before agoraphobia develops, it is one of the most treatable of the anxiety disorders; however, "doctor shopping" and other delaying actions by the PD sufferer often prevent timely and appropriate treatment. In general, treatment usually involves medications in conjunction with psychotherapy in order to address the physical as well as cognitive and behavioral symptoms of PD. One complicating factor is that PD is frequently comorbid (i.e., co-occurs) with conditions such as depression, drug abuse, and alcoholism (McCabe et al. 2006). PD with or without agoraphobia is also associated with a poor overall quality of life as well as with impaired occupational, scholastic, and social functioning. Without treatment, PD and agoraphobia may wax and wane, but both appear to be chronic conditions (Roemer, Erisman, & Orsillo 2009).

Diagnostic Criteria

A diagnosis of PD will specify whether it is with or without agoraphobia, otherwise the criteria are exactly the same. Someone with PD will have at least four of the following symptoms:

1. Rapid heart beat
2. Sweating
3. Shortness of breath
4. Choking feeling or of being smothered
5. Dizziness
6. Nausea
7. Feelings of unreality
8. Numbness
9. Hot flashes or chills
10. Chest pain

11. Fear of dying
12. Fear of going insane

The diagnostic criteria for PD with agoraphobia are:

1. Both (a) and (b):
   a. Recurrent and unexpected panic attacks
   b. At least one of the attacks has been followed by one month or more of:
      i. Persistent concern about having another attack
      ii. Worry about the implications of the attack or its consequences (e.g., losing control, having a heart attack, going crazy)
2. Presence of agoraphobia
3. Panic attacks are not a result of the direct physical effects of a substance (e.g., a drug of abuse or medication) or a general medical condition
4. Panic attacks are not better accounted for by another mental disorder, including other anxiety disorders (American Psychiatric Association 2000)

The diagnostic criteria for agoraphobia are:

1. The individual feels anxiety about being in places or situations from which escape might be difficult or embarrassing, or where help may not be available during a panic attack; and usually fears different clusters of situations and venturing into them, with the number increasing over time.
2. Situations are avoided or endured with marked distress and worry about having a panic attack or similar symptoms. Confronting difficult situations is usually aided by the presence of a companion.
3. Anxiety or avoidance is not better accounted for by another mental disorder (American Psychiatric Association 2000).

One requirement for PD is that unexpected panic attacks occur without any obvious causal factor, however, not all attacks are unexpected (Oei, Wanstall, & Evans 1990). Interestingly, some patients do not experience a fearful response as a result of a panic attack. About 30 percent of panic attacks occur without the fear of dying or going crazy, and they do not differ in terms of age, age of onset, or frequency from those who experience attacks with feelings of fear. Due to the lack of fear, the attacks are rarely associated with shortness of breath, trembling, smothering, and depersonalization, and patients are less likely to experience anticipatory anxiety or be treated with medication, although frequency of attacks leads to the same rate of diagnosis and functional disability. Further, these patients are less likely to develop agoraphobia or other disorders such as major depression. Depending upon how a patient reports their symptoms, the absence of a fear response during panic attacks may lead to the mistaken assumption that the PD is less severe (Keller et al. 1991).

Risk factors for PD include gender, since women are twice as susceptible to developing PD, and marital status, a significant risk factor since the highest lifetime prevalence rates are reported for widowed, separated, or divorced people. No consistent findings relate PD to educational level, and some have found a relationship between smoking and PD, but the causal link is unclear. Sometimes an understandable link between pulmonary disease and PD is reported, since breathing problems can trigger panic attacks.

The most common of comorbid anxiety disorders (not including agoraphobia, as it is an element of the diagnosis) are: social anxiety disorder (social phobia), generalized anxiety disorder, obsessive-compulsive disorder, and posttraumatic stress disorder. Between 30 and 60 percent of patients with PD will also suffer from a depressive disorder, and about 36 percent will suffer from substance abuse, often using alcohol or drugs to self-medicate their fear and anxiety—although recent evidence suggests that substance abuse usually begins prior to the development of panic disorder. Some epidemiology studies demonstrate that major depressive disorder occurs in up to 56 percent of patients with PD at some point in their life, and, in approximately two-thirds of these cases, the symptoms of depression develop along with or secondary to PD. However, since major depression usually precedes the PD, it cannot be assumed that the depression is always a reaction to the PD. Medical conditions that are likely to be comorbid with PD include cardiac, gastrointestinal, respiratory, and neurological diseases (Chen et al. 2009).

Treatment Issues

Experiencing a panic attack is terrifying and is a primary reason that people seek emergency department consultations (Psychiatry.HealthSE 2005). Frequent emergency room visits are one of the reasons why PD sufferers generate high medical expenses, coupled with costly tests, to rule out other medical problems (Weissman 1991). PD is also a leading cause for people seeking mental health services, surpassing both schizophrenia and mood disorders (Katerndahl & Realini 1995). Typically, people do not begin their search for help by contacting mental health professionals, but rather are referred by a physician who has no medical explanation for the patient's symptoms (Boyd 1986).

Seasonal and meteorological changes affect people with PD similarly to patients with seasonal affective disorder (SAD). The frequency of panic attacks varies by month, usually increasing in August and December; although, if a patient peaks in August, they typically will not increase in December and vice versa. Panic attacks are also more likely to occur during cloudy weather, during hot or cold extremes, and when it is humid (Greenberg et al. 1999).

Although PD is a highly treatable condition, especially if diagnosed early, it is not often recognized and diagnosed accurately in the primary care setting, which can lead to unnecessary and costly diagnostic procedures, as well as inappropriate referrals to cardiologists. In one study, medical specialists were given a survey to determine their knowledge of panic attacks and the availability of effective treatments. The results are as listed:

- 51 percent answered the knowledge-based questions correctly.
- Most knew the definition of a panic attack but little about clinical features or treatment.
- 97.4 percent believed medication effectively relieves panic symptoms.
- Only 32.5 percent knew that cognitive-behavioral therapy (CBT) is a first-line treatment for panic disorder.
- Only 6 percent knew how to implement CBT with their patients.
- Only 56.1 percent recognized that psychologists could effectively treat panic disorder (Ohtani et al. 2006).

Although the typical treatment for PD includes medication, it is rarely adequate by itself and must be coupled with other types of psychological treatment to be fully effective. Cognitive-behavioral therapy is the approach that receives the most support, as it offers a variety of behavioral and cognitive strategies to minimize the symptoms of panic and to help the patient cope with the condition.

New types of treatment are being introduced and evaluated, including panic-focused psychodynamic psychotherapy (PFPP), which is based on older forms of treatment dating back to the expansion of Freudian psychoanalysis. Since the traditional psychodynamic approaches often take longer and are difficult to evaluate, they are rarely used. However, newer and briefer forms of psychodynamic treatments such as PFPP are being used and are proving effective in treating PD. With such developments, the psychoanalytic type of therapy can be systematically evaluated in a mode consistent with the principles of evidence-based medicine (Teng et al. 2008).

Identifying what triggers panic attacks is of primary importance to those who experience them. Unfortunately, the proximal cause of a panic attack is rarely found in the immediate situation but rather in the accumulation of many things over time. In response to the question, "What caused my panic attack?" the real answer is, "All of the above." Whether or not a person is diagnosed with PD, it is important to remember that the panic attack itself does not pose any real physical danger. When someone experiences a panic attack, he or she needs to mentally accept the fact that it is happening and not try to fight the symptoms; it will usually subside within 10 to 20 minutes. As simple as this sounds, it is very difficult for a PD sufferer to think rationally while in the middle of a panic attack. However, if the person can ride it out, rather than becoming more upset, the panic attack will subside more quickly. It is also important to recognize the early warning signs of a panic attack, because practicing some effective techniques (e.g., regulated breathing) can actually stop or minimize the attack. Sometimes people can abruptly tell themselves to "Stop It" and immediately focus on something other than themselves as a means of shortening or lessening the impact of an attack—this works best if the reaction is caught early. Nevertheless, if someone experiences four or more attacks during a month, or fears having another attack to the point where that fear disrupts the person's life, it is time for him or her to seek help from a specialist who is experienced in treating PD.

See also Cognitive-Behavioral Therapy; Phobias; Psychodynamic Psychotherapy; Women's Mental Health

Bibliography

American Psychiatric Association. 2000. *Diagnostic and Statistical Manual* (4th ed., text rev.). Washington, DC: American Psychiatric Publishing.

Amir, N., C. Beard, M. Burns, and J. Bomyea. 2009. "Attention Modification Program in Individuals with Generalized Anxiety Disorder." *Journal of Abnormal Psychology* 118(1): 28–33.

Anxiety Disorders Association of America. http://www.adaa.org.

Ballenger, J. C., and A. J. Fryer. 1996. "Panic Disorder and Agoraphobia." In T. A. Widiger, A. J. Frances, H. A. Pincus, R. Ross, M. B. First, and W. W. Davis, eds., *DSM-IV Sourcebook* (pp. 411–471). Washington, DC: American Psychiatric Association.

Boyd, J. H. 1986. "Use of Mental Health Services for the Treatment of Panic Disorder." *American Journal of Psychiatry* 143: 1569–1574.

Brown, T. A., and E. A. Deagle. 1992. "Structured Interview Assessment of Nonclinical Panic." *Behavior Therapy* 23: 75–85.

Chen, J., M. Tschiya, N. Kawakami, and T. A. Funukawa. 2009. "Non-Fearful vs. Fearful Panic Attacks: A General Population Study from the National Comorbidity Survey." *Journal of Affective Disorders* 112: 273–278.

Clark, D. M. 1986. "A Cognitive Approach to Panic." *Behavioral Research and Therapy* 24: 461–470.

Eaton, W. W., R. C. Kessler, H. U. Wittchen, W. J. Magee. 1994. "Panic and Panic Disorder in the United States." *American Journal of Psychiatry* 151: 413–420.

First, M. B., and A. Tasman. 2004. "Anxiety Disorders: Social and Specific Phobias." In M. B. First and A. Tasman, eds., *DSM-IV-TR Mental Disorders: Diagnosis, Etiology, and Treatment* (pp. 867–901). Chichester, England: Wiley.

Greenberg, P. E., T. Sisitsky, R. C. Kessler, S. N. Finkelstein, E. R. Berndt, J. R. T. Davidson, J. C. Ballenger, and A. J. Fyer. 1999. "The Economic Burden of Anxiety Disorders in the 1990's." *The Journal of Clinical Psychiatry* 60(7): 427–435.

Katerndahl, D. A., and J. P. Realini. 1995. "Where Do Panic Attack Sufferers Seek Care?" *Journal of Family Practice* 40: 237–243.

Keller, M. B., K. A. Yonkers, M. G. Warshaw, J. Gollan, A. O. Massion, K. White, A. Swartz, L. Pratt, J. Reich, and P. W. Larori. 1991. "Remission and Relapse in Subjects with Panic Disorder and Panic with Agoraphobia." *Journal of Nervous and Mental Disorders* 182: 290–296.

Markowitz, J. S., M. M. Weissman, R. Oullette, J. D. Lish, and G. Klerman. 1989. "Quality of Life in Panic Disorder." *Archives of General Psychiatry* 46: 984–982.

McCabe, L., J. Cairney, S. Veldhuizen, N. Herrmann, and D. L. Streiner. 2006. "Prevalence and Correlates of Agoraphobia in Older Adults." *American Journal of Geriatric Psychiatry* 14(6): 515.

Norton, P. J. 2009. "Integrated Psychological Treatment of Multiple Anxiety Disorders." In Martin M. Antony and Murray B. Stein, eds., *Oxford Handbook of Anxiety and Related Disorders* (pp. 1159–1171). New York: Oxford University Press.

Oei, T. P. S., K. Wanstall, and L. Evans. 1990. "Sex Differences in Panic Disorder and Agoraphobia." *Journal of Anxiety Disorders* 4: 317–324.

Ohtani, T., H. Kaiya, T. Utsumi, K. Inoue, N. Kato, and T. Sasaki. 2006. "Sensitivity to Seasonal Changes in Panic Disorder Patients." *Psychiatry and Clinical Neurosciences* 60: 379–383.

Pincus, D. 2008. *Mastery of Anxiety and Panic for Adults and Adolescents: Riding the Wave*. New York: Oxford University Press.

Psychiatry.HealthSE.com. 2005. "Panic Disorder and Agoraphobia." *Current Medical Diagnosis & Treatment in Psychiatry.*

Reiss, S., and R. J. McNally. 1985. "The Expectancy Model of Fear." In S. Reiss and R. R. Bootzin, eds., *Theoretical Issues in Behavior Therapy* (pp. 107–121). New York: Academic Press.

Roemer, L., S. M. Erisman, and S. M. Orsillo. 2009. "Mindfulness and Acceptance-Based Treatments for Anxiety Disorders." In M. M. Antony and M. B. Stein, eds., *Oxford Handbook of Anxiety and Related Disorders* (pp. 476–487). New York: Oxford University Press.

Rouillon, F. 1997. "Epidemiology of Panic Disorder." *Human Psychopharmacology* 12: S7–S12.

Teng, E. J., A. D. Chaison, S. D. Bailey, J. D. Hamilton, and N. J. Dunn. 2008. "When Anxiety Symptoms Masquerade as Medical Symptoms: What Medical Specialists Know About Panic Disorder and Available Psychological Treatments." *Journal of Clinical Psychology in Medical Settings* 15(4): 314–321.

Weissman, M. M. 1991. "Panic Disorder: Impact on Quality of Life." *Journal of Clinical Psychiatry* 52: 6–9.

Weissman, M. M., R. C. Bland, G. J. Canino, C. Faravelli, S. Greenwald, H.-G. Hwu, P. R. Joyce, E. G. Karam, C.-K. Lee, J. Lellouch, J.-P. Lépine, S. C. Newman, M. A. Oakley-Browne, M. Rubio-Stipec, J. E. Wells, P. J. Wickramaratne, H.-U. Wittchen, and E.-K. Yeh. 1997. "The Cross-National Epidemiology of Panic Disorder." *Archives of General Psychiatry* 54(4): 305–309.

Paranoia

Martin Kantor

Paranoia is a disorder of the mind, not a flaw in character. In this disorder the individual's characteristic problems with appearance, speech, thought, behavior, mood, insight, judgment, and intelligence when taken together trace a recognizable pattern called the (paranoid) "mental status." But not all paranoid individuals look, think, or act alike. It depends on the subtype of the disorder (e.g., paranoid personality disorder vs. paranoid schizophrenia); the stage of the disorder (early or late); the severity of the problem; and the degree and level of prior treatment.

Some paranoid individuals at most appear to be merely tense; others so alter or neglect their appearance that they look unkempt or bizarre. Thinking may be clear but incorrect, or it may be disorganized. Paranoid individuals can think either too concretely (too literally) or too abstractly—for example, as they brood about such (adversarial) imponderables as "does complimenting a member of a majority group constitute a failure to fully support a member of a minority group?" or even "does complimenting one feature of a member of a minority group constitute a pejorative statement about all other aspects of that individual, and so the group, and therefore overall become a bigoted remark?" Characteristic of paranoid thinking are false ideas ranging from ideas of reference ("the announcer on the television is referring to me personally and specifically") to fixed delusions, which typically are either *persecutory* (involving the usual cadre of so-called adversaries: blacks, Jews, the establishment, or big government), *monomaniacal* (concerned with a single idea or thought), or, commonly, both.

Behaviorally, some paranoid individuals withdraw out of fear and anger, while others involve themselves with their fantasied persecutors to excess, perhaps even stalking them or (rarely) becoming violent. Though paranoid individuals have a *disorder of mood*—e.g., what one researcher calls a "piercing cold paranoid fury" (Cooper 1994, 146)—or display a flatness of affect (emotion), only depressed or bipolar (manic depressive) patients have a pure, classic true mood disorder.

Some paranoid individuals retain a degree of insight, in the sense that they seem to know they are troubled. Others, however, either know they are paranoid but not to

---

Paranoia in Modern History

"Although paranoia today is a diagnosis used to describe patients who exhibit systematized delusions of grandeur and persecution, its original meaning, as the etymology of the word indicates, was 'being out of one's mind.' [J. C. A.] Heinroth in 1818 appears to have equated paranoia with *Verrücktheit* (madness); [K. L.] Kahlbaum in 1863 was the first psychiatrist to give it its modern meaning, and although he regarded paranoia as a persistent, chronic condition, he believed that paranoid patients suffered from a disorder of intellect."

—Charles Rycroft

Source: Charles Rycroft, "Paranoia," in R. L. Gregory, ed., *The Oxford Companion to the Mind*, 2nd ed. (Oxford: Oxford University Press, 2004), 688–698.

what extent, or else become convinced that they are right-thinking individuals who are justified in their beliefs, however unrealistic those beliefs might be (dereism).

Not all paranoid individuals live out their ideas in the form of poor judgment, but there are times when self-destructive antisocial, criminal, or violent activity that is the essence of bad judgment can occur. Legal matters involving paranoia often relate to the complex and typically unclear relationship between paranoia, defective judgment, and culpability.

Intelligence can be enhanced or diminished by paranoid fanaticism. As for enhancement, the paranoid individual's special and often cunning ability to see into the hidden hearts of matters, put a finger on the basics, and then decide what exactly the next right move should be are all parameters of that elusive gift we call "being brilliant."

According to the *Psychodynamic Diagnostic Manual*, or *PDM*, there are several clinical forms of *paranoid psychosis*, including *delusional disorder* and *paranoid schizophrenia* (PDM Task Force 2006, 143). Delusional disorder is an illness characterized by the presence of prominent, relatively fixed, and mostly nonbizarre delusions (nonbizarre delusions are delusions with plausible themes, about plausible situations, that tell an organized story—thus, "I am being followed," or "my therapist is going around spreading a Chinese flu" (Kantor 2006, 725). Such delusions must be extant for at least one month; generally originate from within (as opposed to being "copied" from an external source); be unaccompanied by hallucinations or other symptoms of schizophrenia (unless directly related to the delusion); and involve mood episodes, if present, of a brief nature.

Delusions

The *Diagnostic and Statistical Manual of Mental Disorders* defines a delusion as a "false belief based on incorrect inferences about external reality" (American Psychiatric Association 1994, 765). A delusion may also be defined as "a false unshakable idea or belief which is out of keeping with the patient's educational, cultural, and social background . . . held with extraordinary conviction and subjective certainty . . . indistinguishable from a true belief" (Sims 1988, 82). Finally, delusions can be viewed as persistent forceful ideas or beliefs that, however unlikely, exert "undue influence on [the patient's] life [altering it] to an inexplicable extent" (Munro 1999, 35). However defined, delusions in the case of paranoia tend to be fixed and generally occur in an otherwise clear sensorium (sensory system). They also tend to be vivid, to caricature people and cast them into roles, to be clearly organized, and to be either single or multiple as well as nonbizarre.

Primary or *first-rank* delusions appear to be independent of life's events, coming out of the clear sky with no immediately discernible antecedents (or, as one researcher puts it, without "predisposing features in the personality or situational stresses"; Roth 1989, 1634). *Secondary* delusions have more or less obvious antecedents in the person's life, current circumstances, or personality.

Ideationally, delusions are unquestioningly accepted by the person living with paranoia (or patient); that is, they are minimally subject to correction, so that others attempting to argue with or "talk sense" to the patient are generally met with a hostile secretiveness or suspicion. The abnormal and sometimes violent behaviors that can be the direct product of delusions, though unacceptable to us, are nevertheless comprehensible when understood as arising from delusional beliefs.

Delusions often seem to originate in stress. Some delusions, such as delusions of jealousy, can even have a basis in fact. A clear relationship often exists between a delusion and underlying paranoid personality traits (paranoid personality disorder). Examples of paranoid traits that form the basis of delusions are distrustfulness, hypersensitivity, overreactivity, blaming tendencies, and a "proneness to be biased, judgmental, and rigid" (Shapiro 1994, 54–55).

Some delusions, particularly those having a grandiose component, are the product of more positive than negative ideation (thought and imagination). As such, they can advance worthy causes and can lead to worthwhile social effort or interaction even while, at base, they remain figments.

Subtypes of delusional thinking include the following:

Persecution. Individuals who feel persecuted falsely believe that they might become or currently are the object of a cabal or conspiracy. Central to the idea of persecution is the process of projection, or the reattributing to others tendencies originally located, identified, and challenged and condemned within the self.

Jealousy. Here someone important is believed to be cheating on the individual—sexually, by being personally disloyal, or both. Physical abuse of the perceived cheater, shadowing, or killing are rare but possible consequences.

Somatic/hypochondriacal. Here the individual believes his or her body is somehow being damaged—decaying either spontaneously/within or due to the maliciousness of others.

Grandiose. Here the individual believes that he or she is especially powerful, rich, or famous or has become another person with some or all of these attributes, such as a deity. Often such delusional thinking is accompanied by active proselytizing. Overtly persecutory ideas commonly coexist, contaminating the grandiosity with anger, suspiciousness, and adversarial fantasy and rendering it unjoyful. Dynamically these individuals are often denying sinfulness or badness, suppressing anger toward others, or suppressing self-hatred.

Erotomanic. Here there is either the basic distortive belief that one is loved by an in-fact uninterested stranger, or that one is productively in love with an in-fact unavailable object. In some cases both ideas exist simultaneously.

Litigious. Litigious delusions consist of the belief that one has been treated unjustly and is therefore entitled to compensation by the system. The emotional/physical discomfort of the pain these individuals suffer from is out of proportion to the actual harm done to them. Litigious delusions are conceptually the opposite of delusions of subjugation, such as those characteristic of the "Stockholm syndrome" whereby an actual persecutor is perceived to be one's hero.

Misidentification. In delusional misidentification the individual may misidentify either other people, as in a delusion of a double whereby an individual believes that his wife is not really his wife but a replacement (his real wife being elsewhere); or that the individual him or herself has been replaced by another ("the devil has taken over my body, and I need an exorcism"; or "I am a palatial prince, not a pagan pauper").

Culturally determined. These delusions lie on a continuum between social myth and personal distortion. They have been reported as being more common in the formally uneducated, those with lower IQs, new immigrants to a strange or disorienting place, or in the overscrupulously religious.

Hallucinations

A hallucination is a false perception that can exist in all five senses including taste, smell, and vision, and that may be the product not of an emotional disorder but of an organic disorder such as an endocrine or metabolic disturbance. Auditory hallucinations (hearing voices) are the most common type. The voices heard in such hallucinations may speak to or about the individual. They may or may not elicit a visible/overt response in the patient, and so may or may not be obvious to the casual observer.

Hallucinations may be difficult to differentiate from illusions, which similarly appear in all the senses—but as ordinary, nonbizarre perceptions such as seeing shadows, hearing footsteps, or having religious sightings. Some hallucinations have an intellectual caste, as in the case of a belief that playing a song backwards reveals a secret satanic message.

As with delusions, hallucinations may or may not be subject to self-questioning and challenges from others; and, as with delusions, there may be little or no corrective mechanism available.

Paranoid Personality Disorder

Paranoid personality disorder involves a fixed system of false notions about the world and the people in it that coalesce to become rigid, ongoing interpersonal attitudes of a passionate but perverse nature. The false notions often lead the individual to become overly circumspect, evasive, highly suspicious, and blaming.

Blaming of others tends to originate in excessive guilt of one's own, in turn originating in an excessive, inappropriately rigid morality leading to hypercritical tendencies toward oneself that spread to become thoughts about the immorality of others. There is a tendency to collect injustices around being hurt, sexually abused, or financially taken advantage of, sometimes fueled by retrospective distortion in the form of false memories of early sexual trauma/physical abuse. Feuding with others over injustices believed to have been done, scams perpetrated, and physical assaults initiated is common, as is an associated tendency to expect the worst from people, particularly purportedly unfaithful spouses as well as strangers in environments imagined to be uniquely dangerous, such as a big city.

Some paranoid individuals appear aloof, withdrawn, and shy owing to discomfort with others who attempt to get close. Some closely associate with others but primarily with those who make up fringe groups (cults and militaristic, often Nazi-style organizations) where the members form bonds that are more ideational than interpersonal. Grandiosity is often a compensation for the belief that others are accusing the person of being, and treating him or her as, a nobody. This grandiosity generally has a narcissistic component—e.g., "I am owed, and you are depriving me of my just due."

Cognitive errors drive much of the paranoid individual's distortive thinking as he or she typically operates according to a logic disorder exemplified by statements such as, "I am a virgin, the Virgin Mary is a virgin, therefore I am the Virgin Mary"—thus creating false expectations of disapproval, criticism, and attack. Further examples are, "I am a foreigner, everyone hates foreigners, therefore everyone hates me"; and, "I live in Greenwich Village, homosexuals live in Greenwich Village, therefore I am a homosexual (and people are pointing fingers at me because of it)."

Angry, polemical assertions are common and often founded in selective abstraction—e.g., selective quotations from the Bible to justify homophobia, or selective acknowledgment of the base (negative) motives in complex mental or positively infused behaviors, as in the statement, "You wouldn't have canceled our date using the excuse of illness if you hadn't intended to stand me up all along."

Such individuals often seek or demand consensual validation for their illogical thinking, as much for emotional as for practical reasons. Typically, they ask others to join them in forming antimanagement or other antiestablishment coalitions the reasons for which they concoct more out of perception than out of reality.

Many of these individuals have a tendency to become depressed. Such depression generally occurs in the context of an adversarial relationship with others. Thus while the person's low self-esteem is partly the product of a negative self-view, it is also partly a response to negative things they falsely believe others are saying about or doing to them.

Everyday manifestations of paranoid personality disorder are to be found in contentious, angry, and hypercritical people; muckraking activists; conspiracy theorists; people who are constantly alert to unsuspected dangers such as those from power lines and innocuous vaccines; junk scientists and quacks; terrorists; bigots; serial litigants; those with such shared delusions as the belief that a company logo is satanic; fanatics; eccentrics; and combative individuals prone to violence against adversaries they believe must be defeated at any cost.

Causes

Paranoid symptoms often originate in and develop out of antecedent personality traits such as narcissism, grandiosity, perfectionism, stubbornness, and rebelliousness As Bone and Oldham (1994) suggest, "Paranoid individuals tend to be extremely and intensely aggressive people who as a group feel angrier and get nastier than most" (3). In some patients a delusional disorder is activated by new traumas that specifically bring old traumas to mind.

The progression to violence seems to be most common in individuals subject to past abuse. Violence often flares when the person presently feel, or actually is, rejected, criticized, or dishonored, e.g., when fired from a job. Outbursts such as road rage and mass shootings can often be attributed to feeling helpless in the face of external authority, or, in other cases, they can be understood as a response to unwanted closeness—e.g., a homosexual approach that arouses guilt about newly awakened, unacceptable homoerotic feelings.

A number of observers have commented on the relationships between repressed homosexuality and paranoia, and, certainly, homosexual fantasies do produce some of the content of some of the delusions of some paranoid patients. Thus some paranoid phenomena seem to be explainable as a defense against—that is, as a way to disavow—one's forbidden homosexual desires (as in the example, "the whisperers accuse me of being queer"). In a general way, projection of disavowed anger and sexuality seem central to the process of paranoid symptom formation.

Otto Kernberg (1994) notes that "paranoia typically appears or intensifies as a response to the provocative actions of another" (61). At the same time, there is, arguably, an organic basis to some aspects of paranoia, the discussion of which is beyond the scope of the present entry's focus on psychological roots.

Therapy

For some paranoid individuals, modified insight therapy ("talk therapy") is indicated. As with any other disorder, understanding the intrapsychic and experiential factors that help explain symptoms translates the disorder into human terms, thus making it more understandable and therefore hopefully more manageable.

Cognitive therapeutic approaches involve challenging beliefs, or advancing, as Millon and Davis (1996) suggest, "alternative explanations . . . to shift the weight of probability ... to ... alternative hypotheses [with the goal of introducing] an element of doubt" (725). The specific cognitive error of selective abstraction, whereby the individual sees only the destructive aspects of things or situations, is generally profitably corrected under this approach. Behavioral interventions may involve not asking the patient to attempt to get closer to others but instead stressing preventive or remedial removal from people who appear to be (or actually are) threatening.

Pharmacotherapy consisting of the use of antipsychotic medication can be especially therapeutic for individuals who are nonverbal, noninsightful, extremely angry, or very remote. Antianxiety, antidepressant, and antimanic medication may help in conjunction with antipychotics, but when used alone they may be ineffective or worsen the clinical picture. Antidepressants without antipsychotics can promote suicidal or violent behavior. Proper and sufficient psychotherapy should generally accompany pharmacotherapy. Medication noncompliance is often a complicating factor and may require third-party supervision.

Caretakers ranging from therapists to family members should endeavor always to be supportive. Support tends to revolve around gentle reality testing without crossing the patient whenever that is avoidable, and if possible instead respecting the truthful elements, if any, in his or her ideation. Appropriate limits should be set when accommodation of the person's interests or pursuits is unrealistic. Caretakers and therapists should not deny the more reality-based aspects of paranoid thinking and instead should endeavor to reduce or alter any stressful, hurtful, or dangerous elements in the patient's interpersonal environment.

See also Anger and Aggression; Cognitive-Behavioral Therapy; Depression; Narcissism; Schizophrenia; Violence and Violence-Prone Individuals

Bibliography

American Psychiatric Association. 1994. *Diagnostic and Statistical Manual of Mental Disorders* (4th ed.). Washington, DC: American Psychiatric Publishing.

Bone, Stanley, and John Oldham. 1994. "Paranoia: Historical Considerations." In John M. Oldham and Stanley Bone, eds., *Paranoia: New Psychoanalytic Perspectives* (pp. 3–15). Madison, CT: International Universities Press.

Cooper, Arnold M. 1994. "Paranoia: A Part of Every Analysis." In John M. Oldham and Stanley Bone, eds., *Paranoia: New Psychoanalytic Perspectives* (pp. 133–150). Madison, CT: International Universities Press.

Kantor, Martin. 2008. *Understanding Paranoia: A Guide for Professionals, Families, and Sufferers.* Westport CT, Praeger.

Kernberg, Otto. 1994. "Leadership Styles and Organizational Paranoiagenesis." In John M. Oldham and Stanley Bone, eds., *Paranoia: New Psychoanalytic Perspectives* (pp. 61–79). Madison, CT: International Universities Press.

Millon, Theodore, and Roger D. Davis. 1996. *Disorders of Personality: DSM-IV and Beyond.* New York: Wiley.

Munro, Alistair. 1999. *Delusional Disorder: Paranoia and Relate Illnesses*. New York: Cambridge University Press.

PDM Task Force. 2006. *Psychodynamic Diagnostic Manual*. Silver Spring, MD: Alliance of Psychoanalytic Organizations.

Roth, Martin. 1989. "Delusional (Paranoid) Disorder." In *Treatments of Psychiatric Disorders* (Vol. 2, pp. 1609–1652). Washington, DC: American Psychiatric Association.

Shapiro, David. 1994. "Paranoia from a Characterological Standpoint." In John M. Oldham and Stanley Bone, eds., *Paranoia: New Psychoanalytic Perspectives* (pp. 49–57). Madison, CT: International Universities Press.

Sims, Andrew. 1988. *Symptoms in the Mind: An Introduction to Descriptive Psychopathology*. London: Baillière Tindall.

Paraphilias

See Sexual Disorders and Dysfunctions

Peer Support Groups

Dave Sells and Charles Barber

Peer support groups for mental health typically comprise people who gather together to assist one another in resolving mental health difficulties that they have in common. From humble beginnings in psychiatry, peer support groups have multiplied in size and scope, particularly so within the last 20 years during what has been coined the "self-help revolution" (Norcross 2000); they are now estimated to approach the number of more "traditional" mental health care organizations. The growing appeal of these groups may be related in part to their dual qualities of perceived therapeutic gain and ready social and community networking, with initial outcome studies showing promise as to psychiatric and social rehabilitation.

History of Peer Support Groups

The origins of peer support expressly for mental illness can be traced back to the work of the seminal psychiatrist Harry Stack Sullivan (1892–1949). Like many other psychiatrists in the early 1900s, Sullivan worked in institutions, where his specialty was treatments for men with schizophrenia. Unlike other psychiatrists of his time, however, he invited back former patients who had demonstrated a degree of successful recovery, to serve as aides in helping to mentor current patients within his clinics. Sullivan noted that peer mentoring seemed effective in a variety of ways as an adjunct to his more formal therapeutic approaches.

Interestingly, his early success with treating schizophrenia (paired with the obscurity of his early life) has led some writers to posit that Sullivan himself had at times experienced bouts of psychosis, which enabled a greater empathy and understanding for his patients' experiences, and correspondingly his development of successful therapeutic interventions. In any case, the influence of Sullivan's peer mentoring practices can be seen somewhat later in the 1940s, within more group-oriented settings such as so-called therapeutic communities, in which members could offer to others, through both support and confrontation, knowledge of viable routes to recovery from mental illnesses (Jones 1953). Up until the 1950s and 1960s, however, such group models of peer support for mental illnesses were limited primarily to inpatient care settings.

One of the intended aims of psychiatric deinstitutionalization movements spanning from the 1950s to 1970s, which witnessed mass closings of county and state psychiatric hospitals, was the relocation of formal psychiatric care within the community. While most authorities would argue that community resources for psychiatric care have yet to be adequately addressed, deinstitutionalization did have a strong positive influence on the establishment of community-based mental health peer support groups (also often called "mutual support" groups), notably in two ways. First, formerly institutionalized patients came together to level protest against the often harsh conditions to which they were subjected within psychiatric asylums. The protests took many forms, one of which was mutual support alternatives to treatments offered by the psychiatric establishment, which they regarded with anger and suspicion.

The second way that psychiatric deinstitutionalization spurred the development of peer support groups was through the recognition that, however deleterious the conditions, some qualities of hospital life addressed certain human needs beyond the scope of symptom reduction. One of these qualities, at least at the institutions that fostered it intentionally or otherwise, was a sense of shared community, ironically lacking within community-based psychiatric care. The notion of community required inroads to more generic social networks, beyond the realm of mental health, though arguably still therapeutic in the sense of social rehabilitation. The "Community Support Movement" (Parrish 1989) began to address this need in the 1970s, and in so doing helped set the stage for the development of community-based mutual support groups as hubs to greater community social networks.

The addictions treatment community has long had a strong foothold of mutual support, notably through groups such as Alcoholic Anonymous (AA), which helped spur the formal establishment of peer support groups expressly designed to meet the needs of those with primary mental health concerns. Promoted in the United States during the 1970s, organizations such as GROW (GROW n.d.) and Emotions Anonymous (Kurtz & Chambon 1987) became models for the vast expansion of formal mental health mutual support groups. GROW, for example, was first founded in Australia in the 1950s by a small group of people who were former psychiatric inpatients. Inspired by AA, these persons conceived of peer support programming on the basis of what worked in their own recoveries, and highlighted the maintenance of mutual support networks, cultivation of a supportive community, establishment of programmatic protocols for recovery and personal growth, and operational and legal protocols to help structure the organization.

Variety and Utility of Peer Support Groups

The success of peer support groups like GROW in promoting membership and corresponding testimonies of successful recovery has in the last 20 years triggered a proliferation of mutual support groups for persons with mental health difficulties, ranging from general mental health support such as in Emotional Anonymous, to those addressing specific psychiatric diagnoses (e.g., Avoidant Personality Disorder Support Group, Post-Partum Support International) and including targeted demographics (e.g., Obsessive-Compulsive Disorder Parent Support Group, Child and Adolescent Bipolar Foundation). Presently, a quick search on the Internet for mutual support groups in mental health will yield nearly 3 million hits, many of them linking to mutual support service organizations, the most comprehensive of which, such as "PsychCentral," include mutual support group service directories. Indeed, Goldstrom, Campbell, Rogers, and Lambert (2006) reported that by 2002 the number of national mental health peer support groups (excluding self-help organizations and other consumer-operated services, which may also sponsor support groups) was indexed at 3,315, approaching the total number of more traditional mental health care organizations, estimated at 4,546.

While mental health mutual support groups targeting specific diagnoses and/or other demographic considerations likely offer specialized support components, it is also likely that all mutual support initiatives for mental health share some common salutary characteristics. Davidson and colleagues (1999) summarize some of these common beneficial characteristics in their review of peer support initiatives. First, sharing one's experience with others may trigger personal reflection, leading to greater understanding of one's particular situation and enhanced self-knowledge. This may be particularly true if a member feels predisposed to engaging with another on the basis of some shared experience, which might prompt the speaker's perception of greater empathy, warmth, and understanding on the part of the listener (Sells, Davidson, Jewell, Falzer, & Rowe 2006).

Second, the patterns of social interaction within mutual support groups may allow members to step out of passive recipient roles such as patient, and into more socially valued roles such as caregiver, teacher, and/or role model. This ability to act as provider in addition to recipient has been shown to promote greater life satisfaction and more favorable attitudes toward the notion of both interpersonal giving and receiving (e.g., Maton 1987).

Third, mutual support groups represent distinctive settings in which new information about training, skills, and varying viewpoints on common topics of concern or interest are available, all within a supportive environment. This arrangement may foster greater learning of pertinent coping skills, varying personal and/or conceptual perspectives, and problem-solving strategies than would happen within less purposefully structured environments.

Finally, mental health mutual support groups may offer members tools linked to specific ideology to make better sense out of their experiences. That is, any and all mutual support groups hold some underlying ideology of their approach and operations that explicitly and/or implicitly guide its members' understanding of their roles, difficulties, strengths, behaviors, and recoveries. To the extent that such ideologies prompt a shift in the way members conceive of any these or other such elements, they may garner personal insight and more healthful means for understanding their selves and experiences.

Outcomes of Peer Support Groups

In relation to the estimated number of mental health mutual support groups now available, the number of well-controlled empirical quantitative outcome studies remains rather small; in fact, only seven studies in this category seemed presently worthy of review. Nevertheless, taken together, these studies show promise for mutual support groups to help resolve mental distress, at least at levels equivalent to more traditional therapies as gauged along similar measures (Pistrang, Barker, & Humphreys 2008).

In a relatively early study, Galanter (1988) examined outcomes for persons participating in Recovery International (formerly Recovery Inc.), an earlier mutual support group geared to general mental health difficulties. Galanter compared outcomes for neurotic distress, well-being, and psychiatric treatment usage between long-term group members, new members, and an untreated (control) group, showing that long-term members posted lower on distress and higher on well-being, and received fewer psychiatric treatments than did new members. In another study, Bright, Baker, and Neimeyer (1999) utilized a particularly rigorous randomized control trial design comparing a 10-week mutual support group for depression to group-based cognitive-behavioral therapy (CBT), using varying group leaders (professional or peer) and validated measures of depression. Results showed equivalency between the groups, where all posted significant improvements on depression measures, whether mutual support, CBT, or peer- or professionally led. Roberts and colleagues (1999) examined across several months the benefits from participation in GROW, as described above, showing improvement over time on all symptom-based and adjustment measures. Cheung and Sun (2000) also studied benefits over time from group participation, specifically within a depression and anxiety mutual support group in Hong Kong, but found no change in depression and anxiety measures at 6 and 12 months' time. Powell, Yeaton, Hill, and Silk (2001) conducted a partially randomized trial comparing mutual support groups for depression and manic depression to an untreated control group assessed at 6 and 12 months as to daily functioning and illness management. The study found that group assignment had no effect on outcome but that members' personal involvement with the group led to improved illness management. Houston, Cooper, and Ford (2002) examined the effects of Internet-based mutual support groups for depression over time at 6 and 12 months employing a validated measure of depression, with results showing that 34 percent of participants had significant depressive symptom reductions, and particularly among frequent support users. Finally, Magura, Laudet, Mahmood, Rosenblum, and Knight (2002) studied a 12-step mutual support group for persons with chronic mental illness and co-occurring substance use disorders over 12 months, showing that better attendance was positively associated with more consistent use of prescribed psychiatric medication.

Despite the heterogeneity of this small body of research, results suggest that overall, mental health mutual support groups are effective in reducing members' psychiatric symptoms and increasing salutary behaviors, particularly when members demonstrate felt group connection and more frequent attendance.

Other Benefits of Mutual Support Groups

Effectiveness studies such as the ones mentioned above are generally most concerned with "treatment evaluation" (Humphreys 2004), focusing upon the remediation of psychiatric symptoms, as those symptoms are typically assessed in more formal systems of psychotherapy. As described earlier, however, mental health mutual support groups were, from their origins, never limited in their direct aims to psychiatric remediation but rather were also concerned with the promotion of social connectedness, the resumption (or assumption) of valued roles, and the enhancement of participants' quality of life—regardless of the presence or absence of psychiatric symptoms. Consequently, it is also important to consider the research literature regarding the relation of mutual support participation to these wider potential benefits. With respect to quality of life, Davidson and colleagues' (1999) review noted that participation in mental health mutual support groups is correlated with more positive self-esteem, enhanced social functioning, improved skills for decision making, and the pursuit of educational and employment goals. Moreover, there was preliminary evidence that some forms of mutual support had more favorable effects on participants' self-concept and interpersonal satisfaction over and above that of traditional psychotherapy.

With respect to social connectedness, Rappaport and colleagues (1985) found that long-term participation was associated with larger social networks. This finding seems particularly important in that earlier research strongly suggested that participants who initially attend to mental health mutual support groups tend to have much smaller social networks as compared to those without mental illness.

In terms of valued roles, groups such as GROW tend to purposefully offer roles to new members, in part as a way of expanding their organization's groups, which in turn may have an empowering effect upon its membership (Zimmerman et al. 1991). Other research has shown that the assumption of valued roles builds self-esteem, and that a healthful balance of being the provider (as well as the recipient) of helpful care fosters social adjustment (Davidson et al. 2001).

Conclusion

Mental health peer support groups have quickly gained traction and an expanding membership over the past 20 years, perhaps faster than they could be suitably studied. While further research on their many potential benefits and outcomes is needed, a small literature presently suggests that such groups not only produce therapeutic benefits equivalent to more traditional psychotherapeutic approaches (e.g., CBT) but also seem to directly promote enhanced quality of life, social networking, and the assumption of more valued societal roles. While these things are undoubtedly important, it is yet unclear whether any one of them represents a central feature of the quickly growing appeal of mental health mutual support groups.

Theoretically, it is possible to consider most of the benefits of peer support groups around a common theme of value. That is, mental illness can be painful, its recognition fraught with ambivalence, and its truest resolution forged upon hard work. Beyond the emotional relief that such a resolution may proffer, a person is likely to question the "greater purpose" of all that pain and labor. Whether cast within personal, familial, spiritual, or broader social terms, this can be framed as a question of meaning. It is a question that peer support groups have a unique capacity to address, both explicitly and otherwise, in the sense of felt value for something likely once perceived as a profound burden and liability. More specifically, within the context of mutual support in mental health, persons have something to offer not *despite* their past or present experiences of mental illness but precisely *because* of those experiences. And this transformation from "liability" to "asset," at least within the context of peer support groups, and the hope that such a transformation communicates to other members, might eventually come to be understood as one of the core, and most therapeutic, rewards of participation in such groups.

See also Community Mental Health; Group Therapy; Mental Health Advocacy; Recovery Movement; Rehabilitation Services; Self-Help; Therapeutic Community and Milieu Therapy

Bibliography

Blacklow, Beatrice, Marilyn J. Henderson, and Ronald W. Manderscheid. 2006. "National Estimates for Mental Health Mutual Support Groups, Self-Help Organizations, and Consumer-Operated Services." *Administration and Policy in Mental Health and Mental Health Services Research* 33(1): 92–103.

Bright, J., Kurt Baker, and Robert Neimeyer. 2000. "Professional and Paraprofessional Group Treatments for Depression: A Comparison of Cognitive-Behavioral and Mutual Support Interventions." *Journal of Consulting & Clinical Psychology* 67(4): 491–501.

Cheung, Siu-Kau, and Stephen Y. K. Sun. 2000. "Effects of Self-Efficacy and Social Support on the Mental Health Conditions of Mutual-Aid Organization Members." *Social Behavior and Personality* 28(5): 413–422.

Davidson, Larry, Matthew Chinman, Bret Kloos, Richard Weingarten, David Stayner, and Jacob Kraemer Tebes. 1999. "Peer Support among Individuals with Severe Mental Illness: A Review of the Evidence." *Clinical Psychology: Science and Practice* 6(2): 165–187.

Davidson, L., K. E. Haglund, D. A. Stayner, J. Rakfeldt, M. J. Chinman, and J. Kraemer Tebes. 2001. " 'It was just realizing . . . that life isn't one big horror': A qualitative study of supported socialization." *Psychiatric Rehabilitation Journal* 24(3): 275–292

Galanter, Marc. 1988. "Zealous Self-Help Groups as Adjuncts to Psychiatric Treatment: A Study of Recovery, Inc." *American Journal of Psychiatry* 145(10): 1248–1253.

Goldstrom, Ingrid D., Jean Campbell, Joseph A. Rogers, and David B. Lambert. 2006. "National Estimates for Mental Health Mutual Support Groups, Self-Help Organizations, and Consumer-Operated Services." *Administration and Policy in Mental Health* 33(1): 92–103.

GROW. n.d. "GROW in America: GROW in Detail." Retrieved from http://growinamerica.org/index.php?option=com_content&task=view&id=38&Itemid=35.

Houston, T. K., L. A. Cooper, and D. E. Ford. 2002. "Internet Support Groups for Depression: A 1-Year Prospective Cohort Study." *American Journal of Psychiatry* 159 (12): 2062–2068.

Humphreys, Keith. 2004. *Circles of Recovery: Self-Help Organizations for Addictions.* Cambridge: Cambridge University Press.

Jones, Maxwell. 1953. *The Therapeutic Community.* New York: Basic Books.

Kurtz, L. F., and A. Chambon. 1987. "Comparison of Self-Help Groups for Mental Health." *Health and Social Work* 12(4): 275–283.

Magura, S., A. B. Laudet, D. Mahmood, A. Rosenblum, and E. Knight. 2002. "Adherence to Medication Regimens and Participation in Dual-Focus Self-Help Groups." *Psychiatric Services* 53(3): 310–316.

Maton, Kenneth I. 1987. "Patterns and Psychological Correlates of Material Support within a Religious Setting: The Bidirectional Support Hypothesis." *American Journal of Community Psychology* 15(2): 185–207.

National Alliance on Mental Illness. n.d. "Support & Programs." Retrieved from http://www.nami.org/template.cfm?section=find_support.

Norcross, John C. 2000. "Here Comes the Self-Help Revolution in Mental Health." *Psychotherapy* 37(4): 370–377.

Parrish, Jacqueline. 1989. "The Long Journey Home: Accomplishing the Mission of the Community Support Movement." *Psychosocial Rehabilitation Journal* 12(3): 107–124.

Pistrang, Nancy, Chris Barker, and Keith Humphreys. 2008. "Mutual Help Groups for Mental Health Problems: A Review of Effectiveness Studies." *American Journal of Community Psychology* 42: 110–121.

Powell, T. J., W. H. Yeaton, E. M. Hill, and K. R. Silk. 2001. "Predictors of Psychosocial Outcomes for Patients with Mood Disorders: The Effects of Self-Help Group Participation." *Psychiatric Rehabilitation Journal* 25: 3–11.

PsychCentral. http://psychcentral.com/

Rappaport, Julian, Edward Seidman, Paul A. Toro, L. S. McFadden, Thomas M. Reischl, Linda J. Roberts, Deborah A. Salem, C. H. Stein, and Marc A. Zimmerman. 1985. "Collaborative Research with a Mutual Help Organization." *Social Policy* 15(3): 12–24.

Roberts, Linda J., Deborah Salem, Julian Rappaport, Paul A. Toro, Douglas A. Luke, and Edward Seidman. 1999. "Giving and Receiving Help: Interpersonal Transactions in Mutual-Help Meetings and Psychosocial Adjustment of Members." *American Journal of Community Psychology* 27(6): 841–868.

Sells, Dave, Larry Davidson, Christopher Jewell, Paul Falzer, and Michael Rowe. 2006. "The Treatment Relationship in Peer-Based and Regular Case Management for Clients with Severe Mental Illness." *Psychiatric Services* 57(8): 1179–1184.

Zimmerman, Marc A., Thomas M. Reischl, Edward Seidman, Julian Rappaport, Paul A. Toro, and Deborah A. Salem. 1991. "Expansion Strategies of a Mutual Help Organization." *American Journal of Community Psychology* 19(2): 251–278.

Personality Disorders

See Borderline Personality; Paranoia; Psychopathy and Antisocial Personality Disorder

Pharmaceutical Industry

See Drug Companies

Phobias

Rudy Nydegger

Since most people experience some types of fears, phobia is the most "understandable" of all anxiety conditions. Being afraid of something like poisonous snakes or falling from a tall building is certainly understandable, but sometimes people develop fears of very unusual and obviously not dangerous things or situations. As unusual or common as some of these phobias may be, each has its own, rather impressive-sounding name. For example, a fear of heights is called "acrophobia."

The following list of unusual phobias may be interesting, but the downside is that at some point a patient somewhere had to have presented one or more of these unique symptoms or the phobia would not have been assigned a name.

Ablutophobia: fear of washing or bathing

Alektorophobia: fear of chickens

Anemophobia: fear of air drafts or wind

Arachibutyrophobia: fear of peanut butter sticking to the roof of the mouth

Barophobia: fear of gravity

Bogyphobia: fear of bogies or the bogeyman

Bromidrosiphobia: fear of body smells

Chronophobia: fear of time

Decidophobia: fear of making decisions

Dutchphobia: fear of the Dutch

Hedonophobia: fear of feeling pleasure

Hippopotomonstrosesquippedaliophobia: fear of long words

Lachanophobia: fear of vegetables

Melissaphobia: fear of bees

Opthalmophobia: fear of being stared at

Parthenophobia: fear of virgins

Sophophobia: fear of learning

Teratophobia: fear of giving birth to a monster; or fear of deformed people or monsters

Walloonphobia: fear of Walloons (look this one up—bet you never saw one)

Xylophobia: fear of wooden objects or forests

Many of the fears listed here seem harmless and are perfect examples of how phobias can be acquired. Research has clearly demonstrated that fears can be learned by associating a fear response with a previously neutral stimulus—that is, we can learn to be afraid of something by our own direct experiences or by observing this fear in someone else. The person also learns to avoid the feared object, which may temporarily reduce the anxiety and fear that is experienced but makes it more likely that the person will avoid the feared object or situation in the future. Thus a phobia is born.

Mild fears of certain objects are not unusual or pathological, but irrational or disproportionate fears warrant a diagnosis of phobia, and particularly when the fear causes significant distress and/or impairs the person socially, occupationally, or educationally. Children will pass through different developmental stages, which often include being fearful of various things, but most will gradually outgrow their fears without a problem. This is not unusual—it may simply be a "phase" they are going through—and not something to be concerned about unless it does not go away or otherwise creates significant problems for the child.

Some childhood fears can continue into adulthood and occasionally become diagnostically relevant. To qualify for the diagnosis of phobia, there must be a *persistent, irrational fear* and *avoidance* of the specific thing or activity that elicits the fear. Further, the diagnosis is offered only when the phobia impairs the individual's social, occupational, educational, or other important functioning.

Generally, phobias are listed in three groups: (1) agoraphobia, (2) specific phobia, and (3) social phobia, or, as it also known, social anxiety disorder. Agoraphobia is the fear of being in an unsafe or unfamiliar place, and often results in the person limiting his or her activities and avoiding many places and situations; this is often associated with panic disorder. Specific phobias are common and rarely require treatment as they seldom significantly disrupt a person's life: common types of specific phobias often involve animals such as spiders, snakes, mice, rats, and dogs; other types of specific phobia include fear of flying, heights, injections, public transportation, confined spaces, dentists, storms, tunnels, and bridges. Although some of these fears can be disruptive, it is a testament to a person's creativity that he or she can avoid the feared objects or situations while still managing to function fairly normally.

The last major type of phobia is social phobia (social anxiety disorder), which includes generalized social phobia (GSP) and specific (or discrete) social phobia (SSP). In both cases the person becomes severely anxious while in general or specific types of social situations—that is, situations involving other people. In GSP sufferers are anxious and uncomfortable in almost all social situations, while in SSP sufferers tend to be anxious only in a particular kind of social situation—for example, public speaking.

Agoraphobia

As noted above, agoraphobia is frequently found with panic disorder and involves a person being afraid of leaving his or her "safe" environment to venture into unknown or "threatening" places. One should keep in mind that this fear is not based on realistic appraisals of dangerous situations but rather entails a disproportionate fear based, often on the apprehension of being someplace where a panic attack might occur. Agoraphobia can exist without panic disorder, but this is not the typical case. In any event, the disorder can be a very troublesome and debilitating condition that, nevertheless, is highly treatable *if one can get the patient into a treatment setting*. Unfortunately, for some patients the fear of leaving a safe environment is so frightening that they will not leave and may become entirely "housebound," depending on others to shop for them and to take care of any of their responsibilities that require going out of the house.

Specific Phobias

Phobias are among the most common mental disorders (First & Tasman 2004). Based on a large community sample (part of the so-called Epidemiological Catchment Area study), investigators report that there is a lifetime prevalence of 11 percent for specific phobias (i.e., 11% of the general population can be expected to suffer from specific phobias at some point over the course of a lifetime) and just under 3 percent for social phobia (Eaton, Dryman, & Weissman 1991). Another study (the National Comorbidity Study) found a lifetime prevalence rate of slightly over 11 percent for specific phobias (Kessler et al. 2005). Thus it is estimated that about 19.2 million American adults suffer from some type of phobia, with women being affected about twice as often for specific phobias. This is particularly true of animal phobias, although there are fewer differences between the sexes for acrophobia (fear of heights) and trypanophobia (fear of blood/injections). Typically, phobias emerge in childhood or adolescence and persist into adulthood; they are not, however, the same as normal, developmental childhood fears. Also, phobias tend to run in families and are assumed to be the result of observational or other forms of learning (National Institute of Mental Health [NIMH] 2009).

Specific phobias are circumscribed (i.e., very specific), persistent, and unreasonable fears of a particular object or situation. Although they tend to be less incapacitating than other anxiety disorders, the sufferer usually recognizes the fear as unrealistic, and most are able adjust his or her lifestyle to completely avoid or at least minimize contact with the feared object (Psychiatry.HealthSE 2005). Some intense phobias are so circumscribed that the person can perform certain tasks in specific situations that seem potentially fearful. For example, trained pilots with severe acrophobia are often unable to climb a stepladder, or athletes who ski the highest mountains cannot look off the side of a bridge. While this may seem counterintuitive or irrational, such is the nature of phobias. For most people with any type of anxiety disorder there is usually a significant fear of a loss of control, and this include phobias where the person feels that a certain situation will be out of his or her control and something bad will happen to him or her. If this is true, then it makes more sense that a person might have a fear of heights (acrophobia) and still be able to function in situations where height might appear to be an issue. For example, pilots have control of their plane and skiers are in control of themselves as they head down a slope; therefore they do not notice the heights while they are performing because they feel totally in control of the situation.

A person with a genuine phobia, who is forced to face the feared object or situation, will usually experience acute anxiety and perhaps even a panic attack.

However, if the patient seldom encounters the feared object (e.g., snakes), they may not bother to pursue treatment because the phobia does not adversely affect their daily life. It is encouraging to note that treatment for phobias is usually successful, and specific phobias respond very well to psychotherapies that focus on the fears and ways to reduce them (First & Tasman 2004). Therefore if a person has a phobia that is psychologically distressing or substantially interferes with his or her life, the person should feel optimistic that if treatment is sought with a well-trained professional a good outcome can be expected.

Research during the last decade has resulted in more effective treatments for both social phobia and specific phobias. Investigators have found that specific phobias tend to co-occur with other specific phobias: in one sample, 76 percent of patients with a lifetime history of specific phobia reported one or more co-occurring phobias (Curtis, McGee, Eaton, Wittchen, & Kessler 1998). For example, 70 percent of people with hemophobia (fear of blood) have injection phobias as well (Ost 1992). That does not mean that all people with a phobia will have a second phobia, but many do.

Social Phobia

Social phobia is a relatively common problem that frequently is underdiagnosed and undertreated. It may emerge as a generalized phobia, where people are fearful in most social situations, or it may emerge as a more specific fear involving only one or two situations, usually related to public performance of some kind (Psychiatry.HealthSE 2005). Social phobia affects about 15 million American adults (6.8% of the population). It produces undue embarrassment and anxiety in social situations and is, by definition, extreme enough to impair normal social functioning (Swartz 2007). In this type of phobia, women tend to predominate, but not by much (Antony & Swinson 2000). Men are more fearful than women of urinating in public bathrooms, for example, and of returning items to a store, whereas women are more fearful of talking to people in authority, public speaking, being the center of attention, expressing disagreement, and throwing a party (Turk et al. 1998).

People with social phobia are extremely self-conscious when in social situations; they fear being watched and judged by others and fear doing something embarrassing. They may worry and obsess for days or weeks prior to doing something, regardless of being aware that their fears are unrealistic and unreasonable. Even if they succeed at doing something that is feared, they will worry excessively before the event, be nervous during it, and then worry for hours afterward about what they did, how they did it, and how people may have judged them (NIMH 2009).

Social phobia is an anxiety condition that displays many of the physical symptoms of anxiety. It usually emerges in childhood or adolescence and persists into adulthood. Some researchers have proposed that a genetic factor is involved, but this is still unclear and the mechanisms of action are not well understood (NIMH 2009). Social phobia tends to run in families, at a rate three times higher in patients' families than in nonpatients'. While observational learning and other learning processes may be partly responsible, a higher concordance of social phobia in monozygotic (i.e., identical) twins than in dizygotic (fraternal) twins implies a genetic process ("Social Phobia" 1994).

Questions about the relationship between ordinary shyness and social phobia persist, but the issue is unsettled. One study looked at shy people with and without a diagnosis of social phobia, as well as non-shy people with and without social phobia. In both the shy and non-shy groups, people with social phobia reported more and greater symptoms, more functional impairment, and a lower quality of life than those without social phobia. About one-third of very shy people without social phobia reported no social fears at all. Both shy people without social phobia and socially phobic subjects reported similar levels of anxiety in normal conversation, but the socially phobic group reported more anxiety during the task of giving a speech, and the social phobia subjects performed less effectively than those without the disorder across all tasks (Heiser, Turner, Beidel, & Roberson-Nay 2009). Clearly, then, social phobia is not just a case of severe shyness. There is more to it than that.

The anxiety associated with social phobia can be so intense that it may lead to physical reactions like blushing, stammering, sweating, gastrointestinal upset, racing heart, trembling limbs and even a full-scale panic attack. These physical symptoms can evoke intense emotions that are hidden most of the time, and the physical reactions that are experienced often produce additional embarrassment and humiliation. One of the main challenges for social phobia sufferers is the intrusive nature of the symptoms, which can interfere with important areas of the person's functioning. For example, in one music school 16 percent of the students said that performance anxiety had limited their careers, and, at an international conference of symphony and opera musicians, 24 percent said that they had suffered seriously from stage fright ("Social Phobia" 1994).

Social phobia is a common diagnosis that may affect from 1 to 13 percent of the population, depending on how such phobia is defined. If we look at the most serious variants of the disorder, it is more likely that about 1 to 2 percent of the population experiences significant impairment of work and/or social life. During one phone survey, 21 percent of respondents said that they try to avoid public speaking, and 17 percent said that they try to avoid eating in a restaurant. Another 3 percent try to avoid writing in public, and 0.2 percent said that they consistently avoid urinating in public restrooms. In this sample, 2 percent experienced significant distress during more than one of these situations ("Social Phobia" 1994).

In terms of comorbidities (i.e., co-occurring disorders), social phobia frequently occurs with other disorders: 59 percent of patients with social phobia also had a specific phobia; 49 percent had panic disorder with agoraphobia; 19 percent were alcohol abusers (often self-medicating to reduce the anxiety); 17 percent suffered from major depressive disorder; and 10 to 20 percent of persons in clinics for treatment of anxiety disorders also had social phobia. Major depression is often associated with social phobia, and family members of patients with social phobia also experience a high rate of depression. One study showed that patients with social phobia and panic disorder had a 95 percent risk of also developing major depression, and another study showed that alcoholics have nine times the average rate of social phobia ("Social Phobia" 1994). Generalized social phobia is more often associated with depression, anxiety, general distress, and concerns about negative evaluation from others; and discrete social phobia seems to be associated with greater cardiac reactivity (Turner, Beidel, & Townsley 1992). This means that people with discrete social phobia show more changes in heart rhythms when under stress and this is an indication of how their bodies react to stressful situations. It is also important to determine if a person with a cardiac condition suffers from discrete social phobia, as treatment would be necessary for both conditions if the person were to get the optimal results from his or her treatment(s).

Generalized social phobia is pervasive and persistent and closely resembles avoidant personality disorder (APD), but the qualities of the two disorders are quite different. APD patients are hypersensitive to criticism and rejection and do not express their feelings for fear of ridicule. They want affection and closeness with others but will do nothing to get it. They are afraid to start conversations, ask questions, make friends, or join groups. They consider themselves inept or inferior, and they are often depressed. One major difference between APD and any social phobia is that patients with APD do not have the anxiety component, or if they have anxiety, it is minimally intrusive and not clinically significant ("Social Phobia" 1994).

When a diagnosis of social phobia is suspected, the clinician making the diagnosis must distinguish among other disorders as well as a potential diagnosis of APD, because there are other disorders that involve fear and avoidance of specific situations. For example, panic disorder with agoraphobia can certainly look like social phobia or even a situationally based specific phobia. Postraumatic stress disorder (PTSD) also presents similarly to social or specific phobia in some cases, but the key is that the symptoms of PTSD will follow the traumatic event and would not have been present prior to it. Obsessive-compulsive disorder (OCD) may at first resemble social or specific phobia, but a complete review of symptoms typically reveals a different clinical picture. Finally, to make an appropriate diagnosis, any type of phobia must be separated from normal fears and shyness (First & Tasman 2004).

Summary

Many people experience specific fears, and all of us have certain things or situations that make us uncomfortable. However, to have a clinically relevant phobia these fears must reach a certain level of intensity and must be disruptive to the person's life and functioning. The good news is that there are very good treatments available for all types of phobic disorders. The bad news is that most people who suffer from serious phobias do not get the help they need. For some, it is the stigma of mental health treatment that keeps them from seeking care; for others it is the lack of information and knowledge about the availability of care; and for yet others it is the absence of access to appropriate care. Whatever the scenario in particular cases, the reality is that most people with one or more of these highly treatable conditions do not receive the care that they otherwise could.

See also Panic Disorder; Social Anxiety Disorder; Undiagnosed Mental Illness

Bibliography

Antony, M. M., and R. P. Swinson. 2000. *Phobic Disorders and Panic in Adults: A Guide to Assessment and Treatment*. Washington, DC: American Psychological Association.

Curtis, G. C., W. J. McGee, W. W. Eaton, H. U. Wittchen, and R. C. Kessler. 1998. "Specific Fears and Phobias: Epidemiology and Classification." *British Journal of Psychiatry* 173: 212–217.

Eaton, W. W., A. Dryman, and M. M. Weissman. 1991. "Panic and Phobia: The Diagnosis of Panic Disorder." In L. N. Robins and D. A. Reiger, eds., *Psychiatric Disorders in America: The Epidemiologic Catchment Area Study* (pp. 155–179). New York: Free Press.

First, M. B., and A. Tasman. 2004. "Anxiety Disorders: Social and Specific Phobias." In M. B. First and A. Tasman, eds., *DSM-IV-TR Mental Disorders: Diagnosis, Etiology, and Treatment* (pp. 867–901). Chichester, England: Wiley.

Heiser, N. A., S. M. Turner, D. C. Beidel, and R. Roberson-Nay. 2009. "Differentiating Social Phobia from Shyness." *Journal of Anxiety Disorders* 23(4): 469–476.

Kessler, R. C., P. Berglund, O. Demler, R. Jin, K. R. Merikangas, and E. E. Walters. 2005. "Lifetime Prevalence and Age-of-Onset Distributions of *DSM-IV* Disorders in the National Comorbidity Survey—Replication." *Archives of General Psychiatry* 62: 593–602.

Metcalf, T., and G. Metcalf. 2009. *Phobias*. Farmington Hills, MI: Greenhaven Press.

National Institute of Mental Health. 2009. "Anxiety Disorders." Washington, DC: National Institute of Mental Health.

Ost, L.-G. 1992. "Blood and Injection Phobia: Background and Cognitive, Physiological, and Behavioral Variables." *Journal of Abnormal Psychology* 101: 68–74.

Psychiatry.HealthSE.com. 2005. "Specific Phobias." *Current Medical Diagnosis & Treatment in Psychiatry*. Retrieved from http://psychiatry.healthse.com/psy/more/specific_phobias/.

Scher, C. D., D. Steidtmann, D. Luxton, and R. E. Ingram. 2006. "Specific Phobia: A Common Problem, Rarely Treated." In T. G. Plante, ed., *Mental Disorders of the New Millennium: Vol. 1. Behavioral Issues* (pp. 245–264). Westport, CT: Praeger.

"Social Phobia." 1994. In *Harvard Mental Health Letter*. Cambridge, MA: Harvard Medical School.

Swartz, K. 2007. "Depression and Anxiety." In *The Johns Hopkins White Papers*. Baltimore: Johns Hopkins Medical School.

Turk, C. L., R. G. Heimberg, S. M. Orsillo, C. S. Holt, A. Gitow, L. L. Street, F. R. Schneier, and M. R. Liebowitz. 1998. "An Investigation of Gender Differences in Social Phobia." *Journal of Anxiety Disorders* 12: 209–223.

Turner, S. M., D. C. Beidel, and R. M. Townsley. 1992. "Social Phobia: A Comparison of Specific and Generalized Subtype and Avoidant Personality Disorder." *Journal of Abnormal Psychology* 101: 326–331.

Popular Remedies and Quackery

Timothy Kneeland

The term "quackery" comes from the Dutch word *quacksalver*, the equivalent of quicksilver or mercury, a chemical often used in medical remedies of the eighteenth century. The term not only applies to hucksters who intentionally profit from the practice of medicine or sale of fake remedies, but is also used to identify medical treatments that, in their heyday, were considered highly successful but that were replaced or abandoned as new theories or scientific breakthroughs discredited their curative claims (Porter 1997).

Medical hustlers and medical irregulars are found throughout the history of medicine and mental health care in the United States for three key reasons. First is the intellectual environment in the United States, where a democratic political culture generates a repository of hostility toward all experts and social or economic elites. Thus Americans have often rejected medical hierarchies in order to seek "home remedies" in the treatment of mental ailments plaguing themselves or members of their families. Second, and related to the first, because of the democratic culture there have been fewer restrictions on alternate medicines in the United States than there are in other nations, thus allowing irregular practitioners to flourish. Finally, mental disease has been so little understood from a scientific perspective that both the theoretical construction of mental illness and its treatment have elicited a wide variety of medical paradigms. In the absence of a clear causal agent for the mental ailments afflicting individuals, clinicians and patients have looked to alternative medical options as a last resort for the chronically mentally ill (Porter 1997).

The Rise of Popular Medical Remedies

Throughout the eighteenth and nineteenth centuries, diseases of the mind were presumably tied to somatic dysfunction that was not visible to the naked eye. That is, mental derangement might be traced to poor diet, lack of rest, bodily humors, sexual immorality, and so on, forcing into the mind false perceptions that generated morbid thoughts, hallucinations, or manic behavior. American "nervousness," or the neuroses, were also blamed on unknown, underlying physical problems. Whether the source was located in the brain, the nerves, or the blood, the ideal treatment sought restoration of the body to normal functions. These alternative medical treatments were often promoted by medical sectarians, or people who believed in a single cause of illness and created a therapeutic regimen centered on treatment of that supposed universal source of disease. The treatments might come in the form of diets, spinal readjustment, auto-healing, hydrotherapy, or invasive surgical procedures (Kneeland 1996).

Diet was at the center of the ideas propounded by Sylvester Graham (1794–1851) and John Harvey Kellogg (1852–1943). Graham believed that gastrointestinal ailments led to a host of mental and physical problems, from cholera to mental excitement. He advised people to refrain from meat, alcohol, tobacco, and other harmful substances and to substitute instead his own wholesome Graham crackers (which was a kind of heavy bread made from graham flour, not the kind of sweet cookie/crackers sold today) as the ultimate food for maintaining good health (Nissenbam 1980). John Kellogg treated a host of patients suffering from nervous disease at his Battle Creek Sanitarium, in Michigan. Like Graham a generation earlier, Kellogg traced the ailment to poor diet and lack of exercise. In search of the perfect diet, Kellogg created corn flakes and other cereals as part of natural a regimen to restore the body and mind to wellness (Armstrong & Armstrong 1991). Kellogg and his sanitarium were part of a movement, of sorts, in which hundreds of private rest homes advertised to the fashionable and the nervous to come for restoration and recovery. Silas Weir Mitchell (1829–1914), a leading neurologist of the late nineteenth century, developed the "rest cure," which forced patients to remain in bed and be force-fed for weeks on end. Popular at the time, Mitchell's rest cure is now more likely to be invoked while reading Charlotte Perkins Gilman's short story "The Yellow Wallpaper," which deconstructs the rest cure as owing more to Mitchell's paternalistic nature than to his neurological training (Blackie 2004).

For those who could not afford a trip to an expensive sanitarium in the nineteenth century, mental ease might be restored for men or women by using the medicine available from Samuel Thomson (1764–1843), whose vegetable compounds were often mixed with emetics to cause alternate vomiting and sweating in order to purge the body of toxins. Unlike Graham and Kellogg, who promoted health through diet and restraint, Thomson and his followers sought a means of purging the body of harmful elements and creating an internal heat that was considered beneficial. Thomsonian medicine was popular enough in the nineteenth century to inspire a loyal following: tens of thousands of adherents bought these products and self-medicated; others offered their own, equally questionable versions. Such "puke doctors," as trained physicians called them, even founded their own college, the American Botanico-Medical Institute. Associated with the movement was John Rodes Buchanan (1814–99), who believed there was a natural cause of insanity and tried to find a connection between phrenology (the pseudoscience of personality and character based on skull shape) and diet (Haller 2001).

The water cure or hydrotherapy has a long history going back to European baths and spas. In the United States it was found in expensive resorts such as Saratoga Springs, New York, which offered palliative care in mineral springs for a host of ailments. Until the mid-twentieth century, various forms of hydrotherapy could be found as a tool in every major institution for the mentally ill. Mental health practitioners believed that wrapping patients, especially those displaying aggressive tendencies, in a wet-sheet pack for hours a day would remediate some of their more dangerous behaviors. Another practice was to secure patients into special hydrotherapy tubs. Inside the tub was a tight-fitting hammock that restrained their arms and legs, and on top of the tub was a canvas cover from which their head protruded. Patients were then given alternately cold and hot water treatments of varying pressure until they calmed down and became more lucid. The treatment was believed to work on the patient's nervous system and eliminate "cerebral congestion" or "toxic impurities." As water flowed in and out of the tubs, patients were monitored, with nurses performing regular checks of their vital signs. Hydrotherapy remained a staple of psychiatric treatment in state institutions through the 1950s, but it was abandoned with the advent of electroconvulsive therapy and psychopharmacology (Braslow 1997).

Natural therapies and tonics were derived not only from animal and mineral spirits but also from presumed invisible natural forces and vital fluids operating within the body. One such substance was "innate intelligence," a vital fluid that was said to flow from the brain throughout the rest of the body. When the flow was obstructed, illness resulted. The flow was thought to be disturbed most often by "vertebral subluxation." This concept became the theoretical basis for one of the most successful alternate medical therapies of the mid-nineteenth century, namely, chiropractic. Today, many patients see chiropractors regularly as an established medical treatment, but the field's theory of disease reflects nineteenth-century beliefs that sought a single causal agent for illness and a related system of remediation. Daniel David Palmer (1845–1913), after restoring the hearing of a man by readjusting his spine, suggested that by manipulating the vertebral column by hand, he could restore the normal flow of "innate intelligence" and achieve other cures. Despite being denigrated as a "bone cracker" by regular physicians, Palmer opened a school in Davenport, Iowa, and his theory and practice quickly spread. While today millions of Americans seek relief from chiropractors for physical ailments such as pinched nerves, there are many so-called "straight chiropractors" who continue to claim that their methods will cure a wide variety of illnesses, including generalized anxiety (Martin 1994).

Electricity was also a natural phenomenon employed by mental health practitioners, presumably because it restored tired nerves and the body's natural electrical field from the spine to the brain. In the early nineteenth century, itinerant sellers of putative electrical cures for mental illness included T. Gale who practiced in upstate New York (Kneeland & Warren 2008). Charles Beard (1839–83), who popularized the disorder known as neurasthenia or nervous exhaustion, also promoted the use of electricity to treat it. Beard suggested that applying electricity to the spine or key areas of the body would reinvigorate the cells and restore the patient to health. Electrotherapy was used by regular physicians but also by specialists who were known in their day as electrotherapists. Electrotherapists used a variety of machines from room-sized devices installed in hospitals, clinics, and sanitariums to small bread box-sized boxes that physicians used in their office or took to the homes of wealthy patients. Physicians using electricity claimed that they could cure intractable neuroses such as neurasthenia or hysteria. The practice was popular from the late 1800s until after World War I, when it was identified by Morris Fishbein and the American Medical Association as a form for quackery and quickly abandoned (Kneeland 1996).

Whereas regular physicians sought to cure nervous disease through electricity, hucksters sought to use the public acceptance of electricity for their own gain. They marketed street-corner devices that people could use for the price of one penny, while entire industries were built around selling home electrical remedies to a gullible public. One such company was the J. M. Pulvermacher Company, which profited by selling to the public an assortment of electrical belts, girdles, and the like that claimed to calm nerves, restore vitality, and maintain mental hygiene. One notorious charlatan who brought discredit on electrotherapeutics was Albert Abrams (1863–1924). Abrams was a trained physician who earned medical degrees at the University of Heidelberg and Stanford University and was part of the medical establishment in California, even serving as the vice president of the state medical association. In 1909 he published a book, *Spinal Therapeutics*, that proposed that all disease was caused by problems of the spine. His cure, which he revealed in a follow-up book, *Spondylotherapy*, was to stimulate the key centers of the spine to promote health. Claiming that all disease left an electronic fingerprint, Abrams invented a diagnostic device, the dynamizer, which he said read the electronic signature of the ailment and relayed this information back to the physician. Once the disorder was identified the physician could then stimulate the affected regions of the spine to restore health. Abrams had a large following before his sudden death in 1924, when studies of his machines demonstrated that they measured nothing (Armstrong & Armstrong 1991).

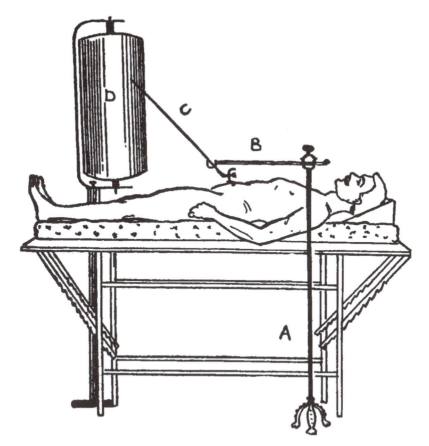

Apparatus for taking a spondylogram, from Albert Abrams's *Spondylotherapy: Spinal Concussion and the Application of Other Methods to the Spine in the Treatment of Disease*, 1910. Spondylotherapy was a diagnostic and curative technique developed by Abrams that used electricity to generate reflexes in the body. (Abrams, Albert. *Spondylotherapy: Spinal Concussion and the Application of Other Methods to the Spine in the Treatment of Disease*, 1910.)

Heavy-Handed Cures

More invasive procedures were also utilized in the struggle to end mental disorder. In the early nineteenth century, Benjamin Rush in his *Medical Inquires and Observations on the Disease of the Mind* (1830) suggested that the cause of mental disorders was an overabundance of blood in the brain. To alleviate this he bled patients, plunged them alternately into very cold and very hot baths, or placed them in a special chair that flung them around to diffuse the blood from the brain (Hall 1944).

Surgery was used to treat mental illness from the nineteenth and into the twentieth century. In the Victorian era, a woman's sexual identity was often conflated with disorderly behavior. The pairing led to the construction of hysteria, a disease that had a multitude of symptoms ranging from mild anxiety to paralysis. Despite the differential symptoms, most physicians believed that hysteria was a precursor to insanity. Hysteria, like neurasthenia, was oftentimes treated with electrotherapy, but some doctors advocated more radical procedures such as cauterization of the clitoris, removal of the ovaries, or blistering the nape of the patient's neck. This practice was used until the late nineteenth century, when hysteria was reconstituted as a psychological disorder rather than a physical one. By the end of World War I, most psychiatrists had all but discarded the concept of hysteria (Shorter 1997).

Henry Cotton (1876–1933), a psychiatrist at Trenton State Hospital, had trained under one of the foremost leaders of modern psychiatry, Adolf Meyer. Cotton believed that insanity and mental illness resulted from infections in the teeth, tonsils, or bowels. To cure his patients, Cotton performed surgeries—over 2,000 of them between 1918 and 1925. Although he reported a high cure rate for his procedure, it came with a staggering loss of life; perhaps as many as one-third of his patients died during or after surgery. Ultimately, outcry over patient abuse led to a legislative investigation and a review of Cotton's findings by other physicians, who rejected his procedure and forced Cotton into retirement (Scull 2005).

The procedure known as lobotomy, a form of psychosurgery, was developed by the Portuguese physician Egas Moniz (1874–1955). Moniz knew that destroying the frontal lobes of chimpanzees eliminated the animals' aggressive behavior. He surmised that he could alleviate violent outbursts in human mental patients by developing a similar surgical procedure. Frontal lobotomy, as it was popularly called, was launched in 1936 when Moniz successfully operated on a patient by drilling two holes in the cranium and dosing the exposed tissues with alcohol. Later, he replaced alcohol with specially crafted tools to cut the fibers of the prefrontal lobes. After the procedure, once-violent and -uncontrollable patients became lethargic and malleable. In the United States, Walter Freeman (1895–1972) popularized this method for treating schizophrenia. Between 1936 and 1958, he performed some 3,400 lobotomies; and an estimated 25,000 lobotomies were performed in the country as a whole. The procedure was discarded in the 1950s when psychiatrists found that they could calm agitated patients with the drug Thorazine (chlorpromazine; Pressman 1998).

Psychological explanations for mental illness have coexisted with somatic ones from the very beginning of metal health practice in the United States. In the early nineteenth century, moral therapy was the preeminent form of therapy used by alienists to cure mental disease. Thomas Kirkbride (1809–83) of the Pennsylvania Hospital for the Insane was one of the key promoters of moral therapy. Kirkbride believed that insanity was caused by the stressful environment, which caused the mental faculties to receive faulty impressions and led to morbid thoughts. Removing the patient from the stressful life situation and placing them in a quiet space,

---

Lobotomy as a Cure

"Clear data on the effectiveness of [lobotomy] are difficult to come by, but even [Walter] Freeman, the procedure's most zealous promoter, only claimed good results for 52 percent of his patients, and he provided no clear standard for what constituted an improvement. Along with inducing violent behavior and hallucinations among some patients, the indiscriminate and imprecise cutting would also damage memory, personality, motivation, language use, and many other functions. Patients often had to relearn basic adaptive skills, such as how to eat or use the bathroom. Obesity and epilepsy would sometimes result, and as many as 3 percent died of the procedure."

—Louis A. Cordón

Source: Louis A. Cordón, *Popular Psychology* (Westport, CT: Greenwood Press, 2005).

---

often called an asylum or a retreat, the mind would gradually heal itself, allowing the patient to return to the outside world (Tomes 1984).

Psychological Therapies

Moral treatment, or the rectifying of personal lapses in morality (thought to cause mental illness), reached its peaks in the decades leading to the Civil War, when it was abruptly abandoned in the face of more severe and chronic mental illnesses (Shorter 1997). Moral therapy, however, was resurrected by Clifford Beers (1876–1943) in the first half of the twentieth century. Beers himself was institutionalized for suicidal ideation, hallucinations, and paranoia, symptoms that were only exacerbated, he claimed, by his treatment. Beers did not begin to recover until he was treated by a physician who cared for him in a humane fashion. Once he was in a climate in which he was given rest and was treated humanely, Beers overcame his symptoms and went on to write a best-selling autobiography, *A Mind That Found Itself* (1908). Beers founded the "mental hygiene" movement, which preached prevention of disease (Dain 1980). A similar approach to healing addictions and treating functional mental illnesses such as neuroses could be found in the Emmanuel movement, led by Elwood Worcester (1862–1940). Worcester advocated humane treatment and spiritual insight, and the movement attracted some notoriety before peaking in the period after World War I (Gardner 1934).

Whereas the moral therapy, mental hygiene, and Emmanuel movements could each lay claim to respectability during the periods when they were active, other psychological approaches clearly were beneficial only to the practitioner. Before the advent of state standards and licensing procedures, it was easy for self-proclaimed "psychologists" or "marriage counselors" to set up shop and ply their trade. Morris Fishbein, the editor of the *Journal of American Medicine*, decried the nearly $400 million spent by consumers on such practitioners, who often made their patients worse not better (Fishbein 1932).

Despite revisions to state medical codes and a greater professional ethos in psychology and psychiatry, alternate mental health therapies continued well after World War II and reached their crescendo in the late 1960s and early 1970s. As many as 130 different psychodynamic therapies were available to patients in the early 1970s. This included standard treatment such as group therapy or family therapy, but also more radical treatments generated by the "human potential" movement and showcased in Erhard Seminars Training (or "est," in which one aggressively "takes responsibility" for one's life); in sensory deprivation chambers; in regression therapy sessions (in which "deep" memories and even past lives are explored); and in primal scream therapy (in which repressed childhood traumas are purged). In a sea of therapeutic anarchy, psychiatrists and psychologists began to question the efficacy of traditional psychoanalysis and the foundation on which it was built. Freudian psychology, a set of ideas that had gripped mental health practice in the United States for three-quarters of a century, was being challenged because of its speculative nature. Researchers tested psychoanalysis against drug therapy and control groups and found that members of control groups often recovered faster than those patients who underwent

Sexual Repression and Orgone Therapy

One controversial theorist and practitioner was the psychoanalyst Wilhelm Reich (1897–1957). Born and trained in Austria, Reich moved to the United States in 1939 and promoted his theory of orgone energy. Reich argued that orgone, a primordial energy, permeated the cosmos, including human beings. By concentrating this energy within the body, a person could increase his or her sexual vitality and overcome repressed sexual urges contributing to neurotic behavior. To produce the desired result, Reich created the orgone box, a lead-lined booth in which the patient sat to accumulate orgone energy.

Reich's ideas influenced members of the Beat generation, such as William S. Burroughs and Jack Kerouac, who believed that sexual repression caused psychological problems and that irrational forces operated in the universe. At the same time, most professional psychologists ridiculed Reich, and he ended up serving two years in prison for making fraudulent claims about his methods.

—*Editor*

Source: Robert S. Corrington, *Wilhelm Reich: Psychoanalyst and Radical Naturalist* (New York: Farrar, Straus and Giroux, 2003); Christopher Turner, *Adventures in the Orgasmatron: How the Sexual Revolution Came to America* (New York: Farrar, Straus and Giroux, 2011).

psychoanalysis. By the late 1980s, psychoanalysis was on the defensive as the psychiatric establishment took up the biomedical model of mental illness.

Conclusion

Reviewing the history of these therapies demonstrates not how scientific mental health treatments have become, but rather the persistence of the American culture to embrace alternate medical strategies. For example, despite the attempt in the late twentieth century to create a scientific approach to mental illness based on biological psychiatry, alternate medical therapies such as aromatherapy and acupuncture are now commonly used to treat posttraumatic stress syndrome, depression, and other functional mental illnesses in American hospitals and clinics.

See also Electroconvulsive Therapy; History of Mental Health Care; Hypnosis and Hypnotherapy; Medical Model of Mental Illness; Mind and Body Approaches to Mental Health; Nutritional Therapies; Self-Help

Bibliography

Armstrong, David, and Elizabeth Metzger Armstrong. 1991. *The Great American Medicine Show: Being an Illustrated history of Hucksters, Healers, Health Evangelists, from Plymouth Rock to the Present.* New York: Prentice Hall.

Beers, Clifford. 1948. *A Mind That Found Itself.* New York: Doubleday.

Blackie, Michael. 2004. "Reading the Rest Cure." *Arizona Quarterly* 60: 57–85.

Braslow, Joel. 1997. *Mental Ills and Bodily Cures: Psychiatric Treatment in the First Half of the Twentieth Century.* Berkeley: University of California Press.

Dain, Norman. 1980. *Clifford Beers, Advocate for the Insane.* Pittsburgh: University of Pittsburgh Press.

Fishbein, Morris. 1932. *Fads and Quackery in Healing: An Analysis of the Foibles of the Healing Cults.* New York: Blue Ribbon Books.

Garrison, Fielding. 1929. *An Introduction to the History of Medicine* (4th ed., rev.). Philadelphia: Saunders.

Green, John Gardner. 1934. "The Emmanuel Movement, 1906–1929," *New England Quarterly* 7: 494–532.

Hall, J. K., ed. 1944. One *Hundred Years of American Psychiatry.* New York: Columbia University Press.

Haller, John S. 2001. *The People's Doctor: Samuel Thomson and the American Botanical Movement, 1790–1860.* Carbondale: Southern Illinois University Press.

Kneeland, Timothy W. 1996. "The Use of Electricity to Treat Mental Illness in the United States, 1870 to Present." Unpublished doctoral dissertation, University of Oklahoma.

Kneeland, Timothy W., and Carol A. B. Warren. 2008. *Pushbutton Psychiatry: A Cultural History of Electric Shock Therapy in America* (updated ed.). Walnut Creek, CA: Left Coast Press.

Martin, Steven C. 1994. " 'The Only Truly Scientific Method of Healing': Chiropractic and American Science, 1895–1990." *Isis* 85: 207–227.

Nissenbaum, Stephen. 1980. *Sex, Diet and Debility in Jacksonian America: Sylvester Graham and Health Reform*. Westport, CT: Greenwood Press.

Porter, Roy. 1997. *Greatest Benefit to Mankind: A Medical History of Humanity*. New York: Norton.

Pressman, Jack. 1998. *Last Resort: Psychosurgery and the Limits of Medicine*. Cambridge: Cambridge University Press.

Rush, Benjamin. 1830. *Medical Inquiries and Observations on Diseases of the Mind*. Philadelphia: John Grigg.

Scull, Andrew. 2005. *Madhouse: A Tragic Tale of Megalomania and Modern Medicine*. New Haven, CT: Yale University Press.

Shorter, Edward. 1997. *A History of Psychiatry: From the Era of the Asylum to the Age of Prozac*. New York: Wiley.

Tomes, Nancy. 1984. *A Generous Confidence: Thomas Story Kirkbride and the Art of Asylum-Keeping, 1840–1883*. New York: Cambridge University Press.

Valenstein, Elliot. 1986. *Great and Desperate Cures: The Rise and Decline of Psychosurgery and Other Radical Cures for Mental Illness*. New York: Basic Books.

Warner, John Harley. 1998. *Against the Spirit of the System: The French Impulse in Nineteenth-Century American Medicine*. Baltimore: Johns Hopkins University Press.

Posttraumatic Stress Disorder

Amber N. Douglas

Traumatic stress reactions as clinical phenomena are deeply rooted within the history of psychology, psychiatry, and general observations of human behavior (Reyes, Elhai, & Ford 2008). Perhaps the first description of a traumatic stress phenomenon was inscribed on clay tablets over 5,000 years ago. Writings describing posttraumatic symptoms consistent with current diagnostic criteria can be found in various texts including the Bible, ancient Greek plays, and Shakespeare's works. Despite these early writings, a formal definition of traumatic stress (disorder) was not articulated until the eighteenth century (Reyes, Elhai, & Ford 2008). The constellation of experiences consistent with our current diagnosis of posttraumatic stress disorder (PTSD) was initially conceptualized by Breuer and Freud (1893). Freud described it primarily as a disorder of memory, in that traumatic experiences become etched upon survivors' memories and cannot be forgotten, resulting in experiences of distress.

PTSD is a psychological disorder occurring within children and adults in response to a severe psychological stressor. Individuals with this syndrome exhibit a core set of symptoms characterized by the reexperiencing of the traumatic event, avoidance of memories of the traumatic event, and (hyper)arousal. While both children and adults experience PTSD, there are specific manifestations of symptoms that are distinct to children. The *Diagnostic and Statistical Manual of*

Psychiatric Disorders (*DSM-IV-TR*; American Psychiatric Association 2000) currently recognizes three subtypes of posttrauma disorders, namely, (1) acute, with symptoms occurring less than three months after the traumatic event; (2) chronic, with symptoms present for more than three months; and (3) delayed onset, with symptoms developing at least six months following exposure to the traumatic stressor. As a diagnosis, PTSD is unique in that it requires an external event, a traumatic stressor, to meet the criteria. It is estimated that almost 7 percent of American adults will experience PTSD at some point in their lives, women being more than twice as likely as men to experience it (National Comorbidity Survey 2005).

What Is Trauma?

Trauma, as it is used within the field of traumatic stress studies, is a broad concept that encompasses both physical and psychological experiences of extreme stress. Weathers and Keane (2008) observe that the term trauma is used to refer to (1) a stressor, (2) an individual appraisal of this stressor, and (3) an individual's response to the stressor. In part, the controversy surrounding the PTSD and trauma itself lies within the accessibility of a broad definition. Interestingly, the current clinical diagnostic classification (criterion A) for PTSD is much narrower than what is commonly used. The criterion requires that a stressful event be or be perceived to be life threatening *and* result in psychological experience of terror, horror, or helplessness. Some critiques of the *DSM* have suggested that the definition of trauma is too narrow and fails to encompass experiences of extreme stress that may not reach the threshold of fear for one's own life or the life of a loved one. Proponents of the criteria contend that the restrictions are necessary to reduce the misuse of the diagnosis.

The *DSM-IV-TR* provides a list of potentially traumatic events that include war, kidnapping, torture, rape, domestic violence, child sexual abuse (without acknowledged fear of death), and terrorism. The inclusion of the term "potentially" indicates the high degree of individual variability in response to stressful events. In fact, far more people will experience extreme stress events and survive more or less intact while only a small minority of those so exposed will go on to experience PTSD. The factors that determine who eventually develops the syndrome are multifaceted.

Etiology of PTSD

Etiology is the study of causation or origin of a disease. There are several factors that are related to the development of PTSD. Magnea and Lanius (2008) classify these factors into three categories that are useful for classification: (1) pretrauma factors, including demographic, family history, and biological predisposition; (2) peritraumatic factors, including emotional processing, cognitive appraisal, and dissociation; and (3) posttrauma factors, including type and availability of social support. Let us look at each of these in turn.

Pretrauma Characteristics

Research on biological differences between individuals with PTSD and those without has produced contradictory findings. Initially, neuroendocrine researchers argued that the hypothalamic-pituitary-adrenal (HPA) axis was involved in the human stress response. Further, findings indicated that cortisol, a hormone secreted at times of stress and fear, was the measureable output of this systemic response. Based on these findings, researchers contended that individuals with PTSD suffered from a hypersensitization of the HPA system, which decreased the levels (inhibited) cortisol secretions as part of the stress response. However, more recent research indicates that in fact there are no differences between the HPA axes or cortisol levels between individuals with PTSD and controls (individuals without PTSD) (Carlson, Dalenberg, & Muhtaide 2008). Behavioral neuroscientists have also examined differences in the hippocampus, a brain structure thought to play a vital role in memory, specifically autobiographical memory. Again, while early studies suggested significantly smaller hippocampi within individuals with PTSD, recent investigations (Carlson, Dalenberg, & Muhtaide 2008) indicate that there are no consistent differences between these individuals and controls. However, research does indicate that despite the failure to observe differences in neurological structures as a result of stress exposure, there are in fact meaningful relationships between genetics and PTSD (Amstadter & Nugent 2008).

The developmental period of when a traumatic event occurs is also an important factor in predicting likelihood of development of PTSD (Carlson, Dalenberg, & Muhtaide 2008). Specifically, those events that occur earlier in development and are chronic have a more substantial impact on individuals' psychological development. Similarly, there is an important relationship between childhood trauma and attachment to primary caregivers that can exacerbate or ameliorate certain types of trauma (see Cloitre, Cohen, & Koenen 2006).

Gender is another preexisting factor that is related to the development of PTSD. While women on the whole are exposed to fewer traumatic events than men, they are more likely to develop PTSD. It is also true that the nature of the traumatic event exposure differs as a function of gender. Theorists posit that differences in rates of PTSD between men and women are a function of the types of trauma and gender roles that place women at greater risk for development of PTSD. As such, treatment interventions have attempted to examine both the nature of traumatic stress in the lives of women survivors and how they interact with gender expectations (Kimerling, Ouimette, & Weitlauf 2007).

Ethno-racial status is a strong predictor of PTSD: higher rates of PTSD have been observed within African American, Latino, American Indian, and some Asian/Pacific Islander American subgroups (Pole & Triffleman 2008). Causal explanations regarding the ethnic disparities are relatively new—at times authors suggest that certain groups experience greater traumatic stress exposure, others indicate a cumulative impact of racial stress and race-based discrimination, and most recently, authors indicate that peritraumatic and posttraumatic processing (Pole & Triffleman 2008) might account for higher rates of PTSD in specific ethno-racial minority groups. In addition to differences in prevalence, ethnic and racial minorities are less likely to utilize existing services as compared to white counterparts. However, when engaged in treatment, it appears that there are little differences in effectiveness as a function of ethnic status (Pole & Triffleman 2008).

Peritraumatic Experiences

Dissociation is the "disruption in the usually integrated functions of consciousness, memory, identity or perception of the environment" (American Psychiatric Association 1994: 477). Peritraumatic dissociation refers to dissociative experiences that occur during or immediately after a traumatic event, and it is linked to the development of PTSD (Van der Hart et al. 2008). Similarly, a growing body of literature indicates that the cognitive and emotional processing during and immediately following a traumatic event mediate the development of PTSD (e.g., Conway & Pleydell-Pearce 2000; Ehlers & Clark 2000; Jobson & O'Kearney 2008; Rubin, Bernsten, & Bohni 2008).

Posttrauma Characteristics

Social support, perceived support, received support, and social embeddedness are important determinants in the development of PTSD. Research on social support suggests that higher levels of each type of social support are predictive of lower posttrauma symptoms. As such, treatment interventions attempt to maximize social networks after trauma exposure to improve psychological adjustment and resiliency (Kaniasty 2008). Treatment is also a factor that determines the likelihood of developing PTSD, as discussed below.

Theoretical Perspectives on PTSD

Brewin and Holmes (2003) provide a thorough and comprehensive review of psychological theory of PTSD. Psychodynamic theory offers one of the oldest perspectives on PTSD. Horowitz's stress response theory indicates that PTSD is the result of two competing processes: the first is motivated to suppress traumatic stimuli and avoid triggers of the trauma; the second is motivated to promote the resolution of the traumatic event. Conflict thereby results as the mind fluctuates between these two modes of processing. Brewin and Holmes (2003) suggest that the psychodynamic stress response theory has been influential in the development of subsequent cognitive processing theories as it was the first to examine the role of underlying schemas, cognitive appraisals, and environmental factors that influence one's response. Psychodynamic approaches to treatment of PTSD focus on the examination of the psychological defense of an unacceptable wish that was triggered by a traumatic event. The goal then for psychodynamic interventions of PTSD is to assist patients toward understanding this wish and working through past conflicts. Trauma according to psychodynamic theory has to be understood within the context of an individual's unique life experiences.

More recently, theories have attempted to isolate mechanisms that maintain core posttraumatic symptoms more explicitly. Foa and Rothbaum's (1998) emotion processing theory (EPT) points to specific cognitive schemas that are disrupted as a result of traumatic stress. At its core EPT is an extension of fear network theories (e.g., Lang 1979), which suggest that trauma memories are typical memories with unique structure (Brewin & Holmes 2003). As such, Foa and her colleagues contend that traumatic events can erode one's previously established sense of safety. According to EPT, core PTSD symptoms are accompanied by a negative belief that is addressed through a treatment of prolonged exposure within a supportive therapeutic context. This approach allows participants to evaluate and examine negative beliefs, confront avoidance behaviors, and reprocessing the traumatic memory.

Exposure therapies are consistent with emotion processing theory. These therapies refer to cognitive and behavioral interventions that, in a systematic, controlled, and measured format, present individuals with images, objects, and in vivo scenarios related to a past trauma to reduce fear response (Rothbaum 2008). Exposure therapies are thought to go beyond extinction responses as observed in traditional learning paradigms and aid in emotion processing of traumatic events. As such, exposure is combined with cognitive training that examines cognitions that are associated with avoidance and fear responses of trauma cues. In addition, the therapeutic context is thought to provide a safe environment to reinterpret and relive past experiences (Rothbaum 2008).

An alternative explanatory theory of PTSD suggests that trauma memories are stored in a unique manner. Dual representation theory posits that traumatic memories are maintained within two parallel memory systems: "verbally accessible memory" and "situationally accessible memory" (Brewin & Holmes 2003). Verbally accessible memory exists within the integrated autobiographical memory systems and can be deliberately retrieved to be accessed. Conversely, situationally accessible memories are flashbacks and triggered by environmental determinants. These memories exist without a verbal code and are not integrated into an individual's life narrative. Treatment according to this theory necessitates the evaluation of negative cognitions and creation of positive associations that build on perceptions of alternative positive possible selves that sometimes develop following a traumatic event.

Finally, Ehlers and Clark (2000) presented a cognitive theory of posttraumatic stress disorder. The theory accounts for pretrauma appraisal processes, peritraumatic evaluations as they predict negative appraisals and subsequent cognitions following a traumatic event. Similar to other theories, Ehlers and Clark stress that the integration of the trauma memory is key but highlight the circumstances that interact to predict the ease and likelihood that this integration and processing will occur. The theory also points to specific therapeutic interventions. Both dual processing and Ehlers and Clark's cognitive theory focus on how trauma has affected one's cognitions and beliefs. The treatment then progresses toward challenging these beliefs and replacing distortions with more accurate and positive cognitive frameworks.

Conclusion

PTSD is associated with difficulty in social and family life, occupational instability, marital problems, and difficulty in parenting, among other things. Mental health care providers need to realize that these difficulties in living are affected not only by the patient's traumatic experiences but also by his or her cultural environment, ethnic background, social relationships, spiritual worldview, and unique neurophysiology.

When individuals experience a life-threatening encounter, they go into a survival and self-protection mode. Persons with PTSD do not readily return to a natural state; rather, they remain in a mode of self-protection and become hyperaware of their surroundings, always looking for the source of the trauma. It is therefore important to understand the processes that keep individuals who remain haunted by their traumas from returning to a state of normalcy. Their usual means of coping (talking with friends, exercise, prayer, and other support methods) do not alleviate the stress for very long. The ability to cope depends as well on the maturity of the individual, his or her personality structure, and previous experiences. Effective treatment considers how a person responds to trauma and manages symptoms to reduce the debilitating effects of PTSD.

See also Dissociative Disorders; Trauma; Veterans' Mental Health

Bibliography

American Psychiatric Association. 1994. *Diagnostic and Statistical Manual of Mental Disorders* (4th ed.). Washington, DC: American Psychiatric Publishing

American Psychiatric Association. 2000. *Diagnostic and Statistical Manual of Mental Disorders* (4th ed., text rev.). Washington, DC: American Psychiatric Publishing.

Amstadter, A., and N. Nugent. 2008. "Genetics." In G. Reyes, J. D. Elhai, and J. D. Ford, eds., *The Encyclopedia of Psychological Trauma* (pp. 294–295). Hoboken, NJ: Wiley.

Breuer, J., and S. Freud. 1893/1955. "On the Psychical Mechanism of Hysterical Phenomenon: Preliminary Communication." In J. Breuer and S. Freud, *Studies on Hysteria* (pp. 3–17). New York: Basic Books.

Brewin, C. R., and E. A. Holmes. 2003. "Psychological Theories of Posttraumatic Stress Disorder." *Clinical Psychology Review* 23: 339–376.

Carlson, E. B., C. Dalenberg, and L. Muhtadie. 2008. "Etiology." In G. Reyes, J. D. Elhai, and J. D. Ford, eds., *The Encyclopedia of Psychological Trauma* (pp. 257–163). Hoboken, NJ: Wiley.

Cloitre, M., L. Cohen, and K. Koenen. 2006. *Treating Survivors of Childhood of Abuse: Psychotherapy for the Interrupted Life*. New York: Guilford Press.

Conway, M. A., and C. W. Pleydell-Pearce. 2000. "The Construction of Autobiographical Memories in the Self-Memory System." *Psychological Review* 107: 261–288.

Ehlers, A., and D. M. Clark. 2000. "A Cognitive Model of Posttraumatic Stress Disorder." *Behaviour Research and Therapy* 38: 319–345.

Foa, E. B., and B. Rothbaum. 1998. *Treating the Trauma of Rape: Cognitive Behavioral Therapy of PTSD*. New York: Guilford Press.

Jobson, L., and R. O'Kearney. 2009. "Impact of Cultural Differences in Self on Cognitive Appraisals in Posttraumatic Stress Disorder." *Behavioural and Cognitive Psychotherapy* 37(3): 249–266.

Kaniasty, K., and F. H. Norris. 2008. "Longitudinal Linkages between Perceived Social Support and Posttraumatic Stress Symptoms: Sequential Roles of Social Causation and Social Selection." *Journal of Traumatic Stress* 21(3): 274–281.

Kimerling, R., P. Ouimette, and J. Weitlauf. 2007. "Gender Issues in PTSD." In M. J. Friedman, T. M Keane, and P. A. Resick, eds., *Handbook of PTSD: Science and Practice* (pp. 207–228). New York: Guilford Press.

Lang, P. J. 1979. "A Bioinformational Theory of Emotional Imagery." *Psychophysiology* 166: 495–512.

Magnea, G., and R. A. Lanius. 2008. "Biology, Brain Structure, and Function, Adult." In G. Reyes, J. D. Elhai, and J. D. Ford, eds., *The Encyclopedia of Psychological Trauma* (pp. 84–90). Hoboken, NJ: Wiley.

National Comorbidity Survey. 2005. NCS-R Appendix Tables: Table 1. Lifetime Prevalence of *DSM-IV*/WMH-CIDI Disorders by Sex and Cohort. Table 2. Twelve-Month Prevalence of *DSM-IV*/WMH-CIDI Disorders by Sex and Cohort. Retrieved from http://www.hcp.med.harvard.edu/ncs/publications.php.

Pole, N., and E. Triffleman. 2008. "Race and Ethnic Factors." In G. Reyes, J. D. Elhai, and J. D. Ford, eds., *The Encyclopedia of Psychological Trauma* (pp. 560–564). Hoboken, NJ: Wiley.

Reyes, G., J. D. Elhai, and J. D. Ford, eds. 2008. *The Encyclopedia of Psychological Trauma*. Hoboken, NJ: Wiley.

Roberts, C. A. 2011. *Coping with Post-Traumatic Stress Disorder: A Guide for Families*. Jefferson, NC: McFarland.

Rosen, G. M., ed. 2004. *Posttraumatic Stress Disorder: Issues and Controversies*. Hoboken, NJ: Wiley.

Rothbaum, B. O. 2008. "Exposure Therapy." In G. Reyes, J. D. Elhai, and J. D. Ford, eds., *The Encyclopedia of Psychological Trauma* (pp. 270–271). Hoboken, NJ: Wiley.

Rubin D. C., D. Berntsen, and M. K. Bohni. 2008. "A Memory-Based Model of Post-traumatic Stress Disorder: Evauluating Basic Assumptions Underlying the PTSD Diagnosis." *Psychological Review* 5(4): 985–1011.

van der Hart, O., J. M. van Ochten, M. J. van Son, K. Steele, and G. Lensvelt-Mulders. 2008. "Relations among Peritraumatic Dissociation and Posttraumatic Stress: A Critical Review." *Journal of Trauma and Dissociation* 9: 481–505.

Weathers, F., and T. M. Keane. 2008. "Trauma, Definition." In G. Reyes, J. D. Elhai, and J. D. Ford, eds., *The Encyclopedia of Psychological Trauma* (pp. 657–660). Hoboken, NJ: Wiley.

Poverty, Unemployment, Economic Inequality, and Mental Health

Deborah Belle and Heather Bullock

Half of the largest economies in the world are corporations, not nations, and globalized corporations today wield tremendous economic power. In search of ever greater profits, they push record numbers of workers into the ranks of the unemployed and the impoverished and shift others into poorly paid, part-time, and insecure jobs that fail to provide the economic and psychological benefits of adequate work. Chief executives of the largest U.S. corporations often earn as much in a day as their employees earn in a year, yet corporations and wealthy individuals have lobbied successfully to reduce their own taxes to record lows while diminishing public and safety net programs. Half of all U.S. children and 90 percent of African American children will depend on food stamps at some point before they reach 18, and the United States has by far the highest level of income inequality among industrialized nations. Such economic realities are at the root of many mental health problems, and effective responses to such problems require an understanding of these causal pathways.

Unemployment

Job loss is associated with elevated rates of mental and physical health problems, increased mortality rates, and detrimental changes in family relationships and in the psychological well-being of partners and children. Compared to stably employed workers, those who have lost their jobs have significantly poorer mental health, lower life satisfaction, less marital or family satisfaction, and poorer subjective physical health (McKee-Ryan et al. 2005). A meta-analysis by Paul and Moser (2009) reinforces these findings—unemployment was associated with depression, anxiety, psychosomatic symptoms, low subjective well-being, and poor self-esteem. Unemployed workers were twice as likely as their employed counterparts to experience psychological problems. Unemployed workers, and even those who had experienced an episode of unemployment 20 years earlier, had a higher risk of dying than did their stably employed peers. Underemployment is associated with decreased self-esteem, increased alcohol use, and elevated rates of depression, as well as low birth weight among babies born to underemployed women.

Research dating back to the Great Depression has found that men who experienced substantial financial loss following unemployment became more irritable, tense, and explosive. Children suffered as these fathers became more punitive and arbitrary in their parenting. Such paternal behavior, in turn, predicted tantrums, irritability, and negativity in children, especially boys, and moodiness, hypersensitivity, feelings of inadequacy, and lowered aspirations in adolescent girls. Subsequent studies continue to find similar pathways from economic loss to father's behavior to children's well-being. Elevated depressive symptomatology has also been documented among unemployed single mothers, with causal links between mothers' dysphoria, negative parenting behaviors, and children's own distress and depression.

The impact of unemployment extends beyond individuals and families to workplaces, communities, and neighborhoods. Coworkers who remain on the job suffer from anxiety that they, too, will soon be fired, and from a heavier workload, as they must now take on the work once done by their former colleagues. Those who retain their jobs in the midst of downsizing may experience comparable physical and emotional effects to workers who lose their jobs. Unemployed workers also report less neighborhood belonging than their employed counterparts, a finding with broad implications for community safety and well-being. Most dramatically, unemployment rates predict both homicide and suicide and also account for much of the racial gap in serious violent crime (Gilligan 2011).

Economic, social, and personal resources cushion the blow of job loss and inadequate employment. Individuals who face unemployment with fewer financial resources report worse mental health and less life satisfaction than those who experience unemployment with greater economic resources (McKee-Ryan et al. 2005). African Americans and Latinos/as are particularly likely to experience unemployment without the cushion of a family home or other resources. In the wake of the housing market crash of the late 2000s and the ensuing Great Recession, communities of color have been devastated by foreclosures and evictions stemming from the targeting of these communities for predatory subprime loans (e.g., adjustable-rate mortgages that move from low to extraordinarily high interest rates).

Countries with stronger systems of protection for the unemployed have lower rates of mental health problems among the unemployed than countries such as the United States, with its relatively weaker supports (Paul & Moser 2009). Poorer outcomes for the unemployed are also found in countries with high rates of income inequality. An economic and cultural climate that is more accepting of collective responsibility for its citizens coupled with the availability of generous unemployment benefits makes job loss less psychologically distressing. Individual-level attributions for unemployment are also important in determining the extent of distress following job loss. Those who blame themselves by making internal attributions for their unemployment report lower life satisfaction and poorer physical health than those who externalize blame for their situation (McKee-Ryan et al. 2005). Unfortunately, negative stereotypes about the unemployed are pervasive and justify the mistreatment of jobless people. For example, discriminatory recruitment and hiring practices that exclude unemployed applicants from being considered for job openings communicate that the unemployed, particularly those who have been out of work for longer periods of time, are flawed and at fault.

Poverty

Poverty is perhaps the most consistent correlate of depression and related mental health problems such as posttraumatic stress disorder (Belle & Doucet 2003; Smith 2010). High levels of depressive symptoms are common among low-income groups, especially mothers with young children. Rates of major depression among homeless and housed low-income mothers are approximately twice as high as in the general population of women. In prospective studies, adults in poverty are twice as likely as nonpoor adults to experience a new episode of major depression, and financial hardship doubles women's risk for the onset of depression. Despite being at great risk for depression, poor women rarely receive mental health services of any kind.

Those in poverty experience more frequent, more threatening, and more uncontrollable life events than does the general population, typically in the context of ongoing, chronic deprivation. Inadequate housing, burdensome responsibilities, and other chronic conditions are even more stressful than acute crises and events, and typically set the stage for acute, stressful material losses. Poverty can also undermine the ability to fulfill important social roles and to maintain personal values. Financial hardship is associated with the perception of success in relatively few domains of life. Such experiences have been demonstrated to constitute risk factors for depression.

Economic hardship tends to increase conflict between partners and to diminish capacity for supportive, attentive, and consistent parenting (McLoyd 1990). Impoverished children also grow up in more dangerous neighborhoods, exposed to more violence, attending inferior schools, breathing more polluted air, and drinking more polluted water (Evans 2004).

Experimental research with nonhuman primates illuminates some of the psychological and physiological consequences of the low social status and lack of power associated with poverty. Shively, Laber-Laird, and Anton (1997) manipulated social status among captive female cynomolgus monkeys and discovered that those monkeys who were placed in a low-status situation were the targets of more aggression from other monkeys, engaged in less affiliative behaviors, spent more time alone and more time fearfully scanning the social environment, and spent more time in a slumped or collapsed body posture, a behavioral indicator of depression. In addition, subordination was associated with suppressed reproductive function and the hypersecretion of cortisol. Because diet and other aspects of the environment were controlled experimentally, these findings can confidently be attributed to low social status.

Although ethical constraints forbid manipulations of social status among humans, nonexperimental research with humans suggests that we, too, endure health-damaging emotional and physiological consequences of low social status. In their study of healthy, nonsmoking white women between 30 and 45 years of age, Adler, Epel, Castallazzo, and Ickovics (2000) found that respondents who reported lower subjective social status experienced higher levels of chronic stress, more negative affect, more pessimism, and less perceived control over life. Although objective indicators of social status (education and income) were associated with some of these psychological variables, subjective social status was a significantly stronger predictor. Subjective social standing was also significantly associated with self-rated health, sleep latency, body fat distribution, resting physiological arousal, and cortisol habituation. Neither education nor income was related to these physical health indicators.

Many poor women create mutual aid networks through which they care for each other in times of stress. Support from family, friends, and other network members is associated with a reduced risk of depression. Yet social networks often serve as conduits of stress, just as they serve as sources of social support (Belle & Doucet 2003). Network members are themselves likely to be poor and stressed, so that considerable stress contagion is likely. Reciprocating the help that is received from network members can be time consuming and emotionally draining, and networks can impede upward mobility and exact emotional costs. For these reasons, the costs associated with social networks often outweigh the benefits they provide impoverished individuals.

Inequality

While poverty exacts a tremendous toll, the negative effects of economic stress are not limited to those who are impoverished. This is because individuals up and down the social and economic gradient experience less well-being in more unequal societies. A striking list of emotional, physical, and social problems are significantly more common in societies that internally are more unequal than in societies in which income levels are less unequal. Comparisons among wealthy nations and among the 50 U.S. states find that inequality is correlated with reduced life expectancy, less trust, lower math and literacy scores among children, and lower levels of economic mobility; and also with higher rates of homicide, infant mortality, high school dropout, obesity, mental illness (including drug and alcohol addiction), fighting, bullying, and unkindness among children, teenage pregnancy and birth rates, and incarceration (Wilkinson & Pickett 2009). Even if the poor were removed from these estimates, the United States' low ranking on measures of life expectancy and many other indicators would remain virtually unchanged because inequality is so great.

Status hierarchies appear to be most harmful to health when they are most extreme. Among industrialized nations it is those with the least unequal income distribution, not those with the greatest wealth, that have the longest-living citizens (Wilkinson & Pickett 2009). The United States, which leads the industrialized world in economic inequality, as well as in per capita income and per capita expenditures on health, ranks behind most of the industrialized nations in life expectancy. Costa Rica, Greece, and Spain, for instance, have citizens who are longer lived.

According to Wilkinson and Pickett (2009, 25), "the view that social problems are caused directly by poor material conditions such as bad housing, poor diets, lack of educational opportunities and so on implies that richer developed societies would do better than the others. But this is a long way from the truth: some of the richest countries do worst. . . . The problems in rich countries are not caused by the society not being rich enough (or even by being too rich) but by the scale of material differences between people within each society being too big. What matters is where we stand in relation to others in our own society." Vast differences between the middle class and the poor and between the very rich and all the rest of us erode trust, destroy community, and lead to debilitating shame and stigmatization among many, as they also skew our political priorities, creating a vicious cycle that sustains economic inequality.

To work effectively with individuals who have been damaged by such dynamics, therapists must be capable of countering the destructive effects of poverty and inequality and the stigmatization of unemployment and poverty that pervade dominant U.S. culture. Increasing societal awareness of the costs of economic inequality is equally important if we are to mobilize politically to challenge the concentration of wealth and power (Lott & Bullock 2007; Wilkinson & Pickett 2009). Inequality kills, and it causes immense human suffering. A small but extremely powerful elite derives wealth from the promotion of inequality and resists every attempt to redistribute resources. It will be a very difficult battle, but one that we as concerned citizens must take on.

See also Ethical Issues; Homelessness and Mental Illness; Public Health Perspectives

Bibliography

Adler, Nancy. E., Thomas Boyce, Margaret A. Chesney, Sheldon Cohen, Susan Folkman, Robert L. Kahn, and S. Leonard Syme. 1994. "Socioeconomic Status and Health: The Challenge of the Gradient." *American Psychologist* 49(1): 15–24.

Adler, Nancy E., Elissa S. Epel, Grace Castallazzo, and Jeanette R. Ickovics. 2000. "Relationship of Subjective and Objective Social Status with Psychological and Physiological Functioning in Preliminary Data in Healthy White Women." *Health Psychology* 19(6): 614–618.

Belle, Deborah, and Joanne Doucet. 2003. "Poverty, Inequality, and Discrimination as Sources of Depression among U.S. Women." *Psychology of Women Quarterly* 27(2): 101–113.

Evans, Gary W. 2004. "The Environment of Childhood Poverty." *American Psychologist* 59(2): 77–92.

Gilligan, James. 2011. *Why Some Politicians Are More Dangerous Than Others*. Cambridge: Polity.

Lott, Bernice, and Heather E. Bullock. 2007. *Psychology and Economic Injustice: Personal, Professional, and Political Intersections*. Washington, DC: American Psychological Association.

McKee-Ryan, Frances. M., Zhaola Song, Connie R. Wanberg, and Angelo J. Kinicki. 2005. "Psychological and Physical Well-being during Unemployment: A Meta-Analytic Study." *Journal of Applied Psychology* 90(1): 53–76.

McLoyd, Vonnie C. 1990. "The Impact of Economic Hardship on Black Families and Children: Psychological Distress, Parenting, and Socioemotional Development." *Child Development* 61(2): 311–346.

Paul, Karsten I., and Klaus Moser. 2009. "Unemployment Impairs Mental Health: Meta-Analyses." *Journal of Vocational Behavior* 74(3): 264–282.

Shively, Carol A., Kathy Laber-Laird, and Raymond F. Anton. 1997. "Behavior and Physiology of Social Stress and Depression in Female Cynomolgus Monkeys." *Biological Psychiatry* 41(8): 871–882.

Smith, Laura. 2010. *Psychology, Poverty, and the End of Social Exclusion: Putting Our Practice to Work*. New York: Teachers College Press.

Wilkinson, Richard, and Kate Pickett. 2009. *The Spirit Level: Why Greater Equality Makes Societies Stronger*. New York: Bloomsbury Press.

Preventative Mental Health Programs

Lisa Rapp

Mental health disorders are a pervasive and significant problem in the United States. It is estimated that every year approximately one-quarter of adults are diagnosed with one or more mental disorders and 6 percent suffer from a serious mental illness (Agency for Healthcare Research and Quality [AHRQ] 2009). The statistics are even more sobering for youth, as 46 percent of adolescents and 13 percent of children have a mental health diagnosis (National Institute for

Mental Health [NIMH] 2011). Mental health disorders often result in grave short- and long-term consequences for individuals, families, and society. Unless accurately diagnosed and effectively treated, mental disorders commencing in childhood continue into adulthood where they often worsen and cause more serious problems. For instance, untreated mental health disorders often precipitate subsequent difficulties in school and employment, impede social relationships, evoke suicide risk, and result in legal problems and economic failure (Rapp-Paglicci, Dulmus, & Wodarski 2004).

Unfortunately, many people do not have adequate access to treatment. It is estimated that in 2008, only half (50.6%) of children and 52 percent of adults diagnosed with a mental disorder had received treatment within the past year (NIMH 2011). Often, transportation barriers and lack of treatment availability are a major impediment to access. Even when treatment is accessed and adequately provided, there are other hurdles such as cost. In 2006, 36.2 million people paid for mental health services totaling $57.5 billion. The average expenditure per person was $1,591. Within this group, 4.6 million children received mental health services totaling $8.9 billion. The average expenditure per child was higher than for adults at $1,931 (National Academy of Sciences 2010). Data taken from the Medical Expenditure Panel Survey of 2006 identified mental disorders as the most costly condition overall, beating cancer and heart conditions.

Unfortunately, by the time treatment is accessed, provided, and paid for it may not be as effectual as was expected. When treatment is delayed there is a risk that the disorder has progressed and become more severe. Consequently, when treatment is finally received, it may not be as potent as earlier intervention could have been and more serious treatment such as inpatient services and medications may now be warranted.

Due to the difficulties regarding mental health treatment access, cost, and effectiveness there has been increasing interest in prevention practices that can intervene early to impede the onset or reduce the severity of mental health disorders (National Academy of Sciences 2010).

Prevention

In the past, prevention was the primary specialty of the field of public health. However, over the past few years, other disciplines have begun to recognize the importance and value of early intervention. The paradigm shift toward prevention first began in the medical field but has since been followed by the mental health disciplines. There are two classifications of prevention and both will be described here as they are both beneficial in understanding mental health prevention programming.

Public Health Prevention Classification

Public health traditionally conceptualized prevention at three times: primary, secondary, and tertiary. According to Jekel, Katz, and Elmore (2001), primary prevention refers to keeping a disease or disorder from occurring and focuses on intervening during the predisease phase and on health promotion. Secondary prevention occurs before symptoms of the disorder are noticed and reduces the number of cases of the disease or disorder (Institute of Medicine [IOM] 1994). Intervention at this stage helps reduce the number of individuals who have the disease and negative outcomes of the disease or disorder (Compton 2010). Tertiary prevention, or what most clinicians would consider treatment, occurs after diagnosis of the disease or disorder and focuses on reducing suffering and impairments from the disorder. Minimizing adverse outcomes and increasing successful rehabilitation are the hallmarks of this type of prevention (Jekel, Katz, & Elmore 2001). The public health prevention model targets differing stages of disease progression, essentially focusing on the *timing* of interventions, while the newer model of prevention developed by the Institute of Medicine targets *who* should receive the interventions.

Institute of Medicine Classification

In 1994, the Institute of Medicine developed a new prevention classification system based primarily on the specific populations who should receive interventions under the primary prevention category (Compton 2010). Three types of populations are targeted: universal, selective, and indicated.

Universal prevention interventions target the general public and are considered positive for the whole population, regardless of one's risk level (Compton 2010; IOM 1994). Examples include the fluoridation of water and laws requiring seat belts. Selective prevention interventions target a subgroup of the population whose risk of disease or disorder is higher than others'. Finally, indicated prevention interventions are those that target high-risk individuals. These individuals may have biological markers and one or more risk factor for a particular disorder (Compton 2010).

Prevention Programs

Currently, there are an infinite number of prevention programs in the area of mental health. They are multifarious in nature, in that they that have been developed and implemented by many different disciplines, intervene at varying critical times, focus on one or more groups that are at risk, and utilize many different intervention components. Prevention programs have also emerged in a variety of settings, including school based, community based, medical settings, and primary care settings. Some programs have even been developed for online delivery.

Despite support from many providers and advocates, funding levels for prevention and mental health promotion services frequently remain low when compared to services for treatment and residential placements (National Academy of Sciences 2010). However, as the medical field continues to persuade the public of the benefits of prevention and health promotion over last-minute treatment, the ideology and emphasis toward early intervention will likely change.

Characteristics of Effective Prevention Programs

Over the past several decades, a scientific database has accumulated that clearly indicates that we can successfully prevent many mental health disorders (Beardslee, Chien, & Bell 2011). Multidisciplinary research has repeatedly proven that early intervention is effective in delaying or fully preventing the onset of disorders and is clearly more cost effective than later interventions (IOM 2009). Most preventive programs are targeted at children, adolescents, and young adults because most mental health problems are diagnosed before age 24, with half beginning by age 14 (Beardslee, Chien, & Bell 2011). This suggests that a developmental approach to early intervention is best.

Solid empirical evidence has indicated that particular risk and protective factors encourage or hinder, respectively, the development of mental health problems. These factors can occur in the biological and genetic systems as well as the familial, parental, and socioeconomic dimensions (Beardslee, Chien, & Bell 2011). Additionally, different risk and protective factors are particularly potent at different stages of development (Rapp-Paglicci & Dulmus 2003). For example, positive peer relationships are extremely important during adolescence. This knowledge has been especially helpful in developing effective prevention programs, since developers are now able to tailor the specific preventive interventions for each age. For instance, since substance abuse problems often begin as early as 15 years of age, many universal prevention programs for substance abuse are initiated during middle school (ages 11–14) and contain interventions directly related to enhancing social skills for positive peer interactions.

Research studies have also indicated that preventive intervention programs that address multiple risk factors and help enhance multiple protective factors are more effective than other, single-focus programs (IOM 2009). This is because individuals who have developed a mental health disorder do not necessarily have the same risk and protective factors. Consequently, programs that are able to target several different risk factors can be effective for a variety of people.

According to Beardslee, Chien, and Bell (2011) prevention programs aimed at young children should focus on general behavioral and emotional wellness, promoting strengths, and advancing parenting skills to support families. Later, as children enter school, programs focusing on academic skills, and enhancing social skills and emotional regulation are particularly helpful. Preventive programs for adolescents should be designed for a particular mental disorder, as adolescents and young adults will benefit more from these. Specific family adversities such as bereavement, parental incarceration, and parental psychopathology, all of which present significant risk factors for youth, should be addressed at any age and as soon as possible to lessen the effects of the stressors.

Evidence-Based Preventive Interventions

In the past few years the amount of research on preventive programs has increased exponentially. It would be impossible to discuss all of the effective programs, however the vast majority of programs that have been deemed evidence based include one or more of the following components, so a summary of these components will be provided.

Skill Enhancement

Skills components are very common preventive interventions as they have been utilized in many effective prevention programs. Studies have found them to be repeatedly efficacious in various settings, with differing cultural groups, and for many types of prevention (primary, secondary, tertiary; and universal, selected, and indicated). They are utilized as early as preschool and through young adulthood and beyond. The most frequently evaluated and effectual skills include: social/communication, problem solving, anger management, self-regulation, and life skills.

Social/communication skills training increases positive interactions, increases appropriate eye contact, and improves youths' self-confidence to engage in conversations. Problem-solving training improves youths' ability to master all of the steps needed to solve problems in any situation. Anger management training decreases aggressive and violent behaviors, by helping youth contain anger and express it appropriately. Self-regulation skills training reduces emotional and behavioral impulsivity and increases self-control and discipline. Life skills training increases competence in time management, organization, money management, interviewing skills, etc.

Skills are often taught and learned in a classroom setting and are modeled and practiced during the program. Youth often gain confidence and an understanding of how and when to use the skills. Parents are often given information about the skills their youth are being taught so that they can encourage the use of the same skills at home.

Skills training has been frequently replicated and found to decrease many different social and mental health problems. For instance, skills training has been effective in reducing aggressive and disruptive behaviors, improving attention, increasing academic achievement, reducing risky behaviors, preventing substance abuse, improving social interactions, reducing impulsivity, and promoting positive mental health (IOM 2009).

Parenting Skills

Parenting programs have repeatedly been shown to be effective in improving parenting techniques such as: increasing positive parent-child interaction, improving disciplinary consistency, and reducing the use of harsh or critical tactics (IOM 2009). The programs often include psychoeducation components, which help parents understand child development and the typical tasks and struggles of each developmental stage. Successful programs often include watching and practicing helpful techniques as well as learning how ineffective tactics such as corporal punishment actually exacerbate problematic behaviors in children. In addition, caregivers also gain social support from others and self-confidence.

Parenting programs have been found beneficial for parents of children in all developmental stages from infancy to young adulthood. They have also been found effective for all types of prevention. In other words, parenting programs can never be delivered too early or too late (IOM 2009).

Parenting components are a frequently researched component of preventive interventions and one of the most, if not the most, efficacious strategies for prevention of multifarious problems. For example, parenting interventions have been found to reduce aggressive and disruptive behaviors, improve academic success, and reduce substance use. These programs have been found effective in multiple settings (schools, community centers, etc.) as well as with various cultural groups, in many different countries (Beardslee, Chien, & Bell 2011).

Strengthening Families

Families are extraordinarily important for intervention success and likewise for prevention program efficacy. Thus many prevention programs include components or services that support or strengthen family members. Family psychoeducation, supportive services, and family interventions have all been indicated as efficacious and incredibly cost-effective approaches to prevention (Beardslee, Chien, & Bell 2011). These programs often include components such as home visitation with supports and education—education regarding health, wellness, and/or specific disorders or social problems. In addition, many free services include health screening and health and mental health services as well as low-cost child care. Beardslee, Chien, and Bell (2011) found that these services were effective across multiple cultural groups and diverse regions.

Modifying Cognitive Processes

Programs that include active components in identifying and transforming cognitive distortions, reframing situations, and positive thinking strategies have been noted as consistently effective in preventing and reducing depression, anxiety, posttraumatic stress disorder, substance abuse, and aggression (National Academy of Sciences 2010). Healthy thinking skills along with cognitive-behavioral therapy (CBT) have often been infused in prevention programs to target specific risk and protective factors. In other words, some programs use CBT as the main interventive technique, while others use it in addition to other components such as skill enhancement or parenting classes. However, there is strong support indicating modifying cognitive processes to be quite effective for children through adults (National Academy of Sciences 2010).

These components are particularly potent because they strive to reduce general risk factors, including poverty and poor parenting skills, that cause or exacerbate multiple social problems and mental health disorders. They also assist in building promotive factors that facilitate resilience and coping skills needed to adapt to adverse situations and prevent the development of mental health disorders. For instance, improving cognitive processes and enhancing skills are significant for resilience but also for preventing anxiety, depression, aggression, and behavioral disorders at all stages of development.

Future of Prevention Programming

The substantial empirical evidence that has been accumulated over the past decade attests to the effectiveness of prevention programs for mental health. It is clear that evidence-based prevention components as well as evidence-based programs in their entirety are now available. Future research is warranted as there are many questions needing further investigation. For example, are different preventive components or programs more or less effective for males and females? Are there differences for programs delivered at school versus the community, etc.?

In addition to more empirical evidence regarding the programs and components, further advocacy is needed at the policy level. For instance, more federal funding needs to be provided to support prevention research, and a long-term prevention plan from NIMH could help advance the idea of prevention beyond public health and the medical fields. In addition, prevention courses need to be mandatory offerings in psychology, social work, and counseling programs.

Prevention programs for mental health have significantly increased in number and have vastly improved in quality. However, there is still work to be done regarding changing the approach and philosophical thinking regarding mental health from treatment to prevention or presymptom intervention. This will require significant efforts, but those efforts will be well worth the result of fewer diagnoses of mental illness, less ancillary consequences of mental illness to individuals and their families, and lowered medical costs. Should the United States focus its health care trajectory on prevention, it is possible that the devastating effects of mental illness could be significantly reduced in the near future.

See also Adolescence and Mental Health; Children and Mental Health; Evidence-Based Practice and Outcome Measurement; Family and Mental Health; Poverty, Unemployment, Economic Inequality, and Mental Health; Primary Care Behavioral Health; Public Awareness and Public Education; Public Health Perspectives; School Mental Health; Undiagnosed Mental Illness

Bibliography

Agency for Healthcare Research and Quality. 2009. *Program Brief: Mental Health Research Findings*. Rockville, MD: Agency for Healthcare Research and Quality.

Beardslee, William, Peter Chien, and Carl Bell. 2011. "Prevention of Mental Disorders, Substance Abuse, and Problem Behaviors: A Developmental Perspective." *Psychiatric Services* 62(3): 247–254.

Compton, Michael. 2010. *Clinical Manual of Prevention in Mental Health*. Washington, DC: American Psychiatric Publishing.

Institute of Medicine. 1994. *Reducing Risks for Mental Disorders: Frontiers for Preventive Intervention Research*. Washington, DC: National Academy Press.

Institute of Medicine. 2001. *Crossing the Quality Chasm: A New Health System for the 21st Century*. Committee on Quality of Health Care in America. Washington, DC: National Academy Press.

Jekel, James, David Katz, and Joann Elmore. 2001. *Epidemiology, Biostatistics, and Preventive Medicine Review*. New York: Saunders.

National Academy of Sciences. 2010. *Preventing Mental, Emotional, and Behavioral Disorders among Young People*. Washington, DC: National Academies Press.

National Institute of Mental Health. 2011. *Any Disorder among Children*. Retrieved from http://www.nimh.nih.gov/statistics/1ANYDIS_CHILD.shtml.

Rapp-Paglicci, Lisa, and Catherine Dulmus. 2003. "Developmental Considerations in Youth Violence Prevention." *School Social Work Journal* 28(1): 21–35.

Rapp-Paglicci, Lisa, Catherine Dulmus, and John Wodarski, eds. 2004. *The Handbook of Preventive Interventions for Children and Adolescents*. New York: Wiley.

Society for Prevention Research. http://www.Preventionresearch.org.

Primary Care Behavioral Health

Christine Runyan

In 2010, dramatic shifts in health care insurance coverage and implementation occurred in the United States. The Patient Protection and Affordable Health Care Act (PPACA) was signed into law in March 2010, the result of highly contentious and laborious deliberations on health care reform. Infused with ideas and funding for pilot programs and demonstration projects, the PPACA is a complex assortment of policies and finance reform that seeks to contain costs, improve access to high-quality health care, and expand insurance coverage. Also in 2010, regulations implementing the Mental Health Parity and Addiction Equity Act of 2008 (MHPAEA) were published. This law requires insurance carriers who offer participants medical/surgical coverage to also allow parity for mental health and substance use disorders (MH/SUD). That is, MHPAEA prevents large group health plans (individual and small-business health plans are not currently bound by this regulation) from imposing financial requirements and treatment limitations on MH/SUD benefits that are more restrictive than the financial requirements and treatment limitations established for the plans' medical/surgical benefits.

Fortunately and collectively, these laws expand opportunities to identify, assess, and treat more people with behavioral health needs than ever before (the term "behavioral health" will be used throughout this entry to include both mental illness and substance use conditions). In doing so, they require changes to and innovations in existing models of service delivery to meet this need. Specifically, the integration of behavioral health into primary care has become the predominant model for increasing screening and access to mental health services in the U.S. health care system, and for good reason. The rationale for integrated care, a working definition of integrated care, and the evidence supporting behavioral health integration into primary care will be summarized in this entry.

The Burden of Illness Requires New Models of Care

The morbidity and economic burden of mental illness in the United States is enormous. The National Comorbidity Survey is conducted among U.S. households every 10 years (it excludes institutionalized and homeless populations) and is a reliable source for epidemiological data about mental illness. In the last survey, 26 percent of respondents reported symptoms sufficient to warrant a mental health diagnosis in the past 12 months, and a lifetime prevalence estimate for any mental health disorder was 46.4 percent (Kessler et al. 2006). Of these, anxiety disorders were most prevalent (18.1%), followed by mood disorders (11.1%). Moreover, in studies examining the prevalence of mental health conditions in primary care clinics, several seminal studies have also documented high rates of mental illness in primary care patients (Mauksch et al. 2001; see the below table).

Another recent study examined the prevalence of specific types of anxiety disorders in a random sample of nearly 1,000 primary care patients and reported that

Prevalence of Mental Illness in Community and Primary Care Samples

	Lifetime Prevalence	Primary Care Setting Current Prevalence
Depression	21%	24%
Anxiety	29%	20%
Alcohol use disorders	15%	17%
Any mental health disorder	46%	52%

Source: Mauksch et al. 2001.

nearly 20 percent of patients (19.5% %) had one or more anxiety conditions (Kroenke et al. 2007). Posttraumatic stress disorder was the most common (8.6%), followed by generalized anxiety disorder (7.6%), panic disorder (6.8%), and social anxiety (6.2%). Despite the scope and severity of conditions, 59 percent of respondents with a mental health condition reported receiving no treatment for their mental illness, and among the 41 percent who did receive treatment, only 44 percent received mental health services. All the others received care only in the primary care clinic, by primary care providers. The reasons for the lack of treatment in general and lack of mental health treatment in particular are many, including access to care. However, stigma remains another common and substantial barrier to seeking mental health care. Based on a survey of 3,239 adults conducted by Roper for the National Mental Health Association in 2000, 42 percent of people with a mental health condition reported that they are embarrassed or ashamed of their symptoms. Thirty-two percent of adults without a mental health condition stated they would likely turn to their primary care provider to help with mental health issues if the need arose; only 4 percent stated they would specifically seek mental health care (National Mental Health Association 2000).

Other data confirm this reality: approximately 50 percent of all behavioral health disorders are treated in primary care, and 48 percent of psychotropic agents are prescribed by nonpsychiatric primary care providers (Kessler et al. 2005). Members of racial and ethnic minorities are even less inclined than whites to seek treatment from mental health specialists (U.S. Department of Health and Human Services 1999). Instead, primary care becomes the point of entry for many minorities. Moreover, of the top five conditions driving overall health care costs in the United States (including utilization costs, lost work-related productivity, and pharmacy costs), clinical depression tops the list (Murray & Lopez 1997).

Particularly for recognizing and treating depression in primary care, numerous studies to date have demonstrated both cost-effectiveness and cost-offset (i.e., lower costs overall following initial investment) when behavioral health care is integrated into primary care settings (Von Korff et al. 1998). Studies have also documented improvements in *medical costs* when behavioral health needs are recognized and treated. For example, in a meta-analysis of 91 studies, medical utilization decreased 15.7 percent for those with a mental health condition who received behavioral health care, while it increased 12.3 percent for those who did not (Chiles, Lambert, & Hatch 1999). Mental health care is and will continue to be delivered in primary care clinics. The data clearly underscore a central role for behavioral health providers to position themselves within primary care clinics, where patients present for care and are willing to receive care in order to best meet these needs.

Models of Integrated Care

The high demand to integrate behavioral health into primary care in the past decade has led to the promulgation of a variety of different models for integration, leading to a plethora of definitions of integrated care (also called collaborative care). However, there is generally insufficient evidence at this time to suggest that one particular model of integrated care is superior to another. Thus a working definition of integrated primary care is suggested here in order to emphasize the critical *elements* of integration as opposed to a particular model (informed by Miller, Kessler, & Peek 2011).

> Integrated care is a *team of trained providers* working in the *same space* (or with a set of working relationships between collaborating clinicians) and from a *shared mission* to care for an *identified and shared population of patients*. In an integrated primary care setting, medical and behavioral health providers use a *clinical and operational system* that allows population-level *screening and identification* as well as *coordinated care plans*, frequent *communication*, and *shared documentation*. In mature integrated care practices, *financial systems* are in place to equitably support medical and behavioral health providers as well as a system that allows for *effective measurement and continuous quality improvement*.

Most models of integration are predicated on the notion of "stepped care," whereby the lowest level of services is offered first and increasingly more resource-intense services are provided only if needed. Thus primary care behavioral health care functions optimally in the context of a larger behavioral health delivery system that includes specialty mental health, substance abuse services, and behavioral services. Just as primary medical care relies on the availability of specialists for consultation and management of complex patients, integrated primary behavioral health care relies on these other types of services and providers. In practice, the demands of a specific primary care setting tend to drive the unique characteristics of how behavioral health might be integrated into the system of care. For example, a community health center in an inner city serves a different patient population than might be found in a rural academic training clinic, thereby necessitating different approaches to best target the clinic's population and needs.

Behavioral health providers positioned in primary care clinics often function in roles and provide services that are different from those provided by traditional psychologists or social workers in mental health settings. They (behavioral health providers) become a member of a larger and interdisciplinary health care team and not only help manage traditional mental health and substance use disorders, but also become involved with the management of psychosocial aspects of chronic and acute diseases. They might work with patients on behavioral change to address lifestyle factors and health risks, such as smoking cessation and weight management. Often, behavioral health providers in primary care settings serve as consultants to the primary care providers and will comanage mental disorders and psychosocial issues alongside the primary care provider. In some models of integrated care, the behavioral health provider might see patients in shorter visits and for fewer visits overall so that he or she is available for a continual stream of patients as opposed to developing a set caseload of patients (which can limit the number of new referrals). To that end, a typical primary care behavioral health service employs a problem-focused assessment and bases treatment on symptom reduction and improvement to individual functioning.

Evidence for Integrated Care

Evidence for integrated care has been accumulated on a variety of clinical outcomes, including: reduced symptoms as well as improved disease management indicators; improved process outcomes (e.g., reduced no-show rates and improved recognition rates); improved economic outcomes (cost-effectiveness and cost-offset); as well as high patient and provider satisfaction. Gilbody, Bower, and Fletcher (2006) published a meta-analysis of 37 randomized studies, which included 12,355 patients with depression in primary care. Results suggested that integrated care improves depression outcomes at 6 months. Furthermore, a sustained benefit was found with clinical improvements after 12 months, 18 months, 24 months, and even up to five years. Bower, Gilbody, Richards, Fletcher, and Sutton (2006) completed a meta-regression of 28 studies of collaborative care reporting outcome data on antidepressant use and 34 studies with data on clinical outcomes; they found that collaborative care had a positive and significant impact on antidepressant use and reduction in depressive symptoms.

Primary care-based studies on the effect of short-term behavioral interventions, and behavioral activation (a kind of therapy) in particular, have demonstrated statistically and clinically meaningful effects on reducing depression at a level comparable to antidepressant medication, with few if any risks (Dimidjian et al. 2006). Moreover, a well-done study on the recognition and treatment of anxiety in primary care using cognitive-behavioral therapy (CBT) and medications also demonstrated that both types of treatment had a significant and sustained (12 months) improvement over treatment as usual (Roy-Byrne 2005). In addition, patients receiving both medication and CBT were less symptomatic at 3 and 12 months on several symptom and functional measures, compared to those receiving medication alone. There is also a sizable and growing body of literature demonstrating the clinical and economic benefits of treating mental health conditions associated with chronic medical conditions (e.g., diabetes or hypertension) in primary care. These studies consistently demonstrate positive effects on clinical outcomes, cost reduction, and decreased fragmentation of care (see Ouwens et al. 2005).

What Conditions to Target in Primary Care

The U.S. Preventive Services Task Force (USPSTF) is an independent panel of nonfederal experts that conducts scientific evidence reviews of a broad range of clinical preventive health care services. Based on these reviews, the USPSTF develops recommendations for primary care clinicians and health systems. The USPSTF focuses on maintenance of health and quality of life and considers the evidence not only in light of the benefits of the service but also in terms of whether the benefits outweigh the harms. Their recommendations are held in high regard by health systems and insurance carriers and often become the coverage and quality benchmarks. Owing to the prevalence and unequivocal evidence regarding the deleterious impact of unrecognized and untreated substance use and depression on physical health status, the USPSTF recommends the following:

- Screening and behavioral counseling interventions to reduce alcohol misuse by adults, including pregnant women, in primary care settings
- Screening of adolescents (12–18 years of age) for major depressive disorder when systems are in place to ensure accurate diagnosis, psychotherapy (cognitive-behavioral or interpersonal), and follow-up
- Screening adults for depression when staff-assisted depression care supports are in place to assure accurate diagnosis, effective treatment, and follow-up

Although there is ample evidence to document the comorbidities of other types of mental illness, such as posttraumatic stress disorder and other anxiety disorders, with medical conditions, the absence of USPSTF recommendations on screening and treatment in primary care screening would be harmful or unhelpful.

The USPSTF does not go beyond the recommendations for screening for depression or alcohol use or advocate for a particular screening tool; however, several well-validated and psychometrically sound instruments exist for screening depression and alcohol use in primary care. Table on p. 559 provides a list of useful screening tools and the associated websites to access these measures where additional details about their scientific integrity can also be found. These tools currently constitute the gold standards for screening and assessment in primary care.

Finally, much of the rationale and evidence for integrating behavioral health providers into primary care settings is also to help address the psychosocial aspects of chronic illness, such as diabetes, and lifestyle habits that portend poor health outcomes, such as smoking. Behavioral health providers working in primary care settings should have substantial and specialized training regarding the biopsychosocial model of health and illness. They work collaboratively with medical providers to offer behavioral change counseling as well as physiological

Screening Tools Available

Symptoms	Screening Tool	Brief Description	Source
ADULTS			
Depression	PHQ-9	(Patient Health Questionnaire Screening for Depression); Self-report; 18+ years	Copyright by Pfizer. No charge. http://www.depression-primarycare.org/clinicians/toolkits/materials/forms/phq9
Anxiety	GAD-2 GAD-7	Seven-item self-report tool for symptoms of generalized anxiety (can use first two items as GAD-2 for even quicker screen)	Copyright by Pfizer. No charge. http://phqscreeners.com/
PTSD	PC-PTSD	Four-item screening tool for core cluster PTSD symptoms	http://www.ptsd.va.gov/professional/pages/assessments/pc-ptsd.asp
Multiple symptoms	M-3 Checklist	Brief, self-rated screen for depressive, bipolar, anxiety, and posttraumatic stress disorders	http://www.annfammed.org/cgi/content/full/8/2/160/DC1
Dementia	(MoCA)	Montreal Cognitive Assessment Clinician-administered screening tool for dementia	www.mocatest.org
Alcohol	AUDIT-C or AUDIT	3- or 10-item screening tool for alcohol use disorders	http://whqlibdoc.who.int/hq/2001/WHO_MSD_MSB_01.6a.pdf
CHILDREN/YOUTH			
Depression	PHQ-A	Modified version of the PHQ-9 for adolescents	http://www.teenscreen.org/
Alcohol/ substance	CRAFFT	Acronym for Car, Relax, Alone, Forget, Friends, Trouble; Screening for substance abuse in ages 11–21 years	Copyright Children's Hospital Boston. No Charge. http://www.ceasar-boston.org/clinicians/crafft.php
ADHD	Vanderbilt ADHD Assessment	Parent and teacher Reports for ADHD symptoms; both initial and follow-up assessments; endorsed by American Academy of Pediatrics	http://www.nccpeds.com/adhd_toolkit.htm (also http://www.brightfutures.org)
Development/ behavior	PEDS	(Parents' Evaluation of Developmental Status) Parent completed; Appropriate for birth to eight years	http://www.pedstest.com

(continued)

Screening Tools Available *(Continued)*

Symptoms	Screening Tool	Brief Description	Source
Developmental	M-CHAT	(Modified Checklist for Autism in Toddlers) Parent-completed checklist; Ages 16–30 months; screens for core symptom of autism	No charge. http://www2.gsu.edu/ ~psydir
General behavior / multiple symptoms	PSC	(Pediatric Symptom Checklist) and YPSC (Pediatric Symptom Checklist–Youth Report) Parent-completed checklists; appropriate for 4–16 years; YPSC for 11+ years and youth completes it	Public domain, no charge. http://www2. massgeneral.org/allpsych/ psc/psc_home.htm

techniques to improve outcomes among patients with chronic medical conditions, with and without concomitant mental health needs.

Conclusions

There is no longer debate about whether integrated care is a good idea, if it works, or if patients and providers like these models of care—the evidence is clear and primary care behavioral health is here to stay. Rather, one of the most pressing unanswered questions is how to effectively fund models of integrated care. Historically, medical and mental health care have both relied on fee-for-service payments, but the two systems have been functionally distinct and financed differently. This presents challenges to care for patients in a single setting and often on the same day with adequate insurance coverage and reimbursements. Movement within the health care reform legislation toward a partially capitated payment system (i.e., one based on set per-patient fees) for both medical and behavioral health care will allow integrated care to prosper. Another issue is that mental health and medical providers are trained in professional and discipline-specific silos with little exposure to or experience with integrated care. Several postgraduate training programs now exist to train behavioral health and medical practitioners of the future to work optimally on interdisciplinary teams in primary care (http://www.umassmed.edu/cipc/index.aspx).

A final issue of note with this new model of care pertains to documentation and data gathering using a shared medical record that captures standardized data of meaningful use. Ultimately, a unified electronic medical record this will allow accurate measurements of health care utilization and effectiveness on both medical and mental health parameters as well as continuous quality improvement. Although these goals are currently unrealized, considerable expertise and effort is being directed toward these topics with a goal of providing high-quality, cost-effective, comprehensive, and integrated health care to all Americans.

See also Culturally Competent Mental Health Care; Evidence-Based Practice and Outcome Measurement; Insurance and Parity Laws; Medical Model of Mental Illness; Preventative Mental Health Programs; Psychotherapy; Stigma; Undiagnosed Mental Illness

Bibliography

Bower, P., S. Gilbody, D. Richards, J. Fletcher, and A. Sutton. 2006. "Making Sense of a Complex Intervention: Systematic Review and Meta Regression." *British Journal of Psychiatry* 189: 484–493.

Chiles, J. A., M. J. Lambert, and A. L. Hatch. 1999. "The Impact of Psychological Intervention on Medical Cost Offset: A Meta-Analytic Review." *Clinical Psychology* 6: 204–220.

Dimidjian, S., S. D. Hollon, K. S. Dobson, K. B. Schmaling, R. J. Kohlenberg, R. Gallop, S. L. Rizvi, J. K. Gollan, D. L. Dunner, and N. S. Jacobson 2006. "Randomized Trial of Behavioral Activation, Cognitive Therapy, and Antidepressant Medication in the Acute Treatment of Adults with Major Depression." *Journal of Consulting and Clinical Psychology* 74(4): 658–670.

Elder, A., and J. Holmes. 2002. *Mental Health in Primary Care*. New York: Oxford University Press.

Gilbody, S., P. Bower, and J. Fletcher. 2006. "Collaborative Care for Depression: A Cumulative Meta-Analysis and Review of Longer-Term Outcomes." *Archives of Internal Medicine* 166(21): 2314–2321.

Kessler, R. C., P. Berglund, O. Demier, R. Jin, K. R. Merikangas, and E. E. Walters. 2006. "Lifetime Prevalence and Age-of-Onset Distributions of *DSM-IV* Disorders in the National Comorbidity Survey Replication." *Archives of General Psychiatry* 62(6): 593–602.

Kessler, R. C., O. Demler, R. G. Frank, M. Olfson, H. A. Pincus, E. E. Walters, P. Wang, K. B. Wells, and A. M. Zaslavsky. 2005. "Prevalence and Treatment of Mental Disorders, 1990 to 2003." *New England Journal of Medicine* 352: 2515–2523.

Kroenke, K., R. L. Spitzer, J. B. W. Williamson, P. O. Monahan, and B. Lowe. 2007. "Anxiety Disorders in Primary Care: Prevalence, Impairment, Comorbidity and Detection." *Annals of Internal Medicine* 146(5): 317–326.

Macarthur Initiative on Depression and Primary Care. http://www.depression-primarycare.org/.

Mauksch, L. B., S. M. Tucker, W. J. Katon, J. Russo, J. Cameron, E. Walker, and R. Spitzer 2001. "Mental Illness, Functional Impairment, and Patient Preferences for Collaborative Care in an Uninsured, Primary Care Population." *Journal of Family Practice* 50(1): 41–47.

Miller, B. F., R. Kessler, and C. J. Peek. 2011. *A National Agenda for Research in Collaborative Care: Papers from the Collaborative Care Research Network Research Development Conference*. AHRQ Publication No. 11-0067. Rockville, MD: Agency for Healthcare Research and Quality.

Murray, C. J., and A. D. Lopez. 1997. "Alternative Projections of Mortality and Disability by Cause 1990–2020: Global Burden of Disease Study." *The Lancet* 349: 1498–1504.

National Council for Community Behavioral Healthcare. Making Integrated Care Work. Retrieved from http://www.thenationalcouncil.org/cs/center_for_integrated _health_solutions.

National Mental Health Association. 2000. "America's Mental Health Survey, May 2000." Conducted by Roper Starch Worldwide, Inc. Retrieved from http://www.roper.com/Newsroom/content/news189.htm.

Ouwens, M., H. Wollersheim, R. Hermens, M. Hulscher, and R. Grol. 2005. "Integrated Care Programmes for Chronically Ill Patients: A Review of Systematic Reviews." *International Journal for Quality in Health Care* (17): 141–146.

Roy-Byrne, P. 2005. "A Randomized Effectiveness Trial of Cognitive Behavioral Therapy and Medication for Primary Care Panic Disorder." *Archives of General Psychiatry* 62(3): 290–298.

Schneider, R., and J. L. Levenson. 2007. *Psychiatry Essentials for Primary Care*. Philadelphia: American College of Physicians.

U.S. Department of Health and Human Services. 1999. "Mental Health: Culture, Race, and Ethnicity. A Supplement to Mental Health: A Report of the Surgeon General." Rockville, MD: U.S. Department of Health and Human Services.

U.S. Preventive Services Task Force. http://www.uspreventiveservicestaskforce.org/index.html.

Von Korff, M., W. Katon, T. Bush, E. H. Lin, G. E. Simon, K. Saunders, E. Ludman, E. Walker, and J. Unutzer 1998. "Treatment Costs, Cost Offset, and Cost-Effectiveness of Collaborative Management of Depression." *Psychosomatic Medicine* 60(2): 143–149.

World Health Organization. 2008. *Integrated Mental Health into Primary Health Care: A Global Perspective*. Geneva: World Health Organization.

Prisons and Mental Health

Steven K. Erickson

A prevailing theme in modern criminal justice is the prevalence of mental illness among people within the correctional system. Epidemiological studies suggest that the proportion of inmates with mental illness in the United States is approximately 15 percent, with some studies estimating much larger numbers. Numerous commentators have decried what is perceived as an epidemic of mental illness within correctional populations based on the assumption that the number of inmates with mental illnesses is historically high compared to the recent past. In addition, scholars and policy officials have expressed concern that many of these inmates do not receive adequate treatment while incarcerated because correctional facilities are often ill-equipped to handle the complex issues that these mentally ill inmates present to the correctional system.

However, the role that mental illness plays in modern correctional practice is not as straightforward as it might appear. Upon closer inspection, it remains uncertain whether the rates of mental illness within the correctional system have increased as dramatically as many proponents claim. Additionally, the reasons for any claimed increase are ambiguous and defy simple explanations. There are a number of competing explanatory theories about the purported rise of mental illness within jails and prisons. Each theory highlights different institutional concerns that warrant varying institutional and societal interventions.

Despite the obscure epidemiological rates, it is quite clear that a sizable number of inmates do receive mental health services with incarceration. However, the quality of those services various tremendously by institution. Some prisons rely simply on segregating inmates with mental health problems from the general prison population while providing access to simple psychiatric care. Others provide more robust treatment, including psychotherapy and integrated discharge planning with community care providers upon an inmate's release from custody.

Rates of Mental Illness in Prison and Jails

In 1999, the U.S. Bureau of Justice Statistics published a study that found that approximately 16 percent of inmates within state and federal jails and prisons suffered from mental illness. This study has been widely cited as evidence that large numbers of inmates across multiple jurisdictions are mentally ill and in need of treatment. But like most similar studies, the methodology utilized was limited. Inmates were counted as mentally ill if they answered affirmatively to one of two questions: whether they had a mental illness or if they had ever spent a night at a psychiatric hospital. These results leave much to be desired because they do not rely upon formal methods of assessment by trained professionals, use different definitions of mental illness, and are prone to numerous reporting biases.

More rigorous studies have arrived at disparate numbers. For instance, a 1990 study that examined 728 jail inmates in Chicago found that 6.4 percent suffered from mental illness. Meanwhile another study found that about a quarter of prison inmates in New York had a functional psychiatric disability (Steadman, Fabisiak, & Dvoskin 1987). Still another federal study found that the rate of inmates with mental health problems approached a whopping 60 percent (James & Glaze 2006). The difference between these studies rests on several factors, including the varying methodologies used to gather the data and, more importantly, the definitions used to define mental illness. Several studies, including the latest federal study, include alcohol and drug abuse. Others include depression and anxiety disorders among those counted as mental illness. Nonetheless, best estimates suggest that about 10 percent of inmates suffer from a major mental disorder and between 2 and 4 percent of those are afflicted with a psychotic disorder such as schizophrenia (Lamb & Weinberger 1998).

Causative Factors

A central question surrounding the rates of mental illness and the correctional system is what might be the putative and genuine causes. Suggestions range from diminishing mental health services to changing legal rules regarding psychiatric hospitalization to changes in social attitudes regarding mental illness. Still others suggest deeper sociological reasons that emphasize the reciprocal nature between prison and mental hospitals.

Lack of Services

Many commentators suggest that the increased number of people with mental illnesses within jails and prisons is attributable to systematic shortage of mental health services within the community. Since the majority of persons with mental illnesses receive their care within the community, adequate outpatient psychiatric services are essential. When services are underfunded or otherwise unavailable, symptoms go untreated and result in calls for assistance from local authorizes, which often includes the police. Since the prevalence of illicit drug abuse occurs at about twice the rate among those with severe mental illnesses than the general population (Bo, Abu-Akel, Kongerslev, Haahr, & Simonsen 2011), high rates of arrests and incarceration are unsurprising.

Deinstitutionalization

Due to several landmark legal cases in the 1970s as well as changing fiscal and social policy, the number of people with mental illnesses who receive their treatment at inpatient settings has decreased dramatically. Some suggest that this change has had the twin effects of placing patients with severe symptoms in the

---

People with Mental Illnesses in Prison

"A prison's purpose is not to prescribe psychiatric medicines and therapy ... [but rather] ... to confine and perhaps reform criminals. To that end it fills the prisoner's days with rigid rules and punishes the disobedient. Typically, those with severe mental disorders are in no position to obey such rules, so they get punished—with or without the medications that they may need. ... On the other hand, if they remain in the company of other prisoners, especially if they draw attention to themselves with bizarre behavior, they become ready targets for brutal beatings, rape, or murder."

—J. A. Hobson and J. A. Leonard

Source: J. A. Hobson and J. A. Leonard, Out of Its Mind: Psychiatry in Crisis (Cambridge, MA: Perseus, 2001), 29–30.

community who are unable to care for themselves while simultaneously removing the most intensive services available for treatment. There is no question that the number of inpatient psychiatric beds has nearly evaporated. In 1955 there were nearly 559,000 people receiving inpatient treatment at a mental hospital whereas presently that number has shrunk to about 72,000 (Lamb & Weinberger 1998). This curtailment of inpatient beds occurred at a time when the general population of the United States has increased by about 100 million. More importantly, it was not uncommon in the past that inpatient hospitalization would entail long, sustained treatment—sometimes for life. Most inpatient treatment nowadays consists mainly of short stays in the psychiatric wing of general hospitals.

Civil Commitment Criteria

Some argue that changing legal criteria for the civil commitment of the mentally ill has focused attention on the dangerousness of behavior associated with their illnesses instead of their disabling effects (Steadman et al. 1984). In the landmark case of *O'Conner v. Donaldson* (1975), the U.S. Supreme Court held that there must be a finding that a person with mental illness is dangerous to not only him or herself but also to others in order justify involuntarily hospitalization. By focusing on dangerousness, it is argued that the court inadvertently emphasized a link between social deviance and mental illness that refocused law enforcement attention on the unlawful activities of persons with mental illness.

The more common explanation, however, is that strict civil commitment criteria prevent effective treatment intervention until behavior becomes dangerous in some fashion (Torrey & Zdanowicz 2001). Since most dangerous behavior is criminalized, it is unsurprising that a sizable number of inmates are mentally ill. This concern has led several states to enact outpatient commitment statutes that provide additional legal leverage to treatment providers while maintaining treatment in the outpatient context (Erickson 2005). Nonetheless, the effect of these new commitment statutes on rates of mental illness among inmates is likely negligible since they are used sparingly and are reserved for persons with extensive histories of severe forms of mental illness.

Criminalization

Another explanatory theory suggests that the increased number of inmates with mental illness is directly caused by law enforcement efforts that target people with mental illness in the community (Engel & Silver 2001). Modeled on social control theory, the criminalization hypothesis holds that broader society is intolerant of social deviance and demands that people who display aberrant behavior be separated from the general community. In the past, long-term psychiatric hospitalization served as the primary mechanism for achieving this result. After deinstitutionalization, people with mental illnesses were merely transferred to the criminal justice system in order to maintain their separation from society. This so-called transinsititutionalization effect posits that the label of mental illness is not really descriptive of any individual psychopathology, but rather is merely a mechanism for segregating people who display social deviancy from the general population. Proponents of this theory point to the fact that the rates of incarceration have risen at the same time the number of long-term psychiatric hospital beds has decreased (Teplin 1984).

Social Attitudes

Analogous to the criminalization hypothesis, another explanation holds that the growth of inmates with mental illness simply reflects society's intolerance of the mentally ill. Whereas in the past when civil commitment was the chief mechanism for handling social deviance that appeared as mental illness, this view suggests that modern social attitudes have grown less paternalistic and perhaps even vengeful toward those with mental illness. As a consequence, society has been less willing to extend treatment as the primary method of handling deviant behavior, but rather insists on law enforcement and punishment as the preferred method for managing behavior that manifests from mental illness.

Mental Health Services in Prison

Irrespective of the cause or rate of mental illness among jail and prison inmates, recognition that a sizable number of people housed within the nation's correctional system has driven systematic changes within the walls of most penal institutions. The first of these changes is the identification and assessment of mental illness by prison staff. While methods and quality of procedures vary, most prisons provide for some initial screening of mental illness upon an inmate's admission into the correctional system. This might merely consist of a series of questions such as whether the inmate has ever received mental health treatment in the past or has had recent thoughts of suicide. Other institutions might administer a roster of questions that are designed to "flag" symptoms of mental illness. In either case, once staff suspect that an inmate has a history of mental illness or is presently suffering from symptoms of mental illness, the case is usual referred to more experienced mental health care staff who conduct formal assessment.

If an inmate is suffering from active symptoms of mental illness, treatment might include placing the inmate in a segregated wing of the prison for observation, medications to help alleviate symptoms, and psychotherapy. While these treatment protocols are similar to the treatment strategies of mental health hospitals and outpatient treatment facilities, numerous institutional factors often frustrate the optimization of care. First, the number of professional mental health staff at most

A counselor leads a wellness self-management class at Fishkill Correctional Facility in Beacon, New York. A prison may not seem like the most obvious place for self-actualization, but a program at Fishkill is trying to help inmates living with mental illness learn more about their conditions, potentially helping to reduce discipline problems and cut down on recidivism. (AP Photo/Mike Groll.)

prisons is small compared to demand. Since prison is by itself a stressful experience, many inmates seek mental health services as an avenue for relief. This often leaves mental health staff overwhelmed with requests for their services.

Other reasons limiting the mental health care within prisons include unsympathetic staff, the stark nature of institutional confinement, and overt manipulation by inmates for services despite an absence of mental illness. The role of the correctional officer is a difficult one. The primary role of correctional officers is to maintain order and safety; yet they are also the frontline staff who interact most on a day-to-day basis with inmates. Insensitivity among prison staff is not uncommon given the inherent dangerousness of the job and the antisocial propensities of many inmates. Adding to this difficulty is the austere environment of prison life. Prisons are almost entirely constructed of concrete, and the personal effects of inmates are strictly regulated. The upshot of this milieu is that excessive noise permeates prison life, privacy is nil, and interpersonal intimidation is widespread.

Another chief limitation of prison mental health treatment is the relative dearth of substance abuse treatment. Most estimates suggest that the vast majority of prison inmates suffer from alcohol and drug abuse (Peters et al. 1998). Given this fact, intensive substance abuse treatment is a rarity within most jails and prisons. Reasons differ, but it is likely that given the sheer number of inmates in need of services, most correctional systems are simply ill-equipped and underfunded to provide sustained and concentrated substance abuse treatment. Additionally, achieving long-term sobriety is a vexing problem even with robustly funded, community-based programs. Various factors seem linked to sustained abstinence from alcohol and drug abuse, but age and internal motivation appear as the most powerful in predicting success (Heyman 2009). Correctional substance abuse treatment programs can provide neither of these factors.

Reentry and Community Care

One of the most promising ventures in managing the population of inmates with mental health problems lies not with treatment within the walls of prison but with programs that target interventions when the inmate is released from custody. The criminal justice system can be viewed as a funnel with many inmates entering the system at the top and a smaller number achieving release at the bottom. Inmates with mental illnesses who are released without planned community care are at risk for arrest and incarceration. Various reasons are posited for this risk factor, but a likely principal reason is that released inmates with mental illness face not only the routine challenges that all released inmates face, including finding employment and employment, but also coping with debilitating mental health symptoms.

Forensic assertive community treatment (FACT) is an example of one model that seeks to integrate comprehensive mental health treatment with established recidivism-reducing strategies in an effort to maximize community tenure among recently released inmates with mental illness (Lamberti, Weisman, & Faden 2004). FACT partners mental health providers and correctional professionals, including parole officers, to identify candidates before release and establishes a planned, comprehensive plan of transition from prison to the community. FACT provides psychiatric treatment, residential housing, and job-training opportunities under a unified team model of treatment. Parole officers are an integral part of the treatment team and provide valuable insight and legal leverage to promote community tenure. FACT-based programs are promising, but they are limited to former inmates with schizophrenia and other psychosis-related mental disorders, which accounts for a small number of mentally ill inmates.

Conclusion

Prison is the primary mechanism society utilizes to handle social deviancy. Distributive theories of punishment justify imprisonment on various grounds, including retribution, deterrence, incapacitation, and rehabilitation. But all of these theories imply that offenders often must be segregated from society in order to achieve their stated purpose. Modern correctional research suggests that a sizable number of inmates housed within the nation's jails and prisons suffer from mental illness. While the precise percentage of inmates suffering from mental illness remains elusive and the exact causative factors remain contested, numerous historical and social forces have transformed the correctional system into a major provider of mental health services. The ability of jails and prisons to provide adequate mental health treatment for this population is an enduring concern of correctional staff, mental health providers, and policy makers. Given the considerable growth in the nation's prison population, this problem is likely to beset correctional policy for years to come.

See also Criminalization and Diversion Programs; Forensic Psychology and Psychiatry; Involuntary Treatment; Violence and Violence-Prone Individuals

Bibliography

Bo, Sune, Ahmad Abu-Akel, Mickey Kongerslev, Ulrik Helt Haahr, and Erik Simonsen. 2011. "Risk Factors for Violence among Patients with Schizophrenia." *Clinical Psychology Review* 31: 711–726.

Ditton, Paula 1999. "Mental Health Treatment of Inmates and Probationers." Retrieved from http://bjs.ojp.usdoj.gov.

Draine, Jeffery. 2002. "Where Is the 'Illness' in the Criminalization of Mental Illness?" *Research in Community Mental Health* 12: 9–21.

Engel, Robin, and Eric Silver. 2001. "Policing Mentally Disordered Suspects: Reexamining the Criminalization Hypothesis." *Criminology* 39: 225–252.

Erickson, Steven K. 2005. "A Retrospective Examination of Outpatient Commitment in New York." *Behavioral Sciences and the Law* 23: 627–645.

Films Media Group. 2009. *The New Asylum*. (Streaming Media). New York: Films Media Group.

Heyman, Gene. 2009. *Addiction: A Disorder of Choice*. Cambridge, MA: Harvard University Press.

James, Doris, and Lauren Glaze. 2006. "Mental Health Problems of Prison and Jail Inmates." Retrieved from http://bjs.ojp.usdoj.gov.

Lamb, Richard, and Linda Weinberger. 1998. "Persons with Severe Mental Illness in Jails and Prisons: A Review." *Psychiatric Services* 49: 483–492.

Lamberti, J. Steven. 2007. "Understanding and Preventing Criminal Recidivism among Adults with Psychotic Disorders." *Psychiatric Services* 58: 773–781.

Lamberti, J. Steven, Robert Weisman, and Dara Faden. 2004. "Forensic Assertive Community Treatment: Preventing Incarceration of Adults with Severe Mental Illness." *Psychiatric Services* 55: 1285–1293.

O'Connor v. Donaldson, 422 U.S. 563 (1975).

Peters, Rogers, Paul Greenbaum, John Edens, Chris Carter, and Madeline Ortiz. 1998. "Prevalence of *DSM-IV* Substance Abuse and Dependence Disorders among Prison Inmates." *The American Journal of Alcohol and Drug Abuse* 24: 573–587.

Pfeiffer, Mary Beth. 2004. "A Death in the Box." *New York Times Magazine*, October 31. Retrieved from http://www.nytimes.com/2004/10/31/magazine/31PRISONER .html?_r=1&scp=2&sq=prisons+mental+health&st=nyt.

Steadman, Hank, Stanford Fabisiak, and Joel Dvoskin. 1987. "A Survey of Mental Disability among State Prison Inmates." *Hospital and Community Psychiatry* 38: 1086–1090.

Steadman, Hank, John Monahan, Barbara Duffee, Eliot Hartstone, and Pamela Clark Robbins. 1984. "The Impact of State Mental Hospital Deinstitutionalization on United States Prison Populations, 1968–1978." *Journal of Criminal Law and Criminology* 75: 474–490.

Teplin, Linda. 1984. "Criminalizing Mental Disorder: The Comparative Arrest Rate of the Mentally Ill." *American Psychologist* 39: 794–803.

Teplin, Linda. 1990. "The Prevalence of Severe Mental Disorder among Male Urban Jail Detainees: Comparison with the Epidemiologic Catchment Area Program." *American Journal of Public Health* 80: 663–669.

Torrey, E. Fuller, and Mary Zdanowicz. 2001. "Outpatient Commitment: What, Why, and for Whom." *Psychiatric Services* 52: 337–341.

Psychiatry

Jia-shin Chen

"Psychiatry," as defined in *Webster's New World College Dictionary* (fourth ed.), refers to "the branch of medicine concerned with the study, treatment, and prevention of disorders of the mind, including psychoses and neuroses, emotional maladjustments, etc." Despite the comprehensiveness of this definition, it does not quite capture the controversies that are embedded in a field that relies heavily on assumptions and assertions of what it is to be normal. As the field continues to grow and to seek new ways to control pathologies, improve pharmaceutical agents and psychotherapeutic approaches, and treat everyday problems medically, it is not merely personal identities but also social norms that are contested, negotiated, and redefined. It is increasingly rare for anybody not to be affected by the various terms, suggestions, and therapies posed by psychiatry or, more broadly, mental health professionals. Psychiatric acronyms such as PTSD (posttraumatic stress disorder), ADHD (attention deficit hyperactivity disorder), and PMS (premenstrual syndrome) have been as much a part of our common vocabulary as the pills such as Prozac, Ambien, and Valium awaiting many of us in our medicine cabinets. The most controversial aspects of the interface of psychiatry and society, therefore, are psychiatric diagnoses, pharmacological treatments, psychological therapies, and biomedicalized preventive strategies.

The Question of Diagnosis

Based on emotional or behavioral symptoms, psychiatric diagnoses are usually classified into several broad categories: psychoses, neuroses, temporary adjustment problems, and in children or adolescents, developmental disorders. Each category is characterized by a different set of major symptoms and defined durations. Sometimes the diagnostic categories may change over time. Adjustment disorders, for instance, last only for a certain period of time. If the symptoms somehow turn into persistent mental conditions, the psychiatric diagnosis will have to change accordingly in order to better describe the clinical features.

The conflicts over diagnoses are rooted in questions of accuracy, especially the accuracy of the identification and coding of clinical symptoms in relation to clinical categories and in relation to predictions of illness courses and outcomes. Issues of accuracy also often call into question the certainty and authority of the diagnostic categories, however. Furthermore, questions of diagnostic accuracy often lead to more fundamental questions: How do psychiatrists acquire knowledge of mental pathology? How "real" or how arbitrary are the diagnostic categories? To what extent does psychiatric knowledge rely on established social norms? Do mental illnesses exist at all? In other words, questions of diagnostic accuracy often lead to questions of epistemology and ontology.

Consider psychoses, for example, characterized by the presence of delusions, hallucinations, and disorganized thinking and usually considered more protracted and destructive than any other kind of mental suffering because psychotic patients usually lose contact with reality. Losing contact with reality is a major distinction between psychoses and neuroses. Such a distinction is not necessarily clear-cut and is often drawn arbitrarily and contestably. Decisions about what constitutes "psychotic" thinking often depend on the range of social norms that guide psychiatrists as they judge the contents of their patients' subjective experiences. Although philosopher and psychopathologist Karl Jasper argued that the criteria of a delusion should be based on form rather than content, most of the time a delusion in clinical settings is merely defined by the bizarreness of its content ("My real mother is kidnapped by aliens that come from Planet X. This one you see is a fake"). Nevertheless, the boundary between purely "bizarre" and simply "extraordinary" is quite arbitrary and sometimes unclear. There is always a gray zone between unrealistic delusions and normal beliefs, just as there is always some ambiguity about vague hallucinations and innocuous misperceptions.

The lack of validation from sources other than direct observation and interviewing often leads to disputes between doctors and patients and among psychiatrists themselves. To standardize diagnostic procedures and minimize possible controversies, the current psychiatric profession in the United States and in most other areas of the world has adopted a set of diagnostic criteria based on large-scale surveys and statistical correlations. The American version is called the *Diagnostic and Statistical Manual of Mental Disorders*, now in its fourth edition (*DSM-IV*) and soon to be in its fifth; the World Health Organization (WHO) has its own version of diagnostic criteria called the *International Classification of Diseases*, now in its 10th edition (*ICD-10*). Except for some minor differences, the structures of the *DSM* and the *ICD* are similar. They catalog manifest emotional and behavioral symptoms, and because they provide a classificatory framework, they both avoid theoretical speculations about the origins of mental illnesses.

In some sense, these diagnostic frameworks are an outcome of long-term debates within the psychiatric profession. Representing not just scientific studies but also expert consensus, they are intended to facilitate global communication among psychiatrists regardless of where they practice. Standardizing communication and diagnostic categories is not always popular, however. Many argue that globalizing psychiatric diagnoses, while disseminating psychiatric knowledge and promoting understanding among psychiatrists and related professionals, ignores the nuances of each diagnostic category in different societies and cultures. Global standards are thus often resisted for the sake of cultural and professional autonomy (Lakoff 2006).

Even with standardized diagnostic categories, many fundamental questions remain unanswered. In psychiatric research on diagnostics, scholars tend to use statistical concepts such as validity and reliability to describe the degree of correctness and consensus regarding psychiatric diagnoses. These increasingly technical approaches do not touch, however, on questions about the existence or the knowledge acquisition of mental disorders. In fact, most controversies around psychiatric diagnosis today focus on the issues of epistemology and ontology.

Consider an imaginary patient, Mike, who is diagnosed with schizophrenia because psychiatrist X finds he exhibits disorganized thinking and behaviors, experiences vivid auditory hallucinations, and possesses a strong delusional belief that his telephone has been wired for some reason. At first glance, we may ask questions of diagnostics: Is Mike correctly diagnosed? Do his symptoms match the criteria of schizophrenia perfectly? But we can also go deeper and ask the more basic questions about psychiatric epistemology: How do we acquire knowledge about what is going on inside the human mind? What does it mean when we say we "know" he is schizophrenic? Finally, there is always the inescapable question: What is schizophrenia? Is there really a disease entity "schizophrenia," with its own specific essence?

Most psychiatrists believe in realism when it comes to the "being" of mental disorders. That is, they think mental illnesses are real and exist in some forms among afflicted patients. Either psychological or biological, pathologies that cause mental agonies are always "out there," identifiable by physical or psychological methods. A notable critic of the idea that diagnostic categories, such as schizophrenia, correspond to real and distinct underlying causes is Thomas Szasz, who began speaking out against the standard psychiatric views in the 1950s and 1960s. In stark contrast to the psychiatric "realists," Szasz, also a psychiatrist, argues that there is no such a thing as mental illness because there has been no decisively identifiable brain pathology accountable for any kind of mental illness (Szasz 1961). Mental illness, Szasz contends, is nothing but a label society puts on its deviant members. Though his claims are often extremely polemical and sometimes rather conspiratorial, he has had a marked influence on the understanding of the social construction of psychiatry.

In more recent times, few people still hold this extremist perspective. Some have critiqued such antipsychiatry positions as contributing to even more rigid divisions of mind and body, society and individual, and norm and pathology than those that psychiatry was accused of upholding. A less extreme version of social constructionism asserts that social convention and social control are indeed involved in shaping the realities of psychiatric diagnoses, but that such social components do not necessarily undermine the reality of psychiatric diseases. Proponents of social constructionist views of psychiatry try to complicate the issue of psychiatric epistemology and ontology by pluralizing the concept of reality that used to be taken for granted. The recognition of sociocultural elements in the making of psychiatric knowledge, they argue, is not a limitation on understanding the truth but an enriching extension of the nature of truth claims. Social constructionists assert that only when the standards of psychiatric truth are expanded to incorporate a broad range of social components can psychiatry become a more robust and reflexive system of knowledge and practice for suffering people (Fee 2000; Wenegrat 2001).

Psychopharmacology

Conflicts about pharmacotherapy are closely related to the problem of diagnosis in psychiatric treatment, including biomedical approaches and psychological interventions. Because treatment always follows diagnosis, disputes about psychiatric diagnoses also apply to therapeutic decisions in clinical settings. Problems of treatment concern much more than considerations of illness management in the clinic, however. Aside from the controversies in psychiatric diagnostics, epistemology, and ontology, what is also at stake is the emergence of a large, new market; pharmaceutical companies, national health services, and psychiatric authorities all contribute to this ever-enlarging market of psychotropic medications around the globe. Controversies arise as the market limits itself to the transactions of therapeutic agents as commodities, as human beings become involved as paid subjects in clinical trials, as medications are smuggled as illegal goods circulating in the underground economy, and as more accessible generic drugs are prohibited or restricted (Petryna, Lakoff, & Kleinman 2006).

Pharmacological approaches are subject to strong criticisms because they are so powerful in changing patients' minds. Just like the so-called illicit psychoactive drugs, anything directed toward mind altering is always tied to certain risks. But in most cases, the underlying question is often not whether they are dangerous, addictive, or irreversible, but whether these agents or interventions may transform the ways we conceive and perceive ourselves. Controversies about the use of medications are often rooted in the fear of losing our original selves and replacing natural identity with one that is chemically contrived.

Owing to the risk of misuse or abuse, psychiatric treatments tend to be used in a very cautious way. Considering the chronic and debilitating nature of certain psychiatric conditions, however, there has been a strong desire among psychiatrists and scientists to witness some therapeutic breakthroughs. Unfortunately, under certain circumstances this well-intentioned enthusiasm may turn into something unthinkably detrimental. Examples from earlier treatment eras still stand as warnings for unbridled enthusiasm. For example, in the early twentieth century, frontal lobotomy (that is, resection or destruction of the frontal lobe) was prevalent among certain psychiatrists as a radical treatment for psychotic patients. The operation was intended to ameliorate psychotic agitation by surgically damaging the frontal lobe responsible for human motivation and abstract thinking. Even though frontal lobotomy was often considered the last resort, the irreversibility of this operation aggravated its negative image and aroused grave concerns about abusing this technique.

The risk of misuse or abuse is often minimized by the joint efforts of regulatory authorities and professional groups. In a society where the idea of patient advocacy is not popular, the imbalance of power and conscience may result in dreadfully undesirable outcomes. In Joao Biehl's ethnography *Vita* (2005), we see how damaging this indiscriminate use of psychotropic medications can be. He traces the life of a poor Brazilian woman, Caterina, who was given various psychiatric medications before a comprehensive neuropsychiatric assessment was made available. This is not an exceptional case. In places where mental health resources are scarce, individuals whose behaviors or emotions are considered pathological are often abandoned and overmedicated without adequate diagnostic evaluation. Their suffering is often silenced and forgotten. In this respect, Caterina's personal tragedy perfectly characterized a depressing dimension of social suffering and everyday violence.

Some view such misuse of psychotropic medications as particular examples that are restricted to times when neither the government nor the medical profession could adequately regulate the distribution of psychiatric medications. The case of Caterina also exposes the social basis of psychiatric practice as indispensable to the welfare of mental patients. Psychiatry, as a segment of health care, cannot escape the tests of financial constraint and social judgment. In the current era of globalization, the socioeconomic impacts on psychiatry as a cultural practice are even more salient.

Psychiatric treatments are provided not merely for therapeutic ends but also for the purposes of clinical experimentation. For example, in some places patients are treated not just because they need medical treatment, but also because the treatment needs them as human subjects to test drug effects. This inherently exploitative practice occurs mostly in developing countries where clinical trials are sometimes the only hope for disenfranchised people to get adequate but overly expensive medications.

The effects of pharmaceutical agents may be scientifically proven, but this fact does not make these psychotropic medications free from being affected by structural forces, such as national public health care services, class stratification, socio-economic configurations, and transnational companies. These structural forces impact the human mind with the millions of tablets and capsules marketed through various venues and channels. The expanding market of psychotropics is reflective of the skyrocketing sale of certain medications such as the anxiolytics Ativan and Valium, the antidepressants Prozac and Wellbutrin, and the hypnotics Ambien and Lunesta, to name a few.

These phenomena create controversy over the adequacy of psychotropic medications. Many people challenge the expansion of pharmacological therapies in psychiatric practice by asking questions such as the following: Are psychotropic medications the only way to liberate mental patients by treating their biological dysfunctions? Are people in danger of losing control and autonomy to chemicals? Are people becoming too vulnerable to overzealous psychiatrists and greedy pharmaceutical companies? Are government regulations sufficient to protect individuals? Are people becoming too likely, given the ever-expanding accessibility of drugs, to use medications for self-change or nonmedical purposes? Are we as a society in danger of losing the distinction between therapeutic medications and pleasurable drugs? All these are difficult questions to answer.

Psychotherapy

The other arm of psychiatric treatment is psychotherapy, which includes any therapeutic efforts based on psychological principles. In clinical settings, this could mean dozens of available approaches for a wide variety of mental illnesses. Most if not all of them are constructed on the foundation of current psychological knowledge about human emotions, motivation, and behavior initiation and modulation, which largely draws on Freudian psychoanalysis and its derivatives. Psychotherapies usually do not distance themselves completely from biological theories, but they tend to pose somewhat different explanations of mental pathology.

In many ways, psychoanalysis is a product of neuropsychiatric theory development in the late nineteenth century. For Sigmund Freud, it was initially intended to explain certain clinical conditions, such as hysteria and paranoia. Its later application to a larger cultural context, illustrated in his works (e.g., *Civilization and Its Discontents*), was an attempt to uncover the shared underlying stratum of individual and collective psychical makeup. When we evaluate the role of psychoanalytic theory in psychiatric practice, we need to bear in mind the fact that the whole theory was situated in the enthusiastic pursuit of a universal structure of human mind. This belief was pervasive in the medical and scientific circles of European intellectual elites of that time but has since been subject to intense criticism.

Psychoanalysis assumes the presence of the unconscious. By definition, the unconscious is a domain of the human mind of which one cannot be directly aware. It is like a warehouse in which we store our memory fragments, emotional impressions, and life experiences in some condensed or distorted forms to elude the censorship of consciousness. It is thus said that these memory fragments are "repressed." Only in dreams or "slips of the tongue" can they emerge transiently, often in condensed and camouflaged forms, into the realm of human consciousness. Repression is the central concept accountable for the etiologies of varying neuroses that Freud studied. In his theory, repressed materials are usually related to one's psychosexual development, and psychoanalysis is the most effective way to unearth these materials. Human beings in this framework are depicted as creatures driven by two major biological instincts: sex and aggression. In Freud's later topographic model of the human mind, a person's psyche is divided into id, ego, and superego, some of which are conscious, whereas some are not.

Current psychotherapies rarely take the form of classical psychoanalysis, which demands that the therapy be carried out almost daily. Despite the intensity of treatment, its efficacy has not been proven because there has been no adequate assessment method for such a therapeutic format. Nonetheless, it is widely accepted that psychoanalytic knowledge about the dynamics of the mind underlies and grounds the theories of many other therapies that aim to modify personality structure and reshape the sense of self. These therapeutic approaches are often clustered under the name of "(psycho-)dynamic psychotherapy." Even if the therapist follows the instructions of a certain school, however, the healing process may still take different and sometimes unexpected routes. For this reason, dynamic psychotherapy is often depicted as a work of art instead of a scientific treatment.

Despite the irregularities in its processes and outcomes, psychoanalysis or its derivative therapies dominated psychiatric thinking as a way to salvage the therapeutic nihilism in the first half of the twentieth century when biological approaches failed to provide satisfactory clinical results. Among these derivative psychotherapeutic approaches were Melanie Klein's object relations theory, Harry Sullivan's interpersonal theory, and Heinz Kohut's self psychology, to name a few. In addition to these British and American theorists, in the 1960s there was Jacques Lacan's "return to Freud" movement that later helped establish a French Freudianism. Lacanian psychoanalysis has been friendly and open to nonphysicians, and its insights have not only benefited psychoanalytic theory but also nourished other academic domains such as literary criticism.

Nevertheless, psychotherapy does not always have to effect changes by exposing and untying unconscious conflicts. In some cases, a direct or indirect instruction or a cognitive reorientation is helpful enough. This psychological approach is called cognitive therapy and has been notably theorized and practiced by Aaron Beck, a former dynamic psychoanalyst. It is frequently used in combination with behavioral therapy (which is based on a wide range of behavioral theories) and termed cognitive-behavioral therapy. Cognitive therapists often lead patients, usually victims of anxiety and depression, to realize and identify their own stereotyped, dysfunctional, and even destructive patterns of thinking. An often-seen example is automatic thought. This refers to a person's habitual ideas usually in the wake of mood changes and life events. For example, when a patient fails an exam, his or her first thought could be "I am *always* a loser" instead of "this could happen *once in a while*, but I will not allow it next time." In this case, automatic thought is characterized by a tendency of overgeneralization, which is typically found among people with low self-esteem or clinical depression.

From the preceding description, we may reach a conclusion that the psychological principles presumed in each psychotherapeutic effort basically fashion the practices taking place within the counseling room. But since there are so many kinds of psychotherapy, it is difficult to know which theoretical orientation is the best match for which patient.

This is where conflicts may arise because there has been no technical standardization for psychotherapy. As a rule, its quality is guaranteed by the disciplinary requirements of intensive supervision and long-term training. Of course, things may still go awry in some cases. Psychotherapies, like psychotropic medications, can be applied inappropriately or under the wrong conditions. Anecdotes about the misuse of psychotherapy abound. In the nonacademic book *Crazy Therapies: What Are They? Do They Work?* (Thaler & Lalich 1996), the two authors talk in a journalistic tone about some psychological interventions that lack sound theoretical bases. Their shocking examples may be rare and exceptional, but these cases signal a widely shared sense of insecurity about sharing the most intimate, private, and perhaps traumatic experiences with the therapist. Professional ethics is especially important in psychotherapy because without it, psychological knowledge that aims to help may become a weapon that tends to hurt.

Biomedicalization

Although psychopharmacology and psychotherapy represent two contested areas of psychiatry, what has been glaring and sometimes alarming in recent years is the trend of biomedicalization in psychiatry (Clarke et al. 2003). Scholars now consider biomedicalization both a quantitative extension of and a qualitative rupture with prior medicalization, which refers to the increased dominance of medicine over diverse areas of life. This trend is, first of all, characterized by the rising importance of genetic knowledge in extricating the long-standing mysteries of mental illnesses. Many warn that it is imprudent and even incorrect to treat contemporary genetic knowledge simply as some twisted reincarnation of old-time degeneration theory because contemporary psychiatric genetics has opened up a space of early prevention and intervention rather than a label of hopeless mental deterioration. Even though it has not been put into routine practice yet, the ideal for psychiatric genetics is to identify those populations at risk for certain mental problems, be they alcoholism or depression, and forestall the development of these diseases. On the other hand, this notion is frequently considered a threat to the belief in individual free will, so it often results in disputes over truth, ethics, and political correctness. The question, therefore, is still open: to what extent are we controlled by biological disposition?

The second aspect of biomedicalization emerges with the dramatic increase of genetic knowledge, as it becomes more and more difficult to identify the line between the normal and the pathological. Genetics involves calculations of probability, and it has turned the definition of normalcy into a question of degree. That is, it is no longer a valid question to ask whether an individual is normal or not; the question is increasingly being articulated as "how normal" the person is. Conceptions of mental health will change when the paradigmatic ideal that people implicitly take as the point of reference has been problematized. This will result in a massive transformation not just in our concept of personhood but also in the ways that people treat others.

The third aspect of biomedicalization in terms of psychiatry is the blurring of boundaries between the biological and the social. Although social and epidemiological studies have repeatedly illustrated the linkages between socioeconomic disenfranchisement and mental suffering, biomedical explanations of mental illnesses are gaining the upper hand. Viewed from a sociological standpoint, this biomedical paradigm is frequently accompanied by the devolution of social responsibility in the afflicted people themselves or their families. Nikolas Rose, a British sociologist, points out the double meanings of this phenomenon (Rose 2007). On the one hand, this development is characteristic of advanced liberal capitalism. It signifies the end of old socialist ideals of the welfare state. The state has withdrawn from the public sphere; now people are left to take care of themselves. On the other hand, it creates a "politics of life itself" by calculating risks and realizing our own molecular (genetic) makeup. This type of politics will in turn shed a new light on ways of reconfiguring collectives and individuals.

Biomedicalization is not necessarily a negative thing. As a phase of the incessant changes in society, it signifies a process in which biomedical technologies, knowledge, and values are increasingly incorporated, both literally and figuratively, into people's lives. Some people embrace these changes; others resist them. Identifying the features of biomedicalization enables us to see more clearly the tensions and conflicts it provokes.

Conclusion

Aside from the antipsychiatry movement in the 1960s and 1970s, psychiatry for the past few decades has been compelled to deal with a plurality of social transformations that challenge the very foundation of psychiatric knowledge and practice. These changes include increased life expectancy (e.g., the aging of baby boomers), unforeseen natural disasters and casualties (e.g., tsunamis, earthquakes, and hurricanes), aggravating large-scale violence (e.g., wars and genocide), and novel technological innovations (e.g., Internet and video game platforms). These changes have created mental and behavioral conditions hardly known before: the emergence of geriatric cognitive problems, proliferation of community mental health issues, reconceptualization of trauma-related disorders (such as the Gulf War Syndrome), and novel diagnostic categories such as Internet and sex addiction. As the experiences of the human mind have been altered, psychiatry has had to align itself more with social demands and act in a preventive and proactive manner. This task takes both scientific rigor and social sensitivity. Although the expanding power of psychiatry may trigger some suspicion about aggravating social control and limiting personal freedom, there is no way to untangle it from the fabric of modern living. Thus what is now most important is to find ways to understand and improve the interactions between psychiatry and society.

See also Culturally Competent Care; *Diagnostic and Statistical Manual of Mental Disorders* (*DSM*); Drug Companies; Ethical Issues; Evidence-Based Practice and Outcome Measurement; Genetics and Mental Health; History of Mental Health Care; Marketing of Drugs; Medical Model of Mental Illness; Neurodiversity; Neuropsychiatry; Psychopharmacology; Psychotherapy; Psychotherapy Integration; State Mental Health Agencies

Bibliography

Bentall, Richard P. 2009. *Doctoring the Mind: Is Our Current Treatment of Mental Illness Really Any Good?* New York: New York University Press.

Biehl, Joao. 2005. *Vita: Life in a Zone of Social Abandonment.* Berkeley: University of California Press.

Carlat, Daniel J. 2010. *Unhinged: The Trouble with Psychiatry.* New York: Free Press.

Clarke, Adele E., Laura Mamo, Jennifer R. Fishman, Janet K. Shim, and Jennifer Ruth Fosket. 2003. "Biomedicalization: Technoscientific Transformations of Health, Illness, and U.S. Biomedicine." *American Sociological Review* 68: 161–194.

Fee, Dwight, ed. 2000. *Pathologies and the Postmodern: Mental Illness as Discourse and Experience.* Thousand Oaks, CA: Sage.

Lakoff, Andrew. 2006. *Pharmaceutical Reason: Knowledge and Value in Global Psychiatry.* Cambridge: Cambridge University Press.

Luhrmann, Tanya. 2000. *Of Two Minds: The Growing Disorder in American Psychiatry.* New York: Knopf.

Petryna, Adriana, Andrew Lakoff, and Arthur Kleinman. 2006. *Global Pharmaceuticals: Ethics, Markets, Practices.* Durham, NC: Duke University Press.

Rose, Nikolas. 2007. *The Politics of Life Itself: Biomedicine, Power, and Subjectivity in the Twenty-First Century*. Princeton, NJ: Princeton University Press.

Shorter, Edward. 1997. *A History of Psychiatry: From the Era of the Asylum to the Age of Prozac*. New York: Wiley.

Singer, Margaret Thaler, and Janja Lalich. 1996. *Crazy Therapies: What Are They? Do They Work?* New York: Jossey-Bass.

Szasz, Thomas. 1961. *The Myth of Mental Illness: Foundation of a Theory of Personal Conduct*. New York: Harper & Row.

Wenegrat, Brant. 2001. *Theater of Disorder: Patients, Doctors, and the Construction of Illness*. New York: Oxford University Press.

Psychoanalysis

Lourdes Mattei and Joan Berzoff

The work by which we bring the repressed mental material into the patient's consciousness has been called by us psycho-analysis.

—S. Freud ("Lines of Advance in Psychoanalytic Therapy," 1919)

What is psychoanalysis? This is a frequently asked question, both inside and outside the field of psychoanalysis. Psychoanalysis is now over 100 years old. As a major contributor to modern Western intellectual tradition, psychoanalysis is a way of thinking about the mind, a way to understand human development, motivation, and suffering. And it is method, a way to know, a way to investigate and a way to practice. One of Freud's earliest definitions of psychoanalysis declares:

Psycho-Analysis is the name (i) of a procedure for the investigation of mental processes which are almost inaccessible in any other ways, (ii) of a method (based upon that investigation) for the treatment of mental disorders and (iii) a collection of psychological information obtained along those lines, which is gradually being accumulated into a new scientific discipline. (Freud 1919, 235)

Ultimately, psychoanalysis sought to understand and "investigate" the *psyche* and as such, it paved the way for one of the major *psychological* ways to understand mental life, its possibilities, and its tragedies. The psychoanalytic understanding of human experience is known for its complexity and depth (for recent meta-analyses of the effectiveness of psychoanalytic psychotherapy for long-term, complex cases, see Leichsenring & Rabung 2008). It has also engendered much criticism. A major source of epistemological, theoretical, and methodological controversy has centered on the challenges posed by the limits of knowing: as

Freud himself claimed, psychoanalysis is a way of "investigating mental processes which are almost inaccessible in any other way." One of Freud's great intellectual/clinical contributions is the concept of the *dynamic unconscious*. But this concept, like all mental process, cannot be observed directly.

Psychoanalysis has evolved into a rich and diverse system of ideas, "a collection of psychological information" that guides our ways of knowing. In this chapter we offer an overview of psychoanalytic theory, or more accurately, theories with a special focus on mental health. As we ask this question, we are reminded of what Lyra, the main character in the fable "The Golden Compass," is encouraged to remember whenever she wants to know:

> Lyra, you mustn't grasp at the answer. Hold the question in your mind, but lightly, like it was something alive.

In the Beginning, There Was Freud

In order to understand psychoanalysis, we need to begin with Freud (1856–1939), whose ideas have formed the basis of psychoanalytic theory and practice for the last century and a quarter. Many of these ideas are so commonplace today that we often forget their origins or simply take them for granted.

Freud himself was a neurologist, trained to think in terms of the brain as made up of parts, often in conflict with each other. Physics shaped his view of the mind as a dynamic system in which excitation and discharge struggled to stay in balance. As is true with hydraulics, Freud conceived of the mind as made up of excessive excitation that once stored up, needed to be discharged. Later he came to think of this excitation as deriving from the drives of sexuality (libido) and aggression. These passions literally "drove" our behaviors in often-inexplicable ways. In order to function within reality and society, the drives need to be neutralized and transformed, which helps us to work and to love effectively.

Freud viewed the mind as governed by passions, then, of love and of hate, which were unruly and bestial and which ultimately needed to be tamed by the family and by society. Freud was influenced not only by physics and neurology but also by embryology. He came to see the drives of libido and aggression emerging at different development periods, which needed to be resolved. He was further influenced by romanticism, a worldview that looked to mythology and Greek tragedy to try to make sense of the human condition. Bettleheim (1983) reminds us that psychoanalysis when translated from the German means "analysis of the soul," and indeed Freud was interested in the mystical side of human behavior. As a Jew in Victorian Vienna, he was also a racial victim of anti-Semitism that kept him marginalized throughout his career. By the end of his life he had to flee Vienna and move to England in order to avoid extermination. His worldview therefore was quite pessimistic. Freud was further influenced by archeology. He viewed the mind as needing to be excavated, its layers needing to come to light in order to understand what motivated human behavior.

Most of mental life, he thought, occurred underground, that is, unconsciously.

Moreover, the powerful instincts of love and hate that resided in the patient's unconscious mind were aroused in the intimacy of the therapeutic relationship. Freud came to identify these feelings as transference and countertransference. Transference involves the ways in which clients brings unconscious past fantasies, feelings, unmet needs, longings, desires, and aggression from their past to their present relationships with their therapists. Likewise, any therapist also brings his or her feelings, longings, desires, aggression and past experiences, memories and desires to his or her relationship with the patient. This is called countertransference. The transference/countertransference matrix is ubiquitous not only in the context of psychoanalytic treatment but also in every relationship.

What have we said so far? First, Freud developed many early ideas: free association, a way of bringing to consciousness that which is unconscious; the idea that symptoms are related to past traumas or experiences that are out of consciousness; the ubiquity of transference and countertransference in every therapeutic relationship; the idea that the mind can be conceived of as in layers that can be excavated. Freud also began to further investigate his new method of psychoanalysis with many more, largely female, patients and began to hypothesize that the mind is often in conflict: that while we might think we want to make conscious that which is unconscious, there are other parts of our minds that resist making conscious what is unconscious. He came to see that traumatized women and men resisted excavating painful memories and that the analysis of resistances was core to understand the unconscious feelings, fantasies, desire, and aggression that drive our behavior. His was a view of the mind in *conflict*.

Freud is called a drive theorist because he saw humans as driven by passions and desires, as well as aggression of which they were unaware. He viewed human beings as driven by forces largely unknown to themselves, which were accessible through dreams, through slips of the tongue, or through the transference phenomenon. These drives of sexuality and aggression are the unruly, often chaotic parts of our minds that both motivate us and that we disavow. Freud thought that the drives were all part of early and unremembered pasts, and that events from the past always affect the present. This means that the contents of our past experiences—our early relationships, our loving, hating feelings, our traumatic experiences—influence our current behavior. While many of the contents within our unconscious minds are inaccessible to us consciously, they influence and shape our behavior in powerful ways. Freud recognized that we keep past desires, passions, and early trauma out of consciousness in order to be able function in the world. Were we to be in touch with the unruly, chaotic, bestial parts of ourselves, we would likely be psychotic, unable to function in everyday life. Therefore Freud believed that we all employ very basic defenses, the most important of which is repression, what keeps what is painful or conflictual out of awareness most of the time. With the relaxation of sleep or with a technique like free association, we often become aware of our unconscious minds. But in conscious life, we resist doing so. In Freud's view, if people could understand what unconsciously motivated their behavior in the present, it could make their behavior more tolerable. Insight into unconscious life, and self- knowledge, were keys to living a freer and more productive life in Freud's view.

As stated earlier, Freud was also deeply influenced by embryology and the belief that psychic life is governed by a developmental progression. He believed that we are all born with an inborn ground plan that unfolds over time and with maturation. Both physical development and psychological development occur in tandem and in relationship with primary caregivers. From birth onward Freud saw us as motivated by sexual and aggressive drives. Normally, these drives have an object, a person to whom they are directed and an aim, which is to discharge their energy at each stage of physical and biological development. From infancy onward, we are driven by biologically based instincts, which "drive" our behavior, of which we are largely unaware. In his view, the mind is a seething cauldron of passion, desire, and aggression. Those sexual and aggressive drives are expressed differently through different predominant biological organs or erogenous zones. For the infant, the erogenous zone is the mouth. A baby expresses her or his love and hate through sucking, biting, screaming, feeding. The baby's drives are directed toward an object, usually the mother or the caregiver. If a caregiver is trustworthy and responsive, the baby's drives can be reduced and biological needs for food and psychological needs for consistency and comfort may be met. But if the caregivers are unable to meet a child's oral needs, because of neglect, inconsistency, abuse, or abandonment, that child is likely to suffer from oral deprivation, which may manifest as a deep psychological hunger that cannot be met, as an urgency that cannot be soothed, and by aggression that cannot be modulated.

At the next stage of development, the anal stage, Freud saw children as governed by sexuality and aggression organized around the primary erogenous zone of the anus. Here, holding onto one's bowels or letting go becomes the predominant struggle directed at caregivers who are trying to train the child to accommodate to family life. As we know, control battles are legion between toddlers and their parents; but where there are sufficient controls and limits in a family that is neither overly punitive nor overly lax, a child eventually internalizes parental controls and prohibitions as her or his own, learning to accommodate her or his own impulses in accordance with the basic rules of the family and the culture. Without controls, children become excessively preoccupied by pleasure in their excrement, or gain pleasure through defiance of social rules. When a child cannot negotiate this period, the consequences are enduring shame and doubt.

At the Oedipal period, Freud saw young children as preoccupied by competitive and sexual feelings toward one parent, and aggressive feelings toward the parent whom the child experiences as a rival for the other parent's affection. Here relationships are triadic, not dyadic, and the child has to negotiate love and hate acted out in a family drama over desire and renunciation. Because a child intensely feels that he or she wants and deserves the exclusive love of one parent or parent substitute, Freud hypothesized, the child wishes to be rid of the parent of the other gender. Given that the grownups are unlikely to allow the child to realize his or her sexual and aggressive desires, the child ultimately must renounce them and does so with the advent of the internal feeling of guilt. Thus romance, longing, and renunciation go underground and an Oedipal child begins to feel guilt for her or his incestuous wishes, competitive and aggressive desires.

While this configuration assumes a heterosexual family arrangement, children from single-parent families, from gay and lesbian families, also express competition and sexual longing and must renounce these feelings in light of reality. For many who do not resolve this period, excessive competitive feelings can become an enduring character trait. The positive achievement of this period is that a child develops a superego, which contains within it the values and ideals of the parent who was the rival with whom a child ultimately identifies. Those values and ideals become internalized as the child's own. The development of a superego also includes the affect of guilt, which keeps children from acting on desires or aggression, which would violate the rules of a civilized society. Instead of accommodating to parental rules, the child now has internalized and identified with the morality of parents, taking inside an ideal of which the child hopes to be. When we do not live up to our ego ideals, we often experience guilt. Thus where once morality was an external concern, enforced by parents, now it is an internal concern. When we violate the rules of society, we feel the discomfort of guilt, an important affect that keeps us from acting on our impulses. We think of those who are motivated by guilt as at the neurotic or the Oedipal level. Those motivated by shame are seen as functioning at the pre-Oedipal level where rules and morality have to be imposed from the outside.

Structural Theory

With the concept of a superego, Freud began to reconfigure the structures of the mind. He came to identify three structures of the mind that he thought were in conflict with each other: the id, the ego, and the superego. The id is the repository of the impulses, the seething cauldron of sexuality and aggression, largely out of consciousness. The ego is the part of the mind, like a rider on horseback, that tries to make the id go where it wants it to go. It tames and neutralizes the drives in order to reharness the id's energy toward purposeful behavior. It disavows unpleasant truths through the use of a range of defenses: projection, dissociation, denial, repression, acting out at the lower level or at the higher level, reaction formation, humor, sublimation, altruism, to name a few. The ego serves to test reality, to employ judgment, to control the impulses, to modulate intense feelings or affects, and it contains within it a drama of early relationships, which Freud referred to as object relations. The superego is the part of the mind that contains prohibitions and morality, which are internalized. But conflict often emerges: between the impulses of the id and the ego. When conflicts arise, the ego will employ defenses to deal with them. The defenses may be early and immature and distort reality or the defenses may be more adaptive, helping a person deal with conflict in ways are purposeful and effective in maintaining reality. The ego's role is to maintain homeostasis, in the face of inevitable conflicts in the mind. When conflicts are intense and irreconcilable, however, the ego is depleted and many of its functions are undermined. This can result in poor judgment, impulsive behaviors, misperceiving reality, impaired relationships, and a loss of equilibrium.

Ego Psychology: Mastery and Competence

Although it was Freud's daughter, Anna Freud (1895–1982), who elaborated on ego psychology, its striving both for reality and for homeostasis, Freud also thought that there were conflict-free parts of the mind. Not everything is embroiled in conflict; often human beings strive to master their environments and often there are parts of the ego that function autonomously. It was Heinz Hartmann (1894–1970) and others, however, who wrote about the ego and its relationship to the environment and the ways in which individuals adapt to their environments by shaping themselves to fit the environment or by finding ways to shape the environment to fit the needs of the individual.

"Economic" Theory

In a very important paper, "Mourning and Melancholia" (1917), Freud developed another set of ideas that led us to understand the first object relations theory. In "Mourning and Melancholia," Freud tried to differentiate normal grief from what we now called complicated grief. Here he described how, after a loss, a person is depleted and empty, and holds intensely onto the memory of the person who has died. The world seems impoverished and the mourner is preoccupied with the lost object. Freud called this preoccupation hypercathexis, and it related to just how intensely we hold onto our memories of the person and of the loss. Over time and with the advent of reality, however, Freud thought that the healthy mourner ultimately was able to reinvest in the world because slowly the mourner identified with aspects of the lost object, taking them inside of the self unconsciously and thus being changed by the experience. He wrote, "The shadow of the object falls upon the ego," showing how are selves are always affected by those whom we have lost and internalized. The shadow of others comes to inhabit our selves.

But for the pathological mourner, Freud thought, there had been a complicated and more problematic relationship with the person who had died. The mourner who has experienced unconscious ambivalence toward the person who has died is ordinarily out of touch with his or her anger at that person. But because the anger and hatred was unconscious, it too comes to be set up inside the self and against the self, in the form of diminished self-esteem, or self-hate. Now aggression, once unconsciously felt toward the lost object, becomes hate turned inward, sometimes even resulting in suicidal ideation.

Freud had a similar idea about narcissism, Here he saw the narcissist as suffering from excessive libido turned inward. For the narcissist, too much love is invested in the self; there is simply not enough energy to love others. Just as the depressive has too much aggression turned inward to be able to see him or herself or others accurately, so too does the narcissist come to be impoverished especially in the capacity to connect to others. Again, whereas aggression turned inward leads to depression, libido or love turned inward leads to narcissism. What is so important about "Mourning and Melancholia," especially, is the idea that with loss, we take in aspects of those whom we have lost; they live inside of us and they become a part of our ego. Here Freud made the case that the ego was made up of abandoned object cathexes by which he meant that the ego is comprised of shadow relationships, or objects, which are the unconscious but nonetheless complicated, intense dramas that live inside of us and that affect our senses of self and of others. Let us turn then to object relations theory to further understand the mysterious inner world made up of representations of parts of others, and parts of the self.

The Relational Turn: The Baby's Needs

One of the main controversies in psychoanalytic theory revolves around the tension commonly known in psychology as the "nature versus nurture" controversy.

In what is now called the classical theory, human nature is conceptualized as an irreducible struggle between a Darwinian biological inheritance (bodily based drives) and society. This battle of forces took place in and through the body—beastly forces that required taming or socializing. The role of the parents as the primary or first taming agents was recognized early in Freudian thinking; its theoretical centrality did not achieve ascendancy until the middle of the twentieth century. Again, in "Mourning and Melancholia" Freud draws our attention to the "shadow of the object" in the ego's development. How does our experience with others shape our psychological development? What types of human environment ("nurture") do we need to grow? To change? How do we "take in" these experiences?

The psychoanalytic concept of "object" remains one of the most fundamental—and confusing—terms in psychoanalytic theorizing. St. Clair (2000) defines object as the "other" in a relationship; whether the relationship is with an actual person (interpersonal) and/or with an "internal" other (intrapsychic). Although the use of the concept at times is ambiguous (partly as a result of theoretical differences), what is undeniable is that a major paradigm shift in our psychoanalytic understanding of human nature and motivation took place. As Fairbairn's (1952) famous quote proclaims: "Libido is not . . . pleasure-seeking; it is object seeking" (137). A group of diverse theories came to group under the umbrella category of "object relations," psychoanalytic perspectives that emphasized the growth and derailment, development and pathology, structure and function of our minds/self in relationship with others. Moore and Fine (1990) define object relations theory in the following way:

> A system of psychological explanation based on the premise that the mind is comprised of elements taken in from outside, primarily aspects of the functioning of other persons. This occurs by means of the process of internalization. This model of the mind explains mental functions in terms of relations between the various elements internalized. (131)

The tension between what in the traditional Freudian view comes from the "inside" (drives) and what comes from the "outside" (people/environment) came to be reformulated both gradually and in revolutionary ways. While some psychoanalytic theorists continued to expand and elaborate on the classical view of the mind, others offered a very different account of the mind's "emergence," function, and structure.

In the United States, this fundamental paradigm shift has been called the "relational turn" or the change from a "one person" to a "two person" psychology. This relational turn makes the boundaries between self and other more fluid and interactive. This "turn" has critical implications for the role and function of the analyst or psychotherapist. Since all psychological growth and health are predicated on the *internalization* of relationships, the transference/countertransference matrix is of vital importance.

One of the first theorists to emphasize the importance of "objects" in our psychological life was Melanie Klein (1882–1960). Her psychoanalytic ideas have had a seminal impact in psychoanalytic thinking, in particular, in the United Kingdom. For Klein our internal world is fully and fiercely populated with objects from early infancy. By contrast to Freud's classical view, in Klein's world "every urge and instinct is bound up with an object. Drives are relational" (St. Clair 2000, 36). For Freud the object is a means to an end, gratification. For Klein, we are "wired" to relate. These internal relationships inhabit our minds in a passionate struggle between love and hate. Kleinians refer to our first psychological relationship as directed to "part objects." Given the baby's developmental mental immaturity, the infant's first experience is with a part of the mother's body, the breast. These early (and subsequent) experiences initially get organized into two broad psychological types of internal objects: "good" (gratifying) and "bad" (depriving/frustrating). Relationships with internal objects are fueled by powerful life and death (loving and destructive) forces that generate psychological anxieties and terrors. The mental (unconscious) strategies to manage and control these forces are what determine psychological life. In a complex cycle of projections and introjections, we both internalize and externalize mental content. Furthermore, Kleinians, as well as most object relations theorists, have come to recognize the critical function of the mechanism of *projective identification* in our mental life. As the term implies, a complex dynamic or interplay between (unconscious) projection and identification shapes our psychological experience. This type of experience is seen both as "generic" and as serving a major function in certain pathological conditions. As Mitchell and Black (1995) tell us,

> A piece of experience, not simply an impulse but a generic dimension of human relatedness, does not register within the boundaries of oneself, but rather is experienced in a dramatically highlighted fashion in others, where it becomes an object of great focus, concern, and effort at control. (102)

A concept originally coined by Klein, the term has been developed to serve a variety of psychological functions such as defense and as a mode of communication (Ogden 1979).

Although Klein's ideas diverged from Freud in important ways, she retained an emphasis on "innate" or biologically rooted forces. Other psychoanalytic theorists/clinicians were heading in a different direction.

Attuned to the Baby's Needs

Thus gradually but unmistakably, psychoanalysis turned its theoretical lens from instinctual forces in conflict with societal demands to an understanding of psychopathology as resulting from lack of psychological nurturing. Both in the United States and in Britain clinicians focused on environmental conditions required for the emergence of psychological capacities indispensable for survival and growth. Mitchell and Black (1995) asked the essential questions posed by this shift:

> If food and other physical needs were not the crucial elements, what exactly *does* involvement with a nurturing person provide? . . . what are the essential features of this environment? How does what is outside affect what develops inside? (39)

Psychoanalysts working with children made significant contributions in this area.

W. R. D. Fairbairn (1889–1964), a Scottish analyst, made a more dramatic shift to what St. Clair (2000) calls a "pure" object relations model, a model that was "purely psychological" (49). Fairbairn completely reversed the motivational thrust in psychological development from instinctual roots to a focus on relationships (internal and external). Fairbairn's clinical work convinced him of the strength and power that relationships to objects have on our psychological life. An abused child will hold on to his relationship to a parent who maltreats him through a series of internal distortions: psychologically speaking, the child *needs* to believe that his parent is good. Consequently, he must bad: the child "takes upon himself the burden of badness which appears to reside in his objects" (Fairbairn 1952, 66). To Fairbairn, ". . . it is better to be a sinner in a world ruled by God, than to live in a world ruled by the Devil" (1952, 66–67). Psychological survival has a high price; not only is there a "reversal" of the child's experience, the relationship to the parent is, paradoxically, intensified. The attachment to the parent becomes stronger and less able to grow.

As psychoanalytic work expanded, other clinicians were making similar observations. The importance of the primary relationship and its first few years became paramount. In contrast to the classical psychoanalytic view of development where the Oedipal psychosexual stage marked the apex of clinical work, object relations theorists emphasized the *pre-Oedipal* period. In contrast to focusing on the child/father/mother triad, the relationship to the mother and its intense dyadic nature became the focus of theorizing. One characteristic feature of the paradigm shift to the "baby's needs" in contrast to the "beastly impulses" is the theoretical and clinical emphasis of the development of a sense of self and other. Two major examples of this shift are the works of two pediatricians who became psychoanalysts, Margaret Mahler (1897–1985) in the United States and D. W. Winnicott (1896–1971) in Britain.

In his felicitous observation, "There is no such thing as a baby," Winnicott captures the irreducible quality of the mother-infant link. Winnicott's unique, almost lyrical, style of writing evokes frequently the paradoxes of development in the experience of becoming a person. Like a reassuring pediatrician, Winnicott reminds us that we do not have to be perfect parents (or therapists) to facilitate psychological growth; we just have to be "good enough." Provided with a nurturing or good-enough "holding environment," the infant not only develops the capacity to feel human and become a self, but the child is able to "play." In his classical book *Playing and Reality*, Winnicott (1971) elaborated an exquisite series of ideas on the relationship between the individual and her environment based on the first relationship. In this relationship *dependence* plays a major role. Confidence on the primary caretaker's reliability forms the basis for a *potential space*. It is in this space that cultural experience happens. And "cultural experience," Winnicott alerts us, "begins with creative living first manifested in play" (1971, 135). And play is a developmental achievement in the psychological progression from what he called *subjective omnipotence* to the awareness of external or objective reality. In a drastically contrasting view of development, Winnicott does not see these experiences as linear stages to be outgrown, but as two types of experiences that remain in dialectical tension. The quintessential example of this phenomenon is the *transitional object* or what most of us identify as the "blankie" or teddy bear. For the child the teddy bear is not inner or outer reality: it exists in the space between both. All human experiences that feel vital, personal, and creative come from this space between. And the capacity to play is central in mental health. Winnicott locates the relationship between the individual and her or his environment in this potential space: "Cultural experience begins with creative living first manifested in play" (1971, 135).

Around the same time in the United States, the psychoanalytic lens also shifted to the earlier years, the pre-Oedipal experience. Margaret Mahler emigrated to New York City after World War II and continued her work with psychotic children. From her research came rich and complex observations about the developmental needs of the mother and infant dyad during the first three years of life. Through the title of their now classic book *The Psychological Birth of the Human Infant*, Mahler, Pine, and Bergman (1975) remind us of a central focus of her work: our psychological birth emerges at a different time than our biological birth. This psychological birth, what we will call our *identity*, has its first major coalescence by the age of three. In optimum conditions, Mahler described this developmental progression as the *separation-individuation* process. The primary caretaker and the new human engage in a complex and nuanced process in which two subjectivities encounter, merge, and e-merge. Mahler's developmental process describes the psychological tension between the infant's growing need for both dependence and autonomy in a series of stages progressing from "normal autism" and "normal symbiosis" through the separation-individuation subphases (differentiation, practicing, rapprochement, and object constancy).

According to Mahler, a person's sense of individuality (identity), her internal sense of herself as being both connected and separate from the primary caretaker, lays the psychological foundation for our sense of self and others. In a superbly rich psychological concept, object constancy, Mahler captures the ideal of psychological maturity in both internal and external relationships using the metaphor of an egg to describe our beginnings as a closed system (St. Clair 2000) at the beginning. Through the "warmth" of the symbiotic period, this closed psychological system begins to open and grow. This hatching launches the infant into the excitement and perils of psychological entry (awareness) of two "worlds" separated by a border ("boundary" between self and other). In this context, Mahler tracks the development of mental representations of self and other. A particular type of anxiety, separation anxiety, shapes the developmental passage. Through this process, the child's internal world is transformed from a closed system through the omnipotent fusion of "oneness" with the world to a time when the world is experienced as sharply divided between "good" and "bad" (part-objects). As psychological maturation unfolds and is properly responded to, the child will achieve a stable and more complex sense of herself and be able to relate to others in a more psychologically complex and stable manner (whole objects). The achievement of *object constancy* is the hallmark of psychological maturity.

Originally introduced by Hartmann, the concept was used to "describe a quality of object relations in the developing child" (in Moore & Fine 1990, 130). Before a certain psychological maturation, the child is unable to relate to another person except as someone who can satisfy her needs (what psychoanalysts called a "need-gratifying" object). In Mahler's theory, with cognitive and emotional maturation in the context of the mother's (or primary caretaker) actual presence and emotional responsiveness, the child comes to develop a positive mental representation of that can sustain her through difficult times. The inability to sustain an internal sense of "goodness" in the face of frustration of need is seen as the hallmark of borderline suffering (e.g., Kernberg 1975).

In contrast to the taming and renunciation of beastly impulses, the importance of the child's developmental needs and its attendant relationship to others or, in psychoanalytic terms, the development of self and object relations became a major focus of theoretical revision. Another major shift in the analytic terrain came from the ideas of a very established psychoanalyst working out of Chicago, Heinz Kohut (1913–81). Kohut's revision of the classical psychoanalytic concept of *narcissism* during the 1970s started a new school of psychoanalysis, *self psychology*. Kohut's interest and analytic work with the previously "unanalyzable" narcissistic personality paved the way for a new way of understanding the relationship between self and other (1971, 1977, 1979, 1984). In the traditional Freudian view, early or primary narcissism is expected to be replaced by object love. In Kohut's view narcissism has its own developmental trajectory. We all need *empathically attuned selfobjects* throughout our lifetime. A *selfobject* is an "object or person undifferentiated from the individual who serves the needs of the self" (St. Clair 2000, 140). Kohut placed *empathy* as a central psychological component in the process of both development and psychotherapy. Empathy, or "vicarious introspection," was "elevated ... to a position of supreme importance" and became the "primary clinical tool" (Flanagan 2011, 165). Kohut's contribution to the psychoanalytic theory paved the way to inclusion of pathologies and revisions of technique that target narcissistic disorders.

To Conclude

The second half of the twentieth century generated many changes, revisions, and expansions in psychoanalytic thought. From Freud's view of human nature and mental illness grounded on our beastly legacy, psychoanalysis continues to debate what makes us human, how we become a person, and how we come to experience suffering. Like all modern psychological theories, psychoanalysis's focus is the *individual*. Nonetheless, the complex relationship between the person and his or her culture is an integral part of psychoanalytic views. We see Freud's *Civilization and Its Discontent* (1930) as one classic example of the psychoanalytic contribution to questions and inquiries more traditionally linked to other disciplines such as sociology and political science. In addition, much debate and controversy has been generated by psychoanalysis's emphasis on sexuality. Psychoanalytic contributions to critical social theory (e.g., Clarke 2003), gender and feminist studies (see for overviews Berzoff 2011; Dimen & Goldner 2005), and race theory (Mattei 2011) are part of a vibrant psychoanalytically informed discourse today. Psychoanalytic presence is also felt in the humanities, the arts (Spitz 2005), and literature (Berman 2005). Outside the English-speaking world, the French psychoanalyst Jacques Lacan (1977), with his emphasis on language, has been a significant influence in academic disciplines such as linguistics. Lastly, psychoanalytic thinking has not been immune to epistemological controversies. Postmodern critiques have influenced psychoanalytic thought in slow but insistent ways. Contemporary debates on intersubjectivity (e.g., Stolorow & Atwood 1992; Frie & Orange 2009) stretch theory to epistemological levels as some psychoanalytic concepts grapple with the nature of psychological knowledge.

In spite of the dominance, currently, of biologically based psychiatric views of mental disorders, psychoanalysis and psychoanalytically informed psychotherapies continue to be vital and flourishing. Paradoxically, during the last decade, psychoanalysis is receiving additional validation from the field Freud started from, neuroscience (e.g., Solms & Turnbull 2002; Cozolino 2010). Hopefully, psychoanalysis will continue to be as controversial as it is alive and thriving.

See also Humanistic Theories and Therapies; Hypnosis and Hypnotherapy; Loss and Grief; Narcissism; Psychiatry; Psychodynamic Psychotherapy; Sexual Disorders and Dysfunctions

Bibliography

Berman, E. 2005. "Literature." In E. S. Person, A. M. Cooper, and G. O. Gabbard, eds., *Textbook of Psychoanalysis* (pp. 491 500). Washington, DC: American Psychiatric Publishing.

Berzoff, J. 2011. "Psychodynamic Theory and Gender." In J. Berzoff, L. F. Flanagan, and P. Hertz, eds., *Inside Out, Outside In: Psychodynamic Clinical Theory in Contemporary Multicultural Contexts* (pp. 241–257). New York: Rowman & Littlefield.

Bettleheim, B. 1983. *Freud and Man's Soul*. New York: Knopf.

Clarke, S. 2003. *Social Theory, Psychoanalysis and Racism*. New York: Palgrave.

Cozolino, L. 2010. *The Neuroscience of Psychotherapy, Healing the Social Brain* (2nd ed.). New York: Norton.

Dimen, M., and V. Goldner. 2005. "Gender and Sexuality." In E. S. Person, A. M. Cooper, and G. O. Gabbard, eds., *Textbook of Psychoanalysis* (pp. 96–113). Washington, DC: American Psychiatric Publishing.

Fairbairn, W. R. D. 1952. *Psychoanalytic Studies of the Personality.* London: Routledge & Kegan Paul.

Flanagan, L. M. 2011. "The Theory of Self Psychology." In J. Berzoff, L. M. Flanagan, and P. Hertz, eds., *Inside Out and Outside In: Psychodynamic Clinical Theory and Psychopathology in Contemporary Multicultural Contexts* (pp. 158–185). Lanham, MD: Rowman & Littlefield.

Freud, S. 1917. "Mourning and Melancholia." *Standard Edition* 14: 237–259.

Freud, S. 1919. "Lines of Advance in Psychoanalytic Therapy." *Standard Edition* 17: 157–168.

Freud, S. 1930/2005. *Civilization and Its Discontents.* New York: Norton.

Frie, R., and D. Orange, eds. 2009. *Beyond Postmodernism: New Dimensions in Clinical Theory and Practice.* New York: Routledge.

Hartmann, H. 1939. *Ego Psychology and the Problem of Adaptation.* New York: International University Press.

Kernberg, O. 1975. *Borderline Conditions and Pathological Narcissism.* New York: Jason Aronson.

Kohut, H. 1971. *The Analysis of the Self.* New York: International University Press.

Kohut, H. 1977. *Restoration of the Self.* New York: International University Press.

Kohut, H. 1978. *The Search for the Self.* New York: International University Press.

Kohut, H. 1984. *How Does Analysis Cure?* Chicago: University of Chicago Press.

Lacan, J. 1977. *Ecrits: A Selection.* Translated by Alan Sheridan. New York: Norton.

Leichsenring, F., and S. Rabung. 2008. "Effectiveness of Long-Term Psychodynamic Psychotherapy, a Meta-Analysis." *Journal of American Medical Association* 300(13): 1551–1565.

Mahler, M. S., E. Pine, and A. Bergman. 1975. *The Psychological Birth of the Human Infant.* New York: Basic Books.

Mattei, M. L. 2011. "Coloring Development: Race and Culture in Psychodynamic Theories." In J. Berzoff, L. F. Flanagan, and P. Hertz, eds., *Inside Out, Outside In, Psychodynamic Clinical Theory in Contemporary Multicultural Contexts* (pp. 258–283). New York: Rowman & Littlefield.

Mitchell, S., and M. Black. 1995. *Freud and Beyond: A History of Modern Psychoanalytic Thought.* New York: Basic Books.

Moore, B. E., and B. D. Fine, eds. 1990. *Psychodynamic Terms and Concepts.* New Haven, CT: American Psychoanalytic Association and Yale University Press.

Ogden, T. H. 1979. "On Projective Identification." *International Journal of Psychoanalysis* 60: 357–373.

Solms, M., and O. Turnbull. 2002. *The Brain and the Inner World: An Introduction to the Neuroscience of Subjective Experience.* New York: Other Press.

Spitz, E. H. 2005. "The Arts." In E. S. Person, A. M. Cooper, and G. O. Gabbard, eds., *Textbook of Psychoanalysis* (pp. 501–511). Washington, DC: American Psychiatric Publishing.

St. Clair, M. 2000. *Object Relations and Self Psychology: An Introduction.* Belmont, CA: Wadsworth/Thomson Learning.

Stolorow, R., and G. Atwood. 1992. *Contexts of Being, The Intersubjective Foundations of Psychological Life.* Hillsdale, NJ: Analytic Press.

Winnicott, D. W. 1971. *Playing and Reality.* New York: Tavistock.

Psychodynamic Psychotherapy

Diana L. Tracy and Jerald Kay

Psychoanalysis is a treatment most people simplistically think of as a patient lying on a couch, facing away from a therapist who interprets free associations and conflict by referencing the patient's childhood sexual fantasies. However, psychoanalysis is actually not only a therapy but also a theory of understanding personality development, the meaning of conflict and emotional pain, and the interplay of a patient's former and current relationships as it unfolds in the context of dialogue between patient and therapist (a phenomenon called transference). As traditional psychoanalytic therapy tends to be quite comprehensive for the patient and requires sometimes years of weekly sessions, four to five times a week, a briefer form of this treatment has evolved over the last 60 years and is commonly known as psychodynamic psychotherapy. This evolution began even in Freud's time (he died in 1939) in the hope that many more patients could be treated effectively by modifying psychoanalytic technique. Beginning in the 1960s, other, shorter-term, efficacious, and psychodynamically influenced therapies (cognitive-behavioral therapy, time-limited psychodynamic psychotherapy, and interpersonal psychotherapy to name but a few) emerged and were strongly supported by both the insurance industry's mission and that of government to contain health care costs.

Overview

Psychoanalysis is a treatment technique first described and implemented by Sigmund Freud at the end of the nineteenth century. His highly original thinking has made a profound and enduring contribution to our understanding of human nature. As a neuropathologist, he appreciated the scientific limits of neurology to explain many medical symptoms and disorders and, instead, began to investigate the mind. Freud's theory is based on the idea that humans experience mental and emotional conflict when they are defending against unacceptable strong, unconscious needs, wishes, and desires.

This is historically explained through different viewpoints, such as the topographical model that describes three levels of mental awareness, called the conscious, preconscious, and the unconscious. Thoughts and feelings may originate in any one of these levels and, if unacceptable or conflicted, a person utilizes defense mechanisms to deal with the thought or feeling in such a way as to prevent emotional discomfort experienced through anxiety (see table on page 595). This is played out universally within the therapeutic relationship between doctor and patient in the form of resistance, when defenses act to protect the patient against pain of awareness of the unacceptable thought or feeling and, hence, may hinder treatment progress unless ultimately brought to the patient's attention. Another explanation of psychological conflict is described through the so-called structural

Some Common Defense Mechanisms*

Denial	Refusal to appreciate information about oneself or others
Projection	Attribution to others of one's own unacceptable thoughts or feelings
Projective identification	Attribution of unacceptable personality characteristics to another followed by an attempt to develop a relationship based on those characteristics
Regression	A partial return to earlier levels of adaptation to avoid conflict
Splitting	Experiencing of others as being all good or all bad, i.e., idealization or devaluation and acting upon it
Conversion	Transformation of unacceptable wishes or thoughts into body sensations
Reaction formation	Transformation of an unwanted thought or feeling into its opposite
Isolation	Divorcing a feeling from its unpleasant idea
Rationalization	Using seemingly logical explanations to make untenable feelings or thoughts more acceptable
Displacement	Redirection of unpleasant feelings or thoughts onto another object
Dissociation	Splitting off thought or feeling from its original source
Sublimation	A mature mechanism whereby unacceptable thought and feelings are channeled into socially acceptable ones

*All defense mechanisms are involuntary and unconscious and are arranged approximately from immature to more mature defenses.

model, or drive theory, consisting of theoretical entities called the id, ego, and superego. The id represents infantile wishes and impulses; the superego represents moral and ethical rules; and the ego represents the mediator between the other two. Defense mechanisms exist within the ego, as does a person's ability to test reality and think logically, and the strength of one's ego refers to the capacity for social and personal competency.

To be precise, there is no single psychoanalytic theory because Freud's work has continued to evolve. Significant psychoanalytic revisions to his original contributions have focused on understanding the importance of interpersonal relationships as explained in, but not limited to, such "offshoots" as object relations theory (individual development in the context of the people and things making up the person's environment), self psychology (the psychology of the self and its unmet needs), relational theory (personality conceived of as the product of early, formative relationships), and attachment theory (concerning infant bonds with primary caregivers).

Above all, psychodynamic psychotherapy assumes that there are specific reasons why humans behave as they do, and that these reasons lie mostly outside of awareness, or, in other words, within the unconscious. Human experiences and memories are never lost from the unconscious and continue to influence a person's current thoughts, feelings, and behaviors (Kay & Kay 2008). Contributions from cognitive neuroscience have supported the significance of Freud's appreciation of the power of both conscious and unconscious memory (explicit and implicit memory). People are compelled to repeat self-defeating behavior patterns in a continuous attempt to overcome or master earlier psychological conflicts.

How Does It Work?

The helpfulness of psychotherapy ultimately depends on the contract and healing power of the therapeutic relationship. The conduct of psychotherapy is challenging and requires specific training most often at the master's or doctoral level. There are three central tasks for the therapist. First, the therapist listens and affirms the patient's current and prior experiences as the patient's conscious memory allows. The therapist then must appreciate and understand both the conscious and unconscious influences on the patient's mental and emotional conflict. Finally, the therapist interprets this understanding to the patient. All of these three operations must occur within the developing alliance between an empathic therapist and trusting patient (Ornstein & Ornstein 1985). This allows the patient to arrive at a deeper understanding of self and the symptoms underlying his or her emotional conflict through reexperiencing unresolved psychological issues. This process cannot occur unless the patient is provided with a safe, predictable, and confidential environment by the therapist to maximize the ability to notice and comment on the thoughts, feelings, and fantasies that come into awareness. The two integral processes of this therapy are transference and resistance. The former refers to those thoughts, feelings, and responses to another person in present time that actually reflect the patient's perceptions and feelings of important people from the past, usually family members. This is encouraged to occur between the patient and therapist so that it can be recognized and interpreted by the therapist for the patient. Once the patient becomes aware of previously hidden thoughts and feelings, healing from previous psychic trauma can take place and the patient experiences relief from symptoms of mental illness. Countertransference, on the other hand, is the therapist's transference reactions to the patient. This was traditionally viewed to be an impediment to progress in therapy but is more currently viewed as a valuable way in which the therapist can better understand the patient. Chances are that the feelings engendered in the therapist by the patient are those that characterize the patient's relationships with others in school, work, marriage, and family.

Resistance, as mentioned previously, is a universal unconscious motivation to suppress the awareness of specific thoughts and feelings. This is accomplished through a panoply of defense mechanisms (see table on page 595 for an abbreviated list). These defense structures are erected early in one's life in reaction to unresolved emotional conflict and serve to protect the patient from the pain of consciously revisiting such conflict. It is important for the therapist to recognize when defense mechanisms are being utilized, to appreciate how the patient is using the defense mechanism as protection from anxiety, to clarify and understand why the patient is unconsciously doing this in the here and now, and, finally, to interpret the resistance to the patient. In sum, the therapist must analyze transference by the interpretation of resistance. Depending on the number and types of negative and/or hurtful experiences in a patient's life, it is a complicated matter to permit the therapist entry into the patient's inner world through the creation of this intimate new relationship. A patient will typically repeat the reliving of prior troublesome experiences via many defense mechanisms over time, begetting self-defeating behaviors and continual unhappiness. The therapist's repeated identification of this tendency in the patient and the patient's emerging self-awareness is called the "working through" stage of psychodynamic treatment. Becoming more self-aware can be a very painful emotional process for the patient; however, the patient finds this tolerable given a supportive, empathic, therapeutic alliance with the therapist (Docherty 1985).

Psychodynamic psychotherapy is an appropriate treatment modality for a vast number of mental disorders, but there are some patient characteristics that lessen effectiveness for this therapy. These include low motivation, low frustration tolerance, low impulse control, significant cognitive deficits, no social support, poor ego strength, and lack of introspective abilities.

Is It Effective?

Many have argued in the past that success in psychodynamic psychotherapy, as in any psychotherapy, is similar to that of a patient's spontaneous remission of symptoms. There is no question at this point in time that psychotherapy is an effective treatment (Lambert, Shapiro, & Bergin 1986; Leichsenrig, Rabung, & Lebling 2004; Smith, Glass, & Miller 1980). Psychodynamic psychotherapy as a short-term treatment (i.e., 12–40 sessions) has reduced the cost of general medical services, has reduced length of hospital stays (Lazar 2010) according to cost-benefit studies, and for some disorders has been shown in highly rigorous studies comparing psychotherapy and medication to be superior to treatment with medication alone (Bateman & Fonagy 2001).

The advent of exciting new research in neurobiology, neuroimaging, genetics, and molecular biology demonstrates the changes psychotherapy effects on brain structure and function and has lent further support for psychotherapy (Lehrer & Kay 2002). For example, sleep architecture, thyroid levels, and neurotransmitter and neural circuitry functioning have been restored in patients with depression after psychotherapy (Kay & Kay 2008). In the not-too-distant future, it is expected that we will gain the ability to predict outcomes of treatment of specific disorders with both psychotherapy and medications (Mayberg et al. 1997).

Current Challenges and Trends in Psychodynamic Psychotherapy

Psychoanalysis is still performed by highly trained professionals, but access to this type of treatment is largely limited to those who can afford self-pay for what tends to be multiple therapy sessions a week for many years. Fortunately, the shorter, yet effective treatment of psychodynamic psychotherapy is usually covered or partially reimbursed by major insurance companies. Many social workers (LISWs, MSWs), psychologists (PsyDs, PhDs), and physicians (MDs) perform this type of therapy, typically on an outpatient basis. Many of the challenges faced in the early twenty-first century by those supportive of psychotherapy revolve around insurance coverage for longer-term therapy, research, and funding for research on psychotherapy. This latter category of research is quite broad as it includes the development of treatment guidelines for specific diagnoses such as personality disorders; the development of reliable, objective measurements for the outcomes of psychotherapy; the search for the most appropriate treatment type for a given patient's personality or stage of development; and the identification of the limits of shorter-term treatment or, in other words, when longer-term treatment is indicated in a given case.

Conclusions and Future Directions

Psychodynamic psychotherapy is a powerful treatment and is best administered by trained professionals to receptive patients with appropriate problems to address. To reiterate, psychotherapy is not indicated for everyone and, as with most treatments, the risks, benefits, adverse effects, and alternatives to psychotherapy should always be explored with the patient during the intake and assessment process.

Research into psychotherapy is growing rapidly from a variety of interfacing scientific fields. For example, exciting work has demonstrated (1) the relationship between the brain region known as the amygdala and types of unconscious memories from childhood; (2) reduced volume of the hippocampus (brain component) in patients with histories of abuse; (3) psychotherapy's influence on neuroimmunology (involving the hypothalamic-pituitary-adrenal system); and (4) the ability to genetically predict risk for major depression and anxiety—to name a few important topics. Taking these studies from the lab bench to the therapist's office will prove crucial. The results of much of this research can profoundly change the way medicine is practiced and the way we will be able to care for each other.

See also Clinical Psychology; Humanistic Theories and Therapies; Psychiatry; Psychoanalysis; Psychotherapy

Bibliography

Bateman, A., and P. Fonagy. 2001. "Treatment of Borderline Personality Disorder with Psychoanalytically Oriented Partial Hospitalization Program: An 18-Month Follow-Up." *American Journal of Psychiatry* 158: 36–42.

Docherty, J. P. (section ed.). 1985. "Therapeutic Alliance and Treatment Outcome." In R. E. Hales and A. J. Francis, eds., *Psychiatry Update: American Psychiatric Association Annual Review* (Vol. 4, pp. 525–633). Washington, DC: American Psychiatric Press.

Kay, J., and R. L. Kay. 2008. "Individual Psychoanalytic Psychotherapy." In A. Tasman, J. Kay, J. A. Lieberman, M. B. First, and M. Maj, eds., *Psychiatry* (3rd ed., pp. 1851–1888). West Sussex, England: Wiley.

Lambert, M. J., D. A. Shapiro, and A. E. Bergin. 1986. "The Effectiveness of Psychotherapy." In S. L. Garfield and A. E. Bergin, eds., *Handbook of Psychotherapy and Behavior Change* (3rd ed., pp. 157–211). New York: Wiley.

Lazar, S. G., ed. 2010. "Psychotherapy Is Worth It: A Comprehensive Review of Its Cost-Effectiveness." The Committee on Psychotherapy Group for the Advancement of Psychiatry. Washington, DC: American Psychiatric Publishing.

Lehrer, D. S., and J. Kay. 2002. "The Neurobiology of Psychotherapy." In M. Hersen and W. Sledge, eds., *The Encyclopedia of Psychotherapy* (pp. 207–221). New York: Academic Press.

Leichsenrig, F., S. Rabung, and E. Lebling. 2004. "The Efficacy of Short-Term Psychodynamic Psychotherapy in Specific Psychiatric Disorders: A Meta-Analysis." *Archives of General Psychiatry* 61: 1208–1216.

Mayberg, H. S., S. K. Brannan, R. K. Mahurrin, P. A. Jerabek, J. S. Brickman, J. L. Takell, J. A. Silva, S. McGinnis, T. G. Glass, C. C. Martin, and P. T. Fox. 1997. "Cingulate Function in Depression: A Potential Predictor of Treatment Response." *Neuroreport* 8: 1057–1061.

Ornstein, P. H., and A. Ornstein. 1985. "Clinical Understanding and Explaining: The Empathic Vantage Point." In A. Goldberg, ed., *Progress in Self Psychology* (Vol. 1, pp. 43–61). New York: Guilford Press.

Shedler, J. 2010. "The Efficacy of Psychodynamic Psychotherapy." *American Psychologist* 65(2): 98–109.

Smith, M. L., G. V. Glass, and T. I. Miller. 1980. *The Benefits of Psychotherapy.* Baltimore: Johns Hopkins University Press.

Thase, M. E., A. L. Fasiczka, S. R. Berman, A. D. Simons, and C. F. Reynolds III. 1998. "Electroencephalographic Sleep Profiles Before and After." *Archives of General Psychiatry* 55: 138–144.

Psychopathy and Antisocial Personality Disorder

Laura E. Drislane and Christopher J. Patrick

Because of its societal costs and its importance to forensic practice and policy, psychopathy ("psychopathic personality") is one of the most widely studied personality disorders. Characterized by a distinct set of affective and interpersonal features accompanied by impulsive, norm-violating behaviors, psychopathy is believed to reflect a chronic condition having a substantial constitutional-genetic basis. Psychopathy in criminal offenders has been linked to heightened levels and severity of criminal deviance, including violent-offense behavior. As such, psychopathy is often discussed hand in hand with the related but distinguishable syndrome of antisocial personality disorder (ASPD) as represented in the current, fourth edition of the *Diagnostic and Statistical Manual of Mental Disorders*

(*DSM-IV*; American Psychiatric Association 2000). While providing extensive coverage of the behavioral deviance features of psychopathy (e.g., impulsivity, irresponsibility, law and rule breaking, in childhood and continuing into adulthood; see the below table), the diagnostic criteria for ASPD in *DSM-IV* provide limited coverage of the affective-interpersonal features such as charm, grandiosity, shallow affect, and callous disregard—all of which are nevertheless central to

Diagnostic Criteria for *DSM-IV* Antisocial Personality Disorder

Criterion Category	Summary Description of Criterion
A. Adult antisocial behavior (three or more of the following since age 15)	1. Repeated participation in illegal acts 2. Deceitfulness 3. Impulsiveness or failure to make plans in advance 4. Hostile-aggressive behavior 5. Engagement in actions that endanger self or others 6. Frequent irresponsible behavior 7. Absence of remorse
B. Age criterion	Current age at least 18
C. Child conduct disorder (three or more of the following before age 15, resulting in impaired social, academic, or occupational function)	*Aggression toward people or animals* 1. Frequent bullying, threatening, or intimidation of others 2. Frequent initiation of physical fights 3. Use of dangerous weapons 4. Physical cruelty toward people 5. Physical cruelty toward animals 6. Theft involving victim confrontation 7. Forced sexual contact *Destroying property* 8. Deliberate fire setting with intent to cause damage 9. Deliberate destruction of property *Deceptiveness or stealing* 10. Breaking/entering (house, building, or vehicle) 11. Frequent lying to acquire things or to avoid duties 12. Nontrivial theft without victim confrontation *Serious rule violations* 13. Frequent violations of parental curfew, starting before age 13 14. Running away from home 15. Frequent truancy, starting before age 13
D. Comorbidity criterion:	Antisocial behavior does not occur exclusively during episodes of schizophrenia or mania.

Source: American Psychiatric Association 2000.

psychopathy. The question of how these disorders should be characterized in relation to one another is at the forefront of current debates in diagnostic classification, as major revisions to ASPD and its child counterpart, conduct disorder, are being considered for the upcoming fifth edition of the *DSM* (expected in 2013).

Historic Conceptions

Historic conceptualizations of psychopathy can be traced to the French physician Philippe Pinel, who applied the term *manie sans delire* ("insanity without delirium") to individuals who exhibited reckless violent behavior while maintaining otherwise intact mental faculties. Following Pinel, the term "psychopathic" grew to encompass a wide variety of conditions considered to arise early in life and persist into adulthood. American psychiatrist Hervey Cleckley sought to clarify and narrow the scope of the disorder in his classic monograph *The Mask of Sanity* (1976/1941), upon which most modern views of psychopathology are based. Influenced by his experiences with psychopathic hospital inpatients, Cleckley described psychopathy as a deep-rooted emotional pathology masked by an outward appearance of robust mental health. Unlike other overtly disturbed

Cleckley's Diagnostic Criteria for Psychopathy, Grouped by Conceptual Category

Conceptual Category	Criterion Number and Label
Appearance of psychological stability	
	1. Superficial charm and good intelligence
	2. Absence of delusions and other signs of irrational thinking
	3. Absence of "nervousness" or psychoneurotic manifestations
	14. Suicide rarely carried out
Chronic behavioral deviance	
	4. Unreliability
	7. Inadequately motivated antisocial behavior
	8. Poor judgment and failure to learn by experience
	13. Fantastic and uninviting behavior with drink and sometimes without
	15. Sex life impersonal, trivial, and poorly integrated
	16. Failure to follow any life plan
Emotional-interpersonal deficits	
	5. Untruthfulness and insincerity
	6. Lack of remorse or shame
	9. Pathologic egocentricity and incapacity for love
	10. General poverty in major affective reactions
	11. Specific loss of insight
	12. Unresponsiveness in general interpersonal relations

Source: Cleckley 1976: 338–339.

psychiatric patients, psychopaths present initially as confident, personable, and well adjusted. However, their underlying disturbance is revealed over time through their attitudes and actions. As a basis for refining diagnosis, Cleckley formulated 16 specific criteria for identifying the disorder. These criteria include indicators of apparent psychological stability, behavioral deviancy, and impaired emotional sensitivity and social relatedness (see table on p. 601).

Of note, Cleckley did not characterize psychopathic patients as saliently cruel, violent, or dangerous. Rather, he viewed the harm they inflicted on others as a secondary consequence of their shallow, feckless natures. As such, Cleckley's case histories included examples of "successful psychopaths" who attained careers as physicians, scholars, or businessmen alongside examples of petty criminals and ne'er-do-wells. In contrast, other writers of Cleckley's era who focused on psychopathy in criminal offenders placed greater emphasis on clinical features such as coldness, viciousness, and exploitativeness. For example, McCord and McCord (1964) described psychopathy in more uniformly pathologic terms, identifying "lovelessness" (inability to form deep attachments) and "guiltlessness" (absence of remorse) as core deficits underlying the disorder. Thus historic conceptions differ to some extent in their portrayals of psychopathic individuals as likeable but untrustworthy "chameleons" (e.g., Cleckley) as opposed to predatory-aggressive "sharks" (e.g., McCord & McCord 1964).

Modern Diagnostic Approaches

Modern approaches to diagnosing psychopathy, consisting of clinician-administered rating instruments and self-report scales, reflect these alternative historic conceptions to varying degrees. Researchers study sample populations of adult criminal offenders, noncriminal adult individuals, and youths diagnosed with conduct disorder, among other subjects.

Psychopathy in Adult Offender Samples

The most widely used measure for assessing psychopathy in incarcerated samples is the Psychopathy Checklist-Revised (PCL-R; Hare 2003), an interview-based inventory developed to systematize the diagnosis of psychopathy in research studies with criminal offenders. The PCL-R consists of 20 items rated on the basis of information derived from a semistructured interview and institutional case records (e.g., social history reports, criminal offenses, etc.). The PCL-R items refer extensively to subjects' criminal histories and attitudes and tap the affective-interpersonal deficits and behavioral deviancy features identified by Cleckley. However, the PCL-R includes only limited, indirect coverage of positive adjustment features of psychopathy highlighted in Cleckley's conception.

The manual for the PCL-R specifies a cutoff score of 30 (out of a possible 40 points) for assigning a diagnosis of psychopathy. High overall scores on the PCL-R are associated with impulsive and aggressive tendencies, low affiliation, low empathy, Machiavellianism, and persistent violent offending. Given these associations, psychopathy as defined by the PCL-R bears greater resemblance to the predatory-aggressive conception advanced by McCord and McCord than to Cleckley's portrayal.

Despite being developed to index psychopathy as a coherent syndrome, the PCL-R contains distinctive components defined by subsets of items: an *affective-interpersonal* component (AI) and an *antisocial deviancy* component (AD). Although distinctive in terms of item content, these components show moderate correlations with one another, reflecting the PCL-R's unitary conception of psychopathy. PCL-AI is associated with pathological tendencies such as high narcissism, low empathy, and use of instrumental aggression (Hare 2003). After controlling for overlap with PCL-AD, PCL-AI also shows some relations with adaptive tendencies, such as social assertiveness and low levels of fear, distress, and depression (Hicks & Patrick 2006). In contrast, PCL-AD is mainly associated with maladaptive tendencies and behaviors, including high impulsivity, sensation seeking, and aggressiveness (in particular, reactive aggression), early and persistent antisocial deviance, and alcohol and drug problems.

Psychopathy in Adult Noncriminal Samples

In noncriminal samples, psychopathy has most often been assessed using self-report measures. Historically, most instruments of this kind have emphasized the antisocial deviancy component of psychopathy. A notable exception is the more recently developed Psychopathic Personality Inventory (PPI; Lilienfeld & Andrews 1996), which does not contain items explicitly tapping antisocial or criminal behavior. Rather, the PPI was designed to comprehensively index personality traits embodied in Cleckley's description of psychopathy. The revised PPI (PPI-R; Lilienfeld & Widows 2005) contains 154 items, organized into eight subscales. Like the PCL-R, the PPI-R's subscales index psychopathy in terms of two broad components: a fearless-dominance component (FD), reflecting social potency, stress immunity, and fearlessness; and a self-centered impulsivity component (SCI), reflecting selfishness, hostility, nonconformity, and lack of planfulness (Benning et al. 2005). In contrast with the PCL-R's correlated components, the two distinct components of the PPI are uncorrelated. Scores on PPI-FD are associated with positive adjustment (e.g., higher well-being; lower anxiousness and depression) as well as tendencies toward narcissism, deficient empathy, and thrill seeking. As such, PPI-FD appears to reflect a purer, more benign expression of dispositional fearlessness (termed "boldness") than PPI-AI—which can be viewed as capturing a more malignant (antagonistic or "mean") expression of fearlessness. Scores on

PPI-SCI, on the other hand, are associated with multiple indicators of deviancy—including impulsivity and aggressiveness, child and adult antisocial behavior, substance problems, heightened distress and dysphoria, and suicidal ideation.

Psychopathy in Conduct-Disordered Youth

In an effort to predict violence and delinquency and to identify youth at elevated risk for developing such problems, various inventories have been developed for assessing psychopathic tendencies in children and adolescents. Efforts have focused in particular on identifying a subset of youth with conduct problems who exhibit severe and persistent antisocial behavior over time. In contrast with earlier research emphasizing age of onset of conduct problems as a crucial predictor (Moffitt 1993, 2006), more recent work has focused on the importance of psychopathic tendencies in predicting severity and persistence of delinquent behavior. Termed "callous-unemotional" traits, these tendencies encompass deficient remorse or guilt, callousness (low empathy), shallow or deficient affect, and a lack of concern about performance (Frick & Moffitt 2010).

One extensively researched inventory that assesses both antisocial tendencies and callous-unemotional traits is the Antisocial Process Screening Device (APSD; cf. Frick & Marsee 2006), designed for use with children (ages 6–13) exhibiting behavioral problems. Patterned after the PCL-R, the APSD consists of 20 items that are completed by parents or teachers. Again, the items of the APSD capture two distinct symptomatic components: a callous-unemotional traits (CU) component, reflecting emotional insensitivity and interpersonal callousness; and an impulsive/conduct problems (I/CP) component, reflecting impulsivity, behavioral deviancy, and inflated self-importance. Children high on the I/CP component but low in CU traits show diminished intellectual ability, high negative emotional reactivity, and frequent reactive (but not premeditated) aggression (Frick & Marsee 2006). In contrast, children high on both APSD-CU and APSD-I/CP exhibit normal intellect, are attracted to activities entailing novelty and risk, report less anxiety and nervousness, and are less reactive to distressing stimuli. They also learn less readily from punishment and engage in high levels of both premeditated and reactive aggression and tend to exhibit more persistent violent behavior across time. Given the apparent importance of CU traits in moderating the expression of conduct disorder, proposed revisions in *DSM-5* include specification of a "callous-unemotional" variant of child conduct disorder.

Building Blocks of Psychopathy: Disinhibition, Boldness, and Meanness

As evident from the foregoing, psychopathy as conceptualized historically and more contemporarily appears to comprise a number of distinct, but in some ways related propensities that vary in their overlap with APSD as currently defined in *DSM-IV.* A model that was recently advanced to organize and make sense of differing conceptions of psychopathy is the triarchic model (Patrick, Fowles, & Krueger 2009). This model conceives of psychopathy as encompassing three distinguishable symptomatic components—disinhibition, boldness, and meanness—that represent thematic building blocks for alternative conceptions of psychopathy.

Disinhibition entails propensities toward impulsivity, weak behavioral restraint, and impaired regulation of emotion. Impulse control problems of various types, including substance use disorders and child and adult symptoms of ASPD, include disinhibition as a strong common element. *Boldness* entails high social efficacy, a capacity to remain calm under pressure and recover quickly from stressors, and a tolerance for unfamiliarity and danger. Correlates of boldness include confidence, interpersonal assertiveness, narcissism and thrill-seeking behavior, and low anxiety and depression (Benning et al. 2005). *Meanness* entails deficient empathy, low social connectedness, rebelliousness, exploitativeness, excitement seeking, and empowerment through cruelty. In contrast with disinhibition, which reflects a general proneness to impulse control problems, meanness involves more specific tendencies toward callous insensitivity, instrumental use of aggression, destructive fun seeking, and predatory manipulation of others.

Recent research suggests differing causal factors underlying the disinhibition component as compared to the boldness and meanness components. With regard to brain mechanisms, disinhibition is hypothesized to arise from dysfunction in anterior brain systems—including the prefrontal cortex and anterior cingulate cortex—that operate to guide decision making and action and regulate emotional reactivity. As a result, highly disinhibited individuals operate in the present moment, failing to moderate their actions and reactions as a function of past experiences or anticipated future outcomes. In contrast, boldness can be conceptualized as an adaptive behavioral (phenotypic) expression of an underlying fearless disposition (genotype). Deviations in the functioning of affective-motivational systems including the amygdala have been posited to play a role in this underlying disposition. Dysfunction of this type is theorized to underlie emotional deficits observed in psychopathy, particularly those related to negative events and stimuli. In addition, experiential factors that promote a sense of personal efficacy and effective top-down regulatory control of emotion may also contribute to individual differences in boldness.

The third thematic component, meanness, may also likewise some contribution of dispositional fearlessness. For example, the external correlates of APSD-CU factor as described earlier are consistent with this hypothesis. However, in contrast with boldness, meanness represents a pathological expression of low fear—one marked by impaired social connectedness and a profound absence of caring. From this perspective, factors that contribute to disaffiliation would be expected to shape fearlessness in the direction of meanness rather than boldness. Some of the environmental influences that may promote meanness include early exposure to physical or sexual abuse and punitive parenting practices. It seems likely that distinctive constitutional-genetic influences contribute as well.

Psychopathy Variants

Given evidence for differing symptomatic components to psychopathy, it might be expected that distinguishable subtypes of psychopathic individuals, reflecting greater prominence of certain symptomatic components relative to others, would exist. Indeed, the idea of psychopathy subtypes has a long history. Benjamin Karpman (1941), a contemporary of Cleckley's, argued for the existence of distinct subtypes that he termed "primary" and "secondary." According to Karpman, the former arises from a constitutional deficit in emotional reactivity, whereas the latter reflects an acquired deficit in the capacity for behavioral control arising from exposure to environmental stressors, such as abuse, severe neglect, or parental rejection. Karpman characterized individuals with secondary psychopathy as highly impulsive and prone to negative emotions and those with primary psychopathy (in line with Cleckley's characterization) as emotionally insensitive and impervious to punishment. Subsequent theorists (Fowles 1980; Lykken 1995) have posited primary and secondary subtypes distinguished by deficient anxiety or fear versus heightened reward sensitivity.

Studies that have used statistical methods to test for subgroups of high-PCL-R offenders with contrasting personality trait or psychopathy symptom profiles (Hicks et al. 2004; Poythress et al. 2010; Skeem et al. 2007) provide evidence for at least two variants, distinguishable in particular on two dispositional dimensions: anxiousness and hostility/aggression. One subgroup of high-PCL-R scorers shows markedly elevated rates of anxiousness along with high levels of aggression, whereas the other is distinguished by very low anxiousness and normative levels of aggressiveness.

Another long-standing distinction in the literature is that of "successful" versus "unsuccessful" psychopathy. The term "successful psychopath" refers to an individual who possesses the core underlying disposition of a psychopath and engages in behaviors that violate social norms and the rights of others, but who refrains from antisocial conduct serious enough to prompt legal consequences (Babiak 1995; Hall & Benning 2006). As noted earlier, Cleckley's case histories included salient examples of such individuals. The concept of boldness, which encompasses some positive-adaptive elements, may be of particular relevance here. Characteristics such as social assertiveness, emotional resiliency, and venturesomeness could well be directly conducive to success, as well as serve to moderate or camouflage co-occurring antisocial propensities. Little is known about successful psychopaths, because most research to date has focused on incarcerated offenders or noninstitutionalized individuals who exhibit salient antisocial-externalizing traits. However, the availability of measures such as the PPI that index the boldness component of psychopathy separately from its meanness and disinhibition components creates new avenues for investigating aspects of psychopathy that may be consistent with (or even contribute to) success in society as opposed to failure.

See also Anger and Aggression; *Diagnostic and Statistical Manual of Mental Disorders (DSM)*; Narcissism; Violence and Violence-Prone Individuals

Bibliography

American Psychiatric Association. 2000. *Diagnostic and Statistical Manual of Mental Disorders*, (4th ed., text rev.). Washington, DC: American Psychiatric Publishing.

Babiak, P. 1995. "Psychopathic Manipulation in Organizations: Pawns, Patrons, and Patsies." *Issues in Criminological & Legal Psychology* 24: 12–17.

Benning, S. D., C. J. Patrick, D. M. Blonigen, B. M. Hicks, and W. G. Iacono. 2005. "Estimating Facets of Psychopathy from Normal Personality Traits: A Step toward Community-Epidemiological Investigations." *Assessment* 12: 3–18.

Cleckley, H. 1941/1976. *The Mask of Sanity* (5th ed.). St. Louis, MO: Mosby.Fowles, D. C. 1980. "The three arousal model: Implications of Gray's two-factor learning theory for heart rate, electrodermal activity and psychopathy." *Psychophysiology* 17: 87–104.

Frick, P. J., and M. A. Marsee. 2006. "Psychopathy and Developmental Pathways to Antisocial Behavior in Youth." In C. J. Patrick, ed., *Handbook of Psychopathy* (pp. 353–374). New York: Guilford Press.

Frick, P. J., and T. E. Moffitt. 2010. "A Proposal to the *DSM-V* Childhood Disorders and the ADHD and Disruptive Behavior Disorders Work Groups to Include a Specifier to the Diagnosis of Conduct Disorder Based on the Presence of Callous-Unemotional Traits." American Psychiatric Association. Retrieved from http://www.dsm5.org/Proposed Revisions/Pages/proposedrevision.aspx?rid=424#

Hall, J. R., and S. D. Benning. 2006. "The 'Successful' Psychopath: Adaptive and Subclinical Manifestations of Psychopathy in the General Population." In C. J. Patrick, ed., *Handbook of Psychopathy* (pp. 459–478). New York: Guilford Press.

Hare, R. D. (2003). *The Hare Psychopathy Checklist* (rev., 2nd ed.). Toronto: Multi-Health Systems.

Hicks, B. M., K. E. Markon, C. J. Patrick, R. F. Krueger, and J. P. Newman. 2004. "Identifying Psychopathy Subtypes on the Basis of Personality Structure." *Psychological Assessment* 16: 276–288.

Hicks, B. M., and C. J. Patrick. 2006. "Psychopathy and Negative Affectivity: Analyses of Suppressor Effects Reveal Distinct Relations with Trait Anxiety, Depression, Fearfulness, and Anger-Hostility." *Journal of Abnormal Psychology* 115: 276–287.

Karpman, B. 1941. "On the Need of Separating Psychopathy into Two Distinct Clinical Types: The Symptomatic and the Idiopathic." *Journal of Criminal Psychopathology* 3: 112–137.

Lilienfeld, S. O., and B. P. Andrews. 1996. "Development and Preliminary Validation of a Self-Report Measure of Psychopathic Personality Traits in Noncriminal Populations." *Journal of Personality Assessment* 66: 488–524.

Lilienfeld, S. O., and M. R. Widows. 2005. *Psychopathic Personality Inventory-Revised (PPI-R) Professional Manual*. Odessa, FL: Psychological Assessment Resources.

Lykken, D. T. 1995. *The Antisocial Personalities*. Hillsdale, NJ: Erlbaum.

McCord, W., and J. McCord. 1964. *The Psychopath: An Essay on the Criminal Mind*. Princeton, NJ: Van Nostrand.

Moffitt, T. E. 1993. "Adolescence-Limited and Life-Course Persistent Antisocial Behavior: A Developmental Taxonomy." *Psychological Review* 100: 674–701.

Moffitt, T. E. 2006. "A Review of Research on the Taxonomy of Lifecourse-Persistent versus Adolescence-Limited Antisocial Behavior." In F. T. Culler, J. P. Wright, and K. R. Blevins, eds., *Taking Stock: The Status of Criminological Theory* (pp. 277–311). New Brunswick, NJ: Transaction.

Patrick, C. J. 2006. *Handbook of Psychopathy*. New York: Guilford Press.

Patrick, C. J., D. C. Fowles, and R. F. Krueger. 2009. "Triarchic Conceptualization of Psychopathy: Developmental Origins of Disinhibition, Boldness, and Meanness." *Development and Psychopathology* 21: 913–938.

Poythress, N. G., J. F. Edens, J. L. Skeem, S. O. Lilienfeld, K. S. Douglas, P. J. Frick, and T. Wang. 2010. "Identifying Subtypes among Offenders with Antisocial Personality Disorder: A Cluster-Analytic Study." *Journal of Abnormal Psychology* 119: 389–400.

Skeem, J. L., P. Johansson, H. Andershed, M. Kerr, and J. E. Louden. 2007. "Two Subtypes of Psychopathic Violent Offenders That Parallel Primary and Secondary Variants." *Journal of Abnormal Psychology* 116: 395–409.

Venables, N. C., and C. J. Patrick. In press. "Validity of the Externalizing Spectrum Inventory in a Criminal Offender Sample: Relations with Disinhibitory Psychopathology, Personality, and Psychopathic Features." *Psychological Assessment*.

Psychopharmacology

William H. Wilson

Medication is a mainstay of current treatment approaches for mood disorders, psychosis, anxiety, and other major disorders of cognition, emotion, and behavior. The term "psychopharmacology" encompasses the study of medications for such problems, and the clinical practice of treating such disorders with medication. The development of psychopharmacology over the past 60 years has dramatically altered the standard treatment of most psychiatric disorders. While many individuals have clearly benefited from medication treatment, the field is fraught with controversy regarding the effects and side effects of medications, the proper role of medications in treatment, the influence of corporate profit motives and governmental regulation on medication development and use, and societal issues such as race and gender.

Psychopharmacology is based on an understanding that a person's ability to perceive, to move, to reason and understand, to love and hate, to work, to have moods and emotions, and to take action is based on the structure and function of the person's brain. The brain, like other organs, is vulnerable to congenital defects and damage from illness or injury. When similar problems affect the heart, the result may be an impairment of blood flow. When problems affect the brain, the result is likely to be impairment in thinking, feeling and/or behaving. Just as proper medication may improve the function of a failing heart, so too particular medications may also improve impaired brain function.

Background and History

Until the mid-twentieth century, there were no specific medication treatments for mental illness. Contemporary psychopharmacology began with the recognition of the antimanic effects of lithium in 1949 and with reports of the effectiveness of medication treatment of psychosis and depression in the early 1950s. The recognition that specific medications could ameliorate particular symptoms of mental illnesses provided a major impetus to the scientific study of the biological basis of mental illness, and gave the pharmaceutical industry an incentive to develop new medications. Technological advances in brain imaging, molecular genetics, and cell biology led to an increasingly sophisticated appreciation of the neurological basis of major psychiatric disorders, and to the development of more effective medications. Nonetheless, knowledge remains partial. For example, in the 1950s brains were largely assessed by light microscopy at autopsy. A variety of brain-scanning techniques now allows detailed assessment of brain structure, metabolic activity, and chemical reactions in living behaving brains. Contemporary imaging techniques (e.g., computed tomography [CAT], magnetic resonance imaging [MRI], functional magnetic resonance [fMRI], spectral fMRI) are still used mainly for research. Their clinical utility is primarily to rule out the presence of neurological disease (e.g., brain tumors, stroke) rather than to diagnose or assess primary psychiatric syndromes.

Today's medication treatments are only somewhat effective and rarely curative. In these respects, medication treatment for psychiatric disorders is analogous to the ongoing medication treatment of diabetes or rheumatoid arthritis rather than to the cures that may come from antibiotic treatment of infections.

Controversies and Challenges

When accompanied by adequate social support for the client or patient and culturally sensitive, "person-centered" services, psychopharmacology provides tools for helping people with mental illnesses to live more stable and more fulfilling lives. However, psychopharmacology has not developed in an ideal manner; rather, it has been confounded by the major societal issues of our times, such as stigma against the poor and ill, economic factors, and the politics of gender, race, culture (Wilson 2011).

The effectiveness of psychopharmacological treatments, and, indeed, the validity of the field in general, is a matter of debate. At stake is the general approach to treatment of millions of individuals as well as the dollars allocated to that treatment. A reasoned middle ground in the debate—one that takes into account the partial but significant effectiveness of medications, on the one hand, and the need to fold these treatments into programs that fully recognize individuals' psychological and social needs, on the other—is often difficult to come by (Kramer 2011).

Tension between the perspectives of scientific psychiatry and commercial interests has permeated psychopharmacology since its inception. With markets in the tens of billions of dollars, there has been sufficient incentive for unscrupulous investigators to inflate or fabricate research data, and for companies to aggressively promote maximal use of their products. With direct-to-consumer advertising, whereby ads for drugs target consumers rather than medical professionals, psychiatrists are at times put in the position of purveyors of consumer goods rather than that of independent scientific practitioners.

The profit motive also leads to a tendency to medicalize problems that could be conceived of as part and parcel of everyday life, and thus create new markets. For example, there is a debate regarding whether or not low sexual desire in women should be regarded as a psychiatric disorder (Jutel 2010).

Basic Principles of Psychopharmacology

Most psychiatric medications work by modulating the activity of neurons (i.e., nerve cells) in the brain (Stahl 2008). Neurons send messages to adjoining neurons by releasing chemicals (neurotransmitters) into the specialized junctions between cells (synapses; see figures on p. 611). The chemical message is received when the neurotransmitter attaches to a large molecule, termed a "receptor," on the next nerve cell, changing the shape of the receptor and thereby turning on a cascade of chemical processes within the cell. Alternatively, a neurotransmitter may cause another type of receptor to open or close a channel through which electrically charged particles can move in and out of the neuron, altering the cell's likelihood of sending on an electrochemical message to other cells.

Many psychiatric medications either inhibit or boost the action of particular neurotransmitters. Most antidepressant and antipsychotic medications affect the "monoamine" neurotransmitters (dopamine, norepinephrine, and serotonin). These small molecules are found in bundles ("tracts") of nerves that run from the brain stem (where the brain meets the spinal cord) to structures throughout the brain. These tracts can be thought of as volume controls for the different parts of the brain. Release of neurotransmitter molecules increases or decreases the activity level of the nerve cells in the areas they innervate. The therapeutic

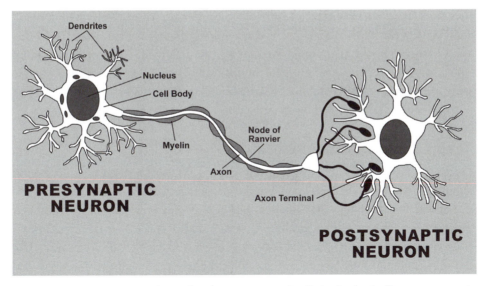

Pathways of electrochemical signaling between neural cells in the brain (from presynaptic to postsynaptic neurons).

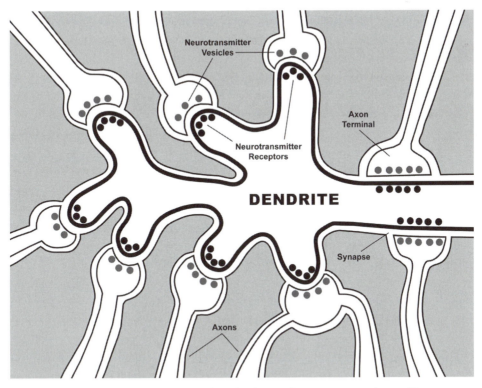

The synapse (between axons and dendrites) where information is exchanged between neural cells.

effects of some medications are immediately evident. More often, symptomatic improvement accrues gradually, over weeks or months, as the brain slowly adjusts to changes in neurotransmission. Antianxiety medications in the benzodiazepine family modulate activity of the neurotransmitter GABA (gamma-amino butyric acid). Lithium and mood stabilizers such as divalproex affect neuronal activity in complex ways that are not directly related to neurotransmitters and receptors.

Major Classes of Medications

The types of psychiatric medications (antipsychotics, antidepressants, mood stabilizers, and the like) are named for the clinical action that is most pronounced or that was first studied. Many medications have broader clinical utility than their name implies. For example, "antidepressants" are also used to treat certain types of anxiety, and "antipsychotics" are also used to treat mood symptoms. The classes of medications covered in the present entry represent the main psycho-pharmacological treatments, but this is not an exhaustive list. Readers are referred to the references below (see Bibliography) for further coverage.

Antipsychotics

The antipsychotic medications were developed after the serendipitous observation that core symptoms of schizophrenia—such as hallucinations, delusions, and thought disorder—improved after a few weeks of treatment with chlorpromazine, which initially had been given as a sedative. This observation led to the development of other similar medications, some of which are less sedating. Together these medications are termed "first-generation" antipsychotics (e.g., chlorpromazine, haloperidol). The therapeutic activity is thought to be due to blockage of dopamine receptors in the brain's limbic system. Dopamine receptors are also blocked in motor-system areas, leading to side effects that mimic Parkinson's disease. Long-term exposure to these medications often leads to uncontrollable tics and writhing motions called "tardive dyskinesia." The second-generation antipsychotics, which came into use in the 1990s, were aimed at reducing motor-system side effects (e.g., clozapine, risperidone). These medications block dopamine receptors and also block the 5-HT2a serotonin receptor. Blockage of the 5-HT2a receptor indirectly increases dopamine activity in motor areas, thereby reducing motor-system side effects. Effectiveness in treating psychosis is similar between first- and second-generation medications. Some of the second-generation medications carry a substantial risk of elevated cholesterol and blood glucose, which are risk factors for cardiovascular disease. Despite the side effects, the antipsychotic medications often give individuals with schizophrenia and related disorders some relief from several of the more troubling symptoms and the chance for improved social functioning.

Antidepressants

Antidepressant medications are used to decrease a range of symptoms in depression, including depressed mood, inability to experience enjoyment, difficulty initiating activity, poor appetite, loss of libido, and more. They do not elevate mood in individuals who are not depressed. The improvement in depression occurs gradually over a period of weeks when the medication is taken consistently. All of the antidepressants work by increasing availability of one or more of the monoamine neurotransmitters (norepinephrine, serotonin, and dopamine), though the mechanism of this varies among the classes for antidepressants. The monoamine oxidase inhibitors (MAOIs, e.g., tranylcypromine) and the tricyclic antidepressants (TCAs, e.g., imipramine) introduced in the 1950s, while effective, have been largely supplanted by newer medications that are less toxic in overdose and may have fewer side effects. These are the selective serotonin reuptake inhibitors (SSRIs, e.g., fluoxetine), serotonin-norepinephrine reuptake inhibitors (SNRIs, e.g., venlafaxine), norepinephrine reuptake inhibitors (NRIs, bupropion), and a handful of medications that work through other mechanisms (e.g., trazodone, mirtazapine). The second-generation antipsychotic aripiprazole is used to boost response to antidepressants.

Antidepressants at times have a paradoxical effect, worsening mood and provoking suicidal behavior. Because of such side effects, antidepressants need to be prescribed judiciously and treatment requires careful professional monitoring. Antidepressants frequently provoke mania in individuals who have bipolar affective disorder and rarely in individuals who do not. Because of this, bipolar depression is usually treated with mood stabilizers (particularly lamotrigine) or the second-generation antipsychotic quetiapine.

Mood Stabilizers

Mood stabilizers are medications that treat mania in bipolar affective disorder and suppress further episodes of both depression and mania. To a lesser extent they are useful in the treatment of the depressed phase of bipolar disorder. Lithium, the original mood stabilizer, is a naturally occurring element similar to sodium. The simplicity of lithium and its natural occurrence make it attractive to some individuals. The doses used therapeutically are much larger than what would be found in nature, and result in a number of short- and long-term side effects, including slow progressive kidney damage. Nonetheless it is an effective medication and has been shown to reduce suicide more than occurs with other mood stabilizers. Several medications developed originally as anticonvulsants are effective mood stabilizers, particularly divalproex, and carbamazepine. The antipsychotics also have mood-stabilizing properties, whether or not psychosis is present.

Antianxiety Medications

Medications for anxiety may be used to quickly avert anxiety in the moment or to continuously reduce overall anxiety. Anxiety is experienced in normal life, and should be treated only when its severity interferes with social functioning. The benzodiazepines (e.g., diazepam, alprazolam) are effective for relief in acute anxiety. Their utility in longer-term treatment is limited by the fact that physical dependence develops rapidly, that there can be a prolonged withdrawal syndrome when they are discontinued, and that they are valued as drugs of abuse. The SSRI antidepressants, and to a lesser extent other antidepressants, are usually the choice for long-term treatment of a variety of anxiety disorders. Buspirone is also used for gradual reduction of anxiety.

Stimulants

Stimulants such as methylphenidate and mixed amphetamines are used to treat attention deficit disorder with and without hyperactivity (ADD, ADHD), in both adults and children. Individuals who do not have a form of ADD experience stimulation from these medications, while individuals with ADD are calmed and show greater ability to focus attention and to function. The nonstimulant atomoxetine is also used for this disorder. For children with ADD or ADHD, medication treatment should be combined with supportive educational approaches that take into account the child's particular needs. Adults need education and training in task management to supplement medication. As with the antidepressants, medications for attention deficit syndrome are often prescribed without sufficient assessment and ongoing monitoring, and without attention to the patient's social and psychological needs. The stimulants are frequently diverted for abuse.

Conclusion

It is clear that many maladies that have been termed "mental illness" are rooted in brain dysfunction. It is equally clear that medications can be helpful, at least when used within the context of skilled professional assessment and monitoring, and with attention to the individual's psychological and social needs. Psychopharmacology should become more rational and more sophisticated as the understanding of the brain improves through advances in neuroscience. It is also clear that the development and use of psychopharmacological agents is confounded by economic and social incentives that tend to distort scientific understanding of medication treatment and to promote overuse at the expense of other approaches. Rational, humane prescription and use of medication for psychiatric problems and the careful scientific advancement of psychopharmacology as a discipline are important societal goals that will be difficult to achieve.

See also Drug Companies; Marketing of Drugs; Medical Model of Mental Illness; Neuropsychiatry; Popular Remedies and Quackery; Psychiatry

Bibliography

American Society of Clinical Psychopharmacology. http://www.ascpp.org.

Diamond, R. J. *Instant Psychopharmacology: Up-to-Date Information about the Most Commonly Prescribed Psychiatric Medications* (3rd ed.). New York: Norton.

Gagnon, M.-A., and J. Lexchin. 2008. "The Cost of Pushing Pills: A New Estimate of Pharmaceutical Promotion Expenditures in the United States." *PLos Med* 5: e1.

Jutel, A. 2010. "Framing Disease: The Example of Female Hypoactive Sexual Desire Disorder." *Social Science & Medicine* 70:1084–1090.

Kramer, Peter. 2011. "In Defense of Antidepressants." *New York Times*, July 9.

Schatzberg, Alan F., Jonathan O. Cole, and Charles DeBattista. 2010. *Manual of Clinical Psychopharmacology* (7th ed.). Washington, DC: American Psychiatric Publishing.

Spielmans, G. I., and P. I. Parry. 2010. "From Evidence-Based Medicine to Marketing-Based Medicine: Evidence from Internal Industry Documents." *Journal of Bioethical Inquiry* 7: 13–29.

Wilson, William H. 2012. "Neuropsychiatric Perspectives for Community Mental Health Theory and Practice." In Jessica Rosenberg and Samuel Rosenberg, eds., *Community Mental Health: New Directions in Policy and Practice* (2nd ed., pp. 238–252). New York: Routledge.

Yudofsky, Stuart C., and Robert E. Hales. 2010. *Essentials of Neuropsychiatry and Behavioral Neurosciences* (2nd ed.). Washington, DC: American Psychiatric Publishing.

Psychosomatic Disorders

Amber N. Douglas and Michael Shally-Jensen

Popular conceptions of psychosomatic illnesses as being "all in your head" or involving individuals suffering from "nervous stomachs" or "tension headaches" are rooted in the notion that psychological distress can and does manifest itself as a physical disorder. In some ways, this process or transformation of the psychological into the physical is fundamental to our understanding and conceptions of psychological health.

The roots of psychosomatic disorders can be traced back to early clinical writers such as Breuer and Freud (1895), who posited that "hysteria" or conversion disorder (the conversion of psychological distress into physical symptoms) was the expression of unconscious psychological conflicts in the bodily sphere (Beutel, Michal, & Subic-Wrana 2008). More recently, Sifneos (1996) expanded on Freud's original theory to explain the conversion of psychological experiences that resist or defy words into physical experiences—most typically pain. Sifneos coined the term "alexithymia," "no words for feelings," as a root experience of psychosomatic disorders. As such, this inability to verbalize psychological experience places the process of "somatization," as the phenomenon is also termed, at the core of disorders of affect or mood (Beutel, Michal, & Subic-Wrana 2008).

At present, there are myriad ailments that colloquially and formally get identified as psychosomatic. These are formally classified by the American Psychiatric Association (APA) as somatoform disorders and include conversion disorder, somatization disorder, pain disorder, hypochondriasis, and body dysmorphic disorder (APA 2000). The diagnostic label was formally accepted by the APA in 1980 and first appeared in the *Diagnostic and Statistical Manual*, third edition (*DSM-III*; APA 1980). The relatively pervasive yet subtle nature of these illnesses has generated several scholarly journals and professional organization as well as numerous self-help groups and self-help books. But what exactly are psychosomatic disorders? And how can one distinguish a psychosomatic illness from a "real" one? Is there truly a difference between psychosomatic illnesses and those that do not have core psychological components?

Characteristics and Types

Individuals who suffer from somatoform disorders report multiple chronic physical complaints in various bodily locations. Similarly, these individuals complain of some type of physical impairment or limitation as a result of their physical pain. Typically, individuals are consumers of medical health care—often demanding costly or invasive medical procedures for diagnosis (Beutel, Michal, & Subic-Wrana 2008). Perhaps the most important and overarching characteristic of all somatoform disorders is the lack of clear medical explanation of symptoms; little or nothing can be shown during the medical exam. At the same time, patients with somatoform disorders often resist a psychological interpretation of their distress; they see the problem as based in the body.

Specifically, the APA describes the various somatoform disorders as follows. *Conversion disorder* includes individuals who report problems with voluntary motor or sensory function without a clear physiological cause. This disorder is estimated to occur in less than 0.5 percent of the general population but close to 3 percent of the population in outpatient mental health clinics. *Somatization disorder* refers to gastrointestinal, sexual, or pseudoneurological problems without a physiological root. *Somatization disorder* is thought to occur in between 0.2 and 2 percent of the population. *Pain disorder* refers to the chronic experience of physical pain without physiological cause. There are substantial challenges in diagnosing pain disorder. It requires the ruling out of countless possible disorders that are associated with pain prior to homing in on a somatoform diagnosis. Because of this, prevalence rates of pain disorder are difficult to estimate. *Hypochondriasis* is the worry of contracting a disease or the fixation on a belief that one might have contracted a disease. This disorder is estimated to occur in between 1 and 5 percent of the general primary care population. There are two subtypes of hypochondriasis, one associated with purely psychological factors, and a second associated with psychological factors and a general medical condition. *Body dysmorphic disorder* refers to the preoccupation on an imagined defect in physical appearance. The APA also recognizes a "not otherwise specified" category and an "undifferentiated" one, both of which are catch-all diagnoses of sorts (APA 2000; Hansell & Damour 2008).

Gender and Culture

Women are more likely than men to be diagnoses with conversion disorder and some other somatoform disorders (APA 2000). This gender difference may be rooted in the tendency for women to externalize emotional distress in either verbal or, in this case, physical expression. Men, on the other hand, are thought to internalize their emotional distress and not express it as such (Hansell & Damour 2008). Of course, it is also possible that, owing to cultural perceptions, the practitioner may be more likely to classify women's experiences as being purely psychological and less likely to aggressively investigate physical causes.

Time and place are particularly important when considering the existence of psychosomatic illnesses. While somoatoform disorders are recognized around the world, it is clear that the expression of ailment is socially and historically constructed. Different peoples in different times and different cultures have different ways of experiencing and communicating psycho-physical distress. Some scholars contend, for example, that the "hysteria" of an earlier era, once characterized by glove anesthesia (numb hands) and convulsions, has not disappeared but changed to fit with the current times; specifically, the experiences of pain, dizziness, or "malaise" can be understood as examples of this type of (Kirmayer & Santhanam 2001). Similarly, when looking across borders, it is important to recognize that standards of health and well-being are culturally defined. There are numerous examples of culturally specific, or "culture bound," psychosomatic disorders.

Treatment

Treatment of somatoform disorders is particularly challenging because people with these disorders often resist psychological interpretations. Individuals may feel that they are not being heard or the severity of their symptoms is not appreciated by their medical provider.

Psychodynamic

Psychodynamic theory posits that somatoform symptoms are tied to an unconscious conflict related to an unfulfilled wish that is converted in physical manifestation. As such, psychodynamic theorists contend that the symptoms reduce anxiety associated with the unconscious conflict and provide a way to obtain attention from others. Psychodynamic treatment explores the use of defense mechanism to explore and illuminate unconscious conflicts that give rise to the reported physical ailment (Beutel, Michal, & Subic-Wrana 2008).

Cognitive-Behavioral

There are some similarities in the way those working from a cognitive-behavioral perspective conceive of psychosomatic disorders and the way those working from a psychodynamic orientation do. Both hold that emotional distress is translated into physical symptoms. However, at the heart of a cognitive-behavioral explanation is the idea that individuals suffering from psychosomatic disorders exhibit distorted cognitive processing. Specifically, such individuals are more likely to "catastrophize" physical symptoms, or believe that relatively minor symptoms signal significant medical conditions. They are also prone to amplification, or the tendency to expand the magnitude of a physical symptom. Treatment therefore focuses on gently challenging these cognitive distortions and working with the individual to test the authenticity of such beliefs (Hansell & Damour 2008).

Conclusion

Psychosomatic illness remains something of an elusive medical and psychological concept, turning, as it does, on the relationship between the mind and the body. It is not clearly understood how mental events can cross the threshold and become physical events or sensations, if one can even speak of such a boundary to begin with. The systems that come into play in psychosomatic illnesses are the same systems that come into play in reactions such as fear, stress, and grief, namely, the autonomic nervous system, the endocrine system, the cardiovascular system, the gastrointestinal system, and others. For this reason, more than any other disorders (with the possible exception of the neuroses), psychosomatic illnesses require practitioners to explore the patient's biography, state of mind, and physiological condition. Often this requires collaboration between medical and psychiatric staffs, sometimes in specialized psychosomatic medicine centers. Research in this area has expanded and is expected to continue to do so in the future.

See also Culturally Competent Mental Health Care; Loss and Grief; Medical Model of Mental Illness; Mind and Body Approaches to Mental Health; Stress and Stress Management; Women's Mental Health

Bibliography

American Psychiatric Association. 1980. *Diagnostic and Statistical Manual of Mental Disorders* (3rd ed). Washington, DC: American Psychiatric Publishing.

American Psychiatric Association. 2000. *Diagnostic and Statistical Manual of Mental Disorders* (4th ed., text rev.). Washington, DC: American Psychiatric Publishing.

Beutel, M. C., M. Michal, and C. Subic-Wrana. 2008. "Psychoanalytically-Oriented Inpatient Psychotherapy of Somatoform Disorders." *Journal of the American Academy of Psychoanalysis and Dynamic Psychiatry* 36(1): 125–142.

Breuer, J., and S. Freud. 1895 (2000). *Studies on Hysteria* (reissue ed.; J. Strachey, trans.). New York: Basic Books.

Freud, S. 1893. "The Neuro-psychoses of Defense." In J. Strachey, ed. and trans., *The Standard Edition of the Complete Psychological Works of Sigmund Freud* (pp. 41–61). London: Hogarth Press.

Hansell, James H., and Lisa K. Damour. 2008. *Abnormal Psychology* (2nd ed.). Hoboken, NJ: Wiley.

Husvedt, Siri. 2009. *The Shaking Woman, or, the History of My Nerves*. New York: Holt.

Kirmayer, L. J., and R. Santhanam. 2001. "The Anthropology of Hysteria." In P. W. Halligan, C. Bass, and J. C. Marshall, eds., *Contemporary Approaches to the Study of Hysteria* (pp. 251–270). Oxford: Oxford University Press.

Shorter, Edward. 1994. *From Mind into the Body: The Cultural Origins of Psychosomatic Symptoms*. Toronto: University of Toronto Press.

Sifneos, PE. 1996. Alexithymia: past and present. *The American Journal of Psychiatry* 153:137–142.

Psychotherapy

Michael J. Constantino and Rebecca M. Ametrano

Psychology is a large discipline with many subdisciplines. The largest subdivision, in terms of degrees granted, is clinical psychology. Clinical psychologists are a heterogeneous group, with their central skills and tasks often centering on assessment/diagnosis, treatment, consultation, research, and/or teaching. As per the American Psychological Association's (APA) Society of Clinical Science, "Clinical Psychology integrates science, theory, and practice to understand, predict, and alleviate maladjustment, disability, and discomfort as well as to promote human adaptation, adjustment, and personal development. Clinical Psychology focuses on the intellectual, emotional, biological, psychological, social, and behavioral aspects of human functioning across the life span, in varying cultures, and at all socioeconomic levels" (http://www.div12.org/about-clinical-psychology). Of clinical psychologists' activities, the most common and time consuming is practicing psychotherapy (Norcross, Karpiak, & Santaro 2005).

Defining Psychotherapy

So what is psychotherapy? Answering this question is difficult, as a consensual definition of this core activity of the clinical psychologist remains elusive. What one authority considers psychotherapy might be vastly different from another respected authority's perspective. In fact, some writers have suggested that it might be easier to practice psychotherapy than to operationalize it (e.g., London 1986)! Depending on one's theoretical orientation, psychotherapy might be viewed as, among many other things, behavioral modification, psychoeducation (i.e., educating a person about the nature of a disorder), coaching, interpersonal persuasion, reparenting, corrective emotional experience, cognitive reattribution (i.e., reviewing and revising patterns of thought and feeling), and/or general health care (Prochaska & Norcross 2010). Some authors have proposed broad, encompassing definitions of psychotherapy; however, even these definitions emphasize different elements and allude to different theoretical assumptions.

For example, Wolberg (1967) referred to psychotherapy as "a form of treatment for problems of an emotional nature in which a trained person deliberately establishes a professional relationship with a patient with the objective of removing, modifying or retarding existing symptoms, of mediating disturbed patterns of behavior, and of promoting positive personality growth and development" (3). In this definition, there seems to be an emphasis on *emotional* problems versus, for example, social or vocational problems. Also, the use of the term "patient" *might* be suggestive of a medical model in which a person has a specific illness to be cured.

Wampold (2001) defined psychotherapy as "a primarily interpersonal treatment that is based on psychological principles and involves a trained therapist and a client who has a mental disorder, problem, or compliant; it is intended by the therapist to be remedial for the clients' disorder, problem, or complaint; and it is adapted or individualized for the particular client and his or her disorder, problem, or complaint" (3). In this definition, there is an emphasis on the relational nature of therapy versus, for example, self-directed therapy (self-help) or impersonal advice giving. Also, the use of the term "client" *might* reflect more of a business-oriented versus medical model. Moreover, a client seeking therapy could have a diagnosable disorder, but he or she could also be seeking help for a less severe problem or compliant. Finally, this definition stresses context and the importance of adapting treatment to the client.

As one final sample definition, Prochaska and Norcross (2010) defined psychotherapy as "the informed and intentional application of clinical methods and interpersonal stances derived from established psychological principles for the purpose of assisting people to modify their behaviors, cognitions, emotions, and/or other personal characteristics in directions that the participants deem desirable" (3–4). This description privileges the multiple dimensions of both distress and psychotherapeutic change. Moreover, it appears to emphasize collaboration among the participants in cocreating and copursuing relevant therapy goals. Finally, these authors circumvent the "patient" versus "client" controversy altogether by simply referring to "people" and "participants."

Clearly, there is no single way to define psychotherapy. However, a connecting thread among the many variations is that psychotherapists tend to rely on theory, or a *system*, to provide an organized, consistent, and coherent perspective on human behavior, psychopathology, and treatment (i.e., the mechanisms through which psychotherapeutic change takes place). Different psychotherapy systems imply that there are different lenses through which people can understand human existence (Messer & Winokur 1980). However, even at this shared level of theory there remain differences. For example, some psychotherapists adhere strictly and rigidly to their theories when practicing psychotherapy. In this sense, they tend to fit their patients to their theory. On the other hand, some psychotherapists are flexible and draw on multiple theories (or components of theories). These clinicians tend to fit their theory, or theories, to their patients. Either way, clinicians need to be thinking about, and conveying to their patients in a credible way, how change takes place through psychotherapy.

There are multiple levels on which one can think about psychotherapy. At a high level of abstraction are global theories of human functioning and change. At a low level are specific clinical techniques or interventions. Finally, at a middle level are principles of change that might cut across various theories and might incorporate various techniques. Some have argued that this middle level might be the most fruitful for understanding how psychotherapy works given that any strategy that emerges across varying theoretical orientations is likely to be robust in that it "survived" the many distortions imposed by therapists' varying biases, allegiances, and lenses on the psychotherapy process (e.g., Goldfried 1980).

Whatever one's take on psychotherapy, most theorists, practitioners, and clinical scientists agree that it is complex and often challenging. Paul Wachtel (1982), a distinguished clinician, provided interesting "food for thought" when he noted that psychotherapy "is rarely as straightforward as textbooks and case reports usually seem to imply ... practicing psychotherapy is a difficult—if also rewarding—way to earn a living. It is no profession for the individual who likes certainty, predictability, or a fairly constant sense that one knows what one is doing. There are few professions in which feeling stupid or stymied is as likely to be part of one's ordinary professional day, even for those at the pinnacle of their field" (xiii). Thus helping others requires not only a guiding theory and a solid understanding of principles of therapeutic change but also humility.

Major Systems of Psychotherapy

Although there are literally hundreds of documented psychosocial treatments, most can be substantially subsumed by several major systems (Gurman & Messer 2003), which we review here with a brief chronological "walk" through history. The earliest roots of the psychotherapy field were perhaps most closely tied to the reform movements of the mid-1800s. Such movements, including Philippe Pinel's moral therapy in France and Eli Todd's retreat program in the United States, centered on more humane treatment of mentally troubled individuals through compassionate and individualized care versus the previously typical inhumane institutionalization (see Cautin 2011). However, in terms of the major psychotherapy systems that remain prominent today (at least in teaching, if not in training and practice), the first phase of evolution involved the emergence of single school models, with each claiming to have arrived at the truth about personality, pathology, and change.

Psychoanalysis and Its Offspring

The first of these models was Freud's (1910) psychoanalysis, which remained the dominant force in the field from the late 1800s to the mid-1900s. According to his *drive theory*, Freud, an Austrian physician, viewed illnesses such as hysteria (psychologically induced bodily problems or disease), sexual perversion, and anxiety, as being the result of conflict between one's primitive, internal sexual and aggressive impulses (drives) and what society deemed acceptable. With self-control as a highly valued trait in the nineteenth-century European Victorian era, people, according to Freud, used defense mechanisms as a way to decrease distress by restraining unacceptable impulses. When such defenses were exacerbated to an extreme level, symptoms would ensue as an indirect expression of an unacceptable wish. Freud became particularly interested in hysteria, and he believed that (1) hysterical symptoms were caused by repression (a psychological removal from awareness) of a real or imagined traumatic experience; (2) the nature of people's symptoms were related to, or symbolic of, the trauma; and (3) symptoms could be relieved through insight—that is, bringing repressed, unconscious material into one's conscious awareness. This latter belief became the basis of psychoanalysis, or the so-called talking cure. The overarching goal of this approach is to bring about personality change by breaking maladaptive patterns through understanding or insight. Psychoanalysts use techniques such as free association (encouraging the patient to say whatever comes to mind) and interpretation (making connections about which the patient was previously unaware) in the service of helping patients give release (catharsis) to what they have deemed, often erroneously, as unacceptable impulses.

At the turn of the century through World War II (1900–39), Freud and psychoanalysis gained significant momentum and a large following, including in the United States. However, some psychologists and psychiatrists (note that psychoanalysis was initially claimed as exclusive to the medical profession) began to struggle with how to account for and how to integrate environmental and social influences with the internal processes that were so central to Freudian psychoanalysis. In this vein, several influential psychoanalysts began to propose modifications to psychoanalysis (some at the expense of remaining in Freud's inner circle). For example, Sullivan (1953) outwardly disagreed with Freud on the basic understanding of the self: whereas Freud posited that the self is comprised of instinctual drives, Sullivan posited that the self is interpersonally constructed through social interactions and larger sociocultural influences. Others attempted to accommodate the importance of social interaction and environment while still maintaining a clear allegiance to core psychoanalytic ideas (e.g., the importance of early experiences, repressed conflict, and unconscious motivation). For example, Klein's (1952) object relations theory was similar to Sullivan's approach in its central focus on social relating; however, her theory maintained Freud's emphasis on the dangers of the defended, repressed self. Reconciling these foci, Klein situated people's social life *within* (vs. between) people. In other words, important people in one's life (especially early caregivers) are "objects" that get mentally internalized. People then carry forward images, emotions, expectations, and conflicts that are connected to their early patterns of relating to others. Object relations treatment, then, focuses on helping patients understand and improve their self-other relations.

Clinical Psychology and Client-Centered Therapy

Following World War II, the entire landscape of psychotherapy changed dramatically. Until 1940, psychotherapy was still relatively unknown to the general public; and to the extent it was known, it was largely synonymous with psychoanalysis and psychiatry. With the war came a markedly greater demand for services, which in turn led to more prominent roles for psychologists, counselors, and social workers (beyond their historically more typical roles of testing and diagnosis). This role expansion also led to the rapid development of government-sponsored training programs in clinical and counseling psychology, and independent practice for psychologists became a reality; no longer was psychotherapy confined to psychoanalysis as practiced by physicians. In additional to the evolving identity of the clinical psychologist, the identity of psychotherapy was expanding as well.

For example, over the 1940s and 1950s, Carl Rogers developed the first radically different perspective from psychoanalysis. Unlike classical psychoanalysis, with its "determined" view of human nature (we are the sum of our urges, desires, and fears), Rogers's *client-centered therapy* adopted a "constructive" view of the human organism (Rogers 1951). Rogers, dismissing the "therapist-as-expert" perspective, emphasized that humans are capable of self-directed growth, which can be facilitated by a therapeutic relationship characterized by genuineness, nonjudgmental caring, and empathy. Thus this humanistic approach to psychotherapy placed the relationship at the center of healing, as opposed to therapist interpretation and the fostering of insight (hallmarks of psychoanalysis). Other humanistic theorists/therapists (e.g., Bugenthal, Maslow, May) followed suit in a rebellion against what they viewed as the mechanistic, impersonal, hierarchical, and elitist psychoanalytic establishment and the overly scientific, cold, and impersonal "behavioral" establishment.

Behavioral Approaches

Regarding that behavioral establishment, the learning theories on which it is based had actually appeared in the 1920s. Following heavily from Watson and Raynor's (1920) work on conditioning, the notion was that people come into the world a blank slate, and that it is the environment that shapes people's behaviors through stimulus and response sequences. However, it was not until the late 1950s that behavioral *treatments* for psychological problems gained momentum. Such treatments were made most noticeable by Wolpe's (1958) publication of *Psychotherapy by Reciprocal Inhibition*. Disenchanted with psychoanalysis and inspired by the likes of Watson and Pavlov, Wolpe used the classical conditioning paradigm to study feeding behavior in cats. He reasoned that if conditioned anxiety could inhibit eating, then he could reverse this pattern by using eating (an inherently pleasurable activity) to inhibit anxiety (i.e., counterconditioning). Based on the success of his work, which capitalized on the physiological incompatibility of relaxation and anxiety, Wolpe promoted the use of progressive muscle relaxation to combat anxiety in humans (a technique referred to as systematic desensitization). On the whole, behavior therapies focus strictly on patient behaviors and situational contingencies, with the therapeutic relationship serving as a social reinforcer (i.e., therapists positively reinforce adaptive behavior change and refrain from reinforcing maladaptive behaviors). These approaches also advocated for an active-directive role for the therapist, a time-limited course, and demonstration of effectiveness.

Cognitive Approaches

The 1960s and '70s saw the emergence of cognitive therapies, which viewed cognition as a mediator of stimulus and response sequences. In other words, whereas purely behavioral theories viewed an activating event as the cause of an emotional or behavioral consequence, cognitive theorists posited a middle step in this chain. For example, being rejected by a lover does not directly cause a consequence, but rather how one processes the event dictates the consequence or outcome. Such processing might be irrational (e.g., "I will never be loved again") leading to one type of emotional or behavioral outcome, or it could be more rational (e.g., "That's sad, but I will love again in time") leading to another type of outcome. Both Ellis's (1973) *rational-emotive behavior therapy* and Beck's (1976) *cognitive therapy* rested on the main tenet that how one thinks about or perceives things has a direct influence on how one feels and acts. This focus represented a shift back to the internal experience of the patient. Cognitive treatments also value a short-term, structured approach, with a therapeutic relationship centered on collaborative empiricism. Although cognitive therapists aspire toward warmth and empathy in their work, these features are viewed (at least traditionally) as neither necessary nor sufficient. Cognitive change, not the relationship, is viewed as the active therapeutic ingredient.

Expansion and Unification of Psychotherapies

Since the 1970s, there has continued to be a proliferation of psychotherapies, which underscores both the growing meaningfulness of psychotherapy as a mental health service and the fact that there is no legal definition of psychotherapy or the exact training required to provide it. With this proliferation also came a second phase in the evolution of psychotherapy—rapprochement. During this phase came attempts at interpreting disparate single-school psychotherapy approaches, if not yet integrating them. For example, Dollard and Miller (1950) attempted to understand and appreciate the commonalities between psychoanalytic and behavioral models. Such rapprochement ultimately led to the third phase in the evolution of psychotherapy, which involved actual attempts to merge commonalities into a stronger therapy amalgam. This rise of psychotherapy integration began in the late 1970s/early 1980s (see Norcross & Goldfried 2005), and remains prominent today. In fact, psychotherapy integration is currently the most widely endorsed orientation among practicing psychotherapists. Furthermore, one primary interpretation of the consistent research finding that different psychotherapies produce largely equivalent outcomes is that factors that are common to these treatments are more responsible for change than factors unique to them. Another interpretation, from a unified psychotherapy perspective (a possible fourth phase in the evolution of psychotherapy), is captured in the following quote: "Each therapeutic approach probably affects the system at a chosen level—cognitive, emotional, behavioral, or interactional—and any specific effect at one level of the system probably reverberates through the highly interconnected levels of the system and produces comparable change in the whole person" (Greenberg 2002, 154).

Several current trends dominate the field. For example, with the explosion of managed health care plans in the 1990s, which operate under the goal of cost containment for health services, the psychotherapy field is squarely within an age of accountability. Virtually gone are the days of clinicians enjoying the freedom to set their own fees, decide their own treatment lengths, and practice whatever type of therapy that they see for a patient's presenting problems. Such days have been replaced by a firm emphasis on *evidenced-based practice in psychology* (EBPP), which the APA has defined as "the integration of best available research with clinical expertise in the context of patient characteristics, culture, and preference" (APA Presidential Task Force on Evidence-Based Practice 2006). Related to this emphasis has been a general movement toward shorter-term, disorder-specific treatments with significant empirical support. There has also been a push for psychologists to gain limited prescription privileges in the service of providing more comprehensive, efficient, and quality mental health care. Such privileges became a reality in 2002 when New Mexico became the first state to give legal prescriptive authority to psychologists undergoing adjunctive psychopharmacology training.

The 1990s and 2000s also saw a growing emphasis on culturally competent treatment; however, this notion is elusive, and there remains a pressing need to understand better how to deliver effective, culturally sensitive therapies. In addition, there is a growing incorporation of technology into mental health practice, and this has become a major initiative of funding agencies. Telehealth, e-therapy, web-based interventions, virtual reality, and smart phone use are just some of the burgeoning technologies being applied in the field. Although the jury is still out on their efficacy, especially when compared to traditional face-to-face psychotherapy, it is inevitable that technology will play an enormous role in psychotherapy of the near future.

Future Trends

Regarding the future of psychotherapy, some authors (e.g., Prochaska & Norcross 2010) have highlighted additional emerging themes, such as (1) a greater focus on the therapeutic relationship, (2) a growing emphasis on self-help resources, (3) incorporation of advances in neuroscience, (4) increased proactive outreach to high risk populations, (5) an increase in faith-based practices, and (6) an integration of psychotherapy and pharmacotherapy. Although the future is impossible to predict, it seems reasonable to believe that it will contain just as many revolutionary breakthroughs and important evolutionary shifts as it has in the past 100+ years.

See also Behavioral Theories and Therapies; Clinical Psychology; Cognitive-Behavioral Therapy; Culturally Competent Care; Group Therapy; Humanistic Theories and Therapies; Mental Health Counseling; Psychoanalysis; Psychodynamic Psychotherapy; Psychotherapy Integration; Therapeutic Community and Milieu Therapy

Bibliography

APA Presidential Task Force on Evidence-Based Practice. 2006. "Evidence-Based Practice in Psychology." *American Psychologist* 61: 271–285.

Beck, Aaron T. 1976. *Cognitive Therapy and the Emotional Disorders*. New York: International Universities Press.

Cautin, Robin L. 2011. "A Century of Psychotherapy, 1860–1960." In John C. Norcross, Gary R. VandenBos, and Donald K. Freedheim, eds., *History of Psychotherapy: Continuity and Change* (2nd ed., pp. 3–38). Washington, DC: American Psychological Association.

Corsini, R. J., and D. Wedding. 2010. *Current Psychotherapies*. Belmont, CA: Brooks Cole.

Dollard, John, and Neil Miller. 1950. *Personality and Psychotherapy: An Analysis in Terms of Learning, Thinking, and Culture*. New York: McGraw-Hill.

Ellis, Albert. 1973. *Humanistic Psychotherapy: The Rational-Emotive Approach*. New York: McGraw-Hill.

Freud, Sigmund. 1910. "The Origins and Development of Psychoanalysis." *The American Journal of Psychology* 21: 181–218.

Goldfried, Marvin R. 1980. "Toward the Delineation of Therapeutic Change Principles." *American Psychologist* 35: 991–999.

Greenberg, Leslie S. 2002. "Integrating an Emotion-Focused Approach to Treatment into Psychotherapy Integration." *Journal of Psychotherapy Integration* 12: 154–189.

Gurman, Alan S., and Stanley B. Messer, eds. 2003. *Essential Psychotherapies: Theory and Practice* (2nd ed.). New York: Guilford Press.

Klein, Melanie. 1952. *Envy and Gratitude and Other Works, 1946–1963*. New York: Delacorte Press.

London, Perry. 1986. *The Modes and Morals of Psychotherapy* (2nd ed.). New York: Hemisphere/Harper & Row.

Messer, Stanley B., and Meir Winokur. 1980. "Some Limits to the Integration of Psychoanalytic and Behavior Therapy." *American Psychologist* 35: 818–827.

National Institute of Mental Health. 2010. "Psychotherapies." Retrieved from http://www.nimh.nih.gov/health/topics/psychotherapies/index.shtml.

Norcross, John C., and Marvin R. Goldfried, eds. 2005. *Handbook of Psychotherapy Integration* (2nd ed.). New York: Oxford University Press, Inc.

Norcross, John C., Christie P. Karpiak, and Shannon O. Santoro. 2005. "Clinical Psychologists across the Years: The Division of Clinical Psychology from 1960 to 2003." *Journal of Clinical Psychology* 61: 1467–1483.

Prochaska, James O., and John C. Norcross. 2010. *Systems of Psychotherapy: A Transtheoretical Analysis* (7th ed.). Belmont, CA: Brooks/Cole, Cengage Learning.

Rogers, Carl R. 1951. *Client-Centered Therapy: Its Current Practice, Implications, and Theory*. Boston: Houghton Mifflin.

Sullivan, Harry Stack. 1953. *The Interpersonal Theory of Psychiatry*. New York: Norton.

Wachtel, Paul L., ed. 1982. *Resistance: Psychodyanmic and Behavioral Approaches*. New York: Plenum Press.

Wampold, Bruce E. 2001. *The Great Psychotherapy Debate: Models, Methods, and Findings*. Mahwah, NJ: Erlbaum.

Watson, John B., and Rosalie Rayner. 1920. "Conditioned Emotional Reactions." *Journal of Experimental Psychology* 3: 1–14.

Wolberg, Lewis R. 1967. *The Technique of Psychotherapy* (2nd ed.). New York: Grune & Stratton.

Wolpe, Joseph. 1958. *Psychotherapy by Reciprocal Inhibition*. Stanford, CA: Stanford University Press.

Psychotherapy Integration

David M. Allen

At present, over 400 different recognized *schools* of psychotherapy treatment are being practiced, each one based on a somewhat different theory about human personality and behavior change (Corsini & Wedding 2007). This number does not even include "biological" interventions. Each school has a different and sometimes contradictory answer to two basic questions addressed by mental health practitioners: (1) Why do people (clients, patients) keep doing the same things over and over again with the same bad results; and (2) How do you get them to change?

The reason for this situation is, first, that psychology is a young science, and in any young science competing theories espoused by dogmatic theorists are the rule rather than the exception. Second, the subject matter of psychology is not amenable to direct observation. We cannot read minds. When you ask people why they do what they do, they may not know, they may lie to you, or they may lie to themselves. We also cannot compare psychotherapy treatments using the touchstone of scientific research, double-blind studies, because doing so would mean that the therapists involved literally would have to *not know* what they were doing in order to make the study "objective."

Many practitioners began to think about how the various schools might be integrated. In the summer of 1983, several therapists began an association that led to the founding of an academic group dedicated to the search for common ground among the two largest schools, psychodynamic and cognitive-behavioral therapy. Gradually, therapists from other major schools joined the group, which was named the Society for the Exploration of Psychotherapy Integration (SEPI).

The group's odd name stemmed from the fact that the founders of the group were fearful that if they actually proposed an integrated model of human behavior and change, they would be in danger of being just one more school. They feared that such a development would lead to the exclusion from the group of both loyal adherents to the existing schools and anyone with a new idea that did not seem to fit in with the new model. Hence, they decided to "explore" only ideas that were conducive to finding areas of agreement between the schools.

Since the organization consisted mostly of nonmedical therapists, psychiatric ideas about the biology of human mental processes were at first not part of the mix of ideas considered by the group. Later, some newer developments in neurobiology were seen by some group members as actually supporting much of what psychotherapists had been saying.

Integrationists, like the theorists before them, began to focus on different modes of integration, and argued among themselves about which mode was most powerful. That is the subject of the next section.

Different Modes of Integrating Psychotherapy Schools

Four general routes to integration are now recognized: common factors, technical eclecticism, theoretical integration, and assimilative integration (Norcross & Goldfried 2005). Let us take a look at each in turn.

Common Factors

This mode of integration "seeks to determine the core ingredients that different therapies share in common" (Norcross 2005, 9). These commonalities include a therapeutic alliance with an empathic therapist; positive expectations of the therapist by the patient; the presentation to patients of a new, internally consistent, and believable way of understanding their problems; and the acquisition and practice of new behaviors, along with an experience of catharsis, or "release" (Grencavage & Norcross 1990). The advantage of a common factors approach is the emphasis on therapeutic actions that have been demonstrated to be effective. The disadvantage is that it overlooks a comparison of the effectiveness of specific techniques that have been developed within particular schools. Proponents of this mode of integration often assert that nonspecific relationship factors, rather than particular therapeutic techniques, are what make psychotherapy successful.

Technical Eclecticism

Arnold Lazarus (2005) is the most famous advocate of this mode of integration. He believes that just because a certain technique may lead to positive behavior change in some patients, the theory behind the technique is not, thereby, proven to be true. Techniques are employed because they are aimed at certain parameters of human psychology and because they seem to work clinically. Technical eclectics (those who pursue this form of integration), then, claim to be atheoretical.

Lazarus identifies several parameters of human psychology that he believes to be important and at which different techniques have been aimed. He uses the acronym BASIC ID, which stands for:

1. **B**ehaviors
2. **A**ffective responses
3. **S**ensory reactions
4. **I**mages
5. **C**ognitions
6. **I**nterpersonal relationships
7. **D**rugs and other biological interventions

Assimilative Integration

"This mode of integration favors a firm grounding in one system of psychotherapy, but with a willingness to incorporate or assimilate, in a considered fashion, perspectives or practices from other schools" (Messer 1992, 151). Most psychotherapists are trained in one or, at most, two theoretical orientations that serve as the basis of their treatment; however, many will also incorporate ideas and strategies from other sources into their practice. This is the essence of assimilative integration.

Theoretical Integration

The last route to integration is theoretical integration: "Two or more therapies are integrated in the hope that the result will be better than the constituent therapies alone" (Norcross 2005, 8). Some models of theoretical integration focus on combining and synthesizing a small number of theories at a deep level, whereas others describe the relationship between several systems of psychotherapy. Examples include Wachtel's model of cyclical psychodynamics (Gold & Wachtel 1993) and Ryle's (2001) model of cognitive analytic therapy.

In the opinion of the present author, theoretic integration is the most comprehensive and promising approach toward a truly complete model. The author's own model is called *unified therapy* (UT) (Allen 1988, 1991, 1993, 2001, 2003, 2005, 2006), and it includes ideas not only from psychodynamic, cognitive-behavioral, and family systems models but also from existential psychotherapy, experiential psychotherapy, neuroscience, linguistics, and social psychology. The attempt to arrive at a unified theory that incorporates ideas not only from psychology but also from a wide variety of other disciplines is also known as *consilience* (Wilson 1998).

Moving Toward Consilience

Many authors have discussed an idea they believe to be key to theoretical integration, namely, the relationship between interacting subsystems at various levels, or between systems and subsystems. The range of subsystems has been termed the "entire matrix of human functioning" (Magnavita 2005, 3) or, alternatively, "foci within the transactional field" (Spiegel 1983, 42). These foci are defined as units within a system that interact to make up larger units that become something more than the sum of their parts. These larger units then interact to form still larger units and so on.

In systems of biological entities such as human beings, these levels are generally thought to start with the gene and move up through the cell, the organ, the organ system (in particular the central nervous system), the individual, the family, the subculture, the predominant culture, and finally the entire ecosystem. Magnavita notes that "none of these domains can be ignored without a loss of clarity and clinical potency" (Magnavita 2005, 3).

Since human beings are biological entities, we should look at the relationship of the structure of the brain and these various levels. The next section looks at our current, but highly primitive, understanding of brain functioning in this regard.

The Neurobiology of the Relationship between the Self and Other People

Within the brain's more primitive part, the limbic system, are areas that are intrinsic to the "fight, flight, or freeze" mechanism that the body goes through when it encounters stimuli that arouse fear. These areas are positioned just beneath the thinking part of the brain—and interconnect with it. Of great importance is the fact that these very same brain areas are also of primary importance in how individuals understand social cues and form attachments to others.

Terror is heavily encoded by a structure called the amygdala, which responds to certain environmental stimuli, many of which have been preset by early learning, before the thinking brain can even perceive the stimulus (Gunderson 2001). We therefore now know that the theories of the early cognitive therapists were somewhat incorrect, in that fear can be a reaction that is not immediately mediated by thought, unlike many other affects (emotional responses). This reaction can, however, later be modified by thought.

Relationship of Fight-and-Flight Responses to Attachment

The psychoanalyst Karen Horney opined that "basic anxiety" requires a sense of isolation from others, helplessness, and of being surrounded by hostility (see Symonds & Symonds 1985). These sorts of perceptions and cognitions are closely related to attachment to others in one's social system. The human brain encodes social events exceptionally well (Brothers 1997). The amygdala is highly involved in and central to this process. Studies have shown that the perception of faces activates specific cells in the amygdala. Different cells respond to different facial features. Certain amygdala cells respond to familiar but not unfamiliar faces (Brothers 1989). Lesions of amygdala in primates are associated with an inability to appraise social signals from other members of same species (Brothers 1989).

In general, the attachment system seems to be one of the most important regulators of arousal. Brain centers other than the amygdala involved in social stimulus appraisal are called the anterior cingulate and the orbital frontal cortex; these areas are also involved in fight-and-flight responses and emotion regulation (Siegel 1999). The amygdala is the first responder within seconds. The signals then go to the other two areas for further evaluation. Information regarding social context directly affects this appraisal process. Increased states of arousal also seem to function as a value system for the brain that leads to enhanced encoding of environmental information as certain connections between brain cells are continuously strengthened, weakened, destroyed, or created in response to environmental stimuli.

Attachment research indicates that the limbic regions use input from the emotional states of attachment figures to regulate both internal and external responses.

Individuals with so-called disorganized attachment have parents who display both frightened and frightening responses. According to Main (1991), parenting that generates multiple, contradictory models of attachment creates a sense of insecurity in the offspring. Problematic reactions can be seen to occur with one parent but not the other (Holmes 2004).

Early learning may be particularly difficult to inhibit; it is much harder to unlearn fear than to learn it in the first place—a fact consistent with the experience of psychotherapists trying to extinguish interpersonal anxiety.

Mental models for behavior within specific social situations, called *schemata* by cognitive-behavior therapists (Young, Klosko, & Weishaar 2003), are also formed early in life through learning in the context of important attachment relationships, and they too may be hard to inhibit. This, of course, does not mean that an individual cannot learn to override them using the thinking parts of the brain, but it does lend credence to the psychoanalytic view of the importance of early attachment figures in determining later personality problems. In UT, it is assumed that the behavior of primary attachment figures is the most powerful environmental reinforcer for cognitive schemata and therefore social behavior—dwarfing the power of other influences, including the behavior of a psychotherapist.

Future Directions for Development and Research in Psychotherapy Integration

Some areas of psychotherapy integration that are currently being developed and researched include the Unified Psychotherapy Project, schema therapy (Young, Klosko, & Weishaar 2003), and UT.

The Unified Psychotherapy Project is led by Jeffrey Magnavita and Steven Sobelman. The group has been compiling the *Psychotherapedia*, a catalog of all of the methods and techniques from all contemporary psychotherapy schools organized according to which domain level (or "foci within the transactional field") they have been applied. The first domain is within the mind of the individual alone; the second domain is the relationship between two individuals, such as a married couple; domain three is the relationship between members of triads and small groups, such as families; domain four is comprised of the interrelationships, structure, function, and hierarchy that span across all levels—that is, the culture, the family, and the individual.

Schema therapy is based on the idea that children form mental models of how to relate to others, called *schemata*, that can become highly ingrained. Schemata can also become self-destructive or self-defeating due to adverse childhood experiences such as abuse or neglect. Schema therapy incorporates ideas and techniques from several diverse therapy paradigms, most prominently guided mental imagery similar to that used by so-called emotion-focused therapists. This treatment has already showed highly promising results in outcome studies of the treatment of one severe personality disorder, namely, borderline personality disorder (Giesen-Bloo et. al 2006).

UT is an individual psychotherapy treatment for self-destructive and self-defeating behavior patterns, similar in many ways to schema therapy, that is based on the idea that ambivalence over role functioning in parents within a patient's family of origin results in a situation in which family members are faced with contradictory demands. Such contradictory demands intermittently and unpredictably trigger and strengthen the patient's internal conflicts and resultant dysfunctional behavior. The conflicted behavior of the affected individuals then simultaneously triggers and strengthens ambivalent, dysfunctional behavior in the rest of the family. The therapy is designed particularly for adults who exhibit self-destructive or self-defeating behavior patterns.

UT accepts the concept of kin selection (Wilson 1998), which posits that individuals within coherent social groups are willing to sacrifice themselves for their kin group in many contexts—as shown, for example, by our willingness to die for our country in a war. Seemingly oppositional behavior, then, results from an individual's perception that his or her family requires oppositionality. In some circumstances, parents may also sacrifice their own children if the group seems to deem it necessary, as evidenced by such cultural traditions as honor killings in the Middle East.

UT posits that ambivalence about the rules by which the family operates are generated by changes in cultural expectations as society evolves. The process of cultural change has sped up to the point at which individuals may learn one set of rules growing up but face a new set by the time they have children themselves. In some families the resultant role confusion becomes amplified (Allen 1988), leading to marked parental instability caused by ambivalence about what they want for themselves. In such cases, children will be induced to attempt to stabilize the parents by whatever means necessary, often at a great cost to themselves.

In order to alter this process, UT first attempts to treat hyperreactivity, anxiety, and depressive symptoms through psychiatric medication. It then aims to achieve the following strategic psychotherapy goals: (1) frame the patient's chief complaint and current difficulties as a response to family-of-origin issues; (2) gather information identifying interpersonal relationship patterns that cue or reinforce self-destructive behavior; (3) gather information about the patient's *genogram* (a relationship-oriented family tree) for the purpose of understanding family misbehavior, so that the patient can develop empathy for targeted family members; (4) make a hypothesis about both the patient's current role in the family and the reasons the family seems to require this role; (5) plan a communicative strategy designed to help the patient confront the problem with his or her family, so that the reinforcing behavior is diminished or extinguished; and (6) implement the strategy and obtain feedback about its effectiveness.

See also Behavioral Theories and Therapies; Borderline Personality Disorder; Cognitive-Behavioral Therapy; Humanistic Theories and Therapies; Medical Model of Mental Illness; Psychodynamic Psychotherapy

Bibliography

Allen, D. M. 1988. *A Family Systems Approach to Individual Psychotherapy* (originally titled *Unifying Individual and Family Therapies*). Northvale, NJ: Jason Aronson.

Allen, D. M. 1991. *Deciphering Motivation in Psychotherapy.* New York: Plenum Press.

Allen, D. M. 1993. "Unified Therapy." In G. Stricker and J. Gold, eds., *Comprehensive Handbook of Psychotherapy Integration* (pp. 125–137). New York: Plenum Press.

Allen, D. M. 2001. "Integrating Individual and Family Systems Psychotherapy to Treat Borderline Personality Disorder." *Journal of Psychotherapy Integration* 11(3): 313–331.

Allen, D. M. 2003. *Psychotherapy with Borderline Patients: An Integrated Approach.* Mahwah, NJ: Erlbaum.

Allen, D. M. 2005. "Unified Therapy with BPD." In A. Freeman, M. H. Stone, and D. Martin, eds., *Comparative Treatments for Borderline Personality Disorder* (pp. 239–258). New York: Springer.

Allen, D. M. 2006. "Unified Therapy: Therapy with a Patient with Multiple Cluster B Personality Traits." In G. Stricker and J. Gold, eds., *A Casebook of Psychotherapy Integration* (pp. 107–120). Washington, DC: American Psychological Association.

Brothers, L. 1989. "A Biological Perspective on Empathy." *American Journal of Psychiatry* 146: 10–19.

Brothers, L. 1997. *Friday's Footprint.* New York: Oxford University Press.

Corsini, R. J., and D. Wedding, eds. 2007. *Current Psychotherapies* (8th ed.). Florence, KY: Brooks/Cole.

Giesen-Bloo, J., R. van Dyck, P. Spinhoven, W. van Tilburg, C. Dirksen, T. van Asselt, I. Kremers, M. Nadort, and A. Arntz. 2006. "Outpatient Psychotherapy for Borderline Personality Disorder: Randomized Trial of Schema-Focused Therapy vs. Transference-Focused Psychotherapy." *Archives of General Psychiatry* 63(6): 649–658.

Gold, J. R., and P. L. Wachtel. 1993. "Cyclical Psychodynamics" In G. Striker and J. R. Gold, eds., *Comprehensive Handbook of Psychotherapy Integration* (pp. 59–72). New York: Plenum Press.

Grencavage, L. M., and J. C. Norcross. 1990. "What Are the Commonalities among the Therapeutic Factors?" *Professional Psychology, Research and Practice* 21: 372–378.

Gunderson, J. G. 2001. *Borderline Personality Disorder: A Clinical Guide.* Washington, DC: American Psychiatric Publishing.

Holmes, J. 2004. "Disorganized Attachment and Borderline Personality Disorder: A Clinical Perspective." *Attachment and Human Development* 6: 181–190.

Lazarus, A. A. 2005. "Multimodal Therapy." In J. C. Norcross and M. R. Goldfried, eds., *Handbook of Psychotherapy Integration* (2nd ed., pp. 105–120). New York: Oxford University Press.

Magnavita, J. J. 2005. *Personality-Guided Relational Psychotherapy: A Unified Approach.* Washington, DC: American Psychological Association.

Main, M. 1991. "Metacognitive Knowledge, Metacognitive Monitoring, and Singular (Coherent) Versus Multiple (Incoherent) Models of Attachment: Findings and Directions for Future Research." In C. M. Parkes, J. Stenson-Hinde, and P. Maris, eds., *Attachment across the Life Cycle* (pp. 127–159). London: Routledge.

Messer, S. B. 1992. "A Critical Examination of Belief Structures in Integrative and Eclectic Psychotherapy." In J. C. Norcross and M. R. Goldfried, eds., *Handbook of Psychotherapy Integration* (pp. 130–165). New York: Basic Books.

Norcross, J. C. 2005. "A Primer on Psychotherapy Integration." In J. C. Norcross and M. R. Goldfried, eds., *Handbook of Psychotherapy Integration* (2nd ed., pp. 3–23). New York: Oxford University Press.

Norcross, J. C., and M. R. Goldfried, eds. 2005. *Handbook of Psychotherapy Integration* (2nd ed.). New York: Oxford University Press.

Ryle, A. 2001. *Introduction to Cognitive-Analytic Therapy: Principles and Practice.* New York: Wiley.

Siegel, D. 1999. *The Developing Mind: Toward a Neurobiology of Interpersonal Experience.* New York: Guilford Press.

Spiegel, J. 1983. *Transactions: The Interplay between Individual, Family, and Society.* New York: Jason Aronson.

Symonds, A., and M. Symonds. 1985. "Karen Horney." In H. I. Kaplan and B. J. Sadock, eds., *Comprehensive Textbook of Psychiatry* (4th ed., pp. 419–426). Baltimore: Williams & Wilkins.

Wilson, E. O. 1998. *Consilience: The Unity of Knowledge.* New York: Knopf.

Young, J. E., J. S. Klosko, and M. E. Weishaar. 2003. *Schema Therapy: A Practitioner's Guide.* New York: Guilford Press.

Public Awareness and Public Education

Ardis Hanson and Bruce Lubotsky Levin

Disease prevention refers to the activities designed to reduce morbidity (rate of occurrence) and mortality by preventing illness and promoting health. Disease prevention is anticipatory, with basic objectives to prevent illness from developing, modifying behavior in promoting a healthier lifestyle, and minimizing the damage if the illness does develop.

Disease prevention is a fundamental principle in public health practice. Historically, it has played important roles in the health of both individuals and communities. The original public health classification system of disease prevention was developed by the Commission on Chronic Illness (1957) and included three types of prevention activities: primary; secondary; and tertiary prevention. Another classification of prevention, conceptualized specifically for mental disorders, also includes three types of interventions: universal prevention; selective prevention; and indicated prevention (Gordon 1983). Like primary prevention, universal prevention includes prevention efforts that are targeted at an entire population. These may include school programs or mass-media campaigns. Selective prevention, similar to secondary prevention, targets individuals who show risk factors for a particular disorder. Indicated prevention, like tertiary prevention, is targeted toward individuals who already have symptoms of a disorder. Since a critical component of prevention is public awareness and public education, effective health communication strategies play an important role in minimizing risk and uncertainty in understanding mental disorders and their treatment, as well as reducing stigma and discrimination of individuals who suffer from mental disorders.

Healthy People

For more than 30 years, Healthy People has provided 10-year national objectives for improving the health of all Americans. A major focus of Healthy People since 1979 has been public awareness and public education concerning physical and mental disorders. In Healthy People 2020, awareness and education is built into almost all areas of the 1,413 objectives. For example, in the topic area of Educational and Community-Based Programs, there are two identified issues: (1) evaluating coordinated school health programs as an intervention to reduce school dropout rates; and (2) establishing an evidence base for community health and education policy interventions to determine their impact and effectiveness, which are critical for improving mental health outcomes across the life span. Both of these objectives are related to the objectives for the topic area of Mental Health and Mental Disorders: increasing treatment and service utilization for persons with mental illnesses or co-occurring disorders across ages and community and school settings. To engage individuals and communities in public awareness and education activities, health communication, social media, and health belief models are utilized to create effective mental health campaigns.

Health Communication

Communication for public health and mental health professionals, for consumers, and to the (mass) media may originate from national, state, and local governments (e.g., health departments). It also may originate from universities (i.e., the results of research studies), professional health societies (e.g., the American Public Health Association), professional mental health associations (e.g., the American Psychiatric Association), and other mental health organizations (e.g., Mental Health America). Some recommendations are specifically targeted to at-risk populations, including campaigns to discourage tobacco use by children and adolescents, or antidrug advertisements that are provided by not-for-profit organizations. Other communications are statewide initiatives, such as the Mental Health Transformation Project to reduce stigma in the state of Washington (discussed later in this entry). Other public health communications are issued at the local and community levels, including those from pharmacies or community health

The National Alliance for the Mentally Ill (NAMI) sponsors a walkathon to raise public awareness about mental illness. (PRNewsFoto/NAMI.)

and mental health centers, where health and mental health counseling and written information is provided to individuals (Levin & Hurd 2004).

The Centers for Disease Control and Prevention (CDC 2007) defines health communication as "the study and use of communication strategies to inform and influence individual decisions that enhance health." Health communication formats range from print (e.g., ads, brochures, posters, and handbooks) to media (e.g., radio, television, online streaming and podcasts, CD-ROMS, and DVDs). There are four stages of the health communication process, which is a recursive process. Each stage feeds into the next stage. When stage 4 is completed, it continues into stage 1, once again passing through each successive stage. This ensures continuous improvement in planning, implementation, and process. The first stage addresses planning and strategy development. Researchers and health communication specialists examine background information to define the problem and set communication objectives. In stage 2, researchers develop and pretest concepts, messages, and materials. This stage is where target audiences are identified, message concepts are developed and pretested, communication channels are selected, and the pretest messages and products are assessed. It is in this stage that the promotion plan is developed. In stage 3, the communication strategies are implemented and the process evaluation is conducted. In stage 4, outcome and impact evaluations are conducted to determine how effective the campaign was and how it may be improved or expanded. Essentially, a health communication campaign needs to answer the following questions:

1. What's out there?
2. What do we want to accomplish?
3. Who do we want to reach?
4. What do we want to say?
5. Where do we want to say it?
6. How do we want to say it?
7. How do we get it used?
8. How do we get it out there?
9. How well did we do?

Social Marketing

In the late 1980s, health promotion campaigns began applying social marketing. Social marketing, as defined by the CDC (2007), is "the use of marketing principles to influence human behavior in order to improve health or benefit society." Using a social marketing approach incorporates the "the four *p*'s of marketing" (product, price, place, and promotion) and allows the provision of health services from the consumer viewpoint (Lefebvre & Flora 1988). Product represents the desired behavior the audience should perform and the information on the associated benefits, objects, and/or services available to support the specific behavior change. Price addresses barriers to change from a broad cost perspective: financial, emotional, psychological, or time. Place encompasses where the audience will perform the desired behavior (e.g., home, workplace, or community facility), where they will access the program products and services (e.g., website, pharmacy, or health center), or where they will think about the campaign. Promotion stands for communication messages, materials, channels, and activities that will effectively reach the identified audience (e.g., print advertisement, bus banner campaign, radio or television public service announcement, and social networking site). The CDC (2007) suggests policy is the "invisible fifth *p*" in social marketing. Policy, after all, creates the laws and regulations that influence the desired behavior (e.g., prohibiting smoking in public spaces).

The CDC uses both health communication practices and social marketing practice in its approach to promoting or "marketing" health and mental health to the public. Viewed as overlapping and complementary, this shared approach utilizes the theoretical underpinnings of social marketing with the outreach communication strategies found in health communications to create effective health and mental health prevention and promotion campaigns. Examples of this approach are found in the CDCynergy training and software applications, such as its Social Marketing and Assessment Response Tool (CDC 2007).

Behavior Change Models

The main issue in health communications and social marketing is to understand how to best change health and mental health behaviors from a population-based perspective. There are many models used to understand behavior change in public health, including the health belief model (HBM), the stages of change theory (SoCT), the theory of reasoned action/theory of planned behavior (TRA), the social cognitive theory (SCT), and the social ecological model (SEM) (Glanz & Rimer 2005). Briefly, consequences of behaviors may lead to change (HBM), change of behavior over time (SofC), the individual's intention toward the behavior and his or her subjective norm (TRA), behavior based upon the interaction of personal, behavioral, and environmental factors (SCT), or levels of personal and social factors that all play a part in the health behavior of a community or population (SEM).

By defining the perceived susceptibility of an individual, both specific at-risk populations and at-risk behaviors are identified. The perceived severity of a behavior helps to determine the specific consequences of the risk(s). The perceived benefits of changing one's behavior identify what action(s) are to be taken as well as where and when the actions occur. Understanding barriers to change identifies incentives, reassurances, and supports that can be created for public awareness and education. These become cues to action, by creating strategies to help individuals make a positive change in their behaviors. Finally, these strategies encourage an individual's belief in his or her ability to change by providing training and guidance in how to change the identified behavior.

Clearly, there are numerous prevention programs and interventions in public health, but the common factor between most of these programs is the recognition of the importance of interactions between several components, including the individual, the environment (social and physical), and human behavior. Different prevention programs and interventions will focus on different factors. While specific interventions focus on individuals, others focus on the environment, and still others focus on the agent or disease. However, it is important not to forget that each of these factors is intertwined with the other factors.

It is also important to remember not all prevention programs are going to be effective with every population. If you are using universal prevention methods, it would be wise to present them in a variety of ways in order to reach the widest possible audience and make the biggest change possible. One of the most well-known examples of universal prevention is the reduction in adult smoking over the past two decades (Cuijpers 2003). However, even though this prevention effort was deemed successful with adult smokers, there was not a corresponding reduction in adolescent smoking. This provides evidence for the argument that the same prevention activity does not necessarily work for all at-risk populations. Behavioral changes are very difficult to achieve and often require intense and more specialized interventions. For example, a selective prevention effort might target children of alcoholic parents. Such a campaign simultaneously may address children's behavioral problems and target children with antidrinking messages.

Addressing the Stigma and Discrimination of Mental Illnesses

One of the largest barriers to utilization of mental health/substance abuse services is the stigma and discrimination that people with mental illnesses and/or substance use disorders face every day in a wide variety of settings, including employment, health care, housing, and education (President's New Freedom Commission on Mental Health 2003). Persons with mental illnesses and substance use disorders experience more difficulty in obtaining jobs if they disclose their mental and/or substance use disorders. Further, persons with mental illnesses and substance use disorders are additionally stigmatized due to a lack of economic productivity and perceived inability to "contribute" to society. Finally, the media emphasizes the dangerousness of persons with mental illnesses and/or substance use disorders and attributes criminal and risky behaviors to persons with mental illnesses and/or substance use disorders.

The "not in my backyard" (NIMBY) viewpoint is one such example of the stigma problem, where people do not want certain buildings near their property and residences, such as mental health housing and treatment facilities in primarily residential neighborhoods. Federal law does not require mental health or substance abuse agencies to inform neighborhoods when establishing supervised housing for individuals with severe mental illnesses/substance use disorders. In fact, within the mental health community, providers, agencies, and persons with severe mental illnesses see this as a positive opportunity for outreach, advocacy, and public education. However, Galster (2003) estimates that neighborhood opposition to special-needs housing and treatment facilities occurs in one-third to one-half of all sites. Neighborhoods cite fears of the effects of such housing on their quality of life, personal and family safety, and property values.

How does one educate the public against NIMBYism and other consequences of stigma and discrimination? Corrigan (2004) suggests three best practices for stigma reduction: (1) contact, (2) education, and (3) protest. In other words: (1) meet people with mental illness; (2) counter misinformation with accurate and up-to-date information; and (3) change prejudicial attitudes and practices. Numerous persons with mental illnesses have written and spoken of their hope for recovery and for the opportunity to live meaningful lives despite their serious mental illness.

Anthony (1993) developed and presented the concept of the recovery model to the mental health community. The recovery model is based on the idea that people with mental illnesses can and do recover and lead productive and fulfilling lives. Learning about the lives of others who have mental illnesses and who have successfully managed their disorder is one way to reduce stigma and discrimination. Hence, a key component in public awareness and public education campaigns is the use of personal stories of mental health recovery.

The National Institute of Mental Health (NIMH) has long encouraged the use of personal stories to give a "face" to individuals with a mental illness and to decrease stigma. In 2003, NIMH launched the "Real Men, Real Depression" campaign. In addition to its print materials, radio and television public service announcements were created that provided personal stories of six men from different age groups and ethnic backgrounds. These personal stories were created in English and in Spanish. The Substance Abuse and Mental Health Services Administration (SAMHSA) also uses personal stories to promote recovery.

More recent initiatives include "Stories that Heal," a national public service advertising partnership campaign with the Ad Council, the "Stay Strong Foundation" targeted to young African Americans, and the "What a Difference a Friend Makes" partnership campaign with the Ad Council and the National Asian American Pacific Islander Empowerment Network. The SAMHSA Resource Center to Promote Acceptance, Dignity, and Social Inclusion Associated with Mental Health (ADS Center) provides a number of resources designed to promote public awareness and public education about mental illnesses, such as the Campaign for Social Inclusion (formerly the Campaign for Mental Health Recovery), free training teleconferences to enhance mental health consumer independence and community participation, an interactive map of campaigns and promotions, and a page of personal accounts.

At a state level, there are various campaigns to reduce stigma. One, in particular, highlights a long-term plan to eradicate stigma. The state of Washington Office of Health Promotion (2006) created a social marketing campaign, the Mental Health Transformation Project, to counteract stigma and promote recovery. Three strategies were identified: contact, education, and protest/reward. The first strategy, contact, was to promote the human side of mental illnesses through the concept of recovery. Out of this strategy, a consumer speakers bureau was created, professional education workshops were given, and strategic speaking engagements were established for persons with mental illnesses to talk publicly about their illnesses.

The second strategy, education, was to educate the public about mental illnesses through understanding how stigma creates irrational fears and misinformation. First, printed and web-based educational materials were created for consumers on mental illnesses, recovery, and treatment options. Persons with mental illnesses need information that is accurate and directs them to treatment options. Next, a print and online compendium of best and promising practices, including the recovery model, was created for providers of services. Policy makers were also targeted with white papers on recovery, resiliency, and stigma, as well as with information on the Mental Health Transformation Project. Materials for the fourth group, the general public, include media toolkits (posters and radio public service announcements) that were distributed to community- and peer-based organizations.

The third strategy was to protest stigmatization of people with mental illnesses. To do this, the Project created an awards program that honored consumers and other individuals, such as providers and policy makers, who contributed significantly to antistigma and advocacy efforts. The Project also created a news bureau to publicize the awards program, to create positive press about persons with mental illnesses who exemplify the recovery model, and to monitor other news sources that continues the stigmatization and discrimination of persons with mental illnesses.

The examples noted above illustrate prevention efforts that may be disseminated in a number of different ways, including through educational initiatives (information dissemination), strengthening prevention factors (e.g., through social support, problem-solving skills, stress reduction, and coping skills), providing greater awareness of risk factors, and informing policy changes.

Social Media

Clearly, the Internet has a major impact on lessening the stigma and isolation of individuals with mental illness. Web 2.0 and social media applications, such as YouTube, Twitter, Flickr, and Facebook, have allowed the creation of numerous online communities and easier access to information on mental illness, treatment, and services delivery. Social media have a number of advantages. They allow people to search for information, share their stories, and decide how much about themselves they want to disclose, such as PatientsLikeMe.com.

Studies by the Pew Internet and American Life Project show that nearly one-third of Internet users in the United States have already "tagged" content using folksonomies and clouds (Rainie 2007) and 6 percent of health information seekers have "tagged" or categorized web health information (Fox & Jones 2009). More important, users may remain anonymous and still receive help and support, as tags created by the users can help pull information to them. Consider the implications for "pushing" targeted prevention and health promotion information anonymously to individuals who have tagged specific sites or disclosed information on health behaviors. As Web 2.0 technologies evolve, there will be greater implementation of personalized interactions based on user specific characteristics. We see this as exciting opportunities to expand public awareness and public education regarding mental illnesses and substance use disorders.

Implications for Mental Health

Public awareness and public education programs are essential tools to effecting changes in population health and societal beliefs surrounding mental illnesses. As discussed in other entries in this volume (see cross-references, below), the stigma attached to individuals with a mental illness is undeserved. Mental illnesses are treatable and are manageable. The effectiveness of treatment for mental illnesses is higher and more sustainable than many other chronic physical diseases. Persons with a mental illness can live integrated and productive lives. However, to disseminate this message requires a variety of strategies and methods. Understanding the mechanisms by which people change their beliefs and behaviors is key. Health communication, social marketing, and the use of social media are examples of tools to utilize in raising public awareness and public education initiatives concerning the prevention of physical and mental illnesses and the promotion of health and mental health.

See also Media Portrayals of Mental Illness; Mental Health Advocacy; Preventative Mental Health Programs; Public Health Perspectives; Public Policy Issues; Recovery Movement; Stigma; Suicide and Suicide Prevention

Bibliography

Anthony, W. A. 1993. "Recovery from Mental Illness: The Guiding Vision of the Mental Health Service System in the 1990s." *Psychosocial Rehabilitation Journal* 16(4): 11–23.

Centers for Disease Control and Prevention. 2007. *CDCynergy Social Marketing Edition* (2nd ed.). Atlanta, GA: Centers for Disease Control and Prevention. Retrieved from http://www.orau.gov/cdcynergy/demo/.

Commission on Chronic Illness. 1957. *Prevention of Chronic Illness*. Cambridge, MA: Harvard University Press, published for the Commonwealth Fund.

Corrigan, P. 2004. "Target-Specific Stigma Change: A Strategy for Impacting Mental Illness Stigma." *Psychiatric Rehabilitation Journal* 28: 113–121.

Cuijpers, Pim. 2003. "Examining the Effects of Prevention Programs on the Incidence of New Cases of Mental Disorders: The Lack of Statistical Power." *American Journal of Psychiatry* 160: 1385–1391.

Fox, S., and S. Jones. 2009. "The Social Life of Health Information." Washington, DC: Pew Internet & American Life Project. Retrieved from http://www.pewinternet.org/~/media//Files/Reports/2009/PIP_Health_2009.pdf.

Galster, George C. 2003. *Why Not in My Backyard? Neighborhood Impacts of Deconcentrating Assisted Housing*. New Brunswick, NJ: Center for Urban Policy Research.

Glanz, Karen, and Barbara K. Rimer. 2005. *Theory at a Glance: A Guide for Health Promotion Practice* (2nd ed.) (NIH Publication No. 05-3896). Bethesda, MD: National Cancer Institute. Retrieved from http://www.cancer.gov/cancertopics/cancerlibrary/theory.pdf.

Gordon, Robert S., Jr. 1983. "An Operational Classification of Disease Prevention." *Public Health Reports* 98: 107–109.

Lefebvre, R. Craig, and June A. Flora. 1988. "Social Marketing and Public Health Intervention." *Health Education Quarterly* 15: 300–301.

Levin, Bruce L., and Peter D. Hurd. 2004. "Public Health: Principles and Practice." In Robert L. McCarthy and Kenneth W. Schafermeyer, eds., *Introduction to Health Care Delivery: A Primer for Pharmacists* (pp. 147–170). Sudbury, MA: Jones and Bartlett.

Office of Health Promotion. 2006. *Plan for Mental Health Social Marketing Anti-Stigma Initiative*. Washington State Department of Health. Retrieved from http://mhtransformation.wa.gov/pdf/mhtg/SocialMarketingPlan.pdf.

President's New Freedom Commission on Mental Health. 2003. *Achieving the Promise: Transforming Mental Health Care in America* (Publication No. SMA-03-3832). Rockville, MD: U.S. Department of Health and Human Services.

Rainie, L. 2007. "Tagging." Washington, DC: Pew Internet & American Life Project. Retrieved from http://www.pewinternet.org/~/media//Files/Reports/2007/PIP_Tagging.pdf.pdf.

Vandiver, Vikki L. 2008. *Integrating Health Promotion and Mental Health: An Introduction to Policies, Principles, and Practices*. New York: Oxford University Press.

Public Health Perspectives

Bruce Lubotsky Levin and Ardis Hanson

The development of public health and health care delivery systems dates back to Europe in the eighteenth century and the United States in the late nineteenth century. Historically, the field of public health has been an intricate combination of many initiatives within a community, including sanitation, immunization, human behavior (particularly personal hygiene), nutrition, genetics, and medical care. As bacteriologic and immunologic advances were discovered and employed to control communicable diseases, the concept of disease prevention was incorporated into public health practice. Eventually, the field of public health evolved into an interdisciplinary collection of public and community health sciences that now incorporates elements from the social, political, and behavioral sciences in health promotion, disease prevention, and early intervention of disease in human populations.

This entry examines the symbiotic nature of the relationship between mental health and public health. Topics covered here include key definitions; prevention; epidemiology; the Healthy People initiative; the differentiation between clinical services and services delivery; systems delivery and policy; health and mental health services integration; and implications for mental health.

Definitions
Public Health

"Public health" has been defined in a variety of ways, but definitions tend to include efforts that promote healthy lifestyles (through health promotion and health education) as well as efforts that contribute to the prevention of diseases in specific at-risk populations.

Public health is the science and art of preventing disease, prolonging life, and promoting physical health and efficiency through organized community efforts . . . which will ensure to every individual a standard of living adequate for the maintenance of health . . . to enable every citizen to realize his [and her] birthright of health and longevity. (Winslow 1920, 6–7)

In 1988, a major report on the status of public health in the United States, the Institute of Medicine's (IOM) *The Future of Public Health* (1988), defined public health as "fulfilling society's interest in assuring conditions in which people can be healthy" (7). Thus the focus on community and social group responses to health promotion and disease prevention is a central component of the definition of public health.

While a medical orientation focuses on the treatment of individuals with acute and chronic illnesses, public health focuses on 10 essential public health services needed to carry out basic public health core functions in a community (Public Health Functions Steering Committee 1994):

1. Monitor health status to identify community health problems.
2. Diagnose and investigate identified health problems and health hazards in the community.
3. Inform, educate, and empower people about health issues.
4. Mobilize community partnerships to identify and solve health problems.
5. Develop policies and plans that support individual and community health efforts.
6. Enforce laws and regulations that protect health and ensure safety.
7. Link people to needed personal health services and assure the provision of health care.
8. Assure a competent public health and personal health care workforce.
9. Assess effectiveness, accessibility, and quality of personal and population-based health.
10. Conduct research for new insights and innovative solutions to health problems.

To perform these functions, public health problems are identified through epidemiologic surveillance. In addition, risk and protective factors are determined for the identified public health problems. Disease prevention, health promotion, and early intervention strategies are developed, implemented, and evaluated. These strategies are then monitored for efficacy and cost-effectiveness.

Mental Health

"Mental health" is a broad term that often includes alcohol abuse and alcoholism, drug use and abuse, mental disorders, developmental and pervasive disabilities, and Alzheimer's and other dementias. Often, the scientific litera-ture uses the term "behavioral health," which collectively represents alcohol, drug abuse, and mental disorders. The *Diagnostic and Statistical Manual of Mental Disorders* (*DSM*), published by the American Psychiatric Association, serves as the definitive American diagnostic tool for mental disorders. In addi-tion, the International Classification of Diseases (ICD) is the global standard diagnostic classification for all diseases, produced by the World Health Organization.

Since different cultures and ethnicities may vary in their definitions of what constitutes "mental health" and "mental illness," a population-based public health perspective offers an innovative and culturally/linguistically appropriate approach to the organization and provision of mental health services.

Prevention

Prevention is the foundation of public health practice. Historically, it has played an important role in the health of both individuals and communities. The original public health classification system of disease prevention was developed by the Commission on Chronic Illness (1957) and included three types of prevention activities: primary; secondary; and tertiary prevention.

The nature, severity, and variety of public health problems in the United States have changed over the past 200 years. Acute illnesses have been superseded by chronic diseases. A variety of local public health issues (e.g., clean air, drinkable water, and waste disposal) have become standardized nationally. In fact, many public health problems have become global concerns rather than specific to single countries or selected at-risk populations. Historically, these changes in public health priorities illustrate the growth and progress of scientific knowledge in the etiology and control of disease in populations. Furthermore, they illustrate the gradual acceptance of health promotion, disease prevention, and early interven-tion as a public responsibility in the United States. Finally, the development of public health practice in the United States also demonstrates that a number of public health issues and problems remain unresolved.

Epidemiology

The basis of public health practice lies in an understanding of the core princi-ples and methods of epidemiology, which may be defined as the study of the fac-tors that determine the frequency, distribution, and etiology of disease in human populations (MacMahon & Pugh 1970). In other words, epidemiologic studies examine the distribution and determinants of disease in populations. "Incidence" and "prevalence" are terms commonly used in the measurement of disease fre-quency. The *incidence* of a disease is the rate of new cases occurring in a popula-tion over a specific time period. The *prevalence* of a disease is the proportion of a population affected by a disease at a specific time. Consider the following prevalence statistics from both global and U.S. perspectives.

Global Perspective

The World Health Organization estimates that 450 million people throughout the world suffer from alcohol, drug use, and mental disorders. Further, over 154 million people globally suffer from depression, 25 million people suffer from schizophrenia, 91 million people are affected by alcohol use disorders, and 15 million people have drug use disorders (World Health Organization 2001).

U.S. Perspective

Mental disorders in the United States are also widespread; approximately one in five adults has a diagnosable mental disorder during any 12-month period (Kessler, Merikangas, & Wang 2010). According to the National Institute of Mental Health (2010), lifetime prevalence of mental disorders among adults in the United States is in excess of 46 percent and the 12-month prevalence rate of adults with mental disorders is approximately 26 percent. Further, over 22 percent of these disorders (nearly 6% of the adult U.S. population) are considered severe. If specific disorders (such as mood disorders) are examined, there is a 12-month prevalence rate of over 9 percent of the adult U.S. population, with 45 percent of these cases (in excess of 4% of the total U.S. population) considered as having a severe mood disorder.

In addition, individuals may have co-occurring disorders: simultaneous physical and mental disorders. An individual may have one or more physical disorders, such as diabetes and high blood pressure; a physical and mental disorder, such as heart disease and depression; or two mental disorders, such as bipolar disorder and alcoholism. Individuals with mental disorders are more at risk for physical illnesses, for communicable and noncommunicable diseases, and for injury. Persons with physical illnesses are also at risk for mental disorders. Appropriate diagnosis of individuals with simultaneous presentations for both physical and mental disorders is difficult. Co-occurring disorders generally complicates as well as worsens both the clinical course and outcomes for individuals with mental disorders.

Approximately one-half of individuals with a serious mental disorder also have an alcohol or other addictive disorder during their lifetime. Approximately 33 percent of individuals who have any type of mental disorder (i.e., not necessarily a severe mental disorder) in their lifetime also have a co-occurring addiction disorder. Furthermore, approximately 3 percent of the U.S. adult population has a co-occurring disorder in any given year (Kessler, Merikangas, & Wang 2010).

Therefore mental disorders, including co-occurring disorders, include some of the most complex problems in public health. This complexity is exacerbated by the lack of integration of physical and mental health services in treatment and services delivery settings. As fundamental changes have occurred within mental health delivery systems over the past 30 years, it is critical to consider mental health care not as an isolated specialty sector but as an important part of public health.

Healthy People 2010/2020

Healthy People is a national public health promotion and disease prevention initiative that establishes evidence-based 10-year national objectives and provides data and tools to enable the assessment and achievement of these national objectives. The *Healthy People* report also monitors national health objectives and measures the impact of prevention activities for the nation. For example, *Healthy People 2010* provided general goals for 10 leading health indicators, such as tobacco use, immunizations, mental disorders, and overweight/obesity (U.S. Department of Health and Human Services 2000). Each publication of *Healthy People* includes objectives for both physical health and mental health.

In the 2010 report, there were three focal areas for mental health: (1) mental health status improvement; (2) treatment expansion; and (3) state activities. Mental health status improvement, for example, addresses suicide reduction overall, reducing adolescent suicide attempts, reducing serious mental illness among adults who are homeless, achieving employment for persons with serious mental illnesses, and reducing eating disorder relapses.

In the 2020 report, the objectives for mental health status improvement are very similar to the 2010 objectives: reducing suicide, reducing suicide attempts by adolescents, reducing eating disorders, and reducing the number of persons (adolescents and adults) who experience a major depressive disorder (U.S. Department of Health and Human Services 2010).

Clinical Services versus Services Delivery

Understanding how public health and mental health intersect may be accomplished by reviewing the difference between clinical services and services delivery. Clinical services focuses on diagnosis, etiology, and treatment of disease in the individual, with the intention of curing, managing, or ameliorating a disease to ensure the best possible outcome for the individual. Clinical services include medication management, therapy, case management, and inpatient and outpatient treatment, with the focus at the individual level.

Services delivery focuses on how best to treat a population within existing service systems. This requires a multitiered perspective, using micro, meso, and macro approaches. Successful services delivery requires understanding the impact of the organization, financing, and management of health services on the quality of, access to, and outcomes of care. It also requires an examination of how to ensure efficient, economic, and equitable delivery of services. Services delivery requires identifying the nature and scope of local needs and matching local services to needs. It also requires structuring integrated care that reaches the consumer; allocating financial resources; understanding the economics and financing of care (cost-efficacy/effectiveness studies); and providing proper protections and incentives to use services appropriately. Services delivery also addresses legal and legislative issues through policy analysis, encompassing scrutiny of outcomes, impact, and implementation, and incorporating new evidence-based treatment paradigms. Services delivery must also develop strategies to change attitudes about the stigma of mental illnesses to increase the treatment-seeking behavior to utilize mental health services.

Mental health within a public health framework encompasses all of these areas, whether it is at a local, state, regional, national, or global level, coordinating all programs and services related to mental health through a common vision. It defines the vision for the future mental health of a population, establishing coordinating mechanisms for programs and services related to mental health across all governmental levels and service providers (Mechanic 2005). Mental health is affected by public health policy, legislation, regulations, and standards for implementation, enforcement, and policy development.

Systems Delivery and Policy

However, to further complicate the issue of mental health services delivery is the multilayered "systems" approach to services delivery. During the 1960s, the publicly financed mental health "system" evolved from state-run hospital settings to a variety of specialty sector services within a number of different organizational settings, largely independent from public health systems. Today, the de facto mental health "system" in the United States is comprised of numerous health and mental health delivery systems intersecting with or tangential to other systems, such as the social welfare, justice, and educational systems. Mental health delivery systems now include both public and private sector services. Each sector (specialty mental health sector, the general medical/primary care sector, and the voluntary care sector) has its own agencies, funding streams, services, and operations, providing acute and long-term care across a variety of care settings (homes, communities, and institutional). Numerous organizations influence how mental health care is accessed, organized, delivered, and financed. These include professional licensing and accreditation organizations, managed care provider entities, insurance companies, advocacy and regulatory agencies, and health care policy-making groups.

Services Integration

The assessment and treatment of individuals with mental disorders often occurs in other health care delivery systems whose primary missions have little to do with the identification of mental disorders (Regier, Goldberg, & Taube 1978). The term "integrated care" includes the integration of screening, prevention, early intervention, and treatment of diseases across service delivery sectors. The Institute of Medicine (Committee on Crossing the Quality Chasm 2006) has repeatedly called for the integration of future public health initiatives with mental health initiatives, particularly in the areas of disease prevention and health promotion. In the IOM report (Committee on Crossing the Quality Chasm 2006), the United States has reached a crisis point where improving the nation's health and resolving the problems of the quality of health care in the United States will require attending equally to the problems associated with health, mental health, and substance use treatment in the United States. Further, there are numerous examples in the scientific literature of the treatment and financial feasibility of services integration, ranging from university hospitals and clinics (Manderscheid, Masi, Rossignol, & Masi 2007) to community-based care (Brousselle et al. 2010).

Recent studies to better understand models of services delivery and their impact on individual health demonstrate that effectiveness is best seen in approaches that bridge the gap between physical and mental health services (Committee on Public Health Strategies to Improve Health 2011). From a services integration level, four factors have been identified as problematic: geographic, financial, organizational, and cultural. Geographic factors address the lack of colocated medical and mental health services. Financial factors are exacerbated by the separate funding streams for physical and mental health services. Organizational factors are concerned with the difficulty in sharing information and expertise across the disparate systems. Cultural issues arise because providers focus on specific symptoms or disorders instead of focusing on the individuals with these problems.

Implications for Mental Health

Levin, Hanson, Hennessey, and Petrila (2010, 10) suggest that "a public health perspective allows one to examine and address the continued fragmentation and gaps in care for children, adults, and the elderly; recovery issues surrounding unemployment, stigma, and disability for people with serious mental disorders; and the lack of a national priority for mental health and suicide prevention." From a population-based, integrative perspective, a public heath approach allows the emphasis on prevention, health promotion, sustaining existing services, and addressing inequalities in health and mental health care. Tools, such as epidemiology and health surveillance, provide information on the effectiveness of integrated primary and specialty health care in order to reduce the increased morbidity and premature mortality from mental and substance use disorders. Finally, a public health approach allows for the awareness of the direct and indirect societal consequences of mental and substance use disorders.

It is important to remember that mental health disorders have been identified in the United States as widespread, severe, and costly. From a public health perspective, two service delivery issues contribute to the problems associated with the adequate and timely identification, assessment, treatment, and recovery of individuals with mental and substance use disorders. First, there has been an increasing recognition of co-occurring disorders, with an accompanying variety of organization, referral pathways to treatment, financing, delivery systems, and outcomes for each type of disorder. Second, the majority of individuals with a diagnosable mental disorder do *not* seek and do *not* receive treatment for a mental disorder. Furthermore, of those individuals who do receive treatment for a mental disorder, over one-half seeks treatment from a primary health care practitioner.

Finally, the continued evolution of health insurance, financing, and services delivery, the explosion of information and communication systems technology, the aging and growing cultural diversity in the U.S. population, and the continued decrease in government support of public health and mental health programs provide significant challenges for mental health services delivery, health promotion, and disease prevention initiatives. Nevertheless, health is not a result of individual medical or clinical care, but if a societal response and commitment to create healthy communities (Committee on Public Health Strategies to Improve Health 2011).

See also Community Mental Health; Evidence-Based Practice and Outcome Measurement; Homelessness and Mental Illness; Preventative Mental Health Programs; Public Awareness and Public Education; Public Policy Issues; State Mental Health Agencies

Bibliography

Brousselle, Astrid, Lise Lamothe, Chantal Sylvain, Anne Foro, and Michel Perreault. 2010. "Integrating Services for Patients with Mental and Substance Use Disorders: What Matters?" *Health Care Management Review* 35: 212–223.

Commission on Chronic Illness. 1957. *Prevention of Chronic Illness*. Cambridge, MA: Harvard University Press, published for the Commonwealth Fund.

Committee on Crossing the Quality Chasm: Adaptation to Mental Health and Addictive Disorders, Institute of Medicine. 2006. *Improving the Quality of Health Care for Mental and Substance-Use Conditions*. Washington, DC: National Academies Press.

Committee on Public Health Strategies to Improve Health, Institute of Medicine. 2011. *For the Public's Health: The Role of Measurement in Action and Accountability*. Washington, DC: National Academies Press.

Institute of Medicine. 1988. *The Future of Public Health*. Washington, DC: Committee for the Study of the Future of Public Health, Division of Health Care Services.

Kessler, Ronald C., Kathleen R. Merikangas, and Philip S. Wang, Philip S. 2010. "The Epidemiology of Mental Disorders." In Bruce L. Levin, Kevin D. Hennessey, and John

Petrila, eds., *Mental Health Services: A Public Health Perspective* (3rd ed., pp. 169–200). New York: Oxford University Press.

Levin, Bruce L., Ardis Hanson, Kevin D. Hennessey, and John Petrila, John. 2010. "A Public Health Approach to Mental Health Services." In Bruce L. Levin, Kevin D. Hennessey, and John Petrila, eds., *Mental Health Services: A Public Health Perspective* (3rd ed., pp. 5–11). New York: Oxford University Press.

MacMahon, Brian, and Thomas F. Pugh. 1970. *Epidemiology: Principles and Methods*. Boston: Little, Brown.

Manderscheid Ronald W., Dale Masi, Charles R. Rossignol, and Daniel A. Masi. 2007. "The Integration of Physical Health and Behavioral Health Services: Three University Case Examples." *Archives of Psychiatric Nursing* 21: 141–149.

Mechanic, David. 2005. *Policy Challenges in Modern Health Care*. New Brunswick, NJ: Rutgers University Press.

National Institute of Mental Health. 2010. "Statistics: Prevalence." Retrieved from http://www.nimh.nih.gov/statistics/ index.shtml.

Public Health Functions Steering Committee. 1994. *Public Health in America*. Washington, DC: U.S. Public Health Services.

Regier, D., I. Goldberg, and C. Taube. 1978. The De Facto U.S. Mental Health Services System: A Public Health Perspective. *Archives of General Psychiatry* 35: 685–693.

U.S. Department of Health and Human Services. 2000. *Healthy People 2010*. Washington, DC: U.S. Department of Health and Human Services.

U.S. Department of Health and Human Services. 2010. *Healthy People 2020*. Washington, DC: U.S. Department of Health and Human Services.

Winslow, Charles-Edward Armory. 1920. "The Untilled Fields of Public Health." *Modern Medicine* 2: 1–9.

World Health Organization. 2001. *The World Health Report, 2001. Mental Health: New Understanding, New Hope*. Geneva, Switzerland: World Health Organization.

World Health Organization. 2010. *World Health Statistics 2010*. Geneva, Switzerland: World Health Organization.

Public Mental Health Systems

See Community Mental Health; History of Mental Health Care; Hospitalization; Public Policy Issues; State Mental Health Agencies

Public Policy Issues

Ardis Hanson and Bruce Lubotsky Levin

As a public policy issue, mental illness has tremendous impact upon society. It affects individuals, families, and communities; it has short- and long-term direct and indirect economic costs to society, families, and individuals; and it is a factor in a number of social issues, such as homelessness, violence and abuse, and human welfare. Since mental health problems present a formidable challenge for health and mental health delivery systems, persons with severe and chronic mental illnesses pose unique challenges in public health and mental health policy making. Fiscal limitations of many private health insurance plans and support services force persons with severe and chronic mental illnesses to rely heavily on public sector health and mental health resources. Further, as the public sector continues to privatize mental health care, a unique combination of issues continue to emerge, including tiers of services, organizational performance, community and consumer input, treatment based upon evidence-based practice and the appropriateness of services, and coordinated planning and services delivery.

Public policy decides who is covered, for what, where, by whom, and under what contingencies. These critical issues mentioned above have far-reaching impacts on access and utilization of services, the quality of available services, and the structure of mental health delivery systems in the United States. For example, it is impossible to understand the effects of insurance coverage for individuals with a mental disorder without examining policy changes that were implemented with the passage of mental health parity legislative initiatives. In addition, in order to understand the effects of deinstitutionalization, one must examine public policy changes in public and private health insurance programs, in welfare and disability entitlements, as well as in societal and civil rights changes over the past half century.

This entry will briefly summarize the public policy-making process, summarize the development of mental health policy in the United States, present key mental health legislative and policy initiatives, and examine the emergence of transition and recovery as important public policy initiatives in mental health services in America.

Public Policy

Public policy making begins with a public recognition of a problem. The problem can be a concern for a city, state, or federal government's mission, objectives, or purpose, the illumination of more encompassing social costs (such as the latent or unintended consequences of government interventions), or the need for consideration of alternatives for unrepresented or disenfranchised populations who participate in public programs. Public policy has the potential to transform social and political institutions. So, how does one make public policy?

Policy making goes through a number of stages. Following the public recognition/identification of a problem, it ideally progresses through a process of seeking expert and citizen input, resulting in the formulation of a policy proposal. The proposal is then presented to the appropriate government authority. The next step is consideration and modification of the proposal. The proposal then is considered for adoption through a decision-making process (passed into law). Finally, after government adoption, administrative modifications are made and the new proposal is implemented and evaluated (Lynn 1978).

Historically, government decision making is a process of advocacy and bargaining guided by power and interests of stakeholders or by a specific political platform. The policy-making process originates at a specific location of a policy institution, such as an agency or a grassroots organization. The policy maker makes a clear statement of intent, often with a list of specific steps and expectations for implementation at every level. A policy maker may be a single individual or a group of stakeholders who, speaking as one, identify the policy problem and propose possible strategies to address the problem. In the case of mental health policy, federal and state governments create numerous commissions, task forces, and legislative committees to address how mental health services should function and for what purpose (Longest 2006).

Mental Health Policy

Mental health policy encompasses a number of areas affecting the organization, financing, services delivery, and outcomes of mental health services. It requires answers from a broad array of mental health services research areas, including epidemiologic (population) studies, information on treatment/clinical services, the organizational structure of services, and examination of the quality and cost of mental health services. From local, state, national, and global perspectives, mental health policy mandates, provides funding, and establishes programs and services related to treating individuals with a variety of mental health problems (alternatively referred to as mental disorders or mental illnesses). In short, mental health policy attempts to define the vision for providing mental health services for at-risk populations.

Often linked to civil and human rights legislation and standards, mental health policy establishes what services will be provided, thereby "assigning" responsibility to government agencies for the implementation, oversight, and evaluation of program quality and success. Rochefort (1994) suggests that "the demands [for mental health policy] are for an approach that is multidisciplinary, sensitive to long-term historical, professional, and ideological forces, wise to the discrepancy between policies and programs, and encompassing in its perspective of the social welfare sector" (659).

National de facto mental health policy affects the agencies, funding streams, services, and operations of public sector and private sector service systems. These service systems include acute and long-term care services in a variety of settings (home based, community based, and institutional care) and across general medical/primary care and specialty mental health settings. Professional licensing and accreditation organizations, managed care provider entities, advocacy and regulatory agencies, and health care policy-making groups influence how local, state, and federal governments deliver and finance mental health care. In addition, state laws, administrative policies, funding priorities, advocates' concerns, and organizational culture and climate create additional "voices" that influence efforts to change the focus of mental health legislation. How a person enters the systems and his or her trajectory into mental health care is potentially influenced by local, state, and national mental health policy.

Historically Important Mental Health Policy Initiatives

Historically, there have been a number of major legislative and policy initiatives in the United States. However, in 1946, the United States affirmed the importance of mental illnesses as a national public health policy issue with passage of the National Mental Health Act (Public Law or Pub. L. 79-487). This law was one of the first major organizational and financial commitments made by the U.S. federal government addressing mental health policy and services research in the United States. This legislation transformed the Public Health Service's Division of Mental Health into the National Institute of Mental Health (NIMH), provided grants-in-aid to state mental health authorities, provided funds for research and training grants, and provided regional consultants for establishing state mental health authorities in each state. Further, this law elevated the level of responsibility and involvement of the federal government in the funding of mental health services, the establishment of mental health programs, the training and education of mental health professionals, the building of mental health facilities, and the provision of a national focus for mental health services in the United States. Alcohol and drug abuse legislation would eventually be passed into law in the 1970s.

In 1955, Congress passed the Mental Health Study Act (Pub. L. 84-182), which established the Joint Commission on Mental Illness and Health. Congress also charged the Joint Commission to evaluate mental disorders in the United States. In 1961, the Joint Commission published *Action for Mental Health*, which called for an expanded federal role in mental health services delivery. It was also one of the first reports to recommend the provision of community-based mental health services, a novel idea at that point in American history.

In 1963, then-President John F. Kennedy's "Bold New Approach" address to Congress called for an intensified search for the etiology of mental disorders, strengthening resources including training more highly skilled professionals in mental health, and improving the funding of programs that served individuals with mental disorders. The Mental Retardation Facilities and Community Mental Health Centers (CMHCs) Construction Act (Pub. L. 88-164) established planning grants to meet specific state mental health needs, to inventory existing state mental health resources, and to create 1,500 community mental health centers throughout the United States.

The overall guiding principle or concept of the CMHC legislation was the establishment of a comprehensive, community-based system of mental health treatment facilities that were accessible to any person in need of mental health care. This was a major policy change in the organization and financing of public mental health services in the United States. Further, state and federal funding of public mental health services, previously supporting only state mental hospitals, would now be available to support community-based mental health facilities. Until this point in time, the only comparable health care delivery system in the United States funded directly by the federal government was tuberculosis (TB) hospitals in early twentieth-century America.

By the early 1970s, the U.S. Congress passed three laws affecting substance use (i.e., alcohol and drug abuse) services in the United States. The Comprehensive Drug Abuse Prevention and Control Act (Pub. L. 91-513) established special grant opportunities for drug abuse, drug dependence, and drug prevention initiatives. In the same year, the Comprehensive Alcohol Abuse and Alcoholism Prevention, Treatment, and Rehabilitation Act (Pub. L. 91-616) established the National Institute of Alcohol Abuse and Alcoholism (NIAAA). This legislation also provided aid directly to states for the prevention and treatment of alcohol abuse and alcoholism. Finally, in 1972 Congress passed the Drug Abuse Office and Treatment Act (Pub. L. 92-255), which authorized the subsequent establishment of the National Institute on Drug Abuse (NIDA).

In 1977, then-President Jimmy Carter established the President's Commission on Mental Health. A year later, the commission (1978) submitted a four-volume report that served as the basis for the Mental Health Systems Act of 1980 (Pub. L. 96-398), which proposed a major reconceptualization of mental health services delivery in the United States. This legislation amended the community mental health centers program and included provisions for the development and support of comprehensive state mental health systems, with a focus on adults with the most severe mental disorders, children and adolescents, the elderly, and other at-risk populations. Public Law 96-398 also established an NIMH unit for prevention, an important step for establishing mental health services within a public health perspective. However, in 1981 then-President Ronald Reagan signed into law the Omnibus Budget Reconciliation Act (Pub. L. 97-35), which largely repealed the Mental Health Systems Act of 1980 prior to its funding and implement.

A number of other mental health policy initiatives were signed during 1980s, including the Child and Adolescent Service System Program (CASSP; NIMH 1983), the Protection and Advocacy for Mentally Ill Individuals Act of 1986 (PAMII; Pub. L. 99-319), and the Stewart B. McKinney Homeless Act of 1987 (Pub. L. 100-77). CASSP established a community-based system of care for an identified underserved population: children and adolescents who had serious emotional disturbances. Due to the CASSP legislation, funding for the Comprehensive

Community Mental Health Services for Children and Their Families Program was authorized by Congress in 1992.

The purpose of PAMII was twofold. Its first goal was to establish advocacy systems on behalf of persons with serious mental illnesses or persons who were institutionalized. Its second goal was to provide emotional, educational, and practical support for persons with serious mental illnesses or memory disorders, such as Alzheimer's disease.

The McKinney Act was important for public policy because it was the first significant federal legislative response to homelessness in the United States. Title VI of the act established a Community Mental Health Services block grant program and two demonstration treatment programs providing mental health, alcohol, and drug abuse services.

In 1990, the Americans with Disabilities Act (ADA; Pub. L. 101-336) became law. Basically a civil rights law, the ADA prohibits, under specific circumstances, discrimination based on disability. What is important from a mental health policy perspective is how the ADA defined disability: "a *physical or mental* impairment that substantially limits a major life activity" (Pub. L. 101-336; italics added).

Also during the 1990s, the Mental Health Parity Act (Pub. L. 104-204) and the Health Insurance Portability and Accountability Act (HIPAA; Pub. L. 104-191) were passed. Title VII in Public Law 104-204 ended the long-held practice of providing unequal insurance coverage for mental illnesses vis-à-vis insurance coverage for physical illnesses. Although the original 1996 act did not provide coverage for substance abuse or chemical dependency, the Mental Health Parity and Addiction Equity Act of 2008 provided parity for coverage of substance abuse and chemical dependency disorders.

HIPAA affected administrative and clinical practices for community treatment providers, consumers, single state agencies, public and private payers of alcohol, substance abuse and mental health services, and professional and trade associations. Not only did it provide regulations that created uniform standards and requirements for the electronic transmission of health information, it also addressed security and privacy concerns in the implementation of the electronic transfer of health records among health care providers.

Influencing Public Policy: The Creation of Public Policy Reports

With the passage of any federal law, there are customary background reports associated with the law. Presidential and U.S. congressional commissions, task forces, and work groups generate numerous reports on the state of the art of a particular topic. In some instances, these reports generate new bills or amendments that may radically change, repeal, or implement services, as previously illustrated with the passage of several public laws noted above. Two important public mental health policy documents prepared during the last 112 years include *Mental*

Health: Report of the Surgeon General and *Achieving the Promise: Report of the President's New Freedom Commission.*

Published in 1999, *Mental Health: Report of the Surgeon General* was the first U.S. Surgeon General's report on mental health (Office of the Surgeon General 1999). It examined the definitions and fundamentals of mental health and mental disorders; mental health and mental illness across age-specific populations; issues in the organization and financing of mental health services; confidentiality of mental health information from legal, ethical, and policy perspectives; and proposed recommendations for the twenty-first century in overcoming barriers to mental health treatment and services delivery in the United States. The U.S. Surgeon General's report issued the following eight major recommendations: (1) continuing to build a more thorough scientific knowledge base in mental health; (2) overcoming stigma of mental disorders in the United States; (3) improving public awareness of effective treatments for mental disorders; (4) ensuring the provision of both mental health providers and services; (5) providing state-of-the-art mental health care; (6) tailoring the treatment of mental disorders to age, gender, race, and culture; (7) assuring access to the treatment of mental disorders; and (8) reducing fiscal and economic barriers to mental health treatment. Many of the recommendations laid the framework for policy initiatives in the United States in the twenty-first century.

In 2003, the President's New Freedom Commission on Mental Health was initiated to study mental health services delivery in the United States and to suggest how to overcome the stigma of mental disorders; the insurance and financial limitations placed upon individuals with mental disorders vis-à-vis physical illnesses; and the multiple, disjointed, and dysfunctional mental health delivery systems across the United States. The commission identified the following six goals as the foundation for transforming mental health care in the United States: (1) understanding mental health as a component of overall (somatic) health and well-being; (2) mental health care should be viewed as consumer and family focused; (3) elimination of disparities in mental health services; (4) implementation of early screening, assessment, and referral to mental health services; (5) prioritizing mental health services delivery and mental health services research initiatives; and (6) the utilization of information technology in mental health practice. The commission also called for "nothing short of [the] *fundamental transformation* of the mental health care delivery system in the United States—from one dictated by outmoded bureaucratic and financial incentives to one driven by consumer and family needs that focuses on building resilience and facilitating recovery" (Goldman, Buck, & Thompson 2009; iv, italics added).

Since the passage of Public Law 102-321 established consumers and family members as members of state mental health planning boards, it is important to note how the passage of this law affected both the *Mental Health: Report of the Surgeon General* and *President's New Freedom Commission on Mental Health* reports. Both reports emphasized the role of persons with mental illnesses and family members in understanding the complexity of mental illnesses, treatment and services delivery, and creating outcomes that focus on quality of life. In *Mental Health: Report of the Surgeon General*, the U.S. Surgeon General (1999, 92) described the consumer role as twofold: "to overcome stigma and prevent discrimination in policies affecting persons with mental illness; to encourage self-help and a focus on recovery from mental illness."

During the 2000s, encouraged by the stance adopted in *Mental Health: A Report of the Surgeon General*, federal agencies required the inclusion of individuals who have mental illnesses and family members on policy-planning initiatives. Currently, there are a variety of stakeholders in public policy making, ranging from researchers, legislators, and academics to persons with mental illnesses/substance use disorders, family members, and advocates. Thus the inclusion of persons with mental illnesses/substance use disorders, family members, and advocates into federal reports, documents, and the law has contributed to paradigmatic shifts in treatment, and has influenced the development of a variety of change in mental health services, including the recovery movement.

In 2003, The President's New Freedom Commission recommended a fundamental transformation of the nation's approach to mental health care, focused on recovery. Recovery refers to the process in which people are able to live, work, learn, and participate fully in their communities. For some individuals, recovery is the ability to live a fulfilling and productive life despite a disability. For others, recovery implies the reduction or complete remission of symptoms. Science has shown that having hope plays an integral role in an individual's recovery (President's New Freedom Commission 2003, 7).

Implications for Mental Health

Despite the plethora of national legislation, mental health policy in the United States has been largely driven by interpretation of those policies by individual states. Thus it is not surprising that significant fragmentation and a lack of coordination occurs across mental health systems. In addition, mental health delivery systems are often disconnected from physical health delivery systems. This is illustrated by various mental health legislation, for example, the CMHC legislation failed to link CMHCs with neighborhood health centers.

In discussing contemporary policy issues in the United States, mental health has not been a significant issue of concern to most citizens, politicians, or policy makers, despite its critical role in the global burden of disease, in terms of morbidity and mortality. However, key policy reports have emerged since the publication of *Achieving the Promise*. In addition, the combination of these reports, with input from national and international agencies and organizations, has been moving toward a more public health-oriented framework when examining the epidemiology, organization, financing, and delivery of mental health services (Levin, Hennessey, & Petrila 2010; World Health Organization 2009; Goldman, Buck, & Thompson 2009).

To effectively transform mental health services in the United States, policy makers will need to address the following crucial issues: the integration of physical and mental health services as well as funding streams; seamless services for adolescents who transition from children's service systems into adult mental health service systems; and integrating the recovery paradigm into services delivery.

See also Disability Rights; Evidence-Based Practice and Outcome Measurement; History of Mental Health Care; Insurance and Parity Laws; Public Health Perspectives; Rights of Patients with Mental Health Conditions; State Mental Health Agencies

Bibliography

Goldman, Howard H, Jeffrey A. Buck, and Kenneth S. Thompson. 2009. *Transforming Mental Health Services: Implementing the Federal Agenda for Change*. Arlington, VA: American Psychiatric Association.

Joint Commission on Mental Illness and Health. 1961. *Action for Mental Health: Final Report*. New York: Basic Books. Retrieved from http://www.questia.com/PM.qst?a=o&d=100859113.

Kennedy, John F. 1963. *Message from the President of the United States Relative to Mental Illness and Mental Retardation* (88th Congress, 1st Session, Doc. 58). Washington, DC: U.S. Government Printing Office. Retrieved from http://www.mnddc.state.mn.us/parallels2/pdf/60s/63/63-MIMR-JFK.pdf.

Levin, Bruce Lubotsky, Kevin D. Hennessey, and John Petrila. 2010. *Mental Health Services: A Public Health Perspective* (3rd ed.). New York: Oxford University Press.

Longest, Beaufort B., Jr. 2005. *Health Policymaking in the United States* (4th ed.). Chicago: Health Administration Press.

Lynn, Lawrence E., Jr. 1978. *Knowledge and Policy: The Uncertain Connection*. Washington, DC: National Academy of Sciences.

National Institute of Mental Health. 1983. Program Announcement: Child and Adolescent Service System Program. Rockville, MD: National Institute of Mental Health.

Office of the Surgeon General. 1999. *Mental Health: A Report of the Surgeon General*. Rockville, MD: U.S. Department of Health and Human Services, U.S. Public Health Service. Retrieved from http://www.surgeongeneral.gov/library/mentalhealth/toc.html.

President's Commission on Mental Health. 1978. *Report to the President from the President's Commission on Mental Health*. Washington, DC: President's Commission on Mental Health. Retrieved from http://www.bookprep.com/read/uc1.b4087616.

President's New Freedom Commission on Mental Health. 2003. *Achieving the Promise: Transforming Mental Health Care in America: Final Report*. Rockville, MD: President's New Freedom Commission on Mental Health. Retrieved from http://store.samhsa.gov/shin/content//SMA03-3831/SMA03-3831.pdf.

Rochefort, David. 1994. "Mental Health Policy Inquiry, Its Importance, and Its Rewards." (Symposium on Studies in Mental Health Policy). *Policy Studies Journal* 22: 653–661.

World Health Organization. 2009. *Improving Health Systems and Services for Mental Health*. Geneva, Switzerland: World Health Organization. Retrieved from http://whqlibdoc.who.int/publications/2009/9789241598774_eng.pdf.

R

Recovery Movement

Charles Barber, Dave Sells, and Sarah Raven

The influential term "recovery" in contemporary mental health has been at times ambiguous and a focus of ongoing debate. Broadly speaking, the recovery approach to mental illness involves people feeling better about their illness; taking the lead in managing their symptoms; living a satisfying life even in the context of their illness; engaging in a holistic approach to treating illness, one that often includes but is not limited to psychiatric medications; reengaging in their communities; at times finding meaning and even positive aspects to their illness; and directing their own psychiatric treatment in conjunction with medical professionals who are viewed more as "expert consultants" than dictatorial providers of care.

A leader and scholar of the Recovery Movement, Larry Davidson (see Davidson et al. 2006) asserts that it is unclear what the word "recovery" means, and indeed many scholars have disagreed on its definition. Traditionally, the term "recovery" is thought to mean that a person would return to a previous, more "pristine" state. Roberts and Wolfson (2004) explain that "recovery" can refer to the movement, a philosophy, a model, a method, and a paradigm. Recovery, for the individual, often has a turning point or low point and is felt to be a process or a journey. As Carpenter (2002) states, "Recovery is not linear" (93).

The recovery model for treatment strongly contrasts with the medical model of psychiatric treatment, which has dominated the field since its inception. The medical model focuses largely if not solely on the patient's illness and not on the patient's life outside of the illness. It is based on the presumption that the clinician's responsibility is to reduce symptoms and, ideally, remove or cure the illness. The means for reducing symptoms, in modern psychiatry, have strongly, and increasingly, been based on psychiatric medications. The Recovery Movement can largely be viewed as a reaction again the medical model, and among its greatest champions are consumers (or patients) and former consumers who feel they were ill-served by the narrowness and rigidity of the biomedical approach.

History of the Recovery Movement

Many scholars have placed the origins of the Recovery Movement in the 1960s and 1970s (Jacobson 2000; Davidson & White 2007; Resnick & Rosenheck 2006;

Schiff 2004). However, Schiff suggests that the roots of this movement can be traced as far back as the mid-1800s, when Elizabeth Packard was institutionalized. Elizabeth Packard was married to a Calvinist minister who had her institutionalized because she announced that she wanted to attend the Methodist church, and he was convinced that she was insane to disagree with him on religious matters. While in the asylum she collected patients' stories and kept a journal. After she was released it took her nine years to gain custody of her children. Packard fought for the rights of people who were accused of being mentally ill until her death, and inspired a law passed in Illinois in 1869 requiring a jury trial before someone was committed. In the 1950s, the height of the inpatient era of psychiatry, state-run institutions became increasingly regarded in negative terms, for by then abuses, such as the rampant use of lobotomy procedures, were better understood by the public at large. By the 1960s, the public became more suspicious of long-term institutional care. This sentiment, coupled with the various civil rights and liberation movements of the 1970s (Schiff 2004), the mental health "consumer/survivor" movement, and the Americans with Disabilities Act, created a sociocultural shift (Davidson & White 2007). The goals of the ex-patient movement included empowerment and liberation. Davidson and White (2007) note that in the 1970s, people who were successfully deinstitutionalized went to urban areas. The highly charged and politicized environment of the 1970s gave an epistemological privilege to individual subjectivity, and accordingly, the new methods and practices in mental health emphasized the rights and preferences of the individual consumer. The Recovery Movement itself was so named around that time and grew markedly in the 1980s and particularly in the 1990s, with additional support from physical disability activists and the increasingly outspoken role of ex-patients (Resnick & Rosenheck 2006).

The Recovery Movement has only gained momentum in the last decade. A major turning point was the President's New Freedom Commission on Mental Health report in 2003, which placed consumers at the center of their mental health care and fully adopted Recovery principles at a federal level. The report also called for parity in physical and mental health care, such that they would be placed on equal footing and be reimbursed in equitable ways by third-party payers. Since that time, individual states and many nonprofit mental health organizations have formally adopted recovery agendas. One of the most visible indicators of the adoption of the recovery approach, for example, has been the hiring of former consumers of psychiatric services to provide support to current patients and work alongside trained professionals.

Philosophy of the Recovery Movement

In the 1980s and 1990s, organizations such as the National Mental Health Consumers' Association were actively involved in advocacy and support for people with mental health diagnoses. The mission of this organization reflected the new paradigm shift in the mental health field:

> Guided by the principles of choice, empowerment, and self-determination, the National Mental Health Consumers' Association is a human rights organization that advocates for employment, housing, benefits, service choice, and the end of discrimination and abuse in the lives of persons who use, have used, or have been used by the mental health systems. (Frese et al. 2001; 1463)

This mission statement used strong human rights language to drive home the point that the liberation of the individual and his or her sense of power and locus of control is of utmost importance. Far from advocating only intangibles, this statement mentions concrete concerns such as jobs and housing.

As noted, the Recovery Movement is diverse and continually evolving, but the following are six consistent tenets of the movement across its many constituents:

• The Recovery Movement utilizes a positive, strengths-based approach that focuses on the strengths of individuals rather than pathologizing people and focusing on their "illnesses" (Resnick & Rosenheck 2006).

• The movement seeks to empower individuals by allowing them greater involvement and choice in their treatment (Frese et al. 2001; Schiff 2004).

• Recovery is best thought of as a nonlinear process whereby the consumer may not ever become completely asymptomatic (Carpenter 2002; Glynn 2004; Roberts & Wolfson 2004).

• The movement is a grassroots one that is often led and championed by consumers/survivors of the mental health system (Frese 2001; Schiff 2004).

• The Recovery Movement promotes mental health advocacy to end the stigmatizing and discrimination of mental health consumers through education and coalition building (Frese et al. 2001; Jacobson 2000).

• The subjectivity of the recovery movement replaces the objectivity of the medical model. Instead of a subject-object relationship, consumers are part of an I-You relationship with medical professionals (Schiff 2004).

Outcomes

Recovery has been called a lot of things, including "magic" (i.e., nonscientific), impractical, not evidence based, and a "fad." However, Fred Frese (Frese et al. 2001), a psychologist who himself is recovering from schizophrenia, and others have sought to counter the claim that there is a lack of evidence-based practices by creating and looking at longitudinal studies concerning the positive as well as the potentially negative results of the recovery method in the lives of consumers. Since the goal of the recovery method is not necessarily to rid the consumer of all symptoms pertaining to his or her mental health diagnosis, the outcomes largely focus on management versus remission.

One of the more contentious illnesses, for example, is schizophrenia. People with a diagnosis of schizophrenia are often stigmatized by society and told they will never recover by mental health professionals (Frese et al. 2001). The *Diagnostic and Statistical Manual* of the American Psychiatric Association (2000) states that schizophrenia leads to deteriorated functioning over time and notes that a cure is rare. However, a longitudinal study led by Courtenay Harding (see Harding & Zahniser 1994) revealed that a majority of people diagnosed with schizophrenia in the 1980s and after recovered. Resnick, Rosenheck, and Lehman (2004) conducted a study of 825 people with schizophrenia diagnoses and found that the recovery method was strongly correlated with a reduction in psychotic systems, an increase in life satisfaction, and individual awareness and knowledge of the illness through direct education. Resnick concluded that the recovery method is of biomedical import. In other words, there is a link between the individual's sense of empowerment, agency, and overall well-being even in cases of serious mental illness.

Other evidence of the strength of the recovery approach comes from the testimonials of consumer-professionals who have "come out" of the mental health closet to show that even serious mental illnesses can be overcome. Individuals sometimes hide their mental health diagnosis due to the stigmatizing effect of labels, the negative depictions in the media of people with serious mental illness (including reports of violent behavior), and the very real consequences of housing and employment discrimination (Byrne 2000, Wahl 1999). Fred Frese's life and work provides a concrete example of someone who shattered people's assumptions about the prognosis of schizophrenia. Frese was diagnosed with schizophrenia at age 25 while serving as a U.S. Marine. He founded the Community and State Hospital Section of the American Psychological Association and has faculty appointments at both Case Western Reserve University and the Northeastern Ohio Universities College of Medicine. He has spent his career studying schizophrenia and advocating for evidence-based practice within the Recovery Movement. Other high-profile contributions to the Recovery Movement have come in the form of revelations by various celebrities who have shared their personal experiences with mental illness. Among them are Jane Pauley (bipolar disorder), Carrie Fisher (bipolar disorder), William Styron (depression), and Mike Wallace (depression). Despite evidence showing that people who have recovered from severe mental illnesses can lead productive and healthy lives, many professionals cannot accept this reality because it flies in the face of conventional medical wisdom (Carpenter 2002).

As noted, the Recovery Movement is a strengths-based approach that is similar in some respects to the positive psychology movement. The positive psychology movement ran a separate yet parallel course to the Recovery Movement (Resnick & Rosenheck 2006). Positive psychologists were often detractors of the Recovery Movement because of the lack of scientific evidence to support the movement and skepticism regarding its grassroots beginnings. However, Resnick argues that positive psychology was able to contribute to the Recovery Movement by establishing strengths surveys, which are now widely utilized in mental health care. Resnick, for example, asked homeless veterans to complete a 240-question survey probing 24 character strengths synthesized from conventional wisdom and American literature as well as international religious and philosophical texts. The respondent's top five positive character traits were generated by this means and recorded on a card that he or she carried. The intervention gave the veterans a sense of pride and accomplishment, and in some cases motivated people to pursue forgotten dreams.

Andresen, Oades, and Caputi (2003) assert that there is a five-stage model to recovery that can be useful for consumers and clinicians in trying to assess outcomes of the recovery method. This model was created by the researchers' exhaustive review of various studies and the literature concerning the Recovery Movement. The stages are (1) moratorium, (2) awareness, (3) preparation, (4) rebuilding, and (5) growth. The moratorium stage is when a consumer is in denial about his or her mental illness or is confused about what to do about it or how to assist in his or her own treatment. This is a familiar stage for anyone trapped inside the mental health "closet"—like Frese before he made his own illness public.

Awareness is characterized by self-reflection and hope, including hope in a possible recovery or in better management of symptoms. This stage is critical for someone needing to know and trust that recovery is possible. Preparation, the third stage, involves a commitment on the part of the consumer to begin working on his or her recovery process, to go to group meetings, to undertake skill building, and to learn about his or her personal strengths and weaknesses. Rebuilding is the stage that involves working toward set goals; it involves the consumer taking responsibility for the costs and benefits (in all senses) of the recovery process. In this fourth stage comes the inevitable rebuilding of one's identity. (Frese, for example, had to transition from viewing himself as an indestructible marine, to a man with an "incurable" mental illness, to a PhD with enormous capacity for growth and self-sufficiency.) The final, growth stage is the outcome of recovery according to Andresen et al. In this stage an individual can manage his or her symptoms even in the face of setbacks and can lead a meaningful and positive life. By then the person has made many overall improvements, including a greater sense of generativity, or looking toward and planning for the future.

Conclusion

The Recovery Movement cannot legitimately be regarded as a fad. In no other time in history have consumers played such an important role in their own recovery (Jacobson 2000). The recovery method has given birth to innovation within mental health care by allowing experiential evidence and consumer feedback to become valid forms of treatment review and measures of progress. Many states are developing recovery curriculums, conducting trainings, and holding state, regional, and national conferences on recovery (Jacobson 2000). Along with recovery-oriented education and training, agencies are adopting consumer-run services, relapse and prevention management, and crisis planning.

More empirical studies need to be done to broaden the body of knowledge and efficacy of the Recovery Movement. But it appears that the widespread adoption of a recovery-oriented paradigm is enduring and will offer consumers increasingly broad-based and diverse services (Roberts & Wolfson 2004). There is a growing recognition in the mainstream of psychiatry, too, that medical professionals need to move away from stigmatizing labels and to respect and empower consumers by treating them as people who live a life well beyond the confines of their illnesses.

See also Advocacy Groups; Chronic Mental Illness; Disability Rights; Medical Model of Psychiatric Illness; Mental Health Advocacy; Neurodiversity; Peer Support Groups; Rehabilitation Services; Stigma

Bibliography

American Psychiatric Association. 2000. *Diagnostic and Statistical Manual of Mental Disorders* (4th ed., text rev.). Washington, DC: American Psychiatric Publishing.

Amering, M., and M. Schmolke. 2009. *The Recovery Movement in Mental Health: Reshaping Scientific and Clinical Responsibilities.* Hoboken, NJ: Wiley-Blackwell.

Andresen, R., L. Oades, and P. Caputi. 2003. "The Experience of Recovery from Schizophrenia: Towards an Empirically-Validated Stage Model." *Australian and New Zealand Journal of Psychiatry* 37: 586–594.

Byrne, P. 2000. "Stigma of Mental Illness and Ways of Diminishing It." *Advances in Psychiatric Treatment* 6: 65–72.

Carpenter, J. 2002. "Mental Health Recovery Paradigm: Implications for Social Work." *Health and Social Work* 27(2): 86–94.

Davidson, L., M. O'Connell, J. Tondora, T. Styron, and K. Kangas. 2006. "The Top Ten Concerns about Recovery Encountered in Mental Health System Transformation." *Psychiatric Services* 57: 640–645.

Davidson, L., and W. White. 2007. "The Concept of Recovery as an Organizing Principle for Integrating Mental Health and Addiction Services." *Journal of Behavioral Health Services and Research* 3(2): 109–120.

Frese, F., J. Stanley, K. Kress, and S. Vogel-Scibilia. 2001. "Integrating Evidence-Based Practices and the Recovery Model." *Psychiatric Services* 52: 1462–1468.

Glynn, S. 2004. "The Potential Impact of the Recovery Movement on Family Interventions for Schizophrenia: Opportunities and Obstacles." *Schizophrenia Bulletin* 32(3): 451–463.

Harding, C., and J. H. Zahniser. 1994. "Empirical Correction of Seven Myths About Schizophrenia with Implications for Treatment," *ACTA Psyciatrica Scandinava* 90 (suppl 384): 140–146.

Jacobson, N. 2000. "Recovery as Policy in Mental Health Services: Strategies Emerging from the States." *Psychosocial Rehabilitation Journal* 23: 333–341.

Kelly, M., and C. Gamble. 2005. "Exploring the Concept of Recovery in Schizophrenia." *Journal of Psychiatric and Mental Health Nursing* 12: 245–251.

Resnick, S., and R. Rosenheck. 2006. "Recovery and Positive Psychology: Parallel Themes and Potential Synergies." *Psychiatric Services* 57: 120–122.

Resnick, S., R. Rosenheck, and A. Lehman. 2004. "An Exploratory Analysis of Correlates of Recovery." *Psychiatric Services* 55: 540–547.

Roberts, G., and P. Wolfson. 2004. "The Rediscovery of Recovery: Open to All." *Advances in Psychiatric Treatment* 10: 37–48.

Schiff, A. 2004. "Recovery and Mental Illness: Analysis and Personal Reflections." *Psychiatric Rehabilitation Journal* 27: 212–218.

Travis, T. 2009. *The Language of the Heart: A Cultural History of the Recovery Movement*. Chapel Hill: University of North Carolina Press.

Wahl, O. F. 1999. "Mental Health Consumers' Experience of Stigma." *Schizophrenia Bulletin* 25: 467–478.

Rehabilitation Services

Lauren Mizock

Psychiatric rehabilitation was conceived in the 1970s and grew as a field in the 1990s (Anthony et al. 2002). The mission of psychiatric rehabilitation is to help people with ongoing psychiatric disabilities increase functioning in their lives with the least professional intervention possible (Farkas & Anthony 1989, 2009). The rehabilitation model developed out of a need for psychiatric disability services that was not focused solely on medication and therapy but on social role functioning in educational, vocational, social, and residential contexts (Pratt et al. 2002).

Psychiatric rehabilitation involves developing skills, strengths, and supports to maximize life satisfaction (Livneh 1984). The focus of this approach is dissimilar to other common modalities such as traditional mental health treatment, which targets symptom relief, or strengths-based case management, which provides resource access (Brun & Rapp 2001). Central assumptions of this model are that rehabilitation can happen without symptom reduction, and role functioning may be as important as symptom eradication for many individuals with psychiatric disabilities (Anthony 2009).

A psychiatric disability is defined as a severe disability from a mental illness and related impairment in functioning (National Institute of Mental Health

[NIMH] 1980). This term has been used to replace labels with more pessimistic connotations such as chronic mental illness (Anthony et al. 2002). A psychiatric disability includes a mental, behavioral, or emotional disorder that results in impairment in at least two areas of functioning in major life activities such as activities of daily living, work, education, social interaction, and finances (NIMH 2008). NIMH has estimated that up to 4.4 percent of the U.S. adult population are affected by mental illnesses or psychiatric disabilities.

Philosophy

Core principles of rehabilitation for individuals with psychiatric disabilities can be delineated (Anthony et al. 2002). Such principles include a focus on improving competencies and abilities, with behavioral improvements taking place in the environment of need (e.g., at home, at school). Rehabilitation seeks to avoid dependence and enable independence from professional involvement. Skills and supports are developed as well as improvements in residential, educational, and vocational outcomes. Active participation and involvement of individuals in the rehabilitation process are facilitated. In contrast to many traditional mental health approaches, long-term drug treatment is seen as a resource that may be needed but is insufficient by itself. Rehabilitation practitioners are encouraged to utilize an eclectic assortment of techniques with a central focus on hope. These principles set basic standards for practitioners in the provision of rehabilitation services.

A number of key rehabilitation values have been identified to guide practitioners in providing rehabilitation-oriented services (Farkas, Anthony, & Cohen 1989). The value of *person orientation* focuses the practitioner on the person as opposed to diagnostic labels. *Functioning* places weight on the person's ability to participate in daily life and roles. *Support* specifies that assistance be made available for as long as needed. *Environmental specificity* directs attention to functioning in the specific daily contexts relevant to the individual. *Involvement* is a value in working collaboratively to integrate the individual's interests and needs in the rehabilitation process. *Choice* emphasizes the preferences of the individual. The value of *outcome orientation* focuses rehabilitation on attaining the individual's goals. Lastly, *growth potential* highlights the individual's potential positive outcome regardless of current challenges. These values are important for providers in maintaining services that fit a rehabilitation model of care.

Psychiatric Rehabilitation and Recovery

The field of psychiatric rehabilitation services has embraced the philosophy of the recovery movement in psychiatric disability (Gagne, White, & Anthony 2007). In this context, recovery does not signify an outcome of symptom elimination but rather refers to a *process* of living a satisfying life of well-being and autonomy (Davidson et al. 2009). Recovery can be supported in rehabilitation

A rehabilitation services coordinator (seated, in background) helps a client with medications he is taking for schizophrenia and bipolar disorder. (AP Photo/M. Spencer Green.)

settings with nonlinear, fail-proof designs that allow multiple points of entry (Deegan 1988).

Psychiatric rehabilitation shares many beliefs and values of the recovery movement and has actively integrated additional recovery principles (Anthony et al. 2002). For example, the recovery movement and psychiatric rehabilitation both see recovery as possible without professional intervention and regardless of how one understands the cause of one's illness. In addition, both believe recovery can happen despite symptoms, although they may diminish in frequency and severity. However, recovery from symptoms and deficits does not signify that one did not have a mental illness to begin with. Recovering from the consequences of the illness is often considered to be more difficult than the experience of the illness itself. Moreover, recovery may not be linear but may include many stops and starts, steps forward as well as steps back (Deegan 1988).

History

In 1972, William A. Anthony and colleagues coined the term "psychiatric rehabilitation" in the seminal article, "Efficacy of Psychiatric Rehabilitation"

(Anthony et al. 1972; Livneh 1984). Psychiatric rehabilitation was popularized in the 1990s after a transition period in the 1980s following deinstitutionalization (Anthony et al. 2002). The deinstitutionalization process began in the 1960s and continued into the 1970s, involving community release of individuals with psychiatric disabilities from their confinement in mental institutions (Pratt et al. 2002).

The ex-patient movement was also important in shaping the mission of rehabilitation and recovery (Chamberlin 1990). The ex-patients' liberation movement had formative years in the 1970s and 1980s, with associated advances dating as far back as the late 1800s. The goals and philosophy of mental patients' liberation emphasized leadership of mental health consumers in reaction to injustices faced in the mental health system at the hands of professionals.

In 1974, the International Association of Psychosocial Rehabilitation Services (IAPSRS) was founded by the leaders of the 13 psychiatric rehabilitation centers in practice at that time (United States Psychiatric Rehabilitation Association [USPRA] n.d.). In 2004, the organization changed names to the United States Psychiatric Rehabilitation Association (USPRA). There are currently 12 states that recognize the Certified Psychiatric Rehabilitation Practitioner certification for mental health providers and over 1,400 members of USPRA.

Intervention Process

The intervention process is divided into five phases, each with a focus on developing individual skills and environmental supports along with a focus on process (Anthony 2003; Anthony et al. 2002). The first phase is *diagnosing and assessing*. In this phase, the practitioner works with the individual to assess and develop rehabilitation readiness, goals, skills, and resources. The latter (resources) may include, for example, a house counselor, food stamps, or a psychosocial club (support group) (Cohen et al. 2010). The diagnostic phase in rehabilitation planning is not concerned with assigning a traditional diagnostic label but rather with conducting an assessment in the context of a specific goal that the individual has identified (Livneh 1984). The diagnosing and assessing phase ensures that rehabilitation planning is tailored to the individual's specific goals and environment.

Goal setting is a primary component of the diagnosing and assessing phase of the intervention, involving multiple steps (Cohen et al. 1991). First, practitioners make a connection with a client by eliciting inspiration and communicating understanding. Practitioners identify personal criteria for a goal based on the individual's experiences and values. Lastly, alternative environments for a goal are identified and the goal is selected, with an outline of the criteria needed for meeting the goal.

The second phase of the psychiatric rehabilitation intervention process is *planning* (Anthony et al. 2002). During this phase, there is a focus on planning for skills and resource development by establishing priorities, objectives, and interventions. Skills may include expressing feelings and opinions, planning, goal setting, problem solving, tracking spending, monitoring prescribed medication, and monitoring symptoms (Cohen et al. 2010; Livneh 1984).

The third phase is *intervening* (Anthony et al. 2002). During this phase, practitioners develop skills in the individual and supports in the community. This phase may include teaching skills, identifying barriers, and supporting the individual's actions as well as coordinating and tailoring the individual's access to resources. Family and other important contacts are involved in this phase to increase support.

Practitioners can facilitate the rehabilitation process by using a variety of technology and assessments that are applicable across a range of contexts (Cohen et al. 1990). This technology has been developed by psychiatric rehabilitation centers based on decades of research. Some examples include technology to facilitate goal setting, planning, skill development, and resource coordination as well as functioning and resource assessments (Anthony et al. 2002).

The overall success of a rehabilitation intervention is measured by the client's reported benefits, demonstrated involvement, and skill enhancement (Livneh 1984). These benefits must be focused within the individual's target goals to ensure that they are being met (Anthony 1982). The rehabilitation intervention focuses on the process of attaining the individual's goals in order to maximize client satisfaction and success.

Programs and Practitioners

The strength of the relationship between the practitioner and recipient has been identified as one of the most important parts of rehabilitation (Goering & Stylianos 1988; Neale & Rosenheck 1995). The title, credentials, and specific role of the rehabilitation practitioner are less relevant than relationships created by practitioners and within rehabilitation programs (Anthony et al. 2002). In addition, the skills of the practitioner are essential. These skills may include a range of abilities in assessing, planning, collaborating, and resource accessing.

Rehabilitation programs should be focused on process as opposed to structure, with a consistent mission of rehabilitation implemented throughout the program (Cohen et al. 2010). The rehabilitation context includes cultural, organizational, and administrative practices that reflect values placed on functioning and support of the individual as well as skill development. Rehabilitation programs may include a grouping of residential, educational, vocational, or social networks. In addition, client services may include treatment, crisis intervention, case management, rehabilitation (skills and supports development), enrichment activities, rights protection, basic support, self-help, and peer support (Davidson et al. 2006).

Aside from the psychiatric rehabilitation centers affiliated through USPRA, there are a range of program models that take a psychiatric rehabilitation approach with varying focuses in goals related to treatment, work, and education. One example of a rehabilitation program is the assertive community treatment (ACT) program model. ACT teams provide services to support individuals with mental illness living satisfying lives in the community, provided by multidisciplinary team who empower individuals in meeting a range of needs (Salyers & Tsemberis 2007).

Another rehabilitation program approach is the choose-get-keep (CGK) model (Rogers, Anthony, & Farkas 2006). This model utilizes Boston University-developed technology that facilitates activities that encourage engagement and collaboration of individuals in recovery. CGK programs include individually tailored assessments, planning, and interventions that foster achievement of personalized rehabilitation goals. These programs may be focused on accessing housing, employment, or education.

Several rehabilitation programs have been developed to provide employment support. The individual placement and support (IPS) model is an example of a rehabilitation-oriented program with an employment focus. The goal of IPS is for employment specialists to provide vocational services by working on an interdisciplinary team of clinicians (Drake et al. 1999). IPS emphasizes the importance of competitive employment as a goal, a quick job search, self-determined job preferences, continuous assessment in a real work situation, and time-unlimited support (Bond 2004). In addition, the supported employment model is another rehabilitation program approach with a vocational focus. The supported employment model was originally developed for people with development disabilities and has been used in the field of psychiatric rehabilitation with a focus on competitive employment and time-unlimited support (Drake et al. 1999). In sum, ACT, CGK, IPS, and supported employment are just a few of the programs that fall within the psychiatric rehabilitation model.

Future Possibilities

The field of psychiatric rehabilitation has grown considerably since its inception in the 1970s. A vision for the future can continue to promote a focus on improving life satisfaction and role functioning for individuals with psychiatric disabilities. Anthony, Cohen, Farkas, and Gagne (2002) have identified a number of goals for future rehabilitation services as provided to individuals with psychiatric disabilities. For one, there is the goal to have mental health systems focus holistically on the person and her or his strengths, not on diagnostic labels. In addition, peers would be well represented among practitioners. Practitioners would come to see people as partners in their care and focus on their skills, not their credentials. In addition, new programs would continue to be developed in educational, social functioning, and vocational areas (Anthony, Cohen, & Farkas 1990). Achieving a vision of recovery would require more comprehensive implementation of psychiatric rehabilitation with the goal of helping people to enjoy ongoing successes and satisfactions within their communities (Farkas & Anthony, 2009). A future vision for psychiatric rehabilitation must be based on consumer input if it is to fit closely with the needs and goals of individual in recovery (Anthony 1993).

Research is an important component of the future of psychiatric rehabilitation. There is a large degree of evidence supporting psychiatric rehabilitation and a need for evidence-based practices that do not overly rely on randomized trials, fail to establish effectiveness for diverse populations, or focus exclusively on program structure rather than on process (Solomon & Stanhope 2004). Research is needed that integrates a recovery- and consumer-centered approach with empirical study. Key components in this respect include the services chosen for study, the methods employed, and outcomes focused on quality of life and psychosocial functioning, not just on symptom reduction.

Conclusion

Psychiatric rehabilitation is a model of services for individuals with psychiatric disabilities that focuses on enhancement of supports and skills with the least "invasive" professional intervention possible. Psychiatric rehabilitation developed out of a need for a new model of services for individuals with psychiatric disabilities that did not concentrate solely on symptom reduction, medication, and mental health treatment. In addition, the focus of rehabilitation services is on process and skills, not specific program structure or practitioner credentials. A large number of research developments and programs continue to implement a rehabilitation model of care for individuals with psychiatric disabilities in order to enhance support, empowerment, and life satisfaction.

See also Chronic Mental Illness; Community Mental Health; Disability Rights; Recovery Movement

Bibliography

Anthony, William A. 1982. "Explaining 'Psychiatric Rehabilitation' by an Analogy to 'Physical Rehabilitation.' " *Psychosocial Rehabilitation Journal* 5: 61–65.

Anthony, William A. 1993. "Recovery from Mental Illness: The Guiding Vision of the Mental Health Service System in the 1990s." *Psychosocial Rehabilitation Journal* 16: 11–23.

Anthony, William, A. 2003. "Studying Evidence-Based Processes, Not Practices." *Psychiatric Services* 54: 7.

Anthony, William, A. 2009. "Psychiatric Rehabilitation: A Key to Prevention." *Psychiatric Services* 60: 3.

Anthony, William A., Gregory J. Buell, Sara S. Sharratt, and Michael E. Althoff. 1972. "Efficacy of Psychiatric Rehabilitation." *Psychological Bulletin* 78: 447–456.

Anthony, William A., Mikal Cohen, and Marianne Farkas. 1990. *Psychiatric Rehabilitation*. Boston: Boston University, Center for Psychiatric Rehabilitation.

Anthony, William A., Mikal Cohen, Marianne Farkas, and Cheryl Gagne. 2002. *Psychiatric Rehabilitation*. Boston: Boston University, Center for Psychiatric Rehabilitation.

Anthony, William A., and Marianne Farkas. 2009. *Primer on the Psychiatric Rehabilitation Process*. Boston: Boston University Center for Psychiatric Rehabilitation.

Bond, Gary R. 2004. "Supported Employment: Evidence for an Evidence-Based Practice." *Psychiatric Rehabilitation Journal* 27: 345–359.

Brun, Carl, and Richard C. Rapp. 2001. "Strengths-Based Case Management: Individuals' Perspectives on Strengths and the Case Manager Relationship." *Social Work* 46: 278–288.

Chamberlin, Judy. 1990. "The Ex-Patients' Movement: Were We've Been and Where We're Going." National Empowerment Center Articles. Retrieved from http://www.Power2u.org.

Cohen, Mikal, Marianne Farkas, Barry Cohen, and Karen Unger. 1991. *Psychiatric Rehabilitation Training Technology: Functional Assessment (Trainer Package)*. Boston: Boston University, Center for Psychiatric Rehabilitation.

Cohen, Mikal, Pat Nemec, Marianne Farkas, and Rick Forbess. 2010. *Psychiatric Rehabilitation Training Technology: Case Management (Trainer Package), Revised Format*. Boston: Boston University, Center for Psychiatric Rehabilitation.

Davidson, Larry, Matthew J. Chinman, David Sells, D., and Michael Rowe. 2006. "Peer Support among Adults with Serious Mental Illness: A Report from the Field." *Schizophrenia Bulletin* 32: 443–450.

Davidson, Larry, Robert E. Drake, Timothy Schmutte, Thomas Dinzeo, and Raquel Andres-Hyman. 2009. "Oil and Water or Oil and Vinegar? Evidence-Based Medicine Meets Recovery." *Community Mental Health Journal* 45: 323–332.

Deegan, Patricia E. 1988. "Recovery: The Lived Experience of Rehabilitation." *Psychosocial Rehabilitation Journal* 11: 11–19.

Drake, Robert E., Deborah R. Becker, Robin E. Clark, and Kim T. Mueser. 1999. "Research on the Individual Placement and Support Model of Supported Employment." *Psychiatric Quarterly* 70: 289–301.

Farkas, Marianne, and William A. Anthony. 1989. *Psychiatric Rehabilitation Programs: Putting Theory into Practice*. Baltimore: Johns Hopkins University Press.

Farkas, Marianne, William A. Anthony, and Mikal Cohen. 1989. "An Overview of Psychiatric Rehabilitation: The Approach and Its Programs." In Marianne Farkas and William A. Anthony, eds., *Psychiatric Programs: Putting Theory into Practice* (pp. 13–16). Baltimore: Johns Hopkins University Press.

Gagne, Cheryl, William White, and William A. Anthony. 2007. "Recovery: A Common Vision for the Fields of Mental Health and Addictions." *Psychiatric Rehabilitation Journal* 31: 32–37.

Goering, Paula M., and Stanley K. Stylianos. 1988. "Exploring the Helping Relationship between the Schizophrenic Client and Rehabilitation Therapist." *American Journal of Orthopsychiatry* 58: 271–280.

Livneh, Hanoch. 1984. "Psychiatric Rehabilitation: A Dialogue with Bill Anthony." *Journal of Counseling and Development* 63: 86–90.

National Institute of Mental Health. "Prevalence of Serious Mental Illness among U.S. Adults by Age, Sex, and Race." Retrieved from http://www.nimh.nih.gov/statistics/SMI_AASR.shtml.

Neale, Michael, and Robert A. Rosenheck. 1995. "Therapeutic Alliance and Outcome in a VA Intensive Case Management Program." *Psychiatric Services* 46: 719–721.

Neale, Michael S., and Robert A. Rosenheck. 2000. "Therapeutic Limit Setting in an Assertive Community Treatment Program." *Psychiatric Services* 51: 499–505.

Pratt, Carlos W., Kenneth J. Gill, Nora M. Barrett, and Melissa M. Roberts. 2002. *Psychiatric Rehabilitation*. San Diego, CA: Academic Press.

Rogers, E. Sally, William A. Anthony, and Marianne Farkas. 2006. "The Choose-Get-Keep Model of Psychiatric Rehabilitation: A Synopsis of Recent Studies." *Rehabilitation Psychology* 51: 247–256

Salyers, Melissa P., and Sam Tsemberis. 2007. "ACT and Recovery: Integrating Evidence-Based Practice and Recovery Orientation on Assertive Community Treatment Teams." *Community Mental Health Journal* 43: 619–641.

Solomon, Phyllis, and Victoria Stanhope. 2004. "Recovery: Expanding the Vision of Evidence-Based Practice." *Brief Treatment and Crisis Intervention* (2004): 311–321.

United States Psychiatric Rehabilitation Association (USPRA). "Our History." Retrieved from http://www.uspra.org.

Religion, Spirituality, and Mental Health

Annemarie Gockel

Since the earliest times, religion has been viewed both as a primary source of madness and as a potential provider of its cure. Tribal shamans with the ability to interpret the spirit world were the first source of healing for people with mental illness, and modern-day spiritual healers continue to play a key curative role in folk traditions in the United States and around the world (Koenig 2005). As the influence of shamans gave way to priests and pastors in the Western world through the Middle Ages, demonic possession became a popular theory about the origins of mental illness, and exorcism remained a key strategy for attempting a cure well into the eighteenth century. Despite the ostracism of the mentally ill that these ideas spurred, religious communities were also the first to provide compassionate care, founding hospitals and asylums and organizing outreach efforts to address the physical, mental, and spiritual needs of those experiencing mental illness in the community (Koenig 2005). With the rise of modern science in the nineteenth century, along with psychoanalysis in the early part of the twentieth century, religion was increasingly dismissed as a source of superstition and a likely cause of disorder. As a consequence, mental health treatment became the province of the medical and psychological establishment. Although many dramatic advances have since been made in the biological and psychological treatment of mental disorders, the question of whether religion and spirituality is helpful or harmful to mental health remains a key controversial issue.

Distinctions between Religion and Spirituality

Definitions of religion and spirituality abound, and there is scant agreement on the precise meaning of spirituality in particular. Traditionally considered to be the "heart and soul" of religion, spirituality has more recently emerged as a construct in its own right (Zinnbauer & Pargament 2005, 36). Scholars following popular trends in the shifting meaning of these terms agree that spirituality is increasingly being used to denote a personal, individual experience of the sacred and one's relationship to it, while religion implies participation in a formal religious institution, with elaborated beliefs, rituals, and practices shared by a community of the faithful. Although spirituality is increasingly being practiced outside of as well as within a religious context, the vast majority of Americans consider themselves to be both spiritual and religious and express their spirituality through an established faith tradition (Zinnbauer & Pargament 2005). According to recent national surveys, the United States is a particularly religious country: 92 percent of Americans believe in God, 84 percent claim a specific religious affiliation, 56 percent say religion is very important in their lives, 58 percent pray daily, and 54 percent attend religious services regularly (Pew Forum on Religion & Public Life 2008). Certainly, the overwhelming majority of the existing research examines spirituality as it is expressed within a religious context. The present entry will therefore also focus on religion and include spirituality primarily as it is expressed with a religious context.

Connecting Religion and Mental Health

Religion has been convincingly connected to a wide variety of indicators of mental health. In a comprehensive review of 100 studies conducted prior to 2000, Koenig (2005) found that almost 80 percent of studies linked religious involvement to greater well-being, increased happiness, higher levels of life satisfaction, and better mood. Religion has not only a direct effect on mental well-being but also an indirect effect. One of the ways that religion is believed to increase mental health is through generating positive emotions. Indeed, religious involvement has been associated with greater levels of optimism, hope, gratitude, altruism, forgiveness, and purpose in life; and many of these positive feelings and states have in turn been linked to lower levels of depression, anxiety, and substance use and to increased happiness, vitality, and life satisfaction (Koenig 2005).

The role of religion may be particularly important to mental health in immigrant or minority communities, where there are fewer external resources and community members may have a reluctance to engage with mainstream mental health services (Miller & Kelley 2005; Pargament 2002), often as the result of previous experiences of oppression. Researchers have shown that Hispanic patients facing a health crisis experienced a greater need for spiritual support than did Caucasians, while African American patients were three times more likely than their Caucasian counterparts to rate spirituality as very important to depression care (Koenig 2005). Religious beliefs and involvement may help to maintain a solid sense of identity in the face of oppression as well as preserve cultural and community ties that would otherwise be lost or eroded. Religious communities can also act as an alternative social support network, and social support has been identified as another central mechanism by which religion may positively impact mental health. Religious social support may be more enduring than secular support and has been shown to predict gains in mental health over and above those accounted for by secular social support, particularly in minority communities (Koenig 2005).

Religion has also been identified as a key factor in preventing mental illness. The vast majority of existing studies on religion and mental health are correlational in nature. These studies overwhelmingly demonstrate that religious involvement is linked to lower levels of depression and anxiety and to lower levels of suicidality among adults and adolescents alike (Koenig 2005; Larson & Larson 2003). Religion is not only a significant factor in protecting against internalizing disorders such as anxiety and depression,; it has also been associated with a lower incidence of externalizing disorders such as substance abuse and behavioral problems. Adults and adolescents who attend services and rate religion as important in their lives are much less likely to suffer from alcohol or drug abuse (Koenig 2005; Larson & Larson 2003). Religious adolescents are less likely to be involved in delinquent and criminal behavior, ranging from truancy and theft to interpersonal violence (Smith & Faris 2002). Religious involvement further appears to contribute to positive health and social behaviors such as reduced alcohol and drug consumption, increased exercise, sleep, healthy eating, and volunteerism, which may be another route to religion's positive effect on mental health (Larson & Larson 2003; Smith & Faris 2002).

Religion may also spur recovery for those actively struggling with mental disorders. Although religious belief has historically been hypothesized to provoke mental illness in those who are vulnerable, this idea may be an artifact of the tendency for people struggling with mental disorders to turn to religion for help in coping. Religion is a primary means of coping for those facing stressful life circumstances, including mental illness, as well as challenges that can precipitate mental health crises such as major life losses, traumatic experiences, and serious physical illness or disability. Religious coping is another possible pathway connecting religious involvement with improved mental health in these circumstances. Recent studies indicate that 80 percent or more of psychiatric patients claim spiritual needs and draw on religion to manage their symptoms, while 48 percent reported that religion increased in importance at times when their symptoms grew more severe (Larson & Larson 2003). Time spent in positive religious coping activities that include collaborating with God to address a problem, drawing on religion to reframe negative events in a positive way, and relying on spiritual support from God, one's clergy, or a congregation member has consistently been related to better mental health and psychosocial adjustment (Pargament, Ano, & Wachholtz 2005). Religious coping among psychiatric patients in particular is associated with lower levels of psychoticism, obsessive compulsiveness, paranoia, anxiety, and interpersonal sensitivity, as well as better overall functioning and shorter hospital stays (Larson & Larson 2003). Although most correlational studies show positive associations between religion and mental health, correlational studies are limited because they can describe the relationship between religion and mental health only at a particular point in time and cannot assess whether becoming religious improves mental health, or better mental health leads to increased religiosity.

Longitudinal studies can further clarify the relationship between religion, spirituality, and mental health by identifying whether religious involvement predicts better or worsened mental health over time. The preponderance of existing longitudinal studies confirm that as people become more involved with religion, their mental health tends to improve and their ability to function more effectively increases. In a 29-year study, Strawbridge, Shema, Cohen, and Kaplan (2001) found that religious service attendance was related to positive changes in mental and physical health behaviors. Frequent service attendees who were single, isolated, and depressed at the start of the study were more likely than those who attended less frequently to have strengthened their interpersonal support network, reduced heavy alcohol consumption, recovered from depression, and developed stable marriages over the duration of the study. Studies of religious coping among the mentally ill further support the idea that religious involvement increases stability and fosters better functioning, even among the highest-risk populations. Koenig (2005) reviewed a prospective study examining predictors for hospital readmission among homeless veterans with co-occurring mental health and substance use disorders. He found that veterans who scored high in religiosity at baseline were readmitted to hospital one-third less of the time during the two-year follow-up period.

Clinical trials offer some of the strongest evidence regarding the effects of religion and spirituality on mental health because they provide a means of assessing the causal impact of religious interventions. Currently, only a small number of randomized trials have been conducted comparing the effects of religiously infused cognitive-behavioral therapy (CBT) or rational-emotive therapy (RET) with standard secular CBT/RET treatments and waitlist controls for religious clients. Religiously oriented CBT/RET incorporated religious imagery, scriptural readings, and Christian theological references. In reviewing these studies and a meta-analysis of their findings, Worthington and Sandage (2001) concluded that religiously oriented CBT/RET was as effective as secular treatment in reducing depression, and indicated that clients in the religious CBT treatment group showed greater gains in spiritual well-being (Worthington & Sandage 2001). Clients in the religiously oriented condition also appeared to recover faster than clients in the secular treatment condition (Koenig 2005). Similarly, when researchers reviewed studies comparing the benefits of adding a religious intervention that involved prayer, reading from the Qur'an, and discussing relevant religious issues to standard secular treatments (supportive psychotherapy plus medication) for Muslim clients with dysthymia, depression, and anxiety, they found that participation in the additional religious treatment alleviated symptoms over and above the gains made with treatment as usual in all three studies (Worthington & Sandage 2001). Far from inclining one to disorder, then, the results of clinical trials indicate that adding a spiritual element to secular interventions may actually facilitate the mental health recovery process for religiously committed clients.

Discrepant Findings

Despite the preponderance of correlational, longitudinal, and experimental evidence testifying to the salutary effects of religion on mental health, positive findings are not universal. Koenig (2005) estimates that 6 percent of the studies prior to 2000 actually showed a negative association between religion and mental health, not to mention the substantial portion of studies that failed to find a significant relationship or that uncovered mixed effects. There are a variety of reasons for this discrepancy. Religion is a complex phenomenon and different aspects of religiosity may have different and even contradictory effects. For example, a wide variety of studies have demonstrated that intrinsic religiosity, which reflects a sincere engagement in religion for its own sake, is related to improved coping, more prosocial behavior, and higher levels of well-being. By contrast, extrinsic religiosity, whereby religion is used as a means to achieve another goal such as enhanced social status, has instead been related to poorer coping, more antisocial behavior, and greater psychological distress (Miller & Kelley 2005). Because studies have historically measured only one or two of the many facets of religion at a time, contradictory findings may result from differing relationships between different aspects of religion and mental health (Hackney & Sanders 2003). Similarly, measures of mental health vary from measures of mental distress, to general indicators of life satisfaction and well-being, to measures of superior functioning. Religion may have a unique relationship to each type of indicator (Hackney & Sanders 2003). Earlier studies, which more frequently found a negative relationship between religion and mental health, often failed to control for other relevant variables in the relationship such as gender, race, or socioeconomic status (Koenig 2005). Thus we find growing evidence of a positive association between religion and mental health in later correlational studies with better controls, or in stronger research designs such as longitudinal studies and clinical trials.

The effects of any form of religion can also vary significantly by context and population. Religious coping seems to be most effective when people face acute and extreme stressors that take them to the limits of their normal coping resources. For example, Maton (1989) found that spiritual support played a greater role in mitigating against depression among parents who had recently lost a child compared to parents who had suffered a prior loss. Effects also vary across denominational lines. Some studies have found that Protestants benefit from religious coping more than Catholics (Pargament, Ano, & Wachholtz 2005). Religious expression also changes over the life course, and different aspects of religiosity may be particularly salient at different points in time. Parental religiosity and being socialized within a religious tradition are key protective factors during childhood, while receiving support from peers who share the same faith and finding one's own internal sense of conviction are more critical to creating positive mental health for adolescents (Miller & Kelley 2005). In general, stronger positive correlations between religion and mental health are found when using proximal measures that reflect one's internalization of religion such as measures of personal devotion, closeness to God, or the subjective importance of religion than when using distal measures of religion such as church attendance or affiliation, which can reflect either intrinsic or extrinsic religious motivations (Hackney & Sanders 2003; Pargament 2002).

Finally, discrepant findings also reflect the fact that certain forms of religion and spirituality can indeed have a negative impact on particular populations at specific times. The negative effects of religion on mental health have been identified in a number of studies. Religious people who are not adhering to the guidelines of their religious tradition have been shown to exhibit poorer mental health (Koenig 2005). Similarly, when people struggle with achieving religious goals such as family harmony, the emphasis placed on these goals by their religious tradition may increase their level of distress (Koenig 2005). People who use negative forms of religious coping such as becoming angry with God or interpreting a life catastrophe as a punishment for sin are much more likely to experience psychological distress and poorer mental and even physical health (Pargament 2002). Although people tend to draw more frequently on positive religious coping strategies (Koenig 2005), spiritual distress, when it occurs, can have a serious impact on mental health and may signal the need for a spiritual or religious intervention to restore well-being and promote adjustment.

Conclusion

There are no simple answers to the question of whether religion and spirituality help or hinder mental health. Rather, the question itself should be revised to ask which forms of religion have what effects on which aspects of mental health, for whom, and in what context? Religion is a complex, multidimensional phenomenon. What is remarkable, given its complexity, is that the vast majority of the hundreds of existing studies in the area offer evidence of multiple positive relationships between various facets of religion and better mental health, lower levels of mental disorder, and more frequent mental health recovery. As future studies grow in sophistication and integrate multidimensional measures of religion, it may become increasingly possible to explain current contradictions in the relationship between religion and mental health. Religion may foster better mental health for the majority of Americans who belong to a faith tradition through promoting positive emotions, fostering social support, encouraging positive health behaviors, and providing an effective means of coping with life's stressors. However, many scholars argue that effects of spirituality and religion cannot be reduced to these intermediary mechanisms alone, but posit a fifth super-empirical factor that, while challenging to measure, represents the impact of religion itself on mental health (Oman & Thoresen 2005). Although a number of preliminary pathways have been identified to explain the effect of religion on mental health, the field awaits a unifying theory that brings the variety of existing hypotheses together with empirical evidence to convincingly explain exactly how religion may be harnessed to promote mental health and well-being.

See also Culturally Competent Mental Health Care; Humanistic Theories and Therapies; Loss and Grief; Mind and Body Approaches to Mental Health

Bibliography

George Washington Institute for Spirituality and Health. http://www.gwish.org/.

Hackney, Charles H., and Glenn S. Sanders. 2003. "Religiosity and Mental Health: A Meta–Analysis of Recent Studies." *Journal for the Scientific Study of Religion* 42(1): 43–55.

Koenig, Harold G. 2005. *Faith and Mental Health: Religious Resources for Healing.* West Conshohocken, PA: Templeton Foundation Press.

Larson, David B., and Susan S. Larson. 2003. "Spirituality's Potential Relevance to Physical and Emotional Health: A Brief Review of Quantitative Research." *Journal of Psychology and Theology* 31(1): 37–51.

Maton, Kenneth I. 1989. "The Stress-Buffering Role of Spiritual Support: Cross-Sectional and Prospective Investigations." *Journal for the Scientific Study of Religion* 28(3): 310–323.

Miller, Lisa, and Brien S. Kelley. 2005. "Relationships of Religiosity and Spirituality with Mental Health and Psychopathology." In Raymond F. Paloutzian and Crystal L. Park, eds., *Handbook of the Psychology of Religion and Spirituality* (pp. 459–478). New York: Guilford Press.

National Study of Youth and Religion. http://www.youthandreligion.org/.

Oman, Doug, and Carl E. Thoresen. 2005. "Do Religion and Spirituality Influence Health?" In Raymond F. Paloutzian and Crystal L. Park, eds., *Handbook of the Psychology of Religion and Spirituality.* New York: Guilford Press.

Pargament, Kenneth I. 2002. "The Bitter and the Sweet: An Evaluation of the Costs and Benefits of Religiousness." *Psychological Inquiry* 13(3): 168–181.

Pargament, Kenneth I., Gene G. Ano, and Amy B. Wachholtz. 2005. "The Religious Dimension of Coping: Advances in Theory, Research, and Practice." In Raymond F. Paloutzian and Crystal L. Park, eds., *Handbook of the Psychology of Religion and Spirituality* (pp. 479–495). New York: Guilford Press.

Pew Forum on Religion & Public Life. 2008. *U.S. Religious Landscape Survey: Diverse and Dynamic*. Washington, DC: Pew Research Center.

Smith, Christian, and Robert Faris. 2002. *Religion and American Adolescent Delinquency, Risk Behaviors and Constructive Social Activities: A Research Report of the National Study of Youth and Religion*. Chapel Hill: University of North Carolina.

Strawbridge, William J., Sarah J. Shema, Richard D. Cohen, and George A. Kaplan. 2001. "Religious Attendance Increases Survival by Improving and Maintaining Good Health Behaviors, Mental Health, and Social Relationships." *Annals of Behavioral Medicine* 23(1): 68–74.

Worthington, Everett L., Jr., and Steven J. Sandage. 2001. "Religion and Spirituality." *Psychotherapy* 38(4): 473–478.

Zinnbauer, Brian, J., and Kenneth I. Pargament. 2005. "Religiousness and Spirituality." In Raymond F. Paloutzian and Crystal L. Park, eds., *Handbook of the Psychology of Religion and Spirituality* (pp. 21–42). New York: Guilford Press.

Residential Treatment for Young People

Katherine Hejtmanek

Residential treatment is a specialized treatment method for young people requiring institutionalization for mental health issues. Over the last century the reasons for institutionalizing youth changed, as have the kinds of care they received. Despite some controversy, residential treatment remains a viable mental health treatment method in the United States. Each institutional setting varies in the details of its structure, staff membership, funding sources, diagnostic criteria of the youth who live there, and treatment models. However, one can establish a general framework that exemplifies residential treatment from various institutional settings and mental health treatments. This framework illustrates how residential treatment is an amalgamation of educational, psychological, social, and family-based programs designed to treat the entire client as well as his or her family. Contemporary research is being conducted on the outcomes of residential treatment as national agencies, scholars, and practitioners question the efficacy of the practice. Critical studies investigate the relationship between child mental health practice, specifically residential treatment, and social inequality in the United States.

History of Residential Treatment

The institutional precursors to residential treatment centers, including orphan asylums and reformatories, were first erected in the United States in the 1820s and a few decades following (Rothman 1971). While reformatories were constructed to house juvenile delinquents, a study in 1858 found that many were not criminals but rather "unfortunates," often the children of poor or socially marginalized parents (Ashby 1997; Courtney & Hughes-Heuring 2009; Rothman 1971). By 1910, over 1,000 child institutions were in operation in the United States and supported financially by state legislatures, city councils, and philanthropic charities (Courtney & Hughes-Heuring 2009). It was during this time that maltreated children were identified, thanks to the new American anticruelty movement, and sent to institutions for care (Courtney & Hughes-Heuring 2009).

Following the 1909 White House Conference on the Care of Dependent Children, a more robust Child Welfare League of America initiated a shift in the institutional settings. At this time, the institutions became more "home-like"; even the names of the institutions changed to "homes," and cottage living quarters were constructed. The first juvenile court was established in 1899 in an effort to separate children from adult criminal populations.

At this time, Christian doctrine was the underlying framework for these kinds of institutions. Creating and maintaining a child's healthy moral constitution was the focus of institutional life and informed the daily routine. Orphanage reformers of the day were concerned that the children living in institutions were not receiving adequate love and affection. It was for these reasons that many reformers pushed for foster care rather than institutional care, initiating the still current debate about effective treatment alternatives to institutional care (Magellan Health Services Children's Services Task Force 2010).

In 1935, the U.S. federal government created the Aid to Dependent Children as Title IV of the Social Security Act, and monetary aid was directly distributed to needy families rather than institutions (Courtney & Hughes-Heuring 2009). This change in legislation resulted in more children living in foster care or with families, and the need for institutions declined. Some institutions remained; however, their names changed to "residential treatment" and they were maintained for children with emotional, behavioral, or psychological disorders (Cotton 1993; Courtney & Hughes-Heuring 2009; Magellan Health Services Children's Services Task Force 2010). Following this shift, children living in institutions were not considered morally flawed as the Christian doctrine had once determined. Rather, these young people had mental health problems requiring therapeutic intervention; institutionalization became an intervention strategy called milieu therapy (see below).

Psychology as a framework for understanding human behavior was rapidly developing at this time, and new ways of understanding asocial behavior were shaping residential treatment practice. August Aichhorn and Anna Freud were two prominent psychologists investigating the benefits of a therapeutic milieu to help "troubled" children create more "adaptive" lives (Aichhorn 1955; Epstein

2005; Freud 1969). Aichhorn (1955) argued that reeducating young people who are mentally ill or delinquent requires a change in environment and institutionalization in new training schools. He argued that these children required love, tenderness, and daily conflict resolution to help treat their "neuroses" and that this treatment was best in an institutional setting. In 1969, Albert Trieschman, Larry Brendtro, and James Whittaker (1969) also argued that institutional living should not be limited to housing young people who receive some therapy. Instead, they argued that a milieu, a therapeutic tool in and of itself, helps treat mentally ill youth (see also Almond 1974; Bettelheim 1955; Bettelheim & Sylvester 1948; Caudill 1958; Noshpitz 1962). Although milieu therapy in residential treatment was becoming popular, not much research was being conducted on its efficacy (see final section, below).

In the 1970s, child and family advocates initiated the permanency planning movement, which sought to make every effort to assist families before removing children from the home (Courtney & Hughes-Heuring 2009). This movement was supported by Public Law 96-272 or the Adoption Assistance and Child Welfare Act of 1980. Following this movement, fewer children were being taken out of the home and placed in residential treatment. This focus on noninstitutional living for children was in tandem with the adult deinstitutionalization movement, in which large psychiatric hospitals were closed or reduced in size and their populations released to the community (Estroff 1981). However, residential treatment remained and today is a relatively robust method of treatment for thousands of young people each year in the United States.

Residential Treatment Today

Residential treatment is considered a milieu therapy with specialized mental health treatment and educational services.

According to the latest numbers collected and distributed in the Adoption and Foster Care Analysis and Reporting System (AFCARS) of the U.S. Department of Health and Human Services (2011), 9 percent of the 408,425 youth in the child welfare system, or roughly 37,000 children, are institutionalized. This number does not include those youth in residential treatment who are not part of the child welfare system (see Funding Sources section below). Unfortunately, demographic information is unknown with the exception of a number for those living in residential treatment. A centralized database that collects and records extensive demographic data on the youth institutionalized in the United States at the present time does not exist.

Despite limits in demographic information of children in residential treatment, residential treatment is considered the end of a long continuum of care for emotionally, behaviorally, and psychologically disordered young people (Foltz 2004). Therefore young people in residential treatment are considered severely behaviorally and emotionally disordered and require intensive, multidisciplinary intervention strategies to treat them (Foltz 2004).

The Structure of Residential Treatment

A milieu in this context is a living space or group home structure where clients live and follow a milieu program. The milieu program structures daily life and is often understood as the key piece of therapeutic management (Cotton 1993). The milieu is where the institutionalized youth spend much of their time, where psychological intervention strategies like behavior management and trauma processing are implemented, and where young people bond with the adults responsible for this kind of treatment. Using a behavior management approach, the program dictates the rules of behavior in the living space. It outlines incentives for positive behavior and consequences for negative behavior. Individuals working with young people in the milieu implement the program as means of therapeutic intervention, to teach young people better behaviors. The milieu is also a place where processing feelings or past traumas takes place (see specialized mental health treatment below), especially when negative behaviors occurring over the course of the day are thought to be symptoms of these past traumas. In addition to behavior management, skill-building activities (e.g., cooking, cleaning) are implemented in the milieu. Institutionalized young people build the strongest kin-like relationships with the adults who work in the milieu as part of their therapy.

In addition to milieu therapy, specialized mental health treatment includes individual therapy, group therapy, recreational therapy, family therapy, and other services. The focus in these therapy sessions is to process feelings and behaviors and to heal from past traumas. Children in residential treatment are required to attend a specific number of sessions each week. Psychopharmacology is used as well as psychotherapy. Children in treatment have one or more mental illness diagnoses outlined in the *Diagnostic and Statistical Manual of Mental Disorders*, fourth edition (*DSM-IV*; American Psychiatric Association 2000). Some youth are treated with medications for their diagnoses and these medications are dispensed in the therapeutic milieu.

The other main component of residential treatment is the education young people receive. Educational services in residential treatment usually include a special education school where special needs are addressed, often through individual education plans (IEP) for each student. These special needs could include a special focus on literacy, below-grade level learning, speech therapy, music therapy, and/or art therapy. The educational services (including elementary through high school) in residential treatment are also unique for the behavior management intervention strategies implemented therein. Much like the milieus, classroom programs outline incentives, privileges, and consequences for various kinds of behavior. Students attend and graduate from these school during their institutionalization.

Adults Who Work with Youth in Residential Treatment

Residential treatment centers hire various kinds of professionals to assist in the treatment process. Psychologists, social workers, counselors, psychotherapists, school psychologists, recreation therapists, music therapists, psychiatrists, and family therapists are responsible for the mental health treatment plans required of each child in residential treatment. They are also responsible for individual therapy, family therapy, group therapy, diagnosing mental illnesses, and determining psychotropic medication needs. These individuals are specially trained in graduate programs in psychology and often hold master's or doctoral degrees.

Teachers with special education degrees or certificates are responsible for the special education needs of the youth in treatment.

The individuals who work with the youth in the milieu or serve as aides to the teachers have the most diverse backgrounds. Some of these staff members hold bachelor's or associate's degrees in various fields. However, staff members responsible for the quotidian practice of residential treatment are trained by the institution itself in the various therapeutic models utilized by the specific institution (see Therapeutic Models section below).

Types of Institutions

Residential treatment treats the gamut of behavioral, emotional, and psychologist disorders affecting young people. Many of the common diagnoses of youth in treatment include conduct disorder, bipolar disorder, and oppositional defiance disorder. However, youth are diagnosed with all kinds of disorders. Residential treatment centers sometimes specialize in treating specific disorders such as autism, substance abuse, sexual predation, and eating disorders.

Funding Sources

Residential treatment centers are funded through the individual clients who are treated there, most often from a public source. If a young person is already a ward of the state, the child welfare system pays for that child's treatment in a center. Other children are funded by the juvenile justice system, school districts, or grants from the department of health and human services. However, some parents have private insurance or pay out of pocket for their child's residential treatment. Children funded by the child welfare system are under the guardianship of the state and have been removed from their homes for reasons of neglect or abuse. The other children are still under the guardianship of their parents or a family member.

Therapeutic Models

As noted above, trends in psychology have influenced residential treatment since the middle of the twentieth century. This influence results in residential treatment centers using various psychotherapeutic models to shape daily life at the institution. Often institutions use different models to inform distinct elements of the treatment process. For example, institutions require a tool to track a child's change or growth in treatment. One assessment tool is the Child and Adolescent Needs and Strengths (CANS) Comprehensive Assessment system developed by John S. Lyons (2009) and his research team at Northwestern University in the early 2000s. Institutions also need a model for dealing with children in crisis. One model is Life Space Crisis Intervention (LSCI), developed by Nicholas J. Long, Mary Wood, and Frank Fescer (2001), which informs how to process and interact with young people who are in crisis. Another model often used is the Therapeutic Crisis Intervention (TCI) system, developed and continually revised by the Family Life Development Center (2001) at Cornell University. TCI was created specifically for residential treatment populations and includes safe and appropriate physical intervention holds (restraints) that are often used to stop violent behavior in residential treatment. Other models are strength-based approaches and focus on enhancing the youths' strengths. One of these models is the Circle of Courage developed by Larry Brendtro, Martin Brokenleg, and Steve Van Bockern (2002) in 1990.

These are only four of various models and tools used by residential treatment centers to measure progress, deal with emotional and physical crises, and develop positive attributes in children. An exhaustive list of the models used in residential treatment is beyond the scope of this entry, as is a more detailed description of the above four models.

While the number and kinds of models used in treatment are considerable, the goals of treatment are few and shared. The main treatment goal is to reduce the child's need for institutionalized care. Improved social functioning and decreased violent or aggressive behavior are the main reasons young people no longer require residential treatment.

Current Research and Continued Questions

Research on the effectiveness of residential treatment is a main concern in contemporary American child mental health practice. The 1999 U.S. Surgeon General's Report on Mental Health maintains that there is little evidence to support the effectiveness of residential treatment. Research to investigate the effectiveness of residential treatment has become more robust in the last decade. Some scholars argue that residential treatment is a viable method of treating troubled adolescents (Bettmann & Jasperson 2009; Hair 2005; Larzelere et al. 2001; Thompson, Hirshberg, & Qiao 2011). Others argue that it is not effective and can even be harmful (Asarnow, Aoki, & Elson 1996; Barth 2002; Hyde & Kammerer 2008). Nonetheless, residential treatment remains a mental health treatment option for thousands of young people every year in the United States.

Continued research on outcomes, or how children fare after they leave residential treatment, is required to assess how effective residential treatment is. Additional research with young people in treatment to determine their experiences of treatment would shed light on improving institutional care (Hejtmanek 2010b; Hyde & Kammerer 2008). Acknowledging American cultural contexts, social inequality, and the overrepresentation of nonwhite populations in American health and foster care (Bell 2007; Billingsley & Giovannoni 1972; Byrd & Clayton 2000; Chibnall et al. 2003; Metzl 2010) and correctional facilities (Alexander 2010; Bureau of Justice Statistics 2003; Mauer 2006) might also provide insight into understanding the practice of residential treatment and how best to contextualize outcomes research (Hejtmanek 2010a).

Continued research on these various topics is required to better inform the practice and effectiveness of residential treatment in the United States today.

See also Adolescence and Mental Health; Mental Health Counseling; Social Work in Mental Health; Therapeutic Community and Milieu Therapy

Bibliography

Aichhorn, August. 1955. *Wayward Youth: A Psychoanalytic Study of Delinquent Children, Illustrated by Actual Case Histories*. New York: Meridian Books.

Alexander, Michelle. 2010. *The New Jim Crow: Mass Incarceration in the Age of Colorblindness*. New York: The New Press.

Almond, Richard. 1974. *The Healing Community: Dynamics of the Therapeutic Milieu*. New York: Aronson.

American Psychiatric Association. 2000. *Diagnostic and Statistical Manual of Mental Disorders* (4th ed., text rev.). Washington, DC: American Psychiatric Publishing.

Asarnow, Joan R., Wayne Akoi, and Steve Elson. 1996. "Children in Residential Treatment: A Follow-Up Study." *Journal of Clinical Child Psychology* 25(2): 209–214.

Ashby, LeRoy. 1997. *Endangered Children: Dependency, Neglect, and Abuse in American History*. New York: Twayne.

Barth, Richard P. 2002. *Institutions vs. Foster Homes: The Empirical Base for the Second Century of Debate*. Chapel Hill: University of North Carolina, School of Social Work, Jordan Institute for Families.

Bell, William. 2007. "How Are the Children?: Foster Care and African-American Boys." In Stephanie J. Jones, ed., *The State of Black America 2007: Portrait of the Black Male. An Official Publication of the National Urban League* (pp. 151–157). Silver Springs, MD: Beckham Publications Group.

Bettelheim, Bruno. 1955. *Truants from Life*. New York: Free Press.

Bettelheim, Bruno, and E. Sylvester. 1948. "A Therapeutic Milieu." *American Journal of Orthopsychiatry* 18: 191–206.

Bettmann, Joanna E., and Rachel A. Jasperson. 2009. "Adolescents in Residential and Inpatient Treatment: A Review of the Outcome Literature." *Child Youth Care Forum* 38(4): 161–183.

Billingsley, Andrew, and Jeanne M. Giovannoni. 1972. *Children of the Storm: Black Children and American Child Welfare*. New York: Harcourt, Brace, Jovanovich.

Brendtro, Larry K., Martin Brokenleg, and Steve Van Brockern. 2002. *Reclaiming Youth At Risk: Our Hope for the Future* (rev. ed.). Bloomington, IN: National Educational Service.

Bureau of Justice Statistics. 2003. *Prisoners in 2003*. Washington, DC: U.S. Department of Justice.

Byrd, W. Michael, and Linda A. Clayton. 2000. *An American Health Dilemma: A Medical History of African Americans and the Problem of Race: Beginnings to 1900*. New York: Routledge.

Caudill, William A. 1958. *The Psychiatric Hospital as a Small Society*. Published for the Commonwealth Fund by Harvard University Press.

Chibnall, Susan, Nicole Dutch, Brenda Jones-Harden, Annie Brown, Ruby Gourdine, Anniglo Boone, and Shelita Snyder. 2003. *Children of Color in the Child Welfare System: Perspectives from the Child Welfare Community*. Caliber and Associates and Howard University School of Social Work for the United States Department of Health and Human Services.

Cotton, Nancy S. 1993. *Lessons from the Lion's Den: Therapeutic Management of Children in Psychiatric Hospitals and Treatment Centers*. San Francisco: Jossey-Bass.

Courtney, Mark E., and Darcy Hughes-Heuring. 2009. "Residential Care in the United States of America: Past, Present, and Future." In Mark E. Courtney and Dorota Iwaniec, eds., *Residential Care of Children: Comparative Perspectives* (pp. 173–190). New York: Oxford University Press.

Epstein, Richard A. 2005. "Beyond the Yellow Door: Outcome and Follow-Up Studies of Students in a Residential Treatment Center." Unpublished doctoral dissertation, University of Chicago.

Estroff, Sue E. 1981. *Making It Crazy: An Ethnography of Psychiatric Clients in an American Community*. Berkeley: University of California Press.

Family Life Development Center. 2001. *The Residential Child Care Project. Therapeutic Crisis Intervention: A Crisis Prevention and Management System*. Ithaca, NY: Cornell University Press.

Foltz, Robert. 2004. "The Efficacy of Residential Treatment: An Overview of the Evidence." *Residential Treatment for Children & Youth* 22(2): 1–19.

Freud, Anna. 1969. *Research at the Hampstead Child-Therapy Clinic and Other Papers: 1956–1965* (Vol. 5). New York: International Universities Press.

Hair, Heather. 2005. "Outcomes for Children and Adolescents after Residential Treatment: A Review of Research from 1993 to 2003." *Journal of Child and Family Studies* 14(4): 551–575.

Hejtmanek, Katie. 2010a. "Caring through Restraint: Violence, Intimacy, and Identity in Mental Health Practice." *Culture, Medicine and Psychiatry* 34: 668–674.

Hejtmanek, Katherine. 2010b. "Mad Love: Life and Change in American Adolescent Residential Treatment Center." Unpublished doctoral dissertation, Washington University, St. Louis.

Hyde, Justine, and Nina Kammerer. 2008. "Adolescents' Perspectives on Placement Moves and Congregate Settings: Complex and Cumulative Instabilities in Out-of-Home Care." *Children and Youth Services Review* 31(2): 265–273.

Larzelere, Robert, Katherine Dinges, M. Diane Schmidt, Douglas Spellman, Thomas R. Criste, and Patrick Connell. 2001. "Outcomes of Residential Treatment: A Study of Adolescent Clients of Girls and Boys Town." *Child and Youth Care Forum* 30(3): 175–185.

Long, Nicholas James, Mary M. Wood, and Frank A. Fecser. 2001. *Life Space Crisis Intervention: Talking with Students in Conflict* (2nd ed.). Austin, TX: Pro-Ed.

Lyons, John S. 2009. *Communimetrics: A Communication Theory of Measurement in Human Services Settings*. New York: Springer.

Magellan Health Services Children's Services Task Force. 2010. *Perspectives on Residential Treatment and Community-Based Treatment for Youth and Families*. 23rd Annual Children's Mental Health Research & Policy Conference.

Mauer, Marc. 2006. *Race to Incarcerate* (2nd ed.). New York: Norton.

Metzl, Jonathan. 2010. *The Protest Psychosis: How Schizophrenia Became a Black Disease*. Boston: Beacon Press.

Noshpitz, J. 1962. "Notes on the Theory of Residential Treatment." *Journal of the American Academy of Child Psychiatry* 1: 284–296.

Rothman, David J. 1971. *The Discovery of the Asylum: Social Order and Disorder in the New Republic*. Boston: Little, Brown.

Thompson, S., D. Hirschberg, and J. Qiao. 2011. "Outcomes for Adoelscent Girls after Long-Term Residential Treatment." *Residential Treatment for Children and Youth* 28: 251–267.

Trieschman, Albert, Larry K. Whittaker, and Larry K. Brendtro. 1969. *The Other 23 Hours: Child-Care Work with Emotionally Disturbed Children in a Therapeutic Milieu*. Chicago: Aldine.

U.S. Department of Health and Human Services. 2011. The AFCARS Report. Retrieved from http://www.acf.hhs.gov/programs/cb/stats_research/afcars/tar/report18 .htm.

U.S. Surgeon General. 1999. *Mental Health: A Report of the Surgeon General*. Rockville, MD: U.S. Department of Health and Human Services, Substance Abuse and Mental Health Services Administration, Center for Mental Health Services, National Institute of Mental Health, National Institute of Health.

Rights of Patients with Mental Health Conditions

Stacey A. Tovino

Traditionally, individuals with mental health conditions had fewer legal rights than individuals with physical health conditions as well as healthy individuals. This entry reviews the trend toward equal rights for individuals with mental health conditions. More specifically, it examines four illustrative (but not exhaustive) sets of rights that are now enjoyed by individuals with mental health conditions, including the right to privacy and confidentiality, the right to be free from restraint and seclusion, the right to give informed consent to treatment, and the substantive and due process rights associated with involuntary civil commitment.

Confidentiality and Privacy

Historically, individuals with mental health conditions did not enjoy rights to personal privacy or health information confidentiality. In the mid-1960s, for example, a filmmaker, Frederick Wiseman, obtained permission from the superintendent of Massachusetts's Bridgewater State Hospital, an inpatient facility for residents with mental health conditions and criminal histories, to film the residents' daily lives (*Commonwealth v. Wiseman* 1969). Wiseman exposed over 80,000 feet of film, including scenes of residents in the nude, residents displaying distressing mental symptoms, and residents in other degrading situations. During fall 1967, Wiseman showed the film to both public and private audiences in New York City.

In addition to breaches of personal privacy, many individuals with mental health conditions also have been subject to breaches of health information confidentiality. Prior to the enactment of federal health information confidentiality regulations, mental health care providers frequently disclosed confidential information to pharmaceutical companies for marketing purposes (Jeffords 1997; O'Harrow 1998). The advent of electronic medical records also facilitated the rapid transmission of confidential information to third parties for purposes unrelated to treatment. The growth of managed care and other cost containment practices led to insurers requiring third-party review and approval of practitioner treatment requests and confidential patient information (U.S. Department of Health and Human Services [HHS] 1999).

Common law and legislation designed to address the privacy and confidentiality concerns of individuals with mental health conditions began to emerge in the last third of the twentieth century. In 1969, the Supreme Judicial Court of Massachusetts reviewed the Bridgewater State Hospital film case and found that "there is a collective, indecent intrusion into the most private aspects of the lives of these unfortunate persons in the Commonwealth's custody" (*Commonwealth v. Wiseman* 1969, 258). In 1980, Congress enacted the Mental Health Patient Bill of Rights, which referenced the recent recommendations of the President's Commission on Mental Health that individuals with mental health conditions should have "the right to a humane treatment environment that affords reasonable protection from harm and appropriate privacy to such person with regard to personal needs" and "the right to confidentiality of such person's records" (42 U.S.C. § 9501(1) (G), (H)). Although the Mental Health Bill of Rights did not contain a private right of action that would allow individuals with mental health conditions to sue for violations, the Bill of Rights did announce "the sense of Congress that each State should review and revise, if necessary, its laws to ensure that mental health patients receive the protection and services they require," including protection from breaches of privacy and confidentiality (42 U.S.C. § 9501).

Many state legislatures responded by passing state bills of rights, which included rights of personal privacy and health information confidentiality. Under Minnesota law, for example, patients with mental health conditions "have the right to respectfulness and privacy as it relates to their medical and personal care program" (Minn. Stat. § 144.651, Subd. 15). The Minnesota law further provides that "privacy shall be respected during toileting, bathing, and other activities of personal hygiene, except as needed for patient or resident safety or assistance" (Minn. Stat. § 144.651, Subd. 15). With respect to confidentiality, Minnesota patients "shall be assured confidential treatment of their personal and medical records, and may approve or refuse their release to any individual outside the facility. [Patients] shall be notified when personal records are requested by any individual outside the facility and may select someone to accompany them when the records or information are the subject of a personal interview" (Minn. Stat. § 144.651, Subd. 16).

Although early federal and state bills of rights prohibited health care providers from disclosing patient information to third parties for purposes unrelated to treatment, these bills typically failed to address whether a mental health professional could testify in a court of law about communications made by the patient. In 1996, the U.S. Supreme Court responded to this lack of authority by recognizing for the first time a psychotherapist-patient testimonial privilege. In *Jaffee v. Redmond*, the Supreme Court held that conversations between a patient and her therapist were confidential, privileged, and protected from compelled disclosure (*Jaffee v. Redmond* 1996).

That same year, Congress enacted the Health Insurance Portability and Accountability Act of 1996 (HIPAA), which directed HHS to adopt regulations protecting the confidentiality of health information (HIPAA 1996). The HHS regulations, which were adopted in final form in 2000 but have been amended several times since, are commonly known as the "HIPAA Privacy Rule" (HHS 2000). The HIPAA Privacy Rule extends a general set of confidentiality protections to all health information, including the health information of individuals with mental health conditions, as well as a special set of confidentiality protections to a class of records known as psychotherapy notes, defined as "notes recorded (in any medium) by a health care provider who is a mental health professional documenting or analyzing the contents of conversation during a private counseling session or a group, joint, or family counseling session and that are separated from the rest of the individual's medical record" (45 C.F.R. § 164.501). Unlike general health information, which the HIPAA Privacy Rule permits to be used for a range of treatment, payment, and health care operations activities without the patient's prior written authorization, psychotherapy notes may be used and disclosed for a very limited set of treatment, training, and litigation purposes.

Restraint and Seclusion

Historically, individuals with severe mental health conditions were subject to physical and mechanical restraints, including handcuffs, wristcuffs, and straitjackets, as well as seclusion, defined as the involuntary confinement of a patient alone in a room or area from which the patient is physically prevented from leaving (Tovino 2007). Although restraint and seclusion may be justified in certain limited emergency situations, mental health professionals and superintendents of mental institutions traditionally used restraint and seclusion as a substitute for patient supervision and as a tool for behavior modification (Tovino 2007). In 1998, the *Hartford Courant* published a series of newspaper articles identifying 142 restraint- and seclusion-related deaths that occurred across the United States between 1988 and 1998 (Weiss 1998). The specific causes of death included asphyxiation, suffocation, strangulation, cardiac causes, pulmonary and respiratory causes, cerebral-related causes, and blood clotting.

In response to these and other public reports of injuries and deaths relating to restraint and seclusion, the federal and state governments began to pass legislation limiting their use. At the federal level, HHS adopted in 1999 regulations giving hospital patients the "right to be free from restraint and seclusion of any form, imposed as a means of coercion, discipline, convenience, or retaliation" (42 C.F.R. § 483.13(e)). Among other requirements, the regulations also provided that restraint and seclusion: (1) may only be imposed to ensure the immediate physical safety of the patient, a staff member, or others, and must be discontinued at the earliest possible time; (2) may be used only when less restrictive interventions have been determined to be ineffective to protect the patient a staff member or others from harm; (3) must be the least restrictive intervention that will be effective to protect the patient, a staff member, or others from harm; (4) must be in accordance with a written modification to the patient's plan of care; (5) must be in accordance with the order of a physician or other licensed independent practitioner who is responsible for the care of the patient and is authorized to order restraint or seclusion by hospital policy in accordance with state law; (6) may never be part of a standing order or ordered on an "as needed" basis; (7) must be limited to four hours for adults 18 years of age or older, two hours for children and adolescents 9 to 17 years of age, and one hour for children under 9 years of age; and (8) must be discontinued at the earliest possible time, regardless of the length of time identified in the order (42 C.F.R. § 483.13(e)). The regulations also require hospital staff members to be trained and able to demonstrate competency in the application of restraint and seclusion (42 C.F.R. § 483.13(f)). Finally, the regulations require hospitals to report to the Centers for Medicare and Medicaid Services each death that occurs while a patient is in restraint or seclusion, each death that occurs within 24 hours after the patient has been removed from restraint or seclusion, and each death known to the hospital that occurs within one week after restraint or seclusion where it is reasonable to assume that use of restraint or placement in seclusion contributed directly or indirectly to a patient's death (42 C.F.R. § 483.13(g)).

In the late 1990s and the early 2000s, states also began to pass legislation specifying the right of individuals with mental health conditions to be free from dangerous methods of restraint and seclusion. Texas, for example, enacted legislation in 2005 prohibiting health care providers and others from administering restraints that obstruct a patient's airway, impair a patient's breathing by putting pressure on the torso, or interfere with a patient's ability to communicate (Tex. Health & Safety Code § 322.051(a)).

Consent to Treatment

Historically, some health care providers imposed treatments on patients with mental health conditions without giving them the prior opportunity to consent or refuse to consent to treatment. The notion of unconsented-to mental health treatment was illustrated most famously in Ken Kesey's *One Flew over the Cuckoo's Nest*, in which mental patient Randle McMurphy was not given the option of refusing to consent to a controversial and dangerous session of electroconvulsive therapy (Kesey 1963).

Federal law now requires all competent adult patients who receive care in Medicare- and Medicaid-certified health care facilities to give their voluntary, informed consent to treatment. In the hospital setting, for example, federal regulations provide that "the patient or his or her representative (as allowed under State law) has the right to make informed decisions regarding his or her care. The patient's rights include being informed of his or her health status, being involved in care planning and treatment, and being able to request or refuse treatment" (42 C.F.R. § 483.13(b)(2)).

In addition, every state now has a statute or regulation that requires all competent adult patients to voluntarily consent to proposed medical treatments and surgical procedures. Nevada, for example, requires all patients to give their prior written informed consent to medical, psychosocial, and rehabilitative care (Nev. Rev. Stat. § 433.484(1)(a)). The patient giving consent must be adequately informed as to the nature and consequences of the procedure; the reasonable risks, benefits, and purposes of the procedure; and available alternative procedures (Nev. Rev. Stat. § 433.484(1)(b)(1)–(3)). The consent of the patient may be withdrawn by the patient in writing at any time with or without cause (Nev. Rev. Stat. § 433.484(1)(c)).

Exceptions to the general rule of voluntary informed consent apply in situations involving incompetent patients, in situations involving involuntarily committed patients, and in emergencies. The state of Washington's informed consent law, for example, classifies an individual as incompetent for purposes of giving informed consent if the individual is "incompetent by reason of mental illness, developmental disability, senility, habitual drunkenness, excessive use of drugs, or other mental incapacity, of either managing his or her property or caring for himself or herself, or both" (Rev. Code Wash. § 7.70.065(1)). In situations involving an incompetent adult patient, consent may be obtained from an individual who is eligible to serve as a surrogate, according to the following priority-ordered list: (1) the appointed guardian of the patient, if any; (2) the individual, if any, to whom the patient has given a durable power of attorney that encompasses the authority to make health care decisions; (3) the patient's spouse or state-registered domestic partner; (4) children of the patient who are at least 18 years of age; (5) parents of the patient; and (6) adult brothers and sisters of the patient (Rev. Code Wash. § 7.70.65(1)(a)(i)–(v)). If the health care provider seeking informed consent from a surrogate makes a reasonable effort to locate and secure authorization from a surrogate in the first or succeeding class and finds no such person available, authorization may be given by any surrogate in the next class in the order of descending priority (Rev. Code Wash. § 7.70.65(b)). Before consenting to a proposed treatment on behalf of a patient, the Washington act requires the surrogate to determine in good faith that the patient, if competent, would have consented to the proposed health care (Rev. Code Wash § 7.70.65(c)). If such a determination cannot be made, the decision to consent to the proposed treatment may be made only after determining that the proposed health care is in the patient's best interests (Rev. Code Wash. § 7.70.65(c)).

Some states have adopted more stringent informed consent procedures that apply to controversial mental health treatments. Texas, for example, has specific informed consent procedures that apply to patients receiving electroconvulsive therapy. First, patients must give their written consent prior to each individual electroconvulsive therapy session (Tex. Admin. Code § 405.108(c)). Second, patients who initially consent to electroconvulsive therapy may revoke their consent for any reason at any time, with such revocation effective immediately (Tex. Admin. Code § 405.108(b)). Third, Texas has developed a mandatory consent form that must be signed by all patients consenting to electroconvulsive therapy (Tex. Admin. Code § 405.117). Among other things, the consent form must include information regarding the indications for the electroconvulsive therapy, the contraindications to the therapy, the results of psychiatric and other medical consultations relevant to the therapy, the nature and seriousness of the mental condition requiring the therapy, the significant risks and side effects of the therapy (including the possibility of permanent memory dysfunction, bone fractures, and significant posttreatment confusion), the fact that there is a division of medical opinion as to the efficacy of the therapy, and an offer to answer any questions regarding the therapy (Tex. Admin. Code §§ 405.108(d), 405.117).

Involuntary Commitment

Some individuals with mental health conditions may not understand the severity of their conditions, may refuse to take prescribed medications, or may be unable to recognize the need for medical assistance. Although family members and friends may try to help, informal social supports may be inadequate to ensure the individual's health, safety, and welfare. Historically, individuals with severe mental health conditions were involuntarily committed to mental health care facilities with little or no substantive justification or procedural due process. Today, every state has a law governing involuntary commitment, defined as the use of legal means to civilly commit a person to a mental health facility or a psychiatric unit of a general hospital against his or her will or over his or her objection. Modern involuntary commitment statutes seek to balance an individual's autonomy with the individual's need for protection and treatment.

Although each state law is slightly different, most state laws address the criteria for involuntary commitment, the amount of evidence that must be presented regarding the need for involuntary commitment, and the procedure for involuntary commitment. In Virginia, for example, an individual with a mental health condition may be involuntary committed for mental health treatment only when a judge or special justice finds by clear and convincing evidence that the individual has a mental illness and there is a substantial likelihood that, as a result of the mental illness, the person will in the near future: (1) cause serious physical harm to him or herself or others as evidenced by recent behavior causing, attempting, or threatening harm and other relevant information, if any, or (2) suffer serious harm due to his or her lack of capacity to protect himself from harm or to provide for his basic human needs (Va. Code Ann. § 37.2-817(C)). The judge or special justice must also find that all less restrictive treatment alternatives to involuntary inpatient treatment that would offer an opportunity for the improvement of the individual's condition have been investigated and determined to be inappropriate. If these criteria have been satisfied, the judge or special justice is permitted to order the individual to be admitted involuntarily to a facility for a period of treatment not to exceed 30 days from the date of the court order. Upon the expiration of the initial order for involuntary commitment, the individual must be released unless he or she is involuntarily admitted for an additional period not to exceed 180 days or the individual voluntarily requests treatment.

Conclusion

Traditionally, individuals with mental health conditions had fewer legal rights than individuals with physical health conditions and healthy individuals. Many individuals with mental health conditions did not enjoy rights of privacy and confidentiality, the right to be free from restraint and seclusion, the right to consent or refuse to consent to proposed medical treatments, or the right to substantive and procedural due process during the involuntary commitment process. During the late 1900s and early 2000s, federal and state lawmakers established a number of legally enforceable rights that can be exercised by individuals with mental health conditions.

See also; Criminalization and Diversion Programs; Disability Rights; Emergency Services; Ethical Issues; History of Mental Health Care; Hospitalization; Involuntary Treatment; Mental Health Advocacy

Bibliography

42 C.F.R. § 483.13 (2011).

42 U.S.C. § 9501 (1980).

45 C.F.R. § 164.501 (2011).

45 C.F.R. § 164.508 (2011).

Commonwealth v. Wiseman, 356 Mass. 251, 249 N.E.2d 610 (1969).

Health Insurance Portability and Accountability Act [HIPAA], Pub. L. No. 104–191, 110 Stat. 1936 (1996).

Jaffee v. Redmond, 518 U.S. 1 (1996).

Jeffords, James. 1997. Statement of Senator James Jefford. Hearing on the Confidentiality of Medical Information. Senate Committee on Labor and Human Resources, 105th Cong.

Kesey, Ken. 1963. *One Flew over the Cuckoo's Nest*. New York: Signet.

Minn. Stat. § 144.651 (2011).

Nev. Rev. Stat. § 433.484 (2011).

O'Harrow, Robert. 1998. "Prescription Sales, Privacy Fears; CVS, Giant Share Customer Records with Drug Marketing Firm." *Washington Post*, February 15, A01.

Rev. Code Wash. § 7.70.065 (2011).

Tex. Admin. Code § 405.108 (2011).

Tex. Admin. Code § 405.117 (2011).

Tex. Health & Safety Code 322.051 (2011).

Tovino, Stacey A. 2007. "Psychiatric Restraint and Seclusion: Resisting Legislative Solution." *Santa Clara Law Review* 47: 511–571.

U.S. Department of Health and Human Services. 1999. *Mental Health: A Report of the Surgeon General*. Rockville, MD: U.S. Department of Health and Human Services.

U.S. Department of Health and Human Services. 2000. *Standards for Privacy of Individually Identifiable Health Information; Final Rule*. 65 Fed. Reg. 82461–82829.

Va. Code Ann. § 37.2-817(C) (2011).

Weiss, Eric M. 1998. "Deadly Restraint: A Hartford Courant Investigative Report." *Harford Courant*, October 11–15, A1.

Rural Mental Health Services

Mary Ann Overcamp-Martini

Rural mental health services are those services available to residents of rural areas with mental health problems or mental illness. Rural areas make up 90 percent of the United States and are those areas with fewer than 2,500 residents, with "population densities as high as 999 per square mile or as low as 1 person per square mile" (Substance Abuse and Mental Health Services Administration 2011). Due to concerns about the impact of such a broad definition on funding initiatives and service provision, "frontier areas" were further defined separately in 1997 in regard to both low population and isolation; in the western states, for instance, a majority of counties are considered "frontier," with fewer than six residents per square mile, which is the current mark of a frontier area (Frontier Education Center 1998). A more descriptive approach to the definition of rural is that of "areas characterized by low population density, limited and fragile economic base, cultural diversity, high level of poverty, limited access to cities" (Sawyer, Gale, & Lambert 2006, 6). Considering both rural and frontier areas, all told, some 25 percent of the population in the United States is considered nonmetropolitan (U.S. Bureau of the Census 2001). In spite of the beliefs and myths regarding the idyllic and stable nature of rural life, the current picture of rural residents is of an isolated and fragmented population becoming increasingly powerless and disenfranchised, and that of rural mental health issues no longer engaging substantial national or professional interest. Rural mental health services are most likely to be located with general health services, which are also underresourced (National Association of Rural Mental Health [NARMH] n.d.).

Barriers

The obstacles and challenges to effective mental health service provision in rural areas are many: distance from urban and medical centers and university services; geography and geographic isolation; weather and travel; high rates of poverty; stigma associated with mental health problems; and the lack of information, accessibility, availability, and acceptance of care and treatment for mental health problems. Of these barriers, the least obvious may be the lack of specialists residing or working in rural areas; although rural residents have been found to have equivalent rates of mental illness as urban residents in the most comprehensive Epidemiologic Catchment Area study, the availability of psychiatrists in rural areas has been found to be only 6 percent or less of practicing psychiatrists nationally (Lambert & Agger 1995). Rural residents are particularly unsupported by employee insurance and even show lower rates of Medicaid enrollment, making them more vulnerable to the instability of health care financing reform initiatives based on Medicaid eligibility as well as market-driven financing based on employee insurance (National Institute of Mental Health [NIMH] 2000). Those "most rural" individuals, living the farthest from metropolitan areas, are 47 percent less likely to receive mental health treatment of any kind than metropolitan residents, and 72 percent less likely to receive any specialized mental health treatment (Hauenstein et al. 2007).

History

Although there has been some increase in research and funding for rural mental health services in the past 35 years, the barriers and challenges of availability and accessibility of rural mental health services remain high, as initially noted in the 1978 *Report to the President* from President Carter's Commission on Mental Health, which said, "The paucity of research in rural mental health is but one manifestation of the mental health resource imbalance in rural America" (President's Commission on Mental Health 1978, 1163). Although there have been many critiques of Carter's President's Commission on Mental Health, it was notably the first time that a presidential commission had been called to deal with the many mental health problems in the nation. One of the milestones of the commission involved this acknowledgment of the long-ignored claim of rural residents for adequately funded and implemented mental health services as addressed by one of the 22 task and subtask panels involved in reviewing specific populations and problems. The *Report to the President* expressly stated, "Other Americans do not receive adequate care because of where they are. . . . this is particularly true of those who live in rural America"—along with the need for the federal government to encourage funding and training for mental health professionals to provide services in rural and other underserved areas (President's Commission on Mental Health 1978, 1:7).

The Mental Health Systems Act passed as congressional legislation in October 1980, providing the first direct involvement of the federal government in the nation's mental health system, including priority on services for the underserved such as rural residents. It was rescinded shortly thereafter, however, in the Omnibus Budget Reconciliation Act the following summer of 1981 after the election of President Reagan. Although the Mental Health Systems Act was not enacted, the commission's recommendation for a national plan of services for those with serious mental illness was implemented in the National Plan for the Chronically Mentally Ill during the 1980s, which provided a blueprint for ongoing incremental change in mental health services, including rural mental health services (Grob 2005; Goldman 2006).

Documentation of the continuing inadequacy of rural mental health services was reinforced in President Bush's 2003 New Freedom Commission on Mental

Health, with particular recommendations for the development of a specialized workforce of mental health professionals for rural mental health services. It was also recommended that a Rural Mental Health Plan be developed that would bridge planning between states' Comprehensive Mental Health Plans and the rural public health system. Clearly, the newer treatment technologies involving intensive treatment teams, psychiatric rehabilitation, the recovery model, and consumer and family participation would provide this integrated treatment with mental health and public health systems. As with the Carter commission recommendations 15 years earlier, sequentialist (planned incrementalist) advances have been made from the New Freedom Commission by slowly implementing the mental health plans in progressive sequence for "quiet success" even when major initiatives do not seem to fit the tenor of the times, currently conservative toward social services in general and mental health in particular (Goldman 2006, 425).

Model Program and New Initiatives

Particularly in the past couple of decades there has been a wide acceptance of the principles of psychiatric rehabilitation and the recovery model for people with serious mental illness, with psychiatric treatment and community supports; however, substantial problems remain in access, availability, and utilization of services in rural areas. In effective urban treatment models, the mental health consumer and family members have come to expect participation in the treatment. As in other areas, the state of treatment is further behind in rural areas, but the participatory models have been found effective and complementary to the needs of consumers, family members, and the social networks and supports that are a part of this treatment technology (Kast 2001). Rural mental health services are often a part of rural health services and rural hospital care, which has seen disruption in the shift in health care services to managed care (Kast 2001) even as the managed care and health maintenance organizations engage more with rural areas. Despite other potential rural models of services, rural mental health services tend to be "smaller, under-resourced versions of their urban counterparts," which retain an office-centered service provision model rather than the newer consumer-driven, team approach to services (NARMH n.d., 4).

The involvement of multidisciplinary treatment teams can be an effective and participatory model for rural mental health services as a way of integrating services for the consumer and the family member. Particularly helpful for those with serious mental disorders who have tended to move frequently between hospital and other settings are those of intensive case management, known by a variety of names but based on the evidence-based program called "PACT" or "ACT," the Program for Assertive Community Treatment with high staff-to-client ratios in a team approach to treatment and care. The PACT programs have been the most studied form of intensive treatment, developed on a team-based approach to providing a "therapeutic umbrella" around a client (Hogarty 1991), and shown to be effective in both urban and rural environments, allowing interagency collaboration in pulling together treatment team members from a variety of agencies with flexibility in funding arrangements (Bond et al. 1990; Stein & Test 1985).

Other newer initiatives include effective evidence-based treatment strategies such as psychoeducational groups and programs for consumers and family members to increase the knowledge and involvement of family members (Hogarty 1991). Targeted outreach programs have more recently been developed, reaching isolated and reluctant individuals, and again increasing the engagement of consumer and family members (Lambert et al. 2001).

Funding Mechanisms

The lifeblood of rural mental health services has historically been public funding by different levels of government. Despite the difficulties in providing rural mental health services, there is some evidence that service provision is actually less expensive than in urban areas, given lowered costs of overhead and personnel, and even in consideration of increased travel, although newer models of treatment would likely raise travel costs if implemented. Managed care and health maintenance organizations have demonstrated effective initiatives in developing behavioral health services for Medicare and Medicaid recipients in rural areas, particularly in integration of rural mental health and substance abuse treatment, long a need in rural treatment services (NARMH n.d.).

The need for additional and targeted outreach services in rural mental health services became clearly evident in the farm crises of the 1980s and 1990s when both farmers and farmworkers were battered by economic instability, loss, and the resulting increase in depression and other mental health problems. Outreach services were initiated by state and federal governments, private foundations, and donations, with the federal Office of Rural Health Policy the main initial sponsor of new outreach programs. Outreach programs sustain their programs by aligning their services with other Medicaid-reimbursable service provision to individual clients when possible to obtain some ongoing reimbursement for services through managed care agencies, yet still generally require constant fund-raising and grant writing for the maintenance of services (Lambert et al. 2001). According to the New Freedom Commission on Mental Health,

> The Commission recognizes that affordable mental health care is a critical issue for rural communities and residents. Federal and State agencies should explore policy options that enable rural individuals and small businesses to enter pools to purchase insurance so that they gain access to more affordable, high quality, health insurance. In addition, Federal agencies should ensure

that new funding announcements do not place unrealistic non-Federal matching fund requirements on rural entities. (President's New Freedom Commission 2003, Recommendation 3.2)

Thus although the impact of the passage of the Patient Protection and Affordable Care Act of 2010 on mental health services in general and rural mental health services in particular is yet to be seen, it is likely that the shift to managed care in behavioral health services will include an increasing number of insurance pools to benefit the uninsured in rural areas.

Telehealth Services

The use of telehealth services (also known as telemental health, telemedicine, telepsychiatry)—electronic strategies of service delivery such as interactive video conferencing, Internet services, e-mail, phone, and fax—has grown tremendously in rural mental health services, and has brought down some of the barriers to service provision. Given the underresourcing of psychiatric care in rural areas, with less than 30 percent of the availability in rural areas as there is in metro areas, and less than 10 percent in frontier areas (Kast 2001), telemental health services have allowed video conferencing between treatment provider and mental health consumer and family members. Even informational and educational resources can be financially inaccessible to rural health and mental health clinics and services, which are now accessible through Internet services. Telemental health services can also serve as a force for centralizing resource information to the client, in a time when services have been found fragmented, underfunded, and inaccessible in the comprehensive framework that supports the greatest efficacy of treatment. *Telehealth World*, the magazine of telehealth, telemedicine, and connected health care, was established in 2007 for medical professionals, health care, technology, and communications providers involved in the remote health care services delivery, including a directory of telehealth organizations and companies (http://www.telehealthworld.com/). They also provide models of exemplary programs with their annual Top 10 list of telehealth programs.

Resources

There are a number of specialized resources regarding rural mental health services. The main journals featuring evidence-based knowledge are the *Journal of Rural Community Psychology* (http://www.marshall.edu/jrcp) and the *Journal of Rural Mental Health* (http://www.narmh.org/publications/jrmh.aspx). The National Institute of Mental Health has a couple of offices most directly involved in rural mental health services, with the central resource being the Office of Rural Mental Health Research (ORMHR) at http://www.nimh.nih.gov/about/organization/od/office-of-rural-mental-health-research-ormhr.shtml. Important organizations include the Frontier Mental Health Services Research Network (http://wiche.edu/MentalHealth/Frontier/frontier.asp) and the National Association for Rural Mental Health (NARMH) at http://www.narmh.org.

Conclusion

Rural mental health services have been the poor stepchild in the development of mental health service models. Although underresourced, rural mental health service providers need to take up the many challenges and demonstrate a particular set of skills and knowledge relative to the separate identity of rural mental health services. Far behind their urban counterparts, implementing the recovery model with consumer and family participation would fit well with the social structure and supports of the rural resident. The specialized knowledge, skills, and professional expertise of the rural mental health professional would assist the long-overdue development of a distinct model of rural mental health services.

See also American Indian and Alaskan Native Mental Health; Community Mental Health; Public Health Perspectives; Recovery Movement; Rehabilitation Services; State Mental Health Agencies; Undiagnosed Mental Illness

Bibliography

Bond, G. R., T. F. Witheridge, J. Dincin, D. Wasmer, J. Webb, and R. DeGraaf-Kaser. 1990. "Assertive Community Treatment for Frequent Users of Psychiatric Hospitals in a Large City: A Controlled Study." *American Journal of Community Psychology* 18(6): 865–891.

Frontier Education Center. 1998. *Consensus Definition—Frontier: A New Definition.* Retrieved from http://www.frontierus.org/documents/consensus_paper.htm#definition.

Goldman, H. H. 2006. "Making Progress in Mental Health Policy in Conservative Times: One Step at a Time." *Schizophrenia Bulletin* 32(3): 424–427.

Grob, G. 2005. "Public Policy and Mental Illnesses: Jimmy Carter's Presidential Commission on Mental Health." *The Milbank Quarterly* 83(3): 425–456.

Hauenstein, E. J., S. Petterson, V. Rovnyak, E. Merwin, E., B. Heise, and D. Wagner. 2007. "Rurality and Mental Health Treatment." *Administration and Policy in Mental Health and Mental Health Services Research* 34(3): 255–267.

Hogarty, G. E. 1991. *Drug and Psychosocial Treatment of Schizophrenia: The State of the Art.* Pittsburgh: University of Pittsburgh.

Kast, B. S. 2001. "Applying Psychiatric Rehabilitation in Rural Areas: A Commissioner's Perspective." *Psychiatric Rehabilitation Skills* 5(2): 321–343.

Lambert, D., and M. S. Agger. 1995. "Access of Rural AFDC Medicaid Beneficiaries to Mental Health Services." *Health Care Financing Review* 17(1): 133–145.

Lambert, D., A. Donahue, M. Mitchell, and R. Strauss. 2001. *Mental Health Outreach: Promising Practices in Rural Areas.* Retrieved from http://www.narmh.org/publications/archives/REVISED_OUTREACH_PAPER.pdf.

National Association of Rural Mental Health. n.d. *Rural Mental Health: 2000 & Beyond.* Retrieved from http://www.narmh.org/publications/archives/vision_paper.pdf.

National Institute of Mental Health. 2000. *Rural Mental Health Research at the National Institute of Mental Health.* Retrieved from http://www.nimh.nih.gov/about/organization/od/office-of-rural-mental-health-research-ormhr.shtml.

President's New Freedom Commission on Mental Health. 2003. *Achieving the Promise: Transforming Health Care in America.* Washington, DC: U.S. Government Printing Office.

Sawyer, D., J. Gale, and D. Lambert. 2006. "Rural and Frontier Mental and Behavioral Health Care: Barriers, Effective Policy Strategies, Best Practices." Waite Park, MN: National Association for Rural Mental Health. Retrieved from http://www.narmh.org/publications/archives/rural_frontier.pdf.

Stein, L. I., and M. A. Test. 1985. "The Evolution of the Training in Community Living Model." In L. I. Stein and M. A. Test, eds., *The Training in Community Living Model: A Decade of Experience* (pp. 7–16). San Francisco: Jossey-Bass.

Substance Abuse and Mental Health Services Administration. n.d. *Rural Communities.* Retrieved from http://promoteacceptance.samhsa.gov/topic/rural/default.aspx.

The President's Commission on Mental Health. 1978. Task Panel Reports (Vol. 3, Appendix). Washington, DC: U.S. Government Printing Office.

U.S. Bureau of the Census. 2001. *Profiles of General Demographic Characteristics 2000: 2000 Census of Population and Housing: United States.* Washington, DC: U.S. Department of Commerce.

S

Schizophrenia

Jeffrey Poland

According to contemporary psychiatry, schizophrenia is a form of mental illness characterized by hallucinations, delusions, bizarre behavior, cognitive deficits, and other symptoms. Its manifestations have been observed across history and culture, and it reportedly affects 1 percent of the population. Viewed as a substantial public health problem, schizophrenia is an object of major research programs as well as considerable clinical and cultural attention. However, although important in modern psychiatric practices, the concept of schizophrenia has been much disputed, as evidenced by considerable variability of the concept over the past 100 years and by current controversy over its scientific validity, clinical utility, and cultural significance. Consequently, whether the concept of schizophrenia is well suited for playing important roles in scientific, clinical, and cultural practices is in question.

History of the Concept of Schizophrenia

Identification of the condition we now call "schizophrenia" is typically credited to Emile Kraepelin (1904), although his term was "dementia praecox." On Kraepelin's view, dementia praecox was clinically distinct from melancholia and mania, and it was characterized by an early onset, a chronic and deteriorating course, and a poor outcome. The central clinical features of dementia praecox included hallucinations, delusions, formal thought disorder, incoherent speech, bizarre behavior, catatonic motor expressions, blunted affect, negativism, and lack of insight. Being sensitive to clinical complexity, Kraepelin observed that the clinical picture in dementia praecox varied over time and its clinical course was episodic. He viewed the condition as a brain disease with an unknown pathology and etiology, and he famously wrote: "The causes of dementia praecox are at the present time still wrapped in impenetrable darkness" (Kraepelin 1919: 223).

Eugen Bleuler (1911) rejected the idea of a dementia with early onset and inevitably deteriorating course, introduced the term "schizophrenia" (splitting of cognitive functions), and talked of the "schizophrenias," thereby suggesting the existence of multiple causes of the disorder. He distinguished between fundamental symptoms, which were always present and constituted the core of the pathology, and accessory symptoms, which were not always present and derived from the fundamental symptoms. According to Bleuler, the fundamental symptoms of schizophrenia were summed up in the so-called "four A's": affect (flat or inappropriate), ambivalence (conflict of affect, will, ideas), association (loosening of associative connections), and autism (isolation, lost in one's own world). The accessory symptoms included hallucinations, delusions, and disturbances of behavior and speech. Like Kraepelin, Bleuler viewed schizophrenia as a brain disease with an essential core pathology and admitting of various subtypes (e.g., simple, latent, paranoid, catatonic, hebephrenic).

Kurt Schneider (1959) subsequently focused more on the psychotic features of schizophrenia and away from course, outcome, and cognition. He distinguished "first rank" and "second rank" symptoms, a distinction with no known theoretical or prognostic significance, but that he believed to be especially significant for diagnosis of the disorder (viz., first-rank symptoms were believed to be "pathognomonic" for schizophrenia). First-rank symptoms included: auditory hallucinations of two or more voices discussing the patient in the third person; thought insertion, thought withdrawal, and thought broadcasting; passivity phenomena in which a person experiences sensations, feelings, impulses, or actions as imposed by an external force; delusional perceptions in which a delusional belief arises suddenly and incomprehensively from a normal perception.

A more recent development in the conceptualization of the symptoms of schizophrenia builds upon the distinction, made by Hughlings Jackson in the nineteenth century, between positive and negative symptoms in neurology: negative symptoms are those that represent losses of function directly due to an anatomical lesion, whereas positive symptoms are those that represent excesses of behavior caused by an intact neurophysiological system not effected by an anatomical lesion (Andreasen 1982; Crow 1980). In schizophrenia, the positive symptoms are supposed to be hallucinations and delusions that are pathological due to an excess of function, whereas the negative symptoms are supposed to include flat affect, avolition (lack of will), and negativity, which are pathological due to an absence of function. Building on this distinction, Crow (1980) hypothesized two distinct disease processes, Type I and Type II schizophrenia.

This distinction between positive and negative symptoms of schizophrenia was extended by Liddle (1987), who identified three symptom clusters (syndromes): psychomotor poverty (poverty of speech, lack of spontaneous movement, blunting of affect), disorganization (inappropriate affect, poverty of content of speech, disturbances of the form of thought), and reality distortion (delusions, hallucinations.) Along similar lines, Andreasen, Arndt, Alliger, Miller, and Flaum (1995) identified three syndromes: negative (avolition, flat affect, anhedonia, asociality), psychotic (hallucinations, delusions), and disorganized (inappropriate affect, thought disorder, bizarre behavior). Empirical studies have found modest support for such clustering, although for the most part it is unclear what theoretical, diagnostic, or prognostic significance these syndromes have. It is generally recognized that a "deficit syndrome" (e.g., Andreasen's negative syndrome) predicts a poor course and outcome.

A different approach to understanding schizophrenia and its manifestations is represented by the idea of "the schizophrenia spectrum": schizophrenia is not to be understood as a unitary disease, but rather as a "spectrum" of diseases related to each other by similarity at some level of analysis (e.g., clinical phenomenology, underlying causal processes). The schizophrenia spectrum typically includes: schizophrenia and its subtypes, schizophreniform disorder, schizoaffective disorder, schizotypal personality disorder, and schizoid personality disorder. In addition, the spectrum has sometimes included alcoholism, bipolar disorder, borderline personality disorder, and other conditions believed to be sufficiently similar to schizophrenia in some important respect.

Parallel to this evolution of the concept of schizophrenia in clinical and research contexts, the diagnostic criteria for schizophrenia, as a category of mental disorder in the *Diagnostic and Statistical Manual* (*DSM*) of the American Psychiatric Association, has taken rather different forms over the past six decades. In the *DSM-I* (American Psychiatric Association 1952) and *DSM-II* (American Psychiatric Association 1968), the diagnostic criteria were loose, psychoanalytically informed, and highly subjective; as a consequence they exhibited low levels of interrater agreement ("reliability") and had little predictive value ("validity"). This approach reflected the dominance of psychoanalysis in psychiatry at the time, and its problems partially set the stage for substantial revisions in subsequent editions of the *DSM*. During a tumultuous period in the 1970s, there was considerable criticism of psychiatry as manifested in the antipsychiatry movement, research demonstrating the substantial lack of reliability and validity of the category of schizophrenia, and apparent failure of the deinstitutionalization movement. In a response designed to restore credibility to psychiatry, the so-called "Neo-Kraepelineans" vigorously pursued a vision of psychiatry as a branch of medicine in which a strong biological approach to understanding disorders such as schizophrenia was favored (Klerman 1978). In the service of this agenda, problems of reliability were aggressively pursued, leading ultimately to the publication of more rigorously defined diagnostic criteria in the *DSM-III* in 1980.

With little change across three more revisions of the *DSM*, the current criteria for diagnosing schizophrenia identify the characteristic symptoms as follows (American Psychiatric Association 1994):

Criterion A. Characteristic symptoms: Two (or more) of the following, each present for a significant portion of time during a one-month period (or less if successfully treated):

　　1. Delusions

　　2. Hallucinations

3. Disorganized speech (e.g., frequent derailment or incoherence)

4. Grossly disorganized or catatonic behavior

5. Negative symptoms, i.e., affective flattening, alogia, or avolition

Note: Only one criterion A symptom is required if delusions are bizarre or hallucinations consist of a voice keeping up a running commentary on the person's behavior or thoughts, or two or more voices conversing with each other.

In addition, current diagnostic criteria include specifications for social and occupational dysfunction, for duration of symptoms, for various exclusions and qualifications related to other disorders (e.g., mood disorders, medical conditions, substance abuse, and developmental disorders), and for longitudinal course. The *DSM-IV* also includes five subtypes of schizophrenia: paranoid, disorganized, catatonic, undifferentiated, and residual.

As the above survey reveals, there has been considerable variation in how schizophrenia has been conceived over the past century, from Kraepelin to the *DSM-IV-TR* (American Psychiatric Association 2000.) For the most part, these conceptualizations were based on clinical observation, speculation, and to some extent political negotiation, largely unguided by scientific research. Despite this variation and despite there being no objective and independent test for the condition, a consensus view that schizophrenia is a brain disease has now emerged in psychiatry.

The Current Consensus View of Schizophrenia

At the core of the current consensus is the belief that schizophrenia exists as a brain disease that is identifiable using *DSM* criteria. This belief provides a conceptual framework for research and clinical practices, and has led to the development of biological models of the disease and medical models for its treatment.

Beginning in the 1960s, biological models of schizophrenia were focused on biochemical hypotheses (e.g., dopamine, glutamate), partly because of the apparent success of psychotropic drugs in controlling some symptoms. Other biological models concerned retroviral and other infections, genetic abnormalities, and neuroanatomical pathologies. However, such single-focus models have given way to more complex neurodevelopmental models, according to which (Insel 2010) schizophrenia is a neurodevelopmental disease that can be broken down into an early risk phase in which genetic and environmental risk factors start to accumulate, a prodromal phase in which early preclinical manifestations of disease become apparent, an acute phase in which signs and symptoms are clinically manifest in episodes of psychosis, and a later stage of chronic disability. Within this broad structure, the disease exhibits a variable presentation across patients and over time, as well as a variable course and outcome. At its core is supposed to be a neural pathology caused by a genetic vulnerability interacting with other genetic and nongenetic factors. On a typical variant of this model (cf., Green 2001; Andreasen 2001) prenatal and perinatal stressors (e.g., malnutrition, infection, injury, stress hormones) interacting with the genetic vulnerabilities of an individual result in disruption of prenatal brain development, which, in turn, initiates a developmental cascade of effects leading to disruptions of neural connectivity and neural miscommunication. Such miscommunication, in turn, is responsible for disrupted brain function, neurocognitive deficits, various patterns of preclinical and clinical signs and symptoms, and disrupted social and adaptive functioning.

Evidence for this model has been developed in a wide range of research programs including clinical phenomenology, epidemiology, genetics, brain pathology and development, and neurocognition. Frequently cited findings include:

- Association of schizophrenia with prenatal exposure to famine, viral infection, stress (cortisol), and poverty, and with perinatal complications
- Tendency of schizophrenia to run in families with risk varying according to genetic relationship
- Identification of genes that appear to confer increased risk
- Association of schizophrenia with physical, motor, psychological, and behavioral anomalies and abnormalities in childhood
- Association of schizophrenia with neurocognitive deficits
- Association of schizophrenia with brain pathologies such as reduced brain volume, ventricular enlargement, and diminished function of the frontal cortex

Defenders of the neurodevelopmental model of schizophrenia view these findings as providing evidence for various components of the model and, hence, as providing support for the model as a whole.

Criticisms of the Consensus View

Despite the apparent consensus concerning the neurodevelopmental model, there is substantial, long-standing, and serious criticism directed at the concept of schizophrenia, biological disease models, and associated clinical and research practices. Such criticisms fall into two broad categories: sociopolitical and scientific.

Sociopolitical Criticisms

More or less radical sociopolitical criticism can be found in the work of Szasz (1988), Scheff (1999), Laing (1983), and many others. Each in different ways argues that the concept of schizophrenia (or the associated label) is a contingent one that has considerable rhetorical power and can play a significant role in managing deviance in the service of dominant social or political forces and vested interests. Such critics highlight the impact of the label on personal, interpersonal, and social processes and they highlight the moral, social, and political significance of its use in a wide variety of contexts. All such critics engage in critical unmasking strategies designed to undermine the credibility of the concept by demonstrating the contingency of the concept and related practices, the interests they serve, and the impact that they have.

Szasz (1988), for example, has famously argued that schizophrenia is not a real mental illness since the concept of mental illness is incoherent. And, because schizophrenia is not known to be associated with a physical pathology, it is not a brain disease either. However, it is not that people with various presentations, problems, and struggles do not exist, it is that these presentations (etc.) are not appropriately conceptualized as either brain diseases or mental illnesses. Rather, such conditions are part of living life and are best conceived of as morally and socially complex problems in living. Consequently, according to Szasz, the psychiatric deployment of the concept of schizophrenia is nothing more than a rhetorically powerful tactic that inappropriately bears on questions of freedom and responsibility, and, more specifically, plays an inappropriate role in questions of excuse from responsibility (e.g., the insanity defense) and deprivations of liberty (e.g., involuntary treatment, involuntary commitment, and suicide prevention).

Scheff (1999) argues that the label "schizophrenia" plays a complex role in social processes related to managing deviant behavior; the label is a normative one that picks out residual social norm violations and that plays a role in psychological, social, and cultural processes for enforcing (or resisting) such norms. On this view, understanding how labeling processes work can help understand chronicity in mental illness as well as the nature of stereotyping and stigma. Importantly, Scheff does not deny that some norm violations might be related to disease processes; rather, he insists that attention to labeling processes has independent importance and that at the time of his writing there was no scientific validation of any disease model of schizophrenia.

Laing (1983) argues that there is no such thing as schizophrenia, although the label "schizophrenia" is real and plays a powerful role in psychosocial contexts that involve power struggles. The experience and behavior of people identified as "schizophrenic" are to be understood as strategies for coping with and living in unlivable situations, whereas the application of the label by others is part of a strategy for controlling the labeled person.

Although, predictably, the above lines of criticism are routinely dismissed by mainstream psychiatry, there are important lessons to be learned from these critics. The first is that the scientific case for the existence of a *disease* called "schizophrenia" has not been made. None of these critics denies the existence of the people or their behaviors, experience, problems, etc.; what they deny is that the most appropriate way of conceptualizing that experience (etc.) is as a brain disease, since that view is not scientifically defensible. The second lesson is that anyone serious about understanding "schizophrenia" or the people who are so labeled should pay close attention to the psychological, social, and moral context in which such persons live and act. One can (and probably should) reject many of the arguments of Szasz, Scheff, and Laing without abandoning the recognition that the persons who are identified as "schizophrenic" are moral agents living a life in the world and that the world is a morally and socially complex place.

Scientific Criticisms

Scientifically based criticisms bearing on schizophrenia have also been widely advanced (e.g., Bentall 2003; Boyle 2002; Carson 1996; Heinrichs 2001). At the heart of these criticisms are concerns about the characteristics of the concept of schizophrenia. As observed above, the concept has varied widely over the past century and has evolved on the basis of clinical observation and speculation, largely unguided by scientific research concerning the disorder. For example, as defined in the *DSM*, the concept of schizophrenia is defined by atheoretical, disjunctive, and arbitrary criteria based upon consensus clinical judgments and political negotiations, and not on research that demonstrates its validity. More specifically, it is a clinical concept that has no scientifically established construct validity (e.g., there is no characteristic pattern of symptoms uniquely associated with schizophrenia; there is no theoretically specifiable core deficit shared by all persons with the condition), and it has very limited, scientifically established predictive validity (e.g., it does not predict clinical course, response to treatment, or outcome; it has no strong associations with causal factors; there are no objective tests that play a role in diagnosis). As a consequence of its atheoretical and disjunctive character and its lack of validity, there is substantial heterogeneity at all levels of analysis of the individuals to whom the concept is applied. Especially significant in this regard is heterogeneity of causal processes. Hence, in addition to lacking scientific validity, the concept masks considerable variation of important characteristics and processes among people with the same diagnosis. Such heterogeneity raises serious concerns about the role of the concept in research and clinical contexts.

With respect to research, critics argue that, because it involves a poorly defined concept that lacks validity and masks substantial heterogeneity of important traits and processes, the research program guided by the concept of schizophrenia is not expected to produce rich and robust findings. And, in fact, there is an emerging recognition that the research program to date has produced findings on important research questions that are typically negative, unreplicated, inconsistent, weak, nonspecific, or uninterpretable. For example, in the context of genetic research, disappointing results have led some researchers to view the trait defined by the schizophrenia concept as a poorly defined phenotype and, hence, ill-suited for genetic research. More generally, there is concern by defenders of the consensus view (e.g., Fischer & Carpenter 2009; Hyman 2010; Insel 2010) that *DSM* categories in general, and the category of schizophrenia in particular, have not provided a framework for a sufficiently progressive research agenda that validates existing categories. Consequently, they recognize that changes in research strategy need to be made.

Parallel criticisms arise with respect to clinical practices organized in terms of the concept of schizophrenia. Despite concerns about the research agenda of the consensus view, most defenders claim that the concept picks out an important class of patients, enables meaningful communication about those patients, and organizes clinical practices of assessment, diagnosis, intervention, and patient education. However, because the category of schizophrenia lacks scientific validity and masks considerable heterogeneity, a diagnosis of schizophrenia provides little useful clinical information. A serious assessment is still required to understand what is wrong and what is likely to help (Spaulding, Sullivan, & Poland 2003; Silverstein, Spaulding, & Menditto 2006); the diagnosis adds nothing of use for these purposes. Further, in addition to not playing a significant role in furthering clinical purposes, it has also been argued (Poland 2003) that the concept of schizophrenia functions as a harmful clinical stereotype that distorts clinician practices of assessment, inference, understanding, and intervention planning and that, because it introduces stigmatizing labels that shape first- and third-person identities, harmfully impacts the psychosocial context of clinical practice. That is, not only does the concept not play a constructive role, it plays a harmful role as well.

Outlook

The prospects for the future of the concept of schizophrenia and the practices based upon it are at best uncertain. Although there are current efforts to revise and improve the *DSM* criteria for schizophrenia as part of the *DSM-5* revision process, these are not likely to lead to any substantial changes in existing diagnostic criteria, since the research base is too weak and any change would be viewed as too disruptive to existing practices. However, there are other approaches on the horizon that hold out more promise. For example, researchers in genetics have recognized the existing problem of phenotypic definition and have proposed research on "endophenotypes," which are more precisely defined traits that offer up better research targets (Thaker 2008.) Such endophenotypes, however, are not likely to be strongly correlated with "schizophrenia," and this research is perhaps best viewed as concerned with severe mental illness and should not be hampered by prior associations with the concept of schizophrenia.

Another research approach, the NIMH Research Domain Criteria initiative (Insel 2010), also similarly recognizes that *DSM* categories have not led to research that validates the categories. This initiative calls for research proposals that do not necessarily rely on *DSM* categories like schizophrenia and that focus instead on well-defined research domains identified in the basic sciences of human functioning (e.g., executive functioning, fear processing, reinforcement learning, etc.) This proposal has promise to the extent that it is able to break from the problematic categories of the *DSM* (especially schizophrenia) and to the extent that it is not restricted to narrow areas of basic science (e.g., genetics and neuroscience). A broad-based research program free of *DSM* categories and drawing on a wide range of sciences at all levels of analysis (from the genetic to the social) is likely required for a better scientific understanding of severe mental illness.

Finally, alternative approaches to clinical practices concerned with severe mental illness (i.e., approaches that depart from practices centered on the schizophrenia concept and the consensus view) are also available. Although it is widely assumed that clinical practice for severe mental illness should take a highly medicalized form, alternative approaches modeled more on rehabilitation paradigms have typically proven to be more successful and have tended to be more in touch with the needs of those seeking help (Spaulding, Sullivan, & Poland 2003; Silverstein, Spaulding, & Menditto 2006.) In such approaches, the concept of schizophrenia plays no substantial role.

In time, the concept of schizophrenia will likely disappear in both research and clinical contexts, as more sophisticated research and clinical programs emerge. Exactly what form such alternatives will eventually take is still open and is a matter of substantial scientific, clinical, and social importance.

See also Chronic Mental Illness; *Diagnostic and Statistical Manual of Mental Disorders (DSM)*; Genetics and Mental Health; History of Mental Health Care; Medical Model of Mental Illness; Recovery Movement

Bibliography

American Psychiatric Association. 1952. *Diagnostic and Statistical Manual of Mental Disorders I*. Washington, DC: American Psychiatric Association.

American Psychiatric Association. 1968. *Diagnostic and Statistical Manual of Mental Disorders II*. Washington, DC: American Psychiatric Association.

American Psychiatric Association. 1980. *Diagnostic and Statistical Manual of Mental Disorders III*. Washington, DC: American Psychiatric Association.

American Psychiatric Association. 1994. *Diagnostic and Statistical Manual of Mental Disorders IV*. Washington, DC: American Psychiatric Association.

American Psychiatric Association. 2000. *Diagnostic and Statistical Manual of Mental Disorders IV-TR*. Washington, DC: American Psychiatric Publishing.

Andreasen, N. 1982. "Negative Symptoms in Schizophrenia: Definition and Reliability." *Archives of General Psychiatry* 39: 784–788.

Andreasen, N. 2001. *Brave New Brain*. New York: Oxford University Press.

Andreasen, N., S. Arndt, R. Alliger, D. Miller, and M. Flaum. 1995. "Symptoms of Schizophrenia: Methods, Meanings, and Mechanisms." *Archives of General Psychiatry* 52: 341–351.

Bentall, R. 2003. *Madness Explained: Psychosis and Human Nature*. London: Allen Lane.

Bleuler, E. 1911. *Dementia Praecox or the Group of Schizophrenias*. Translated by J. Zitkin. New York: International Universities Press.

Boyle, M. 2002. *Schizophrenia: A Scientific Delusion?* (2nd ed.). New York: Routledge.

Carson, R. 1996. "Aristotle, Galileo, and the *DSM* Taxonomy: The Case of Schizophrenia." *Journal of Consulting and Clinical Psychology* 64: 1133–1139.

Crow, T. 1980. "Molecular Pathology of Schizophrenia: More Than One Disease Process?" *British Medical Journal* 280: 66–68.

Fischer, B., and W. Carpenter. 2009. "Will the Kraepelinean Dichotomy Survive *DSM-V?*" *Neuropsychopharmacology* 34: 2081–2087.

Green, M. 2001. *Schizophrenia Revealed*. New York: Norton.

Heinrichs, R. W. 2001. *In Search of Madness*. New York: Oxford University Press.

Hyman, S. 2010. "The Diagnosis of Mental Disorders: The Problem of Reification." *Annual Review of Clinical Psychology* 6: 155–179.

Insel, T. 2010. "Rethinking Schizophrenia." *Nature* 469: 187–193.

Klerman, G. 1978. "The Evolution of a Scientific Nosology." In J. Shershow, ed., *Schizophrenia: Research and Practice* (pp. 99–121). Cambridge, MA: Harvard University Press.

Kraepelin, E. 1896. *Psychiatrie*, (5th ed.). Leipzig: Barth.

Kraepelin, E. 1919. *Dementia Praecox and Paraphrenia*. Translated by R. M. Barclay. Edinburgh: Livingstone. (Originally published in *Psychiatrie*, 8th ed., 1913)

Laing, R. 1983. *The Politics of Experience*. New York: Pantheon.

Liddle, P. 1987. "The Symptoms of Chronic Schizophrenia. A Re-examination of the Positive-Negative Dichotomy." *British Journal of Psychiatry* 151 (August): 145–151.

Poland, J. 2004. "Bias and Schizophrenia." In P. Caplan and L. Cosgrove, eds., *Bias in Psychiatric Diagnosis* (pp. 149–162). Lanham, MD: Jason Aaronson.

Scheff, T. 1999. *Being Mentally Ill* (3rd ed.). New Brunswick, NJ: Aldine Transaction Press.

Schneider, K. 1959. *Clinical Psychopathology* (5th ed.). New York: Grune and Stratton.

Silverstein, S., W. Spaulding, and A. Menditto. 2006. *Schizophrenia*. Cambridge, MA: Hogrefe.

Spaulding, W., M. Sullivan, and J. Poland. 2003. *Treatment and Rehabilitation of Severe Mental Illness*. New York: Guilford Press.

Szasz, T. 1988. *Schizophrenia: The Sacred Symbol of Psychiatry*. Syracuse, NY: Syracuse University Press.

Thaker, G. 2008. "Psychosis Endophenotypes in Schizophrenia and Bipolar Disorder." *Schizophrenia Bulletin* 34: 720–721.

School Mental Health

Donna L. Burton, Ardis Hanson, Bruce Lubotsky Levin, and Oliver T. Massey

The *Report of the Surgeon General's Conference on Children's Mental Health* (2000) identified the growing incidence of mental, emotional, and behavioral disorders in children as well as the unmet need for services to address these concerns. Approximately 1 out of every 10 children faces some degree of impairment in their skills of daily living as a result of mental illnesses, and 5 percent of children experience extreme functional impairment.

This entry explores key topics in school mental health, including common emotional and behavioral disorders in childhood and adolescence, the impact of mental disorders on academic progress, a brief history of legislation and policy making related to mental health services in schools, and the current status of school mental health services delivery systems in the United States. Implications for the implementation of effective school-based mental health programming and notable barriers to implementation will be discussed.

Epidemiology

Reviews of epidemiologic studies over the past decade report on the growing recognition that the onset of mental disorders, including psychosis, mood disorders, and substance-related disorders, are highest between adolescence and early adulthood. In addition, the findings from a review of multiple studies reveal that when a wide range of diagnoses are considered, approximately one-quarter of the child and adolescent population will have some type of mental disorder during any three- to six-month time frame (Green-Hennessy 2010).

Moreover, it is clear that the presence of both internalizing and externalizing mental disorders in childhood predisposes individuals to subsequent mental health and substance use problems in late adolescence and early adulthood. Internalizing disorders manifest as being sad or irritable and withdrawn from others; crying more than usual; seeming fearful, worried, or anxious; expressing guilt; shame or feelings of worthlessness; voicing somatic complaints; being inattentive; being easily distracted; and/or being hyperactive. Externalizing disorders are also referred to as "acting out" or rule-breaking behaviors (e.g., running away, lying, stealing, and truancy) as well as aggressive or oppositional-defiant behaviors (e.g., arguing with others, refusing to follow instructions, having temper tantrums, initiating physical fights, destroying property, or being purposely mean).

While 12 to 22 percent of all persons under the age of 18 years are in need of interventions to address mental, emotional, and behavioral problems, national data have revealed that fully 80 percent of children under the age of 18 years who need services do not receive them (Maternal and Child Health Bureau 2010), despite the numerous policies, regulations, and initiatives the U.S. federal government has created to promote access to mental health services to children and adolescents.

Legislation

When children do receive mental health services, they are most likely to access them in school settings. More than 6 million students receive special education services, with over two-thirds of these students identified as having emotional disabilities, mental retardation, or learning disabilities (Aud et al. 2011). Schools have become critical organizational settings for the delivery of mental health and behavioral services for students and have been described as "the de facto provider" of mental health services for children. As a result, school-based prevention and intervention have become essential strategies for reducing the incidence of emotional and behavioral dysfunction among children.

Legislation initiated in the mid- to late 1960s, in conjunction with deinstitutionalization and the push for delivery of mental health services in community settings, set the stage for the evolution of school health programs to include mental health services. Subsequently, because of the lack of services available to children in traditional community mental health settings over the past 50 years, national policy development and reform have established school settings as a primary venue for child and adolescent mental health interventions.

In 1964, the National Institute of Mental Health (NIMH) published a major monograph on school mental health. *The Protection and Promotion of Mental Health in Schools* (Lambert et al. 1965) became a policy benchmark and served as a catalyst for major efforts and program initiatives to expand clinical and prevention services in schools. Public Law 89-10, the Elementary and Secondary Education Act of 1965 (ESEA), was one of the most far-reaching federal legislative acts affecting education. ESEA emphasized equal access to education by addressing achievement gaps between students by increasing opportunities to achieve education with in-school supports. The notion of expanded services to children who do not have serious emotional disturbances (SEDs) and who do not require special education services was reiterated under the Bush administration in 2001 with passage of Public Law 107-110, the No Child Left Behind Act (NCLB), which expanded and reauthorized the ESEA (Commission on Youth 2011).

Public Law 94-142, the Education for All Handicapped Children Act of 1975 (EHA), was the culmination of significant efforts to enact legislation requiring schools to serve all children with disabilities and among them, children with SEDs. Prior to the EHA, only one out of five children with disabilities received schooling through the public education system. In fact, a number of state laws excluded children with certain disabilities from attending public school, including explicit exclusions for children identified as "emotionally disturbed" or "mentally retarded" (West et al. 2000). EHA was reauthorized with expanded protections in 1997 and in 2004. The important revisions found in the reauthorization included the provision of mental health services to all children, whether or not they had SEDs, and counseling provided to parents to further their understanding of the nature of a child's particular disability (Commission on Youth 2011).

In 1990, Public Law 101-476, the Individuals with Disabilities Education Act (IDEA), provided for governance as to how states and public agencies deliver special education services, including mental health services to children with disabilities. The IDEA and related policy efforts provide for widespread adoption of special education services for all children with disabilities.

In 1995, the Health Resources and Services Administration (HRSA) and the Maternal Child Health Bureau (MCHB) introduced the Mental Health in Schools Program, a concerted effort toward advancement of mental health services in schools. The emphasis of the Mental Health in Schools Program centered on increasing capacity for schools and communities to jointly address the mental health and psychosocial needs of students. Two national centers (Center for School Mental Health Analysis & Action and the Center for Mental Health in Schools) were established in 1995 to provide technical assistance and training (Anglin 2003). Both the Mental Health in Schools Program and its related centers were renewed in 2000 and in 2005. In addition, other organizations, such as the Research and Training Center for Children's Mental Health in the Louis de la Parte Florida Mental Health Institute at the University of South Florida, and the Center for Child and Human Development at Georgetown University, have emerged as major research centers advancing school mental health services. They serve as major hubs for the collection, cataloguing, and dissemination of information on school-based mental health research (Commission on Youth 2011).

In 1999, the U.S. Departments of Education, Health and Human Services, and Justice announced the Safe Schools/Healthy Students Initiative. This federal grant program was developed to promote the health and safety of students by comprehensively addressing the social, behavioral and mental health issues of public school students (U.S. Department of Education et. al. 2012). This program was unique because it involved the cooperation and joint funding of the three U.S. departments and required the use of comprehensive, evidence-based programs to support the healthy development of students. This program also emphasized ongoing cooperation between schools and community providers.

The Impact of SEDs on Academic Success

Schools are a good match for the provision of mental health services to children and adolescents. Perhaps the most notable impact of mental disorders in children is the detrimental effect on the ability to function in school. The relationship between mental health problems and impairments in academic progress and achievement in children is well documented (Reid et al. 2004). Mental illness categorically impairs components of learning, such as concentration, attentiveness, and demonstration of the mastery of newly acquired knowledge and skills. The functional impairments that go hand in hand with mental illness affect all aspects of academic progress. Children with mental illness often experience a pervasive inability to learn even when intellectual deficits, sensory impairments, or other health conditions are not present. Further, mental disorders impact socialization and the capacity of forming supportive relationships with peers, teachers, and other mentors in the school setting that are vital to academic success.

Deleterious effects on school functioning progress as symptoms of a mental illness persist and worsen. A child may recognize his or her own inappropriate behavior in comparison to peers, become increasingly unhappy, moody, or depressed, and begin to manifest anxiety, fear, or physical symptoms in the face of academic and social failures. Low graduation rates, poor grades, high rates of absenteeism, difficulty acquiring the skills needed to progress academically, and deficits in relationships with peers and adults are all associated with children with untreated SEDs. Additionally, for the individual child, untreated mental illness increases the likelihood of suicide and suicide attempts, an accelerated progression of the illness, an increase in risk behaviors and involvement in juvenile justice systems, and damage to brain functioning overall (Commission on Youth 2011).

On the other hand, when schools do adopt practices that support mental health and promote access to mental health interventions, they report higher academic achievement in students, reduced incidence of student absence from school, and an overall reduction in behavioral problems in students. School boards of directors, administrators, and policy makers are becoming increasingly aware of the need to empower teachers and school mental health staff to recognize warning signs and risk factors associated with the emergence of mental illness in children and adolescents. Moreover, to address the needs of students with SED, schools are being increasingly encouraged to create positive environments that enhance children's social and emotional development in healthy learning environments (O'Connell, Boat, & Warner 2009).

Organization of Mental Health Services in the Schools

A significant proportion of all schools provide behavioral health (including alcohol, drug abuse, and mental health) services through some form of agreement with community-based mental health providers, and most schools depend on some form of referral process to these community providers. There are five organizing formats for the delivery of school-based mental health services: (1) classroom-based curricula; (2) school-financed student support services; (3) district-based school clinics or mental health units; (4) formalized, community-based mental health services; and (5) comprehensive and integrated systems of care (SOCs). The most comprehensive organizing formats are models #4 and #5 noted above, which are associated with formal arrangements to provide coordinated care to students with at least minimal collaboration across service entities.

Similar models have been proposed that include expanded school mental health services, comprehensive and interconnected systems of prevention, and early intervention and care (Weist et al. 2010). These approaches are often described as tier models, with the largest number of students served broadly in curricula-based prevention and early intervention programs, and a significantly smaller number served through intensive, individualized care. The Center for Mental Health in Schools at UCLA describes a tier approach that ensures the use of the least intensive intervention needed, but with a clear continuum of programs and services to address progressively complex emotional and behavioral needs. One such formalized, curricula-based model is Response to Intervention (Batsche et al. 2005)

Response to Intervention (RtI) is a team-based model for the early identification of students who are at risk for learning problems. The approach hinges on matching youth to a level of intervention appropriate to their specific needs (Batsche et al. 2005). RtI is a three-tiered model: from core curricula or universal prevention interventions that can conceivably be offered to all students (Tier 1); to targeted group interventions for students who need supplemental help beyond school-wide positive behavior supports (Tier 2); and finally to intensive individualized interventions for those few students with more significant mental health needs. Students may initiate services at any tier, or may progress through levels of care as needed (Batsche et al. 2005). Policy-setting efforts (e.g., the reauthorization of the Individuals with Disabilities Education Improvement Act) encourage school districts toward the utilization of models like RtI that systematically monitor progress and provide for more intensive levels of care and can reduce the incidence of placement in special education.

Even with these successful models of school-based mental health services, it is recognized that there are challenges to successfully operating behavioral health services in schools. Cutting across each of these comprehensive organizing formats is the concern for barriers that prevent the effective implementation, operation, and sustainability of evidence-based programs (EBPs). These barriers often prevent the ability of schools to change or adopt new policies and procedures for the implementation of effective mental health service interventions for children with behavioral health problems. These barriers exist because of a range of contextual issues at the individual, organizational, state, and national levels that influence the effectiveness of behavioral health services in real-world settings. Services may not be of sufficient quality to produce successful outcomes because the services implemented no longer resemble the original evidence-based practices. Interventions may also fail to be responsive to the cultural needs of the local community.

Services Delivery

The successful delivery of mental health services to children in school settings depends a great deal on the broadening of our understanding of the term "mental health." If mental health is conceptualized on a spectrum ranging from health to illness, then the entire spectrum must be considered in the promotion of a well-integrated services delivery system within schools. School mental health services can and should provide for counseling and therapy targeted to those students with diagnosable or identifiable mental illnesses. However, they should also address: the promotion of social development, early detection, and intervention at the onset of learning and behavioral problems; the uncovering of structural and attitudinal barriers to learning and healthy development; promotion of healthy families; enhancement of childhood resilience and protective factors; reductions in systemic issues within schools that affect learning and mental health; and the development of school-community relationships that promote access to health and mental health services (Center for Mental Health in Schools at UCLA 2006).

The provision of mental health services to youth in school settings presents complex problems due to the need to merge two service silos: (1) the general education curricula, and (2) the delivery of mental health services. Moreover, the design and protocols of these fields and the professionals who represent them do not have a long-standing and shared tradition of communication in the interest of program development. Effective approaches to services delivery, however, will necessarily be promulgated in the merging of school and community systems of services delivery. According to the Center for Mental Health in Schools at UCLA (2006), it is critical that "a full continuum of systematically interconnected school and community interventions" should promote health development and emphasize prevention and rapid response to issues as they arise.

Ideally, the range of school mental health services offered includes health promotion and promotion of prosocial development, prevention, early intervention, treatment, and crisis intervention. It is critical that interventions are grounded in evidence-based practice. Models of services delivery have been proposed that encompass these tiers of services.

Implications for Mental Health

The NCLB of 2001 and the IDEA of 2004 emphasize the importance of the schools' role in supporting cognitive and behavioral development in students, particularly those identified with learning problems. However, as schools are asked to support these programs, there are structural, programmatic, and financial challenges to mental health services integration, especially in the implementation of evidence-based practices. Powers, Bowen, and Bowen (2010) suggest there are significant barriers that prevent the implementation of best practices in schools, including the lack of resources, a lack of time available for training, the lack of staff to implement programs in class, and an increasing emphasis on improving test scores.

Problems may also arise because schools are not primarily organized to facilitate the provision of behavioral health services. As a result, these services may not have enough status in the organizational as well as political hierarchy. When the culture of most schools emphasizes instruction and academic outcomes, there may not be structures in place to support a comprehensive approach to mental health services. The emphasis on performance, as dictated by NCLB, may further exacerbate this problem. At the school level, teachers and administrators may resist efforts to provide mental health services for students with significant emotional and behavioral problems because they perceive these efforts as time consuming, difficult to implement, or too costly. Even well-integrated services may not be utilized by students, compromising their effectiveness (Yampolskaya, Massey, & Greenbaum 2006).

Future efforts toward school mental health will necessarily see a restructuring in services delivery and policy reformation toward integrated and collaborative efforts. Emphasis on integrated services, implementation of evidence-based practices, and the collaboration of school and community mental health service delivery systems will help to address the multiple challenges facing implementation of mental health services in schools.

See also Adolescence and Mental Health; Campus Life and Mental Health; Children and Mental Health; Residential Treatment for Young People

Bibliography

American Association of School Administrators. 2011. School Mental Health (Resources). http://www.aasa.org/content.aspx?id=4686

Anglin, Trina Menden. 2003. "Mental Health in School: Program of the Federal Government." In Mark D. Weist, Steven W. Evans, and Nancy A. Lever, eds., *Handbook of School Mental Health Programs: Advancing Practice and Research* (pp. 89–106). Norwell, MA: Kluwer Academic.

Aud, Susan, William Hussar, Grace Kena, Kevin Bianco, Lauren Frohlich, Jana Kemp, Kim Tahan, Katy Mallory, Thomas Nachazel, and Gretchen Hannes. 2011. *The Condition of Education 2011*. Washington, DC: Institute of Education Statistics. Retrieved from http://nces.ed.gov/pubs2011/2011033.pdf

Batsche, George, Judy Elliot, Janet L. Graden, Jeffrey Grimes, Joseph F. Kovaleski, David Prasse, Daniel Reschly, Judy Schrag, and W. David Tilly III. 2005. *Response to Intervention: Policy Considerations and Implementation*. Alexandria, VA: National Association of State Directors of Special Education.

Center for Mental Health in Schools at UCLA. 2006. *The Current Status of Mental Health in Schools: A Policy and Practice Analysis*. Los Angeles: University of California. Retrieved from http://smhp.psych.ucla.edu/pdfdocs/currentstatusmh/Report.pdf.

Commission on Youth. 2011. "School-Based Mental Health Services." In *Collection of Evidence-Based Practices for Children and Adolescents with Mental Health Treatment Needs* (4th ed., pp. 239–245). Richmond: Commonwealth of Virginia, Commission on Youth. Retrieved from http://leg2.state.va.us/dls/h&sdocs.nsf/By+Year/HD92010/$file/HD9.pdf.

Franklin, Cynthia, Mary Beth Harris, and Paula Allen-Meares. 2008. *The School Practitioner's Concise Companion to Mental Health*. New York: Oxford University Press.

Green-Hennessy, Sharon. 2010. "Children and Adolescents." In Bruce Lubotsky Levin, Kevin D. Hennessy, and John Petrila, eds., *Mental Health Services: A Public Health Perspective* (3rd ed., pp. 201–225). New York: Oxford University Press.

Lambert, Nadine M., Eli Michael Bower, George Kaplan, John N. Duggan, William G. Hollister, Donald C. Klein, Nevitt Sanford, and Daniel Schreiber. 1965. *The Protection and Promotion of Mental Health in Schools* (Mental health monograph series, no. 5). Bethesda, MD: National Institute of Mental Health.

Maternal and Child Health Bureau. 2010. *The Mental and Emotional Well-Being of Children: A Portrait of States and the Nation 2007*. Rockville, MD: U.S. Department of Health and Human Services, Health Resources and Services Administration, Maternal and Child Health Bureau. Retrieved from http://www.mchb.hrsa.gov/nsch/07emohealth/moreinfo/pdf/nsch07.pdf.

O'Connell, Mary Ellen, Thomas Boat, and Kenneth E. Warner. 2009. *Preventing Mental, Emotional, and Behavioral Disorders among Young People: Progress and Possibilities*. Washington, DC: National Academies Press. Retrieved from http://www.nap.edu/catalog.php?record_id=12480.

Office of the Surgeon General. 2000. *Report of the Surgeon General's Conference on Children's Mental Health: A National Action Agenda*. Washington, DC: U.S. Department of Health and Human Services, Public Health Service. Retrieved from http://www.surgeongeneral.gov/topics/cmh/childreport.html

Powers, Joelle D., Natasha K. Bowen, and Gary L. Bowen. 2010. "Evidence-Based Programs in School Settings: Barriers and Recent Advances." *Journal of Evidence-Based Social Work* 7: 313–331.

Reid, Robert, Jorge E. Gonzalez, Philip D. Nordess, Alexandra Trout, and Michael H. Epstein. 2004. "A Meta-Analysis of the Academic Status of Students with Emotional/Behavioral Disturbance." *The Journal of Special Education* 38: 130–143.

U.S. Departments of Education, Health and Human Services, and Justice. 2012. "The Safe Schools/Healthy Students Iniatiative." Retrieved from http://www.sshs.samhsa.gov/default.aspx

Weist, Mark D., Robert Burke, Carl Paternite, Julie Goldstein Grumet, and Paul Flaspohler. 2010. "School Mental Health." In Bruce Lubotsky Levin, Kevin D. Hennessy, and John Petrila, eds., *Mental Health Services: A Public Health Perspective* (3rd ed., pp. 201–225). New York: Oxford University Press.

West, Jane, Nancy Mudrick, Mark A. Mlawer, Diane Lipton, Jillian Cutler, Allison Drimmer, Bill Smith, and Chantel Sampogna. 2000. *Back to School on Civil Rights: Advancing the Federal Commitment to Leave No Child Behind*. Washington, DC: National Council on Disability. Retrieved from http://www.eric.ed.gov/PDFS/ED438632.pdf.

Yampolskaya, Svetlana, Oliver T. Massey, and Paul Greenbaum. 2006. "At-Risk High School Students in the Gaining Early Awareness and Readiness Program (GEAR UP): Academic and Behavioral Outcomes." *Journal of Primary Prevention* 27: 457–475.

Self-Help

Victoria E. Kress, Melinda Wolford, and Richard Van Voorhis

While self-help can have many definitions, it is generally defined as the act of helping or improving oneself, typically without the formal assistance of a trained professional (Pratt, Halliday, & Maxwell 2009). According to Pratt and colleagues (2009), self-help interventions in the mental health field tend to be based on professionally developed resources, often drawing on cognitive-behavioral therapy (CBT) techniques, and are typically self-administered or delivered with limited therapeutic contact. Reasons for pursuing self-help treatment typically stem from the person's quest to change in an effort to reach his or her personal goals.

The self-help movement as a whole, long a staple of American life, has exploded in recent decades and is now a large and profitable industry (McGee 2005). As indicated by current best-seller lists, many of those seeking self-improvement (not limited to mental health recovery) turn to works by such self-help gurus as Dale Carnegie (1888–1955), Stephen Covey (1932–), and Eckhart Tolle (1948–). Others, including those seeking help with relationships, personal health, and mental health, follow the lectures of such popular speakers

---

When Self-Help Became Big Business

According to Ian Dowbiggin, author of *The Quest for Mental Health*, the flood of self-help books began in 1976 with Thomas A. Harris's best seller, *I'm Okay—You're Okay*. As Dowbiggin notes further,

> After Harris, authors of such books became virtual gurus, notably "Doctor Phil" McGraw, Tony Robbins, Deepak Chopra, and Robert Fulghum. Daytime television programs, including *Oprah* and *Donahue*, were watched by millions and provided forums in which these self-appointed experts spread their teachings. Mainstream magazines such as *Redbook* and *Ladies' Home Journal* ran countless stories on how to improve the quality of one's emotional life. In 2003 alone, between 3,500 and 4,000 self-help books were published. (Dowbiggin 2011: 191)

Source: Ian Dowbiggin, *The Quest for Mental Health* (Cambridge University Press, 2011), 191.

as Dr. Phil (Phil McGraw; 1950–), Dr. Laura (Laura Schlessinger; 1947–), and John Gray (1951–). Still others utilize online forums or support groups to read posted comments, post topics themselves, and privately communicate with others regarding similar areas of interest and/or need.

Self-help was not a widely studied topic and did not receive significant attention from social scientists until the early 1970s. Since then, however, systematic research on self-help has been more abundant with much of it suggesting that self-help methods can indeed be helpful (Lieberman & Snowden 1994). Self-help is recognized by many in the mental health profession as an integral aspect of successful, sustained mental health treatment.

Self-Help Methods

There are a number of different self-help philosophies and corresponding types of activities. Sometimes, mental health professionals may assign or suggest clients' use of self-help materials. Recently, Nordgreen and Havik (2011) conducted a study to investigate how psychologists in clinical practice perceived and used self-help materials with clients who have anxiety and depression. Results indicated that the majority of the study sample (73.0%) recommended self-help interventions primarily as a supplement to individual or group therapy. Furthermore, 16.6 percent recommended self-help approaches to prevent relapse, 6.8 percent recommended self-help as an alternative to therapist contact, and 1.2 percent recommended it help for clients on waiting list. Written materials in the form of brochures or books were recommended most frequently (79.1%), with CBT-based self-help books being the most common (14.2%). Internet resources were recommended by 41.9 percent, and recorded materials (e.g., videos, CDs, and audiotapes) were recommended by between 6 percent and 10 percent of the sample. Reportedly, the primary aim of such self-help materials was to provide clients with general information about mental health disorders and how to cope with them.

Peer support groups are one type of self-help method that gained increasing popularity over the years. Peer support provides an opportunity for those seeking self-improvement to draw on the collective wisdom of peers to learn coping skills that can assist in recovery. Peer support involves one person supporting another person who has a similar need for change or recovery. Some believe that people who have similar experiences and needs are, in these situations, better able to provide authentic empathy and validation (Campbell 2005). There is a growing body of evidence indicating that peer support provides a solid context for recovery and healing (Mead & Copeland 2000).

Alcoholics Anonymous (AA; established in 1935), is likely the most prominent peer support group in the world, and has been successful in helping millions of people overcome severe alcohol abuse (Makela et al., 1996). Narcotics

Anonymous is another influential self-help group that has as its focus helping people to eliminate their use of drugs. Owing to the perceived benefits of these self-help groups, a myriad of different peer support groups have been developed along similar lines (e.g., Overeaters Anonymous).

In America, three basic types of self-help peer support groups have emerged over time. These include (1) individuals with similar problems, motives, and goals (e.g., AA); (2) groups that are interested in a similar cause and volunteer their services; and (3) groups that include a paid professional and may be more of a mixed population seeking both collaboration and guidance in the self-improvement process (e.g., Weight Watchers, Regional Tobacco Treatment Center programs) (Bairaktaris 1994).

Self-Help Benefits, Drawbacks, and Points to Consider

There are a number of practical benefits to self-help. First, self-help options are both readily available and relatively inexpensive. They also can provide ways to privately explore issues without meeting others face to face. Finally, self-help approaches allow individuals to customize and take responsibility for their own therapeutic plan, which may lead to a sense of ownership and empowerment.

Despite the apparent advantages, when incorporating self-help strategies into a treatment plan, individuals may lack the perspective needed to properly understand the nature of key issues, including the choice of the best self-help strategy for their situation. Lay people may also misunderstand, and consequently incorrectly implement, treatment plans. Furthermore, individuals may lack the motivation to stick with a self-help plan without assistance, especially if they are misled by exaggerated claims about treatment effectiveness. And, to be sure, there is no shortage of such exaggerated or false claims (Salerno 2005).

MacLeod, Martinez, and Williams (2009) caution that exclusive usage of self-help approaches can increase the possibility of misdiagnosis (self-diagnosis). Furthermore, because so many self-help resources are available, it is difficult for those who are untrained and inexperienced in the field to correctly identify and individualize treatment. Finally, unsupervised self-help approaches provide no objective method to detect worsening of clinical symptoms. Thus for those with more severe symptoms and complicated issues, clinical monitoring by a trained professional is generally recommended as a complement to self-help.

See also Mental Health Counseling; Nutritional Therapies; Peer Support Groups; Popular Remedies and Quackery; Psychotherapy; Recovery Movement; Undiagnosed Mental Illness

Bibliography

Bairaktaris, K. 1994. *Mental Health and Social Intervention*. Athens, Greece: Enallaktikes Ekdoseis.

Campbell, J. 2005. *Effectiveness Findings of the COSP Multisite Research Initiative Grading the Evidence for Consumer-Driven Services*. Chicago: UIC NRTC Webcast.

Lieberman, M. A., and L. R. Snowden. 1994. "Problems in Assessing Prevalence and Membership Characteristics of Self-Help Group Participants." In T. J. Powell, ed., *Understanding the Self-Help Organization* (pp. 32–61). Thousand Oaks, CA: Sage.

MacLeod, M., R. Martinez, and C. Williams. 2009. "Cognitive Behaviour Therapy Self-Help: Who Does It Help and What Are Its Drawbacks?" *Behavioral & Cognitive Psychotherapy* 37(1): 61–72.

Mäkelä, K., I. Arminen, K. Bloomfield, I. Eisenbach-Stangl, K. H. Bergmark, N. Kurube, N. Mariolini, H. Ólafsdóttir, J. H. Peterson, M. Phillips, J. Rehm, R. Room, P. Rosenqvist, H. Rosovsky, K. Stenius, G. Światkiewicz, B. Woronowicz, and A. Zielínski. 1996. *Alcoholics Anonymous as a Mutual Help Movement*. Madison: University of Wisconsin Press.

McGee, M. 2005. *Self-Help, Inc.: Makeover Culture in American Life*. New York: Oxford University Press.

Mead, S., and M. E. Copeland. 2000. "What Recovery Means to Us: Consumers' Perspectives." *Community Mental Health Journal* 36(3): 315–328.

National Mental Health Consumers' Self-Help Clearinghouse. http://www.mhselfhelp.org.

Nordgreen, T., and O. Havik. 2011. "Use of Self-Help Materials for Anxiety and Depression in Mental Health Services: A National Survey of Psychologists in Norway." *Professional Psychology: Research and Practice* 42(2): 185–191.

Pratt, R., E. Halliday, and M. Maxwell. 2009. "Professional and Service-User Perception of Self-Help in Primary Care Mental Health Services." *Health and Social Care in the Community* 17(2): 209–215.

Redding, R. E., J. D. Herbert, E. M. Forman, and B. A. Gaudiano. "Popular Self-Help Books for Anxiety, Depression, and Trauma: How Scientifically Grounded and Useful Are They?" *Professional Psychology: Research and Practice* 39(5): 537–545. Retrieved from http://www.ocdhope.com/docs/Self-help-Redding.pdf.

Salerno, Steve. 2005. *SHAM: How the Self-Help Movement Made America Helpless*. New York: Crown.

Self-Injury and Body Image

Margaret Leaf

Self-injury tends to be associated with young women and girls, whereas injuring others is associated with young men and boys. Both behaviors may be understood as forms of gendered violence, directed outward for men and boys and inward for women and girls. While boys learn to act *through* their bodies with physical violence, girls learn to act *on* their bodies with self-inflicted violence.

Background

Adolescence and young adulthood are rife with both physiological transformations (for example, puberty) and social transitions (for example, changing schools, shifting orientation from family to peers) that young people often experience as distressful. However, there is evidence suggesting that the ways people respond to this distress are gendered. Specifically, girls and women are more likely to direct their distress inward, taking it out on themselves, while boys and men are more likely to direct their distress outward, taking it out on others. This can be seen in the higher rates of other-directed violence among boys and young men and higher rates of eating disorders and self-injury among young women.

Of these responses to distress, self-injury has only recently received attention from the media and scientific communities, increasing public attention and debate about the topic. First and foremost, these debates center on the definition of self-injury. Currently, most researchers view self-injury as some type of deliberate harm to one's own body without conscious suicidal intent. However, definitions of the behavior vary greatly in terms of social acceptability, severity, and frequency. For example, some researchers include such behaviors as interfering with wound healing (that is, picking at scabs) and nail biting in their definition, while others specify much more severe and stigmatized behaviors such as self-castration and bone breaking. Additionally, some researchers focus on repetitive self-injurious behaviors, such as head banging or self-hitting, particularly among people who are differently abled. Finally, researchers even disagree about what to call the behavior. While "self-injury" is probably the most common term used, other terms include "cutting," "deliberate self-harm," "self-abuse," "self-injurious behavior," "self-mutilation," and "suicidal" or "parasuicidal behavior."

In addition to disagreement about how to define self-injury, there is also disagreement about who engages in self-injury and how common it is. Estimates of the prevalence of self-injury vary from less than 1 percent to 4 percent in the general population and from 15 percent to 35 percent among adolescent and college-aged samples (Briere & Gil 1998; Favazza 1996; Gratz 2003; Laye-Gindhu & Schonert-Reichl 2005; Whitlock, Powers, & Eckenrode 2006). These differences are mostly due to the fact that there are no nationally representative data on self-injury, so most samples are small or highly specific (for example, students sampled in a university class). Also, while most research has focused on self-injury among white women in the United States, there is a growing body of research on self-injury among other racial groups and in other countries, particularly among Asian women (see Bhardwaj 2001 and Marshall & Yazdani 1991 on self-harm among Asian women; Kinyanda, Hjelmeland, & Musisi 2005 on self-harm in Uganda). Additionally, there is some research suggesting that self-injury is more prevalent among gay, lesbian, and bisexual people (Adler & Adler 2005; Alexander & Clare 2004; Whitlock, Powers, & Eckenrode 2006) as well as among prison populations. One of the few consistencies across most studies is that self-injury typically begins during adolescence or young adulthood and tends to persist for an average of 10 to 15 years, though it may continue for decades (Favazza 1996; Muehlenkamp 2005). Some research indicates that self-injury may be likely

Self-Injury Awareness, Prevention, and Treatment

Awareness of self-injury is increasing, as evidenced by the movement for a Self Injury Awareness Day, set for March 1 of every year, on which people may promote awareness by wearing an orange ribbon.

As awareness increases, prevention becomes easier. First and foremost, self-injurers may be best served by being listened to and encouraged rather than stigmatized or ignored. Building allies in communities and schools, raising awareness, and promoting a sense of power among young people—particularly young women—are all essential steps toward prevention.

Treatment for self-injury is available in many places, in many forms. The S.A.F.E. (Self-Abuse Finally Ends) program supports a national hotline: 1-800-DONTCUT. There are also many therapists, counselors, and other mental health professionals who specialize in treating self-injury. Visit http://www.selfinjury.com for more information.

in some elderly populations, due in part to higher rates of depression and isolation (Dennis, Wakefield, Molloy, Andrews, & Friedman 2005).

For the most part, media depictions of self-injury paint it as a uniquely adolescent and female problem, as evidenced by movies such as *Thirteen* and *Girl, Interrupted*, as well as talk shows such as *Oprah* featuring only female guests who self-injure (Brickman 2004). Yet because there are no nationally representative data on the prevalence of self-injury, it is unclear to what extent women really are likely to self-injure or whether it is a media myth. While a few clinical and community studies have shown that self-injury is as common among men as it is among women (Briere & Gil 1998; Gratz 2003), other studies show that self-injury is less common among men and may be carried out differently among men as well. For example, a study of 2,875 students at Cornell University and Princeton University found that 17 percent had self-injured at some point in their lives, and women were about one and a half times as likely as men to be repeat self-injurers (Whitlock, Powers, & Eckenrode 2006). Additionally, women were more than twice as likely as men to scratch or cut themselves, while men were almost three times as likely as women to punch an object. This difference in the method of injuring reflects a bigger pattern: women and girls may be more likely to act on their bodies—for example, by cutting or scratching themselves with an object—while men and boys may be more likely to act through their bodies by punching someone or something else.

Self-Injury as Gendered Violence

Whether inflicted through punching an object or punching, cutting, scratching, or burning oneself, self-injury can be seen as a form of violence toward oneself and one's body. For instance, James Gilligan (2004, 6) defines violence as the infliction of physical injury on a human being by a human being, whether oneself or another, especially when the injury is lethal, but also when it is life threatening, mutilating, or disabling; and whether it is caused by deliberate, conscious intention or by careless disregard and unconcern for the safety of oneself or others.

This somewhat broad definition of violence differs from more traditional definitions because, although it is limited to physical injury, it includes the act of injuring oneself. Self-injury, according to this definition, is a form of violence, regardless of whether the self-injurer interprets it as such. Self-injury meets all of Gilligan's qualifications: it involves the infliction of physical injury on a human being by a human being (oneself), it is mutilating and sometimes life threatening, and it is done by deliberate, conscious intention. Viewing self-injury as a form of violence allows us to compare it to the other-directed or outward forms of violence more common among men.

James Messerschmidt's study of adolescent boys' violence toward others in *Nine Lives* (2000) is a particularly useful reference. In this book, Messerschmidt considers the social settings—such as family, school, neighborhood, and even one's own body—that influence and are influenced by violence. He also takes an explicitly gendered approach to violence, arguing that social settings also influence and are influenced by gender. In other words, one's family, one's school, and even the larger society (for example, the media) influence how we define masculinity and femininity and how we behave according to these definitions. From this perspective, gender is not just about one's biological male or female status, but instead it is something that we *do* in everyday social interactions, including how we walk and talk, dress, sit, and eat, and even how we do violence.

In *Nine Lives*, Messerschmidt argues that boys are not violent by nature, but they are more likely to become violent if they have been in social settings that define sexually and/or physically fighting back as the appropriate expression of masculinity or the best way to "be a man." For instance, John, a young man who experienced severe sexual abuse at the hands of his father, learned that "dominating someone sexually" was "what a male just did" (37). On the other side of the coin, Sam came from a nonviolent home but was abused by peers at school because of his body size and shape (short and overweight). Lacking the physical resources to fight back, he instead made up for the masculinity threats at school by sexually assaulting the young girls he babysat. As these cases illustrate, the masculinity "lessons" do not come from just one source but can grow out of any one or more of a variety of settings—family, school, neighborhood, or even one's own body.

Within this framework, self-injury can be seen a form of violence that stems from a variety of social sources. Furthermore, self-injury may be as gendered as other forms of violence. While lessons in masculinity taught the boys in

---

Talking about It: Self-Injury Online

A 2006 study by Whitlock, Powers, and Eckenrode identified over 400 online message boards dedicated to the topic of self-injury, with girls and women between the ages of 12 and 20 visiting the boards more than men. The study found that these message boards provide a relatively anonymous forum for self-injurers to share personal stories and problems, voice opinions and ideas, and give and receive support—all of which may be particularly helpful for adolescents and young adults who may have no one else to confide in. However, the study also found that some message boards may encourage self-injury, when, for example, they provide instructions for new self-injury techniques or promote self-injury as a pleasurable, painless behavior.

Messerschmidt's study to inflict violence on others, lessons in femininity lead some women (and fewer men) to inflict violence on themselves. Girls and women learn from various social settings—the media, family, school, peers—that they are inferior, and some women and girls take this out on themselves and their bodies (Brown 2003). This self-inflicted violence is manifested in the various body projects women and girls engage in, from restrictive dieting to starving oneself, and from piercing to cutting (Brumberg 1997). Whereas boys learn to act *through* their bodies with physical violence, girls learn to act *on* their bodies with self-inflicted violence.

Control, Body Image, and Societal Messages

Why are girls and women more likely to act *on* their bodies? Some argue that control is at the center of the picture. Like many self-injurers, some of the boys in Messerschmidt's study had been physically, sexually, and/or emotionally abused at home or at school, resulting in a sense of helplessness and lack of control. In turn, they sought and gained a sense of control by physically and sexually assaulting others, often people whom they viewed as weaker (for example, girls and younger boys). But girls and women sometimes view themselves as weaker or inferior as well, and so instead of trying to control those who are more powerful (that is, men), they try to gain control of girls, including themselves. Lyn Mikel Brown (2003), for example, argues that fighting between girls exists in part because of girls' struggle for power, voice, and legitimacy. The limited power to which girls have access often stems from "qualities they either have little control over, don't earn, or openly disdain," such as their bodies and appearance, and so they take their frustration out on each other and themselves (32).

Furthermore, when this search for control is combined with poor body image and self-esteem, it often results in self-harming practices such as extreme dieting and exercise, disordered eating, and self-injury. From a young age, women and girls are bombarded with images of unrealistically thin and beautiful women in the media. Often these images are so airbrushed and digitally altered that even the models themselves do not measure up. These images, along with other social influences, set a standard of femininity that is thin and beautiful, sexy but sweet, yet relatively passive and powerless. One of the few "appropriate" sources of power regularly advertised to girls and women is sexiness through their bodies and appearance. As a result, girls and women sometimes go to great lengths to fit the sexy media image. Because this image is virtually unattainable, their efforts become self-destructive rather than self-enhancing. Adolescent women and girls may be particularly susceptible to this, given the powerlessness they often feel amid the myriad physical, hormonal, and social changes they have to contend with. While it is difficult, if not impossible, to argue that media images and societal messages directly cause girls and women to engage in self-harming behaviors, they certainly do not help girls and women gain the sense of control and independence they may be seeking.

Conclusion

Although self-injury has only recently received mass media attention, it is not a new problem. People have been self-injuring in cultural and religious rituals, and likely in private as well, for centuries (see Favazza 1996). While the definitions and explanations of self-injury and the responses to it have varied greatly, the practice itself has not changed dramatically: people inflicting violence on themselves without necessarily intending to die. Like violence toward others, violence toward the self results, at least in part, from social surroundings. If boys' and men's violence toward others stems from settings that define fighting back and controlling others as appropriate and valued expressions of masculinity, then perhaps girls' and women's violence toward themselves results from social settings that define fighting back and controlling others as inappropriate. Instead, girls and women are encouraged to control themselves, to be pretty, nice, and quiet, and this results in either turning aggression down—like young girls who learn to lower their voices when fighting—or turning it toward themselves (Brown 2003). Until these messages change, girls and women will continue to find ways to take it out on themselves, with boys and men sometimes taking it out on them too.

See also Adolescence and Mental Health; Borderline Personality; Dissociative Disorders; Eating Disorders; Suicide and Suicide Prevention

Bibliography

Adler, Patricia A., and Peter Adler. 2005. "Self-Injurers as Loners: The Social Organization of Solitary Deviance." *Deviant Behavior* 26: 345–378.

Alexander, Natasha, and Linda Clare. 2004. "You Still Feel Different: The Experience and Meaning of Women's Self-Injury in the Context of a Lesbian or Bisexual Identity." *Journal of Community and Applied Social Psychology* 14: 70–84.

Berman, Jeffrey, and Patricia Hatch Wallace. 2007. *Cutting and the Pedagogy of Self-Disclosure*. Amherst: University of Massachusetts Press.

Bhardwaj, A. 2001. "Growing up Young, Asian and Female in Britain: A Report on Self-Harm and Suicide." *Feminist Review* 68: 52–67.

Bordo, Susan. 2004. *Unbearable Weight: Feminism, Western Culture, and the Body*. Berkeley: University of California Press.

Brickman, Barbara J. 2004. "'Delicate' Cutters: Gendered Self-Mutilation and Attractive Flesh in Medical Discourse." *Body and Society* 10(4): 87–111.

Briere, John, and Eliana Gil. 1998. "Self-Mutilation in Clinical and General Population Samples: Prevalence, Correlates, and Functions." *American Journal of Orthopsychiatry* 68: 609–620.

Brown, Lyn Mikel. 2003. *Girlfighting: Betrayal and Rejection among Girls*. New York: New York University Press.

Brumberg, Joan Jacobs. 1997. *The Body Project: An Intimate History of American Girls*. New York: Random House.

Dennis, Michael, Penny Wakefield, Caroline Molloy, Harry Andrews, and Trevor Friedman. 2005. "Self-Harm in Older People with Depression: Comparison of Social Factors, Life Events and Symptoms." *British Journal of Psychiatry* 186: 538–539.

Favazza, Armando R. 1996. *Bodies under Siege: Self-Mutilation and Body Modification in Culture and Psychiatry*. Baltimore: Johns Hopkins University Press.

Gilligan, James. 2004. "How to Think about Violence." In P. R. Gilbert and K. K. Eby, eds., *Violence and Gender: An Interdisciplinary Reader* (pp. 3–8). Upper Saddle River, NJ: Prentice Hall.

Gratz, Kim L. 2003. "Risk Factors for and Functions of Deliberate Self-Harm: An Empirical and Conceptual Review." *Clinical Psychology: Science and Practice* 10(2): 192–205.

Groves, Abigail. 2004. "Blood on the Walls: Self-Mutilation in Prisons." *Australian and New Zealand Journal of Criminology* 37: 49–65.

Hodgson, Sarah. 2004. "Cutting through the Silence: A Sociological Construction of Self-Injury." *Sociological Inquiry* 74(2): 162–179.

Kinyanda, Eugene, Heidi Hjelmeland, and Seggane Musisi. 2005. "Psychological Factors in Deliberate Self-Harm as Seen in an Urban African Population in Uganda: A Case-Control Study." *Suicide and Life-Threatening Behavior* 35: 468–477.

Laye-Gindhu, Aviva, and Kimberly A. Schonert-Reichl. 2005. "Nonsuicidal Self-Harm among Community Adolescents: Understanding the 'Whats' and 'Whys' of Self-Harm." *Journal of Youth and Adolescence* 34: 447–457.

LifeSIGNS Self-Injury Guidance and Network Support. 2005. *Self-Injury Awareness Booklet* (2nd ed.). Retrieved from http://www.selfharm.org/publications/sia/index.html

Marshall, Harriette, and Anjum Yazdani. 1999. "Locating Culture in Accounting for Self-Harm amongst Asian Young Women." *Journal of Community and Applied Social Psychology* 9: 413–433.

Messerschmidt, James W. 2000. *Nine Lives: Adolescent Masculinities, the Body, and Violence*. Boulder, CO: Westview Press.

Milia, Diana. 2000. *Self-Mutilation and Art Therapy: Violent Creation*. London: Jessica Kingsley.

Miller, Dusty. 1994. *Women Who Hurt Themselves*. New York: Basic Books/HarperCollins.

Muehlenkamp, Jennifer J. 2005. "Self-Injurious Behavior as a Separate Clinical Syndrome." *American Journal of Orthopsychiatry* 75(2): 324–333.

Nixon, Mary K., and Nancy L. Heath, eds. 2009. *Self-Injury in Youth: The Essential Guide to Assessment and Intervention.* New York: Routledge.

S.A.F.E. Alternatives. 2010. "Self Abuse Finally Ends." Retrieved from http://www .selfinjury.com

Strong, Marilee. 1998. *A Bright Red Scream: Self-Mutilation and the Language of Pain.* New York: Penguin.

Whitlock, J. L., J. E. Eckenrode, and D. Silverman. 2006. "The Epidemiology of Self-Injurious Behavior in a College Population." *Pediatrics* 117: 1939–1949.

Whitlock, Janis L., Jane L. Powers, and John Eckenrode. 2006. "The Virtual Cutting Edge: The Internet and Adolescent Self-Injury." *Developmental Psychology* 42: 407–417.

Sexual Disorders and Dysfunctions

Michael Shally-Jensen

Sexual desires and behaviors form an important part of an individual's development prior to adulthood and continue to shape a person's life as an adult. The concept of human sexuality is a broad one that encompasses not only sexual acts and the capabilities and limitations of the body but also thoughts, feelings, fantasies, urges, and an individual's sense of him or herself as masculine or feminine, gay or straight, sexually reserved or adventurous. Given the range and depth of human elements involved in the expression of sexuality, it is not surprising that complications or difficulties can arise, both at the somatic, or bodily, level and at the level of the individual psyche.

Mental health professionals in the United States, drawing on the *Diagnostic and Statistical Manual*, fourth edition (*DSM-IV*) of the American Psychiatric Association, generally divide sexual disorders into three categories: (1) paraphilias, or culturally unusual patterns of sexual activity; (2) sexual dysfunction, or problems having to do with sexual arousal or performance; and (3) gender identity disorder, or discomfort with one's own gender along with a desire to be a person of the opposite sex. The first two categories are the focus of the present entry. (The third is discussed in the entry "Gender Identity Disorder.")

Paraphilias

What used to go by the common name of sexual "perversions" or varieties of sexual "deviance" are, since the publication in 1980 of the third edition of the *Diagnostic and Statistical Manual* (*DSM-III*), referred to as paraphilias by members of the mental health profession. "Paraphilia" is a scientific (New Latin) term meaning "abnormal" (*para*) "love" (*philia*)—although *para* can also mean merely "alongside," the sense that most people today associate with it.

While "paraphilia" is considered a more neutral term than the ones that preceded it, it is still used to refer to sexual *disorders*, or behaviors of a sexual kind that are regarded as culturally unsuitable and that typically cause the individual psychological distress or social impairment. The paraphilias, then, are a set of psychosexual disorders marked by a pattern of recurrent, intensely arousing fantasies, sexual urges, or behaviors involving nonhuman objects, the suffering or humiliation of oneself or one's partner, or the presence of nonconsenting persons. According to the *DSM*, the pattern must occur over a period of at least six months and, in most cases (though not all), be upsetting, embarrassing, distracting, or overwhelming for the individual. The paraphiliac (person living with a paraphilia) is typically aware that the symptoms are negatively impacting his or her life but feels unable to control them. In some cases, the "fetish" object or personal fantasies are necessary for erotic arousal and are deliberately manipulated to that effect, whereas in others the fantasies and behaviors may occur more or less spontaneously, as in situations involving stress or in contexts that serve as triggers. With the exception of sexual masochism (the experiencing of pleasure through the subjection of oneself to pain or humiliation), which occurs in 20 men for every one woman exhibiting the behavior, the paraphilias are hardly ever diagnosed in women.

One question that is often asked by lay people and critics of psychiatry alike is why some of the more harmless paraphilias identified in the *DSM* should be considered mental disorders. Many adults from many different walks of life and many different segments of society enjoy sexual exploration, some of it tending toward the extreme as judged by the practices of the majority of the population. Such persons may not be troubled by their desires or actions and may not exhibit distress or show any impaired functioning. In these cases, the *DSM* definition of mental disorder is not fully met; the behavior is merely "deviant" in the statistical sense, i.e., falling outside the norm. However, there are at least five paraphilias—exhibitionism, frotteurism, pedophilia, sadism, and voyeurism (see below)—that under the *DSM*'s schema do not require a state of distress to be considered disorders. These are regarded both by the populace at large and by clinicians as socially unacceptable (or illegal in the case of pedophilia and a few others) and are treated as evidence of a serious mental or emotional disturbance. The diagnostic criteria have changed over the various editions of the *DSM*, allowing for a greater or lesser degree of psychiatric judgment in the matter, but in *DSM-IV* (2000) these five behaviors are considered disorders regardless of the presence or absence of emotional distress in the subject.

Varieties of Paraphilia

The *DSM-IV* lists nine main categories of paraphilia. Each is described in the sections that follow.

Exhibitionism   The primary symptom for a diagnosis of exhibitionism is the exposure of the genitals to strangers, or, in other words, "flashing." Sometimes masturbation in public is involved as well. The action is directed at strangers and does not lead to mutual sexual activity. This clinical form of exhibitionism thus differs from the practice of having sex with a partner in public, a practice that may be illegal in many jurisdictions but is not regarded as a symptom of a psychiatric disorder.

Fetishism The fetishist is sexually aroused by an inanimate object, such as a woman's undergarment, a high-heeled shoe, or leather clothing. Although many healthy individuals also find such items provocative, the person with a pathological fetish is more interested in the object itself than in the person who wears or uses it. The fetishist can become sexually aroused by touching or smelling the fetish object, with or without a sexual partner present. In the absence of the object the individual may be uninterested in sex altogether or feel generally frustrated and anxious.

Frotteurism Frotteurism, or frottage (both from a French word meaning "to rub"), involves rubbing against or touching a nonconsenting person, typically in a crowded public place. A crowd is preferred because the frotteurist gains satisfaction from the risk involved and from the anonymity of his act. Frottage is not a victimless activity, since the subject of the frotteurist's grope or bodily contact can be at risk for trauma.

Pedophilia Pedophilia involves sexual activity with a child who has not yet passed through puberty, usually someone below the age of 14. The pedophile will likely have fantasized about having sex with children long before acting on the urge. There are two main types of pedophile: the exclusive type is attracted only to children, whereas the nonexclusive type is sometimes attracted to adults as well. Pedophiles tend to prefer either males or females, not both. Those attracted to females generally seek girls 8 to 10 years of age, while those attracted to males tend to prefer slightly older boys. Most pedophiles limit their activities to children whom they know, including their own offspring, stepchildren, relatives, and neighbors. The pedophile often does not see his behavior as wrong. Instead, he rationalizes it as having "educational value" for the child or else claims that the child behaved in a sexually provocative way. Pedophilia is a serious crime in all 50 states, and mental health workers are usually mandated to report it to criminal justice officials when they learn of it in the course of their work. Pedophilia is considered a chronic disorder.

Sexual Masochism In masochism, the individual seeks to be controlled or humiliated by another person during sex. Common masochistic acts include spanking, whipping, being tied up (bondage), piercing, cutting, verbal abuse, groveling, and being urinated or defecated upon. Despite appearances, many masochists are not willing subordinates in other areas of their lives; they may in fact be in positions of authority. (There seems to be an attraction to the idea of losing control.) As with other paraphilias, sexual masochism develops over the long term, the individual masochist tending to prefer a particular type of act and sticking with it. Some individuals act on their masochistic urges while alone, but more commonly a controlling partner (dominatrix) is solicited and instructed as to the masochist's preferences. Partners may be professional sex workers or be identified through websites or social clubs devoted to the practice.

Sexual Sadism   The inverse of masochism, sexual sadism, entails the infliction of pain or humiliation on others. The sadist is aroused by the helplessness, pain, and suffering of the victim. In nonclinical cases involving light role playing among willing partners, sadism can be a sexual game of sorts (spanking, tying up, etc.). In serious cases, however, the sadist seeks to elicit genuine fear in his victim through the use of risky, dangerous, or harmful techniques. In this sense, the disorder shares some traits with that of antisocial personality. As with other paraphilias, sadistic fantasies will likely have been present since childhood. Often, however, the severity of the sadistic acts will increase over time.

Transvestic Fetishism   Transvestism, or transvestic fetishism, involves sexual arousal through cross-dressing. Dressed in women's clothing, the man exhibiting transvestic fetishism may masturbate while fantasizing that he is both the male and the female partner in the sex act. Contrary to popular opinion, this disorder occurs almost exclusively in heterosexual males, and it differs from the cross-dressing that occurs in the case of gender identity disorder. The extent of cross-dressing varies, with some men dressing entirely as women and wearing makeup and jewelry, and others wearing but a single item of women's clothing under their normal attire. Although it is not a common feature, gender dysphoria (dissatisfaction and discomfort with one's gender identity) may also occur. The individual practicing the behavior rarely if ever shares his secret with others, and, indeed, secrecy may play a role in the sexual arousal that comes from the activity. Although in different cultures and in different times and places, men dressing as women was something that was tolerated, in contemporary Western society the behavior is generally frowned upon and, if made known in individual cases, can cause extreme embarrassment and shame.

Voyeurism   Voyeurism is the "looking" disorder, the behavior associated with the "peeping tom." In voyeurism, the individual becomes sexually excited by watching unsuspecting persons, usually strangers, undress or engage in sexual intercourse. Fantasizing about having sex with the person under observation is fairly common, although the situation usually does not go beyond fantasy (and masturbation). There is rarely any contact made or the development of a relationship. Voyeurism, like other paraphilias, begins relatively early in life and becomes more or less part of the individual's makeup (i.e., it is chronic).

Paraphilia Not Otherwise Specified   This category encompasses paraphilias, most of them quite rare, such as coprophilia (arousal by feces), klismaphilia (enemas), necrophilia (dead bodies), partialism (individual parts or areas of the body), and urophilia (urine). Here, too, mental health professionals generally assume that such sexual preferences have been learned in childhood—in other words, some uncommon erotic associations have taken place. Still, the disorder is complex and there is no simple answer for what lies behind it.

Treatments for Paraphilia

As noted, many of the sexual preoccupations that beset paraphiliacs are rooted in childhood or early adolescence and therefore are difficult to redirect in adulthood. Psychoanalysis, or depth psychotherapy, has long had a tradition of handling cases of psychosexual *neurosis* and occasionally more serious cases of mental disorder, but for most paraphiliac disorders today the more common approach is cognitive-behavioral therapy, often in conjunction with medications.

Typically, a therapist treating someone for the disorder is less concerned with trying to *eliminate* the person's unique sexual desires than with helping him or her to *manage* them. The first step is to identify the underlying thoughts and feelings involved and to recognize those situations that compel, trigger, or otherwise facilitate the behavior. It helps, too, to have the client inform loved ones or significant others of his or her status so that they can help provide moral support and possibly steer him or her away from temptations. In this respect the treatment resembles that used for the treatment of addictions, the idea being to limit a person's exposure to the source of the problem and generally manage his or her cravings or urges. In some cases, aversion therapy may be used; the therapist will introduce a variety of negative stimuli (adverse images, noxious smells, mild electric shock) in the context of the client's expressed paraphiliac urges.

Medications that inhibit sexual desire may also be prescribed. A common medication used for this purpose is an antidepressant (an SSRI, or selective serotonin reuptake inhibitor), a side effect of which is blunted sex drive. Technically, this constitutes *off-label* prescription usage, meaning that the drug has been administered for a purpose other than that for which it was designed. The practice, however, is quite common in the medical community and is permitted under current regulatory guidelines. (Some advocates nevertheless oppose it.) A more radical medical approach for treatment of paraphilia is hormone therapy, which involves lowering of testosterone levels by means of a daily pill or a longer-term injection.

Sexual Dysfunctions

A diagnosis of sexual dysfunction is applied in cases where there is a clear and persistent disruption of any of the various stages of human sexual response. These stages include the appetitive stage (the desire to engage in sex), the arousal stage (erotic sensations and physiological responses), the orgasmic stage, and the resolution stage. Such disruptions can result from a variety of factors, among them:

- Anxiety over performance
- Diminished desire stemming from prior adverse sexual encounters
- Preoccupation with judging or evaluating the sex act rather than experiencing it
- Stress or depression
- Feelings of guilt, shame, or embarrassment
- Issues involving self-esteem or body image
- Poor communication between partners (including general marital discord)
- Reliance on standard routines, or, to put it differently, a lack of imagination
- Use of alcohol or drugs (either prescription or illicit drugs)
- The presence of a medical condition

The most common forms of sexual dysfunction, according to data published by the American Psychiatric Association (2000), are hypoactive (lowered) sexual desire (33% of the survey population), premature ejaculation (27%), female orgasmic problems (25%), female sexual arousal problems (20%), painful intercourse among females (15%), male erectile dysfunction (10%), and male orgasm problems (10%).

Treatments for sexual dysfunction range over a wide variety of approaches and methods. Some of the more common ones are

- Cognitive or cognitive-behavioral therapy to deal with false beliefs and unproductive behaviors
- Couples therapy (marital therapy) to deal with anxieties, hostilities, guilt, and fears
- Exercise and behavioral therapy to enhance sexual response at the physiological level
- Sex education and sex therapy (guided performance) to deal with the issue at the psychosomatic (mind-body) level

- Medications such as Viagra, Levitra, and Cialis, which increase blood flow to the sexual organs (and have been shown to be effective in women, in some cases, as well as men)
- Hormonal supplements to increase the levels of testosterone or estrogen (if found to be deficient)

Conclusion

Most research since the time of the famous Kinsey reports (*Sexual Behavior in the Human Male*, 1948; *Sexual Behavior in the Human Female*, 1953) shows that people experience more sex and enjoy a greater variety of sexual partners and sexual behaviors than is commonly acknowledged. Indeed, one proposed addition to the forthcoming fifth edition of the *DSM* (in 2013) is *hypersexual disorder*, or a pathological preoccupation with sex. Though there is a wide range of sexual practices, and an even wider range of sexual fantasies, some patterns of sexual desire can be troublesome. It is difficult to know how many people are involved in these patterns, in part because no comprehensive surveys have been done exactly on this point, and in part because people are not necessarily forthcoming when it comes to discussing their (unusual) sexual preferences. The same observations hold true for sexual dysfunctions, although there the data are somewhat more well founded (American Psychiatric Association 2000). Regardless of the range and scope of the issue, it can be said that the more we learn about sexual disorders and dysfunctions, the better we will understand ourselves as the social and sexual beings that we are and the better we can appreciate the complex and fascinating connections between the mind and the body.

See also Behavioral Theories and Therapies; Cognitive-Behavioral Therapy; Gender Identity Disorder; Psychoanalysis; Psychodynamic Psychotherapy

Bibliography

American Psychiatric Association. 2000. *Diagnostic and Statistical Manual of Mental Disorders* (4th ed., text rev.). Washington, DC: American Psychiatric Publishing.

Balon, Richard, and R. Taylor Segraves. 2005. *Handbook of Sexual Dysfunction*. Boca Raton, FL: Taylor & Francis.

Briken, Peer, Andreas Hill, and Wolfgang Berner. 2007. "Abnormal Attraction." *Scientific American Mind*. February/March: 59–63.

Hazelden Foundation. 1989. *Hope and Recovery: A Twelve-Step Guide for Healing from Compulsive Sexual Behavior*. Center City, MN: Hazelden.

Hock, Roger R. 2007. *Human Sexuality*. Upper Saddle River, NJ: Pearson Prentice-Hall.

Mezzich, Juan E., and Ruben Hernandez-Serrano. 2006. *Psychiatry and Sexual Health: An Integrative Approach*. Lanham, MD: Jason Aronson/World Psychiatric Association.

Roudinesco, Elisabeth. 2009. *Our Dark Side: A History of Perversion*. Malden, MA: Polity.

Westheimer, Ruth. 2001. *Sex for Dummies: A Reference Guide for the Rest of Us*. New York: Wiley.

Sleep and Its Disorders

Michelle Zeidler and Alon Y. Avidan

> If sleep does not serve an absolutely vital function, then it is the biggest mistake the evolutionary process has ever made.
>
> —Allan Rechtschaffen (University of Chicago Sleep Laboratory, 1978)

A Brief History of Sleep Medicine

Sleep has long intrigued humankind. Philosophers, writers, and physicians including Plato, Aristotle, Hippocrates, Maimonides, Dickens, and Freud have pontificated and written about the role of sleep and dreams in human beings. The science of sleep, however, is young and did not embark until 1928 with the observation by German psychiatrist Hans Berger that electrical activity measured from the brain changes significantly between wake and sleep. The characteristics of wake/sleep brain rhythms were well described by 1939. In the 1950s Aserinsky and Kleitman (1953) described REM (rapid eye movement) sleep and concluded correctly that it was associated with dreams. Subsequently, Dement and Kleitman described the normal pattern of sleep stages during the night, including non-REM and REM sleep (see Dement 2005). Narcolepsy (see below) was described by 1960 and obstructive sleep apnea by 1965. The behavioral patterns of sleep were elucidated through sleep deprivation experiments in animals and humans, and the neuroanatomy of sleep was defined through studies in cats to delineate the structures required for the functions of sleep.

Types of Sleep Disorders

Currently, there are more than 80 sleep disorders described in the second edition of the *International Classification of Sleep Disorders* (*ICSD-2*), published in 2005. There are eight main categories of sleep disorders, including insomnia (difficulty with sleeping), sleep-related breathing disorders (including obstructive sleep apnea), hypersomnias (excessive sleepiness), circadian rhythm disorders (sleep out of phase with the 24-hour sleep cycle), parasomnias (unusual behaviors at night), sleep-related movement disorders, isolated symptoms and normal variants, and other sleep disorders.

Sleep Physiology

The regulation of wakefulness and sleep is complex and relies on a delicate balance between homeostatic and circadian processes. The homeostatic factor, Process S, is the pressure to sleep depending on the time spent awake. As Process S increases so does the tendency to fall asleep. A rise in adenosine (a compound that plays a role in neurotransmission) is noted in the central nervous system as sleepiness increases, and declines after sleep. Caffeine antagonizes the effects of adenosine, and thus reduces the propensity to sleep. The circadian factor, Process C, relies on the body's inherent tendency to wake and sleep at specific parts of the 24-hour day. Light, introduced through the retina, is the most important regulator of the circadian clock. Melatonin, secreted by the pineal gland approximately two hours prior to sleep, is also an important regulator of circadian rhythm. Areas of the brain that induce wakefulness include the reticular activating system, which communicates with the thalamus and surrounding regions. Acetylcholine and dopamine are important neurotransmitters associated with wakefulness. The anterior hypothalamus is one of the key anatomic structures responsible for sleep. Neurotransmitters likely responsible for sleep are gamma-aminobutyric acid (GABA), adenosine, and histamine.

Sleep Stages

The study of sleep is classically performed using a polysomnogram (PSG), a continuous recording of multiple parameters during sleep. Parameters include electroencephalogram (EEG), which monitors brain waves; electrooculogram (EOG), which monitors eye movements; electomyelogram (EMG), which measures muscle tone, typically in the chin and legs; electrocardiogram (EKG), which measures heart rate and rhythm; along with nasal flow monitor, respiratory effort monitor, oximetry (blood oxygen levels), and body position. Sleep is differentiated from the awake state using the EEG in conjunction with changes in eye movements, muscle tone, heart rate, and breathing patterns. There are specific rules used to "score" a sleep study, or decide which phase of sleep the individual is in. The original Rechtshaffen and Kales sleep scoring manual of 1968, commonly known as the R and K rules, was used until 2007, at which point the American Academy of Sleep Medicine updated the scoring manual.

Sleep is generally divided into non-REM and REM sleep. Non-REM sleep is further divided into three stages, N1, N2, and N3. N1 and N2 are lighter stages of sleep, and N3 is deep sleep otherwise known as slow-wave sleep. REM is characterized by paralysis of all muscles aside from the diaphragm. REM sleep is split into the tonic phase with complete lack of movement and phasic phase characterized by rapid eye movements and body twitches. It is thought that most dreams occur during REM, with paralysis present to safeguard us from acting out our dreams—although data suggest that dreams can occur in non-REM sleep as well. In normal individuals, sleep follows a characteristic progression starting with stage N1 followed by N2 and N3 and then transitioning to REM sleep. The first period of REM occurs approximately 90 minutes after sleep onset and then repeats every 90 to 120 minutes with three to four REM periods throughout the night. In a normal night's sleep, the first part of the night has the greatest percentage of slow-wave sleep while the second part of the night is spent with increasing periods of REM. Most of sleep is spent in stage N2.

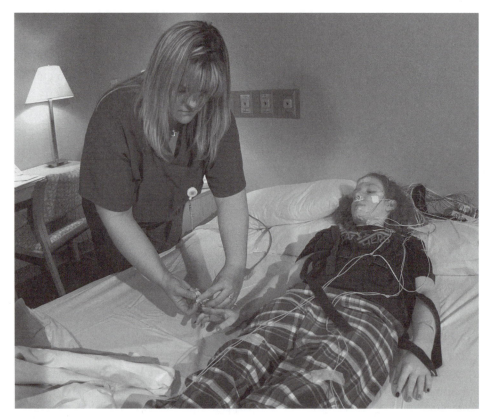

A polysomnographic specialist connects sensors to a patient, who will spend the night at this sleep disorders center. (AP Photo/Charlie Riedel.)

Sleep patterns change markedly with aging. Sleep in an infant younger than three months is defined by sleep onset REM, an occurrence that is highly abnormal in later life, and sleep is described as quiet, active, or intermediate based on EEG, EOG, EMG, and breathing patterns. Non-REM sleep becomes recognizable in infants at around three to six months, but REM and non-REM sleep are equal in frequency. By the first year of life, children have sleep characteristics similar to adults although they retain a high percentage of slow-wave sleep (stage N3), which does not begin to decline until the second decade of life. By young adulthood individuals spend most of their sleep time in stage N2. Predictable changes in sleep architecture with aging include a decrement in slow-wave sleep as well as a decrease in sleep efficiency (the amount of time spent asleep during the bedtime hours). Time in REM sleep remains stable between adolescents and the elderly.

Assessment and Measurement of Sleep

Assessing sleep is done through medical history, physical exam, sleep logs, and questionnaires used to identify and assess sleep patterns and daytime sleepiness and function, and through quantitative measurement of nighttime sleep as well as daytime functioning. These tools are described in the sections that follow.

History and Physical Examination

A comprehensive and detailed sleep history is the cornerstone of the sleep evaluation. Many of the sleep disorders outlined in the *ICSD-2* can be diagnosed by history alone, without further laboratory testing, including diseases such as restless leg syndrome and insomnia. Common presenting symptoms of patients with sleep disturbances include difficulty initiating or maintaining sleep, snoring, abnormal nocturnal motor activities or behaviors, and excessive daytime sleepiness or hypersomnia. The initial visit to the sleep disorders clinic, however, often begins at the request of the bed partner whose sleep is disrupted as well, and much of the history is obtained from the bed partner. Patients themselves can provide important historical facts and details about their sleep patterns and nocturnal arousals, but often the best and most important source of information is the bed partner, since the affected person is asleep and is unaware of his or her sleep patterns at night. This is especially true when inquiring about snoring, apneic or breathing cessation episodes, leg movements, and complex nocturnal movements such as parasomnias (i.e., sleepwalking, REM behavior disorder) or nocturnal seizures.

A detailed inventory of sleep patterns is an important step in the clinical interview. Assessment of sleep habits typically include a description of nighttime rituals before getting to bed during the week and on weekends, the length of time it takes the patient to fall asleep after lights out (described as sleep latency), as well as a description of the bedroom environment to determine whether the environment is conducive or disruptive for sleep onset and maintenance. The number and frequency of awakenings during the night should be elicited from the patient and corroborated by the bed partner if available.

The physical examination is also an important part of the evaluation of sleep disorders, especially for sleep-disordered breathing such as obstructive sleep apnea (OSA). Male gender and a large neck circumference (>17 inches in males and >16 inches in women) have been shown to be independent risk factors for OSA. Obesity, defined as body mass index >30Kg/m^2, is also associated with a higher risk for OSA. Other features that increase suspicion of sleep-disordered breathing include a crowded posterior airspace and retrognathia (abnormal positioning) of the mandible relative to the maxilla. A useful way to grade the openness of the posterior airspace is the Mallampati score, which assesses the relationship between the soft palate and the base of the tongue while the patient protrudes the tongue.

Subjective Assessment of Sleep and Daytime Sleepiness

Sleep logs are completed by patients and provide a wealth of information on sleep habits, including sleep and awake times, nap times, level of energy or fatigue in the morning, and any habits such as caffeine ingestion or use of hypnotic agents, which may affect sleep. Sleep logs are completed for several weeks at a time and brought in for sleep clinic appointments or prior to overnight sleep testing. Sleep logs are helpful in the evaluation and diagnosis of sleep and circadian patterns, and are also helpful in that they assist patients in assessing and monitoring their own sleep patterns.

The Epworth Sleepiness Scale (ESS) is a widely used validated subjective self-assessment questionnaire designed to measure daytime sleepiness. Patients are asked to rate the likelihood of dozing off or falling asleep in eight common situations that are sedentary or involve little activity. The maximum total score attainable is 24, which implies the highest severity of sleepiness, and a score of greater than 10 has been shown to be correlated with significant daytime sleepiness.

It may be difficult for some patients to differentiate between daytime sleepiness and fatigue. Daytime sleepiness is typically characterized by a difficulty staying awake, while daytime fatigue is characterized by a lack of energy or motivation to perform a specific task. Patients may have a low ESS yet still be fatigued.

Quantitative Measurements of Sleep

Overnight polysomnography (as described above) monitors multiple channels continuously over a night of sleep and evaluates the amount of sleep over the course of the night, number of arousals per night, and any sleep abnormalities. This study is performed in a dedicated sleep laboratory with a technician monitoring the ongoing recordings. If sleep apnea (see below) is noted, treatment can be initiated during the night of the study and the response to treatment monitored.

Home sleep testing is currently being employed to diagnose sleep apnea in high-risk patients. This study typically uses only four channels, most often nasal flow, respiratory effort, pulse oximetry, and pulse in addition to a body position sensor. Alternate technologies are also being utilized for home sleep testing to diagnose OSA.

Studies that evaluate the propensity to stay awake or fall asleep are also used in the sleep laboratory. The multiple sleep latency test (MSLT) measures the ability of an individual to fall asleep during five naps occurring every two hours over the course of a day. This study is most often used in diagnosing narcolepsy or idiopathic hypersomnia (sleepiness of unknown origin). The maintenance of wakefulness test (MWT) is used to assess the ability of an individual to stay awake through four naps over the course of a day. This is often used in individuals who have high-risk jobs (for example, commercial pilots) who carry a diagnosis of sleep apnea.

Actigraphy uses an accelerometer to assess the amount of wake and sleep over a 24-hour period. The actigraph is a small, unobtrusive monitor, typically the size of a watch, which is worn on the nondominant hand. It is usually worn over a week's period while the patient concomitantly fills out a sleep diary. The actigraph can differentiate still behavior, such as sitting quietly, from sleep.

Clinical Presentation of Sleep Disorders

Although there are multiple sleep disorders, the most clinically prevalent disorders and their treatment will be discussed in the sections that follow.

Excessive Daytime Sleepiness (EDS)

One of the most common complaints to a sleep physician is EDS, which can be a symptom of many sleep disorders. In the patient with EDS, it is mandatory to investigate whether sleepiness affects driving and has any impact on work environment safety, especially in individuals operating heavy machinery or responsible for public transport. One of the most concerning public health issues is fatigue resulting from sleep disorders leading to motor vehicle accidents and occupational accidents.

Insomnia

Insomnia, the inability to effectively initiate or maintain sleep, can affect up to 10 percent of the population at some point in their life. Insomnia can result from poor sleep habits, start after a stressful life episode, reflect mental illness (most often depression), or, in some individuals, start in childhood. Patients may be increasingly frustrated as they lie awake in bed and spend excessive time planning and worrying about the next day. Watching the time pass as they look at the clock while trying to fall asleep may exacerbate the frustration and may further prolong sleep latency. Insomnia is treated by addressing poor sleep hygiene practices (such as drinking caffeine late in the day or watching TV in bed) or by relaxation techniques, cognitive and behavioral therapy, melatonin receptor agonists (to increase melatonin intake), or H1 histamine receptor antagonists (to inhibit histamine intake).

Obstructive Sleep Apnea (OSA)

Obstructive sleep apnea is the cessation or significant reduction in breathing during sleep associated with a decline in oxygenation. Although the patient attempts to breathe, the airway is collapsed and occluded. OSA affects up to 10 percent of the population, and severe OSA is associated with increased risk for cardiovascular events. Classic signs and symptoms include obesity, large collar size, snoring loudly, waking up multiple times gasping for air at night, witnessed apneas (cessation of breathing) by a bed partner, and excessive daytime sleepiness. OSA is worsened by weight gain, sleep in the supine position (which predisposes patients to airway collapse due to the effect of gravity and easy collapsibility of the tongue on the posterior airway wall), and REM sleep, during which paralysis increases airway collapsibility. Management of obstructive sleep apnea is divided into conservative and nonconservative approaches. Conservative approaches include modification of behavioral factors such as weight loss, avoidance of alcohol and sedating compounds, and smoking cessation. The most commonly accepted conservative mode of therapy includes the use of positive pressure therapy in the form of nasal continuous positive airway pressure (nasal CPAP). Some selected patients may be treated successfully with oral appliances. Nonconservative treatment approaches include the use of surgical management such as uvulopalatopharyngoplasty (removal of tissue in the throat) and maxillo-mandibular advancement (changes to the jaw) and genioglossus advancement (changes to muscles of the tongue).

Central Sleep Apnea (CSA)

CSA is the continuous cycle of cessation of breathing at night. In contrast to the patient with OSA who attempts to breathe, the patient with CSA does not make any attempts to breathe. CSA usually occurs with underlying heart failure, neurologic disease, or high doses of narcotics. Treatment is directed at the underlying medical disorder, such as improving heart function or reducing pain medication usage. Occasionally, nocturnal ventilation is required.

Restless Legs Syndrome (RLS)

RLS, which occurs in up to 10 percent of the population, is diagnosed using four essential criteria:

1. There is an urge to move the lower extremities that may or may not be related to an uncomfortable sensation.
2. The urge to move begins or worsens with inactivity or rest.
3. The urge to move has a circadian predilection, worsening in the evening or night.
4. The urge to move is partially or totally relieved with movement.

A bed partner may provide additional information that the patient is kicking during sleep, suggesting the presence of periodic leg movement disorder (persistent kicking throughout the night), a condition that can be seen in the majority (up to 85%) of patients with RLS. RLS is often reflective of an underlying medical condition such as end-stage kidney disease, iron deficiency, or pregnancy. Treatment includes restoring iron storage levels when low, using hot bath and massages, and medications such as dopamine agonists. RLS of pregnancy resolves after delivery of the baby.

Parasomnias

Parasomnias are complex behaviors that occurs during sleep. Parasomnias can occur in non-REM sleep and include sleep talking, sleep walking, sleep terrors, and sleep eating, or in REM sleep and include REM behavior disorder (RBD). Non-REM parasomnias are very common in childhood as they occur during slow-wave sleep, or deep sleep, a sleep stage this is predominant in childhood. Children generally outgrow these nocturnal behaviors, although they can recur in adulthood especially in times of high stress or sleep deprivation. For example, sleep talking affects up to half of all children but only 5 percent of the adult population. REM behavior disorder is the loss of REM paralysis and the acting out of dream content by the patient. This disorder generally occurs later in life, can affect up to 0.5 percent of the elderly population, and can be a precursor for Parkinson's disease. Complex and purposeful behaviors during sleep may also reflect nocturnal seizures, which must be differentiated from parasomnias through the EEG. Treatment of parasonmias addresses patient and bed-partner safety issues first. The patient may also be treated with benzodiazepines (a psychoactive drug) around bedtime.

Narcolepsy

Narcolepsy is a rare disease affecting up to 0.18 percent of the population. It is a disease of REM intrusion into the awake and sleep cycles. Patients typically present in their teens or early 20s and complain of severe, unremitting sleepiness despite an adequate quantity of sleep. Other REM intrusion phenomena seen in narcolepsy include cataplexy, hypnagogic or hypnopompic hallucinations, sleep paralysis, and disrupted nocturnal sleep. Cataplexy, a sudden and brief loss of muscle tone, is often preceded by a strong emotional trigger such as laughter, sudden surprise, or anger. Patients with cataplexy never lose consciousness, which helps differentiate it from other paroxysmal spells such as seizures or fainting spells. Patients with narcolepsy may describe sensory misperceptions that occur as they fall asleep (hypnogogic) or upon awakening (hypnopompic). Sleep paralysis, a very frightening experience to the patient, occurs as the patient wakes up and consists of a brief inability to move all skeletal muscles while fully awake. A key clinical feature of affected patients is the sensation of overwhelming fear. A history of cataplexy with EDS is diagnostic of narcolepsy. Treatment of narcolepsy is directed at the EDS and the REM intrusion. EDS is addressed with power naps and with wake-promoting agents, including amphetamines, modafinil (an analeptic drug or stimulant), and gamma-hydroxybutyrate (GHB; an anesthetic).

Cataplexy is treated with various antidepressant agents, which inhibit REM, as well as with GHB.

Circadian Rhythm Disorders

Circadian rhythm disorders are awake and sleep times that are shifted out of the natural 24-hour awake-sleep cycle. Individuals can have advanced, delayed, or free-running circadian disorders. In advanced-phase sleep disorders, the individual will have extremely early wake time and bedtimes. This is often seen in geriatric populations. Delayed-phase sleep disorder can affect up to 15 percent of adolescents and is defined by extremely late bedtimes and awakening times. Free-running circadian cycles are seen in blind individuals who cannot entrain light to set their circadian clock and wake and sleep at irregular time intervals. Individuals who are shift workers also have difficulty following a 24-hour sleep-wake cycle. Treatment of circadian sleep disorders is achieved with resynchronization of bed and rise time through the use of timed phototherapy and melatonin.

Conclusion

Sleep is an intriguing phenomenon occupying about a third of human life. The specific reasons why we sleep are poorly understood, but the consequences of poor sleep are serious, leading us to conclude that sleep is indeed a physiologic necessity as important as eating and breathing.

See also Clinical Psychology; Mind and Body Approaches to Mental Health; Neuropsychiatry; Psychopharmacology; Stress and Stress Management

Bibliography

Aldrich, M. S., ed. 1999. *Sleep Medicine*. New York: Oxford University Press.

American Academy of Sleep Medicine. 2000. *International Classification of Sleep Disorders, Revised: Diagnostic and Coding Manual*. Weschester, IL: American Academy of Sleep Medicine.

Aserinsky, E., and N. Kleitman. 1953. "Regularly Occurring Periods of Eye Motility, and Concomitant Phenomena, During Sleep." *Science* 118: 273–274.

Avidan, A. Y., and C. Alessi. 2008. *Geriatric Sleep Medicine*. New York: Informa Healthcare.

Avidan, A. Y., and P. C. Zee, eds. 2006. *Handbook of Sleep Medicine*. Philadelphia: Lippincott Williams & Wilkins.

Chokroverty, S., R. J. Thomas, and M. Bhatt. 2005. *Atlas of Sleep Medicine*. Philadelphia: Elsevier-Heinemann.

Culebras, A. 2007. *Sleep Disorders and Neurologic Diseases* (2nd ed.). New York: Informa Healthcare.

Dement, W. C. 2005. "History of Sleep Physiology and Medicine." In M. H. Kryger, T. Roth, and W. Dement, *Principles and Practice of Sleep Medicine* (4th ed., pp. 1–12). Philadelphia: Elsevier Saunders.

Foldvary-Schaefer, N. 2009. *The Cleveland Clinic Guide to Sleep Disorders*. New York: Kaplan.

Golbin, A. Z., H. M. Kravitz, and L. G. Keith. 2004. *Sleep Psychiatry*. London: Taylor & Francis.

Kryger, Meir H. *Atlas of Clinical Sleep Medicine*. Philadelphia: Saunders/Elsevier, 2010.

Kryger, M. H., T. Roth, and W. C. Dement. 2011. *Principles and Practice of Sleep Medicine* (5th ed.). Philadelphia: Saunders/Elsevier.

Lee-Chiong, T. L. 2006. *Sleep: A Comprehensive Handbook*. Hoboken, NJ: Wiley.

Lee-Chiong, T. L. 2008. *Sleep Medicine: Essentials and Review*. Oxford: Oxford University Press.

Lee-Chiong, T. L. 2009. *Sleep Medicine Essentials*. Hoboken, NJ: Wiley-Blackwell.

Mahowald, M. W. 1999. "Overview of Parasomnias." National Sleep Medicine Course: American Academy of Sleep Medicine, Darien, IL.

Mallampati, S. R., S. P. Gatt, L. D. Gugino, S. P. Desai, B. Waraksa, D. Freiberger, and P. L. Liu. 1985. "A Clinical Sign to Predict Difficult Tracheal Intubation: A Prospective Study." *Canadian Anaesthetists Society Journal* 32(4): 429–434.

Pagel, J. F., and S. R. Pandi-Perumal. 2007. *Primary Care Sleep Medicine: A Practical Guide*. Totowa, NJ.: Humana Press.

Sexton-Radek, K., and G. Graci. 2008. *Combating Sleep Disorders*. Westport, CT: Praeger.

Shneerson, J. 2005. *Sleep Medicine: A Guide to Sleep and Its Disorders* (2nd ed.). Malden, MA: Blackwell.

Social Anxiety Disorder

Michael Shally-Jensen

Everyone is familiar with shyness, either from personal experience or from knowing someone who happens to be shy. Shyness is a normal pattern of behavior involving feelings of nervousness, awkwardness, and inhibition in social settings. Its emotional signature is somewhat similar to that of embarrassment, guilt, or shame. Particularly shy persons, however, can feel such emotions not only following or during social encounters but *in anticipation of* them. They worry about other people judging them negatively or misunderstanding their behavior, and they react accordingly—through avoidance, for example, or through keeping their presence under wraps, as it were. They may prefer to sit at the back of the classroom, not seek out friends beyond a select few, and steer clear of job opportunities that involve public speaking or the meeting of many people. Shyness can be a temporary emotional response in many people, arising from the particulars of a given situation. In others, however, it is more deeply rooted in the personality. People with severe shyness are not able to moderate the behavior well and tend to feel awkward in most social situations. In its most extreme form, shyness is no longer shyness but a debilitating disorder known as social anxiety disorder, or social phobia.

Defining the Disorder

Social anxiety disorder (SAD), one of the anxiety disorders, is a persistent, irrational fear of participating in social situations and of being potentially an object of attention. It is not that persons diagnosed with SAD lack self-esteem, particularly, or have strong feelings of inferiority, though those traits can be present. Persons living with SAD, rather, can be competent and likable, and are comfortable around people they know. When it comes to public speaking, however, or to meeting strangers, conversing in groups, attending parties, and the like, such individuals tend to freeze up, begin to blush, tremble, stammer, sweat, and feel nauseated. They may fear a social event for weeks beforehand, and any mention of it or even planning for it can stir anxieties. Some sufferers may withdraw and become reclusive, but most simply keep to themselves and work to control their involvement with social encounters.

One aspect of the disorder is a kind of meta-awareness, or thoughts about one's own thoughts and behaviors (Clark & Wells 1995). In anxiety-producing situations the individual's nervousness and awkwardness are evident in symptoms such as dry mouth, quivering voice, clammy hands, shakiness, a quickening heartbeat, and dizziness. At the same time, fear that others will witness these physiological responses heightens the sense of nervousness and awkwardness. The same meta-reaction occurs in the realm of cognition, or thinking. Persons with social phobia may worry that something they have said is stupid or inappropriate, or that their body language (posture, gestures, etc.) is out of sync with those around them. The process, moreover, has an exponential quality to it, so that in new or especially uncomfortable situations, persons with severe shyness or social phobia become particularly anxious and self-aware, further exacerbating their symptoms. Additionally, they may selectively remember interactions that seem to reflect negatively on them, castigating themselves for faulty social performance and jealously recalling the ease or directness with which others seemed to move through the same encounter (Scott 2004).

As noted, persons with SAD may rate low in measures of sociability, meaning that their interest in or need for social interaction falls below that which applies to most people. However, this is not always the case. Some persons with social phobia rate relatively high on the sociability scale. Such individuals can experience a tension or conflict between the need for approaching others and the impulse toward avoiding them (Scott 2005). It is in such cases that severe shyness becomes emotionally painful for the individual.

Social anxiety disorder usually begins in adolescence and tends to follow a chronic, unremitting course. The development of perspective—that is, the ability to appreciate differences between the individual's own perceptions and the perceptions of others—is regarded as a key source for the emergence of the disorder at this age (Wells, Clark, & Ahmad 1998). Younger children can show a combination of shyness and anxiety, but most researchers believe that these are contributing factors to the development of the disorder, not symptoms of social phobia per se. Among adults with the disorder, women are slightly more likely than men to be affected, by a ratio of 3:2 (Kessler et al. 2005).

Controversies Regarding SAD

Given the distinction between ordinary shyness, which is reported to occur in about 10 percent of the U.S. population, and social phobia, which is regarded as a serious psychiatric disorder, it is somewhat surprising to learn that SAD is estimated to occur in a full 7 percent of the U.S. population—or an even higher percentage (12%) if one considers lifetime prevalence (Kessler et al. 2005). This makes it one of the most common mental disorders in the United States, behind only depression, alcohol abuse, and specific phobias (e.g., fear of spiders or elevators). Indeed, so common is it, by these estimates, that the popular magazine *Psychology Today* (1993) labeled the illness "disorder of the decade."

The diagnostic criteria for SAD have undergone significant change over the last 25 years, from the time when they first appeared in *DSM-III* (1980) to the publication of *DSM-IV* (1994) and its revision (2000) to the current, ongoing development of *DSM-5* (expected 2013) (Bögels et al. 2010). The reported rates of the illness have risen dramatically during this period, from under 2 percent to their present levels. On the basis of these and other factors, including the heavy involvement of the pharmaceutical industry in promoting SAD as a public health concern, serious questions have been raised. One researcher, for example, who looked at archived letters, transcripts, and memoranda exchanged among the psychiatrists who developed the criteria, found that social phobia remains "the most enigmatic and poorly defined" anxiety disorder (Lane 2007). As a result, doctors and patients too often end up treating ordinary shyness as a disease. The same researcher also found that massive spending on the part of drug companies to promote such drugs as Zoloft, Prozac, and Paxil for the treatment of SAD has caused doctors to over-diagnose the illness and overprescribe these medications.

Shyness, Society, and Culture

Shyness can have both positive and negative aspects. It has been linked, for example, to the positive traits of modesty, sensitivity, and personal warmth (Crozier 1990; Cain 2012). It can be important in terms of maintaining a safe distance from potentially threatening social situations or harmful strangers, allowing individuals to acclimatize to new circumstances, take account of their surroundings, and remain self-focused or "centered" ("Positive Shyness" n.d.). Further, evolutionary psychologists have claimed that shyness has survival value in humans (and animals), serving to advance the practice of appeasement (Marshall 1995).

Benefits of Shyness

According to psychologist Gregory Feist, many creative people in a wide range of fields are introverts who prefer to work alone so that they can focus their attention on the task at hand. Steve Wozniak, for example, cofounder (with Steve Jobs) of Apple, characterizes his own creative process as a form of quiet contemplation. As he writes in his autobiography, *iWoz*, "Most inventors and engineers I've met are like me. They're shy and they live in their heads. They're almost like artists. In fact, the very best of them are artists. And artists work best alone . . . Not on a committee. Not on a team."

Source: Susan Cain, "Shyness: Evolutionary Tactic?" *The New York Times*, June 26, 2011, SR4.

Regardless of its boons, however, shyness is generally negatively perceived in American culture, where the emphasis is on self-confidence, assertiveness, and the extroverted individual. Shy persons or those with social anxiety may not fully realize their potential in school; they may postpone marriage or never marry; they may work at jobs below their level of education or expertise for fear of having to supervise others; and they may take comparatively little satisfaction in life overall (Turk, Heimberg, & Magee 2008). Often, they are drawn to alcohol and drug abuse and, in some cases, suicide.

Cultural factors affect the experience and expression of shyness and social anxiety. In Japan, for example, persons who are socially anxious or phobic are concerned not with public scrutiny of themselves or with personal embarrassment, as in the West, but rather with the prospect of offending others with their behavior or appearance. For the most part, "shyness" (or its cultural equivalent) in Japan is

Fear of Failure and Social Anxiety Disorder

"Canadian journalist Patricia Pearson, writing about her own battle with SAD, argued that the symptoms of anxiety at the end of the twentieth century were due to a culture that celebrates fierce, winner-take-all competition, notably on college campuses, in the information industries, and in the corporate business world. According to Pearson, the message that there is 'no shame in shamelessness' puts a premium on grabbing all the attention we can, thereby fostering an acute fear of failure in countless people who temperamentally find it difficult to emulate the Donald Trumps of the world."

—Ian Dowbiggin

Source: Ian Dowbiggin, *The Quest for Mental Health* (Cambridge: Cambridge University Press, 2011), 184); referring to Patricia Pearson, *A Brief History of Anxiety* (New York: Random House, 2008).

a virtue, linked to the notion of *amae*, or passive dependence. In extreme cases, however, it can lead to the equivalent of social phobia, called *taijin kyofusho*, or even to complete social withdrawal and self-isolation, a condition known as *hikikomori* (Jones 2006).

Treatment Options

Psychotherapeutic methods that can help those with SAD include (1) cognitive therapy, aimed at getting the person to question and ultimately change his or her way of thinking about social interaction; (2) behavioral therapy, aimed at steering the person toward being more assertive and outgoing (often by exposing him or her gradually to situations that bring on fear); and (3) cognitive-behavioral therapy (CBT), which draws on both of these two methods. Additionally, social skills training is sometimes advised, where the therapist can model appropriate behavior, engage the phobic person in role-playing scenarios, and provide feedback. Any steps that reduce anxiety generally, such as regular exercise, relaxation therapy or meditation, and avoiding caffeine, can often help alleviate the symptoms of social phobia.

As noted, antidepressants as well as anxiolytics (antianxiety drugs) are often prescribed for social phobia and other anxiety disorders. The results, overall, are mixed, with some studies showing that CBT is just as or more effective than drug therapy alone and more likely to produce longer-lasting results. Nevertheless, a combination of the two therapies continues to be researched and routinely advised (Ditman 2005).

See also Culturally Competent Mental Health Care; Depression; Marketing of Drugs; Panic Disorder; Phobias

Bibliography

Antony, M. M., and R. P. Swinson. 2008. *The Shyness and Social Anxiety Workbook: Proven, Step-by-Step Techniques for Overcoming Your Fear.* Oakland, CA: New Harbinger.

Beidel, Deborah C., and Samuel M. Turner. 2007. *Shy Children, Phobic Adults: Nature and Treatment of Social Anxiety Disorder.* Washington, DC: American Psychological Association.

Bögels, Susan M., Lynn Alden, Deborah C. Beidel, Lee Anna Clark, Daniel S. Pine, Murray B. Stein, and Marisol Voncken. 2010. "Social Anxiety Disorder: Questions and Answers for the *DSM-V.*" *Depression and Anxiety* 27: 168–189.

Cain, Susan. 2012. *Quiet: The Power of Introverts in a World That Can't Stop Talking.* New York: Crown.

Cheek, J. M., and L. A. Melchior. 1990. "Shyness, Self-Esteem, and Self-Consciousness." In H. Leitenberg, ed., *Handbook of Social and Evaluation Anxiety* (pp. 47–82). New York: Plenum Press.

Clark, D. M., and A. Wells. 1995. "A Cognitive Model of Social Phobia." In R. G. Heimberg, M. R. Liebowitz, D. A. Hope, and F. R. Schneier, eds., *Social Phobia: Diagnosis, Assessment, and Treatment* (pp. 69–93). New York: Guilford Press.

Crozier, W. Ray, ed. 1990. *Shyness and Embarrassment: Perspectives from Social Psychology.* New York: Cambridge University Press.

"Disorder of the Decade: Social Phobia." 1993. *Psychology Today*, July 1.

Ditman, Melissa. 2005. "Stemming Social Phobia." *Monitor on Psychology* 36. Retrieved from http://www.apa.org/monitor/julaug05/stemming.aspx.

Henderson, L., and P. Zimbardo. n.d. "Shyness." The Shyness Institute (Palo Alto, CA). Resources (encyclopedia). Retrieved from http://shyness.com/encyclopedia.html.

Jones, Maggie. 2006. "Shutting Themselves In." *New York Times Magazine*, January 15. Retrieved from http://www.nytimes.com/2006/01/15/magazine/15japanese.html.

Kessler, R. C., P. Berglund, O. Demler, R. Jin, K. R. Merikangas, and E. E. Walters. 2005. "Lifetime Prevalence and Age-of-Onset Distributions of *DSM-IV* Disorders in the National Comorbidity Survey—Replication." *Archives of General Psychiatry* 62: 593–602.

Lane, Christopher. 2007. *Shyness: How Normal Behavior Became a Sickness.* New Haven, CT: Yale University Press.

Marshall, John R. 1995. *Social Phobia: From Shyness to Stage Fright.* New York: Basic Books.

"Positive Shyness: How Shyness Can Work for You." Retrieved from http://shynessonline.com/positive-shyness.html.

Scott, Susie. 2004. "The Shell, the Stranger and the Competent Other: Towards a Sociology of Shyness." *Sociology* 38: 121–137.

Scott, Susie. 2005. "The Red, Shaking Fool: Dramaturgical Dilemmas in Shyness." *Symbolic Interaction* 28: 91–110.

Turk, C. L., R. G. Heimberg, and L. Magee. 2008. "Social Anxiety Disorder." In D. H. Barlow, ed., *Clinical Handbook of Psychological Disorders* (4th ed., pp. 123–163). New York: Guilford Press.

Wells, A., D. M. Clark, and S. Ahmad. 1998. "How Do I Look with My Mind's Eye: Perspective Taking in Social Phobic Imagery." *Behaviour Research and Therapy* 36: 631–634.

Social Work in Mental Health

Jessica Rosenberg

Overview

Social work emerged as a formal profession in the United States in the late nineteenth century, although charitable practices and the moral principle that society is obligated to care for those of its members who cannot care for themselves dates back to early civilizations and is in religion. The guiding mission of the social work profession is to alleviate human suffering and to promote the well-being of others, and the profession primarily formulates this overarching goal through a dual focus in which social workers in direct practice work with individuals, families, and groups. Social workers also work as advocates for just social policies, as community organizers, and engage in political action, research, and education. The core mission is set forth in the preamble to the Code of Ethics of the National Association of Social Workers (1996):

> The primary mission of the social work profession is to enhance human well-being and help meet the basic human needs of all people, with particular attention to the needs and empowerment of people who are vulnerable, oppressed, and living in poverty. A historic and defining feature of social work is the profession's focus on individual wellbeing in a social context and the wellbeing of society. Fundamental to social work is attention to the environmental forces that create, contribute to, and address problems in living.

Social workers specialize in a number of fields of practice. Some of them are addictions, child welfare, health and mental health, aging services, criminal justice, disability services, and school social work.

Origins

The ideological and historical antecedents of the American social work profession are located in the social welfare policies that shaped the treatment of the poor and the ill during the colonial period. Social welfare can be defined as societal policies and programs that are designed to provide for those who cannot care for themselves. The social work profession has always been inextricably linked to the social welfare system; and in fact, the social work profession functions as the mechanism through which social welfare programs are implemented (Popple 1995).

Life in the New World was harsh, and its early settlers were forced to contend with the problem of how to care for those unable to care for themselves. Societies, in order to maintain stability and order, require a system to care for their dependents, lest their sheer numbers and problems threaten the functioning of the community. The New World had many dependent members: the poor, sick, infirm, ill and those described as able-bodied vagrants who were too lazy to work. By the middle of the seventeenth century, the problem of how to care for the large number of destitute was sufficiently pressing as to warrant a community response. The colonists looked across the ocean to England for strategies to control and contain dependency and its related social ills, most importantly crime, and they adapted the English Poor Law of 1601, which became the model for the United States' first organized social welfare program. This established a system of taxation to provide aid to the poor and became the foundation for contemporary systems of public aid and modern social welfare (Reid 1995; Trattner 1999).

Formative History

Social work positions its development as a formal profession within the context of the industrial era of the mid- to late 1880s, a period of rapid socioeconomic change. The mechanical advances of the period—the steam engine, machine-based manufacturing, the development of the railway and the canal—transformed America. Factories were filled with adults and children alike who worked under extremely harsh conditions for low pay as they struggled to keep pace with machines. Americans migrated from rural to urban communities, and a large influx of European immigration contributed to the urbanization of America and its attendant social ills of overcrowding, crime, and poor housing, educational opportunities, and health care (DiNitto 2011). It is at this historical juncture that the social work profession emerges with the development of two major movements: the Charity Organizations Society (COS) and the Settlement House Movement, the leading figure of which is Jane Addams (1860–1935). Jane Addams, who founded Hull House, one of the most famous settlement houses, is affectionately referred to as "the mother of social work," and became the first American woman to receive the Nobel Peace Prize in 1931 (Popple & Leighninger 2011). Both the COS and the Settlement House movements sought to eradicate poverty, however from two distinct philosophical orientations. The COS orientation was informed by conservative and religious ideals, and early social workers, called "friendly visitors," viewed poverty largely as the result of moral failings and sought to help the poor by encouraging them to be independent and to live a moral life. The COS movement sought to infuse social welfare with an organized system of relief that eschewed direct cash, since that was considered an avenue that enabled dependency and drunkenness, in favor of loans and assistance. In contrast, the settlement house movement considered poverty to be caused by structural conditions, such as social inequality, and worked for social reform. These social workers founded settlement houses that were situated in the midst of poor urban neighborhoods and provided services to the community, such as child care, and educational and cultural programs. They worked on behalf of organized labor and fought for political reform (Popple & Leighninger 2011).

Professionalization

In order to establish professional status and to gain acceptance as a discipline that merited educational programs and certification, social workers needed to define a skill set and to develop a knowledge base that uniquely belonged to social work. Although social workers were employed as a salaried occupation by the beginning of the twentieth century, professional development was dealt a severe blow in 1915 when Dr. Abraham Flexner, a leading figure in professional educational programs, asserted in a paper given at the National Conference of Charities and Correction that social work was not a profession because it lacked the defining attribute of a profession, namely, an educationally communicable technique. Social workers were outraged and put on the defensive by this claim, and it galvanized the search for a defined set of skills to call their own.

Mary Richmond's books *Social Diagnosis* (1917) and *What Is Social Casework?* (1922) answered the call, and provided the foundation for the development of generalist social work practice. By 1920, professional programs of social work were growing in number and gaining widespread acceptance. Pivotal to the advancement of professional status was Columbia University School of Social Work, one of the earliest educational social work programs. As of August 2011, there were 473 baccalaureate social work programs and 209 master's social work programs in the United States that are accredited by the Council on Social Work Education (CSWE), a national association that is recognized as the sole accrediting agency for social work education in the United States (http://www.CSWE.org).

Licensing

Regulation, in the form of licensing or certification, is a central component of professional status, and for social work, the passage of regulations has been uneven, with some states, like California, adopting regulatory polices as early as 1929, and other states, such as New York, passing social work licensing in 2003. Currently, in 2011 every state in the United States has some form of licensure or certification, although variation around requirements exists from state to state. The Association of Social Work Boards (ASWB) is the national association that assists states in the regulation of social work practice and helps to develop and implement licensing laws, with four basic tiers of licensure set forth: Bachelors (BSW level), Masters (MSW level), Advanced Generalist (MSW with two years postmaster's supervised experience); and Clinical (MSW with two years postmaster's direct clinical social work experience) (http://www.ASWB.org). To move beyond an entry-level position generally requires an MSW. A clinical license is necessary to engage in private practice in many states.

The National Association of Social Workers (NASW) is the leading professional association. Established in 1955, it is the largest social work organization in the world, representing approximately 145,000 members. NASW seeks to promote social justice through taking a lead role in advocating for sound social policies, it works to improve social work services through a focus on workplace issues, and it creates guiding principles for the profession, including ethical standards.

Selected Fields of Practice

Aging

Gerontology is one of the fastest-growing areas of social work practice, fueled by an increase in the number of older adults and by medical advances that extend life expectancy. By the year 2030, one in five Americans will be age 65 or older (Centers for Disease Control and Prevention 2011), and social workers are essential to ensuring quality of life for this cohort. Screening and assessment, intake and referral, crisis intervention, and individual and family counseling are among the most frequent practice methods utilized in this field. Social workers in aging address psychosocial issues such as depression, isolation, physical decline, and financial problems (Rosenberg 2009; Whitaker, Weismiller, & Clark 2006b).

Child Welfare

Social workers have been in the front lines of child welfare since the beginning of the profession. The mission of social work in child welfare is to promote the well-being of children. Child welfare services utilize preventative interventions (which are directed toward preventing abuse/neglect through early intervention that identifies at-risk children and seeks to keep families together) and protective services (which involve responding to a child who is in danger and removing him or her from harm). Investigations of alleged abuse and neglect are a major function of child welfare social workers. Although social workers have been involved with child welfare for more than 100 years, public confusion about child welfare social workers persists, largely because of negative media coverage that portrays child welfare social workers as intrusive and/or incompetent. When a tragedy, such as a child fatality, occurs, the media coverage frequently vilifies social workers, often erroneously, and always in the absence of any analysis of the system. Structural problems, such as the stress of working in child welfare, high caseloads, low pay, and unsafe working conditions, have led to an extremely high rate of turnover among frontline workers. Frustration from an inability to access appropriate resources to meet the multiple needs of the families with whom they work contributes to job dissatisfaction (Rosenberg 2009; Whitaker, Weismiller, & Clark 2006a).

Medical Social Work

Hospital-based social work holds a central position in the history of the social work profession, and is the second-largest social work practice area among social workers with a master's degree (National Association of Social Workers 2008). Dating back to the turn of the century, social workers were important to hospital-based care. The first hospital social work department was organized in 1905 at Massachusetts General Hospital (Ross 1995). The early hospital social workers worked to better the health of poor people and to improve social conditions associated with illness. In the 1930s, medical social work expanded in the context of federal programs enacted as part of the Social Security Act, such as the Federal Emergency Relief Act of 1933. Psychiatric hospital social work emerged in the 1940s, as the profession adopted a psychoanalytic orientation.

From the 1950s until the end of the of the twentieth century, social work expanded its prominence in health care settings, within the context of societal awareness that health and well-being are related to psychosocial factors (Ross 1995).

The expansion of advent of managed care in the mid-1990s began a period of significant turbulence for social work in health care settings: a reduction in power, scope, and influence (Auerbach, Mason, & LaPorte 2007; Berger et al. 2003). The Clinton's administration failure to establish a national health care program in 1994 set the stage for the growth of market-driven, privatized health care models, subjecting health care to dramatic changes that have significantly affected the social work profession, including downsizing, reengineering, elimination of centralized social work departments, and shifts in social work roles (Globerman, Davies, & Walsh 2002; Mizrahi & Berger 2005; Popple & Leighninger 2011; Rizzo & Abrams 2000). Today, many health care positions have shifted from hospital to community based, accompanied by a decrease in compensation and in status.

Mental Health

Social workers are the largest mental health provider of mental health care in the nation, providing over 60 percent of mental health care in the United States. A clinical licensed is required to practice privately, although practice settings in mental health run the gamut from the small community-based agency to well-established mental health centers. Psychosocial assessment, diagnosis, treatment planning, counseling, referral, and working in multidisciplinary teams are the most common functions. Working in mental health is, in general, one of the highest-paying fields of practice (Rosenberg 2009).

Forensic Social Work

Social work and the law have many areas of commonality as both disciplines work with individuals involved in the legal system. Sometimes referred to as criminal social work (a somewhat punitive term), forensic social workers work with victims and offenders, develop preventive services for persons at risk for incarceration, facilitate reentry for the formerly incarcerated, work with attorneys, provide expert testimony in courts, support alternative programs to incarceration, such as drug courts, and engage in advocacy on issues such as prison reform (Rosenberg 2009).

School Social Work

School social work dates back to 1906 when the first school social work services were offered in the northeast urban areas. The expansion of school social work was greatly advanced by the passage of compulsory school attendance laws.

Currently, approximately 25,000 of the nation's 500,000 social workers are employed in school settings. School social workers work with mainstream and special-needs students, that is, children and youth with an identified developmental or physical disability or a cognitive, emotional, or behavioral disorder. Issues addressed by school social workers include academic difficulty substance abuse, school phobia, bullying, gang violence, family problems, and issues related to sexual orientation and gender development. School social workers work across systems, often referring students for specialized services such as health or mental health services (Freeman 1995; Rosenberg 2009).

Future of the Profession

The Bureau of Labor Statistics (BLS) projects that social work employment is expected to grow faster than the average for all occupations. Demand for social work services is expected to be particularly strong in health care and in aging services, and in rural areas. BLS projects that by 2018 there will be about 22 percent growth in medical and public health social work, 20 percent growth in employment for social workers in mental health and substance abuse, and 12 percent growth in child, family, and school social work (http://www.bls.gov). These robust figures suggest that social work will flourish in the coming decade. Of concern, however, is that social workers work in increasingly challenging environments, with high caseloads, complex cases, limited resources, and low pay more often the case than not. The impact of the recession of 2008, subsequent budget cuts, reduction of entitlements, and a growing population that struggles with multiple social ills related to poverty are factors that pose significant challenges in the workplace. While one can reasonably expect that there will be a strong demand for social work services, many of the available jobs will not be desirable for an extended period of time because of low salaries coupled with intense demands; thus burnout and attrition in the workplace are likely to become increasingly problematic as well.

Such work-based challenges notwithstanding, people are likely to be drawn to the social work profession primarily because of an altruistic desire to help others. Most social work students readily describe a passion for improving the world as their primary motivation for entering the profession. The ideals of charity and care that informed the earliest social workers of the nineteenth century are alive and strong today, and continue to inspire the next generation of social workers.

See also Community Mental Health; Emergency Services; Mental Health Advocacy; Mental Health Counseling; Rehabilitation Services; Residential Treatment for Young People; School Mental Health; State Mental Health Agencies

Bibliography

Association of Social Work Boards. http://www.aswb.org/index.asp.

Auerbach, C., S. Mason, and H. H. LaPorte. 2007. "Evidence That Supports the Value of Social Work in Hospitals." *Social Work in Health Care* 44(4): 17–30.

Berger, C. S., C. Robbins, M. Lewis, T. Mizrahi, and S. Fleit. 2003. "The Impact of Organizational Change on Social Work Staffing in a Hospital Setting: A National, Longitudinal Study of Social Work in Hospitals." *Social Work in Health Care* 37(1): 1–18.

Bureau of Labor Statistics. Occupational Outlook Handbook, 2010–2011 Edition. Retrieved from http://www.bls.gov/oco/ocos060.htm.

Council on Social Work Education. http://www.cswe.org/Accreditation.aspx.

Centers for Disease Control and Prevention, Administration on Aging, Agency for Healthcare Research and Quality, and Centers for Medicare and Medicaid Services. 2011. *Enhancing Use of Clinical Preventive Services among Older Adults*. Washington, DC: AARP.

DiNitto, D. M. 2011. *Social Welfare: Politics and Public Policy* (7th ed.). Boston: Pearson.

Freeman, E. M. 1995. "School Social Work Overview." In R. L. Edwards, ed., *Encyclopedia of Social Work* (19th ed., pp. 2087–2099). Washington, DC: NASW Press.

Globerman, J., J. M. Davies, and S. Walsh. 2002. "Social Work in Restructuring Hospitals:

Meeting the Challenge." *Health and Social Work* 21(3): 178–188.

Mizrahi, T., and C. Berger. 2005. "A Longitudinal Look at Social Work Leadership in Hospitals: The Impact of a Changing Healthcare System on Styles and Strategies over Time." *Heath and Social Work* 30(2): 155–165.

National Association of Social Workers. http://www.socialworkers.org/pressroom/features/general/nasw.asp.

National Association of Social Workers. 2008. Code of Ethics. Retrieved from http://www.socialworkers.org/pubs/code/default.asp.

Popple, P. R. 1995. "Social Work Profession: History." In R. L. Edwards, ed., *Encyclopedia of social work* (19th ed., Vol. 3, pp. 2282–2292). Washington, DC: NASW Press.

Popple, P. R., and L. Leighninger. 2011. *Social Work, Social Welfare, and American Society*. Boston: Allyn & Bacon.

Reid, P. N. 1995. "Social Welfare History." In R. L. Edwards, ed., *Encyclopedia of Social Work* (19th ed., pp. 2206–2225). Washington, DC: NASW Press.

Richmond, M. 1917. *Social Diagnosis*. New York: Russell Sage Foundation.

Richmond, M. 1922. *What Is Social Casework?* New York: Russell Sage Foundation.

Rizzo, V. M., and A. Abrams. 2000. "Utilization Review: A Powerful Social Work Role in Health Care Settings." *Health & Social Work* 25(4): 264–269.

Rosenberg, J. 2009. *Working in Social Work: The Real World Guide to Practice Settings*. New York: Routledge.

Ross, J. W. 1995. "Hospital Social Work." In R. L. Edwards, ed., *Encyclopedia of Social Work* (19th ed., pp. 1365–1376). Washington, DC: NASW Press.

Trattner, W. I. 1999. *From Poor Law to Welfare State: A History of Social Welfare in America* (6th ed.). New York: Free Press.

Whitaker, T., T. Weismiller, and E. Clark. 2006a. *Assuring the Sufficiency of a Frontline Workforce: A National Study of Licensed Social Workers. Special Report: Social Work Services for Children and Families*. Washington, DC: National Association of Social Workers.

Whitaker, T., T. Weismiller, and E. Clark. 2006b. *Assuring the Sufficiency of a Frontline Workforce: A National Study of Licensed Social Workers. Special Report: Social Work Services for Older Adults*. Washington, DC: National Association of Social Workers

State Mental Health Agencies

Donna R. Kemp and Michael Shally-Jensen

Overview

The United States has no national mental health system. Rather, each state has its own distinctive system. This approach allows for adjusting programs to the unique characteristics of different states and communities, but it has the disadvantage of creating disparities and differences in levels of deinstitutionalization (or decentralization) and levels of community services. The private, nonprofit, and public sectors all play major roles in the delivery of services to people with mental illness. The system remains two-tiered, with lower-income people relying on the public sector and higher-income people on the private sector. People with insurance or sufficient income can access private mental health providers, from private psychotherapists, to general hospital psychiatric units in private and nonprofit hospitals, to private psychiatric facilities. The public mental health system remains the provider of last resort for people needing mental health services. However, there is a trend for more of these services to be contracted out to the private sector rather than be provided by the public sector. The missions of most state mental health agencies focus resources on people with the most severe and persistent mental illnesses, such as bipolar disorder and schizophrenia.

The states remain the critical players in the development and maintenance of the public mental health system. In fact, mental health is often singled out for exclusion (i.e., nonfunding or funding restraint) in many federal programs because it is considered to be the domain of the states. In most states, the mental health system is administered by a state mental health agency. This agency may be an independent department, but is most often an agency within a larger department, usually health or social services. About one-third of the states combine mental health and services for people with developmental disabilities in the same agency. About half of the states combine mental health and substance abuse services in the same agency (Lutterman et al. 2010). Almost all states still have state-operated psychiatric hospitals. All state mental health agencies provide funding to community service providers, and many state mental health agencies license private and nonprofit community service providers and monitor their performance. Funding is provided by reimbursement for specific services, contracts for specific programs, and formula grants. As mentioned above, the dividing line between the public and private delivery system is becoming more blurred. As states downsize and close public psychiatric hospitals, particularly in the wake of the recent economic downturn, services provided by private and nonprofit organizations take on increasing importance.

Some state mental health agencies administer mental health benefits under the state's Medicaid plan, especially if they have adopted Medicaid managed care; others pass this function on to counties. Many people who would have been clients of the public mental health system are now seen in the private sector when private providers are able to bill Medicaid or Medicare for reimbursement.

Grading the States

Is more progress being made in providing effective mental health services during the twenty-first century than during the twentieth century? The National Alliance on Mental Illness (NAMI) has continued its evaluation of state mental health services by issuing a recent report, *Grading the States 2009: A Report on America's Health Care System for Adults with Serious Mental Illness*, which as of mid-2012 is the most recent state-by-state assessment of mental health. The report's authors recognize that each state mental health authority (SMHA) has responsibility for administering all mental health services in that state, even though other agencies than mental health agencies, such as Medicaid and agencies involved in vocational rehabilitation, housing, and corrections, are involved in providing mental health services. NAMI defines 10 elements as characterizing a high-quality state mental health system:

1. Comprehensive services and support
2. Integrated systems
3. Sufficient funding
4. Focused on wellness and recovery
5. Safe and respectful treatment environments
6. Accessible information and services
7. Cultural competence
8. Consumer- and family-driven systems
9. Well-staffed and well-trained workforce
10. Transparent and accountable operation

Comprehensive services and supports include affordable and supportive housing, access to medications, assertive community treatment, integrated dual-diagnosis treatment, illness management and recovery, family psychoeducation, supported employment, jail diversion, peer services and supports, and crisis intervention services. Funding through Medicaid, the Federal Mental Health Services Block Grant, or the states should achieve reduced symptoms, increased independence, employment, housing, and increased consumer satisfaction. States also should expect these expenditures to help reduce negative outcomes such as hospitalizations, homelessness, criminal justice involvement, victimization, and suicides (NAMI 2009, 4).

The report does not suggest any improvement in the twenty-first century. Rather, most states either have kept their funding level the same or have reduced funding for mental health services, leaving large numbers of people without access to services and increasing the number of people with mental illness in emergency rooms and jails.

The 2009 NAMI evaluation developed a report card for each state by assessing each state's mental health system relative to three documents: the U.S. Surgeon General's 1999 *Report on Mental Health*, the President's New Freedom Commission on Mental Health's 2003 book *Achieving the Promise: Transforming Mental Healthcare in America*, and the Institute of Medicine of the National Academy of Sciences' 2005 book *Improving the Quality of Health Care for Mental and Substance Abuse Conditions*. The evaluation used five evidence-based practices promoted by the Center for Mental Health Services along with other treatment- and recovery-oriented services. Each state was rated with a letter grade from A to F based on two main sources: a formal questionnaire (2008 Survey of State Mental Health Agencies) and a NAMI staff review of public information and services (called the Consumer and Family Test Drive). Each state was scored on 65 specific criteria in four categories: health promotion and measurement; financing and core services; consumer and family empowerment; and community integration and social inclusion.

The United States scored a D on the national report card, the same score it received in 2006. "Our national mental health care system is in crisis. Long fragile, fragmented, and inadequate, it is now in serious peril . . . States have been working to improve the system, but progress is minimal" (NAMI 2009, ix).

Fourteen states increased their overall score since 2006, while 12 states saw a decline. The rest (23) retained their 2006 score. Oklahoma experienced the most significant improvement, going from a D to a B, whereas South Carolina dropped the farthest, going from a B to a D. No state received an overall grade of A. There were 6 Bs, 18 Cs, 21 Ds, and 6 Fs. (The ranking includes the District of Columbia.)

One state, Connecticut, received an A grade on consumer/family empowerment, while 13 states received a grade of F in that category. Another 13 states received a grade of B for financing and core services, the most for that grade in any category. Contrariwise, only 3 states failed (F) in that category: Mississippi, South Dakota, and West Virginia. The 6 best-performing (B) states overall were Connecticut, Maine, Maryland, Massachusetts, New York, and Oklahoma. The 6 states at the bottom of the overall rankings (F) were Arkansas, Kentucky, Mississippi, South Dakota, West Virginia, and Wyoming.

California is the most populous state in the country, with more than 35 million people. Overall, California received a grade of C from NAMI. The category grades were B for health promotion and measurement, C for financing and core services, D for consumer/family empowerment, and B for community integration and social inclusion. Yet California was 38th in terms of the number of psychiatric hospital beds (8.7 per thousand) it provides to its population. The highest-ranking state entity in this regard was Washington, DC, with 46.1 beds per thousand. Number 2, at 22.3 per thousand, was New Jersey, followed by Mississippi (19.9), New York (17.3), and Delaware (16.1). It should be noted, however, that these beds serve only 3 percent of the total mental health consumer population serviced by SMHAs. The vast majority, *over 95 percent*, are served in community mental health settings (Lutterman et al. 2010). Moreover, of these psychiatric beds, half are often occupied by persons held by state criminal justice systems (National Association of State Mental Health Program Directors 2008). In other words, looking at statistics on inpatient hospital beds is revealing but tells only part of the story.

One useful measure, though by no means the only one, is the amount per capita spent by states on mental health services. The most recent data (for 2005) are shown in the below table. Washington, DC, is ranked number 1 in per capita spending, at $404.40, followed by Alaska at $269.64, New York at $206.21, Pennsylvania a $204.92, and Vermont at $175.16. At the low end are New Mexico (no. 51) at

SMHA Mental Health Actual Dollar and per Capita Expenditures by State, FY 2005

State	SMHA Expenditure Total	Total Rank	2005 Civilian Population	Population Rank	FY 2005 per Capita	Per Capita Rank
Alabama	$273,700,000	27	4,538,375	23	$60.31	42
Alaska	$173,537,901	35	643,593	47	$269.64	2
Arizona	$867,300,000	8	5,931,329	17	$146.22	8
Arkansas (a)	$98,639,615	45	2,770,780	32	$35.60	50
California (b)	$4,270,200,000	1	35,991,095	1	$118.65	17
Colorado	$343,753,830	24	4,627,945	22	$74.28	32
Connecticut (c)	$549,200,000	17	3,493,448	29	$157.21	6
Delaware (a, c)	$74,768,052	46	838,292	45	$89.19	26
District of Columbia (b)	$233,804,705	31	578,151	50	$404.40	1
Florida	$647,169,422	14	17,699,814	4	$36.56	48
Georgia	$443,973,313	21	9,064,226	9	$48.98	45
Hawaii	$192,627,775	33	1,229,552	42	$156.67	7
Idaho	$53,884,900	48	1,425,313	39	$37.81	47
Illinois	$1,021,700,000	6	12,746,732	5	$80.15	29
Indiana	$518,658,624	20	6,264,902	14	$82.79	28
Iowa	$235,552,698	30	2,965,148	30	$79.44	30
Kansas	$253,700,000	29	2,733,483	33	$92.81	25

(continued)

**SMHA Mental Health Actual Dollar and per Capita Expenditures by State,
FY 2005** (*Continued*)

State	SMHA Expenditure Total	Total Rank	2005 Civilian Population	Population Rank	FY 2005 per Capita	Per Capita Rank
Kentucky	$208,442,100	32	4,150,496	26	$50.22	44
Louisiana	$258,500,000	28	4,488,495	24	$57.59	43
Maine (a)	$180,300,000	34	1,314,590	40	$137.15	11
Maryland (b)	$776,500,000	10	5,556,347	19	$139.75	10
Massachusetts (a)	$685,600,000	12	6,429,227	13	$106.64	18
Michigan (b)	$973,500,000	7	10,098,168	8	$96.40	22
Minnesota	$669,275,671	13	5,124,774	21	$130.60	13
Mississippi	$305,899,702	25	2,894,507	31	$105.68	19
Missouri	$414,012,967	23	5,783,136	18	$71.59	34
Montana	$124,816,250	40	931,236	44	$134.03	12
Nebraska	$106,050,000	43	1,751,276	38	$60.56	41
Nevada	$150,500,000	39	2,403,365	35	$62.62	40
New Hampshire	$154,908,224	38	1,305,628	41	$118.65	16
New Jersey (b)	$1,215,827,000	4	8,694,221	10	$139.84	9
New Mexico (a, c)	$46,400,000	51	1,914,935	36	$24.23	51
New York (b)	$3,977,500,000	2	19,288,828	3	$206.21	3
North Carolina	$1,027,800,736	5	8,577,921	11	$119.82	14
North Dakota	$46,760,516	50	628,607	48	$74.39	31
Ohio	$757,733,206	11	11,463,260	7	$66.10	37
Oklahoma	$157,300,000	37	3,521,352	28	$44.67	46
Oregon	$434,558,178	22	3,637,148	27	$119.48	15
Pennsylvania (a, c)	$2,541,278,736	3	12,401,208	6	$204.92	4
Rhode Island (c)	$102,353,080	44	1,071,255	43	$95.55	23
South Carolina	$285,200,000	26	4,212,930	25	$67.70	36
South Dakota	$55,081,896	47	771,677	46	$71.38	35
Tennessee	$522,000,000	19	5,937,718	16	$87.91	27
Texas (b)	$832,200,000	9	22,816,723	2	$36.47	49
Utah	$159,884,700	36	2,485,098	34	$64.34	39
Vermont	$109,000,000	42	622,302	49	$175.16	5
Virginia (b)	$531,500,000	18	7,420,772	12	$71.62	33
Washington	$585,485,304	15	6,230,964	15	$93.96	24
West Virginia (b)	$118,900,000	41	1,813,479	37	$65.56	38
Wisconsin	$579,728,296	16	5,526,732	20	$104.90	20
Wyoming	$49,954,234	49	505,654	51	$98.79	21
Total	$29,396,921,631		$295,316,207		$99.54	
Average (Mean)	$576,410,228		$5,679,158		$103.43	
Median	$285,200,000		$3,893,822		$89.19	
Number of States Reporting	51		51		51	

[a]Medicaid revenues for community programs are not included in SMHA-controlled expenditures.
[b]SMHA-controlled expenditures include funds for mental health services in jails or prisons.
[c]Children's mental health expenditures are not included in SMHA-controlled expenditures.
Source: Center for Mental Health Services, Substance Abuse and Mental Health Services Administration, *Funding and Characteristics of State Mental Health Agencies, 2007* (Washington, DC: CMHS/SAMHSA, 2009).

$24.23, Arkansas (no. 50) at $35.60, Texas (no. 49) at $36.47, Florida (no. 48) at $36.56, and Idaho (no. 47) at $37.81.

In California, for one, there are signs of progress. The passage of Proposition 63, Mental Health Services Act, which raises taxes on those with incomes of $1 million or more, has produced roughly $5 billion in revenues for mental health services. (California provides mental health services through its 58 counties and two city agencies.) Emphasis is being placed on service delivery and workforce development under the Act. "California ... has a workforce development plan that ... clearly identifies goals, objectives, actions, performance indicators, and measurement strategies. It also integrates diversity goals, rather than addressing this issue separately, or as an afterthought" (NAMI 2009, 5). Other states are, similarly, noted in the NAMI report as having strong service delivery and/or workforce development plans (including diversity plans), among them Connecticut, Alaska, Maryland, Massachusetts, and Minnesota.

Who Are the Mentally Ill?

Mental disorders occur across the life span, affecting all people regardless of race, ethnicity, gender, education, or socioeconomic status. The most severe forms of mental disorders, which the NAMI report primarily focuses on, have been estimated to affect 1 in 17 persons, or 6 percent, of those aged 18 years and older during any one year (Kessler et al. 2005). About 15 percent of adults receive help from mental health specialists, while others receive help from general physicians. The majority of people with mental disorders do not receive treatment, and 40 percent of people with a severe mental illness do not look for treatment (Regier et al. 1993). Ronald C. Kessler, principal investigator of the National Comorbidity Survey Replication study, and colleagues (2005b) determined that about half of Americans will meet the criteria for a *DSM-IV* (the American Psychiatric Association's *Diagnostic and Statistical Manual of Mental Disorders*) diagnosis of a mental disorder over the course of their lifetime, with first onset usually in childhood or adolescence. Based on their analysis, lifetime prevalence for the different classes of disorders were anxiety disorders, 28.8 percent; mood disorders 20.8 percent; substance use disorders, 14.6 percent; and any disorder 46.4 percent. Median age of onset is much earlier for anxiety and impulse control disorders (11 years for both) than for substance abuse (20 years) and mood disorders (30 years) (Kessler, Berglund et al., 2005).

The disease model of mental illness remains important in the context of state mental health systems. For the seriously mentally ill, it places a focus on finding and treating the causes of the emotional, behavioral, and/or organic dysfunction, with an approach based on diagnosis, treatment, and cure or recovery. The treatment focus is on short-term inpatient care, with the emphasis on medications and the ability to function in the community. Various services are provided, by state agencies and nonprofits and private organizations, to assist maintenance in the community, including housing, employment, and social services.

The mental health approach to people with less serious emotional disorders is focused on outpatient treatment, often through prescription of medication by a general practitioner. Primary care physicians provide at least 40 percent of mental health care. Employee assistance programs help employees in the workplace with assessment of mental health issues and referral to appropriate treatment sources. Those who are less seriously mentally ill are sometimes referred to in a derogatory way as the "worried well." When resources are short, conflict can arise as those who speak on behalf of the seriously and chronically mentally ill do not wish to see resources expended on the less seriously ill. However, many people at one time need assistance with a mental health problem in their lives, and failure to address their problems can lead to significant costs to society, including suicide.

Studies suggest that the prevalence of mental illness is about equal in urban and rural areas, but access to services is much more difficult in rural areas. Nearly 75 percent of the nation's rural counties do not have access to a psychiatrist, 50 percent do not have access to a psychologist, and 58 percent lack access to trained clinical social workers (Gamm, Seal, & Stone 2002).

Mental Illness and Criminal Justice

Along with homelessness and other negative outcomes of deinstitutionalization, the number of mentally ill in the correctional system has increased sharply. Crime, criminal justice costs, and property loss associated with mental illness cost at least $6 billion per year, and people with mental illnesses are greatly overrepresented in jail populations, in part owing to diversion programs that steer persons with mental illness into the criminal justice system (U.S. Department of Health and Human Services 1999). According to the Bureau of Justice Statistics, 24 percent of state prisoners and 21 percent of local jail inmates have a mental illness (Bureau of Justice Statistics 2006). Many of these inmates do not receive treatment. The percentages are even higher for youth in juvenile justice systems (Skowyra & Cocozza 2007). Costs for state and local governments to arrest, process in court, and hold in jail people with mental illnesses can exceed the total state and local government expenditures on mental health care (California Council of Community Mental Health Agencies n.d.). There are more mentally ill people in U.S. prisons and jails (319,918 in 2005) than in mental hospitals (100,439 in 2005) (Fuller et al. 2010).

Conclusion

As the twenty-first century unfolds, state-based mental health care programs remain complex and cyclical. There is a tug and pull between the many different viewpoints on mental illness. Should people with mental illness be free to manage their lives as they see fit, or should there be social control by the state? Are states adequately prepared to meet the challenge, or are new sources of financing and new models of organization and service delivery needed? What are the best methods of treating the seriously mentally ill, and can these methods be squared with state governments' expectations regarding efficient use of resources? Can the needs of consumers or patients be properly satisfied by large state mental health agencies, or is that asking too much of this type of institution? Is the general public served by diverting mentally ill individuals to jails? Clearly, these issues and others will be debated for decades to come.

See also Community Mental Health; Criminalization and Diversion Programs; History of Mental Health Care; Hospitalization; Insurance and Parity Laws; Prisons and Mental Health

Bibliography

Bureau of Justice Statistics. 2006. "Mental Health Problems of Prison and Jail Inmates." September. Retrieved from http://bjs.ojp.usdoj.gov/content/pub/pdf/mhppji.pdf.

California Council of Community Mental Health Agencies. n.d. *The Development of California's Publicly Funded Mental Health System.* Prepared by S. Naylor Goodwin and R. Selix. Retrieved from http://www.cccmha.org.

Center for Mental Health Services, Substance Abuse and Mental Health Services Administration. 2009. *Funding and Characteristics of State Mental Health Agencies, 2007.* Washington, DC: Center for Mental Health Services and Substance Abuse and Mental Health Services Administration. Retrieved from http://store.samhsa.gov/shin/content//SMA09-4424/SMA09-4424.pdf.

Fuller, E. F., A. D. Kennard, D. Eslinger, R. Lamb, and J. Pavle. 2010. *More Mentally Ill Persons Are in Jails and Prisons Than Hospitals: A Survey of the States.* Arlington, VA: Treatment Advocacy Center.

Gamm, L., M. Tai-Seal, M., and S. Stone. 2002. "White Paper: Meeting the Mental Health Needs of People Living in Rural Areas." College Station: Texas A&M University Health Science Center, School of Rural Public Health, Department of Health Policy & Management.

Institute of Medicine of the National Academy of Sciences. n.d. *Improving the Quality of Health Care for Mental and Substance Abuse Conditions.* Washington, D.C.: Academies Press.

Kelly, Timothy A. 2010. *Healing the Broken Mind: Transforming America's Failed Mental Health System.* New York: New York University Press.

Kemp, Donna R. 2007. *Mental Health in America: A Reference Handbook.* Santa Barbara, CA: ABC-CLIO.

Kessler, R. C., P. A. Berglund, O. Demler, R. Jin, K. R. Merikangas, and E. E. Walters. 2005. "Lifetime Prevalence and Age-of-Onset Distributions of DSM-IV Disorders in the National Comorbidity Survey Replication (NCS-R)." *Archives of General Psychiatry* 62: 593–602.

Kessler, R. C., W. T. Chiu, O. Demler, and E. E. Walters. 2005. "Prevalence, Severity, and Comorbitidy of Twelve-Month *DSM-IV* Disorders in the National Comorbidity Survey Replication (NCS-R)." *Archives of General Psychiatry* 62: 617–627.

Lutterman, Theodore, Michael Hogan, Bernadette E. Phelan, and Noel A. Mazade. 2010. "State Mental Health Agencies." In Bruce Lubotsky Levin, Kevin D. Hennessy, and John Petrila, eds., *Mental Health Services: A Public Health Perspective* (3rd ed., pp. 321–348). New York: Oxford University Press.

National Alliance on Mental Illness. 2009. *Grading the States: A Report on America's Health Care System of Adults with Serious Mental Illness*. Arlington, VA: National Alliance for Mental Illness.

National Association of State Mental Health Program Directors. 2008. State Mental Health Agency Profiling System Results. Retrieved from http://www.nri-inc.org/projects/Profiles/data_search.cfm.

President's New Freedom Commission on Mental Health. 2003. *Achieving the Promise: Transforming Mental Healthcare in America*. Rockville, MD: President's New Freedom Commission on Mental Health.

Regier, D. A., W. Narrow, D. S. Rae, R. W. Manderscheid, B. Z. Locke, and F. K. Goodwin. 1993. "The De Facto U.S. Mental and Addictive Disorders Service System: Epidemiologic Catchment Area Prospective 1-Year Prevalence Rates of Disorders and Services." *Archives of General Psychiatry* 50: 85–94.

Skowyra, Kathleen R., and Joseph J. Cocozza. 2007. *Blueprint for Change: A Comprehensive Model for the Identification and Treatment of Youth with Mental Health Needs in Contact with the Juvenile Justice System*. Delmar, NY: National Center for Mental Health and Juvenile Justice Policy Research Associates, Inc.

U.S. Department of Health and Human Services. 1999. *Mental Health: A Report of the Surgeon General—Executive Summary*. Rockville, MD: U.S. Department of Health and Human Services.

Stigma

Bernice A. Pescosolido

It is often said that individuals with mental illness confront two challenges—the medical and health difficulties associated with the onset of their disease, and the social difficulties associated with the stigma that is attached to mental health problems. While the term "stigma" is thrown around quite loosely in today's society, it has real meaning and impact for persons with mental health problems. Research has documented that the stigma attached to mental health problems has serious consequences that limit a person's social acceptance in society, translating into real, reduced life opportunities in employment, in friendships and marriage, in access to health care, and even in life expectancy (Link & Phelan 2006). In fact, the U.S. Surgeon General, reviewing the state of stigma at the end of the twentieth century, concluded that stigma represents the "foremost obstacle" to the recovery of persons with mental illness (U.S. Department of Health and Human Services 1999).

Of ancient origin, the term "stigma" originally referred to a "mark" that separated individuals one from another (Hinshaw 2006). That mark may be physical (as in various deformities); it may be seen as "blemishes of individual character" (as in mental illness, addiction, unemployment); or it may be as a result of membership in a group that has been targeted at some point, as different (as in the case of ethnic or religious groups). Today, we often refer to the two dominant aspects of stigma: *prejudice*, which produces negative attitudes and beliefs about the person or group, and *discrimination*, which results in negative behavior toward the person or group. Erving Goffman (1963), among the first, and certainly the most well-known person to conceptualize the nature of stigma, defined it as an attribute that marked a person as different, reducing them from being seen as "whole and usual" to "tainted and discounted." When an illness is stigmatized, for example, the person with that illness is devalued by the larger society and is often considered and treated as "less than fully human." According to Goffman's observations in St. Elizabeth's Hospital in the late 1950s and early 1960s, stigma disqualified individuals from full social citizenship, often separating them from others and isolating them as they attempted to participate in social life.

Forms of Stigma

Stigma exists in different "forms," including (1) internalized stigma (or self-stigma), as when a person with mental illness accepts and/or believes the negative stereotypes and/or the dismissive, intolerant actions of others; (2) public stigma, or the larger set of beliefs, attitudes, and behaviors, usually negative, that those in society hold about people with mental illness; (3) treatment stigma, or the negative reactions that derive from others knowing that a person is or has been in mental health treatment; (4) institutionalized stigma, or the negative outcomes produced by persons of authority who deny people with mental illness such items as housing, jobs, and even medical treatment; and (5) so-called courtesy stigma, or stigma directed at family members, friends, and even those who provide treatment simply because of their association with a stigmatized group (Arvaniti et al. 2008; Corrigan, Markowitz, & Watson 2004; Halter 2008; Link et al. 2004; Link & Phelan 2001). For example, some research has shown that doctors and nurses in Intensive Care Units, Emergency Rooms, and other parts of the hospital may indicate an unwillingness to treat people with mental illness (Okazaki 2000).

Stigma, however, can change. Individuals with mental health problems may be unaware of or ignore rejection, they may protest and respond with righteous anger, or they may even accept negative societal judgments, harming their self-esteem (Corrigan, Watson, & Barr 2006). These responses can change across the person's "illness career" (Pescosolido 1991) as their mental health problems ebb and flow, or as other conditions in their lives change. Stigma can also vary across societies and time periods. For example, there have been great improvements in the treatment of mental illness, perhaps not as many improvements as we would like; however, in the United States, we have moved away from treatment in large institutions called "asylums" to community-based care (see Grob 1991).

This has led some leaders in the field of psychiatry to assume that stigma in the United States is "dissipating" (e.g., Goin 2004). Yet we have no firm data on this issue—not, at least, since the path-breaking work by Shirley Star (1955) and the research team for the *Americans View Their Mental Health* project (Gurin, Veroff, & Feld 1960; Veroff, Kulka, & Douvan 1981). The National Stigma Studies were begun in the mid-1990s to provide a scientific examination of the debate about the current state of stigma in the United States. The findings of how the American public responds to individuals described with behaviors consistent with psychiatric diagnoses of major mental illness and substance use disorders were mixed. Unfortunately, as the table on the following page indicates, levels of prejudice continue to be substantial in the United States today.

In the table, the number at the bottom right corner provides an indication of overall levels of stigma. Nearly half of the U.S. population (46.8%) expresses stigmatizing attitudes in the form of "social distance," that is, an unwillingness to interact with or have persons with mental health and addiction problems included in activities. Yet the level of stigma depends on the type of mental health problem and the type of activity described. For example, just over a third of those questioned expressed rejection of persons described with symptoms of depression (37.4%), but nearly half did so regarding schizophrenia (48.4%). Another feature that changed people's responses was the level of intimacy required or implied in the different settings. While not a perfect association, those venues that were more private or intimate (e.g., working closely on the job, marrying into one's family) elicited negative responses from more people. When individuals were asked what the person's problem might be, those who reported they believed the person had a mental illness were even more likely to express a desire for greater social distance (Martin, Pescosolido, & Tuch 2000).

Not all of the findings from the first national studies conducted in nearly 50 years in the United States are discouraging. In fact, the public has become more sophisticated about what mental illness is (Phelan, Stueve, & Pescosolido 2000) and more willing to talk to family and friends about their own mental health issues (Swindle et al. 2000). Americans believe that psychiatric medications are effective (Croghan et al. 2003) and that children and adults who enter treatment will, in fact, improve (Link, Phelan, Bresnahan, Ann Stueve, & Pescosolido 1999; Perry et al. 2007; Pescosolido 2007; Pescosolido et al. 2007a; Pescosolido et al. 2007b). In the 2002 National Stigma Study—Children (NSS-C), the levels of stigma that individuals reported toward children with depression were considerably lower than what had been documented in the adult studies (Martin et al. 2007). However, there was some concern that childhood depression was actually seen as more serious, more likely to predispose adolescents to violence, and more likely a result of poor childrearing (Perry et al. 2007). Further, while treatment was seen as useful, Americans also perceived that children and their families

Percentage of Americans Reporting They Are "Definitely" or "Probably" Unwilling to Interact with an Individual Said to Have a Mental Health Condition

Condition	Type of Social Interaction						
	Move Next Door %	Spend Evening Socializing with %	Make Friends with %	Work Closely with on the Job %	Have a Group Home in Neighborhood %	Marry into Your Family %	Average % by Condition
Alcohol Dependence	45.6	55.8	36.7	74.7	43.4	78.2	55.7
Depression	22.9	37.8	23.1	48.6	31.2	60.6	37.4
Schizophrenia	37.0	49.0	34.0	64.1	33.2	72.2	48.4
Drug Dependence	75.0	72.7	59.1	82.0	52.7	89.0	71.8
Troubled Person	9.5	14.9	10.0	21.0	27.7	41.9	20.8
Average % by Type of Interaction	38.0	55.8	32.6	58.1	37.6	68.4	**46.8**

Source: Adapted from Martin, Pescosolido, and Tuch 2000.

would be affected by the stigma attached to knowing that a person used mental health services (Pescosolido et al. 2007b). Finally, one of the more troubling findings from the National Stigma Studies, overall, is that stigmatizing attitudes and behavioral predispositions seem to pervade society. They are not, contrary to expectations, more likely to be expressed in less educated groups, in groups with more conservative political attitudes, or in any of a range of social and demographic characteristics (e.g., age, gender; Pescosolido et al. 2000). This makes it difficult to target programs strategically.

Addressing the Problem

From the beginning of the twentieth century, there have been both public and private efforts in the United States to reduce stigma. Figure 1 provides an illustrative listing of some of the more prominent organizations established and campaigns mounted in the cause of improving conditions for individuals with mental illness. While this figure provides only a crude count, with some specific events listed for three time periods, it is widely believed, as is shown, that there has been more attention dedicated to stigma reduction in the last two decades, locally, nationally, and even internationally, than previously (Mehta et al. 2009; Sartorius & Schulze 2005). Much of the foundation of these efforts has been predicated on the notion of "a disease like any other"; that is, the idea that when the public becomes more educated about the underlying biological and genetic causes of mental illness, the negative beliefs about people with mental health problems will shift from a moral one of "bad" to a neutral one of "ill." In other words, if mental illness is seen as the result of an underlying brain disease rather than a personal "choice" of some kind, prejudice and discrimination will drop. The National Stigma Study—Replication (NSS-R), which looked at a decade of change over this period of stigma reduction efforts, indicated greater mental health literacy on the part of Americans between 1996 and 2006. Significantly more individuals indicated a belief that genetics or chemical imbalances were root causes of mental health difficulties. Further, more individuals reported that physicians and psychiatrists should be consulted. Unfortunately, the NSS-R was unable to document *any* actual decrease in stigma, as reflected in an ongoing unwillingness to engage in social activities with persons with mental health problems (Pescosolido et al. 2010).

This does not mean that efforts have been ineffective at all levels. In fact, research has indicated that effective public campaigns have been mounted, including the recent "What a Difference a Friend Makes" efforts by the U.S. government's Substance Abuse and Mental Health Services Administration (SAMHSA). Moreover, the science base for stigma reduction efforts is much stronger now than it was a decade or two ago. We now understand that moving from stereotypes of people with mental illness to actually knowing people who have mental health

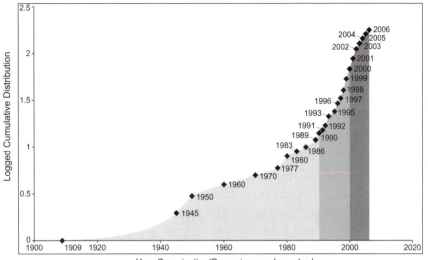

Figure 1. Selected organizations and campaigns addressing mental health issues.

Early 1990's

1909: National Committee for Mental Hygiene (now *Mental Health America*)

1945: Mental Health Foundation formed (U.K.)

1960: Action for Mental Health (U.S. Congress)

1970: National Schizophrenia Fellowship (now *Rethink*) (U.K.)

1979: President's Commission on Mental Health (NAMI, U.S.)

1990's

1991: National Stigma Clearinghouse (U.S.)

1992: World Mental Health Day

1995: "Depression: What Every Woman Should Know" (NIMH, U.S.)

1996: "In Our Own Voice" (NAMI, U.S.)

1997: "Like Minds" (New Zealand)

1998: "There Is Help, There Is Hope" (Canada)

1999: "Open the Doors" (World Psychiatric Assn.); Surgeon General's Report on Mental Health (U.S.)

2000's

2000: "Change Your Mind" (MTV, U.S.); "I Vote, I Count" (NAMI, U.S.); "Beyond Blue" (Australia)

2001: Conference on Stigma and Global Health (NIH, U.S.)

2002: "See Me" (Scotland); "Campaign for the Mind of America" (NAMI, U.S.)

2003: "Real Men, Real Depression" (NIH, U.S.); "Elimination of Barriers" (SAMHSA, U.S.); President's New Freedom Commission on Mental Health (U.S.)

2004: Stigma & Health Disparities (NIH, U.S.); Stigma Busters (Canada)

2005: Voice Awards (SAMHSA, U.S.)

2006: "What A Difference A Friend Makes" (SAMHSA, U.S.)

problems (commonly referred to as "the contact hypothesis") continues to offer great promise (Couture & Penn 2003). In the absence of real-life experiences with persons with mental health problems, individuals may have media images as their only reference point. Since media images tend to portray negative stereotypes of persons with mental illness—for example, the "criminally insane" (Wahl 1995)—individuals who report not knowing anyone with mental health problems tend to report higher levels or prejudice. It is more likely that one will discount these stigmatizing portrayals when one actually knows individuals who have experienced problems (Lang 2000). Since 2006, the Voice Awards have been given in the United States to writers, producers, actors, and directors who incorporate dignified, respectful, and accurate depictions of people living with mental health problems into their programs and films (http://www.whatadifference.samhsa.gov/voiceawards/). Other efforts are under way to work with the media. The Mental Health Media Partnership (MHMP), a joint venture by University of Southern California's Annenberg School for Communication, University of Pennsylvania's Annenberg Public Policy Center, the National Mental Health Awareness Campaign, and the entertainment industry, works with the entertainment industry to promote accuracy and understanding of mental health issues.

Since 1997, former First Lady Rosalynn Carter has sponsored a journalism fellowship program to increase accurate reporting of mental health issues as a way to fight stigma and discrimination against people with mental illnesses. The Rosalynn Carter Fellowships for Mental Health Journalism, an important part of the Carter Center's Mental Health Program, provides awards and training to reporters and writers. In her recent book (Carter 2010), Mrs. Carter offers a frank and insightful assessment of where the United States currently stands in terms of mental health, in terms of the treatment system we have, and about the future. While ultimately optimistic about the progress made to date and the future, she argues that stigma continues to play a significant role in a system that fails to provide the tools for individuals with mental health problems to lead lives that match their potential for recovery and participation in society.

See also Disability Rights; History of Mental Health Care; Media Portrayals of Mental Illness; Medical Model of Mental Illness; Mental Health Advocacy; Neurodiversity; Public Awareness and Public Education

Bibliography

Arvaniti, Aikaterini, Maria Samakouri, Eleni Kalamara, Valentini Bochtsou, Constantinos Bikos, and Miltos Livaditis. 2008. "Health Service Staff's Attitudes towards Patients with Mental Illness." *Social Psychiatry and Psychiatric Epidemiology* 44: 658–665.

Carter, Rosalynn. 2010. *Within Our Reach: Ending the Mental Health Crisis*. New York: Rodale Books.

Corrigan, P. W., F. E. Markowitz, and A. C. Watson. 2004. "Structural Levels of Mental Illness Stigma and Discrimination." *Schizophrenia Bulletin* 30: 481–491.

Corrigan, Patrick W., A. C. Watson, and L. Barr. 2006. "The Self-Stigma of Mental Illness: Implications for Self-Esteem and Self-Efficacy." *Journal of Social and Clinical Psychology* 25: 875–884.

Couture, Shannon, and David L. Penn. 2003. "Interpersonal Contact and the Stigma of Mental Illness: A Review of the Literature." *Journal of Mental Health* 12: 291–305.

Croghan, Thomas W., Molly Tomlin, Bernice A. Pescosolido, Jack K. Martin, Keri M. Lubell, and Ralph Swindle. 2003. "Americans' Knowledge and Attitudes towards and

Their Willingness to Use Psychiatric Medications." *The Journal of Nervous and Mental Disease* 191: 166–174.

Goffman, Erving. 1963. *Stigma: Notes on the Management of Spoiled Identity.* Englewood Cliffs, NJ: Prentice-Hall.

Goin, Marcia Kraft. 2004. "Presidential Address." *American Journal of Psychiatry* 161: 1768–1771.

Grob, Gerald N. 1991. *From Asylum to Community: Mental Health Policy in Modern America.* Princeton, NJ: Princeton University Press.

Gurin, G., J. Veroff, and S. Feld. 1960. *Americans View Their Mental Health: A Nationwide Survey.* New York: Basic Books.

Halter, Margaret J. 2008. "Perceived Characteristics of Psychiatric Nurses: Stigma by Association." *Archives of Psychiatric Nursing* 22: 20–26.

Hinshaw, Stephen P. 2006. *The Mark of Shame: Stigma of Mental Illness and an Agenda for Change.* Oxford: Oxford University Press.

Lang, Annie. 2000. "The Information Processing of Mediated Messages: A Framework for Communication Research." *Journal of Communication* 50: 46–70.

Link, Bruce G., and Jo C. Phelan. 2001. "Conceptualizing Stigma." *Annual Review of Sociology* 27: 363–385.

Link, Bruce G., and Jo C. Phelan. 2006. "Stigma and Its Public Health Implications." *The Lancet* 367: 528–529.

Link, Bruce G., Jo C. Phelan, Michaeline Bresnahan, Ann Stueve, and Bernice A. Pescosolido. 1999. "Public Conceptions of Mental Illness: Labels, Causes, Dangerousness and Social Distance." *American Journal of Public Health* 89: 1328–1333.

Link, Bruce G., Larry Yang, Jo C. Phelan, and Pamela Collins. 2004. "Measuring Mental Illness Stigma." *Schizophrenia Bulletin* 30: 511–541.

Martin, Jack K., Bernice A. Pescosolido, Sigrun Olafsdottir, and Jane D. McLeod. 2007. "The Construction of Fear: Modeling Americans' Preferences for Social Distance from Children and Adolescents with Mental Health Problems." *Journal of Health and Social Behavior* 48: 50–67.

Martin, Jack K., Bernice A. Pescosolido, and Steven A. Tuch. 2000. "Of Fear and Loathing: The Role of Disturbing Behavior, Labels and Causal Attributions in Shaping Public Attitudes Toward Persons with Mental Illness." *Journal of Health and Social Behavior* 41: 208–233.

Mehta, Nisha, Aliya Kassam, Morven Leese, Georgia Butler, and Graham Thornicroft. 2009. "Public Attitudes towards People with Mental Illness in England and Scotland, 1994–2003." *The British Journal of Psychiatry* 194: 278–284.

Okazaki, Sumie. 2000. "Treatment Delay among Asian-American Patients with Severe Mental Illness." *American Journal of Orthopsychiatry* 70: 58–64.

Perry, Brea L., Bernice A. Pescosolido, Jack K. Martin, Jane D. McLeod, and Peter S. Jensen. 2007. "Comparison of Public Attributions, Attitudes, and Stigma in Regard to Depression among Children and Adults." *Psychiatric Services* 58: 632–635.

Pescosolido, Bernice A. 1991. "Illness Careers and Network Ties: A Conceptual Model of Utilization and Compliance." In G. L. Albrecht and J. A. Levy, eds., *Advances in Medical Sociology* (pp. 161–184). Greenwich, CT: JAI Press, 1991.

Pescosolido, Bernice A. 2007. "Culture, Children, and Mental Health Treatment: Special Section on the National Stigma Study—Children." *Psychiatric Services* 58: 611–612.

Pescosolido, Bernice A., Danielle L. Fettes, Jack K. Martin, John Monahan, and Jane D. McLeod. 2007a. "Perceived Dangerousness of Children with Mental Health Problems and Support for Coerced Treatment." *Psychiatric Services* 58: 1–7.

Pescosolido, Bernice A., Jack K. Martin, Bruce G. Link, Saeko Kikuzawa, Giovanni Burgos, and Ralph Swindle. 2000. *Americans' Views of Mental Illness and Health at Century's End: Continuity and Change. Public Report on the MacArthur Mental Health Module, 1996 General Social Survey.* Bloomington: Indiana Consortium for Mental Health Services Research.

Pescosolido, Bernice A., Jack K. Martin, J. Scott Long, Tait R. Medina, Jo C. Phelan, and Bruce G. Link. 2010. " 'A Disease Like Any Other?' A Decade of Change in Public Reactions to Schizophrenia, Depression and Alcohol Dependence." *American Journal of Psychiatry* 167: 1321–1330.

Pescosolido, Bernice A., Brea L. Perry, Jack K. Martin, Jane D. McLeod, and Peter S. Jensen. 2007b. "Stigmatizing Attitudes and Beliefs about Treatment and Psychiatric Medications for Children with Mental Illness." *Psychiatric Services* 58: 613–618.

Phelan, Jo C., Bruce G. Link, Ann Stueve, and Bernice A. Pescosolido. 2000. "Public Conceptions of Mental Illness in 1950 and 1996: What Is Mental Illness and Is It to Be Feared?" *Journal of Health and Social Behavior* 41: 188–207.

Sartorius, Norman, and Hugh Schulze. 2005. *Reducing the Stigma of Mental Illness: A Report from a Global Association.* New York: Cambridge University Press.

Star, Shirley A. 1955. "The Public's Ideas about Mental Illness." National Opinion Research Center, Chicago.

Swindle, R., K. Heller, B.A. Pescosolido, and S. Kikuzawa. 2000. "Responses to 'Nervous Breakdowns' in America over a 40-Year Period: Mental Health Policy Implications." *American Psychologist* 55: 740–749.

U.S. Department of Health and Human Services. 1999. *Mental Health: A Report of the Surgeon General.* Bethesda, MD: U.S. Department of Health and Human Services.

Veroff, J., R. A. Kulka, and E. Douvan. 1981. *Mental Health in America: Patterns of Help-Seeking from 1957 to 1976.* New York: Basic Books.

Wahl, Otto F. 1995. *Media Madness: Public Images of Mental Illness.* New Brunswick, NJ: Rutgers University Press.

Stress and Stress Management

Michael Shally-Jensen

The experience of stress, when it occurs in its most extreme form, is regarded as a debilitating psychiatric condition. For example, persons diagnosed with *posttraumatic stress disorder* (PTSD) or *acute stress disorder* (ASD), both of which arise from exposure to severe, traumatic events, are subject to flashbacks, dissociation, sleep disturbances, depersonalization, "hypervigilance" regarding anything having to do with the original traumatic event, bursts of anger and hostility, hallucinations, and a sense that the future is nonexistent or bleak. Such persons are, of course, advised to remain under the care of medical or mental health professionals and to seek social support as they try to return to a degree of normalcy in their lives. The number of persons in the population that at any given time can be said to fall under a diagnosis of PTSD or ASD is not known precisely, but, clearly, the figure goes up or down depending on the existence of major stressors such as wars and disasters (Cahill & Pontoski 2005).

At the same time, there is a much larger pool of individuals who may be regarded as suffering from "ordinary" stress—the kind related to such circumstances or conditions as work, school, family problems, financial difficulties (including poverty and unemployment), marital discord, poor housing or living conditions, or having a medical condition (including a mental disorder). Indeed, for many people even important social events such as weddings and holidays can be sources of stress. Because of its nature and its source in society, this type of "ordinary" stress is sometimes termed *social stress* (Turner, Wheaton, & Lloyd 1995). As with the more severe, trauma-based forms, social stress can be chronic or acute. It may pass when the situation causing it passes (acute stress), or it may linger and affect an individual's physical and psychological well-being over the long term (chronic stress).

The present entry focuses on stress of this general kind—social stress. (The other, more specific disorders are dealt with elsewhere in the encyclopedia.)

Variable Responses to Stressors

It is a commonly said that some people "thrive on stress." And, indeed, it does seem that certain individuals not only are not bothered by stress but welcome it, within limits, as a way to energize themselves. That is because stress is the body's automatic, protective response to a perceived threat or challenge. It is triggered by those "fight or flight" situations that require a sudden behavioral adjustment. On a physiological level, stress involves changes in many different systems of the body, notably those regulating heart rate, blood pressure, skin sensitivity, and the flow of adrenaline. On a psychological level, stress involves a heightened state of alertness, fear, or anxiety. Although a modest amount of stress is considered harmless, perhaps even beneficial, stress that is excessive or prolonged can take a toll on the individual's physical and mental health.

A stressor is a situation, individual, or environment that causes a state of stress. The stressor need not be present for the stress to be felt, for the individual can think about or worry over the stressor at any time (including during sleep). Moreover, stressors are not necessarily the same for all people. One person, for example, may take an airport delay in stride and use the time to catch up on work, while another may construe it as a personal affront and an example of the ineptitude of the officials in charge. The same stressor is present, but there are two different responses to it.

The body's system for handling stress is designed to remain in a "ready" status most of the time, coming into play only when it is necessary in order to protect the individual. Overuse of the system, so to speak, can cause exhaustion and a host of

Bullying

Bullying at school, at the workplace, or at home is a source of severe stress for those who encounter it. Because bullying takes place in a "closed" situation, with little or no moral or physical support for the victims, the escape, or "flight," course of action is not available to them. Usually, victims are not able to take advantage of the "fight" response either, because of physical or psychological weaknesses they have vis-à-vis the bully. The most common strategy is avoidance, staying away from work or school, with potentially damaging effects. Victims feel that they cannot tell others of their problem, for a variety of reasons. They may, for example, believe that they will be subjected to even harsher abuse, or that others will ridicule them and tell them to "stand up for yourself." (Of course, if they could they would not be bullied to begin with.) Or they may deny, even to themselves, that the problem exists, casting the abuse as a positive form of attention or seeing it as mere jealousy on the part of the bully. These, however, are ineffective coping strategies in the long run. Usually, the victim needs outside help in order to resolve the problem permanently. Domestic violence, or intimate partner violence, is one of the more severe forms of bullying and is known to cause great anxiety, stress, and trauma.

other difficulties. Regardless of these physiological realities, some people do have an overactive stress response that makes them react strongly to even minor provocations. It is possible, according to some researchers, that a genetic predisposition, or genetic dysfunction, exists in individuals who overreact to stressors in this way. It is possible, too, that an exaggerated response is rooted in prolonged or extreme exposure to stress during early childhood, when critical pathways in the brain are still developing (Berger 2005).

Internal conflicts can also be a source of stress. Such conflicts exist, for example, when an individual must decide between two equally compelling but antagonistic options (e.g., take a year off before college or get some prerequisites out of the way?) or between two equally unattractive options (accept a bad job or risk staying unemployed?). Again, some people are better able than others to handle these kinds of situations. Erik Erikson (1980), in his theory of development, notes that often the central internal conflicts revolve around issues of (1) autonomy versus dependence, (2) intimacy versus isolation, or (3) cooperation versus competition. Thought of in that way, it is understandable that some individuals might experience a kind of existential angst in facing important decisions. Most of us, however, experience stress in more prosaic terms and at a more practical level.

Culture, Society, and Stress

Culture and society may shape what situations are perceived as stressful, what coping strategies are acceptable to use, and what institutional mechanisms can be turned to for assistance. In traditional Indian culture, for example, stress is generally understood to be an integral part of life—a kind of energizing principle—not something that needs to be brought to the attention of a mental health professional or other expert. When stress does become a negative force, there are forms of self-healing available, such as meditation and yoga (Laungani 1993).

In Latin American cultures the concept of *nervios* ("nerves") is drawn on to account for symptoms such as headaches ("brain aches"), emotionality, irritability, sleeplessness, dizziness, and so on. *Nervios* is an expression of psychological distress that is more common among women than among men. It is distinguished from a similar disorder, *susto* ("fright," or "soul loss"), in that it is a long-term, or chronic, condition and is more strongly linked to both stress and depression (Weller et al. 2008).

Long ago the sociologist Robert Merton (1957) suggested that society can induce stress by promoting values that conflict with the institutions and social structures through with those values are to be realized. Merton argued that the system of values in the United States promotes attainment of monetary success among more people than can possibly be accommodated by the opportunities available. As a consequence, many of those who have internalized these culturally valued goals are doomed to failure.

There are variations in the prevalence of stress among groups in the United States. For instance, American women are far more likely than American men to be diagnosed with anxiety and stress-related disorders; but this may have to do, in part, with a greater willingness among women to seek professional help for these conditions (Marohn 2003). People who feel marginalized or situated outside the sociocultural mainstream, such as gays and lesbians, people of color, and physically and mentally challenged persons, are also more likely than those from the general population to feel the impact of stress in their lives, a result of discrimination, harassment, economic deprivation, and other factors. Such ongoing adversity can have serious consequences in terms of the individual's neurophysiological health (Krieger 1999).

Addressing Stress

Stress management can refer to any action that helps prevent or reduce the body's stress response. A variety of strategies are available. One of the most common involves relaxation techniques, such as meditation or progressive muscle relaxation, perhaps aided by calming aural and aromatic stimuli. Education about stress is another standard element of most stress management programs. Participants learn how to identify their personal sources of stress, how to recognize the physiological and psychological signs that they are becoming overly stressed (including through biofeedback), and how to avoid or control stressors to the extent that this is possible.

These and other strategies are often part of a cognitive-behavioral approach to stress therapy. Under this approach, individuals are taught to monitor and change stressful thoughts, to reorganize their activities and behaviors in such a way as to minimize stress, to actively schedule "time off" or other pleasant activities, to prioritize and manage their workloads, and to generally adopt a healthy lifestyle. Exercise has also been shown to help reduce stress. Sometimes, however, an antianxiety (anxiolytic) drug may be prescribed in addition to these other techniques.

See also Anger and Aggression; Depression; Posttraumatic Stress Disorder; Poverty, Unemployment, Economic Inequality, and Mental Health; Workplace Issues in Mental Health

Bibliography

American Institute of Stress. http://www.stress.org.

Berger, Kathleen Stassen. 2005. *The Developing Person through Childhood and Adolescence*. New York: Macmillan.

Cahill, Shawn P., and Kristin Ponstoski. 2005. "Post-Traumatic Stress Disorder and Acute Stress Disorder: Their Nature and Assessment Considerations." *Psychiatry* 2: 14–25.

Erikson, Erik. 1980. *Identity and the Life Cycle*. New York: Norton.

Folkman, Susan, ed. 2011. *The Oxford Handbook of Stress, Health, and Coping*. New York: Oxford University Press.

Krieger, N. 1999. "Embodying Inequality: A Review of Concepts, Measures, and Methods for Studying Health Consequences of Discrimination." *International Journal of Social Welfare* 29: 295–352.

Laungani, Pittu. 1993. "Cultural Differences in Stress and Its Management." *Stress Medicine* 9: 37–43.

Marohn, Stephanie. 2003. *The Natural Medicine Guide to Anxiety*. Charlottesville, VA: Hampton Roads.

Merton, Robert K. *Social Theory and Social Structure*. 1957. Glencoe, IL: Free Press.

Turner, R., Blair Wheaton, and Donald A. Lloyd. 1995. "The Epidemiology of Social Stress." *American Sociological Review* 60: 104–125.

University of Massachusetts Center for Mindfulness in Medicine, Health Care, and Society. http://www.umassmed.edu/cfm2/index.aspx.

Weller, S. C., R. D. Baer, J. Garcia de Alba Garcia, and A. L. Salcedo Rocha. 2008. "Susto and Nervios: Expressions for Stress and Depression." *Culture, Medicine, and Psychiatry* 32: 406–420.

Substance Abuse

See Alcohol Abuse, Alcoholism, and Mental Health; Drug Abuse and Mental Health

Suicide and Suicide Prevention

Michael A. Church and Charles I. Brooks

One of the most baffling experiences for many of us to accept is the purposeful taking of one's own life. For those who have never been suicidal, it is difficult to comprehend such an act. In reality, analyses show that there are many different reasons for suicide. Ernest Hemingway took his life after becoming increasingly depressed about overwhelming medical problems. The noted psychiatrist Bruno Bettelheim did not want his family to be encumbered by his chronic and debilitating illness. Still others grow weary of their feelings of depression, hopelessness, drug/alcohol abuse, and/or other practical or psychological problems leading to suicidal behavior. Clearly, this is a very personal act decided upon for varied reasons.

It is estimated that well over 30,000 people commit suicide yearly (Centers for Disease Control and Prevention 2007). However, experts believe that this is a gross underestimate of the actual number, because so many ambiguous deaths are ruled accidental. Moreover, it is estimated that at least 10 persons attempt suicide for every 1 who completes the act.

Some have argued that an individual would have to be psychotic or insane to perform such an act. However, psychological autopsies that involve case study analyses of the histories of those who commit suicide do not support such a contention. Although it is clear that most suicidal individuals usually have one or more psychological disorders, this is not always the case. Moreover, most individuals who commit suicide do not appear to be out of touch with reality (i.e., psychotic). Along these lines, it should be noted that suicide is not classified as a psychological disorder in the most recent diagnostic manual (the American Psychiatry Association's *Diagnostic and Statistical Manual of Mental Disorders*, 4th ed., or *DSM-IV*) used by mental health professionals.

Correlates

Obviously, we cannot perform experiments to delineate factors that cause suicide. Therefore we are left with correlational analyses of these acts. Interestingly, studies have shown that those who attempt suicide are different than those who "succeed." Attempters are likely to be white housewives between 20 and 40 years of age who are experiencing marital or relationship problems and who overdose with pills. Those who actually end their lives tend to be white men over 40 years of age who are suffering from ill health and/or depression, and they shoot or hang themselves (Diekstra, Kienhorts, & de Wilde 1995; Lester 1994; Fremouw, Perczel, & Ellis 1990).

Suicide Statistics

- Suicide is the eighth leading cause of death in U.S. men.
- Married people are less likely to kill themselves than those who are divorced.

- Suicide rates are highest during the spring and summer months.
- The suicide rate among college students is twice as high as those who are not in college, and one in five students admits to suicidal thoughts sometime during college.
- Men commit suicide about three times more often than women, although women attempt it about three times more frequently.
- Physicians, lawyers, law enforcement personnel, and dentists have the highest rates of suicide.
- Socioeconomic status is unrelated to suicide, although a marked drop in socioeconomic status is associated with greater potential for suicide.
- Suicide rates are lower in countries where Catholicism and Islam are a strong influence.
- Native Americans have very high rates of suicide compared with Japanese Americans and Chinese Americans.
- Suicide rates tend to be low during times of war and natural disasters, which tend to create cohesiveness and purpose in a greater percentage of people.
- The majority of people who commit suicide communicated their intent prior to the act.
- Men over 65 years of age are the most likely group to commit suicide.
- Men are more likely to use violent means to kill themselves than women (e.g., firearms vs. pills, respectively), although women are increasing their use of methods more likely to be successful.
- About 60 percent of suicide attempters are under the influence of alcohol, and about 25 percent are legally intoxicated.
- The majority of suicide victims show a primary mood disorder.
- Childhood and adolescent rates of suicide are increasing rapidly, and suicide is the third leading cause of death among teens.
- Although depression is correlated with suicide, hopelessness is more predictive of the act. (For information on this and the other items in the above list, see Berman 2006; Centers for Disease Control and Prevention 2007; Leach 2006; and Shneidman 1993.)

Common Characteristics of Suicide

Suicide victims almost always show ambivalence caused by the built-in desire to survive and avoid death. Still, the goal is to end psychological pain that they see as permanent. They have reached a point of seeing the future as hopeless. Tunnel vision is a common state for the suicidal, wherein they are unable to see the "big picture." Death is viewed as the only way out. Other options and the impact of suicide on significant others are minimally considered, if at all. Thus the act undertaken is one of escape—an act, moreover, that is often typical of their lifelong coping styles.

Theoretical Orientations

Theories of suicide generally focus on sociological, psychodynamic, and biological causes. Sociocultural explanations were originally advanced by the French sociologist Emile Durkheim (1951). He postulated three types of suicide: egoistic, altruistic, and anomic. Egoistic suicide results from an individual's inability to integrate one's self with society. Lack of close ties to the community leaves the individual without support systems during times of stress and strain. Durkheim argues that highly industrialized and technological societies tend to deemphasize connection with community and family life, thereby increasing vulnerability to suicide. Altruistic suicide involves the taking of one's life in order to advance group goals or achieve some higher value or cause. Examples include some terrorist and religious acts. Anomic suicide occurs when dramatic societal events cause an individual's relationship with society to become imbalanced in significant fashion. Higher suicide rates during the Great Depression and among those who were freed from concentration camps after World War II serve as examples.

Psychodynamic explanations were derived from Freudian theory, which says that suicide is anger turned inward. Presumably, the hostility directed toward self is, in actuality, against the love object with whom the person has identified (e.g., the mother, the father, or some other significant relation). Interestingly, research analysis of 165 suicide notes over a 25-year period showed that about one-quarter expressed self-anger. However, the majority either expressed positive self-attitudes or neither. Thus although some suicides may involve anger turned toward oneself, it appears other emotions and factors are also relevant (Tuckman, Kleiner, & Lavell 1959).

Biological explanations have focused on the fact that suicide, like many other psychological phenomena, can run in families. That is, there is evidence that suicide and suicide attempts are higher among parents and close relatives than with nonsuicidal people. Additionally, patients with low levels of the metabolite 5-HIAA (which is involved in the production of serotonin, a brain neurotransmitter) are more likely to commit suicide (Asberg, Traskman, & Thoren 1976; Van Praag 1983). Such persons are more likely to possess histories of impulsive and violent behavior patterns (Edman et al. 1986; Roy 1992). Of course, this evidence is correlational in nature and does not indicate whether low levels of 5-HIAA are the cause or the effect of certain moods and emotions or whether they are directly related.

Children, Adolescents, and College Students

Although suicide almost always leaves one with a deep sense of loss, it is particularly tragic when it occurs with a young person. In many ways, those belonging to the youth population are the most vulnerable to making irreversible decisions (their last) without receiving much, if any, support or help and without fully understanding the ramifications of the suicidal act, including how it will affect others.

There is evidence that family instability and stress is correlated with suicide attempts (Cosand, Bouraqe, & Kraus 1982). Many suicidal children have experienced traumatic events and the loss of a parental figure before age 12. Their parents have frequently been abusers of drugs and/or alcohol. Their families have been found to be under greater economic stress than matched (control group) families. The families of suicide attempters also showed a higher number of medical problems, psychiatric illnesses, and suicides than the control group families.

Carson and Johnson (1985) say that 20 percent of college students have experienced suicidal ideation during their college years. Research has shown that students who commit suicide tend to be men, older than the average student by about four years, more likely to be a graduate as opposed to undergraduate student, more often a foreign or language/literature student, and to have performed better academically as an undergraduate than as a graduate student (Seiden 1966, 1984). Further analyses have shown that, despite excellent academic records, most college undergraduates who commit suicide are dissatisfied with their performances and pessimistic about their abilities to succeed. Along these lines, they tend to show unrealistically high expectations for themselves and perfectionist standards and often feel shame over their perceived failings. Additionally, a frequent stressor is the failure to reach expectations or loss of a close interpersonal relationship. A precipitating factor is often the breakup of a romantic relationship. Also, suicide attempts and suicides are more likely to occur with students who have experienced the separation or divorce of their parents or the death of a parent.

Assessment

Clinical psychologists use various tests, such as the Beck Depression Inventory, Beck Hopelessness Scale (BHS), and Beck Scale for Suicide Ideation, to help assess suicide probability. These and other types of psychological tests can be used to supplement clinical interviews, patient histories, and other information as data that can help determine suicidal risk. These measures depend on the honesty of the respondent because they do not have validity scales that can determine people who are deliberately denying their true feelings and intentions.

A state official talks about a manual to help counselors in community-based suicide prevention programs deal with potential suicides. (AP Photo/Al Grillo.)

Interestingly, Exner's Rorschach system can be used to predict suicide risk. The test includes a suicide constellation score that allows for prediction of those who possess heightened potential for such. Because the Rorschach is comprised of ambiguous stimuli, it is very difficult to fake. Although all of these measures can be used to complement other inputs, the BHS has been found to be particularly helpful in predicting eventual suicide (Beck et al. 1985).

Suicide Prevention

Most suicidal victims display signs of their intent. Families, coworkers, primary care doctors, mental health professionals, and others need to be aware of these signs and then act appropriately in terms of the specific context. Of course, lay-people are not expected to be able to predict the likelihood of a suicide attempt with the accuracy of a trained professional. However, friends, coworkers, and family members are certainly in a better position to see day-to-day changes in potential suicide victims' moods and earlier behaviors in ways a professional cannot. As a result, family members and acquaintances may be able to intervene effectively or get the sufferer needed professional help. For example, knowing that men, particularly the depressed elderly, are more likely to commit suicide than other demographic groups can alert us to warning signs in that group. Suppose we know such a man who lives alone and recently lost his wife after a sustained illness. Add to this information the fact that he seldom sees his family or friends and possesses a gun. Certainly, risk factors are present in that case. Obviously, such factors do not mean that the man *will* attempt to take his life. However, we should be alert to the higher risk of such an act taking place in this situation.

Both laypeople and professionals should be aware that people who have thought out a plan for their suicide are more likely than those without a plan to try it. Generally, the more detail they can provide about their plan, the more serious they are about carrying it out. Also, they often communicate their intent to others and provide indirect behavioral clues. For example, they may make out a will or change insurance policies, give away prized possessions, or go on a lengthy trip. At any rate, their presuicidal behavior in retrospect is often seen as somewhat unusual or peculiar. Of course, previous suicide attempts are often a precursor to a "successful" one and are a major risk factor. Still, we need to keep in mind that some suicide victims have neither tried suicide before nor communicated their intent to anyone.

With respect to suicide prevention, the phenomenon of subtle suicide (Church & Brooks 2009) is relevant. Subtle suicide typically involves a long-term pattern of self-destructive behaviors, thoughts, and feelings that ultimately drag a person down in a self-defeating fashion. As with overt suicide, subtle suicide involves deep ambivalence about living. Sufferers have a desire to live, while, at the same time, there is an equal or greater wish that their life will end. Although not actively suicidal, the subtly suicidal engage in neglectful, self-defeating, risky, and self-destructive behaviors that inevitably lower the quality and sometimes length of their lives. A downward spiraling effect occurs that can eventually lead the subtly suicidal to become overtly suicidal. In other words, some people pass through an extended period of being uncommitted to living before ending their lives. Professional and family interventions may be effective in getting these individuals committed to living more fully and out of a "subtle suicide zone," where they compromise their own physical, psychological, and social well-being.

The main point to emphasize here is that many people take a long, slow slide downhill that may or may not be apparent to those close to them. We need to keep in mind that over half of those who commit suicide have made no previous attempt (Stolberg, Clark, & Bongar 2002; Zahl & Hawton 2004b). Over time, some people who have been subtly suicidal become overtly so, particularly as their lives deteriorate and they become more hopeless in their outlook. Interventions as early in the process as possible stand to save lives and enhance the quality of life for the potential victim and significant others. Thus early detection of people who are becoming or have become suicidal—regardless of whether they suffer from serious psychological disorders—is a first line of defense in the effort to prevent suicide. Many people can avoid the process of dealing with active suicidal ideation and behavior altogether if they get the prerequisite support and help.

A second form of prevention involves crisis intervention. The objective here is to intervene appropriately when an individual calls for help with suicidal ideation, gesture, or attempt. The focus is on maintaining contact with the potential victim. The contact could be on the telephone or in person in a hospital, mental health clinic, or other location. In all instances, the objective is to give helpful support and feedback. Constructive feedback can help in a number of ways, including (but not limited to):

- Bringing calm to the situation
- Minimizing loneliness and alienation
- Reducing the tunnel vision that many suicidal people have in this state
- Combating hopelessness
- Giving empathy
- Offering practical options and choices
- Making referrals to other professionals
- Initiating an involuntary or voluntary psychiatric hospitalization

Follow-up treatments can be crucial in preventing future attempts. Even with treatments, there is an increased risk, as those who have a previous attempt are at a five times greater risk to die by suicide (Stolberg, Clark, & Bongar 2002).

Some successful prevention studies have been done with particular high-risk groups. One program placed older men in roles where they are involved with social and interpersonal activities that help others. These activities have been found to help them cope with feelings of isolation and meaninglessness (Maris, Berman, & Silverman 2000). A similar program involved adolescents with suicidal ideation and behavior and/or mood or substance abuse history (Zahl & Hawton 2004a). Finally, working with adults who had made previous attempts, Brown and colleagues (2005) found that 10 cognitive therapy sessions targeted at suicide prevention reduced subsequent suicide attempts by 50 percent over an 18-month period. The same subjects' feelings of depression and hopelessness, moreover, were lower than the comparison group (Brown et al. 2005). These are just a few of the studies that have shown clear evidence of how suicide prevention can be used effectively.

See also Adolescence and Mental Health; Borderline Personality Disorder; Campus Life and Mental Health; Depression; Self-Injury and Body Image; Preventative Mental Health Programs

Bibliography

Anderson, S. 2008. "The Urge to End It All." *New York Times Magazine*, July 6. Retrieved from http://www.nytimes.com/2008/07/06/magazine/06suicide-t.html.

Asberg, M., L. Traskman, and P. Thoren. 1976. "5HIAA in the Cerebrospinal Fluid: A Biochemical Suicide Predictor?" *Archives of General Psychiatry* 33: 1193–1197.

Beck, A. T., and R. A. Steer. 1987. *Manual for Revised Beck Depression Inventory.* San Antonio, TX: Psychological Corporation.

Beck, A. T., and R. A. Steer. 1988. *Manual for Beck Hopelessness Scale.* San Antonio, TX: Psychological Corporation.

Beck, A. T., R. A. Steer, M. Kovacs, and B. Garrison. 1985. "Hopeless and Eventual Suicide: A 10-Year Prospective Study of Patients Hospitalized with Suicide Ideation." *American Journal of Psychiatry* 142: 559–563.

Beck, A. T., R. A. Steer, and W. F. Ranieri. 1988. "Scale for Suicide Ideation: Psychometric Properties of a Self-Report Version." *Journal of Clinical Psychology* 44: 499–505.

Berman, A. L. 2006. "Risk Management with Suicidal Patients." *Journal of Clinical Psychology: In Session* 62: 1971–1984.

Bertini, K. 2009. *Understanding and Preventing Suicide: The Development of Self-Destructive Patterns and Ways to Alter Them.* Westport, CT: Praeger.

Brown, G. K., T. Have, G. R. Henriques, S. X. Xie, J. E. Hollander, and A. T. Beck. 2005. "Cognitive Therapy for the Prevention of Suicide Attempts: A Randomized Control Trial." *Journal of the American Medical Association* 294(5): 563–570.

Carson, N. D., and R. E. Johnson. 1985. "Suicidal Thoughts and Problem Solving Preparation among College Students." *Journal of College Student Personnel* 26: 484–487.

Centers for Disease Control and Prevention. 2007. *Suicide Facts at a Glance.* Retrieved from http://www.cdc.gov/nipe/dvp/suicide/.

Church, M. A., and C. I. Brooks. 2009. *Subtle Suicide: Our Silent Epidemic over Ambivalence about Living.* Westport, CT: Praeger.

Cosand, B. J., L. B. Bouraqe, and J. F. Kraus. 1982. "Suicide among Adolescents in Sacramento County, California, 1950–1979." *Adolescence* 17: 917–930.

Diekstra, R. F., C. W. M. Kienhorst, and E. J. de Wilde. 1995. "Suicide and Suicidal Behavior among Adolescents." In M. Rutter and D. J. Smith, eds., *Psychological Disorders in Young People* (pp. 686–761). Chichester, England: Wiley.

Durkheim, E. 1951. *Suicide*. New York: Free Press.

Edman, G., M. Adberg, S. Levander, and D. Schalling. 1986. "Skin Conductance Habituation and Cerebrospinal Fluid 5-Hydroxyindeactic Acid in Suicidal Patients." *Archives of General Psychiatry* 43: 586–592.

Exner, J. E., Jr. 1993. *The Rorschach: A Comprehensive System: Vol. 1. Basic Foundations* (3rd ed.). New York: Wiley.

Fremouw, W. J., W. J. Perczel, and T. E. Ellis. 1990. *Suicide Risk: Assessment and Response Guidelines*. Elmsford, NY: Pergamon.

Leach, M. M. 2006. *Cultural diversity and Suicide: Ethnic, Religious, Gender and Sexual Orientation Perspectives*. Binghamton, NY: Haworth Press.

Lester, D. 1994. "Are There Unique Features of Suicide in Adults of Different Ages and Developmental Stages?" *Omega Journal of Death and Dying* 29: 337–348.

Maris, R. W., A. C. Berman, and M. M. Silverman. 2000. *Comprehensive Textbook of Suicidology*. New York: Guilford Press.

Roy, A. 1992. "Suicide in Schizophrenia." *International Review of Psychiatry* 4: 205–209.

Seiden, R. H. 1966. "Campus Tragedy: A Study of Student Suicide." *Journal of Abnormal and Social Psychology* 71: 389–399.

Seiden, R. H. 1984. "The Youthful Suicide Epidemic." *Public Affairs Report* 25: 1.

Shneidman, E. S. 1993. *Suicide as Psychache: A Clinical Approach to Self-Destructive Behavior*. Northvale, NJ: Jason Aronson.

Stolberg, R. A., D. C. Clark, and B. Bongar. 2002. "Epidemiology, Assessment and Management of Suicide in Depressed Patients." In I. H. Gotlib and C. L. Hammen, eds., *Handbook of Depression* (pp. 581–601). New York: Guilford Press.

Tuckman, J., R. Kleiner, and M. Lavell. 1959. "Emotional Content of Suicide Notes." *American Journal of Psychiatry* 16: 59–63.

van Praag, H. M. 1983. "CSF 5-H1AA and Suicide in Nondepressed Schizophrenics." *Lancet* 2: 977–978.

Zahl, D. L., and K. Hawton. 2004a. "Media Influence on Suicidal Behavior: An Interview Study of Young People." *Behavior and Cognitive Psychotherapy* 32(2): 189–198.

Zahl, D. L., and K. Hawton. 2004b. "Repetition of Deliberate Self-Harm and Subsequent Suicide Risk: Long-Term Follow-Up Study of 11,583 Patients." *British Journal of Psychiatry* 185: 70–75.

Survivors' Groups

See Advocacy Groups; Recovery Movement

T

Therapeutic Community and Milieu Therapy

Julie Kipp

Definition

Therapeutic community is a type of milieu therapy, first developed during World War II in military hospitals in Great Britain, that went on to be an important, even ubiquitous, influence in American psychiatry during the mid- to later twentieth century. Although it has faded from the contemporary psychiatric dialogue, therapeutic community continues to have intriguing implications for the milieu settings in which many people with mental illness are still being treated.

Milieu therapy of mental illness refers to a setting where a number of individuals receive treatment, and the interactions between them and their environment are a focus of therapeutic attention. Until the later part of the twentieth century, the setting was the ward of a psychiatric hospital, private or public, large or small. As deinstitutionalization (or downsizing and closing) of the large state psychiatric hospitals in the United States and the rest of the Western world proceeded, milieu therapy moved along with patients to shorter-term wards of smaller, local and private psychiatric hospitals, day programs, and residential settings of various kinds. Not all milieu settings utilize milieu therapy, although many of the principles are now widely accepted and given lip service, at least, even in the bleakest of contemporary settings.

Therapeutic community is an enhancement of milieu therapy in which participants not only are cared for and treated but also are encouraged to take responsibility for as much of the life of the milieu (group or community) as they are able. The therapeutic community philosophically occupies a place midway between the psychiatric hospital and the clubhouse model, as developed in the postwar years in the United States by ex-state hospital patients in New York City's Fountain House. The traditional hospital provides total care delivered according to the standard medical model, with professional staff holding complete responsibility for the care of ill patients. On the opposite end of the spectrum, the clubhouse model, members take all responsibility for their own community, and, historically, are suspicious of professional help. The therapeutic community, on the other hand, occupies a middle ground between these two poles: it operates under the medical model, insofar as members who are professional staff carry responsibility for members who are ill and come for treatment. However, in the therapeutic community the hierarchy is flattened and all members are encouraged to take on responsibility to the best of their ability—and their ability is expected to develop and grow.

In real-life programs and settings, especially contemporary ones, there is a great deal of overlap between models, and currently many medical settings invite patient involvement, while clubhouses employ professional staff.

Three Levels of Care

In understanding the distinctions between therapeutic community and other forms of milieu therapy, it is helpful to refer back to David Clark's 1964 *Administrative Therapy: The Role of the Doctor in the Therapeutic Community.* Although this work is almost 50 years old, Clark's three levels of principles for treatment of mental illness bear repeating: there continue to be incidences of very poor treatment settings in which mentally ill people are offered little more than a place to be "warehoused."

Clark's first level of principles of care of the mentally ill begins with the most basic decent treatment, such as adequate food, clothing, and safe conditions, and a setting in which the needs of the patient are the treating institution's first concern. Over and above these basics, Clark's second level of principles is taken from the 1953 report of the WHO (World Health Organization) Expert Committee on Mental Health, and address the importance of the atmosphere of the hospital setting. The second level principles are (1) preservation of the patient's personality; (2) an assumption of the trustworthiness of patients, at least until proven otherwise; (3) the centrality of activity and work; (4) the importance of staff attitudes and relationships, as affecting the treatment setting; and (5) the use of sanctions to control disturbing behavior. (As a note to this last principle, Clark states that "only with the therapeutic-community concept of peer-group control have we begun to open the possibility of a way of checking deviant behaviour that does not bind the whole institution in paralysing penal rules" [p. 42].)

Beyond basic assurances of life, physical health, and safety, these second-level "modern general principles" begin to emphasize the patient as a person and acknowledge the influence of the institution in which the treatment takes place. "There is no patient 'untreated' by his environment, only patients 'treated' well or ill," Alfred Stanton, author of an influential book of the time, *The Mental Hospital*, stated (Stanton 1962, vii).

Finally, with the ground rules of modern humane treatment in place, Clark (1964) goes on to define the third and highest level of treatment for people with mental illness, namely, the principles of the therapeutic community. These principles are:

• The freeing of communications ("an endless process," as Clark says [1964, 45])

• The analysis of all events

- Provision of learning experiences
- A flattening of the authority pyramid
- Examination of roles
- Use of the community meeting

Each of these is discussed in the section that follows.

The Main Principles of Therapeutic Community

The endless process of *the freeing of communications* involves a "constant effort ... to open communications and to free the many blocks that exist, both between individuals and between different status levels within the community" (Clark 1964, 44). The therapeutic community involves an idealistic commitment to the possibility of communication between human beings, and to the healing power of intimacy. In practice, of course, this is a difficult ideal to achieve, and it is not always true that honesty on every level will be helpful or appropriate for staff or clients. In fact, it has been noted that clients' acculturation into the open communication encouraged by the therapeutic community may not ultimately serve them well in the world at large (see, e.g., Rapoport 1960). However, the therapeutic community values the effort to open communication, and this is surely helpful for many clients isolated in their illness or who have not learned to trust others.

Analysis of all events in the community is another way of saying maintaining a "culture of enquiry," a phrase coined by Tom Main, one of the early military hospital innovators. Main, who also first used the term "therapeutic community" (1946/1996), was referring to a climate of considering all events as important information for the healing work of the community. Of all the third-level principles, this one especially brings the essence of psychoanalysis into the milieu treatment setting. The culture of inquiry directs the therapeutic community practitioner to embrace the daily problems of the life of the community as the stage on which the real work of therapy occurs.

The provision of learning experiences has been noted as an important task of the therapeutic community, and is related to Clark's second-level principle of providing activity and work. While there is something self-evident about providing activity and work to people who have mental illness, the therapeutic community principle of provision of learning experiences spells out how it is part of a therapeutic approach. At the most basic level, activity and work provide daily structure, which is valuable to all humans, and an antidote to the role of ill patient, insofar as the patient can achieve some success. It is also obvious that self-esteem may increase as a client reaffirms him or herself in a past role that is acceptable in the larger community, or learns a new socially valued role in the larger world.

(This emphasis on valued roles as key in recovery from mental illness is a hall-mark of the contemporary psychiatric rehabilitation model [Anthony & Liberman 1986].) But in addition, as a vital component of the therapeutic community, activity and work also provide learning experiences as "grist for the mill," in psychotherapeutic terminology. Activity and work provide the patient an opportunity to come up against reality, in order to learn about him or herself, which will, with support, be healing. Harold Bridger, one of the early innovators in World War II-era Great Britain, noted the importance of activity groups as providing a stage for reality testing. As Bridger pointed out, the traumatized prisoner of war, for example, may have fantasies of a simple life working on a farm, helping to tend the horses. Actual experience, with support and an intention of learning from experience, will help the patients clarify their goals and their current capabilities.

Likewise the importance of a milieu program's daily structure of groups, meetings, and tasks is not only that it makes life easier for the staff, or the program more predictable for regressed patients, or teaches social skills, or imposes order on those whose illness makes it difficult for them to order their own days; the true value of the daily structure is in providing an opportunity for encounters with reality, which all can observe and discuss, and from which all can learn. This knocking-up-against-reality is what is valuable, whether it takes the form of rebellions against reality, overcompliance with others' wishes, or growing abilities to tolerate frustration. Maxwell Jones, the most well known and widely read of the therapeutic community practitioners, referred to this same principle as the "living-learning situation" (Jones 1968).

Flattening of the authority pyramid is an aspect of therapeutic community that is less surprising today but was a radical idea in its time. The originators of the therapeutic community were all psychiatrists and/or military officers, but were able to let go of the reins of power in order that patients might regain agency (or independence, responsibility) in their own lives. In the therapeutic community, it is important not only to consider the effect of staff attitudes and relationships but to question them and to modify them by spreading the power around. However, this does not mean that there is no hierarchy or that all authority resides in the community (as in a pure clubhouse model). Clients with long-standing psychotic disorders may take no responsibility for their own lives, or severely personality-disordered clients may be in an unproductive lifelong battle with authority. In either case, the flattening of the hierarchy invites clients to consider their agency in own lives, and to try out new responses to authority. Some staff authority, ideally, provides the safety necessary for such exploration. The flattening of the pyramid of authority also results in sharing of authority throughout the staff hierarchy, which empowers clinicians, who then can model for clients a more proactive and creative approach to authority.

Role examination is related to the culture of inquiry and to the flattening of the hierarchy; it requires that all in the community

> examine what they are doing, why, and how it affects others. This helps the patients to modify their behaviour towards other people and the staff to modify their way of working. With this often goes some role-blurring so that people become able to do parts of the task of others. (Clark 1964, 46)

The community meeting could be considered a modality in itself, and early therapeutic community innovators were interested in the somewhat different dynamics of the large group as opposed to smaller psychotherapy and activity groups, which have also generally been part of the daily life of therapeutic communities (see Kreeger 1975). Community meetings involve all staff and clients, and offer opportunity for informal, free communication as opposed to some later, watered-down versions that functioned more as a community bulletin board or opportunity for staff to reinforce community rules. Traditionally, a staff review meeting followed the community meeting in order that staff might cull the major themes of the meeting and plan for further intervention, and in order to critique their own participation. Corollary to the community meeting is another sort of staff meeting, namely, the staff support group, whereby staff regularly process their own reactions to the work and work out any difficulties with each other that may get in the way of the work or lead to destructive splitting processes in the community (Hartley & Kennard 2009).

Additional Principles

In addition to the above elements of David Clark's definition of the therapeutic community, there are two other principles that have been highlighted by other authors. These are as follows:

- Patients are able to help one another.
- Innovation in one part of the organization affects other parts of the organization.

Not only is it often the case that *patients are able to help one another*, but in doing so they may be more effective than staff in providing support. Maxwell Jones especially emphasized this principle:

> The therapeutic community is *distinctive* among other comparable treatment centers in the way the institution's total resources, both staff and patients, are self-consciously pooled in furthering treatment. This implies above all a change in the usual status of patients. In collaboration with the staff, they now become active participants in the therapy of other patients, and in other aspects of overall hospital work—in contrast to their relatively more passive recipient role in conventional treatment regimes. (Jones 1959, 200, his italics)

As for the second point—*innovation in one part of the organization affects other parts of the organization*—this concept comes from social psychology. The institution as a whole, from macro to micro levels, from director to janitor, from structured activity to informal encounter, must be considered as impacting treatment to a greater or lesser extent, and an awareness of this helps the community to make use of all the opportunities of daily life.

A Brief History of Therapeutic Community in the United States

As described above, the modern therapeutic community began during World War II in Great Britain in military hospitals treating men found unfit for military service, and later, traumatized soldiers returning from the front (Harrison 2000). Psychoanalysis, particularly as practiced at the Tavistock Institute in London, was an influence as was the social psychology and action research of Kurt Lewin (1890–1947). Psychodynamic group therapy was being developed simultaneously with the therapeutic community, and S. H. Foulkes (1898–1976), one of group therapy's founders, was an officer in one of the first military therapeutic communities.

Karl Menninger (1893–1990), an American psychiatrist, whose family founded the influential Menninger Clinic, was an officer in the U.S. military during World War II and visited the military therapeutic communities in Great Britain late in the war. He brought back the new treatment ideas to the United States, publishing them in the *Bulletin* of the Menninger Clinic. Another American military officer and psychiatrist, Harry Wilmer, also visited British hospitals and returned to start his own therapeutic communities for men with psychiatric casualties from the Pacific and Korea. Wilmer discussed his work in his 1958 book *Social Psychiatry in Action*. Maxwell Jones also came to the United States on several extended occasions and was influential in the growing acceptance of therapeutic community as a treatment for mental illness, starting communities in prisons and community mental health centers. Robert Rapoport, an American anthropologist, researched one of Jones's communities in Great Britain, with the resulting influential book *Community as Doctor* (1960). Loren Mosher, also influenced by the work in Great Britain, especially that of R. D. Laing (1927–89), initiated Soteria House in the early 1970s for young patients experiencing their first psychotic episode. Mosher and his Soteria House experiment went on to influence similar projects in other parts of the United States and in Switzerland. During several decades following World War II, therapeutic community flourished and became widespread in the United States.

Although people with mental illness continued to be treated in milieu settings, therapeutic community per se eventually faded from the professional discourse. One reason why was the late twentieth century's emphasis on pharmacological treatments and its fascination with the new findings of neuroscience, culminating in the Decade of the Brain (1990s). This trend deemphasized all sorts of psychosocial treatments, including therapeutic community, as the bulk of funding and professional research centered on neuroscience and psychopharmacology.

The philosophy of therapeutic community also contributed to its disappearance from the professional dialogue. It was a value of the therapeutic community not to strictly define itself. This was done in order to give members the opportunity to develop independence and responsibility through their own use of the milieu; it was fully expected that each community would be unique to some extent.

Therapeutic community may have also been a victim of its own success since it was the accepted psychiatric canon for several decades of the mid- to late twentieth century, to the point where almost all milieus were called by the name therapeutic community, even if they provided no more than hierarchic business as usual.

Another factor in the fading influence of therapeutic community is that it is a difficult modality to research given its many variables, and it developed at a time when researching the effectiveness of treatments was considered less crucial than it is currently.

Contemporary Therapeutic Community

A few therapeutic communities, consciously identifying themselves as such, continue today. These include Austen Riggs Hospital in Stockbridge, Massachusetts, and the small farm–based communities of Spring Lake Ranch in Vermont and Gould Farm in Massachusetts. Cooper-Riis is a newer, private community in North Carolina. As a *practice* combining self-reflective principles of psychotherapy and community living, on the other hand, therapeutic community continues to be re-created in many settings (not necessarily with reference to its historical culture), especially in areas where staff are still influenced by psychoanalytic or social psychology principles.

The Sanctuary model of Sandra Bloom (1997), for example, is a contemporary, conscious elaboration of therapeutic community. The model both draws on therapeutic community's roots of treating traumatized soldiers returning from war and enhances the earlier paradigm through the addition of recent research on trauma. Bloom has instituted this work in community settings ranging from psychiatric hospitals to children's residential treatment facilities. She has found, as did therapeutic community practitioners before her, that the use of community meetings, giving clients the skills to talk about their feelings, and sharing the responsibility for the daily life and safety of the milieu has led to a much decreased incidence of assaults, and to a secure environment in which healing can take place.

Looking Ahead

Therapeutic community has largely faded from the landscape of mental health treatment in the United States, and yet people with mental illness continue to be treated in milieu settings influenced by its legacy. Therapeutic community provides a seasoned theory and a means of increasing the effectiveness of treatment; it also addresses the inevitable problems and crises that arise when groups of people are thrown together. In contemporary settings for people with mental illness, evidence-based practices such as supported employment, treating substance abuse and mental illness concurrently, and teaching the skills of wellness self-management are in ascendance. While there is research to support such practices, the setting in which they are delivered has not been addressed, and it is often in large outpatient day treatment programs, rehabilitation programs, or vocational programs, where clients attend several days a week, several hours a day. Therapeutic community can provide a healthy milieu in which these evidenced-based interventions can be most successful. For example, workers and clients using supported employment may tend toward frustration as people with mental illness go through the ups and downs of having their abilities, commitment, and focus tested in attaining or sustaining employment. All such persons can benefit from therapeutic community's focus on the importance of analyzing events, including "failures," and its commitment to learning and reality testing in the context of support from others. Similarly, motivational interviewing for the treatment of people with co-occurring mental illness and substance abuse fits well with the therapeutic community principle of encouraging clients to take responsibility for their own lives, as they are ready to do so.

Mental illness continues to be a heart-breaking, draining problem, without easy solutions. Gerald Grob (2000), a historian of American psychiatry, has reflected on the "sobering . . . cyclical pattern alternating between enthusiastic optimism and fatalistic pessimism" (253) as popular treatments have been exalted and then abandoned in disappointment. "Rhetorical claims to the contrary, little is known about the etiology of serious mental disorders. Treatment—whether biological or psychosocial—does not necessarily eliminate the disorder . . . For too long, mental health policy has embodied an elusive dream of magical cures for age-old maladies" (254–255). Therapeutic community is not a magical cure, although it may have been exalted as such by some in its heyday. It is, however, a valid treatment that can still contribute vitally to milieu treatment and related practices.

See also Evidence-Based Practice; Group Therapy; History of Mental Health Care; Humanistic Theories and Therapies; Medical Model of Mental Illness; Neurodiversity; Peer Support Groups; Recovery Movement; Rehabilitation Services; Residential Treatment for Young People

Bibliography

Anthony, William, and R. P. Liberman. 1986. "The Practice of Psychiatric Rehabilitation: Historical, Conceptual, and Research Base." *Schizophrenia Bulletin* 12(4): 542–559.

Bloom, Sandra. 1997. *Creating Sanctuary: Toward the Evolution of Sane Societies.* New York: Routledge.

Bloom, Sandra. 2000. "Creating Sanctuary: Healing from Systematic Abuses of Power." *Therapeutic Communities: The International Journal for Therapeutic and Supportive Organizations* 2(2): 67–91.

Clark, David. 1964. *Administrative Therapy: The Role of the Doctor in the Therapeutic Community.* London: Tavistock.

Foulkes, Elizabeth, ed. 1990. *Selected Papers of S. H. Foulkes: Psychoanalysis and Group Analysis.* London: Karnac.

Grob, Gerald. 2000. "Mental Health Policy in Late Twentieth-Century America." In R. W. Menninger and J. C. Nemiah, eds., *American Psychiatry after World War II (1944–1994)* (pp. 232–258). Washington, DC: American Psychiatric Press.

Harrison, Tom. 2000. *Bion, Rickman, Foulkes and the Northfield Experiments: Advancing on a Different Front* (Vol. 5). Philadelphia: Jessica Kingsley.

Hartley, Phil, and David Kennard. 2009. *Staff Support Groups in the Helping Professions: Principles, Practice and Pitfalls.* London: Routledge.

Jones, Maxwell. 1959. "Toward a Clarification of the Therapeutic Community Concept." *British Journal of Medical Psychology* 32: 200–205.

Jones, Maxwell. 1968. *Beyond the Therapeutic Community: Social Learning and Social Psychiatry.* New Haven, CT: Yale University Press.

Kennard, David. 1998. *An Introduction to Therapeutic Communities* (2nd ed.). Philadelphia: Jessica Kingsley.

Kreeger, Lionel. 1975. *The Large Group: Dynamics and Therapy.* London: Karnac.

Main, Tom. 1996. "The Hospital as a Therapeutic Institution." *Therapeutic Communities: The International Journal for Therapeutic and Supportive Organizations* 17(2): 77–80. (Reprinted from *Bulletin of the Menninger Clinic* 10[3], May 1946)

Menninger, Karl. 1996. "Foreword." *Therapeutic Communities: The International Journal for Therapeutic and Supportive Organizations* 17(2): 75–76. (Reprinted from *Bulletin of the Menninger Clinic* 10[3], May, 1946)

Mosher, Loren. 1996. "Soteria: A Therapeutic Community for Psychotic Persons." In Peter Breggin and E. M. Stern, eds., *Psychosocial Approaches to Deeply Disturbed Persons* (pp. 43–58). New York: Haworth.

Rapoport, Robert. 1960. *Community as Doctor: New Perspectives on a Therapeutic Community.* Springfield, IL: Thomas.

Smith, M. K. 2011. "Kurt Lewin, Groups, Experiential Learning and Action Research." Retrieved from http://www.infed.org/thinkers/et-lewin.htm.

Stanton, Alfred. 1962. "Foreword." In J. Cumming and E. Cumming, eds., *Ego and Milieu.* New York: Atherton Press.

Stanton, Alfred, and Morris Schwartz. 1954. *The Mental Hospital: A Study of Institutional Participation in Psychiatric Illness and Treatment.* New York: Basic Books.

Wilmer, Harry. 1958. *Social Psychiatry in Action.* Springfield, IL: Thomas.

Trauma

Matthew J. Paylo, Nicole Adamson, and Victoria E. Kress

Psychological trauma involves a physical and/or emotional injury, which can have long-lasting effects in terms of the injured person's well-being. A traumatic event is the experience that produces psychological trauma. Trauma can be incited by a singular event or by an enduring traumatic experience. Such events and experiences may threaten an individual's sense of security, leave an individual feeling overwhelmed and isolated, and have a significant impact on an individual's self-worth. Traumatic events create a disruption in normalcy, often impairing an individual's ability to properly think, cope, and process the event and/ or related events. Individuals can have unique reactions to the same event, thus demonstrating the subjectivity inherent in the processing of traumatic events.

Traumatic Events

Although reactions to potentially traumatic events may be subjective, some events have the potential to invite trauma reactions in many, thus affecting one's ability to function at an optimal level. The most common traumatic events that affect an individual's ability to function are natural disasters, physical assault, domestic abuse, serious bodily harm, serious accidents, experiencing or witnessing a horrific injury (or fatalities or carnage), extreme poverty, and sexual assaults including rape, incest, and molestation. Other events that are often less severe yet may invoke trauma reactions include physical injuries, serious illness, verbal exposure to violence, and the death of a loved one.

An individual's reaction to traumatic events is dependent upon his or her personal history, coping skills, values and beliefs, personal reaction, and support from family and friends. The individual's conceptualization of the event and the severity of these events also significantly mediate or moderate the impact of the traumatic event on his or her overall level of functioning.

Childhood Trauma

Childhood trauma can create severe and lasting effects that disrupt a child's sense of security. Many of the trauma experiences that children are exposed to are recurrent (e.g., child abuse, ongoing poverty, exposure to domestic violence), and this can produce a sense that the world is frightening and unsafe. The phenomenon of complex trauma may develop if a child has ongoing exposure to traumatic events. These events may include maltreatment, emotional neglect, sexual abuse, physical abuse, and even witnessing violent acts at home or in the community. These types of trauma can impair a child's ability to form appropriate attachments with caregivers and peers, to control impulsivity, to control aggression and self-destructive behaviors, to regulate executive functioning (i.e., essential cognitive and behavioral actions), and to maintain appropriate self-esteem (Cook, Blaustein, Spinazzola, & Van der Kolk 2005). These ongoing experiences may disrupt a child's ability to grow and explore his or her own world, and as a consequence the child's cognitive and emotional development may be stunted. If childhood trauma is unresolved as an individual enters adulthood, a sense of fear and helplessness may be perpetuated. Childhood trauma reactions can occur secondary to neglect, to abusive or unsafe home environments, to separation from caregivers, and to childhood illnesses.

Symptoms of Trauma

Development of posttraumatic stress disorder (PTSD) and susceptibility to continued PTSD reactions are a function of many different factors including: (1) past life experiences (e.g., a history of prior traumas); (2) developmental level at onset of the trauma; (3) content and intensity of the event (e.g., injured during the attack, threat of being hurt or killed); (4) social support systems available before and after the trauma (e.g., interactions with family, peers, or law enforcement systems); (5) spiritual beliefs and supports; and (6) genetic predisposition (James & Gilliland 2001).

Symptoms of trauma can affect individuals physically, emotionally, and even cognitively. Physical symptoms of trauma, as often noted in individuals' subjective reports, include low energy, sleep disturbances, changes in eating patterns, and disturbances in sexual function. Emotional symptoms of trauma can include changes in mood, increased sense of anxiety, panic attacks, increases in impulsivity or compulsiveness, and social withdrawal. The cognitive symptoms of trauma consist of lapses in memory, difficulties with decision-making skills, concentration issues, and an increase in distractibility.

In addition to the common symptoms of trauma, extreme symptoms also exist. These more extreme symptoms include feelings of depression, a sense of guilt or grief, varieties of amnesia, a tendency toward self-blame, and somatic complaints such as aches and pains along with a sense of hypervigilance or overreaction to external stimulus, heightened levels of anger and/or agitation, an obsession with death and dying, a tendency to mentally and emotionally reexperience the traumatic event (flashbacks, intrusive thoughts), and perhaps a general numbness. Such symptoms often drive individuals to attempt to compensate for the distress experienced through the use of compensatory behaviors, including substance use and abuse, impulsive or reckless actions and choices, dissociation, social withdrawal, and feelings of ineffectiveness, shame, despair. Often, the use of compensatory behaviors clouds an individual's view of him or herself and may leave that individual unaware of the impact of the original trauma on his or her level of functioning, thus leaving him or her susceptible to significant personal and professional impairments.

Mental Illnesses Associated with Trauma

Trauma as a psychological condition becomes a mental illness or a mental disorder when an individual finds the management of normal life activities and events difficult. When the individual's level of dysfunction reaches the point where significant impairment is evidenced at work, at school, and/or in personal

---

What Percentages of Mental Health Clients Have Histories of Trauma?

Individuals with histories of violence, abuse, and neglect from childhood onward make up the majority of clients served by public mental health and substance abuse service systems.

- Of public mental health clients with severe mental illness, including schizophrenia and bipolar disorder, 51 to 98 percent have been exposed to childhood physical and/or sexual abuse. Most have multiple experiences of trauma.

- Seventy-five percent of women and men in substance abuse treatment report abuse and trauma histories.

- Ninety-seven percent of homeless women with mental illness experienced severe physical and/or sexual abuse, and 87 percent experienced this abuse both as children and as adults.

- Nearly 8 out of 10 female offenders diagnosed with a mental illness report histories of physical or sexual abuse.

- Ninety-three percent of psychiatrically hospitalized adolescents had histories of physical and/or sexual and emotional trauma; 32 percent met criteria for PTSD.

- In Massachusetts, 82 percent of all children and adolescents in continuing care inpatient and intensive residential treatment have trauma histories.

- Teenagers with alcohol and drug problems are 6 to 12 times more likely to have a history of being physically abused and 18 to 21 times more likely to have been sexually abused compared with teenagers without alcohol and drug problems.

- Among juvenile girls identified by the courts as delinquent, more than 75 percent have been sexually abused.

- Three years of data from New York State Office of Mental Health showed that only 1 in 200 adult inpatients and only 1 in 10 child/adolescent inpatients carried either a primary or secondary diagnosis of PTSD.

Source: Ann Jennings, *Models for Developing Trauma-Informed Behavioral Health Systems and Trauma-Specific Services* (Alexandria, VA: National Center for Trauma-Informed Care, 2008).

---

relationships, trauma may have reached the level of becoming a mental disorder. This can manifest itself in the form of anxiety, depression, or an increase in compensatory behaviors (as noted above).

The most common and most diagnosed trauma-related mental disorder is PTSD. PTSD is an anxiety disorder that involves a real or perceived threat of security and safety. This typically includes elements of reexperiencing the trauma (e.g., nightmares, flashbacks), avoidance of stimuli associated with the trauma, and an overall increased arousal (e.g., anger, agitation, hypervigilance, difficulties with sleeping or maintaining sleep). The diagnosis of PTSD may be made if the symptoms occur for more than one month.

Basic Treatment Tenets

Although there are differing theories on how to help individuals resolve traumatic events, there are some basic tenets that are fairly consistent throughout all approaches. Owing to the disempowering and disconnecting nature of traumatic events, most approaches are based on, first, establishing a therapeutic relationship with individuals and, thereby, allowing them to feel empowered (Herman 1992). Some of the basic tenets to trauma-focused treatment include establishing a sense of safety, remembering and mourning any loss involved, and reconnecting with the individual's personal world, including reconnecting with others. Additionally, McMackin, Leisen, Sattler, Krinsley, and Riggs (2002) contend that many of the major treatment approaches involve (1) creating a safe environment, (2) providing psychoeducation (i.e., knowledge of the nature of the condition) about trauma and its effects, (3) desensitizing traumatic material through discussion, and (4) developing coping skills to manage trauma. Most approaches to treating trauma address at least these four treatment goals.

Specific Treatments

There are numerous theoretical models that have been applied to treating trauma survivors. Experts in the area of PTSD recommend anxiety management, cognitive therapy, exposure therapy, and psychoeducation when treating trauma survivors (Foa, Davidson, & Frances 1999; Marotta 2000).

A great deal of research has supported cognitive-behavioral therapy (CBT) as being effective relative to other theoretical approaches. Research has also found cognitive therapy approaches to be superior to purely supportive approaches (Bryant, Harvey, Dang, Sackville, & Basten 1998; Foa, Davidson, & Frances 1999).

CBT attempts to assist the client in making connections between his or her thoughts, feelings, and behaviors—connections that can ultimately help clients to change their perceptions and reactions so that they feel better. CBT, with a trauma focus, is a structured model that addresses trauma through the use of psychoeducation, anxiety management, and affective modulation (emotional control), and addresses cognitive distortions, mastery of trauma reminders (e.g., through gradual exposure to the feared stimulus), and future development and safety.

Exposure therapy has been shown to be effective in managing trauma reactions (Foa, Davidson, & Frances 1999). In exposure therapy, clients confront the traumatic stimuli and their fears with respect to it. The repeated exposure is believed to make the stimuli less emotion-laden over time. With exposure therapy, negative reactions and the traumatic event and become increasingly separated, thus decreasing and eventually halting intrusive traumatic recollections and the need to use avoidant behaviors or compensatory behaviors. Exposure to the traumatic material varies in terms of the type of exposure (imagining the trauma event vs. exposure to the feared triggers), the length of exposure (short vs. long), and the client's arousal level during the exposure (Foa, Davidson, & Frances 1999).

Anxiety management training (AMT) has been shown, through controlled studies, to be helpful in treating trauma survivors (Foa & Rothbaum 1998). The most-researched and effective form of AMT has been stress inoculation training, which involves the client becoming more aware of what stimuli are reminders (or "cues") for fear and anxiety. Clients also learn a variety of coping skills that are useful in managing anxiety, such as progressive muscle relaxation and deep-breathing exercises (Meichenbaum 1974). AMT provides ways to manage anxiety when it occurs by having clients develop and apply various cognitive and behavioral skills to their experiences. Examples of coping skills that may help reduce anxiety are positive thinking and self-talk, covert modeling (e.g., clients are asked to use their imagination, visualizing a particular behavior as the therapist describes the imaginary situation in detail), controlled breathing, assertiveness training, guided imagery, and thought stopping (Hensley 2002).

Another approach to dealing with and treating trauma and traumatic events is eye-movement desensitization and reprocessing (EMDR), which is conceptualized by many as a type of exposure therapy. This approach aims at reducing or resolving the symptoms associated with disturbing memories by guiding eye movements. Created by Francine Shapiro (2001), EMDR incorporates eye movement stimulation and direction in the context of the subject's focusing on a traumatic memory and its associated negative emotions and beliefs. An unfreezing of traumatic memory is thought to occur with the facilitation of left-right eye movement in this context. EMDR incorporates components of behaviorism, cognitive approaches, and experiential and somatic therapies.

With regard to treating *specific* trauma reactions, many experts recommend (1) exposure therapy for treating intrusive thoughts, flashbacks, trauma-related factors, and avoidance of trauma-related stimuli; (2) anxiety management for hyperarousal and sleep disturbances; and (3) general cognitive therapy for treating guilt and shame-related experiences (Marotta 2000). Experts identify anxiety management, psychoeducation, and cognitive therapy as both the safest options and the options most preferred by clients (Marotta 2000).

Conclusion

In sum, trauma or traumatic events can have a long-lasting effect on a person's well-being. These events can disrupt normalcy and impair an individual's ability to properly think, cope, and process his or her lived experience. Trauma affects everyone differently and can manifest itself in a host of symptoms and compensatory behaviors. Individuals experiencing impairment in their level of functioning due to a trauma or a traumatic event should seek assistance from a mental health professional immediately.

See also Depression; Disasters and Mental Health; Dissociative Disorders; Posttraumatic Stress Disorder; Women's Mental Health

Bibliography

Bryant, R. A., A. G. Harvey, S. T. Dang, T. Sackville, and C. Basten. 1998. "Treatment of Acute Stress Disorder: A Comparison of Cognitive-Behavioral Therapy and Supportive Counseling." *Journal of Consulting and Clinical Psychology* 66: 862–866.

Carll, E. K. 2007. *Trauma Psychology: Issues in Violence, Disaster, Health, and Illness* (2 vols.). Westport, CT: Praeger.

Cook, A. C., M. Blaustein, J. Spinazzola, and B. van der Kolk, B. 2003. *Complex Trauma in Children and Adolescents*. Retrieved from http://www.nctsnet.org/sites/default/files/assets/pdfs/ComplexTrauma_All.pdf.

Foa, E. B., R. T. Davidson, and A. Frances. 1999. "Expert Consensus Guidelines Series: Treatment of Posttraumatic Stress Disorder." *The Journal of Clinical Psychiatry* 60 (Supplement 16): 1–31.

Foa, E. B., and B. O. Rothbaum. 1998. *Treating the Trauma of Rape: Cognitive Behavioral Therapy for PTSD*. New York: Guilford Press.

Hensley, L. G. 2002. "Treatment for Survivors of Rape: Issues and Interventions." *Journal of Mental Health Counseling* 24: 330–347.

Herman, J. 1992. *Trauma and Recovery*. New York: Basic Books.

James, R. K., and B. E. Gilliland. 2001. *Crisis Intervention Strategies* (4th ed.). Belmont, CA: Brooks/Cole.

Marotta, S. A. 2000. "Best Practices for Counselors Who Treat Posttraumatic Stress Disorder." *Journal of Counseling and Development* 78: 492–495.

McMackin, R. A., M. B. Leisen, L. Sattler, K. Krinsley, and D. S. Riggs. 2002. "Preliminary Development of Trauma-Focused Treatment Groups for Incarcerated Juvenile Offenders." *Journal of Aggression, Maltreatment & Trauma* 6: 175–199.

Meichenbaum, D. 1974. *Cognitive Behavioral Modification*. Morristown, NJ: General Learning Press.

Shapiro, F. 2001. *Eye Movement Desensitization and Reprocessing: Basic Principles, Protocols, and Procedures*. New York: Guilford Press.

U

Undiagnosed Mental Illness

Michael Shally-Jensen

Consider the following set of facts:

- Over 90 percent of suicide victims have a significant psychiatric illness at the time of their death. These illnesses are often undiagnosed, untreated, or both (American Society for Suicide Prevention, n.d.).

- Twelve percent or more of patients seen by primary care physicians have major depression. Often, patients (especially male patients) describe symptoms such as fatigue, sleep problems, headaches, or other vague effects, resulting in the depression going undiagnosed (National Institute of Mental Health 2012).

- Nearly 40 percent of people with major depression could also have a mild form of mania that in some cases indicates bipolar disorder, but the diagnosis is often missed (Beck 2011).

- Ninety-five percent of social phobia (social anxiety) sufferers originally go to the doctor for a different problem, not recognizing or allowing that their symptoms may indicate a psychiatric disorder (Nichols 2008).

- Persons suffering from untreated depression, anxiety, or other serious mental disorders commonly turn to alcohol or some other substance to manage their pain. Mental illness and substance abuse (and addiction) frequently go hand in hand (Kessler, Chieu, et al. 2005).

- It is estimated that of the approximately 2 million homeless adults in the United States, up to one-fourth of them suffer from a serious mental illness (National Coalition for the Homeless 2007).

- More than a half million U.S. teenagers have had an eating disorder, but few have sought treatment for the problem (Swanson et al 2011).

- Twenty percent of people over 55 suffer from a mental disorder, and two-thirds of nursing home residents exhibit mental and behavioral problems; yet less than 3 percent of older adults report seeing a mental health professional (American Psychological Association 2012).

- ADHD affects 4.4 percent of adults in the United States, or over 9 million people; but only 20 percent of those so affected undergo psychiatric evaluation (Kessler, Adler, et al. 2006).

- Girls who fall within the autism spectrum are much more likely than boys to go undiagnosed for a significant period of time (Bazelon 2007).

- Asperger syndrome (an autism spectrum disorder) frequently goes undetected until a child is past the age of eligibility for early intervention services and often remains undiagnosed until adolescence or even adulthood (Gillberg 2002).

- Leading researchers on psychopathic behavior (psychopathy) estimates that 1 out of every 100 men has clear psychopathic tendencies, and 1 out of 300 women (Neumann & Hare 2008).

- People living in low-income, urban communities are at high risk for exposure to traumatic events as well as for symptoms of posttraumatic stress disorder (PTSD), yet the condition often goes undiagnosed (Davis et al. 2008).

If on the basis of the above statements you conclude that the United States has a high prevalence of mental illness and that many individual sufferers go undiagnosed (and untreated), you would be right—at least according to the majority view within the mental health profession. Results from the most recent national survey of mental illness and its treatment suggest that well over half (57.4%) of all U.S. residents have experienced a mental disorder at some point in their lives, and one-third of all residents experience a serious disorder in a given year. On the other hand, only about a third of all those who do have a disorder receive treatment for it (Kessler, Demler et al. 2005).

The National Comorbidity Survey Replication

The survey information regarding prevalence (above) comes from the National Comorbidity Survey Replication (NCS-R), which gathered data between 2001 and 2003 by directing researchers to ask people between the ages of 18 and 54 a series of questions designed to determine whether the interviewees met the criteria for specific mental disorders described in the *Diagnostic and Statistical Manual of Mental Disorders*, fourth edition (*DSM-IV*). These same interviewees were also asked about any treatments (and diagnoses) they may have received. The data so collected were then organized and compared to results from a similar survey that took place between 1990 and 1992—hence the term "replication" in the latest survey's title.

What the survey found was rather astonishing. An earlier study in the 1980s (called the Epidemiologic Catchment Area Study) had found that 29.4 percent of adults had a mental disorder and one-fifth of them received treatment. Ten years later, in the first National Comorbidity Survey (NCS), slightly different results were reported: 30.5 percent of people 15 to 54 years of age had a mental disorder and a fourth of them underwent treatment. In the latest survey, NCS-R, the data showed that 30.5 percent of adults had a mental disorder and one-third of them received treatment. There were no significant differences across demographic categories (age, gender, race or ethnicity, etc.) or socioeconomic categories (education, income, residence, etc.) in the NCS-R, only the single fact that while prevalence rates for mental illness have remained essentially unchanged since the 1980s, the rate of treatment has steadily risen.

And yet the *gap* between the number of persons found to have an identifiable mental disorder (one-third) and the number who have undergone diagnosis and treatment (a third of the third) is notable, according to the study's authors. As they conclude:

> Despite an increase in the rate of treatment, most patients with a mental disorder did not receive treatment. Continued efforts are needed to obtain data on the effectiveness of treatment in order to increase the use of effective treatments. (Kessler, Demler et al. 2005, 2515)

In other words, some *two-thirds* of adults in the United States who can be said to have a mental disorder are not receiving treatment and are likely never to have done so. This is an alarming number. It is only mitigated by the fact that, as shown by the earlier studies, the rate was even higher in decades past: *four-fifths* went untreated in the 1980s, and *three-fourths* went untreated in the 1990s.

Among the cases identified in NCS-R, 18.1 percent were anxiety disorders, 9.5 percent were mood disorders, 8.9 percent were impulse control disorders, 3.8 percent were substance abuse disorders, and 26.2 percent fell into the catch-all category of "any." In terms of severity, 22.3 percent of the individual cases were considered "serious," 37.3 percent were "moderate," and 40.4 percent were "mild." Over half (55%) of all cases involved a single diagnosis, 22 percent involved two co-occurring diagnoses (hence the term "comorbidity"), and 23 percent, nearly a quarter, involved three or more diagnoses (Kessler, Chiu, Demler, & Walters 2005).

Stigma, Fear, and Lack of Access

In examining what lies behind this apparent flood of undiagnosed cases, one can begin by appreciating the roles played by stigma and fear. When a person becomes unwell or his or her relatives or friends notice that he or she is not well, the first steps to deal with this are usually at the personal or folk level. It is only when the matter comes to be seen as involving serious illness (often after simple remedies have failed to produce a cure) that professional, usually medical, help is sought. The route into the mental health care system, in other words, is determined primarily by patients and their families and friends.

There is a difference for most people between being diagnosed with a mental disorder and being diagnosed with a purely somatic (bodily) illness, largely owing to the social stigma attached to mental illness. This stigma is deeply rooted in human history and is evident in many different cultures in varying forms. Humanity attaches great power to the mind while also regarding it as somewhat mysterious, even unknowable. One of our greatest fears as individuals is the loss of control of one's mental capacities and the dissolution of identity that may result (Trad 1991). Even though there is increasing acceptance of the label of mental illness, fostered in part by the growth of the medical model, people who carry the label still face considerable barriers in the form of social bias. The stigma or social fallout associated with serious mental illness can be so detrimental and debilitating in terms of an individual's self-esteem and outlook that many people would rather go undiagnosed and untreated than to subject themselves to the anguish associated with being identified as a mental health consumer.

Moreover, even under the best of circumstances confidentiality cannot be guaranteed. Any number of individuals will have access to a patient's diagnosis, and there are practical consequences that stem from that fact. Employers and insurance companies, though typically barred from discriminating against persons with psychiatric conditions, may nevertheless balk at extending an offer of employment or underwriting a policy for or granting benefits to such an individual.

Access to services is also a factor. Many people are uninsured or have inadequate insurance coverage and are unable to pay for mental health services on their own. Plans with high copayments can have the effect of limiting the number of visits by patients receiving treatment. Location can be an issue as well: many rural areas lack behavioral health services. Even in more populated areas, location and transportation can create hurdles, as can the cultural competence of the staff.

Communities of Color

In the case of cultural minorities, not only is there the usual reluctance to be seen by a mental health professional but also the risk of having one's symptoms misunderstood in the course of the diagnostic interview. Although there is abundant evidence for the utility of the *DSM-IV* in helping to identify psychiatric conditions, its diagnostic schema is based largely on the norms of the dominant culture. Patients who are members of cultural minority groups may express psychosocial distress in ways that are unfamiliar to the clinician.

Among African Americans, there is a well-documented inclination to postpone the receipt of help from majority institutions, particularly when a mental health disorder is at issue (U.S. Department of Health and Human Services 1999). Research shows that among African Americans, self-help strategies and traditional healing practices are preferred over mainline psychiatric services (Theriot, Segal, & Cowsert 2003). There is also a noted lack of services and support systems in many of the lower-income communities where African Americans and other minorities make up the bulk of the population. The facts that African American men remain wary of the criminal justice system and any institutions (including psychiatry) that serve it, and African American women face not only racism but also sexism in their encounters in the public sphere, add to the reluctance of members of this community to seek out help from mental health professionals.

Latinos, too, underutilize available mental health services. Among this population there is a disinclination to accept or even consider mental health explanations for anomalous behaviors, the problem often being described in terms of disturbances within the family, relational issues, problems in making a living, or spiritual disharmony. A likely outcome is consultation with an experienced community member or, at best, treatment for a physiological condition (e.g., headache, stomach pain). In Latino culture, commitment to the group often takes precedence over attention to personal matters, and that applies all the more so in the case of matters of the mind. At the same time, Latinos are often at risk for poverty, unemployment, involvement with the criminal justice system, and many of the health and mental health issues associated with these risks (Gutierrez, Yeakly, & Ortega 2000).

In the case of Asian Americans, here too the tendency is to avoid conceiving the problem in psychological terms. Shame and the stigma associated with mental illness play a significant role. Mental disturbances are often attributed to social or spiritual causes. Moreover, because of an emphasis on mutual assistance within large family networks, Asian Americans may lack comprehensive health insurance and therefore are less likely to seek the services of a behavioral health agency. Add to this the usual language and communications barriers, and it becomes clear why Asian Americans and Pacific Islanders are three times less likely than Caucasians to make use of standard mental health services (Spencer & Chen 2004).

Native Americans and Alaska Natives traditionally have relied on spiritual healing for their health and mental health needs, while at the same time they show statistically higher rates of psychiatric inpatient care than other populations (Snowden & Cheung 1990). Common problems, diagnosed or not, include alcohol abuse, depression, and suicidality in the context of poverty, cultural isolation, lack of economic opportunities, and general awareness of cultural loss. Reluctance on the part of members of this population to seek services from the medical establishment has to be understood in this light. Moreover, in many of the far-flung rural communities where Native Americans and Alaska Natives reside, mental health services are available only on a limited basis, if at all.

Counterview: The Medicalization of Normal Behavior

Critics of NCS-R and other such surveys claim that the reported numbers of untreated cases are artificially high. The main thrust of these counterarguments is that (1) the surveys are flawed methodologically, (2) the predominance of the medical model in the mental health profession causes normal stress and other behavioral responses to be construed as mental illness, and (3) the pharmaceutical industry has a huge stake in the outcome of these studies and has invested heavily in promoting the myth that mental illness is widespread. Let us take a look at each of these points in turn.

As far as survey method goes, critics have pointed out that the standard questions administered by members of the NCS-R survey team do not allow for the appreciation of context. Questions are simply delivered and, if necessary, repeated but are never "explored" in terms of the specifics of the interviewee's situation (Horwitz & Wakefield 2006). Thus the survey process lacks true "clinical judgment," something that only a diagnostician confronted by an actual patient would be capable of providing. Even in the best of circumstances, psychiatric diagnosis is not an exact science and requires follow-up and careful observation over time. These are qualities that a survey cannot deliver.

Because of the survey's methodological limitations, interviewers are said to be unable to distinguish "the normal distress experienced in life from genuinely pathological conditions" (Horwitz & Wakefield 2006, 19). As a result, stressful reactions get recorded as disorders falling under the purview of the biological paradigm, or medical model, in psychiatry. This is the notion of the "medicalization" of ordinary life (or the "pathologizing" of everyday behaviors). Some critics, such as Thomas Szaz (2010), have gone so far as to claim that there is *no such thing* as mental illness, but that is not the view held by most critics of psychiatry today. These critics do, however, argue that too often common "problems in living" are dealt with as though they stemmed from a "chemical imbalance" in the brain, which is a central premise of the medical model.

Finally, it is well documented that the pharmaceutical industry spends large sums of money on the promotion of psychiatric drugs and, more important, on advancing the idea that mental disorders are extremely common in the populace and that the best way to treat them is through the use of prescription medications (Barber 2008; Whitaker 2010). Drug companies fund academic research that up until very recently was under minimal scrutiny, and such research is often intended to show how effective a company's drugs are. Companies also reward clinicians who speak publically about the merits of its drugs, and they reach out to consumers through so-called direct-to-consumer advertisements—those print ads and television commercials that herald the wonders of a particular drug followed by warnings concerning its possible side effects. Strange things happen as a result. For example, one independent study found that the number of children and adolescents diagnosed with bipolar disorder had risen over a nine-year period (1994–2003) by a factor of 40, or 8,000 percent (cited in Carlat 2010, 145)! Clearly, something more than the careful application of medical science was going on in this case. More than likely the spike represents a diagnostic trend fueled by high-stakes research, heavy promotion, consumer interest, and willing psychiatrists.

Conclusion

The question of what the rate of untreated mental illness in the United States is cannot be said to have been fully settled by the National Comorbidity Survey, and it likely will not be settled anytime soon. The one thing that can be safely assumed is that, yes, there are many individuals among us who suffer from mental disorders of varying degrees of severity and duration but who do not receive treatment for them. Barriers to treatment include stigma, fear, alternative (folk) explanations, confidentiality issues, restricted access to care, and problems of cultural competence. The *other* thing that can be safely assumed is that in many instances, estimates of the prevalence of severe mental disorders are probably *unrealistic* and ignore the finer points of psychiatric diagnosis and objective medical science. Flawed research methods, a tendency to yield to the power of the medical model in explaining human behavior, and distortions of knowledge caused by the practices of the pharmaceutical industry are among the factors pointed to by critics of American psychiatry in this context. Somewhere between the two extremes lies the truth of the matter.

See also Diagnostic and Statistical Manual of Mental Disorders (*DSM*); Drug Companies; Marketing of Drugs; Medical Model of Mental Illness; Psychiatry; Public Health Perspectives; Stigma

Bibliography

Alegría, M, N. Mulvaney-Day, M. Torres, A. Polo, Z. Cao, and G. Canino. 2007. "Prevalence of Psychiatric Disorders across Latino Subgroups in the United States." *American Journal of Public Health* 97: 68–75.

American Foundation for Suicide Prevention. n.d. "Facts about Suicide." Retrieved from http://www.afsp.org/files/College_Film/factsheets.pdf.

American Psychological Association. 2012. "Growing Mental and Behavioral Health Concerns Facing Older Americans." Retrieved from http://www.apa.org/about/gr/issues/aging/growing-concerns.aspx.

Barber, Charles. 2008. *Comfortably Numb: How Psychiatry Is Medicating a Nation.* New York: Vintage.

Bazelon, Emily. 2007. "What Autistic Girls Are Made Of." *New York Times Magazine*, August 5. Retrieved from http://www.nytimes.com/2007/08/05/magazine/05autism-t.html?pagewanted=all.

Beck, Melinda. 2011. "When Gray Days Signal a Problem." *Wall Street Journal*, July 26. Retrieved from http://online.wsj.com/article/SB10001424053111904772304576467993357594526.html.

Carlat, Daniel J. 2010. *Unhinged: The Trouble with Psychiatry.* New York: Free Press.

Davis, Regina D., Kerry J. Ressler, Ann C. Schwartz, Kisha James Stephens, and Rebekah G. Bradley. 2008. "Treatment Barriers for Low-Income, Urban African

Americans with Undiagnosed Posttraumatic Stress Disorder." *Journal of Traumatic Stress* 21: 218–222.

Gillberg, Christopher. 2002. *A Guide to Asperger Syndrome*. New York: Cambridge University Press.

Gutierrez, L., A. Yeakly, and R. Ortega. 2000. "Educating Students for Social Work with Latinos: Issues for the New Millennium." *Journal of Social Work Education* 36: 541–557.

Horwitz, Allan V., and Jerome C. Wakefield. 2006. "The Epidemic in Mental Illness: Clinical Fact or Survey Artifact?" *Contexts* 5: 19–23.

Kessler, Ronald C., Lenard Adler, Russell Barkley, Joseph Biederman, C. Keith Conners, Olga Demler, Stephen V. Faraone, Laurence L. Greenhill, Mary J. Howes, Kristina Secnik, Thomas Spencer, T. Bedirhan Ustun, Ellen E. Walters, and Alan M. Zaslavsky. 2006. "The prevalence and correlates of adult ADHD in the United States: Results from the National Comorbidity Survey Replication."American Journal of Psychiatry 163: 716–723.

Kessler, Ronald C., Wai Tat Chiu, Olga Demler, and Ellen E. Walters. 2005. "Prevalence, Severity, and Comorbidity of Twelve-Month *DSM-IV* Disorders in the National Comorbidity Survey Replication (NCS-R)." *Archives of General Psychiatry* 62: 617–627. Retrieved from http://www.ncbi.nlm.nih.gov/pmc/articles/PMC2847357/

Kessler, Ronald C., Olga Demler, Richard G. Frank, Mark Olfson, Harold Alan Pincus, Ellen E. Walters, Philip Wang, Kenneth B. Wells, and Alan M. Zaslavsky. 2005. "Prevalence and Treatment of Mental Disorders, 1990 to 2003." *New England Journal of Medicine* 352: 2515–2523. Available at: http://www.nejm.org/doi/full/10.1056/NEJMsa043266#t=articleDiscussion.

National Coalition for the Homeless. 2007. "How Many People Experience Homelessness?" Retrieved from http://www.nationalhomeless.org/publications/facts/How_Many.pdf.

National Institute of Mental Health. 2012. "Men and Depression." Retrieved from http://www.nimh.nih.gov/health/topics/depression/men-and-depression/men-and-depression-screening-and-treatment-in-primary-care-settings.shtml.

Neumann, Craig S., and Robert D. Hare. 2008. "Psychopathic Traits in a Large Community Study." *Journal of Consulting and Clinical Psychology* 76: 893–899.

Nichols, M. "95% of Social Phobia Sufferers Originally Go to the Doctor for a Different Problem." *Anxiety, Panic, and Health*. Retrieved from http://anxietypanichealth.com/2008/07/11/95-of-social-phobia-sufferers-originally-go-to-doctor-for-another-problem/.

Snowden, L., and F. K. Cheung. 1990. "Use of Inpatient Mental Health Services by Members of Ethnic Minority Groups." *American Psychologist* 45: 347–355.

Spencer, M. S., and J. Chen. 2004. "Effect of Discrimination on Mental Health Service Utilization among Chinese Americans." *American Journal of Public Health* 94: 809–814.

Swanson, S. A., S. J. Crow, D. Le Grange, J. Swendsen, and K. R. Merikangas. 2011. "Prevalence and Correlates of Eating Disorders in Adolescents: Results From the National Comorbidity Survey Replication Adolescent Supplement." *Arch Gen Psychiatry*. 2011;68 (7):714–723.

Szaz, Thomas. 2010. *The Medicalization of Everyday Life: Selected Essays*. Syracuse, NY: Syracuse University Press.

Takeuchi, D. T., N. Zane, S. Hong, David H. Chae, Fang Gong, Gilbert C. Gee, Emily Walton, Stanley Sue, and Margarita Alegría. 2007. "Immigration-Related Factors and

Mental Disorders among Asian Americans." *American Journal of Public Health* 97: 84–90.

Theriot, M. T., S. P. Segal, and M. J. Cowsert. 2003. "African-Americans and Comprehensive Service Use." *Community Mental Health Journal* 39: 225–237.

Trad, P. V. 1991. "The Ultimate Stigma of Mental Illness." *American Journal Psychotherapy* 45: 463–466.

U.S. Department of Health and Human Services. 1999. *Mental Health: A Report of the Surgeon General*. Rockville, MD: U.S. Department of Health and Human Services, Substance Abuse and Mental Health Services Administration, Center for Mental Health Services.

Whitaker, Robert. 2010. *Anatomy of an Epidemic: Magic Bullets, Psychiatric Drugs, and the Astonishing Rise of Mental Illness in America*. New York: Crown.

V

Veterans' Mental Health Care

Daryl S. Paulson and Stanley Krippner

Mental health care provides support and treatment to optimize a person's emotional and psychological well-being. Veterans' mental health care can be conceptualized either as military health care while in the armed services, or as mental health services that are managed by the Veterans Administration (VA) once service members are separated from the armed forces (Slone & Friedman 2008).

Organization of Care

The VA administers various mental health facilities and services to meet veterans' needs. These facilities include community-based outpatient clinics (CBOCs), Veterans Administration Medical Centers (VAMCs), Veterans Administration Hospitals, various Veteran Centers, and some domiciliary care centers (focusing primarily on support for homeless veterans). Medical centers offer some psychiatric and psychological care, along with social work support. Hospitals often provide a broad system of mental health care. Veteran Centers provide mental health treatment for substance abuse, traumatic stress, and sexual trauma support, including military rape. The VA also provides on-call mental health support for veterans and their families, ranging from suicidal thoughts to anger management crises. Periodically, the VA (usually through the Veteran Centers) will offer a community one or more "Stand Down" facilities that supply free counseling, dental checkups, medical support, and services for homeless veterans and those who are unable to access help without assistance. In the event of rural locations distant from a VA facility, the VA will often contract with local providers to provide extended care (in combination with existing VA services).

There are several types of mental health support programs and agencies for veterans that exist at county, state, and local levels. These particular services provide support and treatment similar to what is available at VA facilities, but can often serve those veterans not supported by the VA system such as those with dishonorable and other than honorable discharges.

Veterans often struggle with mental health difficulties, of which posttraumatic stress disorder (PTSD) is the most common, that may require support and treatment. In the case of PTSD, a veteran usually exits military service before beginning a downward spiral of drug and alcohol usage as a way of coping with such

An ex-soldier with posttraumatic stress disorder. The former Army Ranger found himself in what he called a dissociative state surrounded by police on one occasion following his return home from combat. (AP Photo/Jim Mone.)

symptoms as social withdrawal, emotional numbing, hypervigilance, and intrusive memories of the trauma, particularly in nightmares and "flashbacks." Even though there are great individual differences, PTSD has a distinct way of working. It rarely affects the veteran while in the service, but it begins to manifest after the veteran is discharged, because PTSD requires some time to manifest its symptoms. For example, a person might be unable to sleep or is anxious due to a feeling of impending dread. To cope with these feelings, the veteran often drinks or ingests drugs (legal or illegal), acts aggressively, or cuts off social contacts.

Often, one needs to "dry out" before any psychotherapeutic treatment is of value; properly administered medication can be helpful in this phase of treatment. If a veteran is suicidal or overtly aggressive, he or she may be placed under inpatient care, occupying a bed within a VA hospital. Once the crisis has passed, the veteran can be transferred to an inpatient treatment facility where treatment for PTSD is initiated.

PTSD is not the only disorder treated in a mental health facility. Traumatic brain injury (TBI) is often a comorbid (or accompanying) condition. PTSD is related to other anxiety-related syndromes such as panic disorders, social phobias, and acute stress disorders, but may be comorbid with dissociative, bipolar, and antisocial disorders as well. Of course, these syndromes may exist in the absence of PTSD, and the publicity given PTSD may lead to an overdiagnosis of the condition.

Outpatient Care

Most veterans diagnosed with PTSD undergo outpatient care—preferably immediately after the diagnosis or upon being released from inpatient care. They usually visit a psychiatrist monthly and a psychologist once a week. The psychiatrist deals with them on a one-on-one basis, administering medication for PTSD symptom relief. A clinical psychologist or other psychotherapist (such as a psychiatric social worker) usually sees them in one-on-one sessions or in group therapy on a weekly basis. If a veteran requires more support than outpatient services can provide, inpatient care is recommended

Untreated Cases

Often, a veteran in need of mental health care exits the military and rejects all professional help, or terminates treatment after one or two sessions. There are many reasons for avoiding or terminating treatment. Sometimes the veteran fails to "bond" with the mental health care practitioner. At other times, the veteran feels that his or her military record will be blemished if it indicates treatment for a mental disorder. A key reason for avoiding treatment is the veteran's inability to deal with existential here-and-now issues, because these concerns are painful and threaten the veteran's worldview based on fairness, justice, and honor. These issues range from guilt and shame to vulnerability and fear. Many veterans do not understand that there are inner strengths that can be accessed through psychotherapy, but these dividends are attained only if one goes through a painful period, come to terms with it, and then move beyond it. The painful period feels awful—often worse than all the symptoms combined. One way to help a person get through this is to rely on mythology. This is not done in VA hospitals, because it appears "flaky."

There are three aspects of a rite of passage (Campbell 1968): the call, the initiation, and the return. The "call" is the reason a person decides to join the military. The "initiation" is the sum of the experiences from which the veteran suffers. This is where most veterans wind up after they have experienced combat. They remain "betwixt and between" or stuck, with no way to go back or move forward. They feel as if they have become off balance and can only complain of what they feel. They are not comfortable with how they feel now, but they do not see how dealing with their terrifying symptoms will help them. So they get scared and retreat from life. They do not get better.

If they can be told and given reassurance that to get better they must integrate the call and the initiation with the return phase in order to get past the pain. There is no way that they can do this except by connecting with themselves through personal conviction (Keen & Fox 1973).

Also, a veteran may have been told that he or she has been "faking it" or has been put into the "government holding pen," which is the process of waiting for a disability decision. Thus another reaction is the feeling of betrayal and the desire to reject all forms of governmental help. Veterans may then retreat from the world or interact with people in a defensive, guarded manner.

Many untreated veterans will become homeless, spending what money they have on illicit drugs and alcohol (Everson & Figley 2010). As they become dependent on such substances, they become indifferent to work, to socializing, and even to eating, but spend what money they can get on "a better high." This destructive spiral ultimately leads not only to addiction problems but also to detrimental health habits such as ignoring personal hygiene.

Major Disorders Treated

PTSD is the most commonly treated combat-related mental disorder (DeAngelis 2008). People may often be predisposed to PTSD before combat, because they have genetic vulnerabilities in addition to unresolved childhood and adolescent issues (Wilson, Friedman & Lindy 2001). For example, after puberty they may feel sexual attraction but are very insecure about their own worth. Given these difficulties with interpersonal relationships, they may become preoccupied with being "good enough." This lack of self-acceptance is coupled with diminished self-confidence. The net effect is a lack of resiliency, the ability to "bounce back" after a setback of some sort (Conner, Davidson, & Lee 2003). High vulnerability coupled with low resiliency predisposes soldiers to PTSD and other mental disorders during their tenure in the armed forces.

Often, people attempt to grow in the military, thinking that combat will be a proof of their worthiness (Paulson 1994). But their minds are so filled with their predominant insecurities that their combat activities are woefully inept. They cope as well as they can, but the stressors of war put them at risk for developing PTSD or other disorders. For many soldiers, a potentially traumatizing event is assimilated fairly quickly because of their resilience. But resilience and vulnerability engage in a perilous dance; for all too many vulnerable service personnel, this becomes a dance of death, because they cannot assimilate the event and it becomes a traumatic experience, one that is maintained long after the event ends.

Depression and suicide are crucial issues; a 2011 military report noted that an average of one veteran kills him or herself every day, most of them with no history of mental disorders (Dreazen 2011). The suicide rate among veterans has increased each year since 2004 (Abdullah 2010). Veterans make up 8 percent of the U.S. population but account for 20 percent of its suicides (Anonymous 2010). A man or woman returning from combat is often vulnerable to the stresses that are a part of civilian life. If the veteran does not find a job or a supportive relationship, frustration and disappointment may lead to depression, and suicide becomes a very real option. For example, Marla came back from the Gulf in despair because she had lost several friends during insurgent attacks. At the same time, her husband and child now try to reclaim their lost importance. If Marla remains stuck—focusing on her friends' deaths rather than on her family's needs—her family may complain and even threaten to leave. This burdens Marla even more, to the point where she might turn to alcohol or illicit drugs for solace. Marla's situation is not uncommon. As veterans think of what they have lost relative to what they have gained, they may become very depressed. The way out may seem to be to end one's life, and the increasing suicide rate among female soldiers and veterans is of grave concern.

Marla turned her feelings inward, but other veterans have expressed their feelings openly, often directing hostility toward others. For example, if a military person is an adherent of Islam, and his or her coworkers are not Muslims, he or she may feel trapped in a hopeless situation. He or she may identify closely with Islam, while at the same time identifying with the United States and its war against Islamic extremists. This problematic situation may lead to violent behavior if it is unresolved. The 2009 killings at the Fort Hood, Texas, army installation fit this scenario (Geertz 2010). In that case, an army psychiatrist, Major Nidal Hasan, a Muslim himself, became severely stressed while talking to American veterans who had killed people of the Muslim faith in Iraq and Afghanistan. He did not reach out and ask for help, and the American officers who noticed his erratic behavior did nothing to help him for fear that they would be accused of reacting to a stereotype. Major Hasan killed 13 soldiers and wounded 20 others. Some called this "vicarious PTSD," but it is more properly seen as an act of domestic terrorism, one that could have been avoided (Goulston 2009).

Types of Treatment

Psychiatrists, clinical psychologists, psychiatric social workers, counselors, and other mental health practitioners who intend to work with current or former members of the military need to be aware of how military culture influenced their patients. For example, service members leaving the armed forces may have difficulty adjusting to working with civilians, who can be seen as "selfish" and "individualistic" in contrast to the collective spirit promulgated by military culture (Street 2008). The camaraderie and trust that they experienced while on duty may be missing not only at work but in their neighborhood, leaving the veteran disillusioned, depressed, and hostile. If this sense of trust is not established with a psychotherapist, the veteran may not return for his or her second session (Wilson, Friedman, & Lindy 2001).

Current and former members of the American armed forces may be referred to treatment or voluntarily seek it, because they feel depressed or anxious much of the time. They might not realize that these are symptoms of such complex syndromes as PTSD and various personality disorders (Yeoman 2008). It is not unusual for the psychotherapist to face a profusion of symptoms, not knowing which ones to deal with first. No one treatment can meet the needs of every patient, and it is unlikely that a psychotherapist will have mastered a variety of interventions. However, mental health care in the U.S. military services has tilted toward the family of treatments known as cognitive-behavioral therapy (CBT) (Benish, Imel, & Wampold 2008; DeAngelis 2008).

There are several advantages to CBT, one being the active involvement of the patient in the treatment process (Beck & Emery 1985). But for this involvement to be successful, the patient needs to be motivated, a process that can begin in the initial interview when the cognitive-behavioral therapist focuses on what changes are most highly desired. At this point, the therapist becomes directive, indicating where the process needs to begin and how it needs to proceed. The patient's collaboration is sought, but the therapist takes the initiative in the CBT process (Beck 1984). For example, the therapist elicits information that will provide an understanding of a patient's personal, cultural, social, family, age, and gender-related worldviews and rules for living. The West Point motto, "Duty, Honor, Country," is an example of a worldview that may not only help explain a patient's dilemmas but also serve as a therapeutic ally at some point down the road.

The patient's symptoms can be restated as problems or issues that need to be addressed in CBT. Rather than focusing on "depression," the therapist might identify a loss of humor, a lack of sexual desire, and a negative self-concept as issues that will be grist for the therapeutic mill (Wolpe 1982). The therapist helps the patient develop problem-solving strategies and personality traits, such as hardiness, and attitudes, such as self-acceptance, that can resolve the stated problems. It is typical for the therapist to deal with issues that concern the patient in the "here and now," so that any small success can be seen as a milestone in the therapeutic process (Van der Veer 1998). Skill building, skill acquisition, and skill rehearsal—all are parts of the psychoeducational portion of CBT. Many of these skills will be cognitive, involving changing ways of thinking, attitudes, and decision making. Other skills are behavioral and involve activities in the patient's world such as attending 12-step programs to deal with substance abuse, making phone calls or writing e-mails to keep in touch with friends long ignored, and joining social groups for increasing one's level of fun and enjoyment (Snyder & Lopez 2002). Emotion plays a major role in both cognitive and behavioral skill development. Positive emotions stimulate change, while negative emotions stultify it (Rotter & Bovega 1999).

Cognitive concepts can be integrated in different ways into the psychoeducational process by assuming that behavior is determined by worldviews, one aspect of which is rules for living implicit in inner speech or self-instruction. When a person has a traumatic experience, that experience instigates a conditioning process. It includes cognitive representations that result in confirming or challenging current worldviews. These cognitive representations and self-instructions may have been adequate before the time the trauma occurred, but are often inadequate in current, posttraumatic situations and typically result in maladaptive behavior (Scaer 2005). This maladaptive behavior can be changed by altering the cognitive representations that characterize it. For instance, behavior can be altered when new self-instruction is implemented through learning (Runte, Bass, & Yep 2004). Some writers refer to cognitive representations as schemas, themes, cognitive maps, or personal myths (Feinstein & Krippner 1988; Paulson 1994).

The conditioned bio-physiological responses can be changed by exposing the traumatized individual to a variety of stimuli that share conditions similar to the traumatizing events. That is to say, such therapeutic techniques as exposure will work beneficially in a safe situation in which the individual feels protected, respected, and supported. This also requires the person to change his or her cognitive representations (Hayes, Strosahl, & Wilson 1999).

Emanating from both classical behaviorism and the cognitive perspective on conditioning, the effect of traumatic experiences can be described in single terms or have a more complex nature. The traumatic experience is accompanied by bio-physiological reflexes such as sweating, accelerated heartbeat, hyperventilation, and so on (Pine 2000). These reactions can later be triggered by conditioned responses. A soldier who saw his best buddy's head disappear in a mist of pink haze when a mortar shell hit their tank may reexperience the trauma whenever he sees a pink shirt, a pink flower, or a pink bathroom curtain.

According to the cognitive view of conditioning, a conditioned stimulus brings the unconscious memory to conscious awareness (Beck & Emery 1985). A memory of a traumatic experience comes to mind, but unfortunately this memory interferes with other cognitive processes (Roberts & Yeager 2004). Recollections of traumatic events also have a complex structure of accompanying thoughts and feelings. Therapy can be focused on changing the automatic behaviors the individual may undertake to cope with his or her reactions, as well as the accompanying thoughts, sensations, and emotions. The soldier with an aversion to the color pink can begin to associate it with pleasant stimuli, such as pink underwear or pink ice cream. He may also change his thoughts; thus "I wish the shell had hit me instead of my buddy" could be changed to "Terrible things happen in war; I will live my life in a way that brings honor to my buddy and his family" (Krippner & Paulson 2006).

Other Treatment Approaches

Cognitive-behavioral approaches to treatment are just one part of the armamentarium in providing care to veterans' mental health. Another consideration is the role that psychiatrists can play when medication support is required (Davis, Frazier, Williford, & Newell 2006). For example, PTSD involves specific changes in specific neurotransmitter, neurohormonal, and neuroendocrine systems (Thase 2009). The wise use of medication can readjust these imbalances, at least until psychotherapy has led to a long-range stabilization (Sheikh & Nguyen2000; Sussman 2009).

It is important to note that medication management is best used in conjunction with psychotherapeutic approaches. Researched, evidence-based approaches have been identified in several studies (DeAngelis 2008). Most frequently cited treatments were cognitive processing therapy, prolonged exposure therapy, stress inoculation therapy, and eye-movement desensitization and reprocessing (e.g., Hudson 2008; Shapiro 1993). A 2008 study concluded that there was no difference in outcome when all established "bona fide" treatments were compared (Benish, Imel, & Wampold 2008).

What makes an event adverse for one individual does not make that same event adverse for another person. Most personnel exposed to combat or other hazards of military service do not develop PTSD (Hoge, Auchterlonie, & Milliken 2006). One person's ability to successfully and adaptively navigate through a situation may be thought of as resulting from his or her personal construction of the event (Achterberg 2003). Individuals suffering from trauma are often challenged in their ability to create meaning from their experiences (J. L. Solomon 2004). Making sense of the event and why it occurred can determine if that event will become traumatizing or not. The basic premise of existential-humanistic approaches is to help individuals understand who they are and how they can operate in a world that may seem suddenly foreign, requiring a reorganization of their self-concepts and worldviews (S. Solomon, Greenberg, & Pyszczynski 2003; Walsh & McElwain 2001). This is especially necessary for those affected by trauma. In these cases, the humanistic-existential approach attempts to support the individual's challenge of making meaning and understanding from the traumatic experiences, while illuminating the power of choice and responsibility (Paulson 2001, 2003). Like cognitive-behavioral approaches, humanistic-existential interventions focus on the "here and now" and on practical skill-building projects (May 1981). Homework assignments are another common component, and rehearsals are often carried out in the patient's imagination (Gottfried 2004).

Psychodynamic approaches observe the interaction of the environment and the individual with special attention given to early environments and childhood experiences (Allen 2007). In the case of PTSD, the patient is seen as receiving unbearable stimulation that was overwhelming in its effects, evoking unsolved issues such as nurturance and abandonment (McIntyre & Ventura 2003; Roland 2006). The person's usual coping skills or defense mechanisms are no longer able to deal with the events that, as a result, become traumatizing. The individual's affective responses produce an unbearable psychological state, threatening to disorganize and damage the personality structure. This person is like a deer in the headlights of an automobile, unable to escape the glare as it keeps weaving back and forth. He or she often experiences helplessness and lapses into a passive and inhibited state. The process of self-defense and coping skills becomes ever more disorganized. This often results in the marked disappearance of affective reactions, the development of apathy, and the descent of depersonalization into a state of apathy (Paulson & Krippner 2010).

A traumatic experience, from this view, has at least two consequences: psychological damage and a process of separation until one feels completely alone (Angyal 1965). The repeated reliving of a traumatic event can be seen as part of a process in which the emotions experienced during the process of traumatization recur. Psychodynamic psychotherapy resembles CBT approaches in that the ego is bolstered by identifying inner strengths and using them to develop coping skills (Beck 1984).

Many other interventions, most of which can be integrated into the CBT framework, could be cited. These include hypnosis, biofeedback, expressive art and dance therapy, and virtual reality therapy, in which a battleground is reconstructed on a video screen that the patient watches until he or she is desensitized to the event. In eye-movement desensitization and reprocessing, a patient focuses on an aspect of the traumatic experience accompanied by some form of bilateral stimulation (eye movements, tapping, or sound stimulation). Although research studies have not found any of these approaches to be clearly superior to the others, investigations identify the personal qualities of the mental health practitioner and the relationship he or she establishes with the patient as being crucial. This relationship appears to be more important than the nature of the intervention itself (Wolpe 1982).

Evaluation of Services and Psychotherapy

The services offered by the VA and supporting programs are very important and supportive to veterans in developing stable mental health. There are significant areas of treatment being provided that are crucial in meeting veterans' needs. The access to care, however, needs to be improved (Freeman, Moore, & Freeman 2009). The percentage of veterans receiving mental health care is at an appallingly low level, as veterans are often left on waiting lists for months (or longer) just to receive their first appointment. Those who need immediate services, such as individuals confronting difficult responses to traumatic experiences, which can lead to suicidal tendencies, may be missed entirely due to the overwhelming demand for help by so many in the system and the inability to meet this demand. This situation can lead to tragic outcomes. The system is beginning to improve, but much more needs to be done.

Considerable money has been spent trying to find the best psychotherapeutic services for veterans (Foa, Hembree, & Rothbaum 2007). They tend to fall into either cognitive-behavior therapy or medication. They also are under the control of two different factions, as psychologists have the behavior therapy sector, and psychiatrists have the drug therapy area.

The problem is that there is no integration of these treatments. But it is worse than this. Suppose a person is determined to have PTSD. She or he is treated with psychology and perhaps medication. This is a huge step toward healing. But why, then, does the veteran resist change?

To understand this, one can make use of the four-quadrant model. At the top of this figure is a person displaying both subjective and objective aspects of his or her being. On the bottom are cultural and social systems from which individuals attempt to gain reassurance and where their rules of performing originate. Mental health care for veterans often omits the two lower quadrants, both subjective and objective.

Justin, a young veteran who sought mental health care from a VA facility, was able to access the system and became an outpatient. He received weekly psychotherapy as well as prescription medication. But when he returned home, his family ridiculed his visit to a "shrink" and his peers expected him to join them on their weekend alcohol and drug escapades. He described this situation to his psychotherapist as "my group's way of having fun" (lower right-hand quadrant) and excused his family's behavior because "that is the way they were raised" (lower

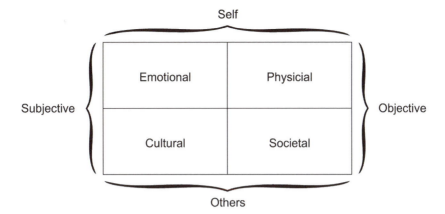

Individual life quadrants.

left-hand quadrant). Justin never gets better because the gains he made at the VA facility were negated when he returned home.

The lower left-hand quadrant can also be used to describe the 2007 Walter Reed Army Medical Center scandal. Long-standing patterns of outpatient neglect and inpatient mistreatment were publicized by two articles in the *Washington Post*, after the same conditions had been identified in 2004 on the Internet and by veterans' complaints to members of Congress, none of which had initiated reform. Once the scandal broke in the newspaper, the secretary of the Army resigned, and the hospital commander was fired, even though he had been on duty for only six months. Walter Reed, the Pentagon's flagship hospital, was accused of mistreating veterans, and not one of the four quadrants escaped criticism. It was claimed that the military culture was self-protective, not self-correcting (upper left-hand quadrant), that medication and psychotherapy (upper right- and left-hand quadrants) were inadequate, and that social support (lower right-hand quadrant) was bypassed, as were cultural and ethnic variables (lower left-hand quadrant). The newspaper articles focused on "Building 18," a former hotel, where proper care (for both physical and mental health issues) was allegedly sabotaged by disengaged clerks, unqualified military personnel, and overworked managers. Hospitalized veterans claimed that they had to cope with cockroaches, rats, and mold inside Building 18, and with drug dealers outside the gate, eager to sell their wares to patients, most of whom had a diagnosis of PTSD.

Some veterans targeted budget cuts and privatization measures that reduced services and staff members not only at Walter Reed but throughout the entire military health care system. The actual providers of health care were spared criticism, but were described as overworked. It was alleged that complex bureaucratic procedures discouraged veterans from applying for help. The typical soldier was asked to fill out 22 documents for eight different commands and three databases, some of which could not communicate with each other because their computer systems were incompatible. Once the Walter Reed scandal broke, a presidential commission was convened that confirmed the charges and suggested reforms, many of which were initiated and resulted in improved conditions. Both the Fort Hood killings and the Walter Reed scandal illustrate the importance of outside monitoring, since internal review and criticism may be insufficient to assure quality in the physical and mental health care that government agencies provide for the nation's injured veterans.

See also Alcohol Abuse, Alcoholism, and Mental Health; Drug Abuse and Mental Health; Homelessness and Mental Illness; Loss and Grief; Marriage, Divorce, and Mental Health; Panic Disorder; Posttraumatic Stress Disorder; Trauma

Bibliography

Abdullah, H. 2010. "Despite Prevention Efforts, U.S. Military Suicides Rise." *Schwartz Report*, January 16, 1.

Achterberg, J. 2003. "Afterword." In S. Krippner and T. M. McIntyre, eds., *The Psychological Impact of War Trauma On Civilians: An International Perspective* (pp. 1–14). Westport, CT: Praeger.

Allen, T. J. 2007. "America's Child Soldier Problem." *In These Times*, May 15, 45.

Angyal, A. 1965. *Neurosis and Treatment*. New York: Wiley.

Anonymous. 2010. "Numbers." *Time*, February 15, 14.

Beck, A. T. 1984. "Cognitive Approaches to Stress." In C. Lehrer and R. Woolfolk, eds., *Clinical Guide to Stress Management* (pp. 255–305). New York: Guilford Press.

Beck, A. T., and G. Emery. 1985. *Anxiety Disorders and Phobias: A Cognitive Perspective*. New York: Basic Books.

Benish, S., Z. Imel, and B. Wampold. 2008. "The Relative Efficacy of Bona Fide Psychotherapies for Treating Post-traumatic Stress Disorder: A Meta-Analysis of Direct Comparisons." *Clinical Psychology Review* 28: 746–758.

Campbell, J. 1968. *Hero with a Thousand Faces* (2nd ed.). Princeton, NJ: Princeton University Press.

Conner, K. M., J. Davidson, and L. Lee. 2003. "Spirituality, Resilience, and Anger in Survivors of Violent Trauma: A Community Survey." *Journal of Traumatic Studies* 16: 487–494.

Davis, L. L., E. G. Frazier, R. B. Williford, and J. M. Newell. 2006. "Long-Term Pharmacotherapy for Post-traumatic Stress Disorder (PTSD)." *Central Nervous System Drugs* 20: 248–260.

DeAngelis, T. 2008. "PTSD Treatments Grow in Evidence, Effectiveness." *Monitor in Psychology*, January, 40–44.

Dreazen, Y. J. 2011. "Army Suicides Rise to Record Levels in July." *National Journal*, August 12, 1–2.

Everson, R. B., and C. R. Figley. 2010. *Families Under Fire*. New York: Routledge.

Feinstein, D., and S. Krippner. 1988. *Personal Mythology*. Los Angeles: Jeremy P. Tarcher.

Foa, E. B., E. A. Hembree, and B. O. Rothbaum. 2007. *Prolonged Exposure Therapy for PTSD*. Oxford: Oxford University Press.

Freeman, S. M., B. A. Moore, and A. Freeman. 2009. *A Psychological Treatment Handbook for Pre- and Post-deployment of Military Personnel*. New York: Routledge.

Geertz, B. 2010. "Muslim Questions Persist in Army Shooting." *Washington Times*, January 25, 24.

Gottfried, J. L. 2004. *The Mild Traumatic Brain Injury Workbook: Your Program for Regaining Cognitive Functioning and Overcoming Emotional Pain*. Oakland, CA: New Harbinger.

Goulston, M. 2009. "The Fort Hood Killer—Guilty but Not Evil." Retrieved from http://www.HuffingtonPost.com/mark-gov/stron-md.

Hayes, S. C., K. D. Strosahl, and K. G. Wilson. 1999. *Acceptance and Commitment Therapy*. New York: Guilford Press.

Hoge, C. W., J. L. Auchterlonie, and C. S. Milliken. 2006. "Mental Health Problems, Use of Mental Health Services, and Attrition from Military Service after Returning from Deployment to Iraq or Afghanistan." *Journal of the American Medical Association* 295: 1023–1032.

Hudson, A. 2008. "VA Grapples with Veterans' Mental Traumas." *Washington Times*, December 28, 12–13.

Keen, S., and A. V. Fox. 1973. *Telling Your Story: A Guide to Who You Are and What You Can Be*. New York: Signet.

Krippner, S., and D. S. Paulson. 2006. "Post-traumatic Stress Disorder among U. S. Combat Veterans." In T. G. Plante, ed., *Mental Disorders of the New Millennium* (Vol. 2, pp. 1–23). Westport, CT: Praeger.

May, R. 1981. *Freedom and Destiny*. New York: Norton.

McIntyre, T. M., and M. Ventura. 2003. "Children of War: Psychosocial Sequelae of Trauma in Angolan Adolescents." In S. Krippner and T. M. McIntyre, eds., *The Psychological Impact of War Trauma on Civilians: An International Perspective* (pp. 40–53). Westport, CT: Praeger.

Paulson, D. S. 1994. *Walking the Point: Male Initiation and the Vietnam Experience*. Plantation, FL: Distinctive Publishing.

Paulson, D. S. 1997. "Participation in Combat Perceived as a Male Rite of Passage." In S. Krippner and H. Kalweit, eds., *Yearbook of Cross-Cultural Medicine and Psychotherapy* (pp. 51–56). Berlin: Verlag for Wissenschaft und Bildung.

Paulson, D. S. 2001. "The Hard Issues of Life." *Pastoral Psychology* 49: 385–394.

Paulson, D. S. 2003. "War and Refugee Suffering." In S. Krippner and T. M. McIntyre, eds., *The Psychological Effects of War Trauma on Civilians: An International Perspective* (pp. 111–122). Westport, CT: Praeger.

Paulson, D. S., and S. Krippner. 2010. *Haunted by Combat*. New York: Rowman & Littlefield.

Pine, D. S. 2000. "Anxiety Disorders: Clinical Features." In B. J. Sadock and V. A. Sadock, eds., *Kaplan & Sadock's Comprehensive Textbook of Psychiatry* (Vol. 1, 7th ed.). Philadelphia: Lippincott, Williams, & Wilkins.

Roberts, A. R., and K. R. Yeager, eds. 2004. *Evidence-Based Practice Manual: Research and Outcome Measures in Health and Human Services*. New York: Oxford University Press.

Roland, A. L. 2006. "Healing Traumatic Memories." Retrieved from http://www .opednews.com/articles/life_a_allen_l_061015_healing_traumatic_me.htm.

Rotter, J. C., and M. E. Bovega. 1999. "Counseling Military Families." *Family Journal* 7: 379–382.

Runte, J. W., D. Bass, and D. Yep, eds. 2004. *Terrorism, Trauma, and Tragedies: A Counselor's Guide to Preparing and Responding* (2nd ed.). Washington, DC: American Counseling Association Foundation.

Scaer, R. 2005. *The Trauma Spectrum: Hidden Wounds and Human Resiliency.* New York: Norton.

Serlin, I., and Cannon, J. T. 2004. "A Humanistic Approach to the Psychology of Trauma." In D. Knafo, ed., *Living with Terror, Working with Trauma* (pp. 313–530). New York: Jason Aaronson.

Shapiro, F. 1993. "Eye movement desensitization and Reprocessing (EMDR) in 1992." *Journal of Traumatic Stress* 6: 417–421.

Sheikh, J. I., and C. T. M. H. Nguyen. 2000. "Psychopharmacology: Anxiety Drugs." In B. J. Sadock and V. A. Sadock, eds., *Kaplan & Sadock's Comprehensive Book of Psychiatry* (7th ed., pp. 3084–3096). Philadelphia: Lippincott, Williams & Wilkins.

Slone, L. B., and M. J. Friedman. 2008. *After the War Zone.* Philadelphia: DaCapo Press.

Snyder, C. R., and S. J. Lopez, eds. 2002. *Handbook of Positive Psychology.* New York: Oxford University Press.

Solomon, J. L. 2004. "Modes of Thought and Meaning Making: The Aftermath of Trauma." *Journal of Humanistic Psychology* 44: 299–319.

Solomon, S., J. Greenberg, and T. Pyszczynski. 2003. "Why War? Fear Is the Mother of Violence." In S. Krippner and T. M. McIntyre, eds., *The Psychological Impact of War Trauma on Civilians: An International Perspective* (pp. 299–309). Westport, CT: Praeger.

Street, N. 2008. "The 'Warrior Mind' of Mental Health." *Search*, November/December, 14–16.

Sussman, N. 2009. "Selective Serotonin Reuptake Inhibitors." In B. J. Sadock, V. A. Sadock, and P. Ruiz, eds., *Kaplan and Sadock's Comprehensive Textbook of Psychiatry* (9th ed., Vol. 2, pp. 3190–3205). Philadelphia: Lippincott, Williams & Wilkins.

Thase, M. E. 2009. "Selective Serotonin-Norepinephrine Reuptake Inhibitors." In B. J. Sadock, V. A. Sadock, and P. Ruiz, eds., *Kaplan and Sadock's Comprehensive Textbook of Psychiatry* (9th ed., Vol. 2, pp. 3184–3190). Philadelphia: Lippincott, Williams & Wilkins.

van der Veer, G. 1998. *Counseling and Therapy with Refugees and Victims of Trauma* (2nd ed.). West Sussex, England: Wiley.

Walsh, R. A., and B. McElwain. 2001. "Existential Psychotherapies." In D. J. Cain, ed., *Humanistic Psychotherapies: Handbook of Research and Practice* (pp. 253–278). Washington, DC: American Psychological Association.

Wilson, J. P., M. Friedman, and J. D. Lindy, eds. 2001. *Treating Psychological Trauma and PTSD.* New York: Guilford Press.

Wolpe, J. 1982. *Behavior Therapy* (4th ed.). New York: Allyn & Bacon.

Yeoman, B. 2008. "When Wounded Vets Come Home." *AARP Newsletter*, 46–53.

Violence and Violence-Prone Individuals

Noah C. Venables and Christopher J. Patrick

Violence is an important topic for scientific study because of the costly toll it exacts on individuals victimized by violent behavior and the widespread impact it has on society as a whole. Some of the most central questions that researchers have sought to address regarding violence and particular individuals who repeatedly engage in acts of aggression are: What is the nature of violent behavior and what are its origins? How do individuals acquire the capacity to engage in heinous acts that appear to strike at the very heart of society? Can we reliably identify persons who are especially likely to commit acts of violence and aggression? If we are able to identify individuals who are violence-prone but who have not yet engaged in acts of violence, how should such information be used?

In the sections that follow, we first provide a description of the nature of violent behavior and then discuss constitutional (genetic) and situational (environmental) factors in violence proneness, the overlap and relevance of such factors with mental disorders, and the various ethical concerns in studying and classifying violent-prone individuals.

The Nature of Violent Behavior

Violent acts occur at all levels of society, and range from mild altercations to military-style assaults resulting in multiple deaths. Epidemiological statistics indicate that the majority of violent acts are perpetrated against known victims, much of the time within families. Partner assaults and physical abuse of children by parents or guardians are among the most destructive forms of violence in terms of their prevalence and persisting effects within and across generations (Frisell, Lichtenstein, & Långström 2011). Although statistically less common, acts of violence against strangers draw substantial attention from the public because they contribute to concerns that no one in society is ever really safe. Indeed, certain extreme acts of violence seem calculated to fuel such fears. A recent disturbing example of this is the attacks in the country of Norway during the summer of 2011 in which right-wing extremist Anders Breivik detonated a car bomb outside government offices in the city of Oslo that killed 8 people, and then two hours later went on a shooting spree at a summer camp on the nearby island of Utøya, killing 69 people and wounding 66 others. While mercifully rare, such events have the power to generate shockwaves of terror that reverberate across the globe.

A formal definition of violent behavior is helpful as a referent for the material presented below. Common themes among alternative definitions of violence that have been proposed include physical (as opposed to verbal or interpersonal) behavior, intentionality on the part of the perpetrator, and the involvement of an immediate recipient (victim). For example, one may define violent behavior as "overt and intentional physically aggressive behavior against another person" (Volavka 1999, 308), or, similarly, as "any behavior directed toward another individual that is carried out with the *proximate* (immediate) intent to cause harm" and that the target individual is motivated to avoid (Anderson & Bushman 2002, 28–29). By these definitions, examples of violent behavior include physical acts such as pushing, grabbing, punching, kicking, or choking another person. Violence can also include the use of objects to inflict harm, such as weapons or thrown items. Acts of violence officially recognized by the criminal justice system include assault, aggravated robbery, rape or other sexual assault, and murder. From some perspectives, self-injury or suicide can be considered acts of violence toward the self—however, this topic falls outside the scope of the present entry. Another form of violent behavior, also beyond the scope of this entry but important to mention, is state-organized (structural) violence involving systematic acts of aggression against specific groups (e.g., ethnic groups) within a society.

Not all acts of violence are equivalent in terms of origins, intention, and functional significance. To accommodate these distinctions, typologies of violent/aggressive behavior have been formulated. One of the major typologies classifies violent acts into *impulsive* (also termed reactive) versus *instrumental* (or proactive) forms. Impulsive or reactive violence occurs in response to an attack or a perceived threat and is reactionary, defensive, and nonpremeditated. In terms of emotional and cognitive systems involved, impulsive violence involves anger and a perceived loss of control along with thoughts of anticipated pending discomfort. Functionally, impulsive/reactive violence and aggression can serve to protect the individual by removing or preempting threat. By contrast, instrumental or proactive forms of violence entail the prospect of gaining some positive or beneficial outcome through purposeful action. Aggressive acts of this sort are offensive in nature and premeditated. Desired outcomes may take the form of tangible objects (money, goods), elevations in group status, or influence over the decisions/actions of others. Rather than heightened negative emotion (typical of impulsive aggression), instrumental aggression entails a positive orientation directed at dominating others and attaining desired goals, and is associated with cognitions related to anticipated mastery and success.

Violence-Prone Individuals

Why are some people more disposed toward or more capable of perpetrating violent acts than others? Are certain individuals *prone to* violence from birth, or is the propensity to behave violently determined by environmental circumstances and experiences? Available scientific evidence indicates that violent behavior most likely results from a combination of constitutional (genetic) and environmental factors. In an unprecedented recent study, a group of researchers utilized registry records for the total population of Sweden (over 12.5 million persons) to investigate familial associations of violent criminal offending (Frisell, Lichtenstein, & Långström 2011). The unique scope of this sample and the comprehensiveness of available records allowed the researchers to examine nearly all violent criminal convictions occurring in the country between 1973 and 2004 (violent offenses included homicide, assault, robbery, threats and violence against an officer, gross violation of a person's integrity [sexual assault], unlawful coercion, unlawful threats, kidnapping, illegal confinement, arson, and intimidation). Further, the authors were able to identify full familial pedigrees within the sample, permitting them to compare individuals who committed violent crimes with their full, half, and adoptive siblings and their biological and/or adoptive parents and grandparents, aunts/uncles, and cousins. The study yielded compelling evidence that violent behavior does indeed run in families, with findings pointing to contributions of both constitutional and experiential factors to family transmission. For example, the researchers reported significantly higher concordance for violent crime between first-degree relatives (who share more genes between them) as compared to biologically more remote relatives (who share fewer genes). First-degree relatives also evidenced higher concordance for violence than did adoptive siblings, who share aspects of their environment but are dissimilar genetically. Nonetheless, a contribution of environment was also indicated by higher concordance between adoptive siblings as compared to matched control pairs.

A crucial question not addressed by this study, however, is the nature of the constitutional propensity that is thought to be transmitted. It is possible, for example, that what is transmitted is not a "violence gene" (unlikely) but rather heritable variations in the capacity to restrain or moderate impulses—with the extent and manner of expression of this inheritance shaped importantly by environmental factors (Patrick & Vaidyanathan 2011; see also Hicks, Krueger, Iacono, McGue, & Patrick 2004; Krueger et al. 2002). From this perspective, certain individuals are born *vulnerable* rather than born violent, the degree of vulnerability varying along a continuum from low to high. The extent to which individuals higher on this continuum express their vulnerability in the form of violent acts is determined importantly by environmental factors such as prenatal events and circumstances, home and neighborhood conditions, illness and injury, and so on.

Violence and Mental Disorders

Outdated notions that severely mentally ill individuals are inherently violent have been and continue to be replaced by newer conceptions that recognize nuanced associations among mental health problems of differing kinds on the one hand and violent behavior on the other. Along these lines, Heather Stuart (2003) has suggested that mental illness is neither sufficient nor necessary for an individual to commit an act of violence. Rather, she argues that demographic and socioeconomic variables (such as being young, male, and from economically disadvantageous background) are more important factors in the prediction of violent behavior than are mental disorders. As discussed further below, Stuart (2003) also highlights research suggesting the role of substance use/abuse as major determinants of violent behavior and recommends targeting treatment interventions for problematic substance use as means to curtail violent behavior.

In a recent review of empirical findings pertaining to mental illness and violence, Bo, Akel, Kongerslev, Helt Haahr, and Simonsen (2011) concluded that, despite contradictory results in many areas, studies of birth cohorts have consistently found that patients with schizophrenia are at higher risk for violence than the general population. Based on their findings, in conjunction with other work, Bo, Akel, Kongerslev, Helt Haahr, and Simonsen suggest two sources for this observed elevation in violent behavior among patients with schizophrenia, namely, (1) a subgroup of patients without prior history of violence or criminal behavior for whom positive symptomatology (delusions and/or hallucinations) appears to explain their violent behavior; and (2) a violent patient group for whom personality disorders, particularly psychopathy (discussed further below), appear to account for the association between schizophrenia and violence.

Another important source of empirical data on the association between mental illness and violent behavior is the MacArthur Violence Risk Assessment Study undertaken in the United States (e.g., Monahan et al. 2005; Steadman et al. 1998). The focus of this large-scale investigation was on systematically evaluating and further elucidating the question of how and under what circumstances mental illness is related to violence. Certain major findings of this study are especially noteworthy. First, individuals diagnosed with a mental disorder *in the absence of a co-occurring substance use disorder* were no more violent than neighborhood-matched controls. However, diagnosed individuals *with* co-occurring substance use disorders were twice as likely to commit violent acts as their matched controls. These results from the McArthur Study, along with findings from subsequent research, highlight the importance of substance problems in the perpetration of violence, even after controlling for demographic variables such as age, gender, marital status, ethnicity, and residential setting (urban vs. rural). One group of researchers, for example, reported that alcohol or drug problems predicted violence above and beyond schizophrenia and other psychotic disorders, even after controlling for demographic variables (Swartz et al. 1998).

Why might a history of substance use be important to consider in evaluating relations between mental disorders and violence? The answer may lie in the phenomenon of systematic co-occurrence (comorbidity) among mental disorders of certain types. Within the current classification system for mental disorders, as represented in the American Psychiatric Association's (APA) *Diagnostic and*

Statistical Manual of Mental Disorders(*DSM-IV-TR*; APA 2000), comorbidity among mental disorders tends to be the norm, with single disorders in isolation occurring more rarely. Studies of patterns of comorbidity among mental disorders defined by *DSM-IV-TR* have revealed two broad thematic dimensions or factors accounting for this phenomenon, namely, (1) an *internalizing* factor, representing the variance in common among fear, anxiety, and unipolar mood disorders; and (2) an *externalizing* factor, reflecting the shared variance of antisocial personality and differing substance-related disorders (Kendler, Prescott, Myers, & Neale 2003; Krueger 1999; Krueger, Caspi, Moffitt, & Silva 1998).

These comorbidity factors have been interpreted as broad symptomatic manifestations of general underlying vulnerabilities contributing to disorders of differing types. In particular, behavior genetic (identical/fraternal twin) research on the second, externalizing comorbidity factor, which is relevant to violent/aggressive behavior, has provided compelling support for this perspective. For example, researchers reported very high (>80%) heritability for externalizing proneness understood as (i.e., operationalized as) the shared variance among child and adult antisocial behavior and substance disorder (alcohol, drug dependence) symptoms along with disinhibitory personality traits (Krueger et al. 2002; similarly high heritability for this common externalizing factor has been reported by others—e.g., Kendler, Prescott, Myers, & Neale 2003; Young, Stallings, Corley, Krauter, & Hewitt 2000). Whereas the general propensity toward externalizing problems appears to be strongly heritable, the specific manner in which this propensity is expressed (e.g., as aggressive behavior, alcohol or drug dependency, or reckless risk taking) is determined substantially by environmental influences (Krueger et al. 2002).

The idea of broad constitutional and specific environmental influences contributing to impulse control problems of various types has been formalized in the *externalizing spectrum model* (Krueger, Markon, Patrick, Benning, & Kramer 2007; Venables & Patrick in press). The model holds that a general underlying constitutional ("genotypic") disposition gives rise, through the conjunctive influence of specific moderating influences (environmental, and perhaps in some cases genetic), to varied behavioral ("phenotypic") expressions in the form of impulsive-disinhibited behaviors, delinquency, substance abuse, and aggression in differing forms. As previously mentioned, research studies (e.g., Monahan et al. 2005; Steadman et al. 1998; Stuart 2003; Swartz et al. 1998) have consistently found that alcohol or drug problems predict violence above and beyond psychotic disorders, even after controlling for demographic variables. From the standpoint of the externalizing spectrum model, this finding may reflect the fact that substance-related problems in individuals with psychotic problems are indicative of an underlying externalizing propensity that is also associated probabilistically with the occurrence of aggressive behavior.

Of course, it must be recognized that violent acts may be potentiated directly in some cases by alcohol or drug use in individuals not otherwise disposed to aggressive behavior. As such, some have argued that treatment intervention targeting problematic substance use may have utility in curtailing violent behavior (e.g., Stuart 2003). However, the externalizing spectrum model suggests that a constitutionally based disposition toward impulsive, unrestrained behavior may account as much or more for violent acts in psychiatric patients as intoxicated states per se. From this perspective, targeting underlying mechanisms related to deficient inhibitory control and emotion regulation may prove more effective in reducing the occurrence of impulse-related problems—including violent and aggressive behaviors. Along these lines, human neuroscience research suggests that aggressive and violent behaviors may be rooted in part in functional impairments in neural circuits related to emotion regulation (e.g., prefrontal cortex, cingulate gyrus, amygdala), and thus treatments directed at improving affective regulatory capacity may be beneficial for preventing violent behavior in at-risk persons (Davidson, Putnam, & Larson 2000).

Violence and Personality Disorders

The above-mentioned externalizing spectrum model encompasses child and adult components of antisocial personality disorder (ASPD) along with substance-related disorders. Within *DSM-IV-TR* (APA 2000), ASPD is one of four personality disorders (the others being histrionic, borderline, and narcissistic) grouped within the "emotional, dramatic, or erratic" category (Cluster B). Disorders in this category, which tend to involve problems with impulse control and emotion regulation, can be viewed as intersecting with the externalizing spectrum of psychopathology. In support of this, Patrick and Bernat (2010) presented evidence that symptom scores for each of the *DSM-IV-TR* cluster B personality disorders show robust positive correlations with scores on a measure of the broad externalizing propensity factor (Krueger, Markon, Patrick, Benning, & Kramer 2007). From this perspective, heightened rates of violent behavior associated with these disorders—most notably ASPD in men and borderline personality disorder in women, which have been conceptualized by some (e.g., Paris 1997) as gender-specific manifestations of a common underlying pathology—may reflect aggression proneness associated with higher levels of externalizing propensity.

Psychopathy is a personality syndrome related to, but distinguishable from, ASPD that also has important implications for identifying violence-prone individuals. Whereas ASPD is defined primarily in terms of impulsive, reckless/destructive, and illicit behaviors, psychopathy is defined by impulsive-antisocial behavior in conjunction with distinctive interpersonal-affective features entailing a dominant and forceful interpersonal style, manipulativeness, callousness/cruelty, and deficient emotional sensitivity. These latter emotional and interpersonal deficits are considered the hallmark of psychopathy, and what differentiates it from *DSM-IV-TR* ASPD.

The most widely used instrument for assessing psychopathy in correctional and forensic settings is Hare's (2003) Psychopathy Checklist-Revised (PCL-R). The PCL-R indexes psychopathy in terms of 20 items rated using information derived from a diagnostic interview and from institutional file records. Analyses of the PCL-R items have yielded evidence for two broad item subsets or "factors" (Harpur, Hare, & Hakstian 1989), each divisible into two lower-order "facets" (Hare 2003; Hare & Neumann 2006). Most research to date on differing symptom components of psychopathy has focused on the two-factor model (Hare 1991; Harpur, Hare, & Hakstian 1989). PCL-R factor 1 taps the core affective-interpersonal features of psychopathy through items dealing with callousness, lack of remorse, shallow affect, blame externalization, glibness and superficial charm, grandiosity, pathological lying, and manipulativeness. PCL-R factor 2 indexes impulsive-antisocial tendencies through items that focus on chronic impulsive and irresponsive behavior, stimulation seeking, poor behavioral controls, failure to establish a life plan, and antisocial behavior beginning in childhood and continuing into adulthood.

As reviewed by Kennealy, Skeem, Walters, and Camp (2010), PCL-R psychopathy is predictive of violent behavior in large part due to the impulsive-antisocial features represented in its factor 2 items. In their meta-analysis, Kennealy, Skeem, Walters, and Camp found that the antisocial deviance factor of the PCL-R (factor 2) was substantially predictive of violence (effect size $d = 0.40$) whereas the affective-interpersonal factor was only mildly predictive of violence ($d = 0.11$). The authors further examined whether the core affective-interpersonal features of psychopathy indexed by PCL-R factor 1 might interact with impulsive-antisocial features to elevate the risk for violence in nonadditive fashion, as some writers have suggested. Their analysis indicated that these two symptomatic factors do not contribute interactively to violence prediction.

In sum, the findings of Kennealy Skeem, Walters, and Camp (2010) indicate that factor 2 of the PCL-R is markedly predictive of violent behavior, whereas the affective-interpersonal features contribute little to the prediction of violence beyond factor 2. The obvious question raised by these results is why factor 2 of the PCL-R in particular seems to be predictive of violent behavior. One plausible explanation is that the items of PCL-R factor 2 deal with symptoms that are largely indicative of externalizing proneness, which in turn predicts aggression. Consistent with this, high scores on factor 2 are associated with greater problems with alcohol and drugs and elevated levels of disinhibitory personality traits (Hare 2003), and recent work confirms a strong association between PCL-R factor 2 and the externalizing comorbidity factor (Patrick, Hicks, Krueger, & Lang 2005). However, an alternative possibility raised by Kennealy, Skeem, Walters, and

Camp (2011) has to do with predictor/criterion overlap. That is, scores on factor 2 of the PCL-R in part reflect the occurrence of aggressive antisocial behavior in childhood as well as adulthood (e.g., through items dealing with early behavior problems, poor behavioral controls, and delinquency). This raises questions as to whether the part of Factor 2 that reflects past aggressiveness may be the key ingredient accounting for the ability of scores on the PCL-R to prospectively predict violence.

Ethical Concerns in Identifying Violence Proneness

As indicated by the foregoing material, our understanding of the roots of violence and factors that dispose certain individuals toward persistent aggressive behavior continues to grow, and it may well be possible in the future to identify those in society who are at high risk to perpetrate violence before they enact it. However, as research in this area continues and knowledge advances, certain ethical concerns must be confronted. Broadly speaking, Ii we become able to reliably identify individuals at risk for violent behavior, how should we use such information, particularly if risk is determined prior to any act of violence or aggression?

One issue in diagnosing or labeling individuals as violence-prone is the concern that the label itself will produce a self-fulfilling prophecy. In social psychology, self-fulfilling prophecies are circumstances in which preconceptions of an individual (whether true or not) operate to "draw out" the expected behavior, and thus to some extent *cause* the behavior. A contemporary illustration of the self-fulfilling prophecy phenomenon, with some relevance to violence, is provided by Madon, Guyll, Spoth, and Willard (2004). These authors prospectively assessed whether parents' beliefs regarding their children's alcohol use in seventh grade would predict drinking behavior one year later. They found that when both parents *overestimated* their child's current use of alcohol, the child engaged in higher rates of alcohol use subsequently. Interestingly, the reverse result was not obtained—that is, future alcohol use was similar when both parents *underestimated* their child's alcohol as compared to when one parent underestimated and the other overestimated. Notably, these findings held even after controlling for a range of variables known to be predictive of alcohol use, such as child gender and past alcohol use. The results of this study are highlighted here to illustrate the potential power of self-fulfilling prophecies, particularly in the case of behaviors that are socially undesirable. Similar concerns need to be considered in labeling individuals as violent or violence-prone.

Another ethical concern involves the potential for discrimination against individuals who are identified as violence-prone. For example, certain demographic and socioeconomic characteristics (e.g., being young, male, economically disadvantaged) are known to be associated with increased violence. Could systematically labeling individuals with these characteristics as "violence-prone" hold the potential for discrimination? This prospect is alarming to some in light of past eugenics movements within the United States and other nations that have focused on subgroups of individuals in society arbitrarily deemed "problematic." Concerns of this type were a major factor in public protests that occurred in reaction to the U.S. Department of Health and Human Services "Violence Initiative," announced in the early 1990s (Touchette 1992).

Even if well intentioned and effective, could preventative programs for violent behavior be administered in an ethically acceptable manner? For example, could mandatory prevention programs ever be implemented—for example, in the way vaccinations are required for entry into public schools? Regardless of their effectiveness, mandated prevention programs for violence clash at some level with our legal system's tenet of "innocent until proven guilty." In particular, given that predictions of future behavior will always be fallible, "false positive" errors (i.e., incorrect identifications of individuals as "at risk") will invariably occur. Beyond the issue of labeling, the possibility that preventative programs could have adverse effects on some mistakenly identified individuals needs to be considered—particularly if the recipients of such programs consist of as-yet innocent children.

Notwithstanding concerns of these types, society cannot shy away from confronting difficult questions like these as our quest to understand the nature and bases of violent behavior continues. While we must always be cognizant of the ethics surrounding diagnostic labeling and prediction of future behavior, violence remains a serious and pressing public health concern that warrants ongoing commitments of societal resources and scientific efforts.

See also Alcohol Abuse, Alcoholism, and Mental Health; Anger and Aggression; Borderline Personality Disorder; Drug Abuse and Mental Health; Ethical Issues; Genetics and Mental Health; Media Portrayals of Mental Illness; Paranoia; Preventative Mental Health Programs; Psychopathy and Antisocial Personality Disorder; Schizophrenia

Bibliography

American Psychiatric Association. 2000. *Diagnostic and Statistical Manual of Mental Disorders* (4th ed., text rev.). Washington, DC: American Psychiatric Publishing.

Anderson, C. A., and B. J. Bushman. 2002. "Human Aggression." *Annual Review of Psychology* 53: 27–51.

Bo, S., A. Abu-Akel, M. Kongerslev, U. Helt Haahr, and E. Simonsen. 2011. "Risk Factors for Violence among Patients with Schizophrenia." *Clinical Psychology Review* 31: 711–726.

Davidson, R. J., K. M. Putnam, and C. L. Larson. 2000. "Dysfunction in the Neural Circuitry of Emotion Regulation: A Possible Prelude to Violence." *Science* 298: 591–594.

Flannery, D., A. Vazsonyi, and I. Waldman. 2007. *Handbook of Violent Behavior.* New York: Cambridge University Press.

Frisell, T., P. Lichtenstein, and N. Långström. 2011. "Violent Crime Runs in Families: A Total Population Study of 12.5 Million Individuals." *Psychological Medicine* 41: 97–105.

Hare, R. D. 1991. *The Hare Psychopathy Checklist-Revised*. Toronto: Multi-Health Systems.

Hare, R. D. 2003. *The Hare Psychopathy Checklist-Revised* (2nd ed.). Toronto: Multi-Health Systems.

Hare, R. D., and C. S. Neumann. 2006. "The PCL-R Assessment of Psychopathy: Development, Structural Properties, and New Directions." In C. J. Patrick, ed., *Handbook of Psychopathy* (pp. 58–88). New York: Guilford Press.

Harpur, T. J., R. D. Hare, and A. R. Hakstian. 1989. "Two-Factor Conceptualization of Psychopathy." *Psychological Assessment* 1: 6–17.

Hicks, B. M., R. F. Krueger, W. G. Iacono, M. K. McGue, and C. J. Patrick. 2004. "The Family Transmission and Heritability of Externalizing Disorders." *Archives of General Psychiatry* 61: 922–928.

Kendler, K. S., C. A. Prescott, J. Myers, and M. Neale. 2003. "The Structure of Genetic and Environmental Risk Factors for Common Psychiatric and Substance Use Disorders in Men and Women." *Archives of General Psychiatry* 60: 929–937.

Kennealy, P. J., J. L. Skeem, G. D. Walters, and J. Camp. 2010. "Do Core Interpersonal and Affective Traits of PCL-R Psychopathy Interact with Antisocial Behavior and Disinhibition to Predict Violence?" *Psychological Assessment* 22: 569–580.

Krueger, R. F. 1999. "The Structure of Common Mental Disorders." *Archives of General Psychiatry* 56: 921–926.

Krueger, R. F., A. Caspi, T. E. Moffitt, and P. A. Silva. 1998. "The Structure and Stability of Common Mental Disorders (*DSM-III-R*): A Longitudinal-Epidemiological Study." *Journal of Abnormal Psychology* 107: 216–227.

Krueger, R. F., B. M. Hicks, C. J. Patrick, S. Carlson, W. G. Iacono, and M. McGue. 2002. "Etiological Connections among Substance Dependence, Antisocial Behavior, and Personality: Modeling the Externalizing Spectrum." *Journal of Abnormal Psychology* 111: 411–424.

Krueger, R. F., K. E. Markon, C. J. Patrick, S. D. Benning, and M. D. Kramer. 2007. "Linking Antisocial Behavior, Substance Use, and Personality: An Integrative Quantitative Model of the adult Externalizing Spectrum." *Journal of Abnormal Psychology* 116: 645–666.

Madon, S., M. Guyll, R. Spoth, and J. Willard. 2004. "The Synergistic Accumulative Effect of Parents' Belief on Children's Drinking Behavior." *Psychological Science* 15: 837–845.

Monahan, J, H. Steadman, P. Robbins, P. Appelbaum, S. Banks, T. Grisso, K. Heilbrun, E. Mulvey, L. Roth, and E. Silver. 2005. "An Actuarial Model of Violence Risk Assessment for Persons with Mental Disorders." *Psychiatric Services* 56: 810–815.

Paris, J. 1997. "Antisocial and Borderline Personality Disorders: Two Separate Diagnoses or Two Aspects of the Same Psychopathology?" *Comprehensive Psychiatry* 38: 237–242.

Patrick, C. J., and E. M. Bernat. 2010. "Neuroscientific Foundations of Psychopathology." In T. Millon, R. F. Krueger, and E. Somonsen, eds., *Contemporary Directions in Psychopathology: Scientific Foundations of the DSM-V and ICD-11* (pp. 419–452). New York: Guilford Press.

Patrick, C. J., B. M. Hicks, R. F. Krueger, and A. R. Lang. 2005. "Relations between Psychopathy Facets and Exetrnalizing in a Criminal Offender Sample." *Journal of Personality Disorders* 19: 339–356.

Patrick, C. J., and U. Vaidyanathan. 2011. "Coming to Grips with the Cycle of Violence." *Psychological Medicine* 41: 41–45.

Steadman, H., E. Mulvey, J. Monahan, P. Robbins, P. Appelbaum, T. Grisso, L. Roth, and E. Silver. 1998. "Violence by People Discharged from Acute Psychiatric Inpatient Facilities and by Others in the Same Neighborhoods." *Archives of General Psychiatry* 55: 393–401.

Stuart, H. 2003. "Violence and Mental Illness: An Overview." *World Psychiatry* 2: 121–124.

Swartz, M. S., J. W. Swanson, V. A. Hiday, R. Borum, H. R. Wagner, and B. J. Burns. 1998. "Violence and Severe Mental Illness: The Effects of Substance Abuse and Nonadherence to Medication." *American Journal of Psychiatry* 155: 226–231.

Touchette, N. 1992. "Cowering Inferno: Clearing the Smoke on Violence Research." *Journal of NIH Research* 4: 31–33.

Venables, N. C., and C. J. Patrick. In press. "Validating Factors of the Externalizing Spectrum Inventory in a Criminal Offender Sample: Relations with Disinhibitory Psychopathology, Personality, and Psychopathic Features." *Psychological Assessment.*

Volavka, J. 1999. "The Neurobiology of Violence: An Update." *The Journal of Neuropsychiatry and Clinical Neurosciences* 11: 307–314.

Young, S. E., M. C. Stallings, R. P. Corley, K. S. Krauter, and J. K. Hewitt. 2000. "Genetic and Environmental Influences on Behavioral Disinhibition." *American Journal of Medical Genetics* 96: 684–695.

W

Women's Mental Health

Amanda Evans and Victoria E. Kress

According to the National Alliance on Mental Illness (NAMI 2011), a mental illness is a "medical condition that disrupts a person's thinking, feeling, mood, ability to relate to others and daily functioning," and often results "in a diminished capacity for coping with the ordinary demands of life" (para. 1). Mental health struggles can be exhibited in individuals of every age, race, gender, religious orientation, sexual orientation, and socioeconomic status, and it is estimated that 1 out of every 17 Americans have a mental health disorder (NAMI 2011). Mental health issues can impact how an individual interacts with family and friends as well as one's ability to secure and maintain employment and educational opportunities. Women may be particularly vulnerable to mental health struggles, the statistics in this area indicating that women are more likely than men to attempt suicide, develop eating disorders (U.S. Department of Health and Human Services 2009), present with symptoms commonly associated with a diagnosis of depression and anxiety, and experience posttraumatic stress disorder secondary to traumatic experiences (Hamdan 2009; McFarlane et al. 2010; Rose et al. 2010).

Risk Factors in Maintaining Mental Health

A variety of sociocultural factors contribute to women's mental health-related struggles. The results of multiple studies suggest that poverty has broad, far-reaching consequences that impact psychological well-being and the quality of one's life across the life span. Poverty and its aftermath are associated with deleterious impacts for all people, but especially women. Because poverty limits access to resources and supports while inviting stress and fatigue, poverty is one of the most consistent predictors of depression in women (Doucet, Letourneau, & Stoppard 2010). Related to poverty, there is a gender disparity in earned wages as women continue to receive about 85 cents to every one dollar earned by their male counterparts (Bureau of Labor Statistics 2012). These salary inequities contribute to poverty as well as psychological stress.

There are also cultural issues that increase the likelihood that a woman will live in poverty and experience mental health struggles as well. Almost a fourth of African American and Hispanic women live in poverty, and one-third of women who head their own households are poor (U.S. Bureau of the Census 2001). In addition

"The . . . concept of premenstrual complaints has undergone some bizarre contortions in the *DSM* series. *DSM-III* in 1980 contained nothing on it. *DSM-III-R* ['revised'] in 1987 proposed in an appendix the diagnosis 'late luteal phase dysphoric disorder,' a 'pattern of clinically significant emotional and behavioral symptoms that occur during the last week of the luteal phase' . . . Nothing was said about PMS [or premenstrual syndrome]. The clunky diagnosis did not catch on. Then, in *DSM-IV* in 1994, the disease designers tried again, with 'premenstrual dysphoric disorder' (quickly abbreviated to PMDD). Although the diagnosis was intended for the mood disorders section of the *Manual*, the American Psychiatric Association once again consigned it to an appendix after a protest campaign by feminist organizations [whose members felt that it 'medicalized' an ordinary body function]."

—Edward Shorter

Source: Edward Shorter, *A Historical Dictionary of Psychiatry* (New York: Oxford University Press, 2005), 227.

to the common stressors that many women experience, women of color and women who are economically deprived are increasingly disadvantaged in receiving adequate mental health treatment (McFarlane et al. 2010). For women, divorce is a significant predictor of poverty, with women who divorce often finding themselves at an increased risk for poverty and consequent mental health struggles.

Women manage multiple roles in their lives, which might include securing employment/educational opportunities, maintaining household responsibilities, and child care, and these can also impact mental health. Doucet, Letorneau, and Stoppard (2010) state that "while it is undeniable that women's roles in the family can be a great source of pleasure for many women, such roles are also a source of stress" (298). Pearson (2008) suggested that women's self-perceived roles, attempting to balance the abundance of roles, and incongruence between the roles can lead to personal difficulties. This expectation to manage professional, personal, and familial obligations whether self-imposed of by society, can lead to increased stress and dissatisfaction. One limitation of balancing multiple life roles is the decrease in probability that all roles will be managed effectively. Women who are not supported in their endeavors to manage multiple life roles may internalize this perceived inability to juggle multiple roles thus leading to additional distresses. As such, women who experience a lack of support by family and friends (secondary to social isolation due to child care responsibilities, divorce, etc.) are also at greater risk of developing self-concept issues that may contribute to mental health problems (Choate & Schwitzer 2009).

In addition to poverty, cultural issues, and a lack of social support, traumatic life experiences (i.e., intimate partner violence, child abuse, sexual assault) may also sharply increase the likelihood of a woman experiencing a mental health disorder

(McFarlane et al. 2010; Rose et al. 2010; U.S. Department of Health and Human Services 2009). Women experience traumatic experiences at alarming rates. Researchers found that approximately 50 percent of women's first sexual experience, before the age of 18, was the result of a sexual assault, and 67 percent reported personal experiences of intimate partner violence (IPV; McFarlane et al. 2010). According to the U.S. Department of Health and Human Services (2009), one out of four women will personally experience physical violence and/ or sexual assault within their lifetimes. For African American women between the ages of 15 and 24 years, partner violence is the leading cause of death and injury from nonlethal causes (Rose et al. 2010). Rose et al. (2010) found that individuals who had experienced IPV were at a higher risk for depression, anxiety, and low self-esteem. Furthermore, women who have experienced IPV reported a high degree of self-blame, and weakened self-esteem and self-concepts, emotional withdrawal, and trauma reactions (Rose et al. 2010).

Biological considerations may also impact women's mental health. Secondary to the ongoing stress and exposure to traumatic events that many women face, biological changes can alter the brains functioning, leaving women vulnerable to depression and anxiety-related struggles. An important advance in women's mental health has been the identification of mood disturbances during specific phases of women's reproductive lives. Researchers have found that many women experience complications as a result of varying hormone levels that decrease/increase neurotransmitter levels (i.e., estrogen, progesterone) and affect the endocrine regulatory system (i.e., chemical regulation, hormone secretion), causing biological imbalances (Doucet, Letorneau, & Stoppard 2010). Relatedly, women are at an even greater risk for mental health disorders during the periods of pregnancy and menopause secondary to not only physical changes but also the demands of managing complex, resource-intensive life adjustments (e.g., raising children; Doucet, Letorneau, & Stoppard 2010; Rose et al. 2010; U.S. Department of Health and Human Services 2009). The U.S. Department of Health and Human Services (2009) reported that 60 to 80 percent of new mothers experience sadness postbirth, and that 1 out of 10 new mothers reported symptoms associated with postpartum depression. Mothers of children under the age of one in residential treatment facilities to treat substance use and abuse disorders are frequently diagnosed with postpartum depression (Brown & Melchior 2008).

Frequently Diagnosed Mental Disorders

Mental health disorders are evidenced in an individual's impairment in one or more of the following areas: thoughts, emotions, behaviors, and ability to maintain relationships (Doucet, Letorneau, & Stoppard 2010). Although mental health disorders seem equally distributed between male and female populations, as previously stated, women are more frequently diagnosed with depression and anxiety-related disorders (Doucet, Letorneau, & Stoppard 2010; Hamdan 2009; U.S. Department of Health and Human Services 2009). As alluded to above, women who have experienced abuse are three to five times more vulnerable to mental health disorders including depression, suicidal ideation, PTSD, and substance use (Golding 1999).

Depression is the most commonly diagnosed mental disorder in women (McFarlane et al. 2010; Rose et al. 2010). Depression is related to physical changes in the brain in which chemical messengers in the brain do not allow nerve cells to communicate with other another as optimally as they should (U.S. Department of Health and Human Services 2009). According to Rose et al. (2010), women diagnosed with depression have frequently experienced child abuse, sexual assault, marriage conflict, and greater numbers of children. Hamdan (2009) reported that approximately one in five women will experience symptoms of depression in their lifetime. For women with depression who have experienced abuse in an intimate relationship, their depressive symptoms coupled with the abusers demand that the individual isolate themselves, can negatively impact the woman's ability to access effective resources including family support (Rose et al. 2010), treatment, and/or medication management.

Women develop eating disorders and eating-disordered behaviors more frequently than men (Choate & Schwitzer 2009). Women experience eating disordered behavior at higher rates than men due in part to societal pressures to remain thin. "Although some are able to resist these pressures, roughly half of all adult women develop some combination of the negative cognitive and affective symptoms that are characterized as body image dissatisfaction (BID)" (Choate & Schwitzer 2009, 165).

Women are also vulnerable to developing substance abuse disorders. Brown and Melchior (2008) found that women who are treated for a mental health disorder (i.e., depression, anxiety, etc.) and substance use at the same time reported more successful treatment outcomes than being treated for just substance abuse. Based on the biological and psychosocial risks that women experience, it is advisable that female clients are screened for co-occurring disorders and substance use (Brown & Melchior 2008).

Prevention and Treatment of Women's Mental Health Disorders

Although one-half of individuals in the United States experience mental health issues at least once in their lifetimes, approximately two out of every five individuals with a diagnosable mental health diagnosis ever seek treatment (U.S. Department of Health and Human Services 2009). Women are more likely to seek mental health services then are men (Hamdan 2009). Information regarding women's mental health has increased throughout the years; however, additional research is needed to effectively prevent and treat mental health disorders in women (Doucet, Letorneau, & Stoppard 2010). Prevention interventions are the strategy of choice when susceptibility to a disorder is possible or probable and an immediate need for treatment does not exist (Choate & Schwitzer 2009). Prevention programs include providing women with psycho-educational materials (i.e., basic information about mental health and illness), networking opportunities, sharing of resources, and an attempt to normalize a previously stigmatized topic. Researchers suggest that effective preventive methods when working with women who are experiencing a mental health disorder include pharmacological intervention for clients to decrease prolonged PTSD symptoms (McCleery & Harvey 2004), providing women with a predisposition toward depression information regarding depressive symptoms and available community resources (Van der Waerden, Hoefnagels, Jansen, & Hosman 2010), and, for women who are experiencing distress related to eating behaviors, the inclusion of health promotion awareness interventions (Choate & Schwitzer 2009). Ultimately, preventive measures are a preferred method of providing knowledge and support to women who are not currently in crisis but are experiencing distress.

Treatment methods for mental health disorders are recommended when someone is experiencing negative reactions to a mental health diagnosis that might impair her or his ability to maintain educational/occupational obligations, family responsibilities, and/or social relationships. Effective treatment methods for individuals who are experiencing a mental health disorder should be tailored to the individual's specific needs and the type of diagnosis (U.S. Department of Health and Human Services 2009). Examples of treatment methods when working with a client who is experiencing a mental health disorder includes individual counseling, group counseling (meeting with a group of people who share similar experiences in a therapeutic environment facilitated by a counselor), inpatient hospitalization, and medication management (Choate & Schwitzer 2009; U.S. Department of Health and Human Services 2009). Effective counseling treatment methods when working with women who are experiencing a mental health disorder include client-focused interventions, motivational interviewing, cognitive-behavioral therapy, mindfulness strategies, safety planning, and emotional regulation techniques (Brown & Melchior 2008; Choate & Schwitzer 2009; NAMI 2011; Rose et al. 2010). McFarlane et al. (2010) found that clients diagnosed with depression and PTSD benefited from receiving counseling services, exploring their personal experiences of abuse, and receiving information on community resources (e.g., legal aide, housing assistance, victims advocate).

Regardless of the specific treatment method utilized, considerations when working with clients who are experiencing a mental health disorder include cultural factors, family structure, and religious orientation (Hamdan 2009). According to NAMI (2011), individuals diagnosed with severe mental health disorders, in addition to therapeutic intervention, benefit from accessible transportation opportunities, a healthy diet, regular exercise, adequate sleep, effective support systems, and opportunities to create meaning in their lives by volunteering in the community. It is important to recognize the individuality of each female client and her specific mental health needs.

Summary

Mental health issues compromise an individual's ability to engage in meaningful activities and utilize effective coping strategies. Impacting individuals of all ages, races, genders, religious orientations, sexual orientations, and socioeconomic statuses, mental illness can severely impact quality of life considerations. Research indicates that women experience mental health disorders at an equal rate as men; however, women are more frequently diagnosed with depression, anxiety, eating disorders, and PTSD (Doucet, Letorneau, & Stoppard 2010; Hamdan 2009; U.S. Department of Health and Human Services 2009). Risk factors for women commonly associated with increased mental health illness vulnerability include previous experiences with trauma, biological factors and psychosocial pressures (Choate & Schwitzer 2009; Doucet, Letorneau, & Stoppard 2010; McFarlane et al. 2010; Rose et al. 2010; U.S. Department of Health and Human Services 2009). Considerations when working with women who experience a mental health disorder include preventative and treatment methods. Preventative interventions might include psychoeducational opportunities and normalizing experiences. Treatment suggestions include individual counseling, group counseling, inpatient hospitalization, and medication management.

See also Depression; Eating Disorders; Lesbian, Gay, Bisexual, and Transgender (LGBT) Mental Health Issues; Marriage, Divorce, and Mental Health; Posttraumatic Stress Disorder; Poverty, Unemployment, Economic Inequality, and Mental Health; Preventative Mental Health Programs

Bibliography

American Psychiatric Association. 2000. *Diagnostic and Statistical Manual of Mental Disorders* (4th ed., text rev.). Washington, DC: American Psychiatric Publishing.

Brown, V. B., and L. A. Melchior. 2008. "Women with Co-occurring Disorders (COD): Treatment Settings and Service Needs." *Journal of Psychoactive Drugs* 5: 365–376.

Bureau of Labor Statistics. 2012. "Usual Weekly Earnings of Wage and Salary Workers, First Quarter 2012." Retrieved from http://www.bls.gov/news.release/pdf/wkyeng.pdf.

Choate, L. H., and A. M. Schwitzer. 2009. "Mental Health Counseling Responses to Eating-Related Concerns in Young Adult Women: A Prevention and Treatment Continuum." *Journal of Mental Health Counseling* 31: 164–183.

Doucet, S. A., N. L. Letourneau, and J. M. Stoppard. 2010. "Contemporary Paradigms for Research Related to Women's Mental Health." *Health Care for Women International* 31: 296–312.

Golding, J. M. 1999. "Intimate Partner Violence as a Risk Factor for Mental Disorders: A Meta-Analysis." *Journal of Family Violence* 14: 99–132.

Hamdan, A. 2009. "Mental Health Needs of Arab Women." *Health Care for Women International* 30: 595–613.

Lundberg-Love, P. K., K. L. Nadal, and M. A. Paludi, eds. 2011. *Women and Mental Disorders*. Santa Barbara, CA: Praeger.

McCleery, J. M., and A. G. Harvey. 2004. "Integration of Psychological and Biological Approaches to Trauma Memory: Implications for Pharmacological Prevention of PTSD." *Journal of Traumatic Stress* 17: 485–496.

McFarlane, J., L. Symes, L. Frazier, G. McGlory, M. C. Henderson-Everhardus, K. Watson, and Y. Liu. 2010. "Connecting the Dots of Heart Disease, Poor Mental Health, and Abuse to Understand Gender Disparities and Promote Women's Health: A Prospective Cohort Analysis." *Health Care for Women International* 31: 313–326.

National Alliance on Mental Health. 2011. *Mental Illness*. Retrieved from http://www.nami.org/template.cfm?section=about_mental_illness.

Pearson, Q. 2008. "Role Overload, Job Satisfaction, Leisure Satisfaction, and Psychological Health among Employed Women." *Journal of Counseling & Development* 86: 57–63.

Rose, L., J. Alhusen, S. Bhandari, K. Soeken, K. Marcatonio, L. Bullock, and P. Sharps. 2010. "Impact of Intimate Partner Violence on Pregnant Women's Mental Health: Mental Distress and Mental Strength." *Issues in Mental Health Nursing* 31: 103–111.

U.S. Bureau of the Census. 2001. *Poverty in the United States: 2000*. Current Population Reports. Series P60-214. Washington, DC: U.S. Census Bureau.

U.S. Bureau of the Census. 2011. "Number, Timing, and Duration of Marriages and Divorces: 2009." *Household Economic Studies* 5: 1–24.

U.S. Department of Health and Human Services, Office of Women's Health. 2009. *Women's Mental Health: What It Means to You*. Washington, DC: U.S. Department of Health and Human Services.

van der Waerden, J. E. B., C. Hoefnagels, M. W. J. Jansen, and C. M. H. Hosman. 2010. "Exploring Recruitment, Willingness to Participate, and Retention of Low-SES Women in Stress and Depression Prevention." *BMC Public Health* 10: 588–595.

Woods, S. 2000. "Prevalence and Patterns of Post Traumatic Stress Disorder in Abused and Post-abused Women." *Issues in Mental Health Nursing* 21: 309–324.

World Health Organization. 2000. *Women's Mental Health: An Evidence Based Review*. Geneva: World Health Organization.

Workplace Issues in Mental Health

Jay C. Thomas and Francesca Piscitelli

A mental health problem can be defined as a disturbance or disruption in interactions between an individual and his or her environment creating a diminished state of mental healthand overall well-being. This disruption can occur in the individual's cognitive, emotional, or behavioral interactions with others, resulting in the potential for problems to arise in the individual's personal and professional life. Stress or problems at work can be responsible for mental health problems experienced by the individual. Employees may also be impacted by the mental health concerns of family members, which can affect employees' productivity in the workplace. Annually, it is estimated that 32.6 million American adults are receiving mental health services, resulting in over $57.5 billion being spent on mental health care needs each year (U.S. Department of Health and Human Services 2006). While there are emotional and financial costs to the individual with a mental health concern, there is also a large cost to employers. Annually, employers may see a reduction in productivity, increased absenteeism, and an increase in office tensions in the workplace.

In the United States, mental health disorders such as depression cost employers billions of dollars each year in lost productivity (see Thomas & Hersen 2004). Depression, anxiety, and bipolar disorder are common mental health problems reported at the workplace, along with learning disorders such as attention deficit hyperactivity disorder (ADHD) and neurological disorders (e.g., Alzheimer's and traumatic brain injury). With the introduction of the American Disabilities Act (ADA) in 1990, employers were prohibited from discriminating against individuals having any form of disability. A disability under the ADA is defined as "a physical or mental impairment that that substantially limits one or more major life activities of such individual; a record of such an impairment; or being regarded has having such an impairment" (ADA 2009). Since its creation, the ADA has been amended a number of times, most recently in January 2009 when it was expanded to include more individuals who qualify as having a disability under its guidelines. Many states and other countries have also passed laws relating to disabilities in general as well as mental health disabilities.

Common Disorders

Mental health diagnoses often present differently in different individuals. Nevertheless, they are commonly considered stigmatizing by the individual and others based on negative stereotypes associated with having a mental health disorder. The most common mental health disorder reported in the workplace is depression, with 6.7 percent of the U.S. adult population having a diagnosis of major depressive disorder at some point in their life (U.S. Department of Health and Human Services 2005). Common symptoms of depression are fatigue, loss or gain of appetite, slowing of physical interactions or thoughts, difficulty in concentrating, and feelings of hopelessness (American Psychiatric Association [APA] 2000). These symptoms can manifest differently across individuals and may show up in the workplace environment as missed days at work, withdrawal from coworkers, reduction in productivity (by not meeting deadlines or completing tasks), overly emotional reactions to situations, and a decreased interest in work (see Thomas & Hersen 2002).

Another commonly encountered mental health disorder experienced in the workplace is anxiety, with over 18 percent of American adults experiencing some form of this disorder in their lifetime (National Institute of Mental Health 2008). With symptoms similar to depression physically, the mental manifestations of anxiety may consist of high levels of agitation or tension, self-consciousness when interacting with others, difficulty concentrating, and generally excessive nervousness. Unlike depression, anxiety disorders can manifest themselves in a variety of different disorders, including social phobia (social anxiety disorder), panic disorder, posttraumatic stress disorder (PTSD), and generalized anxiety disorder (Anxiety Disorders Association of America n.d.; APA 2000)

The third most common mental health problem seen in the workplace is bipolar disorder. While there are different forms of this disorder (e.g., bipolar I and bipolar II) they are best defined as extreme shifts in mood, or "mood swings," where an individual may experience a period of depression followed by periods of elevated mood resulting in irritability or euphoria. Around 5.7 million Americans have been diagnosed with this disorder. Most individuals are able to be productive, innovative, and creative with the aid of medication (see helpguide.org).

In addition to the more common mental health concerns, neurological disorders and learning disorders have increasingly come to employers' attention in recent decades. A neurological disorder can occur from birth or stem from a disease or an injury and can produce physical, cognitive, or more general functional impairments. Traumatic brain injury, for example, is often the result of an accident occurring either on the job or at home. A learning disorder, on the other hand, is a disability in which the individual experiences difficulty in the development, interpretation, and demonstration of language and nonlanguage abilities. The most common symptoms of learning disorders are difficulties in reading, doing mathematics, organizing/coordinating, and displaying consistent and effective reasoning. ADHD, dyslexia, and mathematics disorder (a specific diagnosis) are the most common disorders documented (APA 2000). Often, individuals go undiagnosed in the case of learning disorders unless the disability is documented in school and steps are taken early on to address it.

Finally, mental health problems present differently in individuals based on gender, ethnicity, and cultural context. For example, males with depression may exhibit increased irritability while females may express dysthymic, or "cycling," mood (APA 2000). Individuals from African American, Asian American, and Latino communities are more likely to report somatic complaints such as headaches, digestive concerns, and back pain (APA 2000). Moreover, individuals from these communities are often less likely to seek out professional mental health treatment and may have heightened fears of being stigmatized based on negative stereotypes in their cultural traditions (Mental Health America 2011). According to the World Health Organization (WHO), depression is the leading cause of disability and the fourth leading cause of productivity loss due to disability internationally (WHO 2011). Around 121 million people worldwide suffer with depression but only a quarter of those individuals have access to or seek out effective treatments owing to lack of resources and the social stigma attached to receiving mental health care (WHO 2011).

Addressing the Problem

In some, cases employers may have difficulty in detecting or knowing how to provide services to individuals experiencing difficulties in the workplace. According to the ADA guidelines, if an individual does not disclose or chooses not to disclose his or her disability, he or she is not protected and the employer is not required to provide reasonable accommodations. However, in most cases such difficulties become known, and in any case employers are well advised to have plans in place to provide reasonable accommodations. Reasonable accommodations are often individualized based on the disorder and ensure that there is equal opportunity in the job application process, that disabled employees are able to perform the essential functions of their job, and that they are able to enjoy equal benefits and privileges (Fike 1997).

There are several actions that employers can take to accommodate employees who experience mental disorders. Such actions can have positive effects for both the employee and the employer and deserve to be tried even if they may not be required by the basic federal and state statutes. Frew (2004), for example, recommends that employers follow four steps in working with disabled employees to develop a productive workplace. The first of these steps is assessment and disclosure. The type of assessment involved here has to do with work-related matters such as attendance and productivity, not psychological assessment. In addition, the specific job requirements, tasks, and environment should be examined to determine what can reasonably be changed to make the accommodation. Thus the assessment process should be open and done with the knowledge of the person with a disability. The second of Frew's steps is to make a "work or leave" determination. Unfortunately, there are times when it is not possible to create a modified position or see mental health improvements in a reasonable time, and in such cases the afflicted individual may need to leave the position. Of course, such occasions may be less common than is ordinarily thought. Assuming the individual stays on the job, Frew's third step is to develop a plan of action and implement it. This plan may follow from some of the material presented above or be based on information available from outside sources (see, e.g., Cornell University ILR School n.d.). Finally, Frew notes that motivation and leadership are critical in making the system work. Individuals with mental health problems are particularly influenced by the degree to which they can trust their employer and its representatives (this is true for all employees, of course, but even more so in the case of those with mental disorders/disabilities). If the employer can take the lead in helping employees succeed, the payoff can be significant.

Future Prospects

The future will undoubtedly bring greater awareness of mental health disorders in the workplace. We know, for example, that those who have been exposed to battle in a military environment are prone to serious potential psychological disorders, primarily posttraumatic stress disorder. It is likely that many veterans will have difficulty once they return home and go back to civilian jobs. Employers need to be aware that good services to veterans can literally save lives as well as create a stronger workplace.

The workplace is capable of providing useful mental health information and referral services, and employers should take advantage of this to benefit both workers and businesses. Once an appropriate treatment is available for a mental health-disabled employee, it can generally be expected that work productivity will return or improve and that the employee will remain a valued member of the organization. Even in cases where an employee is no longer able to work owing to the effects of a mental disorder, it is possible for the employer to maintain a positive relationship with the outgoing employee and build a positive reputation throughout the workplace and market by remaining generally open to accommodation and by promoting good mental health practices and programs.

See also Culturally Competent Care; Disability Rights; Mental Health Counseling; Public Awareness and Public Education; Veterans' Mental Health Care

Bibliography

American Psychiatric Association. 2000. *Diagnostic and Statistical Manual of Mental Disorders* (4th ed., text rev.). Washington, DC: American Psychiatric Publishing.

Americans with Disabilities Act of 1990 as Amended, 2009. Retrieved from http://www.ada.gov/pubs/adastatute08.htm.

Anxiety Disorder Association of America. http://www.adaa.org/.

Cornell University ILR School, Employment and Disability Institute. 2011. Disability Policy, Practice, and Research. Retrieved from http://www.ilr.cornell.edu/edi/.

Fike, Hillary Greer. 1997. "Comment: Learning Disabilities in the Workplace." *Seattle University Law Review* 20: 489–541.

Frew, Jon. 2004. "Motivating and Leading Dysfunctional Employees." In Jay C. Thomas and Michel Hersen, eds., *Psychopathology in the Workplace* (pp. 293–312). New York: Bruner-Routledge.

helpguide.org. http://www.helpguide.org/mental/bipolar_disorder_symptoms _treatment.htm.

Mental Health America. 2011. Depression and African Americans. Retrieved from http://www.mentalhealthamerica.net/index.cfm?objectid=C7DF94D0-1372-4D20-C846 4F9E181D55D8.

National Institute of Mental Health. 2008. "The Numbers Count: Mental Disorders in America." Retrieved from http://wwwapps.nimh.nih.gov/health/publications/the -numbers-count-mental-disorders-in-america.shtml#Anxiety.

Partnership for the Workplace of Mental Health. 2007. A Look at Mental Health in Today's Workplace. Retrieved from http://www.workplacementalhealth.org/innerworkings.

Thomas, Jay C., and Michel Hersen, eds. 2002. *Handbook of Mental Health in the Workplace*. Thousand Oaks, CA: Sage.

U.S. Department of Health and Human Services. 2005. *Major Depressive Disorder among Adults*. Retrieved from http://www.nimh.nih.gov/statistics/1MDD_ADULT.shtml.

U.S. Department of Health and Human Services. 2006. Mental Health Care Costs for All Americans. Retrieved from http://www.nimh.nih.gov/statistics/4COST_AM2006 .shtml.

World Health Organization. 2011. WHO Initiative on Depression in Public Health. Retrieved from http://www.who.int/mental_health/management/depression/depressio ninph/en/.

Bibliography

Ethnicity, Race, and Culture

Byrd, W. Michael, and Linda A. Clayton. 2000. *An American Health Dilemma: A Medical History of African Americans and the Problem of Race: Beginnings to 1900.* New York: Routledge.

Cabrera, N. J., F. A. Villarruel, and H. E. Fitzgerald, eds. 2011. *Latina and Latino Children's Mental Health.* Santa Barbara, CA: Praeger.

Castillo, R. J. 1997. *Culture and Mental Illness: A Client-Centered Approach.* Pacific Grove, CA: Brooks/Cole.

Duran, E. 2006. *Healing the Soul: Counseling with American Indians and Other Native Peoples.* New York: Teachers College Press.

Eshun, S., and R. A. R. Gurung, eds. 2009. *Culture and Mental Health: Sociocultural Influences, Theory, and Practice.* Malden, MA: Blackwell.

Fernando, S. 2010. *Mental Health, Race, and Culture.* New York: Palgrave Macmillan.

Hill, N. E., T. L. Mann, and H. E. Fitzgerald, eds. 2011. *African American Children and Mental Health.* Santa Barbara, CA: Praeger.

Kurasaki, K. S., S. Okazaki, and S. Sue. 2002. *Asian American Mental Health: Assessment Theories and Methods.* New York: Kluwer/Plenum.

Leach, M. M. 2006. *Cultural Diversity and Suicide: Ethnic, Religious, Gender and Sexual Orientation Perspectives.* Binghamton, NY: Haworth Press.

Leong, F. T. L., A. G. Inman, A. Ebreo, L. H. Yang, L. Kinoshita, and M. Fu. 2007. *Handbook of Asian American Psychology* (2nd ed.). Thousand Oaks, CA: Sage.

Leong, F. T. L., L. Juang, D. B. Qin, and H. E. Fitzgerald, eds. *Asian American and Pacific Islander Children and Mental Health.* Santa Barbara, CA: Praeger.

Marbley, A. F. 2011. *Multicultural Counseling.* New York: Routledge.

National Latino Behavioral Health Association. http://www.nlbha.org.

Mio, J. S., and G. Y. Iwamasa, eds. 2003. *Culturally Diverse Mental Health: The Challenges of Research and Resistance.* New York: Brunner-Routledge.

Nebelkopf, E., and M. Phillips. 2004. *Healing and Mental Health for Native Americans.* Walnut Creek, CA: AltaMira Press.

Neville, H. A., B. M. Tynes, and S. O. Utsey, eds. 2009. *Handbook of African American Psychology.* Thousand Oaks, CA: SAGE.

Rosenblatt, P. C., and B. R. Wallace. 2005. *African American Grief*. New York: Routledge.

U.S. Surgeon General. 2001. *Mental Health: Culture, Race, and Ethnicity. A Supplement to Mental Health: A Report of the Surgeon General*. Rockville, MD: U.S. Department of Health and Human Services.

Walton, E., K. Berasi, D. Takeuchi, and E. S. Uehara. 2009. "Cultural Diversity and Mental Health." In T. L. Scheid and T. N. Brown, eds., *A Handbook for the Study of Mental Health: Social Contexts, Theories, and Systems* (2nd ed., pp. 439–460). New York: Cambridge University Press.

Watters, E. 2007. "Suffering Differently." *New York Times Magazine*. August 12. Retrieved from http://www.nytimes.com/2007/08/12/magazine/12wwln-idealab-t.html.

Williams, T. M. 2008. *Black Pain: It Just Looks Like We're Not Hurting*. New York: Scribner.

Witko, T. M., ed. 2006. *Mental Health Care for Urban Indians: Clinical Insights from Native Practitioners*. Washington, DC: American Psychological Association.

Institutions, Settings, and Social Contexts

American Association of School Administrators. 2011. School Mental Health (Resources). Retrieved from http://www.aasa.org/content.aspx?id=4686.

Association of Social Work Boards. http://www.aswb.org/index.asp.

Barth, R. P. 2002. *Institutions vs. Foster Homes: The Empirical Base for the Second Century of Debate*. Chapel Hill: University of North Carolina, School of Social Work, Jordan Institute for Families.

Bordo, S. 2004. *Unbearable Weight: Feminism, Western Culture, and the Body*. Berkeley: University of California Press.

Bray, J. H., and M. Stanton, eds. 2009. *The Wiley-Blackwell Handbook of Family Psychology*. Malden, MA: Wiley-Blackwell.

Center for Mental Health in Schools at UCLA. 2006. *The Current Status of Mental Health in Schools: A Policy and Practice Analysis*. Los Angeles: University of California. Retrieved from http://smhp.psych.ucla.edu/pdfdocs/currentstatusmh/Report.pdf.

Cotton, N. S. 1993. *Lessons from the Lion's Den: Therapeutic Management of Children in Psychiatric Hospitals and Treatment Centers*. San Francisco: Jossey-Bass.

Denmark, F., and M. Paludi, eds. 2008. *Psychology of Women: A Handbook of Issues and Theories* (2nd ed.). Westport, CT: Praeger.

Dwyer, E. 1987. *Homes for the Mad: Life Inside Two Nineteenth-Century Asylums*. New Brunswick, NJ: Rutgers University Press.

Estroff, S. E. 1981. *Making It Crazy: An Ethnography of Psychiatric Clients in an American Community*. Berkeley: University of California Press.

Family Life Development Center. 2001. *Therapeutic Crisis Intervention: A Crisis Prevention and Management System*. The Residential Child Care Project. Ithaca, NY: Cornell University.

Franklin, C., M. B. Harris, and P. Allen-Meares. 2008. *The School Practitioner's Concise Companion to Mental Health*. New York: Oxford University Press.

Halpern, J., and M. Tramontin. 2007. *Disaster Mental Health: Theory and Practice*. Belmont, CA: Thomson Learning.

Kadison, R., and T. F. DiGeronimo. 2005. *College of the Overwhelmed: The Campus Mental Health Crisis and What to Do about It*. San Francisco: Jossey-Bass.

Koenig, H. G. 2005. *Faith and Mental Health: Religious Resources for Healing*. West Conshohocken, PA: Templeton Foundation Press.

Loewenthal, K. M. 2007. *Religion, Culture, and Mental Health*. New York: Cambridge University Press.

Lundberg-Love, P. K., K. L. Nadal, and M. A. Paludi, eds. 2011. *Women and Mental Disorders*. Santa Barbara, CA: Praeger.

Mayo, K. R. 2009. *Creativity, Spirituality, and Mental Health: Exploring Connections*. Burlington, VT: Ashgate.

Miccio, S. 2011. *Hospital Diversion Services: A Manual on Assisting in the Development of a Respite/Diversion Service in Your Area*. Poughkeepsie, NY: People Inc.

Miller, J. 2012. *Psychosocial Capacity Building in Response to Disasters*. New York: Columbia University Press.

Nahmiash, D. 2006. "Abuse and Neglect of Older Adults: What Do We Know about It and How Can We Identify It?" In T. G. Plante, ed., *Mental Disorders of the New Millennium: Vol. 2. Public and Social Problems* (pp. 47–67). Westport, CT: Praeger.

National Center on Elder Abuse. http://www.ncea.aoa.gov.

National Empowerment Center. n.d. "Directory of Peer-Run Crisis Respites." Retrieved from http://www.power2u.org/peer-run-crisis-alternatives.html.

O'Connell, M. E., T. Boat, and K. E. Warner. 2009. *Preventing Mental, Emotional, and Behavioral Disorders among Young People: Progress and Possibilities*. Washington, DC: National Academies Press. Retrieved from http://www.nap.edu/catalog.php?record_id=12480.

Penney, D., and P. Stastny. 2008. *The Lives They Left Behind: Suitcases from a State Hospital Attic*. New York: Bellevue Literary Press.

Popple, P. R., and L. Leighninger. 2011. *Social Work, Social Welfare, and American Society*. Boston: Allyn & Bacon.

Reyes, G., and G. A. Jacobs, eds. 2005. *Handbook of International Disaster Psychology*. Westport, CT: Praeger.

Rothman, D. J. 1990. *The Discovery of the Asylum: Social Order and Disorder in the New Republic* (2nd ed.). Boston: Little, Brown.

Runco, M., and R. Richards, eds. 1998. *Eminent Creativity, Everyday Creativity, and Health*. Stamford, CT: Ablex.

Shephard, B. 2000. *A War of Nerves: Soldiers and Psychiatrists in the Twentieth Century*. Cambridge, MA: Harvard University Press.

Sitton, S. 1999. *Life at the Texas State Lunatic Asylum, 1857–1997*. College Station: Texas A&M University Press.

Stefan, S. 2006. *Emergency Department Treatment of the Psychiatric Patient: Policy Issues and Legal Requirements*. Oxford: Oxford University Press.

Tessler, R., and G. M. Gamache. 2000. *Family Experiences with Mental Illness*. Westport, CT: Auburn House.

Thomas, J. C., and M. Hersen, eds. 2002. *Handbook of Mental Health in the Workplace*. Thousand Oaks, CA: Sage.

Vye, C., K. Scholljegerdes, and I. D. Welch. 2007. *Under Pressure and Overwhelmed: Coping with Anxiety in College*. Westport, CT: Praeger.

Williams, K., A. Frech, and D. L. Carlson. 2009. "Marital Status and Mental Health." In T. L. Scheid and T. N. Brown, eds., *A Handbook for the Study of Mental Health: Social Contexts, Theories, and Systems* (2nd ed., pp. 306–320). New York: Cambridge University Press.

Legal and Ethical Issues

Abramsky, S. 2003. *Ill-Equipped: U.S. Prisons and Offenders with Mental Illness*. New York: Human Rights Watch.

Alexander, M. 2010. *The New Jim Crow: Mass Incarceration in the Age of Colorblindness*. New York: New Press.

Bloch, S., and S. Green, eds. *Psychiatric Ethics* (4th ed.). New York: Oxford University Press.

Bureau of Justice Statistics. 2006. "Mental Health Problems of Prison and Jail Inmates." September. Retrieved from http://bjs.ojp.usdoj.gov/content/pub/pdf/mhppji.pdf.

Dennis, D. L., and J. Monahan. 1996. *Coercion and Aggressive Community Treatment: A New Frontier in Mental Health Law*. New York: Plenum Press.

Earley, P. 2006. *Crazy: A Father's Search through America's Mental Health Madness*. New York: G. P. Putnam's.

Erickson, P. E., and S. K. Erickson. 2008. *Crime, Punishment, and Mental Illness: Law and the Behavioral Sciences in Conflict*. New Brunswick, NJ: Rutgers University Press.

Erickson, P., and S. Erickson. 2009. *Crime, Punishment, and Mental Illness: Law and the Behavioral Sciences in Conflict*. Piscataway, NJ: Rutgers University Press.

Films Media Group. 2009. *The New Asylum*. (Streaming Media). New York: Films Media Group.

Goldstein, A., and I. Weiner. 2003. *Handbook of Psychology, Forensic Psychology*. New York: Wiley.

Heilbrum, K. 2009. *Evaluation for Risk of Violence in Adults*. Oxford: Oxford University Press.

Horwitz, A. V. 2002. *Creating Mental Illness*. Chicago: University of Chicago Press.

Malatesti, L., and J. McMillan, eds. 2010. *Responsibility and Psychopathy: Interfacing Law, Psychiatry and Philosophy*. Oxford: Oxford University Press.

Pfeiffer, M. B. 2004. "A Death in the Box." *New York Times Magazine*. October 31. Retrieved from http://www.nytimes.com/2004/10/31/magazine/31PRISONER.html?_r=1&scp=2&sq=prisons+mental+health&st=nyt.

Quincey, V. L., ed. 2006. *Violent Offenders: Appraising and Managing Risk* (2nd ed.). Washington, DC: American Psychological Association.

Robinson, D. 1996. *Wild Beasts and Idle Humors: The Insanity Defense from Antiquity to the Present*. Cambridge, MA: Harvard University Press.

Saks, E. R. 2002. *Refusing Care: Forced Treatment and the Rights of the Mentally Ill*. Chicago: University of Chicago Press.

Slate, R., and W. W. Johnson. 2008. *The Criminalization of Mental Illness: Crisis and Opportunity for the Justice System*. Durham, NC: Carolina Academic Press.

Stefan, S. 2001. *Unequal Right: Discrimination against People with Mental Disabilities and the Americans with Disabilities Act*. Washington, DC: American Psychological Association Press.

Stefan, S. 2002. *Hollow Promises: Employment Discrimination against People with Mental Disabilities*. Washington, DC: American Psychological Association Press.

Szasz, T. S. 1987. *Insanity: The Idea and Its Consequences*. Syracuse, NY: Syracuse University Press.

Valenstein, E. S. 1986. *Great and Desperate Cures: The Rise and Decline of Psychosurgery and Other Radical Treatments for Mental Illness*. New York: Basic Books.

Whitaker, R. 2001. *Mad in America: Bad Science, Bad Medicine, and the Enduring Mistreatment of the Mentally Ill*. New York: Basic Books.

Mental Disorders

Anxiety Disorders

American Institute of Stress. http://www.stress.org.

Antony, M. M., and R. P. Swinson. 2000. *Phobic Disorders and Panic in Adults: A Guide to Assessment and Treatment*. Washington, DC: American Psychological Association.

Antony, M. M., and R. P. Swinson. 2008. *The Shyness and Social Anxiety Workbook: Proven, Step-by-Step Techniques for Overcoming Your Fear*. Oakland, CA: New Harbinger.

Anxiety Disorder Association of America. http://www.adaa.org/.

Beidel, D. C., and S. M. Turner. 2007. *Shy Children, Phobic Adults: Nature and Treatment of Social Anxiety Disorder*. Washington, DC: American Psychological Association.

Bell, J. 2007. *Rewind, Replay, Repeat: A Memoir of Obsessive-Compulsive Disorder*. Center City, MN: Hazelden.

Carll, E. K. 2007. *Trauma Psychology: Issues in Violence, Disaster, Health, and Illness* (2 vols.). Westport, CT: Praeger.

Crozier, W. R., ed. 1990. *Shyness and Embarrassment: Perspectives from Social Psychology*. New York: Cambridge University Press.

Foa, E. B., and B. Rothbaum. 1998. *Treating the Trauma of Rape: Cognitive Behavioral Therapy of PTSD*. New York: Guilford Press.

Folkman, S., ed. 2011. *The Oxford Handbook of Stress, Health, and Coping*. New York: Oxford University Press.

Herman, J. 1992. *Trauma and Recovery*. New York: Basic Books.

International OCD Foundation. http://www.ocfoundation.org.

Kant, J. D., with M. Franklin and L. W. Andrews. 2008. *The Thought That Counts: One Teenager's Experience with Obsessive-Compulsive Disorder*. New York: Oxford University Press.

Lane, C. 2007. *Shyness: How Normal Behavior Became a Sickness*. New Haven, CT: Yale University Press.

Marohn, S. 2003. *The Natural Medicine Guide to Anxiety*. Charlottesville, VA: Hampton Roads.

Marshall, J. R. 1995. *Social Phobia: From Shyness to Stage Fright*. New York: Basic Books.

Metcalf, T., and G. Metcalf. 2009. *Phobias*. Farmington Hills, MI: Greenhaven Press.

Moyer, M. W. 2011. "A New Look at Obsessive-Compulsive Disorder." *Scientific American Mind*. May.

Pincus, D. 2008. *Mastery of Anxiety and Panic for Adults and Adolescents: Riding the Wave*. New York: Oxford University Press.

Roberts, C. A. 2011. *Coping with Post-Traumatic Stress Disorder: A Guide for Families*. Jefferson, NC: McFarland.

Rosen, G. M., ed. 2004. *Posttraumatic Stress Disorder: Issues and Controversies*. Hoboken, NJ: Wiley.

Runte, J. W., D. Bass, and D. Yep, eds. 2004. *Terrorism, Trauma, and Tragedies: A Counselor's Guide to Preparing and Responding* (2nd ed.). Washington, DC: American Counseling Association Foundation.

Scaer, R. 2005. *The Trauma Spectrum: Hidden Wounds and Human Resiliency*. New York: Norton.

Scher, C. D., D. Steidtmann, D. Luxton, and R. E. Ingram. 2006. "Specific Phobia: A Common Problem, Rarely Treated." In T. G. Plante, ed., *Mental Disorders of the New Millennium: Vol. 1. Behavioral Issues* (pp. 245–264). Westport, CT: Praeger.

University of Massachusetts Center for Mindfulness in Medicine, Health Care, and Society. http://www.umassmed.edu/Content.aspx?id=41252.

Child and Adolescent

Ainsworth, P., and P. Baker. 2004. *Understanding Mental Retardation*. Jackson: University of Mississippi Press.

American Association on Intellectual and Developmental Disabilities. 2010. *Intellectual Disability: Definition, Classification, and Systems of Supports* (11th ed.). Washington, DC: American Association on Intellectual and Developmental Disabilities.

Armstrong, T. 2010. *Neurodiversity: Discovering the Extraordinary Gifts of Autism, ADHD, Dyslexia and Other Brain Differences*. New York: Da Capo Lifelong Books.

Barkley, R. A. 2006. *Attention Deficit Hyperactivity Disorder* (3rd ed.). New York: Guilford Press.

Berman, J., and P. H. Wallace. 2007. *Cutting and the Pedagogy of Self-Disclosure*. Amherst: University of Massachusetts Press.

Brown, L. M. 2003. *Girlfighting: Betrayal and Rejection among Girls*. New York: New York University Press.

Carlson, L. 2010. *The Faces of Intellectual Disability: Philosophical Reflections*. Bloomington: Indiana University Press.

Cheng, K., and K. M. Myers. 2011. *Child and Adolescent Psychiatry: The Essentials* (2nd ed.). Philadelphia: Kluwer/Lippincott.

Cooper, M., C. Hooper, and M. Thompson, eds. 2005. *Child and Adolescent Mental Health: Theory and Practice*. London: Hodder Arnold.

Fletcher, J. M., G. R. Lyon, L. S. Fuch, and M. A. Barnes. 2007. *Learning Disabilities: From Identification to Intervention*. New York: Guilford Press.

Garralda, M. E., and J.-P. Reynaud, eds. 2010. *Increasing Awareness of Child and Adolescent Mental Health*. Lanham, MD: Jason Aronson.

Grant, J., and M. N. Potenza. 2010. *Young Adult Mental Health*. New York: Oxford University Press.

Grinkler, R. R. 2008. *Unstrange Minds: Remapping the World of Autism*. Philadelphia: Basic Books.

Harris, J. C. 2006. *Intellectual Disability: Understanding Its Development, Causes, Classification, Evaluation, and Treatment*. New York: Oxford University Press.

National Association on Intellectual and Developmental Disabilities. 2011. National Resources (listing). Retrieved from http://www.aamr.org/content_535.cfm?navID=146.

National Eating Disorders Association. http://www.nationaleatingdisorders.org.

National Institute of Mental Health. 2011. "Eating Disorders." Retrieved from http://www.nimh.nih.gov/health/publications/eating-disorders/complete-index.shtml.

National Research Council. 1998. *Preventing Reading Difficulties in Young Children*. Washington, DC: National Academy Press.

Nigg, J. 2006. *What Causes ADHD? Understanding What Goes Wrong and Why*. New York: Guilford Press.

Olfman, S., ed. 2006. *No Child Left Different*. Westport, CT: Praeger.

Plante, L. G. 2007. *Bleeding to Ease the Pain: Cutting, Self-Injury, and the Adolescent Search for Self*. Westport, CT: Praeger.

Pope, H. G., K. A. Phillips, and R. Olivardia. 2000. *The Adonis Complex: The Secret Crisis of Male Body Obsession*. New York: Free Press.

Shaywitz, S. E. 2003. *Overcoming Dyslexia: A New and Complete Science-Based Program for Reading Problems at Any Level*. New York: Knopf.

Strong, M. 1998. *A Bright Red Scream: Self-Mutilation and the Language of Pain*. New York: Penguin.

Stryer, S. B. *Anorexia*. Westport, CT: Greenwood Press.

Timimi, S., and J. Leo. 2009. *Rethinking ADHD: From Brain to Culture*. New York: Palgrave Macmillan.

Wilmshurst, L. 2009. *Abnormal Child Psychology: A Developmental Perspective*. New York: Routledge.

Dementia and Other Cognitive Disorders

Attix, D. K., and K. A. Welsh-Bohmer. 2006. *Geriatric Neuropsychology*. New York: Guilford Press.

Brain and Behavior Research Foundation. http://bbrfoundation.org/.

Doka, K. J. 2004. *Living with Grief: Alzheimer's Disease*. Washington, DC: Hospice Foundation of America.

Gillings, A. 2008. *How Does Your Memory Work?* (DVD). Princeton, NJ: Films for the Humanities and Sciences.

Kolb, B., and I. Q. Wishaw. 2009. *Fundamentals of Human Neuropsychology* (6th ed.). New York: Worth.

Ogden, J. A. 2005. *Fractured Minds: A Case Study Approach to Clinical Neuropsychology*. Oxford: Oxford University Press.

Dissociative Disorders

Dell, P. F., and J. A. O'Neil. 2009. *Dissociation and the Dissociative Disorders: DSM-V and Beyond*. New York: Routledge.

Hacking, I. 1995. *Rewriting the Soul: Multiple Personality and the Science of Memory*. Princeton, NJ: Princeton University Press.

Hunter, M. E. 2004. *Understanding Dissociative Disorders: A Guide for Family Physicians and Health Care Professionals*. Bethel, CT: Crown House.

Lilienfeld, S. O., and H. Arkowitz. 2011. "Can People Have Multiple Personalities?" *Scientific American Mind* September/October: 64–65.

Simeon, D., and J. Abugel. 2008. *Feeling Unreal: Depersonalization Disorder and the Loss of the Self*. New York: Oxford University Press.

Spanos, N. P. *Multiple Identities and False Memories: A Sociocognitive Perspective*. Washington, DC: American Psychological Association, 1996.

Stout, M. 2002. *The Myth of Sanity: Divided Consciousness and the Promise of Awareness*. New York: Penguin.

Impulse-Control Disorders

Aboujaoude, E., and L. M. Koran, eds. 2010. *Impulse Control Disorders*. New York: Cambridge University Press.

Castelani, B. 2000. *Pathological Gambling: The Making of a Medical Problem*. Albany: State University of New York Press.

Federman, E., C. Drebing, and C. Krebs. 2000. *Don't Leave It to Chance: A Guide for Families of Problem Gamblers*. Oakland, CA: New Harbinger Press.

Gamblers Anonymous. http://www.gamblersanonymous.org.

Grant, J. E. 2008. *Impulse Control Disorders: A Clinician's Guide to Understanding and Treating Behavioral Addictions*. New York: Norton.

Grant, J. E., and S. W. Kim. 2003. *Stop Me Because I Can't Stop Myself: Taking Control of Impulsive Behavior*. New York: McGraw-Hill.

McCown, W., and L. Chamberlain. 2000. *Best Possible Odds; Contemporary Treatment Strategies for Gambling Disorders*. New York: Wiley.

Volberg, R. 2001. *When the Chips Are Down: Problem Gambling in America*. New York: Century Foundation.

Young, K. S., and C. N. de Abreu, eds. 2010. *Internet Addiction: A Handbook and Guide to Evaluation and Treatment*. New York: Wiley.

Mood Disorders

Andrews, L. W. 2010. *Encyclopedia of Depression*. Santa Barbara, CA: Greenwood Press.

Evans, D. L., and L. W. Andrews. 2005. *If Your Adolescent Has Depression or Bipolar Disorder: An Essential Resource for Parents*. New York: Oxford University Press.

Ghaemi, S. N. 2008. *Mood Disorders: A Practical Guide* (2nd ed.). Philadelphia: Kluwer Health/Lippincott, Williams & Wilkins.

Healy, D. 2008. *Mania: A Short History of Bipolar Disorder*. Baltimore: Johns Hopkins University Press.

Jamison, K. R. 1993. *Touched with Fire: Manic-Depressive Illness and the Artistic Temperament*. New York: Free Press.

Martin, E. 2007. *Bipolar Expeditions: Mania and Depression in American Culture*. Princeton, NJ: Princeton University Press.

Miklowitz, D. J. 2010. *The Bipolar Disorder Survival Guide* (2nd ed.). New York: Guilford Press.

Newman, C. F., R. L. Leshy, A. T. Beck, N. Reilly-Harrington, and L. Gyulai. 2002. *Bipolar Disorder: A Cognitive Therapy Approach*. Washington, DC: American Psychological Association.

Nydegger, R. 2008. *Understanding and Treating Depression: Ways to Find Hope and Help*. Westport, CT: Praeger.

Shorter, E. 2009. *Before Prozac: The Troubled History of Mood Disorders in Psychiatry*. New York: Oxford University Press.

Solomon, A. 2001. *The Noonday Demon: An Atlas of Depression*. New York: Scribner.

Personality Disorders

Brown, N. W. 2006. *Coping with Infuriating, Mean, Critical People: The Destructive Narcissistic Pattern*. Westport, CT: Praeger.

Dobbert, D. L. 2007. *Understanding Personality Disorders: An Introduction*. Westport, CT: Praeger.

Films Media Group. 2004. *Should I Live or Should I Die? Understanding Borderline Personality Disorder* (DVD). New York: Films Media Group.

Kantor, M. 2008. *Understanding Paranoia: A Guide for Professionals, Families, and Sufferers*. Westport CT, Praeger

Lackhkar, J. 2008. *How to Talk to a Narcissist*. New York: Routledge.

Linehan, M. M., B. N. Cochran, and C. A. Kehrer, C. A. 2001. "Dialectical Behavior Therapy for Borderline Personality Disorder." In D. H. Barlow, ed., *Clinical Handbook of Psychological Disorders* (3rd ed., pp. 470–522). New York: Guilford Press.

Lykken, D. T. 1995. *The Antisocial Personalities*. Hillsdale, NJ: Erlbaum.

Millon, T., and R. D. Davis. 1996. *Disorders of Personality: DSM-IV and Beyond*. New York: Wiley.

Munro, A. 1999. *Delusional Disorder: Paranoia and Related Illnesses*. New York: Cambridge University Press.

Patrick, C. J. 2006. *Handbook of Psychopathy*. New York: Guilford Press.

Pinsky, D., and S. M. Young. 2009. *The Mirror Effect: How Celebrity Narcissism Is Seducing America*. New York: Harper.

Reiland, R. 2004. *Get Me Out of Here: My Recovery from Borderline Personality Disorder*. Center City, MN: Hazelden.

Ronningstam, E. 2005. *Identifying and Understanding the Narcissistic Personality*. New York: Oxford University Press.

Shapiro, J. L., and S. T. Bernadett-Shapiro. 2006. "Narcissism: Greek Tragedy, Psychological Syndrome, Cultural Norm." In T. Plante, ed., *Mental Disorders of the New Millennium* (Vol. 1, p. 25–52). Westport, CT. Praeger.

Psychosomatic Disorders

Johnson, S. K. 2008. *Medically Unexplained Illness: Gender and Biopsychosocial Implications*. Washington, DC: American Psychological Association.

Sarno, J. E. 2006. *The Divided Mind: The Epidemic of Mindbody Disorders*. New York: HarperCollins.

Shorter, E. 1994. *From Mind into the Body: The Cultural Origins of Psychosomatic Symptoms*. Toronto: University of Toronto Press.

Trimble, M. R. 2004. *Somatoform Disorders: A Medicolegal Guide*. New York: Cambridge University Press.

Schizophrenia

Cockburn, P., and H. Cockburn. 2011. *Henry's Demon: Living with Schizophrenia, a Father and Son's Story*. New York: Scribner.

Green, M. 2001. *Schizophrenia Revealed*. New York: Norton.

Insel, T. 2010. "Rethinking Schizophrenia." *Nature* 469: 187–193.

Silverstein, S., W. Spaulding, and A. Menditto. 2006. *Schizophrenia*. Cambridge, MA: Hogrefe.

Spaulding, W., M. Sullivan, and J. Poland. 2003. *Treatment and Rehabilitation of Severe Mental Illness*. New York: Guilford Press.

Szasz, T. 1988. *Schizophrenia: The Sacred Symbol of Psychiatry*. Syracuse: Syracuse University Press.

Sexual and Gender Identity Disorders

Bering, J. 2010. "The Third Gender." *Scientific American Mind* May/June: 60–63.

Briken, P., A. Hill, and W. Berner. 2007. "Abnormal Attraction." *Scientific American Mind* February/March: 59–63.

Hazelden Foundation. 1989. *Hope and Recovery: A Twelve-Step Guide for Healing from Compulsive Sexual Behavior*. Center City, MN: Hazelden.

Heath, R. A. 2006. *The Praeger Handbook of Transsexuality: Changing Gender to Match Mindset*. Westport, CT: Praeger.

Hock, R. R. 2007. *Human Sexuality*. Upper Saddle River, NJ: Pearson Prentice-Hall.

Lev, A. I. 2004. *Transgender Emergence: Therapeutic Guidelines for Working with Gender-Variant People and Their Families*. New York: Haworth Press.

Mezzich, J. E., and R. Hernandez-Serrano. 2006. *Psychiatry and Sexual Health: An Integrative Approach*. Lanham, MD: Jason Aronson/World Psychiatric Association.

Roudinesco, E. 2009. *Our Dark Side: A History of Perversion*. Malden, MA: Polity.

Sleep Disorders

Foldvary-Schaefer, N. 2009. *The Cleveland Clinic Guide to Sleep Disorders*. New York: Kaplan.

Kroker, K. 2007. *The Sleep of Others and the Transformation of Sleep Research*. Toronto: University of Toronto Press.

Lee-Chiong, T. L. 2009. *Sleep Medicine Essentials*. Hoboken, NJ: Wiley-Blackwell.

Sexton-Radek, K., and G. Graci. 2008. *Combating Sleep Disorders*. Westport, CT: Praeger.

Shneerson, J. 2005. *Sleep Medicine: A Guide to Sleep and Its Disorders* (2nd ed.). Malden, MA: Blackwell.

Substance Abuse

Alcoholics Anonymous. http://www.aa.org.

Brick, J., ed. 2008. *Handbook of the Medical Consequences of Alcohol and Drug Abuse* (2nd ed.). New York: Haworth Press.

Daley, D. C., 2006. *Overcoming Your Alcohol or Drug Problem* (2nd ed.). New York: Oxford University Press.

Erickson, C. K. 2007. *The Science of Addiction: From Neurobiology to Treatment*. New York: Norton.

Myers, P. L., and R. E. Isralowitz. 2011. *Alcohol*. Santa Barbara, CA: Greenwood.

Newton, D. E. 2010. *Substance Abuse: A Reference Handbook*. Santa Barbara, CA: ABC-CLIO/Greenwood.

Ross, D., H. Kincaid, D. Spurrett, and P. Collins, eds. 2010. *What Is Addiction?* Cambridge, MA: MIT Press.

Substance Abuse and Mental Health Services Administration (SAMHSA). http://www.samhsa.gov.

Substance Abuse and Mental Health Services Administration. 2010. *Results from the 2009 National Survey on Drug Use and Health: Vol. 1. Summary of National Findings*. Rockville, MD: U.S. Department of Health and Human Services.

Sussman, S., and S. L. Ames. 2008. *Drug Abuse: Concepts, Prevention, and Cessation*. New York: Cambridge University Press.

Tarter, R. E., and M. M. Vanyukov, eds. 2002. *Etiology of Substance Use Disorder in Children and Adolescents: Emerging Findings from the Center for Education and Drug Abuse Research*. Binghamton, NY: Haworth Press.

Violence and Aggression

DiGuiseppe, R., and R. C. Tafrate. 2007. *Understanding Anger Disorders*. New York: Oxford University Press.

Flannery, D., A. Vazsonyi, and I. Waldman. 2007. *Handbook of Violent Behavior*. New York: Cambridge University Press.

Graham-Bermann, S. A., and A. A. Levendosky. 2011. *How Intimate Partner Violence Affects Children*. Washington, DC: American Psychological Association.

Hare, R. D. 2003. *The Hare Psychopathy Checklist-Revised* (2nd ed.). Toronto: Multi-Health Systems.

Shaver, P. R., and M. Mikulincer. 2011. *Human Aggression and Violence: Causes, Manifestations, and Consequences*. Washington, DC: American Psychological Association.

Sokoloff, N. J., with C. Pratt. 2005. *Domestic Violence at the Margins: Readings on Race, Class, Gender, and Culture*. New Brunswick, NJ: Rutgers University Press.

Tafrate, R. C., and H. Kassinove. 2009. *Anger Management for Everyone: Seven Proven Ways to Control Anger and Live a Happier Life*. Atascadero, CA: Impact.

Psychiatry, Psychology, and Pharmaceuticals

American Psychiatric Association. 2000. *Diagnostic and Statistical Manual of Mental Disorders* (4th ed., text rev.). Washington, DC: American Psychiatric Publishing.

American Psychiatric Association. http://www.psych.org.

American Society of Clinical Psychopharmacology. http://www.ascpp.org.

Angell, M. 2004. *The Truth About the Drug Companies: How They Deceive Us and What to Do About It*. New York: Random House.

Barber, C. 2008. *Comfortably Numb: How Psychiatry Is Medicating a Nation*. New York: Vintage.

Barlow, D. H. 2011. *The Oxford Handbook of Clinical Psychology*. New York: Oxford University Press.

Benjamin, L. T. 2005. "A History of Clinical Psychology as a Profession in America (and a Glimpse at Its Future)." *Annual Review of Clinical Psychology* 1: 1–30.

Bentall, R. P. 2009. *Doctoring the Mind: Is Our Current Treatment of Mental Illness Really Any Good?* New York: New York University Press.

Berrios, G. E. 1996. *The History of Mental Symptoms: Descriptive Psychopathology since the Nineteenth Century*. New York: Cambridge University Press.

Braslow, J. 1997. *Mental Ills and Bodily Cures: Psychiatric Treatment in the First Half of the Twentieth Century*. Berkeley: University of California Press.

Carlat, D. J. 2010. *Unhinged: The Trouble with Psychiatry*. New York: Free Press.

Carter, R. 2010. *Within Our Reach: Ending the Mental Health Crisis*. New York: Rodale Books.

Diamond, R. J. 2009. *Instant Psychopharmacology: Up-to-Date Information about the Most Commonly Prescribed Psychiatric Medications* (3rd ed.). New York: Norton.

Dowbiggin, I. 2011. *The Quest for Mental Health: A Tale of Science, Medicine, Scandal, and Mass Society*. New York: Cambridge University Press.

Drake, R. E., M. Merrens, and D. Lynde, eds. 2005. *Evidence-Based Mental Health: A Textbook*. New York: Wiley.

Elder, A., and J. Holmes. 2002. *Mental Health in Primary Care*. New York: Oxford University Press.

Eriksen, K., and V. E. Kress. 2005. *Beyond the DSM Story: Ethical Quandaries, Challenges, and Best Practices*. Thousand Oaks, CA: Sage.

Ghaemi, S. N. 2010. *The Rise and Fall of the Biopsychosocial Model: Reconciling Art and Science in Psychiatry*. Baltimore: Johns Hopkins University Press.

Glicken, M. D. 2004. *Improving the Effectiveness of the Helping Professions: An Evidence-Based Practice Approach*. Thousand Oaks, CA: Sage.

Grob, G. N. 1983. *Mental Illness and American Society, 1875–1940*. Princeton, NJ: Princeton University Press.

Grob, G. N. 1994. *The Mad among Us: A History of the Care of America's Mentally Ill*. New York: Free Press.

Halgin, R. P., and S. K. Whitbourne. 2009. *Abnormal Psychology: Clinical Perspectives on Psychological Disorders* (6th ed.). New York: McGraw-Hill.

Healy, D. 1999. *The Anti-Depressant Era*. Cambridge, MA: Harvard University Press.

Healy, D. 2004. *The Creation of Psychopharmacology*. Cambridge MA: Harvard University Press.

Hersen, M., and A. M. Gross, eds. 2008. *Handbook of Clinical Psychology*. Hoboken, NJ: Wiley.

Higgins, E. S. 2008. "The New Genetics of Mental Illness." *Scientific American Mind* June/July: 40–47.

Hobson, J. A., and J. A. Leonard. 2002. *Out of Its Mind: Psychiatry in Crisis—a Call for Reform*. New York: Basic Books.

Joseph, J. 2004. *The Gene Illusion: Genetic Research in Psychiatry and Psychology under the Microscope*. New York: Algora.

Joseph, J. 2006. *The Missing Gene: Psychiatry, Heredity, and the Fruitless Search for Genes*. New York: Algora.

Kirk, S. A., & H. Kutchins. 1992. *The Selling of DSM: The Rhetoric of Science in Psychiatry*. New York: Aldine De Gruyter.

Kirsch, I. 2010. *The Emperor's New Drugs: Exploding the Antidepressant Myth*. New York: Basic Books.

Kramer, G. P., D. A. Bernstein, and V. Phares. 2009. *Introduction to Clinical Psychology* (7th ed.). Upper Saddle River, NJ: Prentice-Hall.

Kutchins, H., and S. A. Kirk. 1996. *Making Us Crazy—DSM: The Psychiatric Bible and the Creation of Mental Disorders*. New York: Free Press.

Luhrmann, T. 2000. *Of Two Minds: The Growing Disorder in American Psychiatry*. New York: Knopf.

Lunbeck, E. 1994. *The Psychiatric Persuasion: Knowledge, Gender, and Power in Modern America*. Princeton, NJ: Princeton University Press.

McGovern, C. M. 1985. *Masters of Madness: Social Origins of the American Psychiatric Profession*. Hanover, NH: University Press of New England.

McLeod, J. D., and E. R. Wright. 2010. *The Sociology of Mental Health: A Comprehensive Reader*. New York: Oxford University Press.

Merrens, M. 2005. *Evidence-Based Mental Health Practice*. New York: Norton.

Morrison, J. 2006. *Diagnosis Made Easier: Principles and Techniques for Mental Health Clinicians*. New York: Guilford Press.

Norcross, J. C., and M. R. Goldfried, eds. 2005. *Handbook of Psychotherapy Integration* (2nd ed.). New York: Oxford University Press.

Paris, J. 2005. *Fall of an Icon: Psychoanalysis and Academic Psychiatry*. Toronto: University of Toronto Press.

Peterson, M. 2009. *Our Daily Meds: How the Pharmaceutical Companies Transformed Themselves into Slick Marketing Machines and Hooked the Nation on Prescription Drugs*. New York: Macmillan.

Petryna, A., A. Lakoff, and A. Kleinman. 2006. *Global Pharmaceuticals: Ethics, Markets, Practices*. Durham, NC: Duke University Press.

Pressman, J. 1998. *Last Resort: Psychosurgery and the Limits of Medicine*. Cambridge: Cambridge University Press.

Sadler, J. Z. 2005. *Values and Psychiatric Diagnosis*. Oxford: Oxford University Press.

Schatzberg, A. F., J. O. Cole, and C. DeBattista. 2010. *Manual of Clinical Psychopharmacology* (7th ed.). Washington, DC: American Psychiatric Publishing.

Scheid, T. L., and T. N. Brown, eds. 2010. *A Handbook for the Study of Mental Health: Social Contexts, Theories, and Systems*. New York: Cambridge University Press.

Schneider, R., and J. L. Levenson. 2007. *Psychiatry Essentials for Primary Care*. Philadelphia: American College of Physicians.

Scull, A. 2005. *Madhouse: A Tragic Tale of Megalomania and Modern Medicine*. New Haven, CT: Yale University Press.

Shorter, E. 1997. *A History of Psychiatry: From the Era of the Asylum to the Age of Prozac*. New York: Wiley.

Small, M. 2006. *The Culture of Our Discontent: Beyond the Medical Model of Mental Illness*. Washington, DC: Joseph Henry Press.

Society for the Exploration of Psychotherapy Integration (SEPI). http://www.sepiweb.com.

Szasz, T. 1961. *The Myth of Mental Illness: Foundation of a Theory of Personal Conduct*. New York: Harper & Row.

Szasz, T. 2010. *The Medicalization of Everyday Life: Selected Essays*. Syracuse, NY: Syracuse University Press.

Torrey, E. F. 1997. *Out of the Shadows: Confronting America's Mental Illness Crisis*. New York: Wiley.

Torrey, E. F., and J. Miller. 2001. *The Invisible Plague: The Rise of Mental Illness from 1750 to the Present*. New Brunswick, NJ: Rutgers University Press.

Trent, J. *Inventing the Feeble Mind: A History of Mental Retardation in the United States*. 1994. Berkeley: University of California Press.

Valenstein, E. 1986. *Great and Desperate Cures: The Rise and Decline of Psychosurgery and Other Radical Cures for Mental Illness*. New York: Basic Books.

Wenegrat, B. 2001. *Theater of Disorder: Patients, Doctors, and the Construction of Illness*. New York: Oxford University Press.

Whitaker, R. 2010. *Anatomy of an Epidemic: Magic Bullets, Psychiatric Drugs, and the Astonishing Rise of Mental Illness in America*. New York: Crown.

Wilson, W. H. 2012. "Neuropsychiatric Perspectives for Community Mental Health Theory and Practice." In Jessica Rosenberg and Samuel Rosenberg, eds., *Community Mental Health: New Directions in Policy and Practice* (2nd ed., pp. 238–252). New York: Routledge.

World Health Organization. 2008. *Integrated Mental Health Into Primary Health Care: A Global Perspective*. Geneva, Switzerland: World Health Organization.

Yudofsky, S. C., and R. E. Hales. 2010. *Essentials of Neuropsychiatry and Behavioral Neurosciences* (2nd ed.). Washington, DC: American Psychiatric Publishing.

The Public Sphere

Ashby, L. 1997. *Endangered Children: Dependency, Neglect, and Abuse in American History*. New York: Twayne.

Autistic Self-Advocacy Network (ASAN). http://www.autisticadvocacy.org/.

Baker, D. L. 2011. *The Politics of Neurodiversity: Why Public Policy Matters*. Boulder, Co: Lynne Rienner.

Berlin, R. M., ed. 2008. *Poets on Prozac: Mental Illness, Treatment, and the Creative Process*. Baltimore: Johns Hopkins University Press.

Burns, T., and M. Firn. 2002. *Assertive Outreach in Mental Health: A Manual for Practitioners*. New York: Oxford University Press.

Church, M. A., and C. I. Brooks. 2009. *Subtle Suicide: Our Silent Epidemic over Ambivalence about Living*. Westport, CT: Praeger.

Compton, M. 2010. *Clinical Manual of Prevention in Mental Health*. Washington, DC: American Psychiatric Publishing.

Corrigan, P. W. ed. 2005. *On the Stigma of Mental Illness: Practical Strategies for Research and Social Change*. Washington, DC: American Psychological Association.

Feder, L. 1980. *Madness in Literature*. Princeton, NJ: Princeton University Press.

Frank, R. G., and S. A. Glied. 2006. *Better but Not Well: Mental Health Policy in the United States since 1950*. Baltimore: Johns Hopkins University Press.

Gamwell, L., and L. Tomes. 1995. *Madness in America: Cultural and Medical Perceptions of Mental Illness before 1914*. Ithaca, NY: Cornell University Press.

Goldman, H. H., J. A. Buck, and K. S. Thompson. 2009. *Transforming Mental Health Services: Implementing the Federal Agenda for Change*. Arlington, VA: American Psychiatric Association.

Grob, G. N. 1991. *From Asylum to Community: Mental Health Policy in America*. Princeton: Princeton University Press.

Harper, S. 2009. *Madness, Power, and the Media: Class, Gender, and Race in Popular Representations of Mental Distress*. New York: Palgrave Macmillan.

Hartwell, C. 1980. *Disordered Personalities in Literature*. New York: Longman, 1980.

Hinshaw, S. P. 2006. *The Mark of Shame: Stigma of Mental Illness and an Agenda for Change*. Oxford: Oxford University Press.

Horsley, J. 2009. *The Secret Life of Movies: Schizophrenic and Shamanic Journeys in American Cinema*. Jefferson, NC: McFarland & Co.

Institute of Medicine. 1994. *Reducing Risks for Mental Disorders: Frontiers for Preventive Intervention Research*. Washington, DC: National Academy Press.

Kelly, T. A. 2010. *Healing the Broken Mind: Transforming America's Failed Mental Health System*. New York: New York University Press.

Lamb, H. R., and L. E. Weinberger, eds. 2001. *Deinstitutionalization: Promise and Problems*. San Francisco: Jossey-Bass.

Levin, B. L., K. D. Hennessey, and J. Petrila. 2010. *Mental Health Services: A Public Health Perspective* (3rd ed.). New York: Oxford University Press.

Lott, B., and H. E. Bullock. 2007. *Psychology and Economic Injustice: Personal, Professional, and Political Intersections*. Washington, DC: American Psychological Association.

Ludwig, A. M. 1996. *The Price of Greatness: Resolving the Creativity and Madness Controversy*. New York: Guilford Press.

Mechanic, D. 2008. *Mental Health and Social Policy: Beyond Managed Care*. Boston: Pearson/Allyn & Bacon.

Mental Health America. http://www.nmha.org.

Moffat, M. J. 1992. *In the Midst of Winter: Selections from the Literature of Mourning*. New York: Vintage.

Moniz, C., and S. Gorin. 2010. *Health and Mental Health Care Policy: A Biopsychosocial Perspective* (3rd ed.). Boston: Allyn & Bacon.

National Academy of Sciences. 2010. *Preventing Mental, Emotional, and Behavioral Disorders among Young People*. Washington, DC: The National Academy.

National Alliance on Mental Illness. 2009. *Grading the States: A Report on America's Health Care System of Adults with Serious Mental Illness*. Arlington, VA: National Alliance for Mental Illness.

National Alliance to End Homelessness. n.d. "Mental/Physical Health." Retrieved from http:/www.endhomelessness.org.

National Coalition for the Homeless. n.d. "Why Are People Homeless?" Retrieved from http://www.nationalhomeless.org/factsheets/why.html.

National Institute of Mental Health. http://www.nimh.gov.

Office of the Surgeon General. 1999. *Mental Health: A Report of the Surgeon General*. Rockville, MD: U.S. Department of Health and Human Services, U.S. Public Health Service. Retrieved from http://www.surgeongeneral.gov/library/mentalhealth/toc.html.

President's New Freedom Commission on Mental Health. 2003. *Achieving the Promise: Transforming Mental Health Care in America: Final report*. Rockville, MD: President's New Freedom Commission on Mental Health. Retrieved from http:// store.samhsa.gov/shin/content//SMA03-3831/SMA03-3831.pdf.

Rochefort, D. A. 1993. *From Poorhouses to Homelessness: Policy Analysis and Mental Health Care*. Westport, CT: Auburn House.

Rohrer, G. 2004. *Mental Health in Literature: Literary, Lunacy, and Lucidity*. Chicago: Lyceum Books.

Rosenberg, J., and S. Rosenberg, eds. 2006. *Community Mental Health: Challenges for the 21st Century*. New York: Routledge.

Sartorius, N., and H. Schulze. 2005. *Reducing the Stigma of Mental Illness: A Report from a Global Association*. New York: Cambridge University Press.

Saunders, C., and J. MacNaughton, eds. 2005. *Madness and Creativity in Literature and Culture*. New York: Palgrave Macmillan.

Schutt, R. K., with S. M. Goldfinger. 2011. *Homelessness, Housing, and Mental Illness*. Cambridge, MA: Harvard University Press.

Smith, L. 2010. *Psychology, Poverty, and the End of Social Exclusion: Putting Our Practice to Work*. New York: Teachers College Press.

Society for Prevention Research. http://www.preventionresearch.org.

Thiher, A. 1999. *Revels in Madness: Insanity in Medicine and Literature*. Ann Arbor: University of Michigan Press.

U.S. Department of Health and Human Services. 2010. *Healthy People 2020*. Washington, DC: U.S. Department of Health and Human Services.

Vandiver, V. L. 2008. *Integrating Health Promotion and Mental Health: An Introduction to Policies, Principles, and Practices*. New York: Oxford University Press.

Wahl, O. F. 1997. *Media Madness: Public Images of Mental Illness*. New Brunswick, NJ: Rutgers University Press.

Wedding, D., M. A. Boyd, and R. M. Niemiec. 2005. *Movies and Mental Illness: Using Films to Understand Psychopathology* (2nd ed.). Cambridge, MA: Hogrefe & Huber.

Zimmerman, J. N. 2003. *People Like Ourselves: Portrayals of Mental Illness in the Movies*. Lanham, MD: Scarecrow Press.

Therapies and Approaches

American Counseling Association. 2011. http://www.counseling.org/resources/.

American Group Psychotherapy Association. n.d. "Group Therapy." Retrieved from http://www.agpa.org/group/consumersguide2000.html.

Amering, M., and M. Schmolke. 2009. *The Recovery Movement in Mental Health: Reshaping Scientific and Clinical Responsibilities*. Hoboken, NJ: Wiley-Blackwell.

Anthony, W. A., and M. Farkas. 2009. *Primer on the Psychiatric Rehabilitation Process*. Boston: Boston University Center for Psychiatric Rehabilitation.

Archer, J., and C. J. McCarthy. 2006. *Counseling Theories: Contemporary Applications and Approaches*. Upper Saddle River, NJ: Prentice-Hall.

Association for Humanistic Psychology. 2001. "Humanistic Psychology Overview." Retrieved from http://www.ahpweb.org/aboutahp/whatis.html.

Barrett, D., ed. 2010. *Hypnosis and Hypnotherapy*. Santa Barbara, CA: Praeger.

Beck, A. T., and A. M. Freeman. 1990. *Cognitive Therapy of Personality Disorders*. New York: Guilford Press.

Beck, A. T., G. Emery, and R. Greenberg. 1985. *Anxiety Disorders and Phobias: A Cognitive Perspective*. New York: Basic Books.

Beck, J. S. 1995. *Cognitive Therapy: Basics and Beyond*. New York: Guilford Press.

Bertini, K. 2009. *Understanding and Preventing Suicide: The Development of Self-Destructive Patterns and Ways to Alter Them*. Westport, CT: Praeger.

Bieschke, K., Ra M. Perez, and K. A. Deboard, eds. 2007. *Handbook of Counseling and Psychotherapy with Lesbian, Gay, Bisexual and Transgender Clients* (2nd ed.). Washington, DC: American Psychological Association.

Braslow, J. 1997. *Mental Ills and Bodily Cures: Psychiatric Treatment in the First Half of the Twentieth Century*. Berkeley: University of California Press.

Clarkson, P. 1999. *Gestalt Counseling in Action* (2nd ed.). London: Sage.

Conyne, R. K., ed. 2011. *Oxford Handbook of Group Counseling*. New York: Oxford University Press.

Cooper, J., T. Heron, and W. Heward. 2007. *Applied Behavior Analysis* (2nd ed.). Upper Saddle River, NJ: Prentice-Hall.

Corey, G. 2008. *Theory and Practice of Group Counseling* (7th ed.). Belmont, CA: Thomson Brooks/Cole.

Corey, G. 2009. *Theory and Practice of Counseling and Psychotherapy* (8th ed.). Monterey, CA: Brooks/Cole.

Corrigan, P. C., K. T. Mueser, G. R. Bond, R. E. Drake, and P. Solomon. 2007. *Principles and Practice of Psychiatric Rehabilitation: An Empirical Approach*. New York: Guilford Press.

Corsini, R. J., and D. Wedding. 2010. *Current Psychotherapies*. Belmont, CA: Brooks Cole.

Cozolino, L. 2010. *The Neuroscience of Psychotherapy: Healing the Social Brain* (2nd ed.). New York: Norton.

DeLucia-Waack, D. Gerrity, C. Kalodner, and M. Riva, eds. 2004. *Handbook of Group Counseling and Psychotherapy*. Thousand Oaks, CA: Sage.

Dobson, K. S. 2010. *Handbook of Cognitive-Behavioral Therapies* (3rd ed.). New York: Guilford Press.

Farkas, M., and W. A. Anthony. 1989. *Psychiatric Rehabilitation Programs: Putting Theory into Practice*. Baltimore: Johns Hopkins University Press.

Fink, M. 2002. *Electroshock: Healing Mental Illness*. New York: Oxford University Press.

Freeman, L. 2004. *Mosby's Complementary & Alternative Medicine: A Research-Based Approach* (2nd ed.). St Louis, MO: Mosby.

Frie, R., and D. Orange, eds. 2009. *Beyond Postmodernism: New Dimensions in Clinical Theory and Practice*. New York: Routledge.

Gale, J., A. Realpe, and E. Pedriali, eds. 2008. *Therapeutic Communities for Psychosis: Philosophy, History, and Clinical Practice*. New York: Routledge.

Gladding, S. T., and D. W. Newsome. 2010. *Clinical Mental Health Counseling in Community and Agency Settings* (3rd ed.). Upper Saddle River, NJ: Pearson.

GriefNet. http://www.griefnet.org/.

Gurman, A. S., and S. B. Messer, eds. 2003. *Essential Psychotherapies: Theory and Practice* (2nd ed.). New York: Guilford Press.

Humphreys, K. 2004. *Circles of Recovery: Self-Help Organizations for Addictions*. Cambridge: Cambridge University Press.

Kabat-Zinn, J. 1990 *Full Catastrophe Living: Using the Wisdom of Your Body and Mind to Face Stress, Pain, and Illness*. New York: Dell.

Kennard, D. 1998. *An Introduction to Therapeutic Communities* (2nd ed.). Philadelphia: Jessica Kingsley.

Kneeland, T., and C. Warren. 2008. *Pushbutton Psychiatry: A Cultural History of Electroshock in America*. Walnut Creek, CA: Left Coast Press.

Lazarus, A. A. 1997. *Brief but Comprehensive Psychotherapy*. New York: Springer.

Makela, K., I. Arminen, K. Bloomfield, I. Eisenbach-Stangl, K. H. Bergmark, N. Kurube, N. Mariolini, H. Ólafsdóttir, J. H. Peterson, M. Phillips, J. Rehm, R. Room, P. Rosenqvist, H. Rosovsky, K. Stenius, G. Światkiewicz, B. Woronowicz, and A. Zieliński. 1996. *Alcoholics Anonymous as a Mutual-Help Movement*. Madison: University of Wisconsin Press.

McGee, M. 2005. *Self-Help, Inc.: Makeover Culture in American Life*. New York: Oxford University Press.

Mills, J. A. 1998. *Control: A History of Behavioral Psychology*. New York: New York University Press.

Mitchell, S., and M. Black. 1995. *Freud and Beyond: A History of Modern Psychoanalytic Thought*. New York: Basic Books.

National Institute of Mental Health. 2010. "Psychotherapies." Retrieved from http://www.nimh.nih.gov/health/topics/psychotherapies/index.shtml.

Pratt, C. W., K. J. Gill, N. M. Barrett, and M. M. Roberts. 2002. *Psychiatric Rehabilitation*. San Diego, CA: Academic Press.

Prochaska, J. O., and J. C. Norcross. 2010. *Systems of Psychotherapy: A Transtheoretical Analysis* (7th ed.). Belmont, CA: Brooks/Cole, Cengage Learning.

Rehabilitation Training Technology: Case Management (Trainer Package), Revised Format. Boston: Boston University, Center for Psychiatric Rehabilitation.

Roth, A., and P. Fonagy. 1996. *What Works for Whom? A Critical Review of Psychotherapy Research*. New York: Guilford Press.

Salerno, S. 2005. *SHAM: How the Self-Help Movement Made America Helpless*. New York: Crown.

Shedler, J. 2010. "The Efficacy of Psychodynamic Psychotherapy." *American Psychologist* 65(2): 98–109.

Shorter, E., and D. Healy. 2007. *Shock Therapy: A History of Electroconvulsive Treatment in Mental Illness*. New Brunswick, NJ: Rutgers University Press.

Singer, M. T., and J. Lalich. 1996. *Crazy Therapies: What Are They? Do They Work?* New York: Jossey-Bass.

Sommers, C. H., and S. Satell. 2005. *One Nation under Therapy: How the Helping Culture Is Eroding Self-Reliance*. New York: St. Martin's.

Spaulding, W., M. Sullivan, and J. Poland. 2003. *Treatment and Rehabilitation of Severe Mental Illness*. New York: Guilford Press.

Spurling, L. 2004. *An Introduction to Psychodynamic Counselling*. London: Palgrave Macmillan.

St. Clair, M. 2000. *Object Relations and Self Psychology: An Introduction*. Belmont, CA: Wadsworth/Thompson Learning.

Travis, T. 2009. *The Language of the Heart: A Cultural History of the Recovery Movement*. Chapel Hill: University of North Carolina Press.

Vargas, J. 2009. *Behavior Analysis for Effective Teaching*. New York: Routledge.

Wampold, B. E. 2001. *The Great Psychotherapy Debate: Models, Methods, and Findings*. Mahwah, NJ: Lawrence Erlbaum Associates.

White, M., and D. Epston. 1990. *Narrative Means to Therapeutic Ends*. New York: Norton.

Worden, J. W. 2008. *Grief Counseling and Grief Therapy: A Handbook for the Mental Health Practitioner*. New York: Springer.

Yalom, I. D. (with M. Leszcz). 2005. *Theory and Practice of Group Psychotherapy* (5th ed.). New York: Basic Books.

About the Editor and Contributors

Michael Shally-Jensen is former editor-in-chief of the 30-volume *Encyclopedia Americana*, executive editor of the *Encyclopedia of American Studies*, and editor of numerous other works in the social sciences and social history, including, most recently, ABC-CLIO's *Encyclopedia of Contemporary American Social Issues*. He received his doctorate in cultural anthropology from Princeton University. Currently he works as an independent writer and editor.

Contributors

Nicole A. Adamson is a doctoral candidate at the University of North Carolina at Greensboro and specializes in the treatment of child and adolescent mental health disorders. Her most recent publications and presentations cover topics such as creative counseling techniques, vicarious trauma, and professional advocacy.

Daphne Algaze is a master's degree candidate and dean's fellow at the Simmons College Graduate School of Social Work, in Boston. She has worked as a clinical research coordinator at the Massachusetts General Hospital Schizophrenia Research Program and as a research assistant at McLean Hospital and Harvard University.

David M. Allen is professor of psychiatry at the University of Tennessee and former director of UT's psychiatry residency program. He has published extensively on psychotherapy integration and personality disorders. His latest book is *How Dysfunctional Families Spur Mental Disorders*: *A Balanced Approach to Resolve Problems and Reconcile Relationships*.

Rebecca M. Ametrano is a clinical psychology doctoral student at the University of Massachusetts Amherst. Her research focuses on psychotherapy. A recent publication is, with coauthors, "Expectations," *Journal of Clinical Psychology: In Session* 67 (2011): 1–9.

Linda Wasmer Andrews is a journalist and author with a master's degree in psychology. She is the author of *The Encyclopedia of Depression* (Greenwood, 2010) and specializes in writing about health, psychology, and the mind-body connection. Her entry, "Bipolar Disorder," was originally published in the *Encyclopedia of Depression*.

T. Em Arpawong is a doctoral student in health behavior research at the University of Southern California, Department of Preventive Medicine. Currently, her research focuses on how posttraumatic growth impacts mental well-being and substance use behaviors among adolescents who are at high risk for experiencing trauma and poor health outcomes.

Alon Y. Avidan is a professor in the Department of Neurology at the David Geffen School of Medicine at UCLA. He is director of the UCLA Sleep Disorders Center and director of the UCLA Neurology Residency Program.

Dana Lee Baker is associate professor of political science and director of the Program in Public Affairs at Washington State University. Her research is primarily in the areas of neurology and public policy and comparative disability policy. Her most recent publication is *The Politics of Neurodiversity: Why Public Policy Matters*.

Charles Barber is director of The Connection Institute for Innovative Practice, part of The Connection, Inc., a leading social service agency, and a lecturer in psychiatry at the Yale University School of Medicine. He is the author of *Comfortably Numb: How Psychiatry Is Medicating a Nation* and *Songs from the Black Chair*, among other works.

Deborah Belle is professor of psychology and director of the Women's, Gender, & Sexuality Studies Program at Boston University. Her books include *Lives in Stress: Women and Depression; Children's Social Networks and Social Supports*; and *The After-School Lives of Children: Alone and with Others While Parents Work*.

Joan Berzoff currently teaches in the doctoral, master's, and end-of-life care programs at Smith College School for Social Work. She has coedited six books and written over 25 articles on subjects ranging from women's development and loss and bereavement to psychodynamic theory and practice. She also is in private practice in Northampton, Massachusetts.

Nicole Bradley is a doctoral candidate at Kent State University in the counseling and human development services program and an adjunct faculty member at Youngstown State University in the counseling program. Her areas of interest include wellness and self-care of counselors. Her most recent publication and presentation topics include creative counseling techniques, vicarious trauma, self-care, and ethics.

Thomas Broffman is assistant professor and coordinator of field education in the Department of Sociology, Anthropology, and Social Work at Eastern Connecticut State University in Willimantic, Connecticut. His research interests are problem gambling and motivational interviewing.

Charles I. Brooks is professor and chair of the Department of Psychology, King's College, Wilkes-Barre, Pennsylvania, where he has taught since 1975 and was designated a distinguished service professor in 1993. He has authored or coauthored more than 40 scholarly publications in psychology. His entry, "Suicide and Suicide Prevention," coauthored with Michael A. Church, originally appeared in the *Encyclopedia of Contemporary American Social Issues* (ABC-CLIO, 2010).

Stephanie Brzuzy is director, School of Social Work, Aurora University, Aurora, Illinois. She coauthored *Social Welfare Policy, Programs, and Practice* (1998 with Elizabeth Segal) and has written several articles analyzing the impact of social welfare policy outcomes on vulnerable populations. Dr. Brzuzy is also the coeditor of *Battleground: Women, Gender, and Sexuality* (with Amy Lind, Greenwood Press, 2008), in which the present entry on "Gender Identity Disorder" originally appeared. She has published works on gender identity disorder (GID), transphobia, and same-sex marriage.

Heather Bullock is a professor of psychology at the University of California at Santa Cruz and an affiliate of the Institute for Assets and Social Policy at Brandeis University. A social psychologist, her research examines how members of different socioeconomic groups perceive economic inequality, mobility, and social class.

Donna L. Burton is a PhD candidate in behavioral health at the University of South Florida's College of Public Health. She has more than 20 years of experience in services delivery, planning, and administration of mental health and substance use services for children, adults, and families.

Alma J. Carten is an associate professor of social work at New York University's Silver School of Social Work. She has held a variety of posts in both government and higher education. Her professional interests focus on child welfare and the delivery of culturally competent services.

Kellye S. Carver is a doctoral student in the counseling psychology program at the University of North Texas, where she is specializing in geropsychology and marriage/family issues.

Christine D. Cea is currently a researcher at the New York State Institute for Basic Research in developmental disabilities and a member of the board of regents for the New York State Education Department. She received her doctorate in developmental psychology from the Graduate School of Arts and Sciences at Fordham University and completed a postdoctoral fellowship as associate director of the Developmental Disabilities Project at the Fordham University Center for Ethics Education. A version of her entry on "Intellectual Disability" was originally published in *The Encyclopedia of Human Ecology* (2003, ABC-CLIO), under "Mental Retardation."

Jia-shin Chen is an assistant professor of psychiatry at Taipei Medical University, in Taiwan, and an attending psychiatrist at Shuang Ho Hospital there. His interests include social psychiatry and the history of psychiatry. His entry, "Psychiatry," originally appeared in *Battleground: Science and Technology* (2008, ABC-CLIO).

Kyoung Mi Choi is assistant professor of counseling at Youngstown State University. Her main research interests are third-culture kids (TCKs), intercultural mobility, hybrid identity development, college student friendship, and multiculturalism. She has worked with international students from over 120 countries, providing individual and group counseling to students facing cultural, academic, social, and developmental challenges.

Michael A. Church is associate professor of psychology at King's College in Wilkes-Barre, Pennsylvania, where he has taught since 1976. He has been a licensed clinical psychologist with a private practice since 1980, and is a member of the Council of National Register of Health Service Providers in Psychology. His entry, "Suicide and Suicide Prevention," coauthored with Charles I. Brooks, originally appeared in the *Encyclopedia of Contemporary American Social Issues* (ABC-CLIO, 2010).

Mária I. Cipriani, MA, LCSW, a holistically oriented psychotherapist in private practice in New York, New York, works extensively with lesbian and gay individuals and couples. "Lesbian, Gay, Bisexual, Transgender (LGBT) Mental Health Issues" originally appeared *in LGBTQ America Today: An Encyclopedia*, edited by John C. Hawley (Greenwood, 2008).

Michael J. Constantino is an associate professor of clinical psychology at the University of Massachusetts, Amherst. He has published extensively on psychotherapy process and outcome. He recently received the International Society for Psychotherapy Research's (SPR) 2010 Outstanding Early Career Achievement Award, and was elected president-elect for the North American SPR.

Ruth E. Cook is professor of special education at Santa Clara University, Santa Clara, California. Her primary area of publication is early childhood special education/early intervention. Her book *Adapting Early Childhood Curricula for Children with Special Needs* is now in its eighth edition.

Jennifer Couturier is a child and adolescent psychiatrist, and assistant professor in the Department of Psychiatry and Behavioural Neurosciences at McMaster University, Hamilton, Ontario, Canada. Her research focuses on psychotherapy for eating disorders, with a special interest in family therapy approaches.

Kathleen E. Darbor studies psychology in Texas A&M University's graduate program. Her work focuses on the impact of emotions on cognitive processes, with a particular focus on how emotions such as regret and pride impact people's consumption and ability to regulate.

Carrie DeMarco is a graduate assistant at Youngstown State University, where she is working on research related to self-injury and child abuse and neglect. She has a passion for working with college students and in student affairs.

Sandra DiVitale is a third-year PhD student in clinical psychology at Palo Alto University. She is especially interested in cultural aspects of psychological trauma. Currently, she is a member of the Palo Alto Medical Reserve Corps, providing instruction in psychological first aid to first responders.

Amber N. Douglas is assistant professor of psychology and education at Mount Holyoke College in South Hadley, Massachusetts. Her research interests include psychological trauma and the psychology of ethnic minorities. She is currently working on a pilot study evaluating the effectiveness of a treatment intervention for traumatized children.

Laura E. Drislane is a student in the doctoral program in clinical psychology at Florida State University. Her research applies psychometric and neurobiological approaches to understanding individual differences underlying psychopathy, antisocial behavior, and pathological fear.

Melanie Kautzman-East works as an adjunct faculty member at the Pennsylvania State University and is a graduate student in the counseling program at Youngstown

State University. She has over 10 years of experience working with families and providing multisystemic therapy.

Patricia E. Erickson is professor of criminal justice at Canisius College, Buffalo, New York. She is also an attorney practicing in the area of family law. Her recent publications reflect her concern with critically evaluating law as it relates to the poor, the mentally ill, and other marginalized groups. She is coauthor (with Steven K. Erickson) *of Crime, Punishment, and Mental Illness: Law and the Behavioral Sciences in Conflict.*

Steven K. Erickson is an attorney and forensic psychologist in York, Pennsylvania. He is a distinguished expert in criminal and mental health law, whose work centers on issues of individual responsibility, social intuitions of judgment, and punishment. His latest publication, "Predators and Punishment" (forthcoming, *Psychology, Public Policy and Law*), examines the culpability of the psychopath.

Amanda Evans is an assistant professor in the Special Education, Rehabilitation and Counseling Department at Auburn University. Her research interests include counseling men, preparing competent counseling professionals, and ethics.

Celia B. Fisher is the Marie Ward Doty Chair and professor of psychology, and founding director of the Fordham University Center for Ethics Education. She has published widely in the areas of ethics in medical and social science research and practice and life span development.

Melissa Floyd is an associate professor of social work and director of the bachelor's program in social work at the University of Carolina, Greensboro. Her research interests include social work practice with people with serious mental illness, issues in family substance abuse, and alternatives to involuntary treatment.

Cheryl Fracasso is currently a doctoral candidate at Saybrook University. She serves as a faculty member at University of Phoenix and research assistant at Saybrook University. She also serves as an editorial/advisory board member with the journal *NeuroQuantology* and associate managing editor with the *International Journal of Transpersonal Studies.*

Harris Friedman is research professor (retired) of psychology at University of Florida, and a clinical and consulting psychologist. He is senior editor of *International Journal of Transpersonal Studies* and associate editor of *The Humanistic Psychologist*, as well as a fellow of the American Psychological Association.

Poonam Ghiya is a graduate student at the Pacific Graduate School of Psychology at Palo Alto University, pursuing her PhD in clinical psychology. She has done research focused on children and families, and currently is doing research on adolescents from eastern India.

Annemarie Gockel is an assistant professor of social work at the Smith College School for Social Work, Northampton, Massachusetts. She conducts research and publishes on spirituality in clinical practice and education. Her most recent publication is "Client Perspectives on Spirituality in the Therapeutic Relationship," *Humanistic Psychologist* 32, no. 2 (2011): 154–168.

Joseph P. Gone is an associate professor of psychology and Native American studies at the University of Michigan. In his scholarship, Gone explores the intersection of evidence-based practice and cultural competence in mental health services. He recently completed a residential fellowship (2010–11) at the Center for Advanced Study in the Behavioral Sciences at Stanford University.

Leah Gongola has worked as a public school general and special educator, and she consults and works directly with children with autism and behavioral needs through Proactive Behavior Services, LLC. Dr. Gongola is an assistant professor in the special education department at Youngstown State University.

Richard P. Halgin is a professor of psychology at the University of Massachusetts, Amherst. He has published three textbooks on abnormal psychology, as well as more than 50 articles and chapters in the field of psychology. He is a board-certified clinical psychologist with a part-time psychotherapy practice.

Ardis Hanson is a research coordinator at the College of Behavioral & Community Sciences and a doctoral candidate in the Department of Communication at the University of South Florida. Her research is in health and organizational communication, with particular reference to the discourse of public policymaking in mental health.

William E. Hartmann is a graduate student in clinical psychology at the University of Michigan. His research interests lie in the area of culture and mental health. Currently, he is engaged in work with an urban American Indian community to explore a model of traditional healing.

Bert Hayslip Jr. is a regents professor of psychology at the University of North Texas. His research interests are grandparenting, grandparents raising grandchildren, dementia and caregiving, and spirituality and aging.

Katherine Hejtmanek is an assistant professor in the Children and Youth Studies Program and the Department of Anthropology and Archaeology at Brooklyn College, City University of New York. She is working on a book based on her ethnographic research in a residential treatment center. Her most recent publication is "Caring through Restraint: Violence, Intimacy and Identity in Mental Health Practice," *Culture, Medicine and Psychiatry* 34 (2010): 668–674.

Emily Herman is a graduate student in clinical mental health and school counseling at Youngstown State University. She earned a bachelor's degree in public health from Youngstown State in 2009 and is now a dual-track graduate student in the counseling master's program.

Michelle S. Hinkle is an adjunct professor at both Youngstown State University and Kent State University. Her research interests include counseling pedagogy, creative counseling techniques with children and adolescents, and collaborative supervision.

Kathryn H. Hollen is a freelance science writer and editor who works with her husband, a technical illustrator, out of her rural home west of Washington, DC. She writes for the National Cancer Institute and other organizations engaged in biomedical reporting and research. She is the editor of *The Encyclopedia of Addictions* (Greenwood, 2008), from which the entry "Impulse Control Disorders" is taken.

Marlene E. Hunter is a physician in Victoria, British Columbia. She has worked for many years with adults who were abused as children. The author of seven books and numerous articles, she has worked around the globe, including presentations in 24 countries.

David Jordan is a clinical psychology doctoral candidate at the Pacific Graduate School of Psychology at Palo Alto University. He has focused his studies and research on community mental health, diversity, mental health disparities, substance abuse, and serious mental illness.

Jay Joseph is a licensed psychologist practicing in Oakland, California. He has published numerous reviews of genetic research in psychiatry and psychology. His first book, *The Gene Illusion: Genetic Research in Psychiatry and Psychology under the Microscope*, was published in 2003. In 2006, he published his second book, *The Missing Gene: Psychiatry, Heredity, and the Fruitless Search for Genes*.

Martin Kantor is a Harvard-trained psychiatrist who has been in full private practice and served as an assistant clinical professor of psychiatry. Kantor is now a full-time author whose published works include 19 books, including *Understanding Paranoia*.

Melanie Kautzman is a graduate student in counseling at Youngstown State University. She recently received a DiGiulio Scholarship in recognition of her work in the counseling program and in the community.

Jerald Kay is the Frederick A. White Distinguished Professor and chair of the Department of Psychiatry at Wright State University's Boonshoft School of Medicine in Dayton, Ohio. He was the founding editor of a psychotherapy research journal and has published extensively on the topics of medical and psychiatric education, medical ethics, child psychiatry, psychoanalysis, psychotherapy, and the neurobiology of psychotherapy.

Timothy A. Kelly is director of TAK Consult and chief of behavioral health services for ParkwayHealth Medical Centers in Shanghai, China. He is the former commissioner of Virginia's Department of Mental Health Services and has served on the boards of directors for both the National Association of State Mental Health Program Directors and the National Research Institute. His latest book is *Healing the Broken Mind: Transforming America's Failed Mental Health System.*

Donna R. Kemp is professor of public administration and graduate coordinator of the department of political science at California State University, Chico. Her published works include *Mental Health in America: A Reference Guide* (ABC-CLIO, 2007) and *Mental Health in the Workplace: An Employer's and Manager's Guide* (Praeger, 1994). Versions of her entries "The History of Mental Health Care" and "State Mental Health Agencies" originally appeared in the *Encyclopedia of Contemporary American Social Issues* (ABC-CLIO, 2010; under "Mental Health") and *Mental Health in America*, respectively.

Dennis K. Kinney is a senior research psychologist at McLean Hospital near Boston and associate clinical professor in the psychiatry department at Harvard Medical School. He has published extensively on creativity and liability for mental disorders. A recent publication is "Bipolar Mood Disorders," in M. A. Runco and S. R. Pritzker, eds., *Encyclopedia of Creativity*, 2nd ed. (2011).

Julie Kipp is a practicing mental health social worker in New York City. She received her PhD in social work from New York University. Her research interests include schizophrenia, therapeutic communities, and milieu therapy.

Michele Klimczak is the clinical director of a therapeutic foster care program in Connecticut. She has 20 years of experience in the fields of child welfare and family violence.

Timothy Kneeland is professor of history and political science at Nazareth College, Pittsford, New York. He has published on the history of science, American psychiatry, and American politics. A recent publication is "Robert Hare: Politics, Science and Spiritualism in the Early Republic," *Pennsylvania Magazine of History and Biography* (2008): 245–260.

Victoria E. Kress is professor of counseling at Youngstown State University and serves as the program coordinator of the Clinical Mental Health Counseling program. She has over 50 publications relating to mental health counseling, and has 20 years of experience working in various mental health settings.

Stanley Krippner is professor of psychology and humanistic studies at Saybrook University. In 2002 he received the American Psychological Association's Award for Distinguished Contributions to the International Advancement of Psychology. His several books include *Personal Mythology, Haunted by Combat*, and *Demystifying Shamans and Their World*.

Margaret Leaf is a PhD candidate in sociology at Florida State University. Her research interests include self-injury, rape, and sexual behavior, all of which she has published papers about in professional journals. Her entry, "Self-Injury and Body Image," was originally published in the *Encyclopedia of Contemporary American Social Issues* (ABC-CLIO, 2010).

Fred Leavitt is professor of psychology at California State University, East Bay. He has published extensively on drugs, research methodology, and philosophy. His most recent publication is *Improving Medical Outcomes*, which he cowrote with his daughter, Jessica Leavitt.

Heather C. Lench is assistant professor of psychology at Texas A&M University. Her work focuses on the interactions among cognitive and emotional processes. Her most recent publications deal with discrete emotions in the laboratory and optimism that results from emotion.

Bruce Lubotsky Levin is an associate professor and head of the Graduate Studies in Behavioral Health Program, College of Public Health and College of Community & Behavioral Sciences, at the University of South Florida. He also serves as editor-in-chief of the *Journal of Behavioral Health Services & Research*.

Yue Liao is a doctoral student in health behavior research at the University of Southern California, Department of Preventive Medicine. Her research areas include understanding social influences and substance use in adolescents, evaluating substance use prevention programs, and investigating relationships between the built environment, physical activity, and obesity.

James Lock is professor of child psychiatry and pediatrics at Stanford University School of Medicine, where he also serves as director of the Eating Disorder Program for Children and Adolescents. His current research focuses on interventions for anorexia and bulimia in children and adolescents.

Tessa Lundquist is a clinical psychology doctoral student at the University of Massachusetts, Amherst. She conducts research on attitudes surrounding aging, Alzheimer's disease, and health care decision making in older adults.

Amanda M. Marcotte is an associate professor in the school psychology program at the University of Massachusetts, Amherst. She researches effective assessment practices for instructional planning and psychoeducational evaluations procedures in schools. Recently, she received a grant to investigate methods of formative assessment for reading comprehension problems.

Oliver T. Massey is an associate professor and psychologist in the College of Behavioral & Community Sciences at the University of South Florida. His interests include applied research and evaluation in community-based organizations and the organization and effectiveness of mental health services in public schools.

Lourdes Mattei is associate professor of clinical psychology at Hampshire College, Amherst, Massachusetts. She has worked for many years as a clinical psychologist in a variety of settings such as academia, community mental health, private practice, and the theater. Her interests include psychoanalytic theory and practice, child development, cross-cultural psychology, women's studies, theater, and Puerto Rican culture.

Joshua Miller is a professor at Smith College School for Social Work, Northampton, Massachusetts. His two areas of specialization are antiracism work and helping individuals and communities to recover from disasters. He has responded to many disasters nationally and internationally and his most recent book is *Psychosocial Capacity Building in Response to Disasters* (2012).

Lauren Mizock holds a doctorate in clinical psychology and is research fellow at the Center for Psychiatric Rehabilitation at Boston University. She also teaches courses in undergraduate psychology, provides outpatient therapy, and consults for nonprofit organizations. Her research focuses on psychiatric rehabilitation, racial identity, transgender issues, and size oppression.

Mary Montaldo is a doctoral student at Palo Alto University. She is currently interested in research and practice with children, adolescents, and families.

Rudy Nydegger is a professor of management and psychology at Union Graduate College and Union College, Schenectady, New York, and is also a board-certified clinical psychologist with a private practice and consulting business. In addition, he is chief of psychology at Ellis Hospital, Schenectady.

Mary Ann Overcamp-Martini is the graduate program coordinator in the School of Social Work at the University of Nevada, Las Vegas. Dr. Martini's primary interests are in mental health and disabilities, macro practice, legal issues, and social work education.

Kyle S. Page is a doctoral student in counseling psychology at the University of North Texas. His research, training, and experience emphasize the mental health aspects of aging, fear of dementia, and caregivers.

Christopher J. Patrick, professor of psychology at Florida State University, is the author of over 150 published articles/chapters and editor of the *Handbook of Psychopathy* (2006). He is currently president of the Society for Psychophysiological Research and is a past president of the Society for Scientific Study of Psychopathy.

Daryl S. Paulson is president and chief executive officer of BioScience Laboratories, Inc., a national testing laboratory facility located in Bozeman, Montana. He is board certified by the American College of Forensic Examiners and has published numerous articles on clinical evaluation, psychology, and other topics.

Matthew J. Paylo is an assistant professor and interim director of the student affairs program at Youngstown State University. He has published and presented in the areas of social justice and advocacy. He challenges his students to advocate for the counseling profession as well as for marginalized and discriminated populations.

Carolyn Pender is a licensed psychologist in a private group practice in Raleigh, North Carolina. She earned her PhD in school psychology from the University of South Carolina in 2008. She completed her predoctoral internship and postdoctoral fellowship at Johns Hopkins School of Medicine and the Kennedy Krieger Institute. Her current research interests center around outcomes for children and adolescents with attention deficit hyperactivity disorder.

Christian Perring is chair of philosophy and religious studies at Dowling College, New York, and a member of the Executive Council of the Association for the Advancement of Philosophy and Psychiatry. He edits *Metapsychology Online Reviews*. His main area of research is the philosophy of psychiatry.

Bernice Pescosolido is distinguished professor of sociology and director of the Indiana Consortium for Mental Health Services Research at Indiana University. Her research and teaching focus on how social networks connect individuals to their communities and to institutional structures. She initiated the first major national study of the stigma of mental illness in over 40 years, and, with funding from the Fogarty International Center, led a team of researchers in the first international study of stigma.

Francesca Piscitelli is a graduate student in clinical psychology at Pacific University, Hillsboro, Oregon. She is the student leader of the Pacific University Consulting Team, which provides free consultation to nonprofit organizations. Additional areas of research are posttraumatic stress disorder and cross-cultural review of suicide in militaries.

Alessandro Piselli is completing his doctorate in clinical psychology at the University of Massachusetts, Amherst, where he has conducted research on psychotherapy and psychopathology. His most recent publication is "What Went Wrong? Therapists' Reflections on Their Role in Premature Termination," *Psychotherapy Research* (May 2011): 1–16.

Jeffrey Poland is senior lecturer in the Department of History, Philosophy, and the Social Sciences at the Rhode Island School of Design, in Providence. His areas of specialization include the philosophical foundations of psychiatry, the philosophy of cognitive science, and neuroethics. Among his recent publications is *Treatment and Rehabilitation of Severe Mental Illness* (with W. Spaulding and M. Sullivan).

Jake J. Protivnak is an associate professor and serves as the counseling program coordinator in the Department of Counseling and Special Education at Youngstown State University. His research and professional service focuses is on counselor education, professional advocacy, career development, and the counseling of children and adolescents.

Lisa Rapp is an associate professor and associate director of the University of South Florida's School of Social Work. She was codeveloper and co-principal investigator of the Prodigy Cultural Arts Program, a Florida diversion and prevention project. Her research interests are juvenile crime and violence with an emphasis on prevention and the relationship between mental health and offending.

Sarah Raven taught elementary school for four years in the South Bronx. Currently, as a member of the Episcopal Service Corps, she is working as a Research Associate for The Connection Inc., Middletown, Connecticut, where she is assisting in a study examining the life stories of residents of a halfway house for ex-offenders.

Rebecca Ready is associate professor of psychology and a member of the neuroscience and behavior program at the University of Massachusetts, Amherst. She studies emotional well-being in aging, Alzheimer's disease, and Huntington's disease.

Gretchen Reevy teaches in the Department of Psychology at California State University, East Bay, specializing in personality, stress and coping, and psychological assessment courses. She coedited the *Praeger Handbook on Stress and Coping* and authored (with the assistance of Y. M. Ozer and Y. Ito) the *Encyclopedia of Emotion*. Versions of her entries on "Borderline Personality," "Humanistic Theories and Therapies," "Hypnosis and Hypnotherapy," "Loss and Grief," and Nutrition and Mental Health" originally appeared in the *Encyclopedia of Emotion* (Greenwood, 2010).

Ruth Richards is a professor in the Graduate College of Psychology and Humanistic Studies at Saybrook University in San Francisco. She is a fellow of the American Psychological Association and the 2009 winner of the Arnheim Award for Outstanding Lifetime Achievement in Psychology and the Arts. The author of numerous articles and chapters on creativity, she edited *Everyday Creativity and New Views of Human Nature*.

Glenn Rohrer is director of the School of Justice Studies and Social Work at the University of West Florida (UWF), in Pensacola. Rohrer joined UWF in 2006 to start the master's of social work program after working at East Carolina University for 17 years, where he holds the title of professor emeritus.

Jessica Rosenberg is associate professor of social work at Long Island University. Her books include *Working in Social Work: The Real World Guide to Practice Settings* and *Community Mental Health: Challenges for the 21st Century*, 2nd ed.

Christine Runyan is an associate clinical professor in the Department of Family and Community Medicine at the University of Massachusetts Medical School. She practices clinical health psychology in an academic health center, writes extensively, presents at local, state, and national conferences, teaches, consults, and trains graduate students and medical residents.

Anne Saw is associate director of the Asian American Center on Disparities Research at University of California, Davis. Her research addresses the cultural and structural factors that impact mental and physical health, access to services, and quality of health care for Asian Americans and other racial/ethnic minorities.

Dave Sells is an associate research scientist in the Program for Recovery and Community Health, Department of Psychiatry, at Yale University. His research interests include therapeutic relationships, construction (and reconstruction) of self, symbolic representation, and quantitative and qualitative research strategies.

Laura Shannonhouse is a doctoral student at the University of North Carolina at Greensboro specializing in crisis intervention, disaster response, and multicultural training. She has participated in culture-centered clinical outreach efforts within the United States, Southern Africa, Botswana, Mexico, and Costa Rica.

Jerrold Lee Shapiro is professor of counseling psychology at Santa Clara University, Santa Clara, California, and a licensed clinical psychologist. He is author/editor of 10 books, over 100 articles, and over 200 professional presentations. He is managing partner of Family Business Solutions and a frequent media consultant.

Sherdene Simpson is a doctoral candidate at the University of Akron, where she is working on her degree in counselor education and supervision: marriage and family therapy. Her research interests include assessment, childhood sexual abuse, grief and loss, medical family therapy, religion and spirituality, and supervision.

Sarah C. Sitton is an associate professor of psychology at St. Edward's University, Austin, Texas. Among her publications is *Life at the Texas State Lunatic Asylum, 1857–1997.*

Bradley Smith is an associate professor in the Department of Psychology at the University of South Carolina. From 1993 to 1996, he was the clinical and research supervisor of the adolescent program at the Attention Deficit Disorder Program at the Western Psychiatric Institute and Clinic in the University of Pittsburgh Medical Center. His current scholarly interests are primarily focused on school-based treatment of learning and behavior problems, parenting interventions, and prevention of substance abuse, including studies of college student drinking.

Susan Stefan is an attorney who represents people with psychiatric disabilities in system reform litigation. She has written three books and numerous articles about legal and policy issues involving people with psychiatric disabilities, and served as an expert consultant to the President's New Freedom Commission on Mental Health and to the Institute of Medicine. Most recently, she was a visiting professor of law at the University of Miami School of Law.

Stanley Sue is professor of psychology and director of the Center for Excellence in Diversity, Palo Alto University. He is also emeritus distinguished professor of psychology, University of California, Davis. His research areas include cultural competency, cultural influences on mental health, and Asian Americans and other ethnic minority groups.

Steve Sussman is a professor of preventive medicine and psychology at the University of Southern California. He studies etiology, prevention, and cessation of various addictions, and has over 385 publications. His projects have been used as model programs at numerous agencies.

Richard C. Tessler is a professor of sociology at the University of Massachusetts, Amherst, and the recipient of several research and training grants from the National Institute of Mental Health related to chronic mental illness. He has published widely about mental health services and systems, family experiences, and the psychiatric status of homeless veterans.

Jay C. Thomas is distinguished university professor and assistant dean of professional psychology at Pacific University, Hillsboro, Oregon. He has written and edited several books and articles over the past three decades. He has a special interest in mental disability and successful workplaces.

Stacey A. Tovino is professor of law at the William S. Boyd School of Law at the University of Nevada, Las Vegas. She has published extensively in the areas of health law, bioethics, and the medical humanities. Her most recent publication is "All Illnesses Are (Not) Created Equal: Reforming Federal Mental Health Insurance Law," *Harvard Law School Journal on Legislation* 49, no. 1 (2012): 1–51.

Diana L. Tracy is a third-year psychiatry resident at Wright State University's Boonshoft School of Medicine (Department of Psychiatry) in Dayton, Ohio. She graduated with a BS in psychology from Wright State in 1996, and received her MD from the University of California, Davis, School of Medicine in 2009.

Richard Van Voorhis is an assistant professor in the school psychology program at Youngstown State University. His experience includes full-time employment as a school psychologist in public school settings for 17 years. His current research interests include role and function of school psychologists, career development topics, special education service delivery, low incidence disabilities, and assessment and identification issues.

Noah C. Venables is a graduate student in the clinical psychology doctoral program at Florida State University. His research interests include issues related to the conceptualization, assessment, and neurobiology of externalizing traits and behaviors such as impulsivity, aggression, and criminality.

Danny Wedding is associate dean of management and international programs at the California School of Professional Psychology, Alliant International University, San Diego. Among his publications are *Movies and Mental Illness* and *Current Psychotherapies*.

Linda Wilmshurst is an associate professor of psychology at Elon University, in Elon, North Carolina. She has authored several textbooks, including *Abnormal Child Psychology: A Developmental Perspective* and *Essentials of Child Psychopathology*. With Alan W. Brue she coauthored *A Parent's Guide to Special Education* and *A Complete Guide to Special Education*.

William H. Wilson is a psychiatric educator, investigator, and clinician. Professor of psychiatry at the Oregon Health & Science University, Portland, he is a distinguished fellow of the American Psychiatric Association, and twice received the Exemplary Psychiatrist Award from the National Alliance for the Mentally Ill.

Melinda Wolford has worked as a school psychologist in public schools across the United States. She has applied her specialty training in neuropsychology into practice by supporting children with neurological and behavioral differences. Dr. Wolford is an assistant professor in the Counseling and Special Education Department at Youngstown State University.

Kimberly Young, a licensed psychologist, founded the Center for Internet Addiction in 1995. The author of numerous publications on Internet addiction, including *Caught in the Net* and *Tangled in the Web*, she is a professor of management sciences at St. Bonaventure University, St. Bonaventure, New York. Her work has been widely featured in the media.

Michelle Zeidler is an associate professor of medicine at the David Geffen School of Medicine at UCLA. She is certified in sleep medicine by the American Board of Internal Medicine and is the Associate Sleep Fellowship director at the Greater Los Angeles Veterans Association.

Index